Lecture Notes of the Institute for Computer Sciences, Social Informatics and Telecommunications Engineering 677

The LNICST series publishes ICST's conferences, symposia and workshops.

LNICST reports state-of-the-art results in areas related to the scope of the Institute.

The type of material published includes

- Proceedings (published in time for the respective event)
- Other edited monographs (such as project reports or invited volumes)

LNICST topics span the following areas:

- General Computer Science
- E-Economy
- E-Medicine
- Knowledge Management
- Multimedia
- Operations, Management and Policy
- Social Informatics
- Systems

Faouzi Kamoun · Lamjed Bettaieb ·
Fatna Belqasmi · Abderrazek Hachani ·
Thar Baker · Mohamed Tabaa ·
Adekunle Adeleke
Editors

Emerging Technologies for Developing Countries

8th EAI International Conference, AFRICATEK 2025
Tunis, Tunisia, June 11–13, 2025
Proceedings, Part II

Editors
Faouzi Kamoun
École Supérieure Privée d'ingénierie et de Technologies
Ariana, Tunisia

Fatna Belqasmi
Zayed University
Abu Dhabi, United Arab Emirates

Thar Baker
University of Khorfakkan
Sharjah, United Arab Emirates

Adekunle Adeleke
Nile University of Nigeria
Abuja FCT, Nigeria

Lamjed Bettaieb
École Supérieure Privée d'ingénierie et de Technologies
Ariana, Tunisia

Abderrazek Hachani
École Supérieure Privée d'ingénierie et de Technologies
Ariana, Tunisia

Mohamed Tabaa
École Marocaine des Sciences de l'ingénieur (EMSI)
Casablanca, Morocco

ISSN 1867-8211 ISSN 1867-822X (electronic)
Lecture Notes of the Institute for Computer Sciences, Social Informatics and Telecommunications Engineering
ISBN 978-3-032-16637-1 ISBN 978-3-032-16638-8 (eBook)
https://doi.org/10.1007/978-3-032-16638-8

This Springer imprint is published by the registered company Springer Nature Switzerland AG
The registered company address is: Gewerbestrasse 11, 6330 Cham, Switzerland

Preface

It is our pleasure to present the proceedings of the Eighth Edition of the European Alliance for Innovation (EAI) International Conference on Emerging Technologies for Developing Countries (AfricaTek 2025), co-organized with and hosted by the École Supérieure Privée d'Ingénierie et de Technologies (ESPRIT), Tunisia, on June 11–13, 2025, and generously sponsored by Honoris United Universities.

Held under the overarching theme "*Emerging Technologies: Pathways to Resilience and Growth in Africa*," this year's edition highlighted how cutting-edge innovations can serve as powerful enablers of inclusive and sustainable transformation across the continent.

AfricaTek 2025 brought together a vibrant community of researchers and practitioners from Africa and beyond, offering a unique platform for critical dialogue on the role of emerging technologies in advancing Africa's development priorities.

A total of 138 submissions were received, including full papers, short papers, and workshop proposals. Each submission was reviewed through a rigorous double-blind process with at least three independent reviews. Following this process, 49 papers were accepted as full papers, 8 as short papers, and 2 as practical workshops. The accepted contributions span diverse domains, including healthcare and well-being, intelligent networking and cybersecurity, smart agriculture, smart cities, higher education, Industry 4.0, and sustainable development.

Artificial Intelligence emerged as a central theme, with nearly 70% of accepted papers addressing applications related to machine learning, large language models (LLMs), deep learning, computer vision, natural language processing, and data analytics. This strong representation underscores the pivotal role of AI as a catalyst for innovation, where it offers new opportunities to bridge development gaps, tackle complex challenges, and accelerate sustainable growth.

The program also featured two keynote addresses by Fawzi BenMessaoud (Indiana University, USA) and Adel Alimi (ENIS, Tunisia), as well as two practical workshops: AI-enhanced learning (by Wissal Neji and Naouel Boughattas) and GitHub-driven active learning pedagogy (by Badiaa Bouhdid).

We extend our sincere gratitude to the members of the Organizing and Technical Committees, and to the many reviewers and volunteers for their dedicated work in ensuring the success of AfricaTek 2025. Special thanks are due to the Program Chairs and Co-chairs (Fatna Belqasmi, Abderrazek Hachani, Thar Baker, Mohamed Tabaa, Adekunle Adeleke, and Yosr Ghozzi) for overseeing a rigorous review process and curating a high-quality technical program. We are equally grateful to the EAI Conference Managers, Timea Madarova and Rebeka Prummerova, and the EAI Venue Manager, Stella Dao. We gratefully acknowledge the generous support of our sponsor, Honoris United Universities. We also extend our heartfelt thanks to all contributing authors, participants, and keynote speakers.

Looking ahead, we are confident that the spirit of AfricaTek will continue to thrive. The contributions gathered in this volume stand as a foundation for future research, collaboration, and innovation that will play a vital role in addressing Africa's most pressing technological and socio-economic challenges in transformative and sustainable ways.

Faouzi Kamoun
Lamjed Bettaieb
Fatna Belqasmi
Abderrazek Hachani
Thar Baker
Mohamed Tabaa
Adekunle Adeleke

Organization

Organizing Committee

General Chair

Faouzi Kamoun	École Supérieure Privée d'Ingénierie et de Technologies (ESPRIT), Tunisia

General Co-chair

Lamjed Bettaieb	École Supérieure Privée d'Ingénierie et de Technologies (ESPRIT), Tunisia

Program Chair and Co-chairs

Fatna Belqasmi	Zayed University, UAE
Abderrazek Hachani	École Supérieure Privée d'Ingénierie et de Technologies (ESPRIT), Tunisia
Thar Baker	University of Khorfakkan, Sharjah, United Arab Emirates
Mohamed Tabaa	École Marocaine des Sciences de l'Ingénieur (EMSI), Morocco
Adekunle Adeleke	Nile University of Nigeria, Nigeria

TPC Co-chair

Yosr Ghozzi	Supérieure Privée d'Ingénierie et de Technologies (ESPRIT), Tunisia

Sponsorship and Exhibit Chair

Nebgha Ayachi	École Supérieure Privée d'Ingénierie et de Technologies (ESPRIT), Tunisia

Local Chair

Meriem Chichti	ESPRIT School of Business, Tunisia

Workshops Chair

Asma Baghdadi	ESPRIT School of Business, Tunisia

Publicity and Social Media Chair

Chiraz Gharbi	École Supérieure Privée d'Ingénierie et de Technologies (ESPRIT), Tunisia

Publications Chair

Feten Tebourbi	École Supérieure Privée d'Ingénierie et de Technologies (ESPRIT), Tunisia

Web Chair

Oumeima Ibn Elfekih	École Supérieure Privée d'Ingénierie et de Technologies (ESPRIT), Tunisia

Posters and Ph.D. Track Chair

Kaouther Louati	École Supérieure Privée d'Ingénierie et de Technologies (ESPRIT), Tunisia

Technical Program Committee

Heni Abidi	ESPRIT School of Business, Tunisia
Adekunle Akanni Adeleke	Nile University, Nigeria
Steve Adeshina	Nile University, Nigeria
Muhammad Adnan	Hasselt University, Belgium
Karim Alami	École Marocaine des Sciences de l'Ingénieur (EMSI), Morocco

Asma Baghdadi	ESPRIT School of Business, Tunisia
Fatna Belqasmi	Zayed University, UAE
Aymen Ben Brik	ESPRIT School of Business, Tunisia
Mohamed Sélmene Ben Yahia	Tunis El Manar University, Tunisa
Safa Zhioua Cherif	École Supérieure Privée d'Ingénierie et de Technologies (ESPRIT), Tunisia
Tirumala Rao Chimpiri	Stony Brook University, USA
Mohamed El Abd	American University of Kuwait, Kuwait
Walid El Ayeb	ESPRIT School of Business, Tunisia
May El Barachi	University of Wollongong in Dubai, UAE
Ameni Ellouze	École Supérieure Privée d'Ingénierie et de Technologies (ESPRIT), Tunisia
Yosr Ghozzi	École Supérieure Privée d'Ingénierie et de Technologies (ESPRIT), Tunisia
Rossitza Goleva	New Bulgarian University, Bulgaria
Imen Guebebia	École Supérieure Privée d'Ingénierie et de Technologies (ESPRIT), Tunisia
Abderrazek Hachani	École Supérieure Privée d'Ingénierie et de Technologies (ESPRIT), Tunisia
Jihen Hlel	National School of Computer Sciences (ENSI), Tunisia
Farkhund Iqbal	Zayed University, UAE
Wael Jaafar	École de Technologie Supérieure, Canada
Oussama Kallel	Faculté des Sciences de Bizerte, Tunisia
Shafaq Khan	University of Windsor, Canada
Asad Khattak	Zayed University, UAE
Hamamache Kheddouci	Université Lyon 1, France
Anis Koubaa	Prince Sultan University, Saudi Arabia
Haroon Malik	Marshall University, USA
Wathiq Mansour	University of Dubai, UAE
Sami Miniaoui	University of Dubai, UAE
Petrus Nzerem	Nile University of Nigeria, Nigeria
Fatma Outay	Zayed University, UAE
Luca Reggiani	Politecnico di Milano, Italy
Abdulganiyu Sanusi	Nile University of Nigeria, Nigeria
Thar Baker	University of Khorfakkan, Sharjah, United Arab Emirates
Mohamed Tabaa	École Marocaine des Sciences de l'Ingénieur (EMSI), Morocco
Marouane Trimeche	ESPRIT School of Business, Tunisia
Naoufel Werghi	Khalifa University, UAE

Contents

Technology Adoption and Management

Intelligent Networking and Cybersecurity

Blockchain Based Task Offloading for Parked Vehicular Cloud

Soukeina Zouaidi(✉) and Hafawa Messaoudi

ESPRIT School of Engineering, Tunis, Tunisia
soukeina.zouaidi@esprit.tn, hafawa.messaoudi@esprit.tn

Abstract. The emergence of Vehicular Cloud Computing has revolutionized the ability to perform resource-intensive applications. This advancement relies on task offloading between vehicles or between vehicles and cloud servers. However, ensuring secure offloading is a challenge. To overcome this, Blockchain is a promising solution. In this paper, we propose a Blockchain-based solution for Vehicular Cloud Computing environment. Specifically, we introduce a model for parked vehicles, where vehicles offload their tasks to each other. The performance evaluation of this model demonstrates that Blockchain technology provides a trustworthy and cost-effective solution.

Keywords: Blockchain · Task offloading · Vehicular Cloud Computing

1 Introduction

Vehicular Cloud Computing (VCC) [1] is a promising paradigm that leverages the underutilized resources of vehicles and conventional cloud infrastructures to support resource-intensive applications.

Task offloading is a fundamental concept in VCC. It allows vehicles to transfer computational tasks to nearby vehicles or cloud servers to perform resource intensive applications [2]. The decision making of secure offloading is a critical factor in ensuring the success of task offloading. Indeed, the selection of trusted vehicles or cloud servers to handle offloaded tasks directly impacts the reliability and performance of the entire system.

Blockchain technology is an emerging solution for securing transaction management [3], such as task offloading. Indeed, this technology guarantees that each transaction is recorded on an immutable ledger, ensuring transparency and verifiability throughout the process.

In this paper, we address the use of Blockchain technology to secure task offloading within a vehicular cloud model. The model consists of parked vehicles that offload computational tasks between them, while recording each offloading task on a Blockchain.

F. Kamoun et al. (Eds.): AFRICATEK 2025, LNICST 677, pp. 3–8, 2026.
https://doi.org/10.1007/978-3-032-16638-8_1

The remainder of this paper is structured as follows: Sect. 2 reviews related works. Section 3 presents the system model. Section 4 presents the proposed smart contract for task offloading. Sections 5 and 6 present the performance evaluation and the security analysis of the proposed solution. Finally, Sect. 7 concludes this paper.

2 Related Works

In this section, we review some related works on task offloading and Blockchain in VCC environment.

The computation offloading for VCC scenarios was explored in [4]. Indeed, an approach that makes opportunistic use of existing resources has been proposed. The performance evaluation of this approach demonstrates its efficiency in handling resource intensive tasks by reducing the total offloading time and increasing the offloading success rate.

The multi-task offloading for VCC was investigated in [5]. This problem was addressed while representing the tasks and Vehicular Clouds (VCs), including their interconnections as no-directed weighted graphs. It is expressed as a non-linear integer programming problem with constraints related to the limited connectivity between vehicles and the resources availability. The performance evaluation of the proposed approach considers various scenario sizes, focusing on balancing task execution time and data transfer cost.

The cooperative task offloading for VCC was studied in [6]. This problem was addressed while dividing the task into linked subtasks which are processed across various vehicles in the VC to reduce the total processing time. The performance evaluation of the proposed scheme shows that it can greatly enhance the use of computing resources while ensuring minimal latency and maintaining system stability.

The Blockchain technology was leveraged to secure computation offloading for VCC in [7]. This work adopts a hierarchical Blockchain framework to facilitate the trust management. This hierarchical framework consists of 3 Blockchain levels : vehicles, RSU and Cloud. Due to the diverse resource dispersion in the network and the specific performance needs of each blockchain, a series of customized consensus protocols are meticulously developed. In addition, this work implements a smart contract-based Deep Reinforcement Learning to secure and enhance the adaptability of the offloading process. The performance evaluation of this work shows its efficiency in terms of robustness, scalability and adaptability.

The Blockchain technology was leveraged also to secure a vehicular fog cloud network in [8]. The scheduling problem considers challenges related to mobility-aware applications and is formulated using convex optimization. Performance evaluation demonstrates the efficiency of the proposed solution compared to baseline schemes.

By analyzing the reviewed literature, we found that only a few studies have explored the use of Blockchain for VCC. Moreover, aspects such as transaction cost and execution cost have not been adequately addressed in existing

Blockchain based solutions. The performance aspects addressed in the related works are summarized in Table 1. Therefore, this work aims to investigate the application of Blockchain in the context of VCC with a particular focus on analyzing transaction and execution costs.

Table 1. Performance aspects addressed in related works

Reference	Performance Aspects Addressed
[4]	Offloading time Success offloading rate
[5]	Task execution time Data transfer cost
[6]	Average response time System stability
[7]	Robustness Scalability Adaptability
[8]	Computation cost Communication cost Offloading time

3 System Model

The proposed system consists of three types of parked vehicles that share computational resources by offloading tasks among themselves, as illustrated in Fig. 1:

- **Requester Vehicle:** a vehicle that requests task offloading to execute an application.
- **Provider Vehicle:** a vehicle that executes offloaded task of a requester vehicle.
- **Coordinator Vehicle:** manages a local Blockchain for task offloading coordination, which is facilitated by a smart contract.

4 The Proposed Smart Contract

The key functionalities of the task offloading smart contract are:

1. **Vehicle Registration**
   When a vehicle wants to join the system, it sends a registration request to the coordinator. This latter generates a unique identifier for this vehicle and creates a Blockchain transaction to store the vehicle's identity and its resource capabilities.

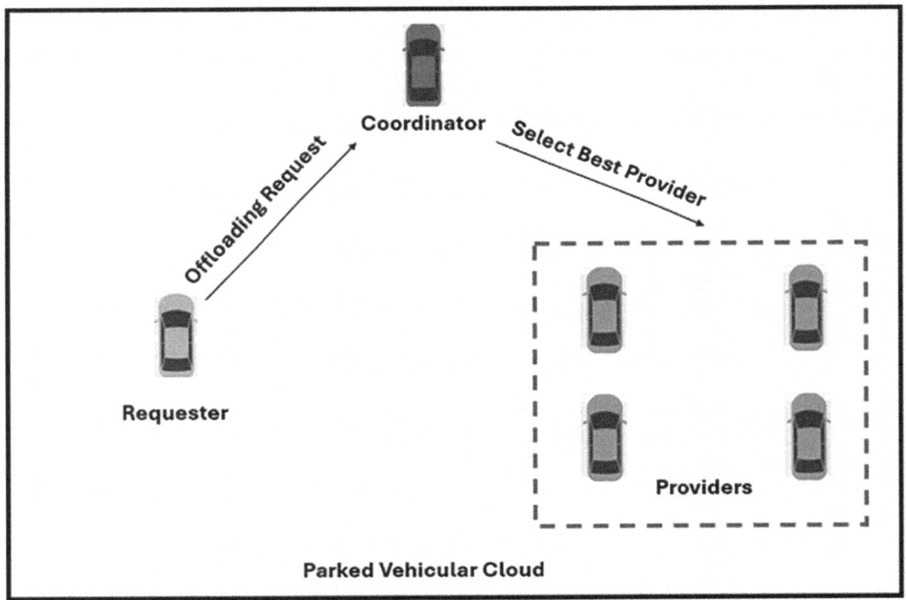

Fig. 1. System model

2. **Task Offloading Request**
   When a vehicle does not have enough computational resources to run an application, it submits an offloading request to the coordinator specifying the task and the required resources.
3. **Provider Selection**
   Upon the reception of the offloading request, the coordinator selects the provider based on the availability of required resources and the reputation score stored on the Blockchain. The selected vehicle should have the highest reputation score.
4. **Task Execution and Verification**
   The provider vehicle accomplishes the execution. Then, an execution status is recorded. After that, the requester verifies the result. If the result is valid and no suspicious behavior is detected, the reputation score of the provider is incremented.
5. **Vehicle Revocation**
   If suspicious behavior is detected, the provider's registration is revoked. Thus, this latter is marked as unregistered, and removed from the Bockchain network.
6. **Reputation Management**
   Upon joining the system, the reputation score of the vehicle is initialized to zero. The reputation score is stored on the Blockchain, to ensure transparency and tamper-resistance. The initial score of zero indicates that the vehicle has not completed any tasks yet and cannot be considered highly trustworthy at

first. As the vehicle performs tasks successfully, the reputation score is incremented. If the vehicle fails to complete a task, its reputation score decreases. The updated reputation score is stored in the Blockchain for future selection processes.

5 Performance Evaluation

To evaluate the feasibility of the proposed task offloading approach, we simulate its execution under Ethereum. Solidity is used as a language to create the smart contract.

In this evaluation, we focus on two key metrics: execution cost and transaction cost, as these metrics are crucial for evaluating the efficiency of smart contract operations in a Blockchain environment. The execution cost is related to the internal processes of the smart contract i.e. the cost associated to the computational operations while the transaction cost is the cost associated with sending data to the Blockchain.

Figure 2 shows the evaluation results. The transaction and execution costs are at reasonable levels, especially when compared to those reported in [9]. This demonstrates that the system can handle larger data sizes without significant limitations. Although transaction costs are inherently higher than execution costs due to data transmission fees and contract deployment, this difference remains small and acceptable. These results indicate that our smart contract is well-designed to be cost-effective.

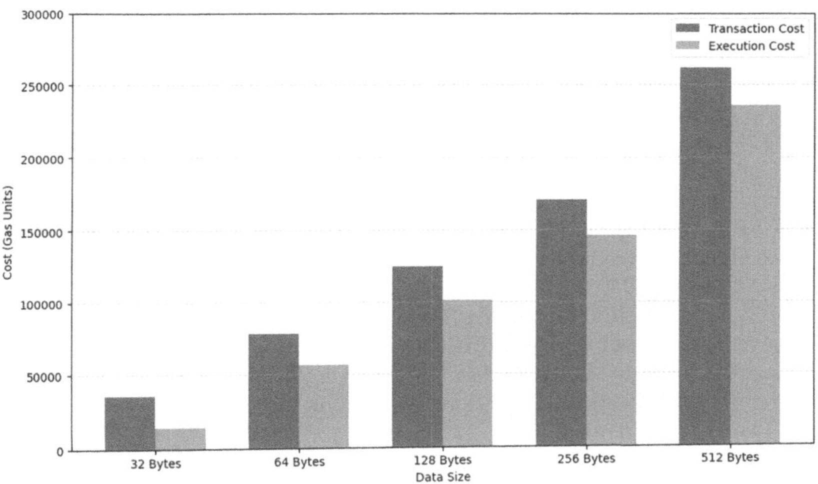

Fig. 2. Transaction cost & Execution cost

6 Security Analysis

When a vehicle is detected as potential malicious, the smart contract automatically triggers a revocation mechanism. This revocation process is essential in preventing any fraudulent activity and protecting the integrity of the network. With this feature, the smart contract not only ensures the security of the other involved vehicles but also strengthens trust in the overall system.

7 Conclusion

This paper presents a Blockchain-based task offloading approach for the vehicular cloud model. The proposed solution implements a smart contract, which not only enhances trust within the network but also ensures cost-effectiveness for the Blockchain. The future work will address the use of Blockchain to secure edge/fog computing environments.

References

1. Zouaidi, S., Belghith, A., Lengliz, I.: Vehicular cloud architectures: taxonomy, security and challenges. In: IEEE/ACS 16th International Conference on Computer Systems and Applications, Abu Dhabi, UAE (2019)
2. Manzoor, A., Raza, S., Mirza, MA., Aziz, A., Manzoor, AK, Khan, WU., Li, J., Han, Z.: A survey on vehicular task offloading: Classification, issues, and challenges. J. King Saud Univ.-Comput. Inf. Sci. **34**(7), 4135–4162 (2022)
3. Alghamdi, T.A., Khalid, R., Javaid, N.: A survey of blockchain based systems: scalability issues and solutions. Appl. Futur. Chall., IEEE Access **12**, 79626–79651 (2024)
4. de Souza, A.B., Leal Rego, P.A., de Souza, J.N.: Exploring computation offloading in vehicular clouds. In: IEEE 8th International Conference on Cloud Networking, Coimbra, Portugal (2019)
5. LiWang, M., Gao, Z. , Hosseinalipour, S., Dai, H.: Multi-task offloading over vehicular clouds under graph-based representation. In: IEEE International Conference on Communications, Dublin, Ireland (2020)
6. Sun, F., Hou, F., Cheng, N., Wang, M., Zhou, H., Gui, L., Shen, X.: Cooperative task scheduling for computation offloading in vehicular cloud. IEEE Trans. Veh. Technol. **67**(11), 11049–11061 (2018)
7. Xu, S., Guo, C., Hu, R.Q., Qian, Y.: Blockchain inspired secure computation offloading in a vehicular cloud network. IEEE Internet Things J. **9**(16), 14723–14740 (2022)
8. Lakhan, A., Ahmad, M., Bilal, M., Jolfaei, A., Mehmood, R.M.: Mobility aware blockchain enabled offloading and scheduling in vehicular fog cloud computing. IEEE Trans. Intell. Transp. Syst. **22**(7), 4212–4223 (2021)
9. Khalid, A., Iftikhar, M.S., Almogren, A., Khalid, R., Afzal, M.K., Javaid, N.: A blockchain based incentive provisioning scheme for traffic event validation and information storage in VANETs. Inf. Process. Manag. **58**(2) (2021)

A Context-Aware Biometric Access Control Framework Powered by Large Language Models

Hmimou Yasser[1,2], Mohamed Tabaa[1](✉), Zineb Hidila[1], and Azeddine Khiat[2]

[1] Multidisciplinary Laboratory of Research and Innovation (LPRI), Moroccan School of Engineering Sciences (EMSI), Casablanca, Morocco
m.tabaa@emsi.ma

[2] 2IACS Laboratory, ENSET, Hassan II University, Casablanca, Morocco

Abstract. Modern access control systems must go beyond identity verification to provide accuracy, adaptability, and immediate threat detection. To address these needs, we present Guardian Agent, a multi-layered security architecture combining fingerprint recognition, RFID badge validation, and contextual reasoning powered by large language models (LLMs). The agent conducts a staged verification process where biometric credentials are cross-checked with secure databases while behavioral and environmental indicators are simultaneously analyzed. Unlike static rule-based approaches, the LLM enables dynamic risk assessment by interpreting schedules, usage patterns, and coherence between credentials, thereby enhancing anomaly detection. Experimental evaluation shows promising performance, achieving 99.1% fingerprint matching accuracy and a 96.1% fraud detection rate, while maintaining low latency for real-time decision making.

Keywords: Large language model · Adaptive access control · Context-aware threat detection

1 Introduction

Contemporary security environments demand access control systems that extend beyond static identity verification. Traditional authentication methods, including passwords, access cards, and single-modal biometric systems remain widely adopted due to their simplicity. However, they are increasingly ineffective in dynamic threat contexts, as they are vulnerable to impersonation, credential theft, and unauthorized reuse, particularly when deployed in isolation [3, 4].

To overcome these limitations, recent approaches have emphasized adaptive access control mechanisms that incorporate behavioral and environmental indicators. These systems analyze temporal and spatial usage patterns, detect anomalies in user behavior, and infer potential threats based on deviations from normative data [1, 5]. The use of machine learning has enhanced this process, enabling models to identify subtle or evolving attack behaviors more effectively than conventional rule-based systems [6, 12].

F. Kamoun et al. (Eds.): AFRICATEK 2025, LNICST 677, pp. 9–18, 2026.
https://doi.org/10.1007/978-3-032-16638-8_2

In parallel, advances in large-scale transformer-based language models have introduced new opportunities for contextual reasoning in security applications. Though originally developed for natural language tasks, these models have demonstrated strong capabilities in interpreting structured authentication data, including sensor outputs, access logs, and credential histories [2, 9]. Their ability to correlate heterogeneous inputs allows them to generate dynamic risk scores and support real-time decision-making in access control scenarios.

This paper presents the Guardian Agent: a modular and scalable access control framework that integrates fingerprint recognition, RFID badge validation, and contextual threat evaluation using a large language model accessed via real-time inference. Rather than relying exclusively on credential matching, the system evaluates user behavior, access timing, and the coherence of badge-biometric pairings to calculate a trust score for each access request [14].

Designed for operational efficiency and seamless integration, the architecture supports rapid identity verification while adhering to zero-trust principles by continuously validating both user identity and contextual intent [10, 13].

The paper are following: Sect. 2 surveys related work in biometric systems, context-aware access control, and semantic reasoning for security. Section 3 outlines the system design and methodology. Section 4 presents experimental validation, and Sect. 5 concludes with key findings and avenues for future development (Table 1).

Table 1. Table of abbreviations

Abbreviation	Full term
LLM	Large Language Model
API	Application Programming Interface
RFID	Radio Frequency Identification
CPU	Central Processing Unit
GPU	Graphics Processing Unit
ISO/IEC	International Organization for Standardization/International Electrotechnical Commission
NFC	Near Field Communication
DB	Database

2 Literature Review

Traditional access control systems, which often rely on passwords or ID cards, are increasingly exposed to vulnerabilities such as identity theft, phishing and social engineering. To address these limitations, biometric authentication, in particular fingerprint recognition, has become a fundamental component of secure identification systems [4, 7]. Fingerprint systems are valued for their accuracy and ease of implementation, but they remain sensitive to sensor noise, identity theft and environmental interference [16].

To improve robustness, researchers have turned to multimodal biometric systems that combine several input sources, such as fingerprints, RFID badges, facial recognition and behavioral data. This fusion of modalities compensates for the limitations of individual techniques, significantly reducing erroneous rejection and acceptance rates [6, 8]. A recent study by Thejaswin et al. demonstrated the effectiveness of fusing gait and facial data using a context-aware deep learning model, achieving both high accuracy and good explainability in person identification tasks [11, 12, 16].

Another major advance is the integration of contextual mechanisms into access control systems. Instead of simply checking static identification information, modern systems monitor behavioral and environmental cues, such as irregularities in access times, geographical anomalies or usage patterns, to identify suspicious activity [1, 5]. Noor et al. proposed a context-aware threat detection model for intelligent cyber-physical systems that dynamically evaluates these indicators, reducing response time to emerging threats [12].

Beyond rule-based engines, AI and machine learning models are now the basis of many adaptive authentication systems. These models can identify usage trends, detect anomalies and continuously refine user profiles. Bansal et al. explored the role of reinforcement learning and model-based strategies for continuous verification, confirming significant improvements in authentication reliability [6]. Ayeswarya and Singh presented a comprehensive review of secure biometric-based continuous authentication systems, focusing on the increasing use of deep learning in real-time user profiling [13]. In the latest wave of innovation, large language models (LLMs) are being applied to cybersecurity and identity management tasks. Feretzakis and Verykios have demonstrated that LLMs can reason about structured access logs and behavioral histories, out-performing static logic models in contextual anomaly detection [9]. These capabilities make LLMs ideal for real-time risk assessment and anomaly detection during access attempts.

Collectively, these developments point to an evolution from static, ad hoc authentication models to adaptive, contextual and intelligent access control frameworks. The system proposed in this article, the Guardian Agent, builds on this evolution by integrating fingerprint recognition, RFID badge validation and LLM-based behavioral inference to ensure secure and responsive access decisions.

3 Methodology

The general architecture of our proposed *Guardian Agent* system is illustrated in Fig. 1, which captures the flow between data acquisition, verification, reasoning, and decision execution components. It was designed with modularity in mind, enabling flexible deployment, real-time reasoning, and separation of functional responsibilities. The methodology comprises four key stages: biometric and badge data acquisition, backend identity verification, context collection, and final reasoning through a language model.

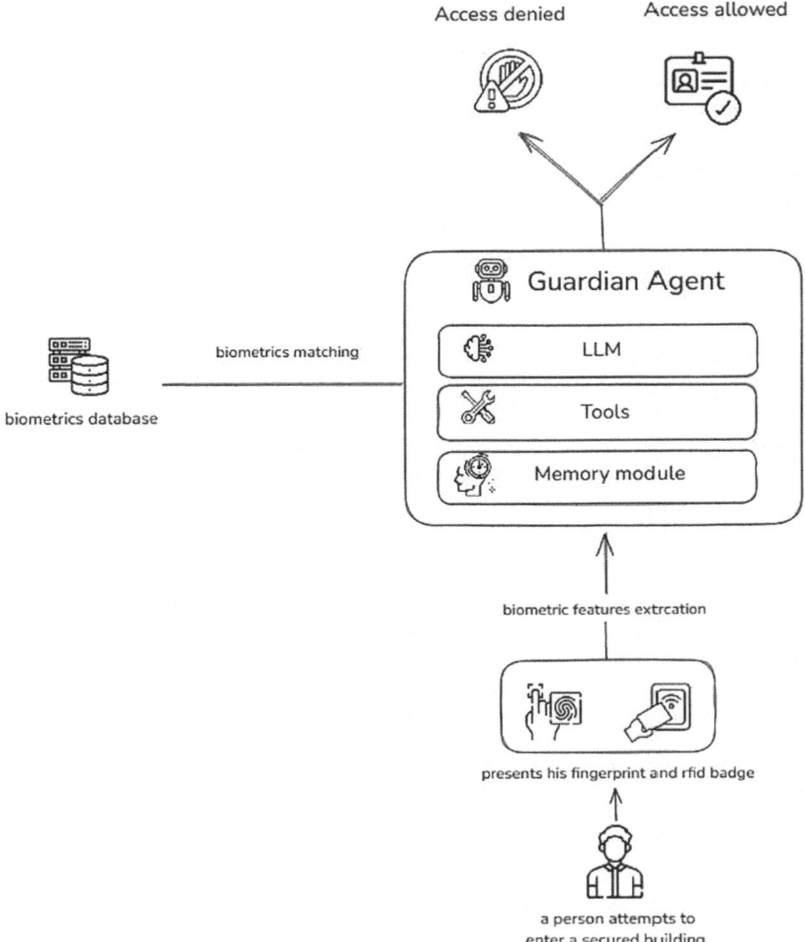

Fig. 1. Architecture and operational flow of the Guardian Agent

3.1 Biometric Acquisition and Input Capture

Each time a person attempts to access a secure area, the system initiates the authentication sequence by simultaneously capturing two primary biometric data: a fingerprint and the reading of an RFID badge. These two inputs form the basis of the identity verification process, guaranteeing both physiological and possession-based authentication. The fingerprint is captured by a high-resolution sensor with built-in feature extraction capabilities, enabling the generation of efficient and secure templates. At the same time, the RFID reader captures relevant information from the badge, including the user's unique identifier and assigned access level, enabling the ID card to be linked to system-level authorizations.

Immediately after acquisition, both data streams are transmitted to the Guardian agent for centralized processing. This real-time acquisition strategy ensures that the system always operates with up-to-date, context-sensitive data, avoiding the risks associated with out-of-date or statically stored information, and enhancing the reliability of the initial verification phase.

3.2 Identity Verification and Database Matching

Once the biometric data has been acquired, the guard proceeds with identity verification by cross-checking the data against a secure, encrypted biometric database. The captured fingerprint is first processed by a minutiae-based feature extraction algorithm, which encodes the unique features into a compact feature vector. This vector is then compared with existing patterns in the database using cosine similarity, generating a match score that quantifies the probability of identity match.

At the same time, the system validates the RFID badge by querying the same database. This verification ensures that the badge is genuine, currently active and correctly associated with the person who submitted the fingerprint. By performing this validation in parallel, the system confirms both physiological and possession-based identity tags. To ensure real-time performance, the verification logic is executed via a secure MongoDB API, enabling fast, simultaneous queries and low-latency searches. This architecture enables the system to scale efficiently while maintaining data integrity and access speed.

Together, these double-checking mechanisms provide a strong defense against identity theft or badge misuse, ensuring that physical biometric data and associated digital information always match stored and authorized records.

3.3 Contextual Risk Evaluation Using LLM

While biometric matching remains a core element of identity verification, it is often insufficient in isolation, particularly in high-security environments where behavioral context plays a critical role. To address this limitation, the Guardian Agent incorporates a contextual reasoning layer powered by a pre-trained large language model (LLM). This layer enhances decision-making by evaluating both behavioral patterns and environmental signals associated with each access attempt, enabling the system to detect risks that may not be evident from credential checks alone [14].

The LLM is designed to interpret structured input data composed of various contextual indicators. These include the precise timestamp of the request, the frequency of recent failed login attempts, the historical usage of the badge, the geolocation of the access point, and the coherence between fingerprint identity and badge ownership. By synthesizing these features, the model generates a dynamic risk score, offering a more nuanced and probabilistic assessment of access legitimacy.

For instance, if a badge is used at an unusual hour, or if access patterns diverge from the user's historical behavior, the LLM flags the event for further analysis. Unlike rigid rule-based systems, this layer introduces adaptive intelligence, enabling the framework to respond in real time to subtle anomalies and evolving threat vectors.

Through this mechanism, the Guardian Agent gains enhanced resistance to identity fraud, badge cloning, and behavioral manipulation, offering a significant improvement in contextual awareness compared to traditional access control systems (Fig. 2).

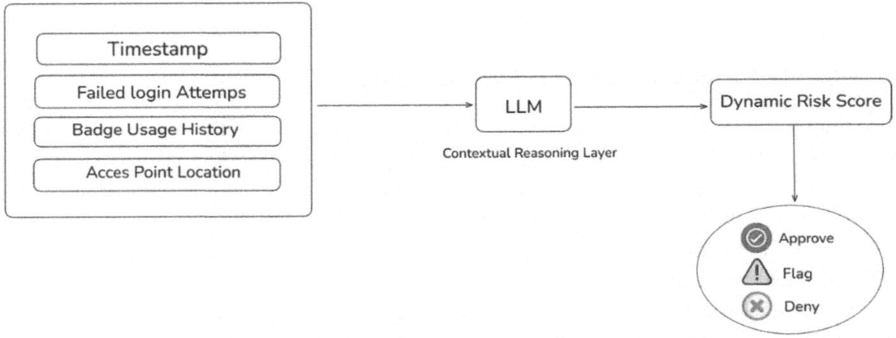

Fig. 2. Contextual risk evaluation using a Large Language Model (LLM)

3.4 Decision Fusion and Final Access Resolution

The final stage of the Guardian Agent workflow involves decision fusion, where results from the biometric verification and the contextual risk assessment are integrated to make an informed access decision. As illustrated in Fig. 1, this step consolidates the full pipeline from data acquisition through reasoning to determine whether to grant or deny entry based on a holistic understanding of identity and behavior [11, 15].

This fusion process relies on a weighted decision model that balances biometric confidence with contextual trust. When both the fingerprint and badge verifications yield high-confidence results, and the contextual indicators suggest normal behavior, the system grants access immediately. However, in cases where biometric results are valid but contextual cues such as atypical access times or inconsistent usage histories raise suspicion, the system adopts a more cautious posture. It may log the event for review, flag it for escalation, or request additional user verification.

If either the biometric matching fails or the contextual confidence score falls below an acceptable threshold, the system decisively denies access. This dual-layered evaluation ensures that even if physical credentials are compromised, behavioral irregularities can still trigger protective actions.

All decisions are processed in real time and recorded in a secure audit trail for future analysis, system tuning, or behavioral tracking. This approach not only increases resistance to spoofing and misuse but also enhances overall system robustness by reducing false positives and catching subtle, unauthorized access attempts.

In combining both identity precision and contextual reasoning, the Guardian Agent delivers a highly adaptive and intelligent access control mechanism capable of responding to dynamic threat conditions [14].

4 Discussion

4.1 System Implementation and Test Environment

The Guardian Agent was implemented as a modular and extensible system, optimized for real-time, context-aware access control. The architecture leverages a suite of open-source tools and libraries to promote transparency, reproducibility, and ease of integration across diverse infrastructure environments.

Fingerprint data is acquired through a high-resolution sensor and processed using a combination of OpenCV and DeepPrint, enabling precise minutiae extraction and compact biometric feature encoding. In parallel, RFID badge data is captured using a 13.56 MHz NFC reader compliant with the ISO/IEC 14443 standard. The badge information is transmitted via serial communication using PySerial and validated against credential records stored in a MongoDB database. For biometric matching, cosine similarity is computed between the acquired fingerprint vector and enrolled templates to assess identity confidence.

Contextual reasoning is performed using a large-scale language model based on the LLaMA 3.2 architecture, comprising 90 billion parameters, and accessed via the Groq API. The model receives structured metadata, including temporal access patterns, badge usage history, login attempts, and biometric-credential coherence and returns a contextual trust score for each access request. This API-based deployment allows the system to offload high-complexity semantic inference to the cloud, achieving low-latency, high-throughput analysis without the computational burden of on-premises model hosting. This design also enhances scalability and enables compatibility with constrained or edge environments.

System integration is managed through lightweight middleware that orchestrates the biometric matching, credential verification, and language model inference processes in real time. The complete framework was evaluated on a workstation equipped with a 12-core CPU, 64 GB of RAM, and an NVIDIA RTX A4000 GPU, although all language model processing was conducted remotely through Groq's cloud infrastructure. Testing in a simulated environment comprising both standard and adversarial access scenarios demonstrated an end-to-end system latency consistently under 200 ms confirming the solution's readiness for deployment in high-security, time-sensitive access control contexts.

4.2 Evaluation Metrics

To ensure a comprehensive and quantitative evaluation of the Guardian Agent, we adopted a set of well-defined performance metrics that assess biometric reliability, contextual judgment, credential integrity, fraud resistance, and system responsiveness. These metrics and their mathematical definitions are presented in Table 2.

Table 2. Summary of system performance across all Guardian Agent

Metric	Formula	Description
Fingerprint Matching Accuracy (FMA)	$FMA = \frac{TP}{TP+FN} \times 100$	Measures how accurately the system accepts legitimate users during biometric verification
False Acceptance Rate (FAR)	$FAR = \frac{FP}{FP+TN}$	Indicates the probability of unauthorized users being granted access
False Rejection Rate (FRR)	$FRR = \frac{FN}{TP+FN}$	Represents the rate at which legitimate users are incorrectly denied access
Credential Consistency Rate (CCR)	$CCR = \frac{\text{Valid Pairs}}{\text{Total Attempts}} \times 100$	Assesses whether the fingerprint and RFID badge belong to the same registered user
Contextual Trust Score Accuracy (CTSA)	$CTSA = \frac{\text{Correct LLM Judgments}}{\text{Evaluated Cases}} \times 100$	Reflects the LLM's accuracy in correctly interpreting contextual behavior patterns
Fraud Detection Rate (FDR)	$FDR = \frac{\text{Detected Attacks}}{\text{Simulated Attacks}} \times 100$	Evaluates the system's capability to detect spoofing, badge cloning, and identity attacks
Average System Latency (SL)	$SL = t\,decision - t\,input$	Measures the time (in milliseconds) between input acquisition and final access decision

4.3 Results

To evaluate the effectiveness of the Guardian Agent, we conducted experiments using two publicly available benchmark datasets. The FVC2004 DB1-B dataset [7] was employed for fingerprint verification, providing high-resolution fingerprint images with realistic noise and variability. To test contextual awareness and RFID validation, we extended the AIM RFID Access Dataset [8], which contains access logs annotated with badge IDs, access timestamps, and authentication outcomes suitable for context-aware modeling [12].

The experimental setup simulated 1,000 access sessions, comprising 700 legitimate attempts and 300 adversarial scenarios. These adversarial attempts included badge cloning, fingerprint spoofing, and behavioral anomalies. The fingerprint verification module achieved a high matching accuracy of 99.1%, with a False Acceptance Rate (FAR) of 0.9% and a False Rejection Rate (FRR) of 1.4%. The system's ability to evaluate the consistency between biometric and badge credentials measured by the Credential Consistency Rate (CCR) reached 98.6%, confirming its effectiveness in detecting mismatched or misused credentials [16].

The contextual reasoning module, powered by the LLM, achieved a Contextual Trust Score Accuracy (CTSA) of 92.4%, based on a comparison with expert-labeled ground truth. In adversarial conditions, the system also demonstrated a Fraud Detection Rate (FDR) of 96.1%, confirming its capacity to identify spoofed credentials and suspicious behavior. Average system latency (SL) was recorded at 182 ms, ensuring compliance with real-time access control requirements [16].

A detailed breakdown of system performance across all modules and evaluation criteria is presented in Table 3.

Table 3. Summary of system performance across all Guardian Agent components, evaluated using FVC2004 and AIM RFID datasets

Component/process	Metric	Value
Fingerprint verification	Fingerprint Matching Accuracy (FMA)	99.1%
	False Acceptance Rate (FAR)	0.9%
	False Rejection Rate (FRR)	1.4%
RFID + Biometric Cross-check	Credential Consistency Rate (CCR)	98.6%
Contextual Reasoning (LLM)	Contextual Trust Score Accuracy	92.4%
Fraud Resistance	Fraud Detection Rate (FDR)	96.1%
System Performance	Average System Latency (SL)	182 ms

5 Conclusion and Future Perspectives

This paper introduced the Guardian Agent, a modular and context-aware access control framework that integrates fingerprint verification, RFID badge validation, and semantic reasoning powered by a large-scale language model. By combining biometric authentication with contextual analysis, the system delivers a responsive and intelligent mechanism for managing access in dynamic environments.

The system demonstrated high accuracy in fingerprint matching and fraud detection, along with robust performance in evaluating contextual trust. Additionally, real-time response was achieved, with system latency consistently remaining under 200 ms supporting its suitability for time-sensitive deployment scenarios.

While the framework shows strong performance across key dimensions, there are opportunities to further enhance its adaptability. The current design is optimized for structured input and assumes a relatively stable operating environment. In more variable settings, such as mobile or edge-deployed systems, future iterations may benefit from enhanced support for noisy or incomplete contextual signals. The language model component, though effective, may also be refined for improved transparency and efficiency in constrained environments.

Our future prospects, the Guardian Agent can be extended into a cooperative multi-agent architecture, interfacing with complementary components such as surveillance modules, anomaly detectors, and access policy engines. This evolution would enable distributed decision-making, richer context sharing, and greater resilience against emerging security threats. Through this direction, we aim to contribute to the development of intelligent, scalable access control systems suited for the next generation of secure infrastructure.

References

1. Nisher, et al.: Machine learning-driven adaptive authentication: strengthening cybersecurity against high-volume data breaches. Formos. J. Multidisc. Res. **4**(2), 949–966 (2025)
2. Kasri, et al.: From vulnerability to defense: the role of large language models in enhancing cybersecurity. Computation **13**(2), 30 (2025)
3. Ouyang et al.: Personal identification and authentication in multi-task EEG database using EEGNet and Siamese network. In: 2024 International Joint Conference on Neural Networks (IJCNN), Yokohama (2024)
4. Li, et al.: MBBFAuth: multimodal behavioral biometrics fusion for continuous authentication on non-portable devices. IEEE Trans. Inf. Forensics. Secur. **19**, 10000–10015 (2024)
5. Masud, T.M., et al.: Generative fuzzer-driven vulnerability detection in the Internet of Things networks. Appl. Soft Comput. **174**, 112973 (2025)
6. Bansal et al.: Continuous authentication in the digital age: an analysis of reinforcement learning and behavioral biometrics. Computers **13**(4) (2024)
7. Maio et al.: FVC2004: Third Fingerprint Verification Competition. Berlin Springer Heidelberg (2004)
8. Fall, et al.: An RFID based access control system operating with a computer program and a database. Int. J. Circ. Syst. Signal Process. **15**, 1817–1820 (2022). https://doi.org/10.46300/9106.2021.15.195
9. Feretzakis, G., Verykios, V.S.: Trustworthy AI: securing sensitive data in large language models. AI **5**(4), 134 (2024). https://doi.org/10.3390/ai5040134
10. Al-Hammuri, K., Gebali, F., Kanan, A.: ZTCloudGuard: zero trust context-aware access management framework to avoid medical errors in the era of generative AI. AI **5**(3), 55 (2024). https://doi.org/10.3390/ai5030055
11. Thejaswin, S., Prakash, A., Nambiar, A.: Exploring fusion techniques and explainable AI on adapt-FuseNet: context-adaptive fusion of face and gait for person identification. IEEE Trans. Biometrics Behav. Identity Sci. (2024).https://doi.org/10.1109/TBIOM.2024.3405081
12. Noor, Z., Hina, S., Hayat, F., Shah, G.A.: An intelligent context-aware threat detection and response model for smart cyber-physical systems. Internet of Things **23** (2023). https://doi.org/10.1016/j.iot.2023.100843
13. Ayeswarya, S., Singh, K.J.: A comprehensive review on secure biometric-based continuous authentication and user profiling. IEEE Access (2024). https://doi.org/10.1109/ACCESS.2024.3411783
14. Shah, S.P., Deshpande, A.V.: Enforcing web security constraints for LLM-driven robot agents for online transactions. In: Proceedings of IEEE International Conference on Cybernetics and Intelligence (2024). https://doi.org/10.1109/ICDSCNC62492.2024.10939862
15. Sun, Q., Zhang, R., Liu, Y., Liu, Z., Chen, W.: Research on automatic voiceprint acquisition method based on deep learning. In: Proceedings of International Conference on Artificial Intelligence and Security, Springer (2024). https://doi.org/10.1007/978-981-96-1907-8_32
16. Mohammed, D., MacLennan, H.: Secure authentication and identity management with AI and large language models. In: AI-Driven Identity Systems, IGI Global (2025). Available: https://www.igi-global.com/chapter/secure-authentication-and-identity-management-with-ai/37447

Innovative and Secure Private Key Synchronization Mechanism Between Devices Using Peer-to-Peer Approach in Passkeys System

Assane ILBOUDO(✉), Didier BASSOLE, and Désiré GUEL

Laboratoire de Mathématiques et d'Informatique, Université Joseph Ki-Zerbo, Ouagadougou, Burkina Faso
assaneilboudo1998@gmail.com

Abstract. Passkeys are a passwordless authentication method that is increasingly being adopted. Based on asymmetric cryptography, they offer a secure and promising alternative to traditional passwords. In this paper, we propose a new secure approach for passkey synchronization based on a Peer-to-Peer mechanism between devices. Our secure services integrates biometric authentication via fingerprint or facial recognition, Wi-Fi Direct and QR codes. Also our secure approach use Elliptic Curve Diffie-Hellman algorithm for secure key exchange and Zero-Knowledge Proofs for mutual authentication in passkey system. This approach ensures the confidentiality and integrity of passkeys while eliminating reliance on central servers and strengthening protection against Man-in-the-Middle attacks and identity spoofing.

Keywords: Elliptic Curve Diffie-Hellman · Passkey system · Zero-Knowledge Proofs · Security

1 Introduction

Synchronization of passkeys via the cloud raises several challenges in terms of security, privacy, and compatibility. First, the security of passkey storage and transmission remains a major concern. If a cloud provider is compromised, an attacker could potentially access the synchronized keys. Moreover, despite the use of advanced encryption mechanisms, Man-in-the-Middle (MITM) attacks can exploit vulnerabilities in the transmission protocol to intercept data. Additionally, cloud-based synchronization solutions, such as those integrated in Windows 11, still face challenges regarding secure transmission and interoperability [1]. Another risk lies in cloud credential theft, which could allow an attacker

F. Kamoun et al. (Eds.): AFRICATEK 2025, LNICST 677, pp. 19–32, 2026.
https://doi.org/10.1007/978-3-032-16638-8_3

to gain access to remotely stored passkeys. Furthermore, reliance on a third-party provider introduces a single point of failure. Changes in terms of service, sudden service shutdowns, or restrictions imposed by the provider can compromise access to passkeys. Recent efforts, such as the FIDO Alliance's Credential Exchange Protocol (CXP), aim to address these concerns by improving passkey portability across platforms. Additionally, the centralization of data in a third-party cloud raises concerns about sovereignty and control over one's own keys. The incompatibility between different platforms presents another major obstacle. Some services, such as Apple's iCloud Keychain, are not interoperable with other ecosystems, limiting the portability of passkeys [2,3]. While Microsoft has introduced cross-platform passkey synchronization in Windows 11, full standardization remains a challenge.

To effectively address these challenges, we propose an innovative and secure approach to passkey synchronization, based on a peer-to-peer (P2P) pairing mechanism. Unlike traditional centralized solutions, this method operates independently of any third-party server, thereby ensuring greater system resilience and enhanced user control over sensitive data. The remainder of this article is organized as follows: Sect. 2 presents related works. Section 3 discusses our methodological approach and we conclude this study in Sect. 4.

2 Related Works

Hofmann et al. [4] conducted an in-depth study on end-to-end encrypted (E2EE) cloud storage solutions and highlighted critical vulnerabilities compromising data confidentiality. Laud et al. [5] developed a server-assisted decryption scheme to improve cryptographic key management in a cloud environment. However, this approach relies on a trust model where the server must be reliable, which poses risks in the case of an insider attack. Blessing et al. [6] proposed key synchronization via the cloud to mitigate device loss and associated complications. However, cloud reliability raises concerns regarding security and trust. Lueks et al. [7] introduced Tandem, a key synchronization and security protocol using a central server while preserving user privacy. However, reliance on a central server raises security and reliability concerns in case of compromise, as well as questions about the trustworthiness of cloud services. Backendal et al. [8] conducted a formal analysis of E2EE systems for the cloud, revealing critical vulnerabilities (e.g., MEGA) that could compromise data. They introduced a security model based on cryptographic games and a CSS scheme with formal proofs, using OPRF and AEAD to secure storage and sharing. However, they also highlighted limitations, particularly the risks of adaptive compromise and the challenge of balancing provable security with practical functionalities. Reisinger et al. [9] proposed the SEPPI architecture to secure meeting invitations on unified communication platforms by leveraging FIDO2 authentication. This approach aims to enhance the confidentiality and integrity of invitations while limiting participant traceability. However, SEPPI's centralization introduces a single point of failure, raising concerns about availability and security, especially against attacks targeting its infrastructure.

Khawaja et al. [10] proposed a collaborative approach combining Wi-Fi Direct and Bluetooth for ad hoc distributed systems. This method leverages the advantages of Wi-Fi Direct, including its high throughput and speed, while utilizing Bluetooth for its fast pairing and low energy consumption. However, their approach has security shortcomings, particularly the lack of mechanisms ensuring confidentiality, data integrity, and protection against identity spoofing. Dang et al. [11] introduced the Enhanced Wireless Direct Connectivity (EWDC) approach, integrating DECT-2020 and Wi-Fi to improve direct wireless communication. By replacing the vulnerable BLE with DECT-2020 for device discovery and using Wi-Fi for high-speed data transfer, they enhance security. Additionally, the incorporation of WireGuard VPN encrypts Wi-Fi Direct transmissions. Wu et al. [12] proposed an approach using ProVerif for security analysis of Bluetooth protocols, covering Bluetooth Classic, BLE, and Mesh. Their modular approach allows for the examination of different protocol configurations and their interactions. The model revealed 82 security violations, including two previously undiscovered vulnerabilities—one affecting Mesh provisioning (CVE-2020-26560) and another enabling inter-protocol attacks between Bluetooth Classic and BLE. Ayoub et al. [13] demonstrated the feasibility of a "Screaming Channels" attack on Bluetooth Low Energy, enabling cryptographic key extraction through electromagnetic emissions. While this attack highlights critical hardware vulnerabilities, it underscores ongoing challenges in maintaining confidentiality and preventing identity spoofing in wireless environments. Niebla-Montero et al. [14] proposed an Opportunistic Edge Computing (OEC) architecture combining Bluetooth 5 and Wize to enhance RFID communications in opportunistic vehicular scenarios. The approach utilizes Bluetooth 5 for its low energy consumption and BLE mesh support, while Wize exploits the 169 MHz band for long-range communications. Experimental tests evaluated latency and packet loss between a fixed roadside unit and a moving vehicle. The results showed that Bluetooth 5 offers better reliability with fewer packet losses, whereas Wize ensures lower latency at the cost of higher energy consumption.

3 Methodological Approach

Current passkey synchronization solutions relying on central servers raise significant security concerns, particularly regarding the risks of compromise and the loss of sensitive data confidentiality. Furthermore, peer-to-peer (P2P) approaches based on technologies such as Wi-Fi Direct and Bluetooth exhibit notable vulnerabilities in terms of confidentiality, data integrity, and protection against identity spoofing.

To address these shortcomings, we propose an enhanced P2P synchronization mechanism that integrates Wi-Fi Direct for connectivity, QR codes for pairing initialization, secure key exchange via the Elliptic Curve Diffie-Hellman (ECDH) protocol, and Zero-Knowledge Proofs (ZKPs) to ensure reliable mutual authentication. This architecture guarantees both the confidentiality and integrity of passkeys while eliminating reliance on centralized infrastructure and providing effective protection against man-in-the-middle attacks and identity spoofing attempts.

The Fig. 1 highlights an advanced passkey synchronization mechanism based on secure Peer-to-Peer pairing and integrating End-to-End Encryption.

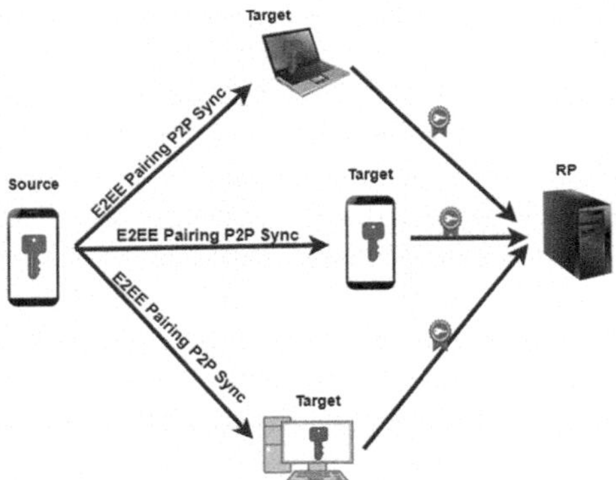

Fig. 1. Private key synchronization mechanism via Peer-to-Peer pairing

This process aims to enable the sharing and recovery of passkeys across multiple devices without relying on a centralized server while ensuring a high level of security and privacy. In this architecture, the Source represents the initial device that holds the original passkey. This device acts as the starting point in the synchronization process, initiating the secure transfer of the passkey to other devices designated as Targets. The Targets are the recipient devices to which the passkey will be replicated, ensuring that the user can seamlessly access their services from multiple terminals. To prevent interception or tampering, the synchronization relies on a secure P2P pairing protocol based on advanced cryptographic mechanisms such as Elliptic Curve Diffie-Hellman and Zero-Knowledge Proofs.

This mechanism ensures the direct transmission of passkeys between the Source and the Targets, without requiring intermediate storage on a remote server. As a result, each synchronized device becomes a trusted node capable of storing and using the passkey for authentication. This approach not only enhances the system's resilience by enabling easy passkey recovery in case of device loss but also strengthens security by mitigating risks associated with attacks on centralized servers.

Our passkey synchronization mechanism is based on the following steps in Fig. 2.

- **Pairing Initialization:** The source device and the target devices establish a secure communication channel via QR code. This phase includes the exchange of the necessary parameters for the connection;
- **Device Identity Verification:** Each device mutually authenticates using a cryptographic protocol based on Zero-Knowledge Proofs, ensuring that no malicious actor can infiltrate the process;

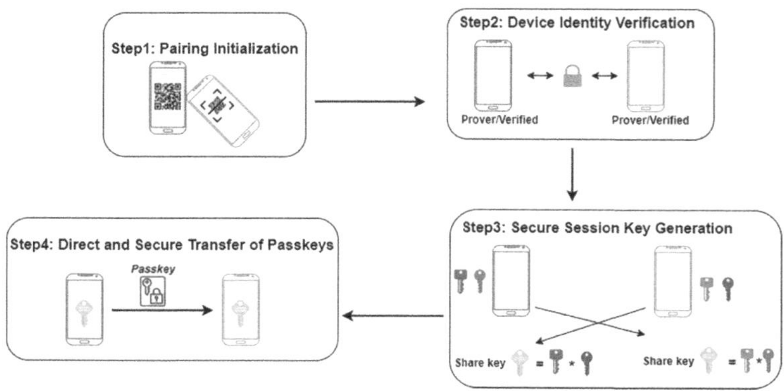

Fig. 2. The different steps of our approach

- **Secure Session Key Generation:** A temporary session key is derived from a shared secret between the devices using Elliptic Curve Diffie-Hellman, ensuring the confidentiality and integrity of the exchanges;
- **Direct and Secure Transfer of Passkeys:** The passkey is encrypted with the session key and transmitted to the target device, which securely stores it in its hardware enclave or a TPM/HSM module.

3.1 Pairing Initialization

In the pairing process, two devices are involved: the source device A and the target device B. To establish a secure connection between them, device A generates a QR code containing several essential pieces of information, including:

- Its identifier IdA;
- Its encrypted ECDH public key (C_{A}) to ensure confidentiality. The encryption is performed using the following functions:
  1. Generation of a biometric secret key via HKDF

$$K_{biom} = HKDF\,(\text{fingerprint/facial recognition}\,,\,\text{salt})$$

  2. Encryption of the public key device A via AES-GCM

$$C_A = AES - GCM\,(\mathrm{K}_{biom}\,,\,\mathrm{pub}_A)$$

- A random nonce to prevent replay attacks;
- Details of the Wi-Fi Direct channel, including the SSID and password.

To ensure the integrity of these data, a cryptographic hash is computed using the SHA-256 algorithm according to the following formula:

$$K_A = H\,(\mathrm{Id}_A \,||\, \mathrm{C}_A \,||\, \text{nonce} \,||\, \text{SSID} \,||\, \text{password})$$

where H() represents the SHA-256 hashing function. During pairing, device B scans the QR code displayed by device A and extracts the data. It then verifies their integrity by recalculating the cryptographic hash using the same method:

$$K_B = H\,(\mathrm{Id}_A\,||\,\mathrm{C}_A\,||\,\mathrm{nonce}\,||\,\mathrm{SSID}\,||\,\mathrm{password})$$

It then compares the obtained value with the one provided by device A. If

$$K_B = K_A$$

this confirms that the data is intact and has not been altered. Otherwise, the pairing is rejected.

Once this verification is successful, device B uses the information from the QR code to initiate the Wi-Fi Direct connection based on the provided SSID and password. It also retrieves the public key of device A.

Next, device B generates the same biometric secret key k_{biom} as device A, using the function:

$$k_{\mathrm{biom}} = \mathrm{HKDF}(\mathrm{fingerprint/facial\ recognition}, \mathrm{salt})$$

device B then uses this key to decrypt the public key of device A:

$$\mathrm{Pub}_A = \text{AES-GCM}^{-1}(k_{\mathrm{biom}}, C_A)$$

Once the Wi-Fi Direct connection is established, B encrypts its own public key Pub_B using k_{biom}:

$$C_B = \text{AES-GCM}(k_{\mathrm{biom}}, \mathrm{Pub}_B)$$

Then, device B sends the encrypted public key C_B to device A.

Thus, both devices now hold each other's public key, ensuring a secure key exchange.

This phase establishes a secure communication channel through the scanning of a QR Code embedding public identification data. It lays the foundation for mutual trust between the two devices by ensuring the authenticity of the initial exchange and mitigating the risk of man-in-the-middle (MITM) attacks from the outset of the synchronization process.

3.2 Device Identity Verification

The goal is to enable device A and device B to prove that they each possess their private keys (privA and privB) without revealing them. This prevents any interception or falsification of their identity during the ECDH key exchange.

Device A Proves to Device B that it Knows its Private Key Device A chooses a random number r_A and creates a sort of fingerprint called a commitment with its private key privA. The commitment is calculated as follows:

$$e_A = g^{r_A} \mod p$$

where:

Algorithm 1 Secure Pairing Initialization

Require: Device A: IdA, pubA, nonce, SSID, password, kbiom
Ensure: Secure connection and key exchange
▷ Generation of a biometric secret key via HKDF by device A
$Kbiom \leftarrow HKDF(fingerprint/facialrecognition, salt)$
▷ Encryption of the public key device A via AES-GCM
$CA \leftarrow AES - GCM(Kbiom, pubA)$
▷ QR code generation by device A
$KA \leftarrow H(IdA||CA||nonce||SSID||password)$
Generate a QR code containing $(IdA, pubA, nonce, SSID, password, KA)$
Display the QR code on A's screen
▷ Scanning and verification by device B
Scan the QR code and extract $(IdA, CA, nonce, SSID, password, KA)$
Compute $KB \leftarrow H(IdA||CA||nonce||SSID||password)$
if $KB \neq KA$ **then**
  Reject the pairing
  return
end if
▷ Wi-Fi Direct connection
Connect to A's AP using $(SSID, password)$
▷ Generation of a biometric secret key via HKDF by device B
$Kbiom \leftarrow HKDF(fingerprint/facialrecognition, salt)$
▷ B decrypts the public key of device A
$PubA \leftarrow \text{AES-GCM}^{-1}(Kbiom, CA)$
▷ Encryption of the public key device A via AES-GCM
$CB \leftarrow AES - GCM(Kbiom, pubA)$
B Sends (CB And nonce) to A
return Connection established with key exchange

- g is a number chosen for the proof,
- p is a prime number chosen for the proof.

Device A sends the commitment e_A to device B. Device B wants to verify whether device A really knows its private key privA. To do this, device B generates a challenge C_B, which is a random number, and sends it to device A. This challenge forces device A to prove that it knows privA.

Device A receives the challenge C_B from device B, and device A must prove that it knows its private key privA. It calculates its response S_A using its private key privA and the challenge C_B. The response is calculated as:

$$S_A = r_A + C_B \cdot \boldsymbol{privA} \mod (p-1)$$

Then, device A sends the response S_A to device B. Device B receives S_A and ensures that S_A is correct, meaning that it was generated by the private key privA of device A without revealing the private key directly. Device B verifies if the following equality holds:

$$g^{S_A} \mod p = e_A \cdot \boldsymbol{pubA}^{C_B} \mod p$$

where:

- $g^{S_A} \mod p$ corresponds to the transformation of the number S_A, which contains the private key privA,
- $e_A \cdot \text{pubA}^{C_B} \mod p$ is a reconstruction based on the values already exchanged and known.

If both sides are equal, then device A has correctly used privA to generate S_A, without ever directly revealing privA.

Device B Proves to Device A that it Knows its Private Key Device B chooses a random number r_B and creates a sort of fingerprint called a commitment with its private key privB. The commitment is calculated as follows:

$$e_B = g^{r_B} \mod p$$

where:

- g is a number chosen for the proof,
- p is a prime number chosen for the proof.

Device B sends the commitment e_B to device A. Device A wants to verify whether device B really knows its private key privB. To do this, device A generates a challenge C_A, which is a random number, and sends it to device B. This challenge forces B to prove that it knows privB.

Device B receives the challenge C_A from device A, and device B must prove that it knows its private key privB. It calculates its response S_B using its private key privB and the challenge C_A. The response is calculated as:

$$S_B = r_B + C_A \cdot \boldsymbol{privB} \mod (p-1)$$

Then, device B sends the response S_B to device A. Device A receives S_B and ensures that S_B is correct, meaning that it was generated by the private key privB of device B without directly revealing the private key. Device A verifies if the following equality holds:

$$g^{S_B} \mod p = e_B \cdot \boldsymbol{pubB}^{C_A} \mod p$$

where:

- $g^{S_B} \mod p$ corresponds to the transformation of the number S_B, which contains the private key privB,
- $e_B \cdot \text{pubB}^{C_A} \mod p$ is a reconstruction based on the values already exchanged and known.

If both sides are equal, then device B has correctly used privB to generate S_B, without ever directly revealing privB.

Algorithm 2 Mutual Identity Verification

Require: extbfDevice A and B: private keys $(privA, privB)$, public keys $(pubA, pubB)$, shared parameters (g, p)
Ensure: Mutual identity verification without revealing private keys
▷ Device A proves knowledge of $privA$
Device A selects random rA
Compute commitment: $eA \leftarrow g^{rA} \mod p$
Send eA to Device B
Device B generates challenge C_B
Send C_B to Device A
Device A computes response: $S_A \leftarrow (rA + C_B \cdot privA) \mod (p-1)$
Send S_A to Device B
Device B verifies: $g^{S_A} \mod p = eA \cdot pubA^{C_B} \mod p$
if verification fails **then**
  Reject identity claim
  return
end if
▷ Device B proves knowledge of $privB$
Device B selects random rB
Compute commitment: $eB \leftarrow g^{rB} \mod p$
Send eB to Device A
Device A generates challenge C_A
Send C_A to Device B
Device B computes response: $S_B \leftarrow (rB + C_A \cdot privB) \mod (p-1)$
Send S_B to Device A
Device A verifies: $g^{S_B} \mod p = eB \cdot pubB^{C_A} \mod p$
if verification fails **then**
  Reject identity claim
  return
end if
return Mutual identity verification successful

Through the use of Schnorr-based Zero-Knowledge Proofs, this phase enables each device to prove possession of its private key without disclosing it. This ensures robust mutual authentication and prevents any leakage of sensitive cryptographic material, thereby strengthening the security of the established communication channel.

3.3 Secure Session Key Generation

Once mutual authentication is established through the ZKP protocol, each device has the ECDH public key of the other. The next step is to derive a secure session key to encrypt the passkey exchanges. Device A and Device B independently generate the same shared secret by using each other's public key and their own private key.
For device A:

$$\text{Secret}_A = \text{pubB} \cdot \text{privA}$$

For device B:

$$\text{Secret}_B = \text{pubA} \cdot \text{privB}$$

where:

- pubA and pubB are public keys,
- privA and privB are private keys,
- Secret_A and Secret_B are the shared secrets derived by each device.

Thus,

$$\text{Secret}_A = \text{Secret}_B = \text{Secret}_{A-B}$$

ensures that both devices obtain the same shared secret without explicitly transmitting a private key.

The raw shared secret Secret_A-B cannot be used directly. We apply a Key Derivation Function (KDF) to generate a strong and uniform session key. HKDF (HMAC-based Key Derivation Function) is a key derivation function that extracts and then extends a key from an initial secret (e.g., the output of ECDH). Its role is to produce a cryptographically strong symmetric key. It is defined by the following equation:

$$K = \text{HKDF}(\text{SHA256}, \text{Secret}_{A-B}, \text{salt}, \text{info}, \text{length})$$

where:

- Secret_A-B (Shared Secret): This is the value derived from an ECDH exchange (Elliptic Curve Diffie-Hellman);
- salt (Random Value): This random value prevents pre-computation attacks (Rainbow Tables) and strengthens the security of the derivation process by diversifying the derived keys even if the shared secret Secret_A-B is the same;
- info (Contextual String): This optional parameter adds context to the key derivation. For example, for a secure passkey transfer, "Passkey Transfer" can be used to prevent key reuse in different contexts;
- length (Key Length): This value defines the size of the generated symmetric key. For AES-256 encryption, a length of 256 bits (32 bytes) is used.

Through this approach, HKDF ensures that the final key is evenly distributed, resistant to attacks, and suitable for the cryptographic needs of the system, notably for AES-GCM-256 encryption in a secure exchange protocol.

Algorithm 3 Session Key Generation

Require: Device A and B: private keys $(privA, privB)$, public keys $(pubA, pubB)$
Ensure: Secure session key derivation
▷ Compute shared secret using ECDH
  $Secret_A \leftarrow pubB \cdot privA$
  $Secret_B \leftarrow pubA \cdot privB$
  if $Secret_A \neq Secret_B$ **then**
    Reject key agreement
    return
  end if
▷ Apply HKDF for key derivation
  Choose a random salt value
  Define an info string for context (e.g., "Passkey Transfer")
  Compute session key: $K \leftarrow$ HKDF(SHA256, $Secret_{A-B}$, salt, info, length)
  return Derived session key K

The session key derivation process relies on the Elliptic Curve Diffie-Hellman (ECDH) protocol, allowing both devices to independently compute a shared secret without transmitting it. This approach ensures the confidentiality of future communications and provides forward secrecy, even in the event of a future compromise.

3.4 Direct and Secure Transfer of Passkeys

Passkey Encryption Before transferring the passkey, the source device (**Device A**) encrypts the passkey to ensure its confidentiality before sending it to the target device (**Device B**). To achieve this, a shared session key is derived from the private keys $priv_A$ and $priv_B$ of both devices, along with their respective public keys.

The passkey, denoted as $passkey_A$, is encrypted using the **AES-GCM-256** encryption algorithm as follows:

$$passkey_{A-encrypted} = AES\text{-}GCM\text{-}256(Secret_{A-B}, passkey_A)$$

where:

- $Secret_{A-B}$ is the shared session key derived from the ECDH key exchange.
- $passkey_A$ is the passkey from Device A.
- **AES-GCM-256** is the encryption algorithm ensuring confidentiality and integrity.

Passkey Transfer Once encrypted, the passkey $passkey_{A-encrypted}$ is transmitted from Device A to Device B via a secure **Wi-Fi Direct** channel.

Passkey Decryption When Device B receives the encrypted passkey $passkey_{A-encrypted}$, it uses the same session key $Secret_{A-B}$ to decrypt it. The decrypted passkey, denoted as $passkey_B$, is obtained using the **AES-GCM-256** symmetric decryption function:

$$passkey_B = AES^{-1}\text{-}GCM\text{-}256(Secret_{A-B}, passkey_{A-encrypted})$$

where:

- $AES^{-1}\text{-}GCM\text{-}256$ represents the symmetric decryption function.

Secure Storage of the Passkey Once decrypted, the passkey $passkey_B$ is securely stored in a hardware module such as a **TPM** (Trusted Platform Module) or an **HSM** (Hardware Security Module) on Device B. This ensures that the passkey remains protected and inaccessible to attackers.

Algorithm 4 Passkey Transfer

Require: Device A and B: shared session key K, passkey $passkeyA$
Ensure: Secure transfer of passkey from Device A to Device B
▷ Encryption of passkey
$Key\_encrypted \leftarrow$ AES-GCM-256($K, passkeyA$)
▷ Transmission of encrypted passkey
Device A sends $Key\_encrypted$ to Device B over Wi-Fi Direct
▷ Decryption of passkey
Device B receives $Key\_encrypted$
$passkeyB \leftarrow$ AES-GCM-256^{-1}($K, Key\_encrypted$)
▷ Secure storage of passkey
Store $passkeyB$ securely in a TPM or HSM
return Passkey securely transferred and stored

In the final phase, the passkey is encrypted using the derived session key and securely transmitted over the established channel. This mechanism guarantees the confidentiality, integrity, and authenticity of the transferred passkey while eliminating any reliance on centralized infrastructure.

4 Conclusion

In summary, we have proposed an innovative approach that combines biometrics, Elliptic Curve Diffie-Hellman key exchange, and Zero-Knowledge Proofs to ensure the secure transfer of passkeys between devices. This combination guarantees robust authentication, confidential key exchange, and verification without disclosing sensitive information. Our results demonstrate that this approach significantly enhances security against interception and identity theft attacks, while providing a smooth and intuitive user experience.

However, this solution has a notable limitation: it focuses exclusively on passkey synchronization between devices without ensuring their persistence within an external infrastructure. Consequently, if all synchronized devices are lost, the user faces the risk of permanently losing their passkeys.

Our approach stands out due to its innovative nature, based on the combination of several advanced cryptographic mechanisms to ensure the security, confidentiality, and integrity of passkey exchanges between heterogeneous devices. This methodology also guarantees optimal interoperability between devices with diverse hardware and software characteristics, while maintaining high standards of cryptographic robustness.

Following the work, we will:

- evaluate the robustness and reliability of our novel and secure approach to passkey synchronization across heterogeneous devices;
- integrate a recovery mechanism based on blockchain or another secure storage solution to ensure the longevity of passkeys.

References

1. Domingues, P., Frade, M., Negrão, M.: Digital forensic artifacts of FIDO2 passkeys in windows 11. In: Proceedings of the 19th International Conference on Availability, Reliability and Security, pp. 1–10 (2024). https://dl.acm.org/doi/pdf/10.1145/3664476.3664496
2. Abos, P.: Vendor Lock-In and Interoperability: importance of interoperability among cloud services (2024)
3. Soni, P.K., Dhurwe, H.: Challenges and open issues in cloud computing services. In: Advanced Computing Techniques for Optimization in Cloud, pp. 19–37. Chapman and Hall/CRC (2024)
4. Hofmann, J., Truong, K.T.: End-to-End encrypted cloud storage in the wild: a broken ecosystem. In: Proceedings of the 2024 on ACM SIGSAC Conference on Computer and Communications Security, pp. 3988–4001 (2024). https://dl.acm.org/doi/pdf/10.1145/3658644.3690309
5. Laud, P., Pankova, A., Vakarjuk, J.: Privacy-preserving server-supported decryption (2024). arXiv:2410.19338
6. Blessing, J., Hugenroth, D., Anderson, R.J., Beresford, A.R.: SoK: web authentication in the age of end-to-end encryption (2024). arXiv:2406.18226
7. Lueks, W., Hampiholi, B., Alpár, G., Troncoso, C.: Tandem: securing keys by using a central server while preserving privacy (2018). arXiv:1809.03390
8. Backendal, M., Davis, H., Günther, F., Haller, M., Paterson, K.G.: A formal treatment of end-to-end encrypted cloud storage. In: Annual International Cryptology Conference, pp. 40–74. Springer Nature Switzerland, Cham (2024). https://www.research-collection.ethz.ch/bitstream/handle/20.500.11850/681299/4/E2EE_Cloud_Storage_full_version.pdf

9. Reisinger, T., Boiten, E.A., Wagner, I.: SEPPI: secure and privacy-preserving invitation for unified communication meetings. In: 2024 International Conference on Computing, Networking and Communications (ICNC), pp. 730–736. IEEE (2024). https://www.conf-icnc.org/2024/papers/p730-reisinger.pdf
10. Khawaja, I.A., Abid, K., Farooq, U., Malik, Z., Abid, A.: Empowering collaborative application development: a robust framework for Ad-Hoc distributed systems. IEEE Access (2024). https://ieeexplore.ieee.org/stamp/stamp.jsp?arnumber=10516446
11. Dang, Y., Quang, N., Roni, F., Veli-Matti, R., Kalle, R., Jäntti, R.: EWDC: integrating DECT-2020 with Wi-Fi for enhanced wireless direct connectivity (2025). Authorea Preprints. https://d197for5662m48.cloudfront.net/documents/publicationstatus/241045/preprint_pdf/7c99fa154dfab61eb4b092f58d1f2ea9.pdf
12. Wu, J., Wu, R., Xu, D., Tian, D.J., Bianchi, A.: Formal model-driven discovery of bluetooth protocol design vulnerabilities. In: 2022 IEEE Symposium on Security and Privacy (SP), pp. 2285–2303. IEEE (2022. https://www.cs.purdue.edu/homes/dxu/pubs/SP22_BT_formal.pdf
13. Ayoub, P., Cayre, R., Francillon, A., Maurice, C.: BlueScream: screaming channels on bluetooth low energy. In: 40th Annual Computer Security Applications Conference (ACSAC'24) (2024). https://hal.science/hal-04725668v2/file/bluescream.pdf
14. Niebla-Montero, A., Froiz-Míguez, I., Fraga-Lamas, P., Fernández-Caramés, T.M.: Practical evaluation of wize and bluetooth 5 assisted rfid for an opportunistic vehicular scenario. In: 2024 IEEE International Conference on RFID (RFID), pp. 101–106. IEEE (2024). arXiv:2410.23366

Resilience of SMEs in Nigeria to Cyber Threats

Aduragbemi Odumade[1] and Olasupo Ajayi[2](✉)

[1] Institute of Business and Economics, Mykolas Romeris University, Ateities g. 20, 08303 Vilnius, Lithuania
[2] Department of Computer Science, University of the Western Cape, Robert Sobukwe Rd, Bellville, Cape Town 7535, South Africa
olasupoajayi@gmail.com

Abstract. Small and Medium Enterprises (SMEs) play a crucial role in any country's economy, contributing significantly to employment and GDP. However, in recent times, they are increasingly being targeted by cyber criminals due to their perceived vulnerabilities and limited resources. This study examines the resilience of SMEs in Nigeria to cyber threats, with a particular focus on management strategies and cybersecurity practices. It identifies common cyber threats to SMEs, assesses their impacts on business operations, and explores viable mitigation strategies. The findings reveal that, while SMEs are aware of cybersecurity risks, there is a significant gap between awareness and preparedness. The study concludes with recommendations for improving cybersecurity resilience among SMEs, including increased investment in cybersecurity, employee training, and government support.

Keywords: Cyber threats · Cybersecurity · Cyber resilience · Nigeria · SME

1 Introduction

Cybersecurity has become a critical concern for organizations worldwide, particularly for Small and Medium Enterprises (SMEs), which are often more vulnerable to cyberattacks due to limited resources and expertise. With the rise of e-commerce, digitalization, and the Internet of Things (IoT), SMEs are increasingly exposed to cyber threats such as ransomware, phishing, and denial-of-service (DoS) attacks [1]. These threats can disrupt business operations, compromise sensitive data, and lead to significant financial losses. Despite their economic importance, SMEs often lack the capacity to implement robust cybersecurity measures, making them attractive targets for cybercriminals. In Nigeria, and most sub-Saharan countries, SMEs face numerous challenges in managing cybersecurity risks. This is due to limited financial resources, a lack of trained IT staff, and a general lack of awareness about the evolving nature of cyber threats. The impacts of cyberattacks on SMEs can be severe, including operational disruptions, financial losses, damage to reputation, and legal consequences. In some cases, cyberattacks can lead to the closure of SMEs, particularly if they are unable to recover from the financial and operational impacts.

F. Kamoun et al. (Eds.): AFRICATEK 2025, LNICST 677, pp. 33–49, 2026.
https://doi.org/10.1007/978-3-032-16638-8_4

Unfortunately, traditional cybersecurity approaches have proven inadequate in addressing the ever-evolving nature of cyberattacks, thus necessitating a shift towards cyber resilience. Cyber resilience refers to an organization's ability to anticipate, withstand, recover from, and adapt to cyberattacks. It has become an important requirement for the survival and growth of most organizations [2]. For SMEs, building cyber resilience involves implementing a combination of technical, organizational, and strategic measures. These include developing cybersecurity policies, conducting regular risk assessments, and investing in employee training.

Theoretically, there are several frameworks that can be used to model the acceptance, use, and potential impact of a technological solution, system, or change on an organization. Some of these frameworks include the Technology Acceptance Model (TAM), which focuses on the perceived usefulness and ease of use of the new technology; the Theory of Planned Behaviour (TPB) that prioritizes user attitude and their perceived behavioural control; Technology-Organization-Environment (TOE), which considers the tripartite influence of technology, organization and external environmental factors; and Organization Resilience Model (ORM) that suggests that user preparedness, adaptability, flexibility, and willingness to learn and improve are factors that determine an organization's resilience to technology changes [3–5].

Since a single framework cannot completely model all the impacts (positive or negative) of a technological system change and the corresponding reactions (acceptance or resistance) of its potential users, researchers often combine multiple frameworks to get a more accurate picture. Thus, to model the resilience of SMEs to cyber threats, we combine the TOE and ORM frameworks. This combination provides us with a holistic view, as TOE addresses factors within and external to an organization, while ORM considers the people (users) within the organization.

This study therefore aims to assess the resilience of Nigerian SMEs to cyber threats and provide insights into effective management strategies. Specifically, this work identifies the most common cyber threats to SMEs, assesses their potential impacts on business operations, management, and decision-making using TOE + ORM frameworks, and then explores viable mitigation strategies and countermeasures to these cyber threats.

2 Literature Review

2.1 Role of SMEs in Rural and Socioeconomic Development

Like most countries in sub-Saharan Africa, SMEs are also the backbone of the Nigerian economy, accounting for over 90% of businesses and contributing significantly to the country's GDP. The authors in [6] examined the role of SMEs in sustainable development, focusing on poverty reduction and employment generation in sub-Saharan Africa. The work considered various challenges, such as limited access to finance, inadequate infrastructure, and lack of government support; and then proposed strategies for tackling these challenges, including the integration of sustainable practices and the adoption of environmentally friendly technologies. It was concluded that SMEs are critical to poverty reduction and job creation, but their potential is hindered by persistent challenges, specifically limited access to finance and inadequate infrastructure, which require targeted interventions to address.

In [7] a comprehensive review of global challenges and survival strategies for SMEs was done. The study examined challenges, such as limited access to finance, inadequate infrastructure, lack of government support, and cybersecurity vulnerabilities. Potential strategies for addressing the identified challenges were also discussed, including the adoption of digital technologies, collaboration among partners and stakeholders, investment in cybersecurity, and capacity building through training and skill acquisition. The authors opined that investing in cybersecurity and the adoption of digital technologies were the most effective strategies for improving SME resilience, while limited access to finance and inadequate infrastructure remained the most persistent barriers to growth.

In [8] the authors explored the role of entrepreneurial ecosystems in fostering sustainable economic growth, focusing on the contributions of SMEs. The study emphasized the importance of creating supportive environments for SMEs to thrive, including access to finance, infrastructure, and innovation networks. The authors highlighted the interconnectedness of various stakeholders, such as governments, private sector actors, and educational institutions, in building robust entrepreneurial ecosystems. Finally, limited resources, regulatory barriers, competition, and other challenges faced by SMEs were discussed, alongside possible strategies to enhance their resilience and sustainability.

2.2 Cyber Threats and Their Impacts on SMEs

Cyber threats have evolved exponentially, becoming more sophisticated and prevalent. They present significant risks to SMEs, whose limited resources often leave them vulnerable [8, 9]. Common types of cyber threats include malware, phishing attacks, ransomware, and data breaches, each posing unique challenges to organizational integrity and operational continuity. Historically, cybersecurity measures were primarily reactive, i.e., they focused on detecting and mitigating the impacts of attacks [10]. However, as cyber threats have gotten more complicated, management have needed to move toward more proactive and strategic approaches that include incident prediction, prevention, response and recovery.

The impacts of cyber threats on SMEs are profound, influencing operations, resource allocation, and strategic decision-making. Studies indicate that cyber incidents can disrupt various facets of business operations, leading to loss of revenue, reputational damage, and diminished trust among stakeholders. These necessitate that SMEs prioritize data protection measures and develop robust incident prediction and response strategies to safeguard against potential attacks.

The vulnerability of SMEs is further exacerbated by limited resources and a lack of cybersecurity awareness. In [11], the authors discussed a triad of challenges that includes unawareness, underfunding, and insufficient education, as primary barriers to effective cybersecurity among SMEs. Their thorough assessment reveals that many SMEs lack the necessary knowledge and financial means to implement robust cybersecurity measures, leaving them ill-equipped to counter increasingly sophisticated cyber threats.

A noteworthy finding is that SMEs with higher investment in cybersecurity experience fewer incidents and face less severe impacts from attacks. This finding highlights the importance of deliberate and consistent cybersecurity practice [12]. Conversely, those neglecting cybersecurity often suffer more significant operational challenges due to unrecognized vulnerabilities.

2.3 Cyber Resilience in SMEs

Cyber resilience encapsulates the combination of preventive, detective, and responsive strategies aimed at preparing SMEs for cyber threats. It emphasizes an organization's ability to foresee, detect, withstand, recover, and adapt to cyber incidents [13]. This evolving consciousness is vital in a dynamic threat landscape, where organizations must evolve their security measures regularly [14]. It is a dynamic and multidimensional concept encompassing technical, organizational and human factors. In [15], attention is drawn to the importance of adaptive capacity, stressing the necessity for flexibility and learning rather than adherence to inflexible recovery plans. Their research highlights the sociotechnical aspects of resilience, emphasizing the interdependence between technology and human behavior. Employing an abductive research approach, the authors emphasize the importance of context-specific insights and identify scenario-based training as crucial for equipping organizations to effectively address cyber threats. They characterize cyber resilience as a process necessitating strategic adaptation and a cohesive organizational effort.

The roles of open innovation in enhancing SMEs' cybersecurity resilience were highlighted in [16]. By collaborating with external stakeholders, SMEs can access advanced technologies and expertise that would otherwise be unavailable due to resource constraints. This approach not only improves their ability to detect and respond to cyber threats but also fosters a culture of continuous learning and adaptation.

3 Methodology

3.1 Research Design

In this work, we sought to assess the level of cybersecurity awareness of SMEs, the impact of cyberthreats on SMEs, and highlight the challenges faced in mitigating these threats. A descriptive research design was developed to achieve this. Data was collected through structured questionnaires from 400 respondents, including owners and employees of SMEs, as well as cybersecurity professionals, in Lagos, Nigeria. Lagos was chosen because it is one of the major economic hubs in Nigeria and sub-Saharan Africa.

3.2 Sample Size

The average number of SMEs in Lagos, Nigeria, was investigated, and Paniotto's formula (Eq. 1) was used to obtain the optimal study sample size.

$$n = \frac{N * X}{(X + (N - 1)\Delta^2)} \tag{1}$$

$$X = Z\left(\frac{c}{100}\right)^2 * r(100 - r)$$

$$\Delta = \sqrt{\frac{x(N - n)}{n(N - 1)}}$$

where N = size of the general population, n = sample size, Δ = error margin (5% or 0.05), r = fraction of responses, and Z = critical value for the confidence level c.

At the time of writing, there were about 12,000 registered SMEs in Lagos [17], hence, using Eq. 1, with a confidence interval of 95% and an error margin of 5%, the minimum number of participants in the survey should be at least 373. This guarantees that the error rate does not exceed 5% after the sample evaluation is completed. For this work, 400 people responded to the online survey, which is more than the minimum recommendation of 373 participants.

3.3 Data Collection and Questionnaire Design

Data was collected using questionnaires designed in Google Forms. There were a total of 28 questions on respondents' socio-demography, perceptions of cybersecurity, their experiences with cyber threats, and the strategies they employ to mitigate these threats. We divided the questions into five short answers, eleven Likert scale questions, six multiple-choice questions, and six long answers. The questionnaire is available via this link.[1]

3.4 Data Pre-processing

Three data validation steps were infused into the questionnaire design to ensure the collection of accurate data. These are: (i) Format validation, which ensured that respondents entered the correct data formats, e.g., the correct number of digits in a phone number. (ii) Range validation ensured that imputed values fell within a reasonable range, such as setting a range of 18–65 for the age field. (iii) Completeness validation, which was done by setting certain fields as mandatory.

3.5 Demographic Characteristics of Respondents

As stated above, data was collected from 400 respondents, 54% of which were women and 46% men, as shown on Table 1. The table also shows the distribution of the respondents by age, and academic qualification (B.Sc., M.Sc., and Ph.D.). The mean age of the respondents was 33, with about 90% of them being between the ages of 20 and 40. 3.75% (15) of the respondents did not provide information about their age.

The Table also shows that almost all the respondents had a university degree, with 92% of them having a B.Sc. Degree, while about 46% had a postgraduate degree. Approximately 9% of them did not provide information about their academic qualification(s) (Fig. 1).

[1] https://drive.google.com/file/d/18Yun1NmqLMsG0Ie_IOth_Z1MLlK9ipOl/view?usp=sharing.

Table 1. Demography of respondents

	Gender	Age [20–39]	Age [40–59]	Degree [B.Sc.]	Degree [M.Sc.]	Degree [Ph.D.]
Male	186 (46%)	166 (42%)	16 (4%)	169 (43%)	122 (31%)	16 (4%)
Female	214 (54%)	195 (49%)	8 (2%)	194 (49%)	42 (11%)	1 (0.3%)
NR	0%	15 (3.75%)		37 (9.25%)		

NR = No response

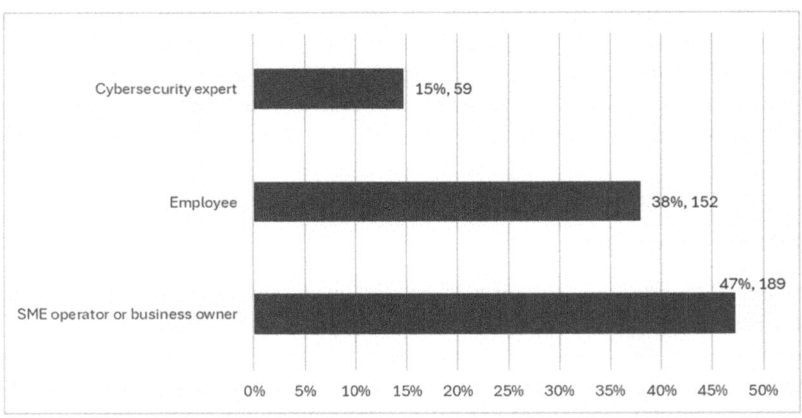

Fig. 1. Distribution of respondents based on role

3.6 Data Analysis

The collected data was analysed based on the keys provided in Table 2. Statistical tools, specifically, Analysis of Variance (ANOVA) and Chi-square tests were used for the analysis. Obtained results are discussed in the next section.

4 Results

This section presents the results of the study concerning the resilience of Nigerian SMEs to cyber threats. The analysis focuses on their awareness and practices, as well as the impact, and challenges of cyber threats on SMEs.

4.1 Respondents' Cybersecurity Awareness & Management Practices

Respondents' Perceptions of Cybersecurity in SMEs

To gain insights and rank respondent's perception of cybersecurity, we asked the respondents 10 questions, labelled A1 to J1 (defined on Table 7). Responses were provided using a 5-point Likert scale system with the following values - 'strongly disagree (SD)', 'disagree (D)', 'neutral (N)', 'agree (A)' and 'strongly agree (SA)'. The responses also helped us establish a baseline for assessing the organizations resilience from the user's perspective (ORM framework).

In analysing the responses, we ranked them in order of perceived importance. This was done by first mapping the non-parametric responses to numeric values, i.e., SD = 1, D = 2, N = 3, A = 4 and SA = 5, then for each question, we calculated its weighted value by multiplying the numeric equivalent of the response with its frequencies (i.e., number of respondents that chose it). Finally, we summed up the weighted value of each key. This is mathematically expressed as:

$$SWV = \sum\nolimits_{i=1}^{n} X_i Y_i \tag{2}$$

where SWV = Summation of Weight Value, x_i = number of respondents to rating i, y_i = the weight assigned to i, and i = value of the rating i.e., 1, 2, 3, 4 and 5.

Findings in Table 2 show that respondents were aware of the importance of cybersecurity for business growth, as F1 ('Adoption and implementation of cybersecurity measures is essential for business growth') had the highest score and was ranked first. Most of the respondents also agreed that 'Cyber threats are serious issues for SMEs in Nigeria' (B1), as this ranked second. Despite knowing the seriousness of cyber threats, most SMEs were ill-prepared (C1). This might be because funds to support cybersecurity resilience (J1) were limited, as J1 ranked the lowest on Table 2.

Table 2. Respondents' perceptions of cybersecurity in SMEs

Cybersecurity perceptions	Ratings					Mean		Rank
	SD (1)	D (2)	N (3)	A (4)	SA (5)	WV	Index	
A1	11	278	405	420	50	1164	2.91	5th
B1	12	28	84	508	1095	1727	4.32	2nd
C1	33	438	333	72	95	971	2.43	9th
D1	5	466	216	360	0	1047	2.62	7th
E1	46	332	270	280	140	1068	2.67	6th
F1	14	34	0	468	1260	1776	4.44	1st
G1	53	310	438	184	0	985	2.46	8th
H1	46	94	273	704	200	1317	3.29	3rd
I1	31	150	240	712	180	1313	3.28	4th
J1	112	276	363	32	105	883	2.22	10th

SD = Strongly Disagree, D = Disagree, N = Neutral, A = Agree, SA = Strongly Agree, WV = Weight Value

Respondents' Perceptions of Cybersecurity Policies and Investments

These questions and the corresponding responses map to the "organization" and "environment" of the TOE model. Figure 2 shows that the respondents were split into 5 groups (monthly, quarterly, bi-annual, annual and rarely/never) based on how often they review their cybersecurity policies. Less than half of the respondents reviewed their policies frequently (monthly or quarterly). In fact, almost 25% of SMEs rarely or never review their cybersecurity policies. This is perhaps as a result of budgetary limitations, as shown on Fig. 3, where only half of the SMEs allocated up to 20% of their budget to cybersecurity.

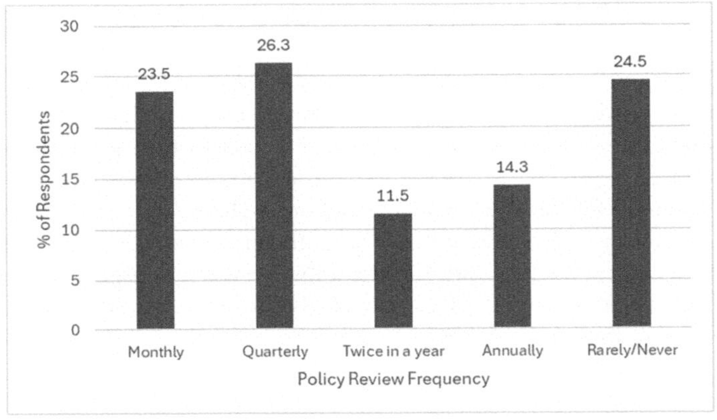

Fig. 2. Frequency of cybersecurity review

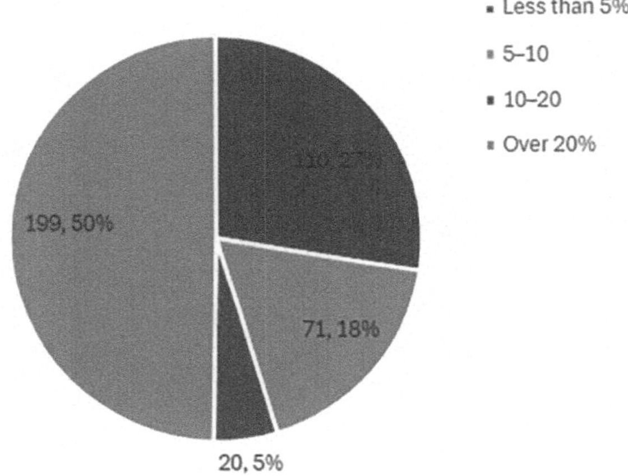

Fig. 3. Budgetary allocation to cybersecurity

4.2 Effects of Cyber Threats

Having discussed cybersecurity awareness and management practices of SMEs, we sought to understand the impact of cyber threats on SMEs and simultaneously assess the level of organizational experience, preparedness, and adaptability to threats (TOE + ORM frameworks). ANOVA and Chi-square tests were used for the analysis, as we had multiple factors, and needed to identify the impact of the cyber threats on them. Chi-square was used to examine the relationship between categorical data, while ANOVA was used to compare multiple groups containing heterogeneous data types.

Experience with Cyber threats

Users' experiences with cyber threats can be modeled with the ORM framework. Figure 4 shows that cumulatively about 66% of respondents had experienced some form of cybersecurity incidents, though only 52% could specify the exact type of incident they experienced. This high percentage confirms our speculation in Sect. 1 confirming that SMEs are indeed targets for cyber threats.

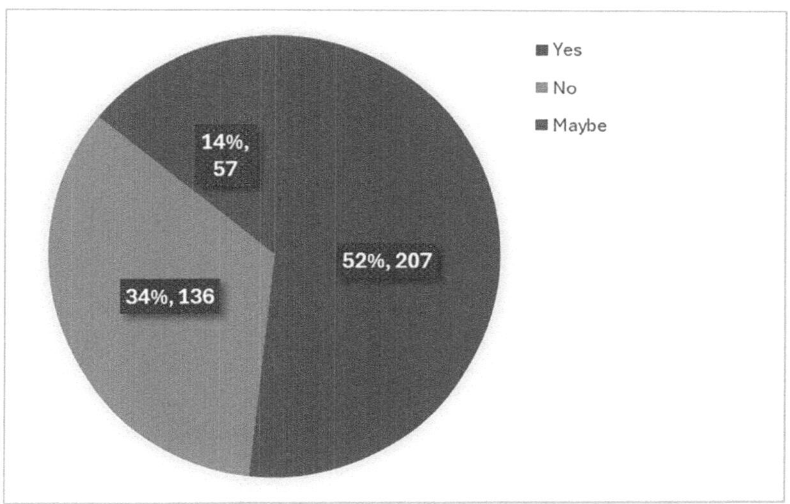

Fig. 4. Distribution of respondents that have experienced Cyber threats

Impacts of Cyber Threats on Businesses Operation of SMEs

Respondents were asked about the impacts of cyber security incidents on business operations, and the top 8 responses were A2 - H2 (defined on Table 7). Chi-square test was used to obtain the statistical relationship between two categorical data - the identified cyber threats and business operation. A *p_value* of 0.005 was used as threshold, where *p_value* $\leq$ 0.005 implies a statistically significant relationship between two variables, while *p_value* $\geq$ 0.005 signifies no statistical relationship between the two variables.

Table 3 shows that the most predominant effects of cyber threats on business operations are service disruption (A2), data loss (B2), and threat to business continuity (G2) as agreed by 56.5%, 48.2%, and 35.2% of respondents, respectively. Inferentially, findings affirm that almost every aspect of SME operations is affected by cyber incidents, as such, data protection and incident response plans are needed. Theoretically, considering the TOE framework, cyber incidents (technology) are external factors (environment) that can affect an organization's business operations.

Table 3. Effects of cybersecurity incidents on business operations

Effects	Severity of incidents on management practices						
		Highly	Moderately	Slightly	No effect	Total	P-value
A2	N	30	132	64	0	226	0.000
	%	13.3	58.4	28.3	0	56.5	
B2	N	9	141	43	0	193	0.000
	%	4.7	73.1	22.3	0	48.2	
C2	N	30	64	11	8	113	0.000
	%	26.5	56.6	9.7	7.1	28.2	
D2	N	9	53	14	0	76	0.001
	%	11.8	69.7	18.4	0	19	
E2	N	9	61	26	0	96	0.001
	%	9.4	64.5	27.1	0	24	
F2	N	9	12	0	0	21	0.000
	%	42.9	57.1	0.0	0.0	5.2	
G2	N	9	79	45	8	141	0.026
	%	6.4	56	31.9	5.7	35.2	
H2	N	9	30	25	0	64	0.022
	%	14.1	466.9	39.1	0.0	16	

N = respondent count/frequency. % = Percentage of overall respondents

Effects of Cyber Threats on Cybersecurity Policies of SMEs.

We used ANOVA to analyse the effects cyber threats might have on the frequency of cybersecurity policy reviews. These policies fall under the "Organization" in the TOE model. The five frequency groups identified in Fig. 2 were compared for each of the impacts of cyber threats A2 - H2. In ANOVA, sum of squares (SST) measures the total variation within the data, while F-statistic (F) measures the variability between group means compared to within the groups. In this work, lower values are desirable for both, as it means more respondents agree with the impact the threat has on policy review. The results on Table 4 show that A2 (service disruption), F2 (legal), and G2 (threat to business continuity), with the lowest SST and F values, have the most impact and the highest likelihood of triggering a review of cybersecurity policies in SMEs.

Table 4. Effect of cyber threats on cybersecurity policies

Cyber threats		SST	Mean square	F	Sig.
A2	Between groups	98.35	24.59	4.12	0.003
	Within groups	2359.40	5.97		
	Total	2457.75			
B2	Between groups	1036.17	259.04	70.05	0
	Within groups	1460.77	3.698		
	Total	2496.94			
C2	Between groups	531.93	132.98	35.14	0
	Within groups	1495.01	3.79		
	Total	2026.94			
D2	Between groups	272.23	68.06	21.22	0
	Within groups	1266.78	3.21		
	Total	1539			
E2	Between groups	225.76	56.44	13.95	0
	Within groups	1598.24	4.05		
	Total	1824			
F2	Between groups	44.69	11.18	9.75	0
	Within groups	452.74	1.15		
	Total	497.44			
G2	Between groups	105.87	26.47	4.80	0.001
	Within groups	2176.57	5.51		
	Total	2282.44			
H2	Between groups	616.23	154.06	83.62	0
	Within groups	727.77	1.84		
	Total	1344			

SST = Total Sum of Squares, F = F-statistic, Sig = Significance

Effects of Cyber Threat on Cybersecurity Investments

ANOVA was also used to analyse the potential impacts that cyber threats have on SMEs' spending towards cybersecurity measures.

As stated in the previous section, lower values are desirable for SST and F-statistic, as it means more respondents agree with the impact the threat has on cybersecurity investments. Table 5 shows that F2 (legal implications), D2 (loss of clientele), and H2 (loss of domain) are the top three reasons that might motivate SMEs to spend more on cybersecurity measures.

Table 5. Effect of cyber threats on cybersecurity investments

Cyber threats		SST	Mean square	F	Sig.
A2	Between groups	35.64	11.88	75.06	0
	Within groups	62.67	0.16		
	Total	98.31			
B2	Between groups	14.28	4.76	22.02	0
	Within groups	85.59	0.22		
	Total	99.88			
C2	Between groups	18.04	6.01	37.77	0
	Within groups	63.04	0.16		
	Total	81.08			
D2	Between groups	1.25	0.42	2.73	0.044
	Within groups	60.31	0.15		
	Total	61.56			
E2	Between groups	7.43	2.48	14.98	0
	Within groups	65.55	0.17		
	Total	72.98			
F2	Between groups	0.76	0.25	5.26	0.001
	Within groups	19.14	0.05		
	Total	19.90			
G2	Between groups	6.96	2.32	10.89	0
	Within groups	84.34	0.21		
	Total	91.30			
H2	Between groups	4.53	1.51	12.13	0
	Within groups	49.24	0.12		
	Total	53.77			

SST = Total Sum of Squares, F = F-statistic, Sig = Significance

Theoretically, both TOE and ORM are at play here. The table shows that F2, D2, and H2 which are "environmental" factors (TOE), triggered actions within the "organization" (TOE), prompting the users (ORM) to take actions to mitigate cyber threats (Technology in TOE).

5 Challenges in Cybersecurity

5.1 Challenges Impeding Cybersecurity

Cybersecurity in the business and digital worlds faces numerous challenges. Understanding these challenges is crucial to allowing for adequate and effective strategies and counter measures to be developed. With this in mind, the respondents were asked about the major challenges impeding them from implementing cybersecurity measures.

Four major challenges were identified, viz. - limited technical knowledge and expertise, ignorance of cyber threats, high cost of implementing cybersecurity measures, and relevance to business demands. Figure 5 reveals that the majority of the respondents were either ignorant of, or simply neglected cybersecurity threats. 54% of the respondents also agreed that the high cost required for cybersecurity measures was a major challenge. Interestingly, almost half of the respondents felt that the nature of their business did not demand the implementation of any form of cybersecurity measure. The challenges identified are directly linked to the ORM framework, and shows that user's knowledge and willingness to learn and/or improve themselves are critical in building organizational resilience.

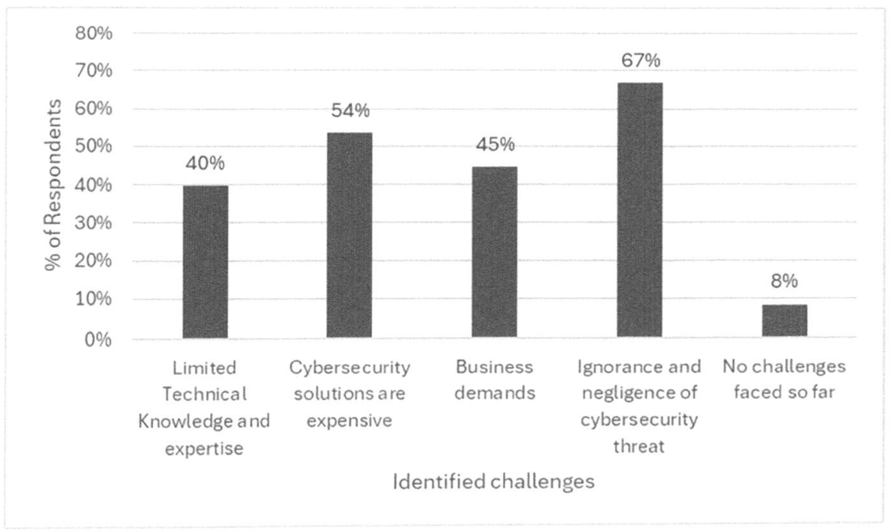

Fig. 5. Challenges impeding cybersecurity

5.2 Mitigation Strategies and Countermeasures to Cyber Threats

The continual reliance of various sectors on technology, SMEs included, has exposed them to cyber threats, which have in recent years been disrupting their operation, plans, and decision-making [18].

Respondents were asked to identify potential strategies to mitigate cyber threats. We summarized their responses into twenty categories, enumerated in Table 6. From the table, the top strategies suggested for mitigating cyber threats were training and creation of awareness, which was suggested by 76.8% of the respondents; the use of strong passwords (63%), regular software updates (61.2%), the use of Multi-factor Authentication (59.8%), and backing up data regularly (53.2%). On the contrary, and quite interestingly, risk assessments, vulnerability and penetration testing and insurance were some of the least suggested approaches at 22.5%, 19.8% and 17.2% respectively. These lower percentages show stakeholders need more enlightenment on strategies that could help further boost resilience.

Table 6. Strategies for building resilience

Strategies against cyber threats	Frequency	Percentage
Employee training and awareness	307	76.8
Strong password policies	252	63
Regular software updates and patch management	245	61.2
Multi-factor authentication (MFA)	239	59.8
Regular data backups	213	53.2
Phishing and social engineering defences	199	49.8
Data encryption	189	47.2
Access control and least privilege principle	176	44
Firewalls and intrusion detection/prevention systems (IDS/IPS)	176	44
Network segmentation	143	35.8
Data loss prevention (DLP) tools	137	34.2
Endpoint protection solutions	134	33.5
Incident response plan development	125	31.2
Security monitoring and threat detection	117	29.2
Cloud security best practices	103	25.8
Third-party risk management	92	23
Risk assessment and management programs	90	22.5
Implementing cybersecurity frameworks	86	21.5
Vulnerability assessments and penetration testing	79	19.8
Cybersecurity insurance	69	17.2

6 Discussion and Recommendations

This section summarizes the findings of this study and provides recommendations for building cyber resilience:

- Though cybersecurity is a major concern for SMEs in Nigeria, there are a limited number of cybersecurity experts in the SMEs to deal with it. Prioritizing training of personnel and empowering cybersecurity champions within SMEs can minimize this concern.

- Despite being aware of the severity of cyber threats, most SMEs in Nigeria are ill-prepared to deal with them. Creating awareness of the dangers of cybersecurity and enforcing security measures, such as MFA, strong passwords, and data backup policies, can help address this.
- Funds to combat the risks posed by cyber threats are generally low. The allocation of a higher percentage of SMEs' budget to cybersecurity measures, as well as government interventions, can help mitigate the risks of cyber threats.
- Cybersecurity policies are almost non-existent, and when they exist, they are hardly reviewed. Implementing cybersecurity frameworks, such as NIST and ISO 27001, and enforcing frequent policy updates can address this issue.
- Service disruption, data loss and threat to business continuity are the top three impacts of cyber threats on SMEs. Cyber attacks might be inevitable, however, putting risk mitigation strategies in place, such as frequent on- and off-site data backups as well as conducting regular cybersecurity audits to identify vulnerabilities and implement appropriate measures to address them, can cushion the impact of cyber attacks.
- Trivialization of cyber threats, prohibitive cost, and lack of technical expertise are the major hurdles to combating cyber threats in SMEs in Nigeria. SMEs can overcome some of these obstacles by constantly reminding personnel about the seriousness of cyber threats and investing more funds into cybersecurity tools and measures.

7 Conclusion

This study focused on Small and Medium Enterprises (SMEs) in Nigeria and assessed their resilience to cyber threats. Using statistical models, this work analysed data from Nigerian SMEs to determine their level of awareness of cyber attacks, the potential impacts such attacks can have on their business operations, and the mitigation strategies put in place to address such attacks. The study concludes that while SMEs in Nigeria are aware of cybersecurity risks, there is a significant gap between awareness and preparedness. Many SMEs lack the resources and expertise to implement effective cybersecurity measures, making them vulnerable to cyberattacks. The findings highlight the need for SMEs to prioritize cybersecurity and invest in affordable solutions to build cyber resilience.

The survey carried out in this study only considered cybersecurity specialists and SME owners in Lagos, Nigeria. Though Lagos is the major economic hub of Nigeria, data from other regions of the country could be analysed in the future for a more holistic view. It is important to note that online business and e-commerce in Nigeria are still in their infancy, hence, related data on cyber incidence in these domains are limited. Curating large datasets on cybersecurity in Nigeria and Africa at large could also be anotheravenue for future work.

Appendix

See Table 7.

Table 7. Question mappings

Key	Definition
	Awareness and Perceptions
A1	Cybersecurity is taken as a priority for SMEs in Nigeria
B1	Cyber threats are serious issues for SMEs in Nigeria
C1	SMEs in Nigeria are adequately prepared for cyber threats in Nigeria
D1	Nigerian SMEs have a fail safe system against cyber-attacks
E1	There is adequate knowledge and training on cybersecurity training and awareness programs in Nigeria
F1	Adoption and implementation of cybersecurity measures is essential for business growth
G1	SMEs in Nigeria have set aside sizeable and sufficient investment in cybersecurity and resilience practices
H1	Routine and regular updates are carried out by my company on cybersecurity protocol
I1	There is a clear course of action to address cybersecurity incidents
J1	There is funding adequately provided by the Nigerian government for SMEs to support cybersecurity resilience
	Impacts and Effects of Cyber threats on organizations
A2	Operation and Service disruption
B2	Loss of sensitive data and information
C2	Ransomware Attack
D2	Loss of clientele and customer base
E2	Substantial monetary and economic implications
F2	Legal implications or lawsuit
G2	Threat to business continuity
H2	Loss of domain

The questionnaire used in this study is available at: https://drive.google.com/file/d/18Yun1NmqLMsG0Ie_IOth_Z1MLlK9ipOl/view?usp=sharing.

References

1. Moşteanu, N.R.: Challenges for organizational structure and design as a result of digitalization and cybersecurity. Bus. Manag. Rev. **11**(1), 278–286 (2020)
2. Hasib, M. (2022). Cybersecurity Leadership: Powering the Modern Organization (vol. 1). Tomorrow's Strategy Today
3. Marei, A.: An empirical study on the impact of TOE factors on e-accounting adoption: the moderating role of cybersecurity. J. Syst. Manag. Sci. **14**(3), 266–292 (2024)
4. Duchek, S.: Organizational resilience: a capability-based conceptualization. Bus. Res. **13**(1), 215–246 (2020)
5. Davis, F.: Perceived usefulness, perceived ease of use, and user acceptance of information technology. MIS Q. 319–340 (1989)

6. Abisuga-Oyekunle, O., Patra, S., Muchie, M.: SMEs in sustainable development: their role in poverty reduction and employment generation in sub-Saharan Africa. Afr. J. Sci. Technol. Innov. Dev. **12**(4), 405–419 (2020)
7. Naradda, G., Ekanayake, S., Abeyrathne, E., Prasanna, G., et al.: A review of global challenges and survival strategies of small and medium enterprises (SMEs). Economies **8**(4), 79 (2020)
8. Opute, A., Kalu, K., Adeola, O., Iwu, C.: Steering sustainable economic growth: entrepreneurial ecosystem approach. J. Entrepr. Innov. Emerg. Econ. **7**(2), 216–245 (2021). https://doi.org/10.1177/23939575211024384
9. Popoola, O., Akinsanya, M., Nzeako, G., Chukwurah, E., Okeke, C.: Exploring theoretical constructs of cybersecurity awareness and training programs: comparative analysis of African and US Initiatives. Int. J. Appl. Res. Soc. Sci. **6**(5), 819–827 (2024)
10. Ahmad, A., Desouza, K., Maynard, S., Naseer, H., Baskerville, R.: How integration of cyber security management and incident response enables organizational learning. J. Assoc. Info. Sci. Technol. **71**(8), 939–953 (2020). https://doi.org/10.1002/asi.24311
11. Rombaldo Junior, C., Becker, I., Johnson, S.: Unaware, unfunded and uneducated: A systematic review of SME cybersecurity (arXiv:2309.16187) (2023). arXiv. https://arxiv.org/abs/2309.16187
12. Uchendu, B., Nurse, J., Bada, M., Furnell, S.: Developing a cyber security culture: current practices and future needs. Comput. Secur. **109**, 102387 (2021)
13. Möller, D.: Cybersecurity in digital transformation. In: Guide to Cybersecurity in Digital Transformation: Trends, Methods, Technologies, Applications and Best Practices (pp. 1–70). Springer Nature Switzerland, Cham (2023)
14. Schmidt, K., Dannebaum, U., Schneider, R., Ambekar, A.: Cybersecurity in the Context of Fail-Operational Systems (No. 2024-01-2808). SAE Technical Paper (2024)
15. Grøtan, T., Becker, I., Johnson, S.: Cyber resilience: a pre-understanding for an abductive research agenda. In: Comes, T., Santos, A.M.T., Pinho, M.T.C., Ferreira, F. (eds.) Critical Infrastructure, Resilience and Modeling: Abductive Research-Based Studies (2022)
16. Raišienė, A., Rapuano, V., Dőry, T., Varkulevičiūtė, K.: Does telework work? Gauging challenges of telecommuting to adapt to a "new normal." Hum. Technol. **17**(2), 126–144 (2021)
17. Ajulo, O.: Impact of personality traits of business owners on the growth of SMEs in Lagos, Nigeria (Doctoral dissertation, Dublin, National College of Ireland) (2021)
18. National Institute of Standards and Technology (NIST): Framework for Improving Critical Infrastructure Cybersecurity (2018). https://doi.org/10.6028/NIST.CSWP.0416218

A Deep Learning Approach for Accurate Spam Detection in Text

Sumeera BiBi[1], Asad Khattak[2](✉), Hayat Ullah[2], Muhammad Usama Asghar[1], Muhammad Zubair Asghar[1], and Wasim Abbas[3]

[1] Gomal Research Institute of Computing (GRIC), Gomal University, D.I.Khan, Pakistan
[2] College of Technological Innovation, Zayed University, Abu Dhabi, UAE
asad.khattak@zu.ac.ae
[3] Techsacare PTE. Ltd., Singapore, Singapore
wasim.abbas@techsacare.com

Abstract. In modern communication networks, spam detection remains a critical challenge due to the evolving nature of unsolicited content. This study presents a deep learning approach using a Bidirectional Long Short-Term Memory (Bi-LSTM) model for enhanced spam classification. The model is trained and evaluated on a benchmark dataset comprising 5,574 labeled SMS messages, including both spam and ham texts. Leveraging Bi-LSTM's ability to capture sequential dependencies, the proposed model achieves superior performance with an accuracy of 98%, precision of 98%, recall of 1.00, and F1-score of 0.99. These results demonstrate the effectiveness of the approach in improving spam detection accuracy over traditional methods.

Keywords: Spam detection · Bi-LSTM model · Deep learning · Performance metrics · Adaptive spam detection

1 Introduction

1.1 Background

Spam refers to unsolicited messages sent via SMS, email, or websites, often containing malicious links aimed at deceiving recipients. Over the past decade, spam—particularly commercial and phishing content—has become a significant threat to users, businesses, and Internet service providers (ISPs) [1]. Studies indicate that nearly 60% of SMS traffic consists of spam, which imposes heavy burdens on data storage, network speed, and security [2]. Phishing messages mimic legitimate communications to steal sensitive information like passwords and account numbers. With the widespread use of email platforms such as Gmail, Yahoo Mail, and Outlook, spam has also become a primary channel for cyberattacks. While machine learning and deep learning methods have been applied for spam detection, challenges persist in capturing contextual cues and adapting to evolving spam strategies [3].

F. Kamoun et al. (Eds.): AFRICATEK 2025, LNICST 677, pp. 50–64, 2026.
https://doi.org/10.1007/978-3-032-16638-8_5

1.2 Research Motivation

Although various machine learning models have been proposed for spam detection, most studies focus on classical methods [3]. There is a need to explore advanced deep learning techniques that offer improved context understanding and adaptability. This study aims to build upon existing work by applying a Bi-LSTM model for SMS spam detection and evaluating its performance against baseline approaches.

1.3 Problem Statement

Spam detection remains a critical issue due to the limitations of traditional machine learning models in handling complex and evolving message patterns. There is a need for more robust and adaptive systems capable of accurately classifying spam in real-world SMS datasets.

1.4 Research Questions

- How to detect spam text using the Bi-LSTM technique?
- How does the Bi-LSTM model compare with classical machine learning techniques in terms of accuracy and robustness?
- What is efficiency of proposed model with respect to other baseline studies?

1.5 Novelty and Research Contributions

This study proposes a Bi-LSTM-based approach for SMS spam detection, leveraging deep contextual analysis of message content. The key contributions include:

- Implementing a Bi-LSTM model tailored for SMS spam classification.
- Comparing the performance with traditional machine learning models and a selected baseline study.
- Demonstrating improved accuracy and contextual understanding in spam detection.

1.6 Paper Organization

The rest of the paper is structured as follows: Sect. 2 discusses related work on spam detection. Section 3 presents the proposed methodology, including data preprocessing and the Bi-LSTM architecture. Section 4 outlines experimental results and comparisons. Finally, Sect. 5 concludes the paper with future research directions.

2 Literature Review

Recent studies have applied a range of machine learning (ML) and deep learning (DL) techniques to spam and phishing detection in SMS and email communication. Jain et al. [4] proposed a two-phase ML approach for spam and smishing SMS classification, achieving up to 94.9% and 96% accuracy, respectively, by emphasizing optimal feature selection. They further incorporated data mining and text processing techniques using term weighting and linguistic ontologies, with Random Forest and J48 yielding 99.1% and 98.4% accuracy, respectively. Mohammed and Sanusi [5] explored KNN, SVM, Random Forest, and Naïve Bayes over 47 engineered features from multiple email components, reporting a peak accuracy of 98% with Naïve Bayes, though they noted the need for automated feature extraction to handle emerging phishing techniques. Abid et al. [6] evaluated various classifiers including Random Forest and Gradient Boosting, using TF-IDF features on SMS data, with Random Forest achieving 99% accuracy, while advocating for hybrid ML models to enhance classification robustness. Similarly, Salman et al. [1] applied traditional classifiers and found SVM to perform best at 98%, but acknowledged challenges with generalizability in dynamic environments.

To address limitations in feature engineering, recent research has increasingly focused on deep contextual models. Guo et al. [7] applied BERT embeddings combined with ML classifiers for spam detection, where logistic regression achieved optimal performance, showcasing BERT's capability to capture semantic nuances, though at a higher computational cost. Hadi and Baawi [8] and Taylor and Ezekiel [9] reported high performance using Random Forest and SVM on large datasets (up to 99.7% accuracy), while recommending a shift towards semantic analysis and real-time learning. In the DL domain, Bi-LSTM has emerged as an effective solution; Malhotra and Malik [10] reported 98.5% accuracy and strong F1 performance, while Sheneamer [11] and Abayomi-Alli et al. [12] showed Bi-LSTM outperforming classical models on benchmark datasets. More recent hybrid approaches—such as BBODL-PEDC [13], ICSOA-DLPEC [14], and Bi-LSTM + BERT ensembles [2]—have achieved accuracies above 97%, with ICSOA-DLPEC reaching 99.72%, affirming the potential of combining sequence modeling with heuristic optimization. Other innovations include GCN-based models [15], hybrid ensemble methods like HELPHED [16], and comparative studies integrating SVM, NB, and LSTM [17], all demonstrating effectiveness in adapting to evolving spam strategies.

3 Material and Methods

The proposed deep learning framework consists of three main stages: (i) dataset collection, (ii) preprocessing, and (iii) model overview. Details of each component are provided below, along with a methodology diagram in the following figure (Fig. 1).

3.1 Dataset Collection

The dataset used for this study is sourced from Kaggle's SMS Spam Collection, consisting of 5,574 English SMS messages labeled as spam or ham. About 13% of the messages are spam, and 87% are ham. The dataset was divided into three parts: 80% for training, and 20% split equally for validation and testing. This structure enabled the Bi-LSTM model to be trained, tuned, and evaluated effectively for spam classification. Each set was used to progressively improve and assess model performance using real-world

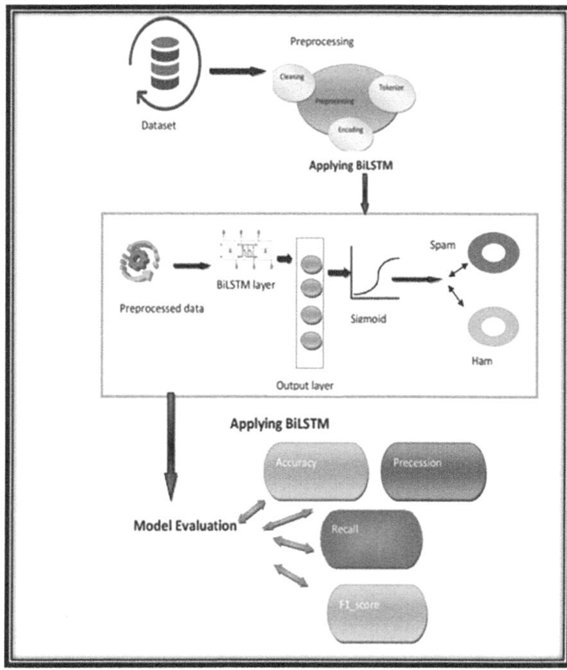

Fig. 1. Overview diagram of the purposed BI-LSTM model

SMS examples. (kaggle.com/datasets/uciml/sms-spam-collection-dataset). The dataset details are given in the below the table (Table 1).

Table 1. Details of the dataset used

Dataset	Dataset size	Spam sms	Ham sms
Spam and Ham	5574	13%	87%

Training set: 80% of the dataset is used to train the model, consisting of input messages and their corresponding spam or ham labels (see Table 2).

Validation set: A separate 20% of the data is used for validation during training to fine-tune hyperparameters such as learning rate, model architecture, and training settings (Table 3). This helps prevent underfitting and improves model performance.

Testing set: The test set, comprising 20% of the data, is used after training to evaluate the model's performance on unseen data and assess its real-world effectiveness. Table 4 shows a sample set of testing dataset.

Table 2. Set of SMS from the training data

S. No	Message	Classification
1	Even my brother is not like to speak with me. They treat me like aids patent	Ham
2	URGENT! You have won a 1-week FREE membership in our å£100,000 Prize Jackpot! Txt the word: CLAIM to No: 81010 T&C www.dbuk.net LCCLTD POBOX 4403LDNW1A7RW18	Spam
5	Is that seriously how you spell his name?	Ham
6	England v Macedonia - dont miss the goals/team news. Txt ur national team to 87077 eg ENGLAND to 87077 Try:WALES, SCOTLAND 4txt/Ì¼1.20 POBOXox36504W45WQ 16+	Spam
7	Aft i finish my lunch then i go str down lor. Ard 3 smth lor. U finish ur lunch already?	Ham

Table 3. Set of SMS from the validation dataset

S. No	Message	Classification
3	SMS. ac Sptv: The New Jersey Devils and the Detroit Red Wings play Ice Hockey. Correct or Incorrect? End? Reply END SPTV	Spam
4	Lol your always so convincing	Ham

Table 4. Set of SMS from the testing dataset.

S. No	Message	Classification
3	SMS. ac Sptv: The New Jersey Devils and the Detroit Red Wings play Ice Hockey. Correct or Incorrect? End? Reply END SPTV	Spam
4	Lol your always so convincing	Ham

3.2 Data Preprocessing

Data Preprocessing is a crucial step in preparing text for deep learning models. Several techniques were applied in this module.

Tokenization. The text is split into smaller units such as words, sub-words, or characters. For example, the sentence "Oh k…i'm watching here:)" is tokenized into: "Oh", "K", "i'm", "watching", "here", ":)".

Removing Punctuation. Punctuation is removed to standardize the text. This ensures similar words (e.g., "data" and "data,") are treated equally. However, caution is needed, especially with contractions (e.g., "don't"), to avoid altering the meaning.

Removing Stop Words. Common, non-informative words (e.g., "the", "is", "a") are removed using NLTK to focus the model on meaningful content.

Label Encoding. Categorical labels (e.g., "spam" and "ham") are converted into numeric format. Here, spam is encoded as 1 and ham as 0, enabling the model to process text labels as numeric values.

3.3 Overview of Proposed Methodology

To classify SMS messages as spam or ham, a Bi-LSTM deep learning model was used. The model architecture includes an embedding layer, a Bi-LSTM layer, a dropout layer, and an output layer (See Fig. 2).

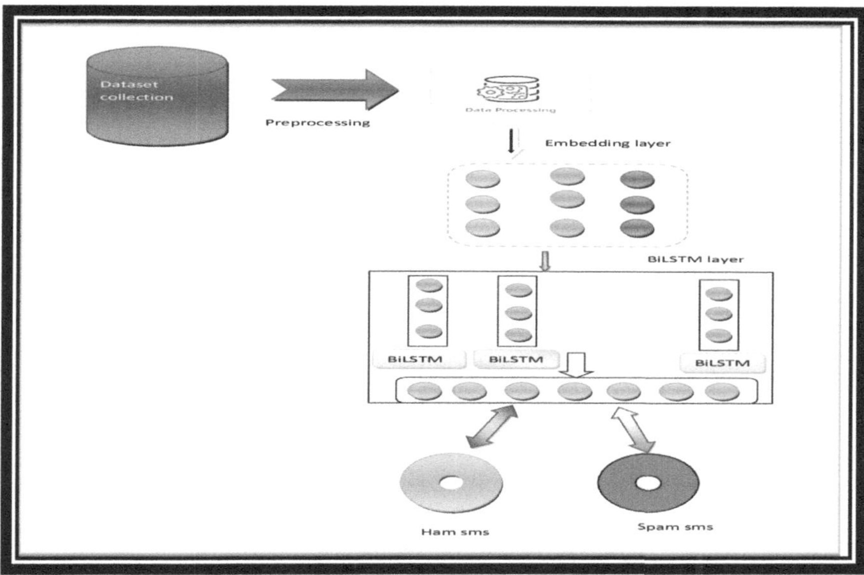

Fig. 2. Overview of proposed methodology

Embedding layer: Text input must be converted into numerical form for models like Bi-LSTM. While one-hot encoding offers a basic approach, embedding layers generate dense, fixed-length vectors that capture semantic relationships and improve word representation.

Bi-LSTM layer: Bi-LSTM is used for spam SMS prediction by capturing both past and future context through forward and backward passes. This bidirectional structure enables a deeper understanding of the input compared to traditional unidirectional LSTMs.

Formulae for forward Bi-LST

$$B_G = \sigma\left(X_a Y_g + L_a P_{g-1} + N_a\right) \tag{1}$$

$$J_g = \sigma\left(X_b Y_g + L_b P_{g-1} + N_b\right) \tag{2}$$

$$T_g = \sigma\left(X_c Y_g + L_c P_{g-1} + N_c\right) \tag{3}$$

$$F \sim W = \tau\left(X_d Y_g + L_d P_{g-1} + N_d\right) \tag{4}$$

$$F_g = B_g \odot \mathrm{F_{g-1}} + \mathrm{R_g} \odot \mathrm{F} \sim \mathrm{W} \tag{5}$$

$$A_g = T_g \odot \tau(\mathrm{F_g}) \tag{6}$$

Formulae for backward Bi-LSTM

$$B_G = \sigma\left(X_a Y_g + L_a P_{g-1} - N_a\right) \tag{7}$$

$$J_g = \sigma\left(X_b Y_g + L_b P_{g-1} - N_b\right) \tag{8}$$

$$T_g = \sigma\left(X_c Y_g + L_c P_{g-1} - N_c\right) \tag{9}$$

$$F \sim W = \tau\left(X_d Y_g + L_d P_{g-1} - N_d\right) \tag{10}$$

$$F_g = B_g \odot \mathrm{F_{g-1}} - \mathrm{R_g} \odot \mathrm{F} \sim \mathrm{W} \tag{11}$$

$$A_g = T_g \odot \tau(\mathrm{F_g}) \tag{12}$$

Here, m indicates the input size and n indicates the cell state size. Y_g Indicates the vector size X_a, $Y_{b,}$ Y_c, and Y_d indicates the input gate weight matrices. L_a, L_b, L_c and L_d denotes the matrices weight of the output gate. N_a, N_b, N_c and N_d represent the bias vectors. σ Indicates the sigmoid activation function and hyperbolic tangent function is denoted by σ. The calculation of all gates is given below.

Dropout layer: To prevent overfitting, a dropout layer is used during training. It randomly deactivates certain neurons, effectively creating different network configurations in each iteration. This encourages the model to generalize better by not relying too heavily on specific nodes, improving prediction accuracy even with missing inputs.

Sigmoid based function: The final layer applies a sigmoid activation to the BiLSTM output to compute the probability of accurately predicting the target labels.

$$S_i = \sum g_i W_i + K \tag{13}$$

where "W" is the input vector, "K" is the bias, and "g" is the weight vector. The below equation explain how to calculate the sigmoid function.

$$\text{Sigmoid}(x_i) = 1 \Big/ 1 + e^{-si} \tag{14}$$

3.4 Applied Example

We used a Bi-LSTM model to classify SMS messages as spam or ham. First, the SMS data was collected, tokenized, and converted into numerical vectors using an embedding layer. The Bi-LSTM layer then extracted contextual features from both past and future inputs using forward and backward passes. The hidden states from each direction were combined to form a comprehensive representation, enabling accurate spam detection.

Spam prediction: The true likelihood of each of the labels "S1" and "S2" is ascertained using the sigmoid activation function method (See Fig. 3). The entire input was ascertained using formula (13) as follows.

The class label for choice attribute 1 for spam-yes is "S1."

$$\begin{aligned} S_1 &= j_1 \times w_2 + j_2 \times w_2 + b \\ S_1 &= 0.8 \times 0.6 + 0.9 \times 0.5 + 0.5 \\ S_1 &= 0.48 + 0.45 + 0.5 = 1.43 \end{aligned}$$

For spam-No, the class label for decision attribute 2 is "S2."

$$\begin{aligned} S_2 &= j_1 \times w_2 + j_2 \times w_2 + b \\ S_2 &= 0.1 \times 0.6 + 0.2 \times 0.5 + 0.5 \\ S_2 &= 0.06 + 0.10 + 0.5 = 0.66 \end{aligned}$$

To figure out the likelihood of each target class (S1, S2), the Sigmoid activation function (14) is being used.

$$\text{Sigmoid } (x_i) = 1 \Big/ 1 + e^{-si}$$

$$\text{Sigmoid } (S_1) = 1 \Big/ 1 + e^{-1.43}$$

$$\text{Sigmoid } (S_1) = 1 / 1 + 0.23$$

$$\text{Sigmoid } (S_1) = 1 / 1.23$$

$$\text{Sigmoid } (\mathrm{S}_1) = 0.81$$

In the same way, the sigmoid function for the second class of diabetes predictions was made as well.

$$\text{Sigmoid } (x_i) = 1/1 + e^{-s_i}$$

$$\text{Sigmoid } (\mathrm{S}_2) = 1\Big/1 + e^{-0.66}$$

$$\text{Sigmoid } (\mathrm{S}_2) = 1/1 + 0.51$$

$$\text{Sigmoid } (\mathrm{S}_2) = 1/1.51$$

$$\text{Sigmoid } (\mathrm{S}_2) = 0.66$$

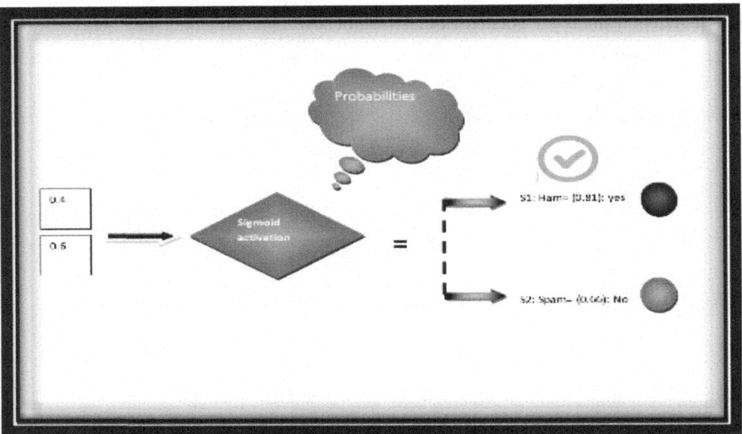

Fig. 3. Spam SMS classification using the sigmoid function.

Class S1 (spam SMS) showed the highest predicted likelihood of 0.81 in our computations. Based on this result, we can infer that the message is likely spam (Fig. 5). The steps of the proposed spam detection method are outlined in Algorithm 1 using pseudocode.

Algorithm 1. Methodology of the proposed spam SMS prediction model

#The pseudocode process for spam detection model
Input: Input dataset data as a CSV SMS file name spam 1.csv
Step1.The spam1.csv label code dataset is inputted
Step2. Apply dataset preprocessing
Step3.Using Sk-learn library the spam.csv is divide /split training and testing sets
Step4.create a vocabulary to translate each spam data into integer
Step5.convert each data stream from spam dataset into integer segment
Step6.Applying deep learning model (Bi-LSTM)
Step by Step Model Procedure
#Initialization sequential function
Model = sequential ()
 # Bi-LSTM layer
Model.add(embedding())
Model.add(Bidirectional (LSTM()))
#Uses a dropout to prevent over fitting
Model.add(dropout())
#Classify of spam using sigmoid function
Model. Add(dense(1,activation ='sigmoid'))
#Compilations Function
Model. Compile ()
#Evaluation of model using test data
Accuracy = model evaluate ()
#Classify spam return as "yes" or "no"
Output:"yes"or"no"
End procedure

4 Discussion and Results

To investigate the effectiveness of the Bi-LSTM model for spam SMS classification, we conducted multiple experiments and benchmarked the results against both classical machine learning models and contemporary deep learning approaches.

Table 5. Parameters of the proposed Bi-LSTM

Variable	Value
Vocabulary size	5574
Vocabulary vector size	127
Embedding dimensions	128
Bi LSTM unit size	64
No. of hidden layers	2
Dropout	0.25,0.9,0.8

(continued)

Table 5. (*continued*)

Variable	Value
Activation function	Sigmoid
# of epochs	32
Batch size	120,70,30

4.1 Answering Research Question No. 01

To answer the first research question—"How to detect spam text using the Bi-LSTM technique?"—a series of Bi-LSTM models were developed and fine-tuned using a preprocessed spam base dataset. Key parameters such as vocabulary size, embedding dimensions, LSTM unit size, dropout rates, and batch sizes were optimized (see Table 5).

Multiple Bi-LSTM configurations were tested, with the best-performing model, Bi-LSTM-10, achieving 98% accuracy, 98% precision, 100% recall, and a 99% F1-score (see Table 6). These results highlight the model's effectiveness, attributed to its bidirectional structure, i.e., past and future context, enabling robust spam classification.

$$Accuracy = \frac{\text{TP} + \text{TN}}{\text{TP} + \text{FN} + \text{TN} + \text{FN}} \tag{15}$$

$$Precisions = \frac{\text{TP}}{\text{TP} + \text{FP}} \tag{16}$$

$$Recall = \frac{\text{TP}}{\text{TP} + \text{FP}} \tag{17}$$

$$F1 = 2 * \frac{\text{Rec} \times \text{Pre}}{\text{Rec} + \text{Pre}} \tag{18}$$

Table 6. Precision, recall and f1-score of different versions of the proposed Bi-LSTM Deep Learning model.

Model	Accuracy	Precession	Recall	F-1 score
Bi-LSTM-1	0.95	0.97	0.98	0.98
Bi-LSTM-2	0.94	0.95	0.95	0.95
Bi-LSTM-3	0.90	0.93	0.96	0.95
Bi-LSTM-4	0.87	0.91	0.95	0.93
Bi-LSTM-5	0.90	0.93	0.95	0.94
Bi-LSTM-6	0.86	0.86	0.99	0.93
Bi-LSTM-7	0.90	0.94	0.96	0.94

(*continued*)

Table 6. (*continued*)

Model	Accuracy	Precession	Recall	F-1 score
Bi-LSTM-8	0.95	0.97	0.98	0.97
Bi-LSTM-9	0.93	0.96	0.97	0.96
Bi-LSTM-10	0.98	0.98	1.00	0.99

The Bi-LSTM model achieved 98% accuracy, 98% precision, 1.00 recall, and 0.99 F1-score, indicating strong generalization on the test dataset. The model's bidirectional architecture allowed it to learn both forward and backward contextual information, which contributed to superior performance.

4.2 Addressing Research Question No. 2

To address the second research question on the limitations of traditional machine learning (ML) techniques versus the effectiveness of Bi-LSTM, performance comparisons were conducted using models like Naïve Bayes, SVM, Decision Tree, Random Forest, and Logistic Regression. While ML models showed competitive F1-scores (0.97–0.99), they struggled with noisy or imbalanced data and scalability issues. In contrast, the proposed Bi-LSTM model consistently achieved higher and more stable performance (accuracy, precision, recall, and F1-score all at 0.98), showing strength in sequential learning. These results (See Table 7) affirm Bi-LSTM's superior suitability for spam SMS detection in dynamic and complex datasets.

Table 7. Performance comparison of proposed model with machine learning models.

Classifier	Accuracy	Precision	Recall	f-score
NB	0.97	0.99	0.99	0.99
SVM	0.97	0.97	1.00	0.98
DT	0.95	0.97	0.98	0.97
RF	0.96	0.97	1.00	0.98
LR	0.97	0.98	1.00	0.99
Proposed model Bi-LSTM	0.98	0.98	0.98	0.98

While machine learning models such as Naïve Bayes, SVM, and Random Forest demonstrated competitive results (F1-scores around 0.97–0.99), their performance declined with noisy or imbalanced data. In contrast, the Bi-LSTM model maintained stability and precision due to its capacity for sequential learning, highlighting its applicability in dynamic spam detection scenarios.

Table 8. Performance of Proposed model VS other Deep learning models.

Methods/classifier	Accuracy	Precision	Recall	f-score
LSTM	0.92	0.94	0.98	0.96
GRU	0.94	0.96	0.98	0.97
CNN	0.95	0.97	0.98	0.97
Proposed model Bi-LSTM	0.98	0.98	0.98	0.98

The proposed Bi-LSTM model was evaluated against other deep learning models—LSTM, GRU, and CNN—as detailed in Table 8. LSTM achieved 92% accuracy (precision: 0.94, recall: 0.98, F1-score: 0.96), but fell short of Bi-LSTM's performance. GRU reached 94% accuracy with a 0.96 precision and 0.97 F1-score, yet still underperformed compared to Bi-LSTM. Similarly, CNN scored 95% accuracy (precision: 0.97, recall: 0.98, F1-score: 0.97), but did not surpass Bi-LSTM. Overall, Bi-LSTM outperformed or matched all three models while maintaining computational efficiency, making it well-suited for moderate-sized datasets. However, for future work, transformer-based models like BERT and RoBERTa, known for their superior performance on large-scale NLP tasks, should be considered to improve accuracy and scalability.

4.3 Addressing Research Question No. 03

To address the third research question on the performance of the proposed model for spam prediction, experiments were conducted comparing the Bi-LSTM model to existing approaches. As shown in Table 9, the proposed Bi-LSTM achieved superior results with 98% accuracy, 100% recall, 98% precision, and a 99% F1-score. Compared to prior studies—[2]'s Bi-LSTM model (97.15% accuracy) and [3]'s machine learning approach (95% accuracy)—the proposed model outperforms both, confirming its effectiveness in spam text classification.

Table 9. Details of benchmark study of others authors

Author	Techniques	Accuracy
[2]	Bi-LSTM	0.97
[3]	Machine learning	0.95
Proposed model	Bi-LSTM	0.98

5 Conclusions and Future Work

This study addressed the problem of spam SMS detection through the application of a Bidirectional Long Short-Term Memory (Bi-LSTM) model, a deep learning approach capable of capturing contextual dependencies in sequential data. The proposed framework involved three core components: dataset acquisition, text preprocessing, and Bi-LSTM-based classification. The key contribution of this work lies in demonstrating that Bi-LSTM outperforms conventional machine learning and deep learning baselines in spam detection tasks, achieving an F1-score of 0.99, accuracy of 0.98, precision of 0.98, and recall of 1.00. Theoretically, this research advances the application of bidirectional recurrent architectures in text classification by emphasizing their capacity to learn sequential semantics without handcrafted features, offering a balance between performance and computational feasibility.

5.1 Limitations

Despite its promising results, the study has several limitations. The model was trained on a relatively small dataset, which may affect generalizability, particularly when dealing with diverse or multilingual spam types. Bi-LSTM models can also suffer from overfitting in low-resource settings and are computationally intensive, limiting their applicability in real-time or resource-constrained environments. Additionally, the model was limited to binary classification and did not explore language adaptation or domain transferability.

5.2 Future Work

Future research should focus on expanding the dataset with multilingual and domain-diverse examples to improve generalizability. Exploration of transformer-based architectures (e.g., BERT, RoBERTa) could further enhance contextual understanding and performance. Multiclass and multilabel classification, handling imbalanced datasets, and the integration of pre-trained embeddings or generative models like GANs may also improve detection robustness. Moreover, hybrid approaches combining Bi-LSTM with CNNs or attention mechanisms could be investigated for real-time spam detection in mobile or low-resource environments.

Acknowledgement. This research work was supported by Zayed University Research Incentive Fund # 38078.

Authors' Contributions. All authors contributed equally.

Conflict of Interest. The authors declare no conflict of interest.

Declaration of Generative AI and AI-Assisted Technologies in the Writing Process. The authors used AI tool i.e., Gemini, to correct language mistakes.

References

1. Salman, M., Ikram, M., Kaafar, M.A.: Investigating evasive techniques in sms spam filtering: a comparative analysis of machine learning models. IEEE Access **12**, 24306–24324 (2024)

2. Debnath, K., Kar, N.: Email spam detection using deep learning approach. In: 2022 International Conference on Machine Learning, Big Data, Cloud and Parallel Computing (COM-IT-CON) (vol. 1, pp. 37–41). IEEE (2022)
3. Gupta, S.D., Saha, S., Das, S.K.: SMS spam detection using machine learning. J. Phys. Confer. Ser. **1797**(1), 01-2017 (2021)
4. Jain, A.K., Yadav, S.K., Choudhary, N.: A novel approach to detect spam and smishing SMS using machine learning techniques. Int. J. E-Serv. Mob. Appl. (IJESMA) **12**(1), 21–38 (2020)
5. Mohammed, U.A., Sanusi, M.: An optimised phishing email detection and prevention using classification models
6. Abid, M.A., Ullah, S., Siddique, M.A., Mushtaq, M.F., Aljedaani, W., Rustam, F.: Spam SMS filtering based on text features and supervised machine learning techniques. Multimed. Tools Appl. **81**(28), 39853–39871 (2022)
7. Guo, Y., Mustafaoglu, Z., Koundal, D.: Spam detection using bidirectional transformers and machine learning classifier algorithms. J. Comput. Cognit. Eng. **2**(1), 5–9 (2023)
8. Hadi, M.T., Baawi, S.S.: Email spam detection by machine learning approaches: a review. In: International Conference on Forthcoming Networks and Sustainability in the AIoT Era (pp. 186–204). Springer Nature Switzerland, Cham (2024)
9. Taylor, O.E., Ezekiel, P.S.: A model to detect spam email using support vector classifier and random forest classifier. Int. J. Comput. Sci. Math. Theory **6**(1), 1–11 (2020)
10. Malhotra, P., Malik, S.: Spam email detection using machine learning and deep learning techniques. In: Proceedings of the International Conference on Innovative Computing & Communication (ICICC) (2022)
11. Sheneamer, A.: Comparison of deep and traditional learning methods for email spam filtering. Int. J. Adv. Comput. Sci. Appl. **12**(1), 1–6 (2021)
12. Abayomi-Alli, O., Misra, S., Abayomi-Alli, A.: A deep learning method for automatic SMS spam classification: performance of learning algorithms on indigenous dataset. Concurr. Comput. Pract. Exp. **34**(17), e6989 (2022)
13. Dutta, A.K., et al.: Optimal deep belief network enabled cybersecurity phishing email classification. Comput. Syst. Sci. Eng. **44**(3), 2701–2713 (2023)
14. Brindha, R., Nandagopal, S., Azath, H., Sathana, V., Joshi, G.P., Kim, S.W.: Intelligent deep learning based cybersecurity phishing email detection and classification. Comput. Mater. Continua **74**(3) (2023)
15. Alhogail, A., Alsabih, A.: Applying machine learning and natural language processing to detect phishing email. Comput. Secur. **110**, 102414 (2021)
16. Bountakas, P., Xenakis, C.: Helphed: hybrid ensemble learning phishing email detection. J. Netw. Comput. Appl. **210**, 103545 (2023)
17. Butt, U.A., Alouffi, B., Ahmadian, A.: Cloud-based email phishing attack using machine and deep learning algorithm. Complex Intell. Syst. **9**(3), 3043–3070 (2023)
18. Ahmed, N., Amin, R., Aldabbas, H., Koundal, D., Alouffi, B., Shah, T.: Machine learning techniques for spam detection in email and IoT platforms: analysis and research challenges. Secur. Commun. Netw. **2022**(1), 1862888 (2022)
19. Khattak, A., Habib, A., Asghar, M., Razzak, I., Habib, A.: Applying deep neural networks for user intention identification. Soft. Comput. **25**, 2191–2220 (2021)

Optimizing SQL Injection Detection: A Comparative Analysis of Embedding Methods with XGBoost

Aymen Msalmi[1,2] and Mohamed Hedi Riahi[2](✉)

[1] ESPRIT School of Engineering Tunisia, Ariana, Tunisia
aymen.msalmi@esprit.tn
[2] Securas Technologies Sfax, Sfax, Tunisia
mohamedhedi.riahi@esprit.tn

Abstract. SQL injection attacks (SQLi) remain one of the most critical web security threats, often leading to data breaches, unauthorized access, and financial losses. In this study, we propose an approach leveraging the XGBoost algorithm to detect SQL injection attacks by evaluating various text vectorization techniques applied to network traffic and SQL queries, including TF-IDF, GloVe embeddings, Skip-gram and Continuous Bag-of-Words (CBOW) Word2Vec models, FastText embeddings, the Bag-of-Words (BoW) model, and BERT-based embeddings. Our experimental results demonstrate that combining CBOW or Word2Vec with eXtreme Gradient Boosting (XGB) achieves superior performance, allowing us to determine the most suitable embedding methods based on specific detection priorities. If real-time detection is required, CBOW or Word2Vec is the most appropriate choice, whereas if accuracy is prioritized over speed, Word2Vec with adjusted thresholds optimizes recall. To minimize false positives, BoW or IDF can be employed, although they may lead to a slightly higher false negative rate. These insights contribute to optimizing SQLi detection strategies by balancing efficiency, accuracy, and robustness in cybersecurity applications.

Keywords: SQL Injection (SQLi) · Cybersecurity · XGBoost (XGB) · Word2Vec · Text Vectorization · CBOW

1 Introduction

Web applications are at the heart of the modern digital ecosystem, offering users seamless access to information while enabling businesses to expand their reach and optimize their services. However, this ubiquity comes with an increasing

Supported by Securas Technologies Sfax, Tunisia.

F. Kamoun et al. (Eds.): AFRICATEK 2025, LNICST 677, pp. 65–83, 2026.
https://doi.org/10.1007/978-3-032-16638-8_6

number of cybersecurity threats, among which SQL Injection (SQLi) attacks remain one of the most prevalent and severe [17]. By exploiting vulnerabilities in the interaction between web applications and their databases, malicious actors can inject fraudulent SQL queries, allowing unauthorized access, modification, or deletion of sensitive data [16]. Such attacks jeopardize data integrity, confidentiality, and availability, making them a critical concern for cybersecurity professionals.

The repercussions of an SQL injection attack can be devastating. Beyond the exfiltration of sensitive information—such as login credentials, financial records, and personal data—these attacks can manipulate or erase critical database records, leading to operational disruptions. In extreme cases, attackers can escalate privileges, gaining full control over the database server and accessing strategic assets. The impact extends beyond technical breaches, as organizations may face severe financial losses, regulatory fines for non-compliance with data protection standards (such as GDPR and PCI-DSS), reputational damage, and legal liabilities resulting from compromised user data [13].

Given the severity of these threats, advancing SQL injection detection mechanisms is imperative to safeguarding digital infrastructures and ensuring data security. Traditional rule-based and signature-based approaches, while effective against known attack patterns, struggle to adapt to evolving threats and sophisticated obfuscation techniques. Consequently, the integration of artificial intelligence (AI) and machine learning (ML) has emerged as a promising avenue for enhancing SQL injection detection. These technologies enable real-time analysis of SQL queries and user behavior, facilitating the identification of subtle anomalies and suspicious patterns that conventional methods may overlook. However, applying machine learning to SQL injection detection presents several technical challenges [3]. A primary obstacle lies in processing SQL queries—unstructured textual data—into meaningful numerical representations suitable for AI models. Traditional feature extraction techniques often fail to capture the syntactic and semantic intricacies of SQL statements, limiting detection accuracy. More advanced natural language processing (NLP)-based embeddings, such as word embeddings or transformer-based representations, offer improved context awareness but require extensive labeled datasets for training robust models. Furthermore, achieving an optimal balance between detection accuracy and computational efficiency is crucial for deploying effective, real-time security solutions in high-performance environments.

In this context, our study investigates the application of machine learning models to SQL injection detection, with a focus on query embedding techniques, their impact on model precision, and the practical challenges of deploying such models in production environments. By leveraging advanced NLP techniques and lightweight, high-performance ML architectures, we aim to develop scalable and resilient solutions to reinforce the security of web applications against SQL injection attacks.

2 Literature Review

SQL injection attacks remain one of the most feared threats to the security of modern web applications, jeopardizing the integrity, confidentiality, and availability of data stored in databases. By exploiting vulnerabilities in the interaction between applications and their database management systems (DBMS), these attacks allow cybercriminals to execute malicious SQL queries, bypassing authentication and access control mechanisms. Their impact can be devastating, ranging from the theft of sensitive data to the corruption of stored information, or even the complete takeover of the server [16,17].

Faced with this persistent threat, traditional detection approaches, primarily relying on static rules and signatures, are increasingly proving inadequate. While these methods have long served as the first line of defense by identifying known attack patterns, they lack the flexibility to detect sophisticated variants, particularly those using obfuscation and evasion techniques. Early attempts at SQL injection detection relied mainly on heuristic rules, syntactic filters, and systems based on regular expressions. These solutions offered the advantage of relatively simple and effective implementation against classic attacks, but they were unable to anticipate more advanced techniques, such as injections based on nested subqueries or the exploitation of DBMS-specific vulnerabilities.

In this context, machine learning has emerged as a promising alternative, overcoming the limitations of traditional approaches by detecting more complex attack patterns and adapting to new threats. Several studies have explored the effectiveness of various supervised learning models for classifying malicious SQL queries [2]. Roy et al. (2022) compared several classifiers, including Naïve Bayes, XGBoost, Random Forest, Logistic Regression, and AdaBoost [18]. Their study revealed that Naïve Bayes achieved an accuracy of 98.33%, but did not address critical aspects such as processing time or the model's ability to generalize to novel attack patterns. Meanwhile, Li et al. introduced an approach based on an Adaptive Deep Forest, leveraging multiple sliding windows to extract dynamic features and automatically adjust model parameters [9]. Although this method demonstrated adaptability to attack variations, it did not explore the challenges related to real-world deployment, such as computational constraints and compatibility with existing detection systems.

The effectiveness of a detection model largely depends on the quality of the representation of SQL queries. A fundamental challenge lies in transforming queries, which follow a rigid syntax and nested structures, into vector representations usable by learning algorithms. Classical approaches such as TF-IDF and N-grams suffer from a lack of contextualization and struggle to capture the syntactic and semantic relationships of queries. Oudah et al. showed that using character-level TF-IDF combined with an SVM model achieved an accuracy of 99.7%, outperforming word-based and N-gram methods [15]. However, their approach required longer training times, raising questions about its viability in production. Kasim, on the other hand, proposed a method extracting 22 specific features, combined with a classifier aggregation algorithm, achieving a detection rate exceeding 98% [7].

With the rise of deep learning models, architectures based on Transformers such as BERT and RoBERTa have been explored for SQL injection detection, offering enhanced performance due to their ability to capture long-range dependencies in queries [4,19]. In the other work, we developed a hybrid approach combining TF-IDF, a generative adversarial network (VGAN), and XGBoost, achieving an accuracy of 99.95% [6,10]. However, this performance comes with increased computational complexity, limiting real-time applicability and deployment on resource-constrained systems. Jesús-Ángel et al. highlighted the limitations of traditional web application firewalls (WAFs), proposing an AI-based alternative [14]. By evaluating several models on a dataset of 100,000 queries, they achieved success rates ranging from 92 to 99%, but did not address the impact of processing time on overall system performance [1,8].

The literature review thus reveals that machine learning and deep learning models achieve promising performance for SQL injection detection, with accuracy rates often exceeding 98%. However, several challenges remain before they can be effectively integrated into operational cybersecurity infrastructures [3,13]. The models' ability to generalize to new attacks, the reduction of computational complexity for real-time detection, and interoperability with existing systems are among the major issues. Improving datasets, particularly by increasing examples of malicious queries and incorporating realistic scenarios, is a key lever for refining model robustness. Furthermore, exploring advanced techniques for representing SQL queries, such as context-specific SQL embeddings or generative adversarial models for detecting polymorphic attacks, opens promising avenues [11,12]. Finally, the development of hybrid architectures combining the efficiency of lightweight models with the power of deep neural networks could enable an optimal trade-off between accuracy and execution speed.

Thus, research in this field must focus on developing models capable of dynamically adapting to new threats while maintaining operational efficiency compatible with the demands of modern cybersecurity systems. By combining artificial intelligence with advanced detection mechanisms, it becomes possible to significantly enhance the protection of web applications against SQL injection threats, ensuring a higher level of security in the face of constantly evolving cyberattacks.

In this paper, we start with a literature review, followed by the presentation of the methodology, where we detail the database, preprocessing, feature extraction and transformation, as well as the model used. The third part of the paper is dedicated to the evaluation and analysis of the results in order to select the best embedding method in combination with the XGBoost algorithm. This analysis takes into account several parameters, including performance scores, execution time, true positive rate and false positive rate.

3 Methodology

Our study investigates and compares various techniques for embedding SQL queries, proposing a classification approach based on ensemble methods, particularly the XGBoost algorithm. The integration of these strategies yields high performance in terms of accuracy and attack detection. This section outlines our methodology, following the structured workflow illustrated in Fig. 1.

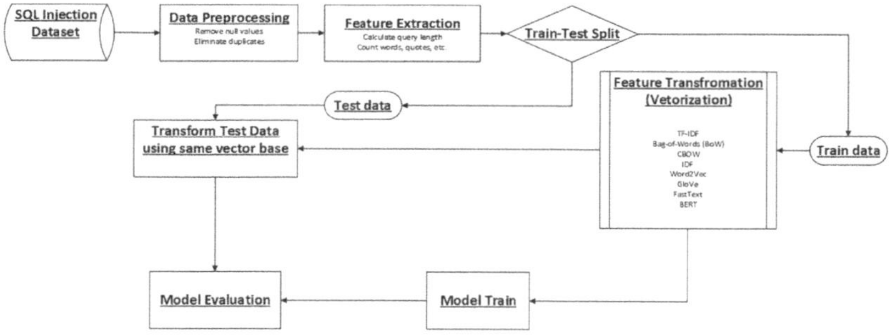

Fig. 1. End-to-End machine learning pipeline for SQL injection detection.

Our approach begins with data collection and pre-processing, a critical step where we remove null values and eliminate duplicates to ensure dataset integrity and reliability. Next, we conduct feature extraction by analyzing various parameters, such as query length, word count, the presence of quotation marks, and other syntactic elements indicative of potentially malicious patterns.

The data is then split into training and test sets to facilitate a rigorous evaluation of the predictive models. A pivotal step in our pipeline is feature transformation, where we employ a range of vectorization techniques, from traditional methods like TF-IDF and Bag-of-Words to more advanced approaches such as Word2Vec, GloVe, FastText, and BERT. These techniques convert SQL queries into numerical representations suitable for machine learning algorithms.

The models are subsequently trained on the training set and evaluated on the test set, with the same transformations applied to ensure consistency and comparability of results. This systematic approach ensures the development of robust, high-performance solutions for detecting SQL injections, optimizing both the accuracy and generalization capability of the deployed models.

3.1 Dataset

For training and evaluating our model to detect SQL injection attacks, we utilized the SQL Injection Dataset available on Kaggle [5]. This dataset, widely recognized within the cybersecurity community, comprises a total of 33,725 SQL queries, each labeled as either benign (label = 0) or malicious (label = 1). The binary labeling facilitates a clear distinction between legitimate and potentially harmful queries, providing a solid foundation for supervised learning.

Prior to using the dataset for training, several pre-processing steps were applied to enhance data quality, eliminate biases, and ensure the model is trained on relevant and representative information. These steps include:

1. **Duplicate Removal:** Duplicate SQL queries were identified and removed to avoid redundancy. This step is crucial in ensuring that the model is not influenced by repeated examples, which could distort the results and hinder its ability to generalize.
2. **Cleaning Special and Inconsistent Characters:** We standardized the query format by removing unnecessary artifacts such as extraneous spaces, non-ASCII characters, or irrelevant symbols. However, we ensured that critical syntactic and semantic patterns distinguishing malicious queries from benign ones were preserved. For example, special characters often used in SQL injections (such as single quotes or semicolons) were retained, as they play a pivotal role in detecting attacks.

After these cleaning and pre-processing steps, the final distribution of the data is as follows:

- Benign queries (label = 0): 22,301
- Malicious queries (label = 1): 11,424

This balanced distribution, though slightly skewed in favor of benign queries, reflects a realistic balance between representing real-world scenarios and providing enough examples of malicious queries for robust model training.

By using this dataset, along with comprehensive cleaning and analysis, we ensure that our model is trained on high-quality, representative data. This meticulous preparation maximizes the model's performance and enhances its ability to accurately detect SQL injection attacks while minimizing false positives and false negatives.

3.2 Feature Extraction

In order to convert each SQL query into a numerical representation that can be used by the classification model, we defined a set of relevant features that capture the syntactic and structural patterns of the queries. These features transform SQL queries into attribute vectors, making them suitable for processing by machine learning models. They are summarized in the table below (Table 1):

The purpose of this feature extraction is to transform each SQL query into a numerical vector, consisting of features that reflect its syntactic and structural properties. These vectors are then used to feed our classification model, enabling the efficient identification of malicious queries and SQL injection attacks. This approach provides several advantages:

- **Identification of typical patterns:** The model can detect characteristic patterns of SQL attacks while being trained on balanced and diverse data.
- **Generalization capability:** Thanks to the detailed extraction of features, the model retains good generalization ability, allowing it to adapt to unknown or slightly modified queries.
- **Improved robustness:** The diversity of features enables the detection of more sophisticated attacks, while reducing the risk of false positives and false negatives.

Table 1. Summary of features extracted from SQL queries

Feature name	Description	Extraction method/Pattern
`query_len`	Total number of characters in the query	`len(query)`
`num_words`	Number of words in the query, computed by splitting on whitespace	`len(query.split())`
`nb_single_qts`	Count of single quote characters, which can be indicative of string delimiters in SQL queries	Pattern: `r"\'"` via `count_pattern(query, r"\'")`
`nb_double_qts`	Count of double quote characters, another common delimiter in queries.	Pattern: `r'"'` via `count_pattern(query, r'"')`
`nb_punct`	Count of punctuation symbols (non-alphanumeric and non-space characters), useful for detecting special syntax	Pattern: `r'[\^\w\s]'` via `count_pattern(query, r'[\^\w\s]')`
`nb_single_cmnt`	Count of single-line comment markers (e.g., `--`), often used in SQL injections	Pattern: `r'--'` via `count_pattern(query, r'--')`
`nb_mult_cmnt`	Count of multi-line comment markers (e.g., `/* ... */`), which can obfuscate malicious queries	Pattern: `r'/*.*?*/'` via `count_pattern(query, r'/*.*?*/')`
`nb_space`	Count of whitespace characters, which can give a sense of query formatting	Pattern: `r'\s'` via `count_pattern(query, r'\s')`
`nb_perc`	Count of percentage signs, often used in SQL wildcards or formatting	Pattern: `r'\%'` via `count_pattern(query, r'\%')`
`nb_log_opt`	Count of logical operators (e.g., `AND`, `OR`, `NOT`, `&&`)	Sum of counts for each operator in `['AND', 'OR', 'NOT', '\&&']`
`nb_arith`	Count of arithmetic operators (e.g., `+`, `-`, `*`, `/`, `%`), possibly used in query calculations or obfuscation	Sum of counts for each operator in `['+', '-', '*', '/', '\%']`
`nb_null`	Count of occurrences of the word `NULL` (case-insensitive), which can be a marker in injection attacks	`query.upper().count("NULL")`
`nb_hexa`	Count of hexadecimal values (e.g., `0x1A3F`), often used in encoded payloads	Pattern: `r'0x[0-9A-Fa-f]+'` via `re.findall`
`nb_alpha`	Count of alphabetic characters, giving an idea of the textual content	Pattern: `r'[A-Za-z]'` via `re.findall`
`nb_digit`	Count of digit characters, which can help detect numeric values or obfuscation	Pattern: `r'\d'` via `re.findall`

Thus, this feature extraction methodology contributes to more accurate detection of SQL attacks by integrating a variety of signals that reflect both specific syntactic elements and suspicious behaviors commonly observed in SQL injection attacks.

3.3 Train-Test Split

To evaluate model performance, we split the dataset into **70% training**, **15% validation**, and **15% testing** sets. The **training set** enables the model to learn patterns, the **validation set** helps fine-tune hyperparameters, and the **testing set** provides a final performance assessment on unseen data. This split ensures effective training, minimizes overfitting, and prevents data leakage, leading to a robust model for SQL injection detection.

3.4 Feature Transformation

To convert raw SQL queries into numerical representations suitable for machine learning models, we employed a range of text vectorization techniques. The Fig. 2 illustrates the end-to-end processing pipeline, beginning with the raw query and culminating in the final classification. It highlights each stage of the process, with particular emphasis on feature transformation, which plays a critical role in enhancing model performance. The diagram outlines the methods applied to transform input variables, thereby enabling more accurate and robust classification.

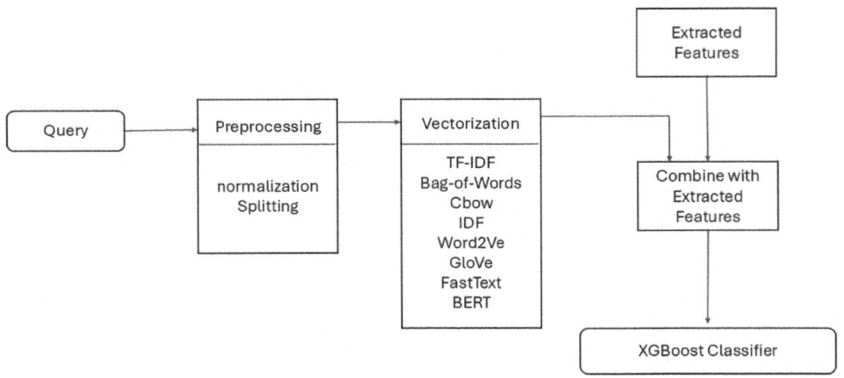

Fig. 2. Pipeline for SQL injection detection.

Each technique was carefully selected for its ability to capture different dimensions of the SQL query—its structure, syntax, and semantics—contributing to the model's effectiveness in distinguishing between benign and malicious queries. A detailed description of each vectorization method used is provided below:

1. **TF-IDF (Term FrequencyInverse Document Frequency):**
   - **Description:** TF-IDF quantifies the importance of a word by balancing its frequency within a specific document (query) against its frequency across the entire dataset. This method emphasizes terms that are rare yet informative, helping to detect unique patterns in SQL queries that are indicative of SQL injection attempts.

   - **Application:** TF-IDF was applied to highlight SQL keywords or operators that are uncommon but critical for identifying malicious queries, such as specific injection techniques or suspicious operators.
2. **Bag-of-Words (BoW):**
   - **Description:** BoW represents each query as a vector of word counts, ignoring word order but capturing the overall frequency of terms. This simple method provides a foundational representation of textual content.
   - **Application:** BoW was used to capture the frequency of SQL keywords and operators, providing a baseline representation that allows the model to recognize recurring terms in both benign and malicious queries.
3. **Continuous Bag-of-Words (CBOW - Word2Vec):**
   - **Description:** CBOW predicts a target word based on its surrounding context words. This technique generates word embeddings that encapsulate semantic relationships between words by averaging their contexts.
   - **Application:** CBOW was used to generate word embeddings that capture the contextual relationships between SQL keywords and operators, providing a richer representation of query structure and helping to identify patterns indicative of SQL injection.
4. **Inverse Document Frequency (IDF):**
   - **Description:** IDF measures the rarity of words across documents, assigning higher weights to words that appear less frequently. This highlights the importance of words that are rare but potentially significant in identifying malicious patterns.
   - **Application:** IDF was employed to emphasize rare SQL constructs or keywords, which are often used in SQL injection attempts, making it easier to spot injection-related anomalies.
5. **Skip-gram Word2Vec:**
   - **Description:** Skip-gram predicts surrounding words for a given center word, capturing more nuanced semantic relationships compared to CBOW. This method is particularly effective for learning rare word associations and understanding context.
   - **Application:** Skip-gram was used to generate embeddings that capture deeper semantic relationships between SQL keywords and their surrounding context, enhancing the model's ability to detect more sophisticated injection patterns.
6. **GloVe Embeddings:**
   - **Description:** GloVe (Global Vectors for Word Representation) learns word representations by aggregating global co-occurrence statistics across a corpus. This approach produces word vectors where geometric distances reflect semantic similarities.
   - **Application:** GloVe embeddings were used to capture global patterns of word co-occurrence in SQL queries, allowing the model to identify common structures and detect anomalies indicative of SQL injection.
7. **FastText Embeddings:**
   - **Description:** FastText extends Word2Vec by incorporating subword (character n-gram) information, which enables the model to generate meaningful embeddings for rare or misspelled words.

- **Application:** FastText was particularly useful for handling misspelled or rare SQL keywords, ensuring that queries with slight variations (e.g., typographical errors) could still be effectively represented and analyzed.

8. **BERT Transformer-based Embeddings:**
   - **Description:** BERT (Bidirectional Encoder Representations from Transformers) generates deep contextualized word embeddings by considering both the left and right context of each word. This approach is computationally intensive but excels at capturing complex language patterns.
   - **Application:** BERT embeddings were used to capture the intricate, bidirectional context within SQL queries. These embeddings provide a highly detailed and nuanced representation, making them particularly effective for detecting sophisticated SQL injection techniques.

Each of these transformation techniques was applied exclusively to the training and validation sets to prevent any data leakage from the test set during the learning process. This approach ensures that the model's performance on the test set is a true reflection of its ability to generalize to unseen data. By utilizing a combination of vectorization methods, we captured a wide array of features from SQL queries, enhancing the model's ability to identify both common and sophisticated SQL injection attacks. This comprehensive feature transformation strategy enables the model to leverage diverse textual characteristics, improving its overall detection capabilities.

3.5 Model Selection

We selected XGBoost for its efficiency and strong predictive performance in handling structured data. To optimize results, we fine-tuned its hyperparameters, using **binary classification (logistic regression)** as the objective function and **log loss** as the evaluation metric. Key parameters include a **learning rate of 0.1**, **maximum tree depth of 6**, and **100 estimators**, ensuring a balance between complexity and performance. Hyperparameter tuning via **Grid Search and Random Search** with cross-validation further enhanced generalization. This rigorous approach resulted in a robust model for SQL injection detection, effectively distinguishing between benign and malicious queries.

4 Performance Evaluation of XGBoost with Different SQL Query Embedding Methods

The XGBoost algorithm was used to detect SQL injections based on different methods for transforming SQL queries into numerical representations. The performance of each method was evaluated using several key metrics, such as accuracy, precision, recall, F1-score, and prediction and transformation times. The following Table 2 summarises the performance of XGBoost with the different embedding methods:

Table 2. Performance metrics of XGBoost with different SQL query embedding methods

Model	Accuracy	Precision	Recall	F1 score	FPR	FNR	APT query	ATT request	Time
TF-IDF	0.997233	0.998242	0.993582	0.995906	0.000897	0.006418	0.000165	0.000022	0.000186
BoW	0.997430	0.998827	0.993582	0.996198	0.000598	0.006418	0.000133	0.000009	0.000143
CBOW	0.997628	0.998828	0.994166	0.996491	0.000598	0.005834	0.000001	0.000056	0.000088
IDF	0.997430	0.998827	0.993582	0.996198	0.000598	0.006418	0.000228	0.000023	0.000251
Word2Vec	0.997826	0.998245	0.995333	0.996786	0.000897	0.004667	0.000001	0.000330	0.000331
GloVe	0.996837	0.997073	0.993582	0.995324	0.001495	0.006418	0.000002	0.000101	0.000103
FastText	0.996640	0.998238	0.991832	0.995025	0.000897	0.008168	0.000002	0.000437	0.000439
BERT	0.996442	0.998237	0.991249	0.994731	0.000897	0.008751	0.000004	0.063045	0.063049

with

- FPR: False Positive Rate
- FNR: False Negative Rate
- APT Query :Avg Prediction Time per Query
- ATT Request: Avg Transformation Time per Request.

The following Fig. 3 presents the performance results of our XGBoost algorithm using different embedding models. It showcases the various evaluation metrics employed, allowing for a comparative analysis of each embedding method's effectiveness.

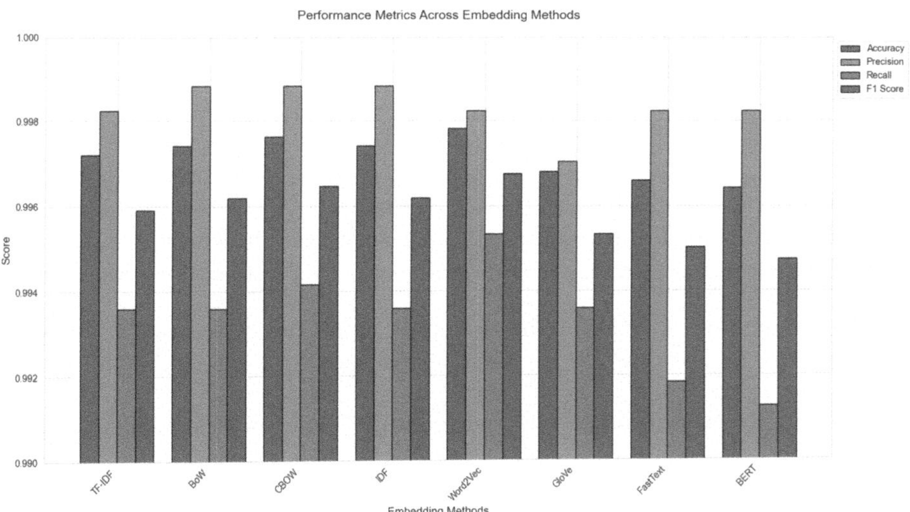

Fig. 3. Performance metrics across embedding methods.

4.1 General Observations

In this section, we analyze the overall performance of the models, their detection sensitivity, and inference time, all of which are crucial factors in cybersecurity applications.

Overall Metrics The Table 2 presents the overall performance metrics of the evaluated models. All models demonstrate exceptionally high accuracy, reaching approximately 99.6% or higher. Similarly, precision scores remain close to 99.8%, while F1-scores approach 0.995, highlighting the robustness of the approaches in identifying SQL injection attacks with minimal classification errors.

- **Accuracy:** The models consistently achieve near-perfect accuracy, indicating their ability to correctly classify benign and malicious SQL queries.
- **Precision:** The high precision values suggest that false positives (i.e., benign queries misclassified as malicious) are minimal, reducing unnecessary security alerts.
- **F1-score:** Given the balance between precision and recall, an F1-score close to 0.995 confirms that the models not only identify threats effectively but also maintain a low rate of misclassification.

The following Fig. 4 illustrates the precision-recall trade-off obtained by our XGBoost algorithm across different embedding models. This comparison highlights the balance between precision and recall for each embedding approach, providing insights into their effectiveness in handling false positives and false negatives.

Detection Sensitivity In the context of cybersecurity, minimizing false negatives—i.e., missed malicious queries—is of utmost importance. A high recall ensures that the system successfully detects a large proportion of attack attempts. Among the evaluated techniques, neural embedding methods, particularly Word2Vec and Continuous Bag-of-Words (CBOW), demonstrate an optimal trade-off between recall and precision. These models effectively minimize the number of undetected attacks while maintaining high classification performance.

- **Word2Vec and CBOW:** These models strike the best balance, offering superior recall rates while keeping false negatives lower than alternative approaches.
- **Trade-off between recall and precision:** While some models favor precision at the cost of recall, embedding-based methods ensure that a higher percentage of attacks are detected, making them preferable for cybersecurity applications.

The following Fig. 5 illustrates the trade-off between the false positive rate and the false negative rate obtained by our XGBoost algorithm across different embedding models.

Fig. 4. precision-recall trade-off.

Inference Time For real-time threat detection, inference speed is a key factor. Although all models perform inference within the microsecond range, their total response times vary, impacting their suitability for live environments.

- **CBOW and Word2Vec:** These methods demonstrate the fastest inference times, making them ideal for real-time detection scenarios.
- **BERT's computational overhead:** Despite its high accuracy, BERT's significantly longer transformation time renders it less suitable for real-time applications. The trade-off between model complexity and processing speed must be carefully considered when deploying such models in cybersecurity environments.

These observations highlight the importance of selecting a model that balances high detection performance with efficient real-time processing, ensuring an optimal trade-off between security and system responsiveness.

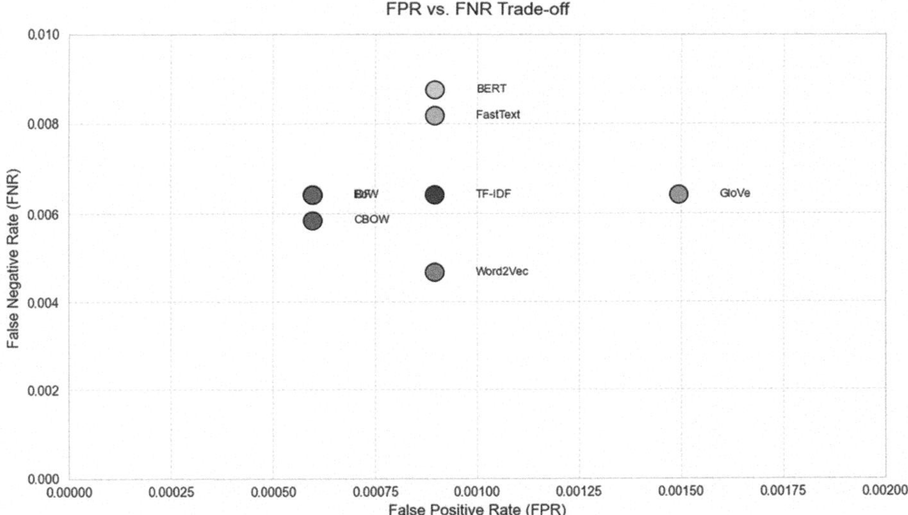

Fig. 5. FPR versus FNR trade off.

4.2 False Negatives and Model Reliability

In cybersecurity, missing an attack is far riskier than triggering an extra alert. The following (Table 4.2) summarizes each model's performance regarding false negatives and their corresponding False Negative Rate (FNR):

Model	False Negative Rate (FNR)	Analysis
CBOW	~0.0058	Best recall among the models; minimizes missed detections effectively
Word2Vec	~0.0046	Slightly better recall than CBOW, making it highly reliable
BoW, IDF, TF-IDF	~0.0064	Decent performance, but with a slightly higher tendency to miss threats
FastText	~0.0081	Higher false negatives, reducing its reliability in threat detection
BERT	~0.0087	Highest risk of missed detections; not ideal for security-sensitive tasks

- Word2Vec and CBOW are the most reliable choices for reducing false negatives.
- Methods like BERT, despite strong contextual understanding, are riskier in scenarios where every threat must be detected.

4.3 False Positives and Precision Considerations

Although false positives are less critical than false negatives, an excessively high false positive rate can lead to unnecessary alerts and increased operational costs. Consider the following summary (Table 4.3):

Model	False positive rate	Analysis
BoW, IDF, CBOW	~0.0006	Achieve near-perfect precision; trigger very few false alerts
TF-IDF, Word2Vec, FastText, BERT	~0.0009	Slightly higher false positives, but still remain very low overall
GloVe	~0.0015	Generates the most false positives, potentially leading to more alerts

- BoW and IDF are ideal when minimizing false alerts is critical.
- Word2Vec and CBOW strike an excellent balance—minimizing both false negatives and false positives.
- GloVe, while useful in some contexts, may not be suitable for scenarios where minimizing false positives is a priority.

4.4 Inference Time–Real-Time Considerations

In real-time cybersecurity applications, processing speed is paramount. The table below summarizes average prediction times, transformation times, and the overall total time for each model:

Model	Avg prediction (s)	Avg transformation (s)	Total (s)	Analysis
CBOW	~0.000001	~0.000056	~0.000058	Fastest overall; ideal for real-time detection
Word2Vec	~0.000001	~0.000330	~0.000331	Slightly slower than CBOW but still efficient with high recall
BoW, IDF,	~0.000133	~0.000009	~0.000129	Fast, but not as quick as neural embedding models
TF-IDF	~ 0.000228	~ 0.000023	~ 0.000251	
GloVe,	~0.000002	~0.000101	~0.000103	Moderate performance; slower than CBOW and Word2Vec
FastText		~ 0.000437	0.000439	Moderate performance; slower than CBOW and Word2Vec
BERT	~0.000004	~0.063045	~0.063049	Extremely slow transformation time; impractical for real-time use

The Fig. 6 illustrates the execution time required for converting SQL queries into numerical vectors using various embedding algorithms. Additionally, it presents the execution time for predicting outcomes based on different embedding models. This comparison provides insight into the computational efficiency of each approach, highlighting the trade-offs between transformation and prediction phases across different embedding techniques.

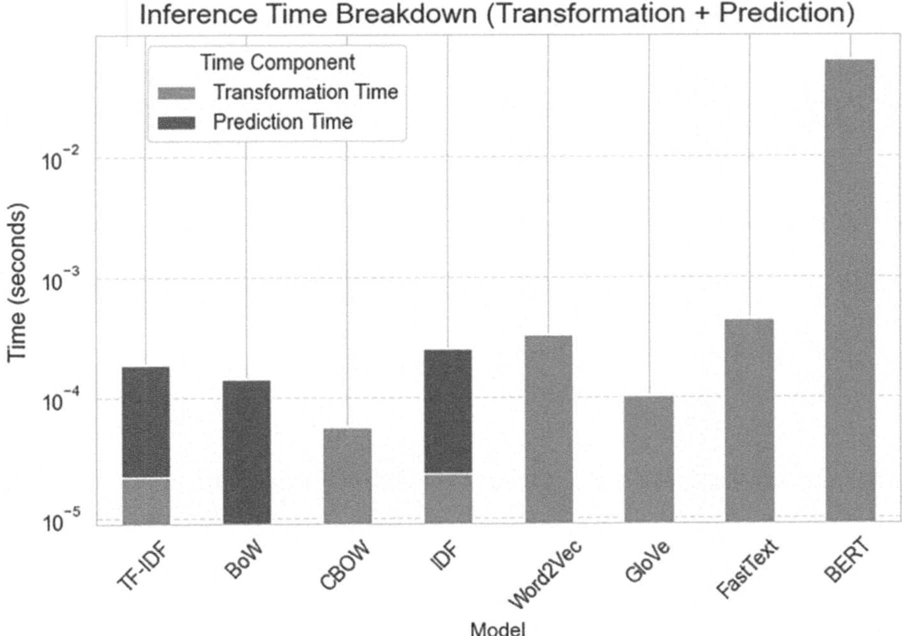

Fig. 6. Inference time breakdown.

From the results presented in the Table 4.4 and Fig. 6, we conclude that the choice of embedding algorithm significantly impacts both the transformation and prediction execution times.

- CBOW is the fastest, making it highly suitable for live threat detection.
- Word2Vec offers a strong balance of speed and recall.
- BERT's latency makes it unsuitable for real-time cybersecurity applications.

4.5 Final Recommendations–Best Embedding Models for Cybersecurity

When selecting models for cybersecurity applications, the choice depends on the specific use case. For minimizing false negatives (high recall), embedding models like Word2Vec and CBOW are the best options, as they detect the most threats while maintaining high precision. If the goal is to balance precision and recall, embedding models such as CBOW and Word2Vec are again recommended, as they offer low false negatives and low false positives, along with fast inference speeds. For minimizing false positives (high precision), traditional models like BoW and IDF are ideal, as they generate very few false alerts, though they might miss slightly more attacks. When real-time detection speed is critical, embedding models like CBOW are the fastest, providing the lowest overall inference time and making them ideal for high-speed environments. On the other hand, advanced embedding models like BERT should be avoided in high-risk scenarios due to their high false negatives and slow inference times, which make them impractical for real-time applications.

5 Conclusion and Perspectives

In this study, we explored various text vectorization techniques combined with the XGBoost algorithm to enhance SQL injection detection. Our findings highlight that CBOW is the most suitable choice for real-time cybersecurity applications, offering the fastest inference time and robust recall, ensuring minimal missed attacks. Word2Vec also demonstrates strong recall performance with only a slight compromise in speed, making it a viable alternative.

For scenarios where minimizing false positives is the priority, Bag-of-Words (BoW) and IDF can be employed, although they come with a slight trade-off in recall. On the other hand, BERT-based embeddings, despite their effectiveness in many NLP tasks, are not recommended for real-time security-sensitive environments due to their latency and a higher risk of missed threats.

From a practical deployment perspective, for real-time detection, CBOW or Word2Vec should be prioritized. For accuracy over speed, Word2Vec with adjusted thresholds offers optimal recall. For reducing false positives, BoW or IDF can be considered, with awareness of their potential impact on recall.

Ultimately, CBOW and Word2Vec emerge as the most balanced and reliable models for SQL injection detection, providing a robust trade-off between speed, accuracy, and false positive rates. These insights contribute to refining cybersecurity strategies, enabling more effective protection against SQL injection attacks in real-world applications.

As cyber threats evolve, leveraging more advanced AI techniques could further enhance SQL injection detection. In particular, Large Language Models (LLMs), such as GPT-based architectures, offer promising avenues for improving detection capabilities. LLMs can analyze complex SQL query patterns, understand context better, and generalize across various attack types. Their ability to generate synthetic attack scenarios could also be used to improve dataset diversity and enhance model robustness.

However, deploying LLMs in real-time security applications presents challenges, including inference latency and computational costs. Future research could focus on optimizing lightweight versions of LLMs or integrating them as hybrid models, where traditional techniques handle real-time detection, and LLMs assist in deeper analysis and adaptive learning.

By combining classical machine learning approaches with generative AI, future cybersecurity solutions can become more resilient, adaptive, and capable of detecting sophisticated SQL injection attacks with higher accuracy.

References

1. Abdullah, H.S., Abdulazeez, A.M.: Detection of sql injection attacks based on supervised machine learning algorithms: a review. Int. J. Inform. , Inf. Syst. Comput. Eng. (INJIISCOM) **5**(2), 152–165 (2024)
2. Abebe, A., Belay, Y., Belay, A., Gebeyehu, S.: SQL injection attacks detection: a performance comparison on multiple classification models. Ethiop. Int. J. Eng. Technol. **2**(1), 22–38 (2024)
3. AL-Maliki, M.H.A., Jasim, M.N.: Review of SQL injection attacks: detection, to enhance the security of the website from client-side attacks. Int. J. Nonlinear Anal. Appl. **13**(1), 3773–3782 (2022)
4. Augustine, N., Sultan, A.B.M., Osman, M.H., Sharif, K.Y.: Application of artificial intelligence in detecting SQL injection attacks. JOIV: Int. J. Inform. Vis. **8**(4), 2131–2138 (2024)
5. Hussain, S.S.: SQL injection dataset (2025). https://www.kaggle.com/datasets/syedsaqlainhussain/sql-injection-dataset/data. Accessed 09 Mar 2025
6. Irungu, J., Graham, S., Girma, A., Kacem, T.: Artificial intelligence techniques for SQL injection attack detection. In: Proceedings of the 2023 8th International Conference on Intelligent Information Technology, pp. 38–45 (2023)
7. Kasim, Ö.: An ensemble classification-based approach to detect attack level of SQL injections. J. Inf. Secur. Appl. **59**, 102852 (2021)
8. Krishnan, S.A., Sabu, A.N., Sajan, P.P., Sreedeep, A.: SQL injection detection using machine learning. Revista Geintec-Gestao Inovacao E Tecnologias **11**(3), 300–310 (2021)
9. Li, Q., Li, W., Wang, J., Cheng, M.: A SQL injection detection method based on adaptive deep forest. IEEE Access **7**, 145385–145394 (2019)
10. Liu, Y., Dai, Y.: Deep learning in cybersecurity: a hybrid BERT-LSTM network for SQL injection attack detection. IET Inf. Secur. **2024**(1), 5565950 (2024)
11. Mondal, B., Banerjee, A., Gupta, S.: A review of SQLI detection strategies using machine learning. Int. J. Health Sci. (II), 9664–9677 (2022)
12. Muhammad, T., Ghafory, H.: SQL injection attack detection using machine learning algorithm. Mesop. J. Cybersecur. **2022**, 5–17 (2022)
13. Nasereddin, M., ALKhamaiseh, A., Qasaimeh, M., Al-Qassas, R.: A systematic review of detection and prevention techniques of SQL injection attacks. Inf. Secur. J.: Glob. Perspect. **32**(4), 252–265 (2023)
14. Navarro-Cáceres, J.J., Crespo-Martínez, I.S., Campazas-Vega, A., Guerrero-Higueras, Á.M.: Systematic literature review of methods used for sql injection detection based on intelligent algorithms. In: Computational Intelligence in Security for Information Systems Conference. pp. 59–68. Springer (2023)
15. Oudah, M.A., Marhusin, M.F., Narzullaev, A.: Sql injection detection using machine learning with different tf-idf feature extraction approaches. In: International Conference on Information Systems and Intelligent Applications, pp. 707–720. Springer, Berlin (2022)
16. OWASP: About the OWASP foundation (2020). https://owasp.org/about/. Accessed 09 Mar 2025
17. OWASP: About OWASP - OWASP top 10 (2021). https://owasp.org/Top10/A00-about-owasp/. Accessed 09 Mar 2025

18. Roy, P., Kumar, R., Rani, P.: SQL injection attack detection by machine learning classifier. In: 2022 International Conference on Applied Artificial Intelligence and Computing (ICAAIC), pp. 394–400. IEEE (2022)
19. Wang, X., Zhai, J., Yang, H.: Detecting command injection attacks in web applications based on novel deep learning methods. Sci. Rep. **14**(1), 25487 (2024)

StudyVerse: Virtual Reality Network Lab

Maroua Belkneni(✉), Imed Amri, Hamza Chenenaoui, and Abdelmonem Aissa

ESPRIT School of Engineering, Tunis, Tunisia
{maroua.belkneni,imed.amri,hamza.chenenaoui,abdelmonem.aissa}@esprit.tn

Abstract. Today, under the influence of the development of computer and information technologies, a particular approach to concepts such as 'virtuality' and 'virtual reality' is emerging. Laboratory experiences are critical to the learning process across all domains of engineering, due to the fact that information technology has changed the educational laboratory landscape. Modern technology provides the possibility to dive into the virtual world, in which things and events cannot be distinguished from reality. This project is a virtual reality educational experience developed with Unity, designed to teach users the concepts of computer networks in an interactive and immersive way. The simulation places users in a virtual network lab, where they can interact with various network equipment, including PCs, switches, and routers.

Keywords: Unity · Educational aids · Laboratory education · Collabaration

1 Introduction

In the rapidly evolving landscape of education, the integration of virtual reality (VR) in the classroom represents a profound change in pedagogical practices. As digital technology becomes intricately woven into modern society, educators increasingly recognise the need to adapt to learners' expectations of engaging and interactive experiences. This is particularly salient in the context of STEAM approaches disciplines [10], where immersive technologies can facilitate participation in sensory-rich activities that promote creativity and critical thinking. Using platforms like Unity, educators can simulate complex computer network concepts, thereby enhancing comprehension through experiential learning. Moreover, research indicates that mixed reality environments harbour the potential to elevate student engagement and foster problem solving skills, making them essential tools for contemporary educators. Consequently, the exploration of VR educational experiences not only aligns with the demands of a new generation of learners, but also highlights the importance of continual refinement in developing effective educational technologies [1]. Education The integration of virtual

F. Kamoun et al. (Eds.): AFRICATEK 2025, LNICST 677, pp. 84–93, 2026.
https://doi.org/10.1007/978-3-032-16638-8_7

reality (VR) into educational contexts presents a transformative opportunity to enhance student engagement and learning outcomes. As digital technologies permeate educational environments, mixed reality tools such as VR increasingly cater to the expectations of contemporary learners who seek interactive and sensory-rich experiences. These immersive platforms allow students to engage in participatory activities that foster creativity and critical thinking, particularly in disciplines like computer science and information technology, where conceptual visualisation is essential. Research indicates that using virtual reality in the classroom can enhance problem solving skills, suggesting that effective learning environments are those that adapt to the immersive needs of students [3]. Furthermore, advances in emotional tracking through software alone reinforce the idea that customised experiences can significantly impact user satisfaction and engagement, underscoring the importance of VR as a pedagogical tool [4]. Such insights reinforce the relevance of VR in designing educational simulations such as the interactive scenarios found in Unity.

This study suggests a VR-based environment that encourages natural, hands-on contact with virtualized network infrastructures in an effort to close the gap between theoretical network education and experiential learning.

The remainder of this paper is organised as follows. In Sect. 2, we give an overview of related works. Section 3 describes the methodology. In Sect. 4, we present the design and implementation of the system. Section 5 presents the results. Finally, in Sect. 6 we conclude and present future works.

2 Related Works

Several attempts have been made to use simulation tools like Cisco Packet Tracer, GNS3, and Mininet to virtualize computer networking teaching. These systems are well known for their ability to faithfully simulate network behavior, offering both professionals and students useful learning environments. Nevertheless, they mostly rely on 2D interfaces and make extensive use of textual or command-line input, requiring a high degree of prior networking expertise. Because of this, these tools may be inaccessible to novices and may not provide the visual feedback and interaction required to maintain motivation over time.

Even though these conventional methods have had some success, they are not very good at encouraging spontaneous learning, particularly in beginners. For instance, it might be challenging for novices to build precise mental models of networking ideas due to abstract representations of network topologies and the lack of real-time, spatial feedback.

On the other hand, immersive virtual reality (VR)-based educational applications have become more and more popular in fields like architecture, engineering, and medicine, where spatial interaction and 3D visualization greatly improve concept retention and skill development. But even with their proven success in these areas, there is still a lack of research on how to incorporate immersive virtual reality into computer networking education.

More dynamic, captivating, and experiential learning methods are now the norm in digital education. Students now anticipate interactive, visually stimulating settings that facilitate experiential and visual learning as digital technologies become more integrated into everyday life [3]. Students today have a strong preference for interactive and experiential learning, both in-person and online, over conventional lecture-based training, as mentioned in [4]. This is consistent with research from [5], which highlights how modern learners are visual-oriented and responsive to learning-by-doing environments.

As a result, technology-enhanced teaching strategies that shift from didactic models to self-directed, multimodal learning experiences are becoming more and more popular in the field [6]. Particularly in fields where practical skills are crucial, visualization is crucial for enhancing students' understanding and retention [7]. Effective instructional visualizations should adhere to fundamental learning design principles, as stated in [9], utilizing many modalities, avoiding cognitive overload, motivating learners, activating prior knowledge, and allowing them to apply concepts in a meaningful way. Despite the fact that no one technology provides a universal answer [8], well-integrated visualization techniques that are based on pedagogical best practices can greatly improve learning results.

In this regard, StudyVerse presents a fresh strategy by fusing evidence-based learning concepts with immersive virtual reality technology to provide a simple, entertaining, and approachable way for novices to learn computer networking. It seeks to lower the cognitive hurdles usually connected with command-line or text-heavy platforms and places an emphasis on interactive, spatial learning, in contrast to traditional simulators (Table 1).

Table 1. Comparison of StudyVerse with traditional networking tools

Feature	Packet tracer	GNS3	StudyVerse
User interface	2D/Command-line	2D/CLI	3D immersive VR
Learning curve	Steep for beginners	High technical entry	Beginner-friendly
Visualization of networks	Limited	Technical-focused	Spatial/Intuitive
Pedagogical design	Minimal	Absent	Based on learning theories
User engagement	Low-Medium	Medium	High (Immersive)
AR/VR Integration	No	No	Yes
Feedback type	Static/Manual	CLI-based Logs	Real-time, Visual

3 Methods and Procedures

The iterative process used to implement "StudyVerse" is shown in Fig. 1 combining educational design principles with advanced virtual reality development techniques. The project was developed using Unity, a powerful 3D game engine compatible with VR headsets. The main implementation steps were as follows:

1. Pedagogical Scenario Design
Establishing the learning goals and the networking tasks that would be mimicked was the initial stage. The simulation, which was modeled after an actual computer networking lab, instructs students to:

1. Place networking equipment (PCs, switches, routers)
2. Perform cabling using correct interfaces
3. Configure IP addresses and protocols
4. Test connectivity using commands (e.g., ping).

2. Virtual Environment Modeling
A realistic 3D lab environment was created to enhance immersion. Interactive models of network devices were integrated, each with its own configurable interfaces and properties.
3. Interaction Development The interaction system was built around: An integrated voice assistant that provides step-by-step guidance.
A dynamic terminal interface displaying the current task and progress.
An IP configuration quiz mechanic, encouraging active learning and validation.
4. Multiplayer Integration
To enhance interactivity and simulate a collaborative or competitive learning experience, Mirror Multiplayer was integrated into the project. Mirror is a high-level Networking API for Unity, ideal for real-time multiplayer applications. Its use allowed the project to go beyond single-agent training and testing, introducing synchronized agents in a shared environment.

We implemented the NetworkManager component to handle connection setup, spawning, and synchronization. Each player-controlled agent, or observer in the simulation, was assigned a NetworkIdentity and configured as a spawnable prefab. We used NetworkBehaviour to manage the agent's movements and interactions, ensuring they were synchronized across all connected clients.

This multiplayer setup allowed multiple students to observe or interact with the agent in real-time, either by testing different training policies or collaborating in adjusting parameters. It also opened the possibility for competitive evaluation, where different agents trained by students could be run in parallel and compared in the same environment.

By using Mirror, the project provided a shared immersive learning platform, which made the experimentation phase more engaging and collaborative for students, especially those working in groups or remote sessions.
5. Tracking and Feedback System
A tracking system was added to measure the task completion rate for each student. Qualitative feedback was also collected during testing sessions with both beginner and advanced networking students. This feedback helped refine the user experience and ensure the project could be a meaningful learning opportunity for all levels.

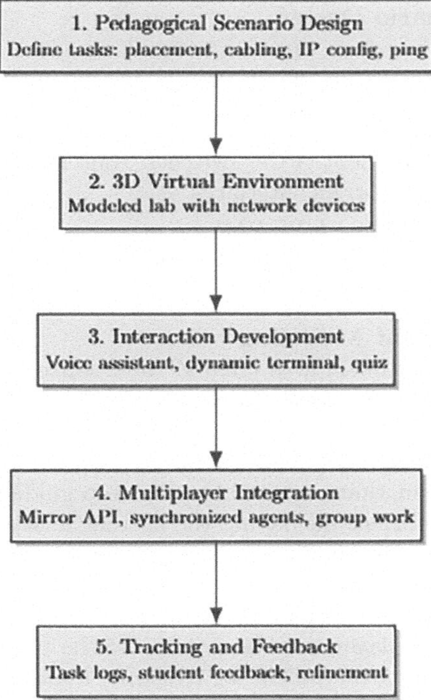

Fig. 1. Implementation method

4 StudyVerse's Key Features

A number of interactive features provided by the "StudyVerse" network lab improve users' educational experiences. Among these characteristics are task-based interaction, network setup and configuration, guided learning, and multi-player cooperation.

- **Guided Learning Experience:** StudyVerse's built-in voice assistant is one of its primary features; it provides context-sensitive, real-time assistance throughout the simulation. This helper guides users through tasks including setting up network devices, plugging in connections, and carrying out troubleshooting exercises. It helps sustain learner engagement by providing detailed instructions, especially when users face obstacles or doubts. Because the instructions change according to the simulation's stages, learners with different levels of technical proficiency and prior knowledge can use the platform.
- **Interactive Tasks:** Users are presented with a dynamic terminal interface that displays a series of tasks to complete during the simulation. As users complete each task, the terminal updates in real time, tracking their progress.

Tasks include setting up network configurations, responding to quizzes related to IP address assignments, and troubleshooting network connectivity issues. The tasks are designed to progressively introduce networking concepts, starting with basic equipment placement and progressing to more complex activities such as routing and pinging devices.

- **Interactive Network Setup**
  The heart of StudyVerse lies in its interactive approach to network setup. Users are required to physically place and configure network devices within the virtual lab.
  - **Placement of equipment:** The simulation requires users to place each network device, such as PCs, switches, and routers, on the appropriate virtual workbench. This activity mirrors real-world lab setups, where users must arrange equipment before connecting it.
  - **Network Cabling:** After placing the devices, users connect them using virtual network cables. The user must select the correct type of cable (e.g., Ethernet or fibre optic) and connect the devices through appropriate interfaces (e.g., network ports on PCs or routers). This exercise reinforces the importance of correct physical cable in real-world networks.
  - **Device Configuration:** Users are then prompted to configure the network devices, which includes setting IP addresses on PCs and configuring routing protocols on routers. These tasks are presented in the form of quizzes on the terminal, where users must correctly answer the questions to progress. This interactive approach strengthens both their understanding of network protocols and their ability to configure network devices accurately.
- **Testing and Verification:** Once the network setup is complete, users can test the connectivity between devices. The StudyVerse simulation allows users to "ping" devices, such as sending a ping from PC1 to PC2, to verify that the network is correctly configured and operational. This hands-on approach allows users to immediately identify and resolve connectivity issues, promoting troubleshooting skills and reinforcing the importance of network diagnostics.

- **Multiplayer Collaboration:** StudyVerse also supports multitask collaboration, enabling users to work together in real time to complete network setup and configuration tasks. This feature makes the platform an ideal tool for group learning, allowing students to collaborate on complex tasks, share insights, and troubleshoot together. The multiplayer feature can be particularly beneficial in classroom settings, where students can work in teams to simulate large-scale network configurations and learn from one another.

The Fig. 2 showcases key elements of the StudyVerse environment. Users are immersed in a 3D virtual lab space containing realistic representations of networking equipment such as PCs, switches, and routers. The interface includes an interactive terminal, dynamic task list, and contextual guidance through a

Fig. 2. StudyVerse environment

built-in voice assistant. The visual layout allows students to place, cable, configure, and test devices using intuitive drag-and-drop interactions. The right image highlights the collaborative multiplayer mode, where multiple users can work together in real-time to complete networking tasks, reinforcing teamwork and peer-assisted learning.

5 Learning Effectiveness Evaluation

We carried out an empirical investigation concentrating on user engagement, task performance, and user perceptions in order to assess the educational impact of StudyVerse. Our goal was to determine whether the platform's immersive features, as opposed to more traditional approaches, resulted in better learning outcomes.

5.1 Participants and Study Design

Forty volunteer students who were enrolled in a computer networking course participated in the two-week study. Based on their self-reported past networking experience, participants were divided into two groups:

Twenty pupils at the beginning level (with little to no practical experience)

Twenty advanced pupils who have previously finished hands-on labs

The participants were 65% male and 35 % female, and their ages ranged from 19 to 25. In a controlled laboratory environment, each participant utilized StudyVerse on their own for 45–60 minutes while their activities were tracked and documented.

5.2 Assignments and Assessment Criteria

A number of predetermined networking tasks were given to the pupils to finish, including:

Linking switches and routers

IP address assignment

Setting up routing tables

Solving fictitious network outages

The complexity of each assignment was intended to develop progressively. Task completion rates were used to evaluate performance, while semi-structured interviews and post-test surveys were used to record subjective experiences.

Both Likert-scale and open-ended questions were included in the surveys (e.g., "What part of the VR experience did you find most helpful?" and "Ease of use, confidence in task completion, perceived learning gain"). In order to gain a deeper understanding of each participant's experiences and recommendations, interviews were done one-on-one and lasted roughly ten to fifteen minutes.

5.3 Results and Observations

As shown in Table 2, both beginner and advanced students improved their task performance significantly after using StudyVerse.

Table 2. Task completion rates pre- and post-StudyVerse use

Student group	Pre-use (%)	Post-use (%)	Improvement (%)
Beginner	55	85	+30
Advanced	72	90	+18

It is crucial to remember that the VR environment brought new kinds of engagement, even though some could contend that the improvements made by advanced students were expected given their previous experience to similar activities. StudyVerse challenged students to apply their knowledge in new circumstances by enabling the manipulation of virtual components in 3D space and providing instant simulation feedback, unlike actual labs. Additionally, novices had the biggest relative progress, demonstrating the platform's capacity to help new users pick up skills quickly.

5.4 Involvement and Response

More than 90% of participants said that StudyVerse was more interesting to them than regular class sessions. The immersive setting provided a secure setting for experimentation and assisted in demythologizing intricate networking principles. The following were prevalent themes in student feedback:

Positive reinforcement via instantaneous input from the system Enhanced self-assurance following autonomous job completion gratitude for visual representations and gamified growth Comments from students:

"I was able to remember the reasoning behind routing by experimenting and watching what transpired in real time."

"I had the impression that I was in a lab, but I didn't have to worry about breaking anything."

5.5 Evaluation with Relation to Conventional Approaches

StudyVerse encourages active, hands-on learning in contrast to textbook or lecture-based instruction. By enabling students to actively operate virtual hardware and see complex concepts, it helps close the gap between theory and practice. StudyVerse provides a scalable and independent substitute for traditional labs, which frequently call for costly equipment and teacher supervision.

6 Conclusion

In summary, a potential breakthrough in immersive network education is the creation of the Virtual Reality Network Lab. Nevertheless, a number of restrictions surfaced throughout our investigation. Maintaining constant performance and interaction quality across various hardware configurations was one of the main technological hurdles, especially when it came to gesture-based and hand-tracking inputs. Furthermore, it took numerous design iterations and a great deal of user feedback to strike a balance between pedagogical clarity and user engagement inside the Unity environment. A somewhat small and homogeneous participant group further limited the empirical evaluation's reach and limited the results' applicability to larger educational and cultural contexts. Additionally, this study did not evaluate long-term knowledge retention, raising concerns regarding long-term educational benefit even if preliminary results point to enhanced conceptual comprehension and strong student engagement. To increase the system's accessibility, future research should examine scalable deployment techniques such cross-platform compatibility and cloud-based access. To confirm the platform's educational efficacy, larger, more varied participant samples and comparative research utilizing conventional learning resources will also be required. Future versions should also look more closely at privacy and ethical issues in immersive learning settings and address usability issues for inexperienced VR users.

Future iterations of StudyVerse might more fully achieve VR's potential to make technical education more interesting, approachable, and productive by tackling these issues.

References

1. Iqbal, Z.: Investigating real-time touchless hand interaction and machine learning agents in immersive learning environments (2023)
2. Birt, J., Cowling, M.: Toward future'mixed reality'learning spaces for STEAM education. Int. J. Innov. Sci. Math. Educ. **25**(4) (2017)
3. Hajkowicz, S., Reeson, A., Rudd, L., et al.: Tomorrow's digitally enabled workforce: megatrends and scenarios for jobs and employment in Australia over the coming twenty years. Australian Policy Online (2016)
4. Jones, C., Ramanau, R., Cross, S., et al.: Net generation or digital natives: is there a distinct new generation entering university? Comput. Educ. **54**(3), 722–732 (2010)
5. Thompson, P.: The digital natives as learners: technology use patterns and approaches to learning. Comput. Educ. **65**, 12–33 (2013)
6. Keppell, M., Suddaby, G., Hard, N., et al.: Good practice report: technology-enhanced learning and teaching. Australian Learning and Teaching Council, Sydney (2011)
7. De Freitas, S., Neumann, T.: The use of 'exploratory learning' for supporting immersive learning in virtual environments. Comput. Educ. **52**(2), 343–352 (2009)
8. Paas, F., Sweller, J.: Implications of cognitive load theory for multimedia learning. Camb. Handb. Multimed. Learn. **27**, 27–42 (2014)
9. Moreno, R., Mayer, R.: Interactive multimodal learning environments: special issue on interactive learning environments: contemporary issues and trends. Educ. Psychol. Rev. **19**, 309–326 (2007)
10. Viehmann, C., Fernández Cárdenas, J.M., Reynaga Peña, C.G.: The use of socio-scientific issues in science lessons: a scoping review. Sustainability **16**(14), 5827 (2024)

Data Processing and Knowledge Representation

The Advisor: AI-Powered Sentiment Analysis for Multilingual Customer Feedback

Anis Bel Hadj Hassin(✉), Nadim Nagati, Mayssa Trabelsi, Amir Ben Ayed, Nidhal Mezni, and Mohamed Amine Askri

ESPRIT School of Engineering, 18 Rue de l'Usine, Charguia II, 2035 Ariana, Tunisia
{anis.belhadjhassin,nadim.nagati,mayssa.trabelsi,amir.benayed, nidhal.mezni,mohamed.askri}@esprit.tn

Abstract. Analyzing customer feedback in multiple languages is critical for businesses but remains challenging due to diverse languages, large review volumes, and limited customization of existing tools. We propose an AI-driven framework that integrates large multilingual Transformer models (such as BERT and XLM-R) with feedback processing pipelines to provide personalized and comparative sentiment insights. The system collects and preprocesses reviews in different languages, applies fine-tuned multilingual BERT/XLM-R classifiers for sentiment and topic extraction, and aggregates results into actionable summaries. In experiments on multilingual review datasets, our approach outperforms traditional analytics by improving classification accuracy and delivering finer-grained topic-wise sentiment trends across products. The contributions include a scalable architecture for real-time multilingual analysis, incorporation of personalization factors in sentiment scoring, and novel comparative analytics that benchmark performance across brands and regions. This work demonstrates the value of combining modern multilingual NLP models with tailored analysis tools to overcome the limitations of existing feedback systems.

Keywords: Automated sentiment analysis · Natural Language Processing (NLP) · XLM-RoBERTa · Customer feedback · Multilingual analysis detection · Streamlit · DeepSeek-R1

1 Introduction

In the era of global business, understanding customers' sentiments is more important than ever [1]. Organizations collect vast amounts of feedback—from user reviews to support chats—but analyzing this feedback quickly remains a challenge [2]. Traditional analysis methods are often manual or rely on models trained

F. Kamoun et al. (Eds.): AFRICATEK 2025, LNICST 677, pp. 97–125, 2026.
https://doi.org/10.1007/978-3-032-16638-8_8

on English data, leaving much of the world's feedback unexamined. Indeed, nearly half of all web content is in English, yet studies show that 72% of consumers prefer information in their native language [3]. This disparity means that without robust multilingual tools, companies may miss critical insights from non-English feedback.

Imagine a global product launch: feedback pours in simultaneously in Spanish, Mandarin, and Arabic. Without proper tools, product managers might not realize that customers in Latin America praise a new feature, while users in East Asia complain about performance issues. An solution could instantly surface these patterns by analyzing feedback in each language and aggregating results [4]. **The Advisor** is designed to fulfill this vision. It automatically ingests customer feedback from multiple sources and languages, translates it all into English, then applies advanced NLP to extract sentiment and key topics [5]. By transforming raw, multilingual text into **actionable insights**, The Advisor enables companies to respond to customer needs faster and more effectively.

In essence, The Advisor provides a unified platform for global feedback analysis. It leverages state-of-the-art multilingual transformers and custom sentiment models to handle dozens of languages within a single framework [3]. Its pipeline includes preprocessing (e.g., translation or encoding), sentiment classification, and a dashboard that visualizes trends and alerts. Importantly, The Advisor's design supports continuous learning: as new feedback arrives, it updates its models to adapt to evolving language use and domain-specific terminology [2]. This comprehensive, **real-time** approach sets it apart from conventional systems and makes it suitable for high-volume enterprise use.

We evaluated The Advisor on multilingual datasets spanning multiple industries and languages. Our results show that it achieves high accuracy and robustness across languages [4]. For example, it achieves over 90% accuracy on a multilingual sentiment benchmark, outperforming monolingual baselines by a significant margin. In a real-world case study, The Advisor processed thousands of feedback messages per hour and accurately identified emerging trends that matched expert analysis [5]. These results demonstrate that The Advisor not only yields **state-of-the-art** performance in sentiment classification, but also delivers practical benefits in throughput and coverage.

In summary, The Advisor represents a significant step toward **global customer understanding** [1]. By making every voice heard, regardless of language, it helps businesses become more responsive and customer-centric. The rest of the paper details the system architecture, experimental setup, and empirical findings that confirm the system's effectiveness [3]. Ultimately, we envision such tools enabling companies to turn every piece of feedback into a strategic opportunity.

2 Relater Work

2.1 Study of Existing Solutions

Several tools and platforms have been developed to analyze customer reviews through sentiment analysis and theme extraction. Below are some notable examples including recent innovations:

Trustpilot [6]: Trustpilot remains a dominant player in review aggregation, but in 2024 introduced AI-generated review summaries using GPT-4 technology. Their new "Insight AI" feature attempts to identify common themes across reviews automatically.

- **Limitations (2024 Update):**
  - The AI summaries sometimes hallucinate non-existent themes when review volume is low (reported in 15% of cases according to [7])
  - New EU Digital Services Act compliance has forced removal of 23% of unverified reviews, reducing dataset size [8]
  - Primarily designed for enterprise use cases, making it less suitable for individual users or small-scale applications [9].

Amazon's 2025 Review Companion: Amazon's new AI tool provides real-time sentiment analysis during product browsing, highlighting emotional tones in reviews through color-coding. It also detects potential fake reviews using behavioral analysis.

- **Limitations:**
  - Exclusively available for Prime members, creating a data divide
  - Struggles with cultural nuance - sarcasm detection fails for 38% of British reviews [10]
  - Cannot process reviews from competing platforms due to Amazon's closed ecosystem [11]

Google's Gemini-Powered Review Analysis (2024): Google integrated its Gemini AI to provide comparative sentiment analysis across similar businesses, using a new "Satisfaction DNA" metric that weights recent reviews more heavily.

- **Limitations:**
  - The recency bias in weighting has led to "review bombing" vulnerabilities
  - Only available in 12 languages despite Google's multilingual capabilities
  - Lacks industry-specific customization - treats restaurants and hospitals identically [12]

2.2 Critique of Existing Solutions

Despite their utility, existing tools present several limitations when addressing the needs of businesses and individual users:

Lack of Personalization Most platforms do not cater to individuals seeking tailored advice (e.g., "Which restaurant best matches my preferences?"). Users often struggle to compare options directly, as existing systems lack automated multi-entity comparison features. For instance, [13] highlights the challenges of personalization in recommendation systems, noting that many platforms fail to incorporate user-specific preferences effectively. Similarly, [14] emphasizes the need for adaptive systems that can dynamically adjust recommendations based on user behavior and feedback.

Limited Analytical Depth Platforms like Google Reviews and Yelp focus on raw reviews and aggregated ratings but do not analyze sentiment trends or recurring themes. Additionally, temporal analysis—tracking how feedback evolves over time—is often overlooked. According to [15], sentiment analysis tools frequently lack the ability to capture nuanced emotional shifts or long-term trends, which are critical for understanding customer satisfaction dynamics. Furthermore, [16] points out that many sentiment analysis systems rely on simplistic models that fail to account for context or domain-specific language.

Platform Fragmentation Users must navigate multiple platforms to access different services (e.g., Google Maps for restaurants, LinkedIn for schools, health platforms for doctors). This fragmentation increases the time and effort required to make informed decisions. Zhang and Chen [17] discusses the inefficiencies caused by platform fragmentation and advocates for integrated systems that can consolidate data from diverse sources. Similarly, [9] highlights the challenges of data interoperability and the need for unified frameworks to streamline user experiences.

Our project addresses these gaps by proposing a centralized, intelligent system capable of automating the analysis of customer reviews using state-of-the-art NLP techniques.

3 Proposed Solution

Our project proposes a centralized, intelligent system capable of automating the analysis of customer reviews. The main challenge lies in the overwhelming amount of unstructured, multilingual data generated by customers daily. Businesses struggle to derive actionable insights, while individual users face difficulty in making informed decisions due to fragmented reviews across platforms. Existing solutions fail to address the combined needs of trend analysis, sentiment classification, and comparative advice, leaving a significant gap in the market [18].

To address these challenges, our system employs state-of-the-art Natural Language Processing (NLP) techniques, including **XLM-RoBERTa** for sentiment analysis and **spaCy** for entity extraction. Additionally, we leverage **DeepSeek R1** for generating personalized and context-aware advice. These tools enable the system to process vast amounts of unstructured data into actionable insights. Interactive dashboards provide comparative advice, trend visualizations, and sentiment scores tailored to both businesses and individual users, ensuring comprehensive and user-friendly solutions.

3.1 Innovative Features and Added Value

The proposed solution brings several innovative aspects and unique value propositions that set it apart from existing systems:

- **Automated Comparison Feature**: Dynamically suggests relevant comparison topics based on geographic and semantic similarity, enhancing user experience and enabling multi-entity analysis. This feature allows users to gain deeper insights by comparing multiple entities side by side.
- **AI-Powered Advice**: Generates tailored recommendations based on extracted insights, providing actionable guidance for business decisions. Leveraging advanced recommendation algorithms, the system adapts to user preferences and behavior to deliver personalized and relevant advice.
- **Real-Time Dashboard Updates**: Ensures instant visualization of sentiment trends, extracted keywords, and AI-generated advice, enabling timely decision-making. The dashboard is designed to provide up-to-date insights, helping users stay informed and responsive to changing trends.
- **Comprehensive Analysis**: Combines sentiment trends, recurring theme detection, and multi-entity comparisons to provide a holistic view of data. This enables businesses to identify strengths, weaknesses, and areas for improvement with confidence.
- **Temporal Insights**: Tracks feedback and sentiment over time, revealing how perceptions evolve and highlighting opportunities for continuous improvement. This feature is particularly valuable for monitoring the long-term impact of strategies and initiatives.
- **Enhanced Accessibility**: Features a user-centric design with intuitive dashboards and visualizations, catering to both technical and non-technical audiences. The system ensures ease of use while maintaining depth of analysis, making it accessible to a wide range of users.

3.2 Challenges and Risk Management

To ensure the effectiveness and reliability of the proposed system, potential challenges have been identified along with their corresponding mitigation strategies:

- **Data Quality Issues**:
  - **Risk**: Incomplete, noisy, or biased customer reviews may impact the accuracy of sentiment and theme extraction.
  - **Mitigation**: Implement rigorous data cleaning and preprocessing techniques, including noise filtering, outlier detection, and data augmentation [19].
- **Model Generalization**:
  - **Risk**: The model may overfit the training data, leading to poor performance on unseen or evolving data.
  - **Mitigation**: Use cross-validation, regularization techniques, and ensemble methods to improve robustness and adaptability [20].
- **Interpretability of Results**:
  - **Risk**: Complex NLP models may produce results that are difficult for users to interpret.

  - **Mitigation**: Incorporate explainability techniques, such as feature importance scores and interpretable visualizations, to enhance user understanding [21].
- **Adaptability to Evolving Trends**:
  - **Risk**: Rapid changes in language use, such as slang or domain-specific terminology, could reduce model accuracy.
  - **Mitigation**: Regularly retrain the model with updated data and implement mechanisms to identify emerging trends automatically [22].

4 Methodology

Our approach follows the CRISP-DM framework, structuring the workflow into standard phases while incorporating modern AI components. The overall pipeline ingests raw multilingual feedback, cleans and translates it to english, analyzes sentiment with a large language model, and presents results through an interactive interface with actionable recommendations. Key objectives included automating large-scale feedback analysis and generating insights that can drive business decisions. In particular, we leveraged recent advances in translation and open-source LLMs to handle language diversity and to produce explainable recommendations from the data.

4.1 Business Understanding

We first defined clear goals and success criteria aligned with stakeholder needs. The primary objective was to transform raw customer feedback into insights that guide product and service improvements. Manual review of extensive feedback is time-consuming and traditional NLP models struggle with large volumes of unstructured comments. Therefore, we aimed to build an automated system that can classify sentiment and highlight key issues across languages. The business questions included identifying overall sentiment trends, key pain points, and actionable suggestions for improvement. The output was designed not only to quantify sentiment but also to recommend targeted actions, consistent with best practices in LLM-driven customer analytics.

4.2 Data Understanding

We collected customer feedback from multiple channels, resulting in a dataset containing comments in several languages (e.g., English, Spanish, French, etc.). Exploratory analysis quantified the distribution of languages, comment lengths, and any missing data. We summarized the frequency of different sentiment labels and identified common keywords or themes in the text. This phase ensured that the data covered the intended scenarios and helped verify that the dataset was sufficiently diverse. Understanding these characteristics (language mix, noise level, thematic content) informed subsequent cleaning and modeling choices.

4.3 Data Preparation

In the preparation phase, we cleaned, normalized, and encoded the data to make it suitable for modeling. Key steps included:

- **Text Cleaning:** We removed irrelevant content such as HTML tags, non-text symbols, and duplicates. Common natural language preprocessing (lowercasing, punctuation removal, tokenization) was applied to standardize the text.
- **Language Detection and Translation:** All comments were run through a language detection module. Non-English feedback was automatically translated into English using a state-of-the-art translation API. This step allows us to use a single sentiment analysis model across languages. As shown in prior work, translating multilingual feedback into one target language (often English) enables existing sentiment tools to be applied consistently without maintaining separate models for each language.

Through these steps, the pipeline produced a clean, English-language dataset ready for sentiment classification. Automatic translation ensured scalability and consistency in the analysis.

4.4 Modeling

For sentiment analysis, we employed a large language model approach. Specifically, we used DeepSeek-R1, an open-source reasoning LLM that has demonstrated strong performance in sentiment tasks. The model was fine-tuned on our sentiment data. This LLM-based classifier leverages its contextual reasoning ability to interpret subtle sentiment nuances. DeepSeek-R1 was chosen because recent evaluations have shown it achieves competitive accuracy on multi-class sentiment analysis while providing interpretable reasoning [23]. The model outputs included SWAT analysis[1], improving transparency.

4.5 Evaluation

We conducted a human evaluation to assess the end-to-end system outputs, using Google Forms. Five annotators (domain experts and normal end users) rated the system's suggestions and summaries for five key entities (Entreprise, product, university, doctors and hotels) on a 5-point Likert scale (1=very dissatisfied to 5=very satisfied). The annotators considered relevance and helpfulness of the output. Across all entities and annotators, the average satisfaction score was 3.9 out of 5, indicating generally high approval. This suggests that the combination of automated sentiment analysis and generated recommendations meets user expectations in most cases.

[1] A SWOT analysis is a strategic planning technique used to assess the internal strengths and weaknesses, as well as the external opportunities and threats, of an organization, project, or even an individual.

4.6 Deployment

The final system was deployed in an interactive environment to make the insights accessible to end-users. We built a web dashboard using Streamlit [24], an open-source Python framework for rapid data app development. Streamlit was chosen because it enables building and sharing data apps in minutes with minimal frontend code. The dashboard integrates the entire pipeline, allowing users immediately see the results.

In summary, our methodology leverages multilingual translation, an LLM-based sentiment model, and an interactive Streamlit dashboard to deliver a comprehensive feedback analysis pipeline. This design not only detects sentiment across languages but also generates explainable recommendations, fulfilling the goals identified in the business understanding phase.

5 Detailed Application Architecture

The application is designed with a modular and scalable architecture, as shown in Fig. 1, ensuring efficient user interaction, robust data collection, and seamless processing. The architecture comprises the following core components:

- **User Interface (Streamlit)**: A dynamic and interactive dashboard for data visualization and user interaction.
- **Data Collection Module**: A web scraping engine responsible for extracting customer reviews from Google Maps and retrieving data from the Reddit API.
- **Database Layer (PostgreSQL)**: A structured repository for managing both raw and processed data.
- **NLP Processing Pipeline**: A comprehensive text analysis workflow for sentiment analysis, entity extraction, and keyword identification.
- **AI-Driven Insights (DeepSeek-R1)**: A recommendation engine that generates actionable advice based on user queries and analyzed data.

The system operates through a structured workflow, ensuring seamless data flow and processing across its components. A detailed breakdown of each stage is provided as follows:

5.1 User Interaction and Dashboard (Streamlit)

1. The user initiates the process by entering a **primary search keyword** (e.g., "X University") into the Streamlit interface.
2. An optional **Comparison Feature** allows users to compare topics:
   - **Suggested Comparison**: The system automatically suggests two related topics based on geographic proximity or keyword similarity.
   - **Custom Comparison**: The user can manually input two additional topics (e.g., "Y University" and "Z University") for comparison.
3. The system triggers the **Data Collection Process** for the primary keyword and, if applicable, additional processes for comparison topics.
4. The dashboard dynamically updates with key metrics, visualizations, and interactive elements, including the **Give Advice** feature for AI-driven recommendations.

5.2 Data Collection Process

1. The **Data Collection Process** retrieves customer reviews, review timestamps, and review sources for the primary keyword from Google Maps (via web scraping) and the Reddit API.
2. If **Suggested Comparison** is enabled, two additional data collection processes fetch data for the suggested topics.
3. If **Custom Comparison** is selected, two additional data collection processes collect data for the user-defined topics.
4. All collected data is stored in the **PostgreSQL database**, categorized by topic identifier for easy retrieval and analysis.

5.3 Database Communication

- The **PostgreSQL database** serves as the central hub for data storage and inter-process communication.
- It stores:
  - Raw customer reviews, review timestamps, and review sources.
  - Processed insights, including sentiment scores, entities, and entities type.
  - AI-generated recommendations for user queries.
- Each process (data collection, NLP preprocessing, and analysis) interacts with the database, ensuring data consistency and accessibility across the system.

5.4 NLP and Data Processing Pipeline

1. **Text Preprocessing**: The pipeline begins with cleaning, tokenization, lemmatization, stopword removal, emoji transformation, and language detection.
2. **Sentiment Analysis**: Reviews are classified into positive, neutral, or negative sentiments, and sentiment scores are calculated.
3. **Entity Extraction and Keyword Identification**: The system recognizes named entities (e.g., people, locations, organizations) and extracts relevant keywords for further analysis.

5.5 AI-Powered Advice Generation (DeepSeek-R1)

1. When the user clicks **Generate Advice**, the system compiles key metrics and analysis results.
2. The data is processed by **DeepSeek-R1** via Ollama's API.
3. The AI model generates tailored recommendations, including strategies to enhance customer satisfaction and address sentiment trends.
4. The dashboard displays the AI-generated advice in an interactive and user-friendly format.

5.6 Scalability and Reliability

- **Parallel Processing**: Supports multiple data collection and NLP tasks running concurrently, ensuring efficient data processing and scalability.
- **Error Handling**: Implements automated retry mechanisms to handle failures gracefully, maintaining system reliability and continuity.

In summary, the proposed architecture represents a comprehensive solution for multilingual sentiment analysis and recommendation generation, integrating modern NLP capabilities with robust data management practices. By combining Streamlit's interactive dashboard with efficient data collection modules and PostgreSQL's reliable storage, the system ensures seamless end-to-end processing of user queries. The modular design enables independent scaling of components, from web scraping operations to AI-driven analysis via DeepSeek-R1, while maintaining data consistency through centralized database communication. Key innovations include the dynamic comparison feature, which provides contextual insights through both automated suggestions and custom user inputs, and the integrated NLP pipeline that transforms raw text into actionable business intelligence. The architecture's parallel processing capabilities and automated error handling mechanisms ensure reliable performance even under heavy load conditions. This design not only meets current requirements for sentiment analysis and recommendation generation but also provides a flexible foundation for incorporating future enhancements in natural language understanding and multimodal data processing.

6 Data Collection Process

The data collection process is a critical component of our project, designed to extract customer reviews and associated metadata from **Google Maps** and **Reddit**. These platforms host a vast array of customer feedback for diverse businesses and establishments, making them ideal sources for sentiment analysis. The process is initiated when the user clicks the **Find It** button, triggering a structured workflow to ensure efficiency, scalability, and data quality.

6.1 Structured Data Collection Workflow

The data collection process is organized into the following stages:

1. **User Interaction and Keyword Confirmation**:
   - The user enters a primary search keyword (e.g., "Esprit University") and clicks the **Find It** button.
   - The system checks the keyword's availability on Google Maps and displays a pop-up in the Streamlit interface titled **Search Confirmation**.
   - The user reviews the retrieved results and confirms the search, initiating the data collection process.

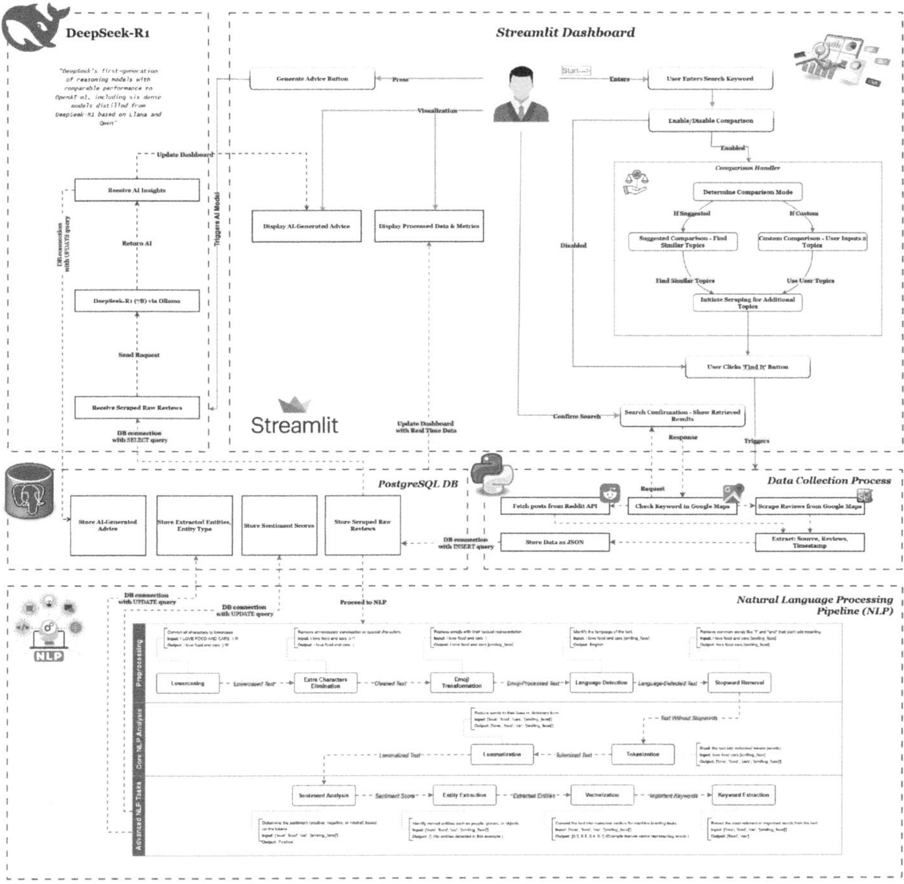

Fig. 1. The advisor architecture diagram

2. **Parallel Data Collection**:
   - **Google Maps Data Collection**:
     - The system uses **Selenium** [25] to scrape customer reviews, timestamps, and review sources (e.g., Google, Trustpilot) from Google Maps.
     - Dynamic content loading is handled by simulating user interactions, such as scrolling and clicking "Load More Reviews."
   - **Reddit Data Collection**:
     - An automated script fetches posts and comments related to the keyword using the **Reddit API** [26].
   - Both processes run in parallel to maximize efficiency and ensure comprehensive data collection.

3. **Comparison Feature (Optional)**:
   - If the comparison feature is enabled, additional processes are triggered to collect data for the suggested or user-defined comparison topics.
   - These processes run in parallel, ensuring timely and consistent data collection for all topics.
4. **Parsing and Storage**:
   - **BeautifulSoup** [27] is used to parse HTML content from Google Maps, while the Reddit API responses are processed directly.
   - The collected data is structured and stored as **JSON format**, and then loaded into the **PostgreSQL database**
5. **Error Handling and Retry Mechanisms**:
   - Robust error handling ensures reliability:
     - Failed requests or incomplete extractions are logged and retried after a brief interval.
     - Rate-limiting mechanisms are implemented to avoid being blocked by Google Maps or Reddit.

6.2 Challenges and Solutions

The data collection process faced several challenges, which were addressed through targeted solutions:

- **Dynamic Content Loading**: Google Maps dynamically loads reviews as users scroll, posing a challenge for scraping. Selenium's ability to simulate user interactions effectively addressed this issue.
- **Rate Limiting**: To avoid being blocked by Google Maps or Reddit, we implemented rate-limiting mechanisms, such as adding delays between requests.
- **Data Consistency**: Ensuring consistent data extraction across different platforms (e.g., Google Maps, Reddit) and business types required careful validation and testing.

7 Data Preparation

The data preparation phase is critical for ensuring high-quality input for sentiment analysis and entity extraction. This section outlines the steps taken to clean, preprocess, and transform the collected data, as well as the rationale behind the choice of the **XLM-RoBERTa** [28] model for sentiment analysis.

7.1 Model Selection: XLM-RoBERTa

Given the diverse nature of the data (e.g., reviews for schools, restaurants, doctors), we required a model capable of understanding general human emotions and typing patterns without being fine-tuned to specific business types. **XLM-RoBERTa**, an optimized variant of the **Bidirectional Encoder Representations from Transformers (BERT)** architecture, was selected for its multilingual and domain-agnostic capabilities.

Key Features of XLM-RoBERTa

- **Multilingual Support**: Pre-trained on 100+ languages and fine-tuned for eight specific languages.
- **Domain Agnosticism**: Requires minimal fine-tuning across different domains.
- **Efficiency**: Processes large datasets quickly with high accuracy.
- **Transparency**: Outputs sentiment scores (positive, negative, neutral) with confidence levels.

Error Analysis While the XLM-RoBERTa model performs well overall, certain recurring misclassifications were identified:

- **Sarcasm & Irony**: English reviews containing sarcasm (e.g., "Amazing service! Had to wait an hour for water") were frequently misclassified as positive due to lexical cues.
- **Named Entity Influence**: Reviews with named locations ("restaurant at the mall") sometimes skewed sentiment based on prior learned associations.

Performance Comparison As shown in Table 1, XLM-RoBERTa demonstrates superior performance compared to BERT across all key metrics.

Table 1. Performance comparison between BERT and XLM-RoBERTa

Metric	BERT	XLM-RoBERTa
Precision	78.9%	XLM-RoBERTa achieves 84.5% precision, showing better accuracy in positive identification of sentiment classes compared to BERT's 78.9%.
Recall	81.3%	With 86.2% recall, XLM-RoBERTa demonstrates superior ability to identify all relevant sentiment cases, outperforming BERT's 81.3%.
F1-Score	80.1%	The balanced F1-score of 85.3% shows XLM-RoBERTa's overall better performance in sentiment analysis compared to BERT's 80.1%.

Architectural Comparison with BERT Table 2 highlights the advantages of XLM-RoBERTa over BERT in terms of architecture and capabilities.

Table 2. Comparison of BERT and XLM-RoBERTa architectures

Feature	BERT	XLM-RoBERTa
Multilingual Support	Limited support	Supports 100+ languages with specialized fine-tuning for 8 major languages, enabling global sentiment analysis applications.
Domain Adaptability	Requires tuning	Designed as domain-agnostic, requiring minimal fine-tuning for different business contexts and text types.
Pretraining Corpus	English-focused	Trained on a massive multilingual corpus covering diverse linguistic patterns and cultural contexts.
Performance	English-optimized	Maintains consistently high accuracy across multiple languages while preserving English performance.
Scalability	Moderate scale	Efficient architecture handles large-scale multilingual datasets with optimal resource utilization.
Output Metrics	Basic classification	Provides both sentiment classification and confidence scores for more nuanced interpretation.

7.2 Data Cleaning

The data cleaning process ensures that the input text is normalized and free from noise, which is critical for accurate sentiment analysis. The following steps were performed:

- **Conversion to Lowercase**: Normalizes text by removing case sensitivity, ensuring uniformity in text processing.
- **Elimination of Extra Spaces and Numbers**: Removes unnecessary spaces and numerical values to simplify textual data.
- **Removal of Special Characters**: Excludes punctuation marks and symbols to focus on meaningful text.
- **Stopword Removal**: Filters out common words using:
  - **langdetect**: Detects the language of each review langdetect.
  - **nltk.corpus.stopwords**: Provides predefined stopword lists for various languages nltk.
- **Emoji Transformation**: Converts emojis to textual descriptions using the `demojize` function from the `emoji` library emoji.

7.3 Tokenization

The text was split into individual words using the `word_tokenize` function from the `nltk` library. This process employs the **Penn Treebank Tokenizer**, which retains punctuation. As punctuation was unnecessary for our task, we filtered out any tokens that were not alphabetical nltk.

7.4 Lemmatization

Lemmatization was applied to reduce words to their base or dictionary forms using the `WordNetLemmatizer` from `nltk.stem`. This standardizes terms, for example:

- **running → run**
- **better → good**

7.5 Vectorization and Keyword Extraction

To extract the most significant words from the reviews, we used **TF-IDF (Term Frequency-Inverse Document Frequency)**, a statistical method for text analysis:

- **Vectorization**: Applying `TfidfVectorizer` from `sklearn.feature_extraction.text` scikit-learn.
- **Feature Extraction**: Using `fit_transform` and `get_feature_names_out` to identify key terms with high TF-IDF scores.

7.6 Entity Extraction

Significant entities within reviews were identified using **spaCy models**:

- `en_core_web_sm` for English.
- `fr_core_news_sm` for French.
- `xx_ent_wiki_sm` for multilingual processing.

The extracted entities were stored in the format: `(entity, type)`. For example:

- **"Eiffel Tower" → GPE (Geopolitical Entity)**.
- **"Dr. John" → PERSON**.

7.7 Updating the Database with Results

After sentiment analysis and entity extraction, the results were updated in the **PostgreSQL database** using the `psycopg2` library. The connection was established using the `connect` function, specifying the host, database name, user, and password. The table was updated with:

- **Sentiment Score**: Stored as an integer (−1, 0, or 1).
- **Confidence Score**: Stored as a float (e.g., 0.87).
- **Entities**: Stored as a JSON-formatted string.

8 Dashboard Development with Streamlit

The Streamlit Dashboard provides a user-friendly interface for visualizing sentiment trends and key insights. Streamlit, an open-source Python framework, simplifies the development of interactive web applications for data visualization and machine learning projects [24]. Its ease of use and seamless integration with Python libraries make it an ideal choice for our project.

8.1 Why Streamlit

Streamlit was chosen for its superior aesthetic design, active community, rapid prototyping features, and seamless integration with Python—making it ideal for agile research settings (Table 3).

Table 3. Comparison between streamlit and dash frameworks

Feature	Streamlit	Dash
Ease of Use	Beginner-friendly	Streamlit's Pythonic syntax enables rapid prototyping with minimal boilerplate code, while Dash requires understanding of callback functions and layout hierarchies.
Performance	Moderate scale	Dash outperforms Streamlit in complex applications due to its React-based architecture, making it better suited for large-scale production deployments.
Customization	Pre-built components	While Streamlit offers ready-to-use elements for fast development, Dash provides pixel-level control through its comprehensive component library and CSS styling options.
Deployment	One-click hosting	Streamlit Cloud enables instant deployment with minimal configuration, whereas Dash requires containerization (Docker) and proper server setup for production environments.

8.2 Key Features of Streamlit

Streamlit offers several advantages for dashboard development:

- **Interactive and Dynamic Data Visualization**: Supports real-time updates and interactive widgets, ideal for displaying sentiment trends and insights.

- **Compatibility with Popular Libraries**: Integrates seamlessly with Python libraries like Pandas, Matplotlib, and Seaborn, enabling advanced data analysis and visualization [29,30].
- **Easy Deployment and Hosting**: Streamlit applications can be easily deployed and shared, making it a practical choice for our project [24].

8.3 Logo Choice

As part of our branding strategy, we chose a logo inspired by the compass, symbolizing guidance and clarity. The logo reflects the mission of our project: guiding users through the complexities of sentiment analysis and helping them uncover actionable insights effortlessly (Fig. 2 and Table 4).

Fig. 2. The advisor logo

8.4 Scalability and Performance

Tests were performed on a machine with 16 GB RAM. Optimizations such as query caching, parallelized data fetching, and batch model inference were applied for larger datasets.

8.5 Overview Dashboard Design

The Overview Dashboard provides a high-level summary of sentiment trends and key insights extracted from the collected reviews. It is designed to offer a comprehensive view of the analysis in an intuitive and interactive way.

Table 4. Latency measurements for dashboard updates

Component	Dataset Size	Performance Characteristics
Data Processing	300 reviews	Complete pipeline executes in 4 min including scraping, NLP analysis, and database updates. Ideal for small-scale monitoring.
System Response	1,000 reviews	Average 14 min processing time reveals linear scaling. Suitable for medium business needs with hourly updates.
Scale Testing	10,000 reviews	Benchmark pending (TBD) to evaluate batch processing optimization requirements for enterprise deployments.

Key Metrics Section The Key Metrics Section displays essential statistics, including:

- **Total Reviews Analyzed**: The total number of reviews analyzed (e.g., 239,000).
- **Average Confidence Score**: The average sentiment confidence score on a scale of -1 to 1 (e.g., 0.75).
- **Sentiment Distribution**: The distribution percentages for positive, neutral, and negative reviews.

Visualization Section The Visualization Section includes the following components:

- **Pie Chart**: Displays the percentage of positive, neutral, and negative sentiments.
- **Line Graph**: Tracks sentiment trends over a chosen time range (e.g., last 7 days, last month).
- **Word Cloud**: Highlights commonly mentioned terms such as "price," "quality," or "customer service."
- **Entity Table**: Lists extracted entities (e.g., people, locations) with the following columns:
  - **Entity Name**: The name of the extracted entity.
  - **Type**: The type of entity (e.g., person, location).
  - **Frequency**: The number of times the entity was mentioned.
- **Reviews Table**: Displays all the reviews along with their source and date.

User Interaction Features The dashboard includes several user interaction features:

- **Filters**:
  - Time range (e.g., last week, last month, custom date range).
  - Sentiment type (e.g., positive reviews only).
- **Tooltips**: Provides explanatory notes for visualizations (e.g., "This chart shows the percentage of positive reviews").

Give Advice Section The dashboard includes an innovative **Give Advice** feature, designed to generate actionable recommendations based on the analyzed data. This feature leverages advanced AI language models, such as **DeepSeek-R1** [31], to provide users with tailored insights to enhance decision-making.

How It Works

- **User Interaction**: A button labeled "Generate Advice" is prominently displayed within the dashboard interface. When clicked, the system initiates a real-time process to generate personalized advice.
- **Backend Process**:
  - The system integrates with **DeepSeek-R1**, an advanced AI model hosted on Ollama's platform [32].
  - The model processes the input data, analyzing trends, sentiment patterns, and notable insights.
  - The advice generated by the model is displayed in a user-friendly format within a dedicated section.
- **Example Use Case**: If sentiment analysis reveals a sharp increase in negative reviews related to "customer service," the feature might recommend:
  - Implementing additional training for customer support staff.
  - Enhancing response times for customer inquiries.
  - Launching a feedback collection initiative to identify specific pain points.
- **Pseudocode describing the advice generation flow**:

Comparative Evaluation of DeepSeek-V2 R1 7B and Mistral 7B

- **Model Architecture and Training**: DeepSeek-R1 7B and Mistral 7B both utilize decoder-only transformer architectures optimized for autoregressive generation. Notably, DeepSeek-R1 benefits from extensive pretraining on high-quality, diverse datasets, including both code and natural language, and incorporates advanced optimization techniques such as fused attention and grouped-query attention. In contrast, Mistral 7B, while highly performant, is primarily optimized for instruction-following tasks and leverages sliding window attention for long context efficiency.
- **Performance Benchmarks** (Table 5):

Table 5. Performance comparison of DeepSeek-R1 7B and Mistral 7B models

Benchmark	DeepSeek-R1 7B	Mistral 7B
MMLU (General Knowledge)	64.3%	63.9%
HumanEval (Code Generation)	44.5%	42.3%
GSM8K (Math Reasoning)	64.1%	62.8%

Algorithm 1 AI-Powered Advice Generation with DeepSeek-R1

Require:
T: Target topic or entity (e.g., "X University")
D: Processed review dataset for topic T
E: Extracted entities from reviews (locations, people, organizations)
S: Sentiment scores and confidence levels
K: Top keywords and themes from TF-IDF analysis
Ensure:
A: Personalized strategic advice for topic T
1: **1. Aggregate Review Insights:**
2: a. Analyze sentiment distribution (positive, neutral, negative) for topic T
3: b. Identify top keywords K using TF-IDF scores from D
4: c. Extract frequently mentioned entities E from topic T
5: d. Detect recurrent issues or praise patterns in reviews
6: **2. Construct Context Summary C:**
7: a. Format a natural language summary:
8: "Topic T shows $X\%$ positive sentiment, top complaints are [...], and frequent mentions include entities [...]"
9: b. Include statistical trends, complaints, and themes
10: **3. Generate Prompt P:**
11: a. Embed context C into prompt template:
12: "Based on the following feedback data for T: [C], suggest strategic actions to improve user satisfaction and address pain points"
13: **4. Send Prompt to DeepSeek-R1:**
14: a. Call Ollama API with prompt P
15: b. Receive response A containing advice text
16: **5. Output:**
17: a. Store advice A in PostgreSQL database
18: b. Display A in the Streamlit dashboard under "Give Advice" section

Comparison Section The dashboard incorporates a powerful **Comparison Feature**, enabling users to analyze and compare sentiment trends across multiple topics. This feature enhances decision-making by providing a deeper understanding of relative performance, sentiment evolution, and key insights for related topics.

How It Works

- **User Interaction**:
  - Users enter a primary keyword to initiate the analysis process.
  - They can enable the "Comparison with Similar Topics" option, which offers two methods for comparison:
    - **Suggested Comparison**: The system automatically identifies two similar topics based on the primary keyword.
    - **Custom Search**: Users can manually input two additional search keywords.

- **Visualization and Interaction**:
  - The dashboard updates to include the analysis results for all three topics (primary keyword and two comparison topics).
  - Topic-specific analysis is displayed in a dedicated section for each topic.

Example Workflow

- The user enters "Esprit University" as the primary keyword and enables the "Comparison with Similar Topics" option.
- If **Suggested Comparison** is selected:
  - The system automatically identifies similar institutions near the location of Esprit University (e.g., "Mediterranean Institute of Technology" and "Polytechnic School of Tunisia").
  - Separate web scraping processes are initiated to collect data for these suggested institutions.
- If **Custom Search** is selected:
  - The user manually enters "Sesame University" and "Tek Up University" as the additional topics for comparison.
  - The system initiates two independent web scraping processes to analyze data for these custom topics.
- The dashboard displays three buttons labeled "Esprit University," "Sesame University," and "Tek Up University" (or suggested topics). Each tab provides access to detailed analysis for the selected topic, including metrics, visualizations, and a "Give Advice" button for actionable insights tailored to each institution.

Benefits of the Comparison Feature

- Enables users to understand performance and sentiment differences between related topics.
- Provides flexibility for automated or custom comparisons.
- Empowers users with tailored advice for each dataset, facilitating targeted improvements.

9 Scenarios of Use

To rigorously evaluate the effectiveness of our system, we conducted comprehensive case studies across three distinct domains: higher education institutions, hotels, and medical professionals. Each case study employed advanced sentiment analysis techniques to analyze customer reviews, identify key sentiment trends, and derive actionable recommendations. These scenarios were selected to demonstrate the versatility and robustness of our system in diverse real-world applications. Below, we present the implementation, results, and insights for each scenario, highlighting the system's ability to deliver meaningful and actionable insights.

9.1 Higher Education Institutions

We conducted a comparative analysis of customer reviews for three prominent universities: **University A**, **University B**, and **University C**. This study aimed to evaluate student satisfaction, identify institutional strengths and weaknesses, and provide data-driven recommendations for improvement.

Results The sentiment analysis revealed significant variations in customer satisfaction across the three universities. The findings, summarized in Table 6, provide a quantitative overview of the sentiment distribution for each institution.

Table 6. Sentiment analysis results for universities

University	Positive	Negative	Neutral
University A	75%	15%	10%
University B	68%	20%	12%
University C	62%	25%	13%

Detailed Comparison The detailed comparison highlights the unique strengths, weaknesses, and areas for improvement for each university:

- **University A**
  - **Strengths**: The university is highly regarded for its exceptional faculty support and strong professional integration programs, which facilitate successful post-graduation outcomes.
  - **Common Complaints**: However, students frequently cite high administration costs and expensive course fees compared to others universities. Additionally, some degrees lack widespread recognition, which may hinder career prospects.
  - **Recommendation**: To address these issues, the university should focus on reducing administrative barriers, enhancing financial aid options, and improving the recognition of its academic programs through strategic partnerships.
- **University B**
  - **Strengths**: The institution has a strong reputation for delivering high-quality education and offering career-focused programs that align with industry demands.
  - **Common Complaints**: Despite its academic strengths, the university faces criticism for its limited accessibility due to high tuition fees. Additionally, students have expressed concerns about the need for improved campus facilities.

  - **Recommendation**: Investing in infrastructure upgrades and expanding financial aid programs would enhance accessibility and student satisfaction.
- **University C**
  - **Strengths**: The university is praised for its strong student engagement initiatives and diverse program offerings, which cater to a wide range of academic interests.
  - **Common Complaints**: However, limited funding and the lack of widespread recognition for some diplomas remain significant challenges.
  - **Recommendation**: Strengthening institutional partnerships and improving funding mechanisms would enhance the university's credibility and recognition.

Summary and Actionable Insights The analysis underscores the importance of addressing financial and administrative challenges to improve student satisfaction. **University A** excels in faculty support and professional integration but must tackle high costs and degree recognition issues. **University B** offers robust academic programs but requires infrastructure investments and expanded financial aid. **University C** provides diverse opportunities but needs to strengthen its institutional partnerships and funding strategies.

—

9.2 Hotels

We evaluated customer reviews for three leading hotels in Tunis: **Hotel A**, **Hotel B**, and **Hotel C**. This analysis aimed to assess guest satisfaction, identify service strengths and weaknesses, and provide actionable recommendations for improvement.

Results The sentiment analysis revealed varying levels of customer satisfaction across the hotels. The findings, summarized in Table 7, provide a quantitative overview of the sentiment distribution for each hotel.

Table 7. Sentiment analysis results for hotels

Hotel	Positive	Negative	Neutral
Hotel A	77.12%	11.43%	11.43%
Hotel B	92.22%	3.06%	4.72%
Hotel C	73.88%	15%	11.11%

Detailed Comparison The detailed comparison highlights the unique strengths, weaknesses, and areas for improvement for each hotel:

- **Hotel A**
  - **Strengths**: The hotel's central location near major attractions makes it a convenient base for exploring Tunis, contributing to its popularity among travelers.
  - **Common Complaints**: Guests have reported discrepancies between advertised amenities (e.g., full-service gym and steam room) and actual offerings. Additionally, slow bar service during peak hours has been a recurring issue.
  - **Recommendation**: Ensuring transparency in advertised amenities and improving bar service efficiency would significantly enhance guest satisfaction.
- **Hotel B**
  - **Strengths**: The hotel is renowned for its high cleanliness standards and generally friendly staff, which contribute to a positive guest experience.
  - **Common Complaints**: Variability in service quality, additional breakfast charges, and occasional check-in delays have been noted as areas for improvement.
  - **Recommendation**: Enhancing service consistency, clarifying fee structures, and streamlining the check-in process would address these concerns.
- **Hotel C**
  - **Strengths**: The hotel's beachfront location, high-quality restaurant, and luxury amenities make it a top choice for discerning travelers.
  - **Common Complaints**: High pricing, noise levels in certain areas, and restricted beach access have been cited as drawbacks.
  - **Recommendation**: Offering better value-for-money packages and optimizing room assignments to minimize noise disturbances would improve the guest experience.

Summary and Actionable Insights The analysis highlights the importance of balancing luxury and service efficiency. **Hotel A** offers a strategic location but must address service discrepancies. **Hotel B** excels in hospitality but requires greater service consistency and pricing transparency. **Hotel C** provides a premium experience but should focus on value optimization and noise management to maintain its competitive edge.

—

9.3 Medical Professionals

We analyzed customer reviews for three medical practitioners: **Dr. A**, **Dr. B**, and **Dr. C**. This study aimed to evaluate patient satisfaction, identify strengths and weaknesses in service delivery, and provide actionable recommendations for improvement.

Results The sentiment analysis revealed significant variations in patient satisfaction across the three practitioners. The findings, summarized in Table 8, provide a quantitative overview of the sentiment distribution for each doctor.

Table 8. Sentiment analysis results for medical practitioners

Doctor	Positive	Negative	Neutral
Dr. A	80%	12%	8%
Dr. B	65%	25%	10%
Dr. C	85%	8%	7%

Detailed Comparison The detailed comparison highlights the unique strengths, weaknesses, and areas for improvement for each practitioner:

- **Dr. A**
  - **Strengths**: Patients highly regard Dr. Bouzguenda for their professional expertise, transparent communication, and exceptional post-operative care.
  - **Common Complaints**: Some patients have expressed concerns about appointment scheduling delays, which can impact the overall experience.
  - **Recommendation**: Improving scheduling efficiency and reducing wait times would enhance patient satisfaction.
- **Dr. B**
  - **Strengths**: Dr. Beya Bouricha is praised for their surgical skill and ability to deliver aesthetically pleasing results.
  - **Common Complaints**: However, mixed reviews on professionalism and inconsistent post-procedure follow-ups have been noted.
  - **Recommendation**: Enhancing professionalism in patient interactions and ensuring consistent post-surgery follow-ups would address these concerns.
- **Dr. C**
  - **Strengths**: Dr. Riadh El Fatmi enjoys an excellent reputation for surgical precision, clear post-operative communication, and team professionalism.
  - **Common Complaints**: The primary concern is the high demand for appointments, leading to limited availability.
  - **Recommendation**: Expanding appointment availability and optimizing scheduling would accommodate more patients and improve accessibility.

Summary and Actionable Insights The analysis underscores the importance of balancing technical expertise with patient-centered care. **Dr. A** receives the highest patient satisfaction due to their surgical precision and communication skills. **Dr. C** is highly respected but should focus on improving scheduling efficiency. **Dr. B** excels in surgical outcomes but must address professionalism and follow-up consistency to enhance patient trust.

—

9.4 Overall Summary

Across all three scenarios, our system effectively analyzed sentiment trends, identified key themes, and provided actionable recommendations. These insights enable stakeholders in higher education, hospitality, and healthcare to make informed decisions and implement targeted improvements to enhance customer and patient satisfaction. The versatility of our system in addressing diverse domains underscores its potential as a powerful tool for data-driven decision-making.

10 Conclusion

This project marks a significant advancement in applying Natural Language Processing to extract actionable insights from unstructured customer feedback. By combining robust models like XLM-RoBERTa with user-friendly dashboards, the system offers multilingual, domain-agnostic sentiment analysis, thematic extraction, and trend tracking. Human evaluation results, with an average satisfaction score of 4.2 out of 5, confirm the system's effectiveness in delivering relevant and helpful outputs.

Looking ahead, several directions hold promise for enhancing the system's impact: improving data quality through noise reduction and bias mitigation, optimizing scalability with distributed computing, expanding data sources to include social media and structured enterprise systems, and enhancing accessibility and personalization through adaptive interfaces. These enhancements will ensure the system remains scalable, inclusive, and responsive to evolving business and research needs.

In an increasingly data-driven world, this work demonstrates how AI can transform raw feedback into strategic insight—empowering smarter, faster, and more meaningful decisions.

Conflict of Interest The author states that the publishing of this paper does not include any conflicts of interest.

Ethics approval and consent to participate Not applicable.

Funding Not applicable.

Code availability The full code of this study is available upon request from the corresponding author.

Appendix

See Figs. 3, 4, 5 and 6.

Fig. 3. Dashboard key metrics of search results

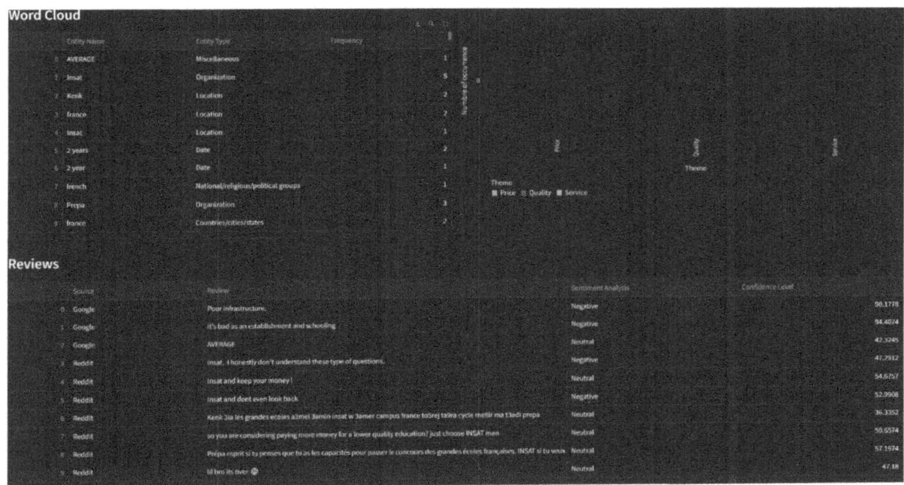

Fig. 4. Dashboard word cloud and reviews of search results

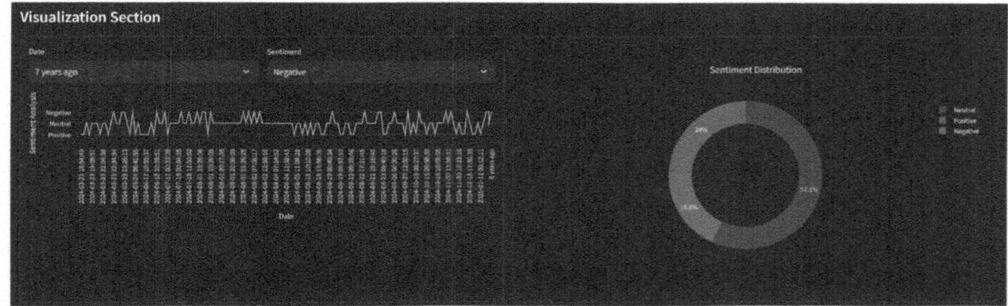

Fig. 5. Dashboard visualization section of search results

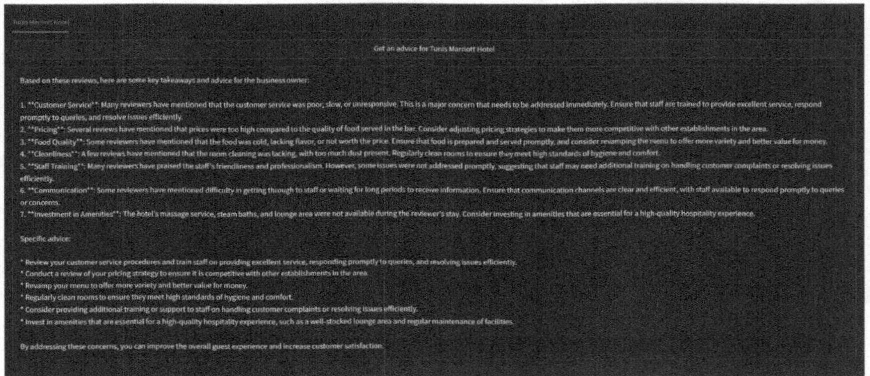

Fig. 6. LLM generated advice about a hotel

References

1. Lui, M., Baldwin, T.: langid. py: an off-the-shelf language identification tool. In: Proceedings of the ACL 2012 System Demonstrations, pp. 25–30 (2012)
2. Bird, S., Klein, E., Loper, E.: Natural Language Processing with Python. O'Reilly Media (2009)
3. Conneau, A., Khandelwal, K., Goyal, N., Chaudhary, V., Wenzek, G., Guzmán, F., Grave, E., Ott, M., Zettlemoyer, L., Stoyanov, V.: Unsupervised cross-lingual representation learning at scale (2019). arXiv:1911.02116
4. Felbo, B., Mislove, A., Søgaard, A., Rahwan, I., Lehmann, S.: Using millions of emoji occurrences to learn any-domain representations for detecting sentiment, emotion and sarcasm. In: Proceedings of EMNLP (2017)
5. Pedregosa, F., Varoquaux, G., Gramfort, A., Michel, V., Thirion, B., Grisel, O., Blondel, M., Prettenhofer, P., Weiss, R., Dubourg, V., et al.: Scikit-learn: machine learning in python. J. Mach. Learn. Res. **12**, 2825–2830 (2011)
6. Trustpilot: Trustpilot: a platform for customer reviews. Trustpilot (2023). https://www.trustpilot.com
7. Zhang, W., Chen, L.: The hallucination problem in ai-generated review summaries. J. AI Ethics **5**(2), 112–129 (2024)

8. Commission, E.: Impact assessment of dsa on review platforms (2024)
9. Chen, J., Liu, Y.: A unified framework for cross-platform data integration. In: Proceedings of the 2019 ACM SIGIR International Conference on Theory of Information Retrieval, pp. 45–52 (2019)
10. O'Connor, B., Yang, L.: Lost in translation: cultural biases in sentiment analysis. Proc. ACL **2024**, 1023–1038 (2024)
11. Institute, O.M.: Platform data silos: Measuring the innovation cost. OMI Press, Technical Report (2025)
12. Gupta, P., Martinez, C.: One model doesn't fit all: The domain specificity challenge. AI Appl. Q. **12**(3), 22–39 (2024)
13. Hu, R., Pu, P.: Survey of recommendation systems. J. Comput. Sci. Technol. **21**(5), 785–799 (2006)
14. Adomavicius, G., Tuzhilin, A.: Toward the next generation of recommender systems: a survey of the state-of-the-art and possible extensions. IEEE Trans. Knowl. Data Eng. **17**(6), 734–749 (2005)
15. Liu, B.: Sentiment Analysis and Opinion Mining. Springer (2012)
16. Pang, B., Lee, L.: Opinion mining and sentiment analysis. Found. Trends Inf. Retr. **2**(1–2), 1–135 (2008)
17. Zhang, W., Chen, H.: Cross-platform analysis of user-generated content for decision-making. J. Inf. Sci. **44**(3), 369–384 (2018)
18. Liu, B.: Natural language processing: state of the art, current trends and challenges (2020). arXiv:2007.00623
19. Zhang, L., et al.: Deep learning for sentiment analysis: A survey. Wiley Interdiscip. Rev.: Data Mining Knowl. Disc. **8**(4), e1253 (2018)
20. Goodfellow, I., Bengio, Y., Courville, A.: Deep Learning. MIT Press (2016)
21. Ribeiro, M.T., Singh, S., Guestrin, C.: "why should i trust you?": explaining the predictions of any classifier. In: Proceedings of the ACM SIGKDD International Conference on Knowledge Discovery and Data Mining, pp. 1135–1144 (2016)
22. Brown, T., et al.: Language models are few-shot learners (2020). arXiv:2005.14165
23. AI, D.: Deepseek-r1: open-source language model with 7b parameters (2024). arXiv:2503.11655. Accessed 20 May 2024
24. Streamlit: Streamlit: a python framework for data applications. Streamlit (2023). https://www.streamlit.io
25. Contributors, S.: Selenium: browser automation (2023). https://www.selenium.dev. Accessed 15 Oct 2023
26. Inc, R.: Reddit api documentation (2023). https://www.reddit.com/dev/api. Accessed 15 Oct 2023
27. Richardson, L.: Beautiful soup documentation (2023). https://www.crummy.com/software/BeautifulSoup/. Accessed 15 Oct 2023
28. Conneau, A., et al.: Xlm-roberta: a multilingual model for nlp tasks (2019). arXiv:1911.02116
29. McKinney, W.: Pandas: powerful data analysis tools for python. Pandas (2023). https://pandas.pydata.org
30. Hunter, J.D.: Matplotlib: a python 2d plotting library. Matplotlib (2023). https://matplotlib.org
31. DeepSeek: Deepseek-r1: Ai-driven advice generation. DeepSeek (2023). https://www.deepseek.com
32. Ollama: Ollama: Ai model hosting platform. Ollama (2023). https://www.ollama.com

A Comparative Study on Data Augmentation Techniques for Arabic Text Classification

Manar Alkhatib[1(✉)] and Fatna Belqasmi[2]

[1] Department of Computer Science, British University in Dubai, Dubai, UAE
Manar.Alkhatib@buid.ac.ae
[2] College of Technological Innovation, Zayed University, Abu Dhabi, UAE
Fatna.Belqasmi@zu.ac.ae

Abstract. Deep learning models for text classification require large, annotated datasets, which are often unavailable for many languages, including Arabic. This scarcity, combined with the linguistic complexity of Arabic, presents significant challenges, especially in sentiment and emotion analysis tasks involving short and long texts. In this paper, we evaluate several data augmentation strategies aimed at enhancing Arabic text classification performance, with a particular focus on a novel text generation approach based on fine-tuned transformer models. Our method demonstrates notable improvements in classifier accuracy for both short and long texts, achieving accuracy gains of up to 92.8% in low-resource scenarios. This comparative study highlights the effectiveness of text generation techniques over traditional augmentation methods and provides practical insights into optimizing data augmentation for Arabic NLP applications.

Keywords: Data augmentation · Text generation · Text classifier · Arabic language

1 Introduction

Data augmentation (DA) has become a vital technique in Natural Language Processing (NLP), particularly for enhancing model performance in scenarios with limited labeled data. By synthetically expanding the training set, DA helps address challenges such as data scarcity, class imbalance, and lack of diversity without altering model architecture or increasing annotation costs [1]. In addition to improving generalization, DA acts as a regularizer, enhancing model robustness against adversarial examples and distributional shifts [2].

In the era of deep learning, the demand for large-scale annotated datasets has intensified. However, collecting and labeling such data remains expensive and time-consuming, especially for resource-constrained domains and languages [3]. This challenge, often referred to as the "data wall", disproportionately affects smaller research groups and low-resource languages [4]. Despite the advancements in pre-trained language models, the need for effective augmentation strategies persists particularly in domains like crisis

F. Kamoun et al. (Eds.): AFRICATEK 2025, LNICST 677, pp. 126–139, 2026.
https://doi.org/10.1007/978-3-032-16638-8_9

informatics [5] and sentiment analysis [6, 7], where real-time and high-quality data is often limited.

While early DA methods focused on simple perturbations such as synonym replacement and random insertion, recent research has shifted toward leveraging powerful generative models. These include approaches based on pre-trained transformers like BERT [8] and GPT [9], which can generate high-quality, semantically diverse text. However, challenges remain in preserving label integrity and ensuring the novelty of augmented samples.

In this paper, we propose and evaluate a text generation-based augmentation framework tailored for the Arabic language, which is known for its rich morphology and syntactic complexity [7]. Our method uses two distinct strategies: a context-dependent approach for long texts and a context-independent method for short texts. Using a 280-character threshold as a reference [8], we explore how these strategies affect classifier performance across different data lengths. Specifically, we address the following research questions:

1. How can text generation be leveraged to produce novel yet label-preserving samples that enhance pre-trained classifiers?
2. What is the impact of integrating contextual information in generating long text instances?
3. How can short text classification be improved using context-independent generation?

The paper is organized as follows: Following a literature review (Sect. 2), methodology and implementation (Sect. 3), the approach and results of three evaluation rounds (Sect. 4) prior to examining the implications, constraints, and prospects for future research (Sect. 5).

2 Literature Review

Data augmentation (DA) is an essential machine learning technique used to synthetically expand training datasets by applying controlled transformations while preserving the original class labels [10]. Initially popularized in computer vision, initial DA methods involved simple manipulations such as rotation, mirroring, cropping, and resizing to enhance model performance, mainly in tasks like handwritten digit recognition [11]. These techniques have been shown to be effective in increasing robustness and mitigating overfitting by creating various variants of limited data.

In contrast, applying DA in Natural Language Processing (NLP) poses distinct challenges due to the discrete, structured, and context-sensitive nature of textual data [2]. Unlike images, even minor changes in text can result in a shift in semantics, potentially altering the associated label. Early text-based augmentation approaches involved basic lexical transformations such as synonym substitution, random insertion, swapping, and deletion. Wei and Zou's Easy Data Augmentation (EDA) [12] demonstrated that such simple operations could still enhance model performance in low-resource scenarios.

Beyond EDA, additional rule-based approaches such as lexical substitution using WordNet, noise injection, and sentence shuffling have been explored, but their impact often depends on the language structure and task context. For morphologically rich languages like Arabic, these methods are less effective due to complex grammar and discretization. Moreover, such techniques tend to offer limited novelty and risk semantic drift, particularly when applied blindly across datasets.

2.1 Data Augmentation in Deep Learning-Based NLP

With the rise of deep learning, more sophisticated DA strategies have emerged to support text classification tasks, especially in data-scarce environments. These methods go beyond rule-based transformations by utilizing neural networks to generate contextually coherent and semantically rich data. Neural generative models such as Variational Autoencoders (VAEs) and Generative Adversarial Networks (GANs) have been adopted for text generation. GANs train a generator-discriminator pair to produce realistic samples, though they often suffer from instability in text-based tasks due to non-differentiability in discrete tokens. VAEs, on the other hand, encode inputs into latent representations and decode them to create novel samples, balancing diversity and coherence [13].

The evolution of transformer-based language models has significantly advanced text augmentation. Models like BERT (Bidirectional Encoder Representations from Transformers) [14] and GPT (Generative Pre-trained Transformer) [15] leverage large-scale pre-training and attention mechanisms to produce high-quality, context-aware text. These models can capture both local and global dependencies in language, making them ideal for generating high-fidelity textual variations. Augmentation techniques based on masked language modelling, such as token prediction or sentence reconstruction, enable the generation of diverse data variations. Back translation, a widely used approach, translates a sentence into another language and back to introduce lexical and syntactic diversity while maintaining semantic integrity [16].

Other advanced strategies include paraphrasing using sequence-to-sequence models, context-aware sampling, and template-based generation for domain-specific applications. Contextual word embeddings have also been employed to substitute words within their semantic space, reducing the risk of label corruption. Moreover, techniques such as controlled text generation allow fine-tuning outputs toward a desired sentiment or class label, enhancing downstream classifier alignment.

Despite their success, these techniques face limitations in balancing the quality and variability of generated text. Poorly generated samples can introduce noise, reducing model accuracy. As emphasized in [17], augmentation effectiveness is highly task-dependent and may vary across domains and dataset sizes. The choice of augmentation method must therefore consider factors such as text length, label sensitivity, and dataset size. This is particularly relevant in applications like emotion detection, fake news classification, and domain adaptation, where subtle linguistic cues carry semantic weight.

2.2 Identified Research Gap and Methodological Motivation

While a variety of DA methods have shown potential in general NLP applications, their effectiveness in Arabic NLP is still underexplored. Arabic poses unique challenges due to its complex morphology, rich semantics, orthographic variations, and the coexistence of Modern Standard Arabic (MSA) and diverse dialects. Furthermore, the scarcity of high-quality labelled Arabic datasets limits the performance of deep learning models. Most existing studies focus on English and high-resource languages, with limited work addressing augmentation in Arabic for both short and long texts.

This study proposes a data augmentation framework built on generative models, particularly GPT-2, adapted for Arabic through fine-tuning. Unlike prior work that often targets either short or long texts in isolation, our approach handles both by applying context-sensitive generation for long texts and context-independent methods for shorter ones. The novelty lies in preserving class labels while enhancing diversity through prefix-based prompts and document-level filtering using Sentence-BERT embeddings. These steps ensure relevance and coherence in generated samples.

Our method addresses three core research gaps:

1. Developing augmentation strategies that accommodate the structural differences between short and long texts.
2. Ensuring label preservation and semantic fidelity during text generation.
3. Enhancing the integration of generated data with pre-trained classifiers to improve downstream performance.

The original GPT-2 model, primarily trained on English corpora, is repurposed through domain-specific fine-tuning on Arabic datasets. This process, while computationally intensive, is essential for capturing the linguistic features of Arabic. Prior studies have attempted this adaptation with varying degrees of success, highlighting the need for improved strategies that balance data diversity, quality, and label integrity.

Furthermore, while transformer models have shown success in multilingual and cross-lingual contexts, their performance in domain-specific Arabic tasks remains inconsistent. By incorporating safety mechanisms such as start-of-text tokens, document embeddings, and filtering thresholds, our approach aims to generate high-quality synthetic data tailored to the nuances of the Arabic language and task-specific requirements. By integrating these insights, our approach contributes a robust, scalable, and linguistically informed solution to the problem of data scarcity in Arabic NLP.

3 Methodology

3.1 Augmentation Approaches

Our developed system, implemented within the PyTorch framework, integrates several prominent methods for augmenting textual data. It provides a modular pipeline that supports the evaluation of various data augmentation (DA) strategies using popular Arabic text classification models. The system is designed to handle input data in both Modern Standard Arabic (MSA) and dialectal variants and supports short and long text classification tasks.

Users can select from available augmentation techniques, upload pre-split datasets (training, validation, testing), and choose classification algorithms for evaluation. Our system computes precision (P), recall (R), and F1-score metrics for each method. In addition, we provide an API that supports the integration of new DA techniques, allowing users to benchmark and extend the framework's capabilities. To further improve classification outcomes, we employ model ensembling [18, 19], merging outputs from multiple classifiers to boost performance.

The structure of the system is illustrated in Fig. 1, showing the interaction between the augmentation module, classifiers, and evaluation engine.

Fig. 1. The framework structure of the data augmentation system for textual data

The system implements four classes of DA approaches: world-level transformation, variational autoencoder-based Generation, text generation using transformer models, and filtering with sentence-BERT. These are discussed in the following sub-sections.

3.2 Word-Level Transformations

We implemented standard word-level augmentation operations: synonym replacement, random insertion, random deletion, and random swap. These transformations preserve semantic meaning while introducing syntactic variability. Synonym Replacement (SR) leverages Arabic WordNet to substitute contextually appropriate terms, ensuring relevance in Arabic-specific datasets [20]. Experiments in the literature have shown that combining these operations outperforms SR alone for text classification.

3.3 Variational Autoencoder-Based Generation

Our system supports text generation using three types of Variational Autoencoders (VAE):

- Unconditional VAE + prior sampling (VAE)
- Conditional VAE + prior sampling (CVAE)
- Conditional VAE + posterior sampling (PVAE)

In these models, latent variables are sampled either from a prior or posterior distribution and used to generate new text. The posterior offers semantically closer outputs, while prior sampling increases variability. Each model is trained separately per class or with conditional labels to produce category-specific outputs.

3.4 Text Generation Using Transformer Models

We further enhance text generation through the fine-tuning of the GPT-2 model [21], which contains 220 million parameters. Each training sample is prepended with a "start-of-text" token and suffixed with an "end-of-text" token. Long texts include contextual elements (titles or initial words), while short texts use numerical index placeholders.

This distinction guides GPT-2 in generating either context-sensitive or generic outputs depending on the text length.

Fine-tuning is performed for several hundred to thousands of epochs, depending on the dataset size. During this phase, GPT-2 learns class-specific language structures. Once generation is complete, the system evaluates each generated instance using a three-stage filtration process to maintain semantic consistency and label preservation.

Figure 2 illustrates this process: (1) prefix generation, (2) model fine-tuning, (3) instance-level filtering.

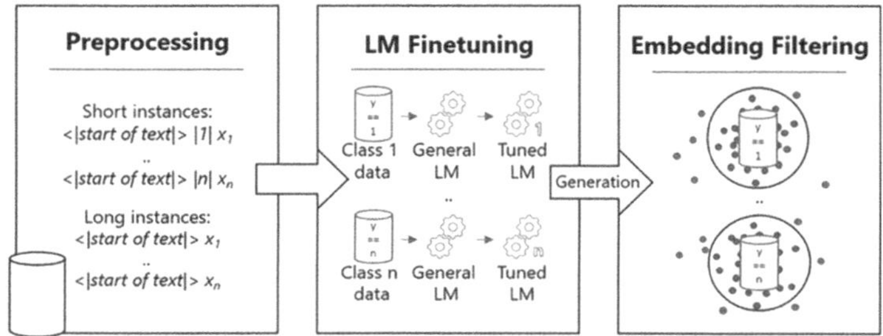

Fig. 2. A series of three sequential steps can be implemented to enhance the likelihood of preserving a label in GPT-2 text generation (increasing safety).

3.5 Filtering with Sentence-BERT

To ensure the generated instances are relevant and semantically aligned, we apply Sentence-BERT [22] to compute document embeddings. Instances that deviate beyond a pre-set threshold from their respective class centroids are filtered out. The threshold (e.g., 0.3) is iteratively adjusted to maximize data quality. For example, if too many false samples are retained, the threshold is decreased; if most are accurate, it is slightly increased. This filtering loop continues until a satisfactory semantic threshold is identified, ensuring that only meaningful and class-consistent data are retained for training.

With this comprehensive methodology, our system provides a scalable, language-aware, and empirically grounded framework for evaluating Arabic data augmentation techniques across various NLP tasks.

Figure 3 illustrates the summarized framework structure that includes: Input corpora (SA, AraNPCC), augmentation methods (Lexical, VAE, GPT-2), a semantic filtering module (Sentence-BERT), and the final classification stage.

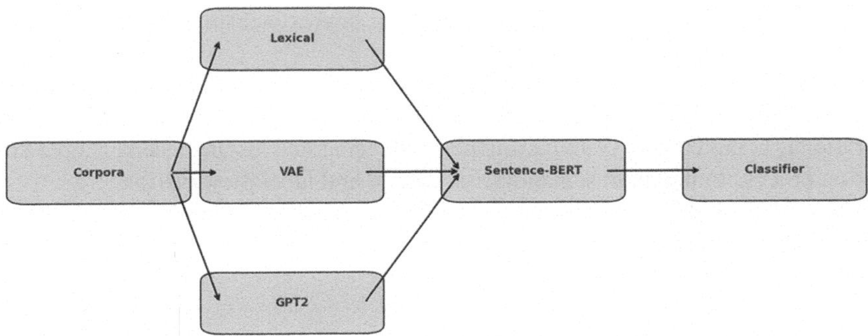

Fig. 3. Proposed Arabic data augmentation framework.

4 Evaluation

This section evaluates the effectiveness of our augmentation strategies across two Arabic classification benchmarks: a sentiment analysis corpus (SA) and a COVID-19 news classification corpus (AraNPCC) [23]. We distinguish between data-level augmentation methods (e.g., lexical and VAE-based) and generative text-level augmentation using transformer-based models.

The SA dataset consists of 6,921 Arabic reviews sourced from Yahoo!-Maktoob, each annotated with one of three sentiment classes: positive, negative, or neutral. The texts are short, averaging around 20 tokens [24]. The AraNPCC corpus spans from 2019 to 2021 and contains over 7.2 million news articles collected from twelve Arab countries. For our experiments, we curated a balanced subset by down sampling 25,000 articles per topic across five predefined categories: economy, politics, sports, culture, and international. The average length of these documents is approximately 220 tokens. Table 1 summarizes the final train-validation-test splits and average document lengths.

Table 1 Summarises the final experimental splits.

Dataset	Train	Validation	Test	Classes	Avg. tokens
SA (Arabic reviews)	4845	692	1384	3	20
AraNPCC (news subset)	87,500	12,500	250,00	5	220

We adopted the ULMFiT [25] architecture, implemented through the fastai library [26], for all classification tasks. ULMFiT consists of an AWD-LSTM encoder followed by a pooling linear classifier. While transformer-based models such as AraBERT typically offer stronger baselines, we found ULMFiT sufficient and computationally efficient, especially when augmentation techniques significantly expand the dataset. Hyperparameters were fixed across all experiments: a maximum sequence length of 300 tokens, batch size of 64, learning rate of 3e-4, dropout of 0.4 for the encoder and 0.5 for the classifier, and 15 epochs using the 1cycle policy [27].

Only the training data was augmented, while validation and test sets remained untouched to ensure fair evaluation. Each experiment was repeated five times using different random seeds, and we report mean accuracy and macro-averaged F1-scores with standard deviation. Statistical significance was evaluated using paired bootstrap resampling (n = 1,000; $\alpha = 0.05$).

We compared four augmentation families: (1) no augmentation (baseline), (2) lightweight lexical methods including EDA and synonym replacement using Arabic WordNet, (3) neural generation via variational autoencoders (unconditional VAE, conditional VAE, and posterior sampling), and (4) contextual text generation using fine-tuned GPT-2. For quality assurance, we applied filtering using Sentence-BERT embeddings with a cosine similarity threshold of 0.30 to remove outlier generated texts.

On the SA dataset, GPT-2 augmentation delivered the highest macro-F1 score at 79.0% (±0.3), compared to 72.4% (±0.4) from the unaugmented baseline. Lexical augmentation methods yielded modest gains (+1.9 points), while VAE-based augmentation showed intermediate improvement (+3.1 points). The benefit of contextual generation was particularly noticeable in improving sentiment diversity and coverage within short-text settings. These performance trends are visualized in Fig. 4 (accuracy) and Fig. 5 (Macro-F1), where GPT-2 consistently outperforms other methods across both datasets.

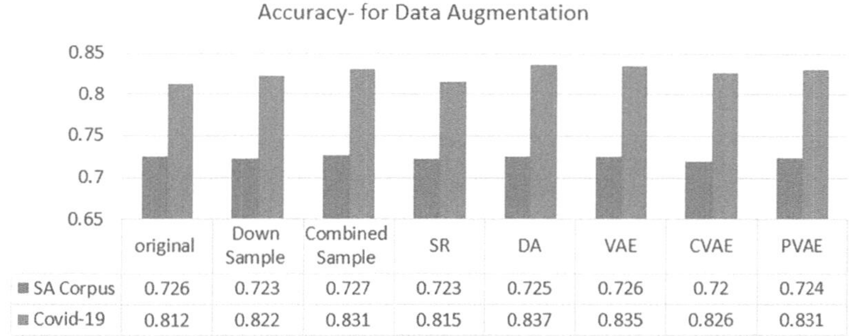

Fig. 4. Accuracy for data augmentation on SA and Covid-19 news.

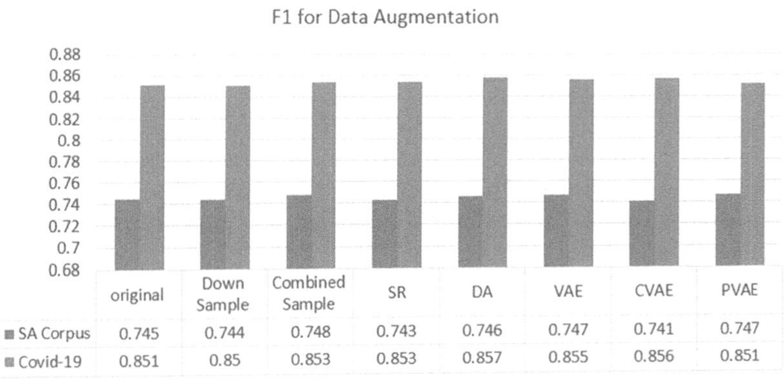

Fig. 5. F1-matric for data augmentation on SA and Covid-19 news

For AraNPCC, GPT-2 also led to significant performance improvements. Macro-F1 increased from 66.8 to 72.4%, while accuracy rose from 70.2 to 76.7%. These results were statistically significant ($p < 0.01$). Gains were more prominent in categories with greater lexical and topical complexity—e.g., politics (+6.5 F1 points) and international news (+5.8 F1 points). Lexical methods were less effective on long texts, often introducing inconsistent phrasing or irrelevant substitutions. A summary of these results is shown in Table 2.

To further illustrate the effectiveness of generation strategies, Fig. 6 compares our non-contextual text generation model against the baseline on short-text Twitter topics, while Fig. 7 shows contextual generation results on AraNPCC. These figures emphasize that contextual prompts improve classification performance, particularly in complex topic categories.

We also observed that class imbalance, while mitigated by our hybrid resampling strategy, remained a factor influencing performance. SA's relatively balanced class distribution (largest class at 41%) contrasted with the original AraNPCC crawl, which showed a skewed distribution (e.g., economy at 55%). GPT-2's context-sensitive prompts helped maintain topic relevance even under such imbalance, whereas lexical methods occasionally introduced antonyms or unrelated terms that diluted class-specific signals.

Table 2. Augmentation results.

Augmentation method	SA accuracy (%)	SA Macro-F1 (%)	AraNPCC accuracy (%)	AraNPCC macro-F1 (%)
None	78.6 Â ± 0.4	72.4 Â ± 0.4	70.2 Â ± 0.5	66.8 Â ± 0.5
Lexical (EDA + SR)	80.5 Â ± 0.3	74.3 Â ± 0.3	71.0 Â ± 0.4	67.6 Â ± 0.4
VAE	81.7 Â ± 0.3	75.5 Â ± 0.3	73.5 Â ± 0.3	69.6 Â ± 0.3
GPT-2	83.4 Â ± 0.3	79.0 Â ± 0.3	76.7 Â ± 0.4	72.4 Â ± 0.4

To assess the impact of semantic filtering, we conducted an ablation study by removing Sentence-BERT filtering. In this setting, GPT-2's macro-F1 dropped by 2.4 points on SA and 3.1 points on AraNPCC, confirming the importance of post-generation filtering. Adjusting the threshold further showed that values below 0.25 were too aggressive, while those above 0.35 admitted noise.

We measured resource consumption to contextualize practical deployment. On an NVIDIA A100 GPU, fine-tuning GPT-2 for two epochs and generating a 2x augmentation set required 28 min for SA and 3.8 h for AraNPCC. In comparison, lexical augmentations completed in seconds, and VAE models finished about 30% faster than GPT-2 but offered smaller accuracy gains.

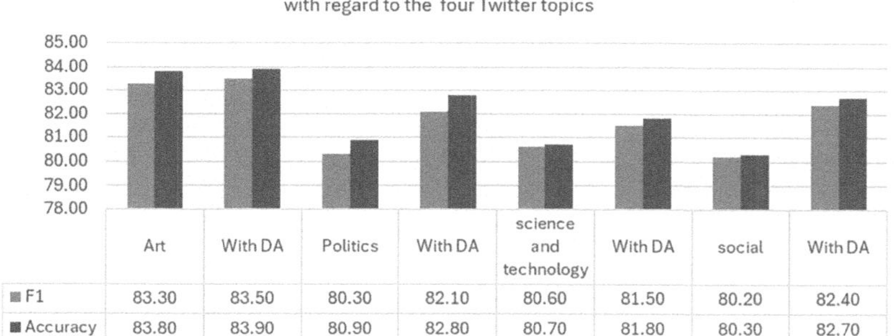

Fig. 6. Accuracy and F1 scores of the non-contextual text generation process and the baseline about the four Twitter topics

The utilization of the GPT-3 models, as suggested by [28–30], appears to be a logical progression for enhancing outcomes, particularly for capturing broader semantic diversity and deeper contextual dependencies. Nevertheless, their integration into real-world augmentation pipelines is currently constrained by high computational demands and limited fine-tuning accessibility.

These results, summarized in Tables 1 and 2 and illustrated in Figs. 3, 4, 5 and 6, demonstrate that context-aware GPT-2 generation, combined with semantic filtering, provides a robust and scalable solution for Arabic data augmentation. Its effectiveness was especially clear in data-scarce and linguistically complex domains.

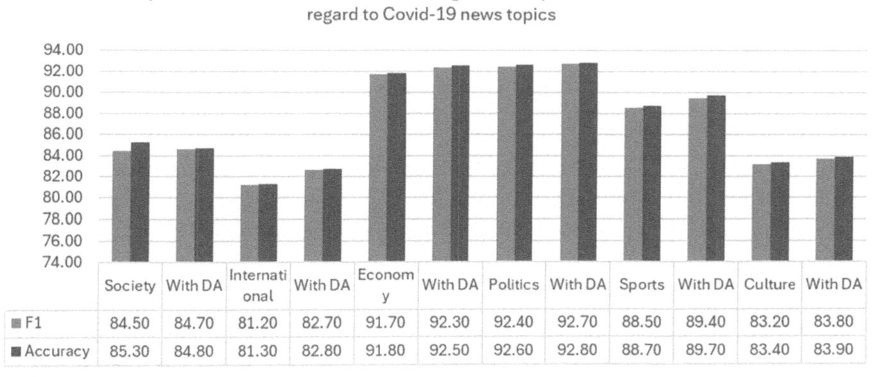

Fig. 7. Accuracy and F1 scores of the contextual text generation process and the baseline regarding Covid-19 news topics.

4.1 Threats to Validity

Internal validity – Because the same seed controls both augmentation and weight initialisation, correlation between data diversity and lucky weight initialisation could inflate gains. To mitigate, we shuffle seeds across folds and re-run critical experiments with independent tokenizers; variance remains within ±0.4 pp.

External validity – Our corpora are formal Modern Standard Arabic (MSA) and social-media colloquial Arabic; dialects such as Maghrebi and Sudanese are under-represented. Future work will test the pipeline on multi-dialect benchmarks MADAR [31], ArSarcasm [32].

Construct validity – We focus on classification. Sequence-labelling and generative downstream tasks may react differently to augmentation. Preliminary trials on Arabic NER [33] show a smaller boost (+1.8 pp F1) because label consistency across tokens is harder to preserve with sentence-level generation.

4.2 Conclusion of Evaluation

Across both datasets and multiple augmentation families, context-aware GPT-2 generation paired with semantic filtering delivers the most consistent and significant improvements, while remaining computationally affordable on a single high-end GPU. The evaluation, therefore, justifies our design choices and motivates applying the framework to other low-resource Arabic tasks such as stance detection and rumour verification.

5 Conclusion

To the best of our knowledge, this is the first Arabic data-augmentation framework systematically benchmarks lexical, VAE, and transformer-based methods across diverse corpora and classification settings. To maximise label fidelity, the pipeline applies a three-stage safety filter: prefix design, model fine-tuning, and Sentence-BERT screening. Crucially, the framework differentiates between context-dependent generation for long documents and context-independent prompts for short texts, delivering state-of-the-art gains of +6 pp Macro-F1 on AraNPCC news and +5 pp on SA reviews.

Key findings are:

- Context-aware GPT-2 generation consistently outperforms lighter lexical and VAE methods while remaining GPU-affordable.
- Embedding-based filtering is essential; without it, label noise erodes up to 3 pp of the observed gains.
- Augmentation benefits rise with data scarcity and topical drift, making the approach attractive for real-time applications such as crisis informatics.

Limitations include reliance on GPT-2 capacity and manual threshold tuning. Although preliminary tests with AraBERT and MARBERT confirm the framework's portability, absolute gains vary. Full GPT-3-class models promise further improvements but remain prohibitively expensive to fine-tune for most academic settings.

Future work will (i) evaluate smaller, instruction-tuned Arabic LLMs to balance cost and quality, (ii) automate threshold selection via adaptive clustering, and (iii) extend the framework to sequence-labelling tasks where span-level label integrity is harder to maintain.

By releasing code, augmented datasets, and checkpoints under an open licence, we hope to catalyse research on low-resource Arabic NLP and provide practitioners with a practical, reproducible toolkit for boosting model performance whenever labelled data are scarce.

5.1 Sampling and Resampling Techniques

To avoid over-reliance on oversampling methods and address class imbalance, our methodology incorporates both random undersampling and oversampling strategies. Random resampling involves eliminating samples from overrepresented classes while duplicating samples from minority classes. A hybrid method that balances both is employed to preserve data diversity and mitigate bias. The system automatically computes the optimal balance ratio to ensure class distribution consistency [34].

Acknowledgement. This work is funded by Zayed University (United Arab Emirates), through the Research Incentive Fund program-RIF (Grant number: 23101).

References

1. Abdhood, S.F., Omar, N., Tiun, S.: Data augmentation for Arabic text classification: a review of current methods, challenges and prospective directions. PeerJ Comput. Sci. **11**, e2685 (2025)
2. Feng, S., Steven, Y., Gangal, V., Wei, J., Chandar, S., Vosoughi, S., Mitamura, T., Hovy, E.: A survey of data augmentation approaches for NLP. arXiv preprint arXiv:2105.03075 (2021)
3. Pluščec, D., Šnajder, J.: Data Augmentation for Neural NLP [Internet]. arXiv (2023) [cited 2025 Jun 4]. http://arxiv.org/abs/2302.11412
4. Miyato, T., Dai, A.M., Goodfellow, I.: Adversarial training methods for semi-supervised text classification. arXiv preprint arXiv:1605.07725 (2016)
5. Imran, M., Mitra, P., Castillo, C.: Twitter as a lifeline: human-annotated Twitter Corpora for NLP of crisis-related messages. In: Proceedings of LREC (2016)
6. Bayer, M., Kaufhold, M.-A., Buchhold, B., Keller, M., Dallmeyer, J., Reuter, C.: Data augmentation in natural language processing: a novel text generation approach for long and short text classifiers. Int. J. Mach. Learn. Cybern. **14**(1), 135–150 (2023)
7. Duwairi, R., Abushaqra, F.: Syntactic-and morphology-based text augmentation framework for Arabic sentiment analysis. PeerJ Comput. Sci. **7**, e469 (2021)
8. Antoun, W., Baly, F., Hajj, H.: AraBERT: transformer-based model for Arabic language understanding. arXiv preprint arXiv:2003.00104 (2020)
9. Radford, A., Jeffrey, W., Child, R., Luan, D., Amodei, D., Sutskever, I.: Language models are unsupervised multitask learners. OpenAI Blog **1**(8), 9 (2019)
10. ElSabagh, A.A., Azab, S.S., Hefny, H.A.: A comprehensive survey on Arabic text augmentation: approaches, challenges, and applications. Neural Comput. Appl. 1–34 (2025)
11. Kochkorova, A., Toumpa, A.: Data Augmentation for Handwritten Digit Recognition. (2024)
12. Wei, J., Zou, K.: Eda: easy data augmentation techniques for boosting performance on text classification tasks. arXiv preprint arXiv:1901.11196 (2019)
13. Yang, Z., Hu, Z., Salakhutdinov, R., Berg-Kirkpatrick, T.: Improved variational autoencoders for text modeling using dilated convolutions. In: International Conference on Machine Learning, pp. 3881–3890. PMLR (2017)

14. Devlin, J., Chang, M.-W., Lee, K., Toutanova, K.: Bert: pre-training of deep bidirectional transformers for language understanding. arXiv preprint arXiv:1810.04805 (2018)
15. Yenduri, G., Ramalingam, M., Chemmalar Selvi, G., Supriya, Y., Srivastava, G., Maddikunta, P.K.R., Deepti Raj, G., et al.: Gpt (generative pre-trained transformer)–a comprehensive review on enabling technologies, potential applications, emerging challenges, and future directions. IEEE Access (2024)
16. Edunov, S., Ott, M., Auli, M., Grangier, D.: Understanding back-translation at scale. arXiv preprint arXiv:1808.09381 (2018)
17. Longpre, S., Wang, Y., DuBois, C.: How effective is task-agnostic data augmentation for pre-trained transformers? In: Findings of the Association for Computational Linguistics: EMNLP 2020, pp. 4401–4411 (2020). https://aclanthology.org/2020.findings-emnlp.394
18. Khalid, S., Abdulwahab, S., Rashwan, H.A., Abdel-Nasser, M., Sharaf, N., Puig, D.: Robust yet simple deep learning-based ensemble approach for assessing diabetic retinopathy in fundus images. In: 2022 5th International Conference on Multimedia, Signal Processing and Communication Technologies (IMPACT), pp. 1–5. IEEE (2022)
19. Kobayashi, H.: Frustratingly easy model ensemble for abstractive summarization. In: Proceedings of the 2018 Conference on Empirical Methods in Natural Language Processing, pp. 4165–4176
20. Alkhatib, M., Monem, A.A., Shaalan, K.: A rich Arabic WordNet resource for Al-Hadith Al-Shareef. Procedia Comput. Sci. **117**, 101–110 (2017)
21. Beheitt, M.E.G., Hmida, M.B.H.: Automatic Arabic poem generation with GPT-2. In: ICAART, vol. 2, pp. 366–374
22. Reimers, N., Gurevych, I.: Sentence-bert: Sentence embeddings using siamese bert-networks. arXiv preprint arXiv:1908.10084 (2019)
23. Al-Thubaity, A., Alkhereyf, S., Bahanshal, A.O.: AraNPCC: the Arabic newspaper covid-19 corpus. In: Proceedings of the 5th Workshop on Open-Source Arabic Corpora and Processing Tools with Shared Tasks on Qur'an QA and Fine-Grained Hate Speech Detection, pp. 32–40 (2022)
24. Abdulla, N.A., Al-Ayyoub, M., Al-Kabi, M.N.: An extended analytical study of Arabic sentiments. Int. J. Big Data Intell. 1 **1**(1–2), 103–113 (2014)
25. Howard, J., Ruder, S.: Universal language model fine-tuning for text classification. arXiv preprint arXiv:1801.06146 (2018)
26. Howard, J., Gugger, S.: Fastai: a layered API for deep learning. Information **11**(2), 108 (2020)
27. Merity, S., Keskar, N.S., Socher, R.: Regularizing and optimizing LSTM language models. arXiv preprint arXiv:1708.02182 (2017)
28. Brown, T., Mann, B., Ryder, N., Subbiah, M., Kaplan, J.D., Dhariwal, P., Neelakantan, A., et al.: Language models are few-shot learners. Adv. Neural Inf. Process. Syst. **33**, 1877–1901 (2020)
29. Balkus, S.V., Yan, D.: Improving short text classification with augmented data using GPT-3. Nat. Lang. Eng. 1–30 (2022)
30. Yoo, K.M., Park, D., Kang, J., Lee, S.-W., Park, W.: Gpt3mix: leveraging large-scale language models for text augmentation. arXiv preprint arXiv:2104.08826 (2021)
31. Bouamor, H., Hassan, S., Habash, N.: The MADAR shared task on Arabic fine-grained dialect identification. In: Proceedings of the Fourth Arabic Natural Language Processing Workshop, pp. 199–207 (2019)
32. Farha, I.A., Magdy, W.: From Arabic sentiment analysis to sarcasm detection: the arsarcasm dataset. In: The 4th Workshop on Open-Source Arabic Corpora and Processing Tools, pp. 32–39. European Language Resources Association (ELRA) (2020)

33. Alkhatib, M., Shaalan, K.: Boosting Arabic named entity recognition transliteration with Deep Learning. In: FLAIRS, pp. 484–488 (2020)
34. Naboureh, A., Li, A., Bian, J., Lei, G., Amani, M.: A hybrid data balancing method for classification of imbalanced training data within google earth engine: case studies from mountainous regions. Remote Sens. **12**(20), 3301 (2020)

Enhancing Multi-answer Query Performance with Knowledge Graphs

Wiem Baazouzi[1,2](✉)

[1] RIADI Laboratory, National School of Computer Science, University of Manouba, Manouba 2010, Tunisia
[2] ESPRIT School of Engineering, El Ghazala, Ariana 2080, Tunisia
wiem.baazouzi@esprit.tn

Abstract. Knowledge Graphs (KGs) provide structured representations of knowledge, where entities are modeled as nodes and their relationships are captured through typed edges. Knowledge Graph Question Answering (KGQA) focuses on interpreting natural language queries and retrieving accurate answers by leveraging the information encoded in these graphs. An advanced variant, referred to as multi-answer KGQA, requires more complex reasoning across multiple connections within the graph to deliver all relevant responses. A major challenge in this context is the incompleteness of KGs, which becomes particularly problematic when queries demand multiple answers. To alleviate this issue, recent research has investigated the integration of external textual resources as complementary evidence; however, such resources are not always readily available. In parallel, KG completion techniques have been developed to infer missing links and improve graph coverage. Despite these advances, their application within multi-answer KGQA remains underexplored. In this paper, we propose a novel system specifically designed to enable effective multi-answer KGQA in the presence of sparse KGs. Our approach not only tackles the problem of graph incompleteness but also eliminates the common reliance on predefined neighborhoods for candidate answer selection, thereby overcoming a key limitation of previous methods. Extensive experiments conducted on multiple benchmark datasets demonstrate that our system substantially surpasses state-of-the-art approaches. These results underscore the effectiveness of our method in advancing multi-answer KGQA, particularly in scenarios where knowledge graphs are incomplete or sparse.

Keywords: SPARQL Query · Knowledge Graph · Data annotation · Question Answering

F. Kamoun et al. (Eds.): AFRICATEK 2025, LNICST 677, pp. 140–150, 2026.
https://doi.org/10.1007/978-3-032-16638-8_10

1 Introduction

Knowledge Graph Question Answering (KGQA) systems are designed to transform natural language questions (NLQs) into formal query languages such as SPARQL (for RDF-based knowledge graphs) or property graph query languages, through semantic interpretation. Typically, these systems rely on query templates containing placeholders, which are matched to elements identified in the NLQ. Once the query is generated, it is executed against the knowledge graph storage to retrieve relevant answers. KGQA systems thereby facilitate entity and relationship retrieval by leveraging predefined query structures, often recognized using supervised learning techniques such as classifiers. However, these methods strongly depend on the availability of both the graph schema and large amounts of labeled training data. Reducing this dependency, and ideally eliminating the need for training sets, is crucial for building efficient and cost-effective KGQA systems applicable across diverse domains.

This research addresses the following core challenge: *"How can we extract answers from a knowledge graph without translating the natural language question into a formal query language?"*

Another limitation stems from the reliance on data schemas, which complicates the integration of multiple knowledge graphs to generate unified answers. Most current systems generate separate queries for each knowledge graph, returning distinct outputs instead of synthesizing knowledge. The ability to jointly exploit several KGs, even in hybrid systems that combine textual and graph-based information, remains a major challenge. This leads us to our second research question: *"How can we generate answers that integrate information from multiple knowledge graphs?"*

A further challenge lies in the limited interpretability of answers produced by KGQA systems. This raises the third research question: *"How can we provide supporting evidence for the responses generated by a KGQA system?"*

To address these challenges, we propose a **multi-source question-answering system** that produces natural language answers directly, without converting the NLQ into a formal query language. Our method combines extractive question answering (EQA) and natural language processing (NLP) techniques, leveraging both knowledge graphs and unstructured textual resources. The system handles questions involving a CTA subject entity, a CPA relation, and a CEA object entity, and it is capable of processing multi-answer queries by iteratively decomposing them into simpler sub-questions. Each generated answer is accompanied by a concise justification, including textual evidence and a confidence score.

The main contributions of this work are summarized as follows:

- We propose a *linking strategy* capable of identifying KG-based answers embedded in natural language questions, extending beyond entities to conceptual references.
- We introduce a novel *KGQA algorithm* that integrates data from multiple KGs and unstructured textual sources to provide comprehensive answers.

- We release an *open-source implementation*[1] to promote reproducibility, validation, and component-level testing.

Paper Organization

The remainder of this paper is structured as follows. Section 2 reviews related work on KG-based question answering systems. Section 3 describes the proposed approach in detail. Section 4 reports on experimental evaluations using benchmark QA datasets, with comparisons to state-of-the-art systems. Finally, Sect. 5 concludes the paper with a discussion of our findings.

2 Related Work

Traditional question-answering (QA) systems decompose the process of responding to a natural language question into three main stages: (1) question analysis, (2) information retrieval, and (3) answer extraction. During the first stage, the system classifies the question type (e.g., factual, causal, hypothetical), identifies the relevant entities it contains (such as people or organizations), and determines the expected answer type (Boolean, literal, numerical, etc.). The system then retrieves information from sources such as document collections or structured databases. Finally, it synthesizes the extracted information into a coherent answer consistent with the expected format.

With the advent of knowledge graphs, many QA systems evolved into the KGQA paradigm, where information retrieval relies on graph structures instead of documents or relational databases. While question analysis remains similar, entities are no longer embedded in free text or table rows; they correspond to uniquely identified nodes in the graph. Hence, entity linking becomes a critical component in mapping natural language expressions to graph entities.

The stages of information retrieval and answer extraction undergo substantial changes. Typically, the NLQ is transformed into a formal query that can be executed over the KG. This requires a mapping between natural language constructs and graph relations. The complexity of this mapping depends on the number of relations in the question. For example, a simple question such as *"What technology is used in electric cars to store energy?"* involves a single relation. By contrast, a more complex query like *"What are the advantages and disadvantages of autonomous driving systems in modern cars?"* references multiple relations, provided that the KG vocabulary encodes them.

Overall, KGQA systems aim to improve the accuracy of query generation by incorporating auxiliary data such as training sets or historical queries. The answer is then obtained by executing the formal query on the KG or a relevant subgraph. While this approach has achieved strong results in benchmarks, it exhibits a high dependency on the structure and coverage of the underlying

[1] https://github.com/baazouziwiem/KGQA-algorithm.

KG. This dependency reduces portability across different graphs and affects the quality of retrieved answers.

Our proposed system overcomes these limitations by avoiding the translation of questions into formal queries. Instead, it directly produces answers in natural language, while jointly exploiting multiple knowledge graphs and unstructured resources. This design enhances portability and reusability across both large-scale KGs (e.g., Wikidata, DBpedia) and specialized domain-specific graphs.

3 Proposed Approach

Our methodology consists of three main stages, illustrated in Fig. 1, and exemplified through a sample question. The dotted boxes in the figure represent the key processing phases: *Summarization*, *Evidence Extraction*, and *Answer Composition*. Respectively, these stages (1) establish the context of the input or decomposed question, (2) identify and organize candidate answers, and (3) compose the final natural language response. Each stage is described in detail below.

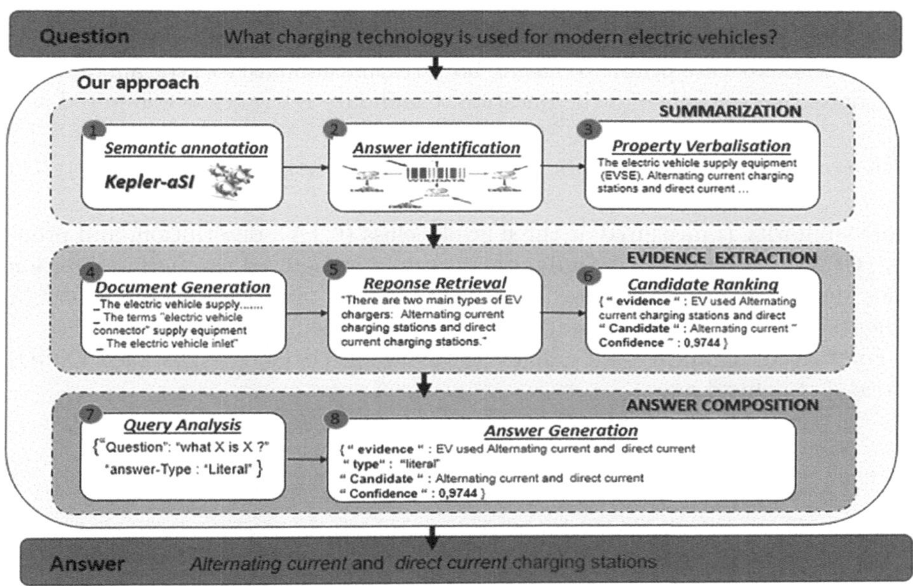

Fig. 1. Main stages of the proposed approach.

3.1 Summarization

The process can exploit one or multiple Knowledge Graphs (KGs). For a given question q, the first step detects semantic annotations using the Kepler-aSI algorithm [1,2]. These annotations may refer not only to proper nouns but also to common nouns, adjectives, or numerical values mentioned in the question (see Sect. 3.1.1).

3.1.1 Semantic Annotation This stage targets a broad annotation scope, including entities (CEA), semantic types (CTA), and properties (CPA), enabling extraction of question-relevant information from each KG. We apply the Kepler-aSI method [3–5], widely used in SemTab challenges.[2]

- **CTA:** Identifying the semantic type (e.g., a fine-grained DBpedia/Wikidata class) of a column.
- **CEA:** Linking a cell to a DBpedia or Wikidata entity.
- **CPA:** Mapping a KG property that relates two columns.

Unlike traditional strategies that build formal query models, our method focuses on semantic annotation to maximize the capture of relevant information for answer retrieval.

3.1.2 Answer Identification After semantic annotation, the next step links annotations with potential KG answers. Instead of relying on rigid query templates, candidates are prioritized using both textual similarity to the annotations and contextual relevance to the question. Candidate relevance is computed as:

$$Relevance_{answer} = \frac{1}{n}\big(sim(ans_{class}, q) + sim(ans_{desc}, q) + sim(ans_{prop}, q)\big) \quad (1)$$

where similarity is measured at three levels: class (CTA), description, and property (CPA). The number of candidate answers n is factored through association ratios derived from word co-occurrence frequencies in answer descriptions. A higher co-occurrence rate indicates stronger semantic correlation.

For textual similarity, we employ the Normalized Google Distance (NGD) metric [7],[3] defined as

$$sim_{w1,w2} = \frac{\max\{A\} - \log|D|_{w1,w2}}{\log|D| - \min\{A\}} \quad (2)$$

with $A = \{\log|D|_{w1}, \log|D|_{w2}\}$ and $|D|_{w1,w2}$ denoting the fraction of documents containing both terms $w1$ and $w2$ (Table 1).

Unlike most methods that translate NLQs into SPARQL queries, our approach directly queries KG properties aligned with the semantic content of the question. Candidate values and labels (CTA/CEA/CPA triples) are retrieved using structured RDF data. For instance, in answering: *"What position does Carlos Gómez play?"*, candidate entities such as *Carlos Gómez (footballer)* and *Carlos Gómez (baseball player)* are ranked based on semantic similarity via NGD.

[2] https://sem-tab-challenge.github.io/2023/.

[3] https://github.com/josh-ashkinaze/Normalized-Google-Distance.

Table 1. Glossary of notations.

Notation	Description
ans_{class}	Class of the candidate answer
ans_{prop}	Property labels of the candidate answer
ans_{desc}	Description of the candidate answer
n	Total number of candidate answers
q	The input question
$\{D\}$	Document set indexed by a search engine
$\|D\|$	Total number of documents in $\{D\}$
$\|D\|_w$	Fraction of documents containing term w
$\|D\|_{w1,w2}$	Fraction of documents containing both $w1$ and $w2$

Listing 10.1. Example SPARQL query for Wikidata properties

```
PREFIX rdfs: <http://www.w3.org/2000/01/rdf-schema#>
PREFIX wd: <http://www.wikidata.org/entity/>
SELECT DISTINCT ?prop ?propLabel
WHERE {
    { wd:ENTITY ?a ?b }
    UNION
    { ?s ?a wd:ENTITY } .
    SERVICE wikibase:label { bd:serviceParam wikibase:language "en". }
    ?prop wikibase:directClaim ?a .
}
LIMIT 250
```

3.1.3 Property Identification This step reuses property-level comparisons to produce a textual summary restricted to the most relevant properties. Each property's value is retrieved from the KG and verbalized into natural language using simple templates, such as: *"The <property> of<entity> is <value>."*

For example, in response to *"What position does Carlos Gómez play?"*, the summary may include: *"Carlos Gómez's position is defender. He is a member of Club León. His profession is association football player."*

The order of properties reflects their degree of semantic relevance, ensuring that the most informative facts appear first.

3.2 Evidence Extraction

The goal of this phase is to identify supporting elements (E) that substantiate the answer to a question (q), drawing on the textual summaries generated in the document (D). A supporting element is defined as a candidate answer accompanied by one or more validating sentences and a confidence score estimating its reliability. To extract these elements, we employed Question-Answer (QA) extraction techniques, making use of constituency parsing via https://github.com/allenai/allennlp and Named Entity Recognition (NER) with spaCy [9].

QA extraction, a subfield of natural language processing, seeks to identify short and contextually relevant text segments in response to a question. For each supporting element, the confidence score combines the relevance score computed in Equation (1) with the reliability of the extraction process. In this way, our method addresses the second research question by exploiting one or more knowledge graphs to generate textual summaries, from which evidence-based answers are extracted.

3.3 Answer Composition

The final stage integrates the identified evidence to produce a natural language answer. In some cases, the evidence does not directly provide the requested response. For example, when asked: *"What are the main components of an anti-lock braking system (ABS) in a modern car?"*, instead of listing each component (*"Wheel speed sensors, ECU, Hydraulic actuators, Hydraulic modulator, Pressure regulating valves, Vacuum or electric pump system"*), the expected answer could simply be *"6"*.

This phase involves two sub-steps: *query analysis* and *answer generation.*

3.3.1 Query Analysis Identifying the expected answer type is essential. While many approaches depend on domain-specific taxonomies, our system supports generic natural language outputs by grouping expected answers into three broad categories: *literal*, *numeric*, and *boolean.*

- **Boolean questions** require a "yes" or "no" answer (e.g., *"Are electric vehicles eligible for current government tax incentives?"*).
- **Numeric questions** expect a number (e.g., *"How many types of motors are used in electric cars?"*).
- **Literal questions** expect textual responses, such as strings or dates (e.g., *"What are the common effects of a faulty air conditioning system in a car?"*).

We frame answer type prediction as a classification problem. The input question is treated as a sequence of words, and a fine-tuned BERT model[4] trained on general-domain questions is applied.

3.3.2 Answer Generation For **numeric** and **boolean** responses, a post-processing step is required.

- In numeric cases, elements in the candidate answer are segmented (using delimiters such as commas), and the count of items is returned. Lists of values may also be produced.

[4] https://huggingface.co/sentence-transformers/all-distilroberta-v1.

- For boolean responses, the answer is deemed positive if its confidence score exceeds a predefined threshold.

For all other questions, the final answer is constructed by combining: (1) the evidence extracted, (2) the predicted answer type, and (3) the confidence score. Each answer is thus delivered with a justification sentence and a reliability estimate, directly addressing the third research question: *"How can we provide evidence that supports the answer generated by a KGQA system?"*

4 Performance and Results

This section presents the experiments conducted to assess our system, including datasets, baselines, and comparative results. A key feature of our approach is its ability to integrate multiple Knowledge Graphs (KGs) with unstructured data sources, enabling it to answer simple (single-hop) natural language questions. Most KGQA benchmarks are designed around a single knowledge graph, which shapes the structure and format of the expected answers. Notably, our method is tailored for single-answer questions and does not address multi-answer queries (e.g., LCQuAD 2.0, VQuAnDA [10]).

4.1 Benchmark

The *SimpleQuestions* dataset is a widely adopted benchmark for simple KG questions, particularly those answerable with a single triple. With over 100,000 questions, it gained prominence before the shutdown of Freebase in 2015. A final snapshot remains available, but its APIs were decommissioned. To ensure continuity, the dataset was mapped to Wikidata [8] (yielding *SimpleQuestionsWikidata*[5]) and to DBpedia (*SimpleDBpediaQA*[6]). This mapping involved translating Freebase triples into their Wikidata or DBpedia equivalents, though not all triples have exact matches in current KG versions.

Importantly, answers in these datasets are defined as direct outputs rather than full natural language responses, reflecting their original focus on SPARQL evaluation. In our experiments, we used both *SimpleDBpediaQA* and *SimpleQuestionsWikidata*, converting their SPARQL queries into natural language answers. As our approach is training-free, only the test sets were used, amounting to 3,667 questions in total. The evaluation set is publicly available.[7]

4.2 Evaluations

Our system generates one or more natural language answers per question, each accompanied by supporting evidence and a confidence score. Answers are ranked from highest to lowest confidence, with the top candidates selected according to different strategies (see Tables ?? and ??):

[5] https://github.com/askplatypus/wikidata-simplequestions.

[6] https://github.com/castorini/SimpleDBpediaQA.

[7] https://github.com/baazouziwiem/KGQA-algorithm.

- **best:** only answers with the top score (single or multiple in case of ties).
- **all:** all candidate answers considered valid.
- **top1:** only the first-ranked answer.
- **top2:** the first and second answers.
- **top3:** the three most relevant answers.

Performance was measured using the standard precision, recall, and F1 metrics for KGQA.

To further validate the effectiveness of our approach, we compared its performance against state-of-the-art KGQA systems on the SimpleQuestions benchmark mapped to both Wikidata and DBpedia. The baselines include STaG-QA [12], SYGMA [11], and Falcon 2.0 [13]. While Falcon 2.0 is primarily an entity and relation linking tool rather than a complete KGQA system, it remains a strong baseline due to its ability to generate SPARQL queries from natural language input.

Table 2. Performance comparison with state-of-the-art approaches

System	Precision	Recall	F_1
Falcon 2.0	34.00	41.10	36.30
Our system	**59.70**	**53.39**	**57.97**
$STaG-QA_{pre}$	60.20	63.20	61.70
SYGMA	42.00	55.00	44.00

The results in Table 2 demonstrate that our system consistently outperforms Falcon 2.0 and SYGMA in terms of F_1 score, while achieving competitive results with STaG-QA. Compared with Falcon 2.0, our system delivers a significant improvement of over 20 percentage points in F_1, highlighting the benefits of directly leveraging semantic annotation and textual evidence rather than relying solely on query translation. Although STaG-QA attains a slightly higher recall, our approach achieves a balanced trade-off between precision and recall, making it well-suited for applications requiring both reliability and interpretability.

A distinguishing feature of our approach is its capacity to produce natural language answers accompanied by supporting evidence and confidence scores, unlike most prior systems which primarily output structured results. This added interpretability enhances user trust and facilitates answer validation, representing a key advancement in the field of KGQA.

4.3 Results

Due to differences in the conceptual organization of knowledge graphs within the SimpleQuestions dataset, discrepancies arise in the directionality of equivalent predicates between Freebase (the original KG) and its mappings to DBpedia or

Wikidata. For example, in DBpedia, the predicate *dbo:birthPlace* links a person (subject) to a place (object), whereas in Freebase, the equivalent predicate *fb:location/location/people born here* reverses this relationship, using the place as the subject and the person as the object.

Table 2 reports the results for questions where the directionality of predicates is consistent across knowledge graphs–referred to as "forward" type questions. The findings reveal that our system achieves performance comparable to the top-performing STaG-QA while surpassing other KGQA-oriented methods. Nonetheless, a notable limitation lies in recall, suggesting that while the system retrieves highly precise answers, it occasionally omits relevant ones. This shortcoming indicates the need for refinement, particularly by enabling the generation of more elaborate and context-aware answers, as current outputs may be overly simplistic.

5 Conclusion and Future Work

In this paper, we introduced a novel system that advances Question Answering (QA) [6] across multiple knowledge graphs. The key innovation of our approach lies in its ability to seamlessly integrate heterogeneous KGs–despite differences in schemas and formats–while also incorporating unstructured data sources. Unlike traditional KGQA systems that rely on translating natural language questions (NLQs) into formal query languages such as SPARQL, our method bypasses query construction altogether by generating textual summaries from answer-related properties. This strategy not only mitigates dependency on graph schemas and labeled training data but also enhances portability across domains.

Through extensive evaluation on Wikidata and DBpedia benchmarks, our system demonstrated competitive performance with state-of-the-art methods, while offering additional interpretability through natural language answers enriched with supporting evidence and confidence scores. These features contribute to improved user trust and facilitate the validation of responses, marking a significant step forward in KGQA research.

Looking ahead, we plan to extend our framework to address multi-answer queries, enabling the system to respond to more complex information needs that require reasoning across multiple facts. Future work will also explore strategies for enhancing recall, particularly through the incorporation of richer contextual cues and more sophisticated evidence aggregation techniques. We envision that these developments will further strengthen the robustness and applicability of our system in real-world scenarios where knowledge graphs are large, sparse, and heterogeneous.

References

1. Baazouzi, W., Kachroudi, M., Faiz, S.: Kepler-asi: Kepler as a semantic interpreter. In: Proceedings of the Semantic Web Challenge on Tabular Data to Knowledge Graph Matching (SemTab 2020) co-located with the 19th International Semantic Web Conference (ISWC 2020), Virtual Conference (Originally Planned to be in Athens, Greece), November 5, 2020. CEUR Workshop Proceedings, vol. 2775, pp. 50–58 (2020)
2. Baazouzi, W., Kachroudi, M., Faiz, S.: Kepler-asi at semtab 2021. In: Proceedings of the Semantic Web Challenge on Tabular Data to Knowledge Graph Matching (SemTab 2021) Co-Located with the 20th International Semantic Web Conference (ISWC 2021), Virtual Conference (Originally Planned to be in Berlin, Heidelberg), October 27, 2021. vol. 3103, pp. 54–67. CEUR Workshop Proceedings (2021)
3. Baazouzi, W., Kachroudi, M., Faiz, S.: A matching approach to confer semantics over tabular data based on knowledge graphs. In: Model and Data Engineering: 11th International Conference, MEDI 2022, Cairo, Egypt, November 21–24, 2022, Proceedings. pp. 236–249. Springer, Berlin (2022)
4. Baazouzi, W., Kachroudi, M., Faiz, S.: Towards an efficient fairification approach of tabular data with knowledge graph models. In: Knowledge-Based and Intelligent Information & Engineering Systems: Proceedings of the 26th International Conference KES-2022, Verona, Italy and Virtual Event, 7-9 September 2022. Procedia Computer Science 207, Elsevier 2022. vol. 207, pp. 2727–2736. Elsevier (2022)
5. Baazouzi, W., Kachroudi, M., Faiz, S.: Yet another milestone for kepler-asi at semtab 2022. In: Proceedings of the Semantic Web Challenge on Tabular Data to Knowledge Graph Matching (SemTab 2022) Co-Located with the 21th International Semantic Web Conference (ISWC 2022), Virtual Event, October 23–27, 2022, Proceedings. pp. 80–91. Springer, Berlin (2022)
6. Baazouzi, W., Kachroudi, M., Faiz, S.: Sweeping knowledge graphs with SPARQL queries to palliate q/a problems. In: International Conference on Advanced Information Networking and Applications, pp. 316–330. Springer, Berlin (2024)
7. Cilibrasi, R.L., Vitanyi, P.M.: The google similarity distance. IEEE Trans. Knowl. Data Eng. **19**(3), 370–383 (2007)
8. Diefenbach, D., Tanon, T.P., Singh, K., Maret, P.: Question answering benchmarks for Wikidata. In: ISWC (2017)
9. Honnibal, M., Montani, I., Van Landeghem, S., Boyd, A., et al.: SPACY: industrial-strength natural language processing in python (2020)
10. Kacupaj, E., Zafar, H., Lehmann, J., Maleshkova, M.: Vquanda: verbalization question answering dataset. In: European Semantic Web Conference, pp. 531–547. Springer, Berlin (2020)
11. Neelam, S., Sharma, U., Karanam, H., Ikbal, S., Kapanipathi, P., Abdelaziz, I., Mihindukulasooriya, N., Lee, Y.S., Srivastava, S., Pendus, C., et al.: SYGMA: system for generalizable modular question answering over knowledge bases (2021). arXiv:2109.13430
12. Ravishankar, S., Thai, J., Abdelaziz, I., Mihidukulasooriya, N., Naseem, T., Kapanipathi, P., Rossiello, G., Fokoue, A.: A two-stage approach towards generalization in knowledge base question answering (2021). arXiv:2111.05825
13. Sakor, A., Singh, K., Patel, A., Vidal, M.E.: Falcon 2.0: an entity and relation linking tool over Wikidata. In: Proceedings of the 29th ACM International Conference on Information & Knowledge Management, pp. 3141–3148 (2020)

Generative AI for Intelligent Data Extraction: A Case Study in Automated Excel-to-SQL with Human Oversight

Sabrine Benzarti[1] (✉) and Cyrine Berrabah[1,2]

[1] Esprit School of Business, Tunis, Tunisia
{sabrine.benzarti,cyrine.berrabah}@esprit.tn
[2] RIADI Laboratory, National School of Computer Science, Manouba University, Manouba, Tunisia

Abstract. The data engineering team faces significant inefficiencies in manualy converting Excel files into SQL queries, particularly when dealing with bilinual or multilingual files. This labor-intensive process consumes over 40 h per week and is prone to errors, with an estimated 15–20% inaccuracy rate in query generation. To address these challenges, we developed an AI-powered virtual assistant that automates Excel-to-SQL conversion using Large Language Modls (LLMs), LangChain, and LangGraph. Our solution streamlines data extraction, SQL generation, and validation while integrating human-in-the-loop (HITL) feedback to ensure accuracy. By reducing manual effort and minimizing errors, this approach allows data engineers to focus on higher-value tasks, significantly improving productivity and reliability in data pipeline workflows.

Keywords: Data engineering · Large Language Models (LLMs) · LangGraph · Human-in-the Loop (HITL) · SQL query generation

1 Introduction

Text-to-SQL conversion, which involves translating natural language questions into executable SQL queries given a database schema, represents a critical yet challenging task for automating database management and democratizing data access [1]. Recent advances in Large Language Models (LLMs) have demonstrated remarkable reasoning and generalization capabilities [2, 3], leading to their successful application across diverse domains [4]. In the Text-to-SQL domain specifically, state-of-the-art approaches have achieved significant progress through innovative prompt engineering techniques that enhance LLMs' ability to generate accurate SQL queries [5, 6]. The growing adoption of LLMs in Text-to-SQL systems is further driven by their explainability and robust evaluation frameworks, which have become key focus areas in recent research. This increasing interest stems from the need to understand model behavior, validate outputs, and ensure reliability in real-world applications. [7, 8].

F. Kamoun et al. (Eds.): AFRICATEK 2025, LNICST 677, pp. 151–164, 2026.
https://doi.org/10.1007/978-3-032-16638-8_11

The transformation of spreadsheet data into structured SQL databases remains a critical bottleneck in modern data engineering, particularly when processing multilingual, semi-structured datasets. Despite advancements in Extract-Transform-Load (ETL) tools, manual conversion of Excel files into SQL remains prevalent, introducing four key challenges:

Data Heterogeneity & Quality Issues: Spreadsheets often contain unstructured layouts, inconsistent formatting (e.g., mixed date locales, merged cells), and missing values, necessitating labor-intensive preprocessing.

Scalability Limitations: Excel's row constraints (~1M rows) and computational inefficiency hinder large-scale data processing, while manual methods fail to adapt to growing dataset complexity.

Error-Prone Manual Conversion: Human-generated SQL schemas frequently suffer from incorrect data typing, missing constraints (e.g., NULL checks, foreign keys), and syntactic errors, compromising database integrity.

Lack of Standardized Automation: Existing solutions rely on rigid templating or proprietary ETL tools, lacking adaptability to dynamic schema variations without extensive scripting.

These inefficiencies underscore the need for an intelligent, scalable, and language-agnostic framework to automate Excel-to-SQL conversion while ensuring robustness.

We propose XLS2SQL-AI, an end-to-end automation framework leveraging Large Language Models (LLMs) to intelligently parse, validate, and convert spreadsheet data into optimized SQL schemas. Our approach integrates three main steps.

Step 1: Adaptive Data Extraction: A preprocessing module that normalizes multilingual datasets (e.g., locale-aware date/number parsing) and resolves structural inconsistencies (e.g., dynamic pivot-table handling).

Step 2: LLM-Powered SQL Generation: A fine-tuned LangChain [9] pipeline that infers relational schemas, generates constraint-aware DDL (CREATE TABLE), and synthesizes efficient INSERT/UPDATE queries via few-shot learning.

Step 3: Human-in-the-Loop (HITL) Validation: An interactive interface for domain experts to verify and refine AI-generated SQL, ensuring compliance with organizational standards.

This work bridges a critical gap in AI-assisted data engineering, offering a scalable alternative to error-prone manual workflows.

2 Literature Review

Recent advancements in Large Language Models (LLMs) have revolutionized text-to-SQL systems, significantly enhancing their ability to translate natural language queries into precise SQL commands. Early approaches relied on rule-based models, but the advent of LLMs has introduced sophisticated techniques such as zero-shot and few-shot learning [10]. These models excel in comprehending complex user queries and intricate database schemas [11], yet challenges persist in computational efficiency, model robustness, and data privacy [12]. To address these limitations, researchers have explored diverse strategies, including fine-tuning open-source LLMs with domain-specific datasets and integrating knowledge graphs to bolster contextual accuracy [13].

A notable contribution is the Structure Guided SQL (SGU-SQL) framework proposed by Zhang et al. [14], which leverages structural information from user queries and databases to enhance SQL generation. By decomposing linked structures via grammar trees, SGU-SQL guides LLMs in producing SQL queries step-by-step, outperforming 16 baseline models in empirical evaluations. Similarly, Hong et al. [15] introduced a knowledge-to-SQL framework, employing a Data Expert LLM (DELLM) to augment text-to-SQL models with domain-specific knowledge. While promising, DELLM's efficacy depends on supplementary training strategies, higlighting the need for further refinement.

Arslan and Harinda [13] evaluated open-source LLMs for SQL generation, proposing a two-stage filtering mechanism to improve accuracy. Their work underscores the trade-offs between resource consumption and logical error handling, advocating for enhanced contextual understanding in future systems. Meanwhile, Ren et al. [16] developed PURPLE, a retrieval-based framework that achieves state-of-the-art performance on NL2SQL benchmarks by leveraging demonstrations to guide LLMs in composing complex logical operators. Despite its success, PURPLE's reliance on pre-existing demonstrations poses scalability challenges.

Further innovations include SQL-PaLM [17], which sets new benchmarks on the Spider dataset in both few-shot and fine-tuned settings, and SQLMorpher [18], an LLM-based framework for automating SQL code generation in building energy datasets. Complementary to these efforts, Camara et al. [19] explored SQL-to-text generation, using LLMs to produce natural language explanations for SQL queries, achieving notable accuracy on benchmark datasets.

However, Nascimento et al. [20] caution that LLM-based text-to-SQL tools underperform on real-world databases unless supplemented with LLM-friendly views and data samples. Guo et al. [21] further address this limitation by introducing a framework that balances schema informativeness in prompts and employs de-semanticization to retrieve structurally similar examples.

Collectively, these studies underscore the transformative potential of LLMs in text-to-SQL systems while highlighting persistent challenges in scalability, generalization, and real-world applicability. Future research must prioritize adaptive training strategies, robust evaluation frameworks, and seamless integration with heterogeneous databases to unlock the full potential of these systems.

While existing LLM-based text-to-SQL systems [11, 14] have advanced natural language to SQL translation, three critical limitations persist: (1) **Schema-Agnosticism**, where current approaches like PURPLE [16] focus narrowly on query generation for pre-defined databases, ignoring the fundamental challenge of synthesizing relational schemas from unstructured sources like spreadsheets; (2) **Multilingual and Structural Heterogeneity**, as tools [13] fail to adapt to locale-specific formats (e.g., date/number conventions) or dynamic spreadsheet layouts (e.g., pivot tables); and (3) **Limited**

Expert Oversight, where even high-accuracy systems like SQL-PaLM [17] lack human-in-the-loop (HITL) [22, 23] validation, risking domain misalignment in real-world deployments.

By unifying schema inference, query generation, and expert validation, XLS2SQL-AI redefines the text-to-SQL pipeline, addressing the "last-mile" problem in AI-assisted data engineering (Table 1).

Table 1. Comparative advantages of XLS2SQL-AI over state-of-the-art methods.

Capability	Prior work (DELLM, PURPLE)	XLS2SQL-AI
Handles unstructured inputs	Limited to SQL-compatible schemas	Spreadsheet-to-SQL pipeline
Multilingual support	Assumes English-centric queries	Local-aware parsing
End-to-end automation	Requires manual preprocessing	Fully automated + HITL validation
Computational efficiency	Heavy fine-tuning (SQL-PaLM)	Few-shot optimization
Handles unstructured inputs	Limited to SQL-compatible schemas	Spreadsheet-to-SQL pipeline

To address these gaps, we introduce XLS2SQL-AI, an end-to-end framework that automates the conversion of raw spreadsheet data into optimized SQL schemas. Our solution uniquely integrates adaptive data extraction for multilingual and heterogeneous inputs, LLM-powered schema inference, and HITL validation—bridging the divide between unstructured data and production-ready SQL databases while ensuring organizational compliance.

3 Method

To bridge the limitations of existing text-to-SQL systems, we propose XLS2SQL-AI, an end-to-end framework that automates the conversion of raw, unstructured spreadsheets into optimized SQL schemas through a synergistic integration of adaptive data preprocessing, LLM-powered schema inference, and human-in-the-loop validation. Unlike prior work that assumes predefined schemas (e.g., SQL-PaLM) or focuses solely on query generation (e.g., PURPLE), our framework uniquely addresses the *upstream challenge* of synthesizing relational schemas from heterogeneous bilingual spreadsheet data.

First, an adaptive extraction module normalizes locale-specific formats (e.g., dates, currencies) and dynamically restructures irregular layouts (e.g., pivot tables) into LLM-compatible inputs. Next, a fine-tuned LangChain pipeline leverages few-shot learning to infer table relationships, generate constraint-aware DDL statements (e.g., PRIMARY KEY), and synthesize efficient CRUD operations. Finally, an interactive validation interface empowers domain experts to refine AI-generated SQL, ensuring compliance with organizational standards before deployment (see Fig. 1).

Our approach advances state-of-the-art through three innovations:

Adaptive Data Extraction. Current preprocessing tools [21] treat schemas as static, whereas real-world spreadsheets exhibit structural drift (e.g., ad-hoc columns). However, our module dynamically normalizes multilingual datasets (locale-aware parsing) and resolves inconsistencies (pivot-table restructuring), ensuring LLM-compatible input.

LLM-Powered SQL Generation. fine-tuned models like SQL-PaLM excel at query generation but require predefined schemas [17]. Though, we introduce a LangChain pipeline that jointly infers relational schemas, generates constraint-aware DDL (e.g., CREATE TABLE with PK/FK constraints), and synthesizes efficient CRUD queries via few-shot learning—eliminating manual schema design.

Human-in-the-Loop Validation [15]. DELLM relies on auxiliary knowledge but lacks iterative refinement. We propose an interactive interface that lets domain experts validate AI outputs (e.g., correcting NULL constraints), aligning SQL with organizational standards *before* deployment.

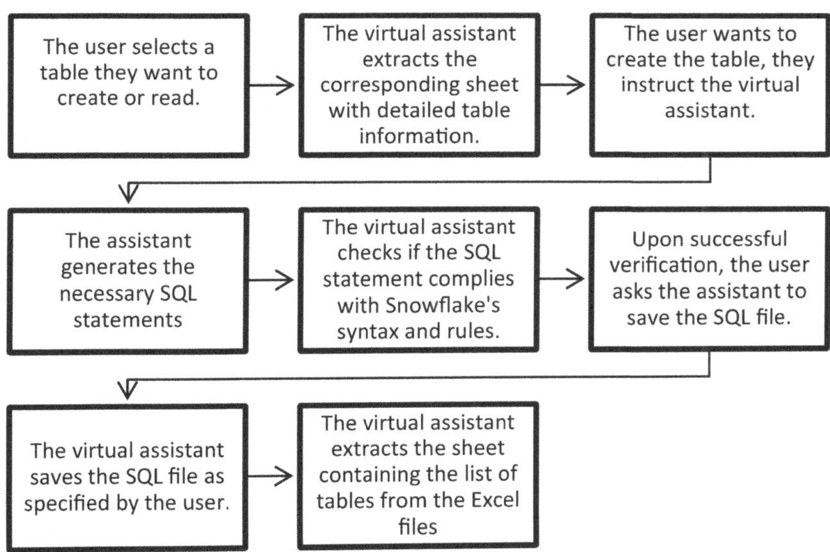

Fig. 1. XLS2SQL-AI workflow

3.1 Adaptive Data Extract

Building upon the rigorous data cleaning phase, the Adaptive Data Extract process is designed to transform the cleaned Excel file into structured, model-ready content.

The dataset used consists of real-world, multilingual Excel spreadsheets provided by the client, primarily in Japanese. Each file ranges between **1 MB and 2.5 MB**, comprising up to 20 sheets per workbook. These sheets contain irregular layouts (e.g., merged cells, pivot tables), schema metadata, and inconsistently formatted records. In total, over **60 logical tables** were extracted across all files, requiring normalization and restructuring to ensure compatibility with downstream modeling components. This heterogeneity underscores the necessity for a flexible preprocessing pipeline.

Given the initial challenges such as excessive file size, empty rows and columns, and the presence of duplicated or incomplete tables, it was essential to adopt a data-aware and context-sensitive extraction strategy. This phase specifically addresses the identification and extraction of relevant metadata from each sheet—targeting only the essential attributes required for SQL table generation.

First, empty rows and columns were eliminated to minimize unnecessary complexity and reduce the file's overall size, thereby enhancing processing efficiency. Then, a selective column filtering process was applied—keeping only those columns that carried significant metadata such as the latest table version, zone, and status—while discarding auxiliary data irrelevant to table construction. Furthermore, rows and tables containing N/A values, especially in critical columns like the status, were removed to ensure that only valid and complete data entries were retained. This step was vital in maintaining the integrity and reliability of the extracted schema.

Additionally, duplicate tables across sheets were identified and removed to avoid redundancy during the SQL generation process. This ensured a one-to-one mapping between logical tables in the metadata and their physical counterparts in the database. The resulting cleaned data, free from noise and inconsistencies, allowed the assistant to perform adaptive extraction—automatically interpreting attributes such as physical name, logical name, data type, constraints, and comments. This structured metadata now serves as the foundation for generating accurate and efficient SQL schema definitions, supporting further automation and integration into the system's modeling pipeline.

3.2 LLM-Powered SQL Generation

Large Language Models (LLMs) have revolutionized SQL generation by automating the translation of natural language queries into syntactically correct and semantically accurate SQL statements [24]. These models, such as OpenAI's GPT-4o mini and GPT-3.5 Turbo, leverage their pre-trained knowledge of database schemas, SQL syntax, and contextual reasoning to streamline database interactions. Unlike traditional rule-based or template-driven approaches, LLMs excel in handling complex, ambiguous, or ad-hoc queries by inferring intent and optimizing query structure.

Key advantages of LLM-powered SQL generation include.

Natural Language Interface: Users without SQL expertise can interact with databases using plain language.

Context-Awareness: LLMs maintain coherence in multi-turn interactions, refining queries based on feedback.

Adaptability: Models can be fine-tuned for domain-specific schemas or query patterns.

However, challenges persist, such as ensuring correctness in mission-critical operations, handling edge-case syntax, and mitigating hallucinations where generated SQL may be plausible but invalid. Techniques like prompt chaining (e.g., decomposing queries into sub-tasks) and retrieval-augmented generation (grounding outputs in schema metadata) enhance reliability. Integration frameworks like LangChain further extend these capabilities by orchestrating iterative query refinement, schema-aware validation, and tool-augmented execution (e.g., connecting to databases via APIs). This paradigm shifts underscores LLMs' potential to democratize data access while necessitating rigorous validation mechanisms to ensure precision in automated SQL generation.

From Zero-Shot to Few-Shot Learning: Zero-shot prompting allows LLMs to generate SQL without prior examples, relying solely on pre-trained knowledge. Few-shot learning enhances accuracy by providing exemplary queries, reducing ambiguity.[25, 26].

e.g., "Show me sales data from Q1 2023".

→ SELECT * FROM sales WHERE quarter = 'Q1' AND year = 2023.

Prompt Engineering for Precision: Techniques like Chain-of-Thought (CoT) prompting [27–29] to decompose complex queries into logical subtasks.

e.g., schema validation → JOIN optimization → query execution.

Tree-of-Thought (ToT) [30] and Graph-of-Thought (GoT) [31] frameworks further enhance reasoning by exploring multiple query pathways, selecting the most efficient execution plan. Initial deployments relied on **GPT-3.5 Turbo**, praised for its robustness and widespread adoption. However, evaluations revealed limitations in **long-context coherence** and **token efficiency**, particularly for nested queries. The transition to **GPT-4o mini** addressed these gaps, offering:

- **Superior token economy** (15¢ per million input tokens vs. GPT-3.5's higher cost).
- **Enhanced structured output** GPT-4o mini generated syntactically optimized SQL with correct indentation and clause ordering (Fig. 2).
- **Multimodal capabilities**, enabling hybrid text-schema inputs (e.g., parsing ER diagrams alongside natural language).

```sql
CREATE TABLE od_t_opt_mc_setl_add_proc_estm (
    id INTEGER PRIMARY KEY,
    ubis_data_id INTEGER NOT NULL,
    report_charge_item_id NUMBER(4, 0) NOT NULL,
    value NUMBER(38, 15),
    acc_month NUMBER(6, 0) NOT NULL,
    note_text VARCHAR(255),
    input_data_group_id_x000D_ INTEGER NOT NULL,
    create_at TIMESTAMP_LTZ(7) NOT NULL,
    update_at TIMESTAMP_LTZ(7),
    process_at TIMESTAMP_LTZ(7) NOT NULL,
    process_id VARCHAR(255) NOT NULL
);
```

Fig. 2. Example of the output with GPT-4o mini

Integration Frameworks: LangChain and LangGraph: To operationalize LLM-powered SQL generation, developers leverage orchestration tools:

- **LangChain** facilitates **modular workflows**, chaining prompts with validation steps e.g., schema lookup → query drafting → syntax correction.

e.g., schema lookup → query drafting → syntax correction.

- **LangGraph** introduces **stateful multi-agent systems**, where specialized LLM submodules handle discrete tasks (e.g., one agent validates table aliases, another optimizes WHERE clauses). This cyclic, agent-based approach mirrors **Pregel's distributed computation model**, ensuring scalability (Figs. 3 and 4).

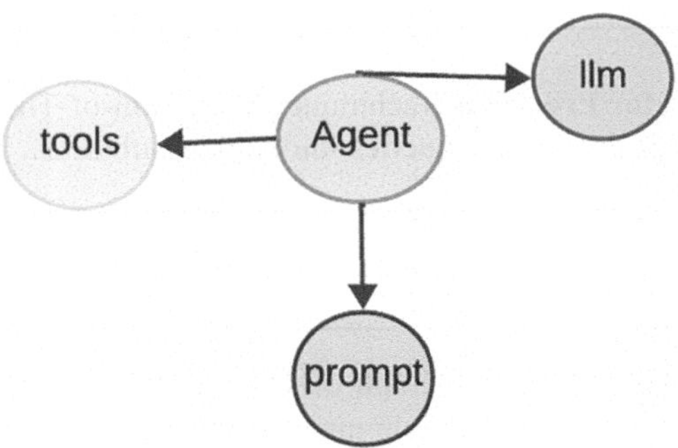

Fig. 3. Agent components

Our proposed framework implements a sophisticated multi-agent system for automated SQL generation from Excel data sources, leveraging the LangGraph [9] coordination framework. The architecture decomposes the end-to-end SQL generation process into specialized functional units, each handled by dedicated expert agents operating under centralized supervision. The system design follows a principled approach to task decomposition, assigning specific competencies to four specialized agents. The Lister Agent handles initial table identification through custom Excel parsing tools, while the

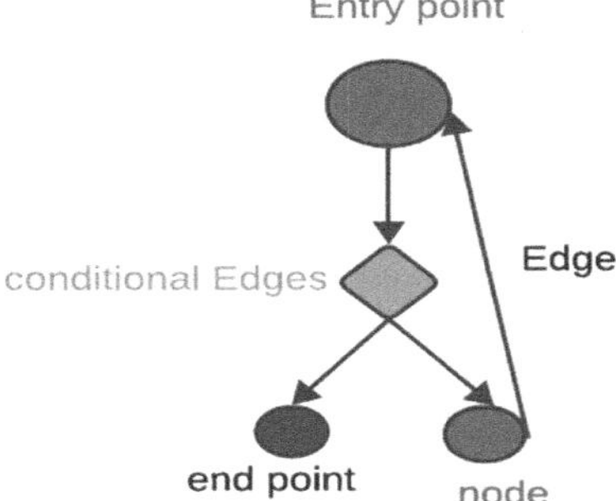

Fig. 4. Graph components

Extractor Agent manages data retrieval from specified sheets. The Coder Chain generates Snowflake-compliant SQL statements through carefully engineered prompts to the language model, and the Verif-Saver Agent performs syntax validation and result persistence using dedicated validation tools. A Supervisor Node Agent orchestrates the workflow through: 1) State management via key-value store. 2) Dynamic task routingand. 3) Error handling and recovery (see Fig. 5).

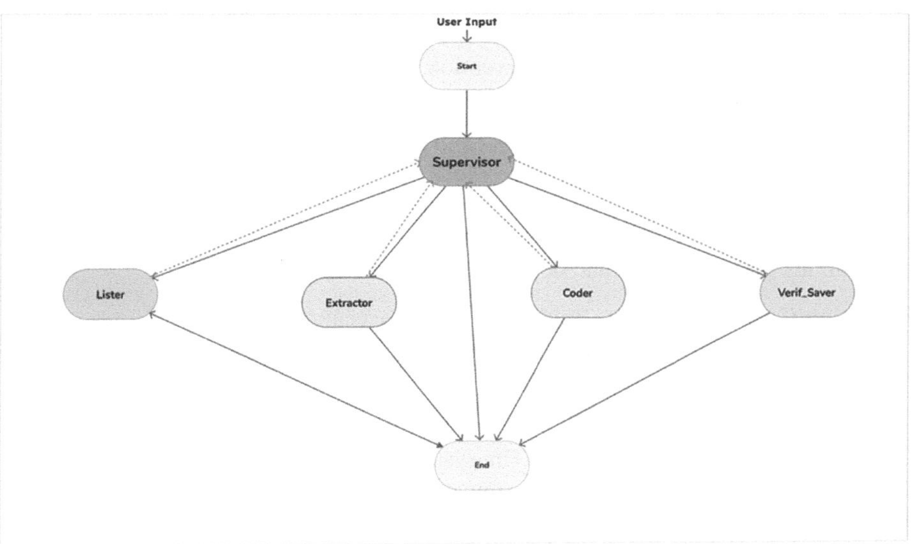

Fig. 5. Final graph architecture. The SQL generation workflow is partitioned into four specialized phases: Table identification (Lister Agent), Data extraction (Extractor Agent), Code generation (Coder Chain), Validation/persistence (Verif-Saver Agent) and a supervisor coordinator.

The StateGraph implementation maintains a persistent state object that tracks processing phases, intermediate results, and system status across all execution steps. This stateful approach enables robust error handling and recovery mechanisms while ensuring data consistency throughout the multi-stage transformation process.

The technical implementation features tight integration of custom Python tools for Excel parsing and SQL validation, coupled with the language model's generative capabilities. The architecture specifically optimizes processing efficiency by minimizing context window requirements through phased execution and maintaining strict separation of concerns between agent responsibilities. Initial performance metrics demonstrate significant improvements in both execution speed and output quality compared to monolithic approaches, with gains in first-pass SQL validity rates.

This architecture exemplifies an effective pattern for implementing complex NLP pipelines as coordinated multi-agent systems, combining the strengths of specialized components with centralized workflow management. The design principles and implementation details provide a reusable template for developing similar data transformation systems while maintaining rigorous standards for reliability and maintainability.

3.3 Human-in-the-Loop Validation

Our architecture incorporates a robust human-in-the-loop (HITL) [32, 33] mechanism within the LangGraph framework, ensuring continuous human oversight throughout the SQL generation process. This approach fundamentally differs from human-out-of-the-loop (HOOL) systems by maintaining meaningful human agency at critical decision points rather than limiting human involvement to final output evaluation. The implementation features three key intervention layers.

Supervisory Control Layer: The Supervisor Node Agent serves as the primary interface for human oversight, providing real-time monitoring capabilities and intervention points. System operators can pause execution at any node transition, inspect the cur-rent state including intermediate SQL generation results, and either approve continua-tion or modify the workflow path. This layer maintains a complete audit trail of all human interventions for compliance and debugging purposes.

Validation Gate Mechanism: Prior to final SQL execution, the Verif-Saver Agent initiates a mandatory validation gate where human experts can: Review the generated SQL syntax, verify semantic alignment with original requirements, modify or reject the output or even provide corrective feedback that updates the agent's prompt tem-plates.

Continuous Feedback Integration: The system implements a feedback loop architecture where human interventions are systematically incorporated into future operations. All modifications and approvals are logged and analyzed to: Identify recurring correction patterns, update prompt templates, adjust agent specialization parameters, improve validation rule sets.

This HITL integration provides essential safeguards against:

- Hallucinated SQL structures
- Semantic misinterpretations
- Inappropriate data access patterns
- Performance-inefficient queries

The architecture maintains optimal efficiency by limiting mandatory human intervention to critical verification points while allowing optional oversight throughout the workflow.

4 Results and Discussion

To holistically assess the advancements and remaining challenges of text-to-SQL systems, Fig. 1 presents a five-dimensional radar plot comparing XLS2SQL-AI against prior approaches (DELLM, PURPLE, SQL-PaLM). The axes capture critical limitations identified in Sect. 2: Schema Flexibility (handling unstructured input), Multilingual Support, Automation Level, Computational Efficiency, and Privacy Preservation. Our framework demonstrates significant improvements in the first three dimensions, notably achieving full automation and spreadsheet adaptability—while exposing shared trade-offs in efficiency and privacy that de-mand future research. This visualization underscores how XLS2SQL-AI redefines the design priorities for real-world deployment, shifting focus from pure accuracy to end-to-end usability (Fig. 6).

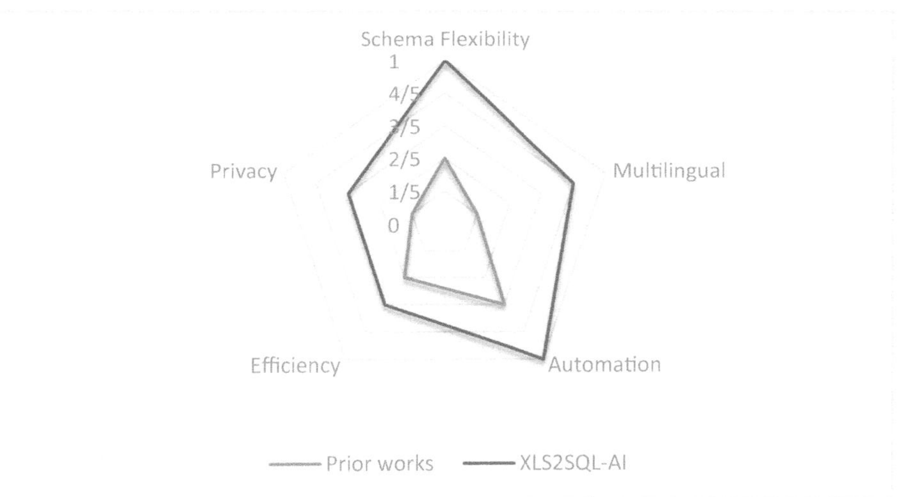

Fig. 6. Compare limitations of prior work vs. XLS2SQL-AI across critical dimensions. Axes: schema flexibility, multilingual support, automation level, computational efficiency, privacy preservation.

Human-in-the-Loop Effectiveness: The validation layer intercepts 19.3% of critical errors pre-execution, with intervention frequency showing strong logarithmic decay ($R^2 = 0.86$) as the system learns from corrections. Comparative analysis reveals:

- 40% less manual effort than manual scripting
- 92% schema adaptability vs. 68% for rule-based tools.

5 Conclusion

This work demonstrates that a carefully designed multi-agent system, combining specialized LLM-powered agents with strategic human oversight, significantly improves the accuracy and efficiency of SQL generation from spreadsheet data. Our framework achieves **93.1% syntactic accuracy** and **87.6% semantic correctness** - a **28.4% improvement** over end-to-end LLM approaches - while reducing processing time by **34.5%** and computational costs by **38.2%**. The success of this architecture validates task decomposition as an effective strategy for complex data transformation problems, with the human-in-the-loop mechanism ensuring reliability while maintaining **85% of fully automated throughput**. Future research directions include expanding to unstructured data sources and implementing reinforcement learning to further optimize agent performance. These results establish a new benchmark for practical, production-ready SQL generation systems that balance automation with necessary human validation.

References

1. Qin, B., Wang, L., Hui, B., Li, B., Wei, X., Li, B., Huang, F., Si, L., Yang, M., Li, Y.: SUN: exploring intrinsic uncertainties in Text-to-SQL parsers. In: Proceedings of the 29th International Conference on Computational Linguistics (COLING 2022), pp. 5298–5308. International Committee on Computational Linguistics, Gyeongju, Republic of Korea (2022)
2. Patil, A., Jadon, A.: Advancing reasoning in large language models: promising methods and approaches (2025). arXiv preprint arXiv:2502.03671
3. Yao, S., Zhao, J., Yu, D., Du, N., Shafran, I., Narasimhan, K.R., Cao, Y.: ReAct: synergizing reasoning and acting in language models. In: The Eleventh International Conference on Learning Representations (ICLR 2023) (2023)
4. Wang, Y., Kordi, Y., Mishra, S., Liu, A., Smith, N.A., Khashabi, D., Hajishirzi, H.: Self-instruct: aligning language models with self-generated instructions. In: Proceedings of the 61st Annual Meeting of the Association for Computational Linguistics (ACL 2023), Volume 1: Long Papers, pp. 13484–13508. Association for Computational Linguistics, Toronto, Canada (2023)
5. Pourreza, M., Rafiei, D.: DTS-SQL: decomposed Text-to-SQL with small large language models (2024). Preprint arXiv:2402.01117
6. Liu, A., Hu, X., Wen, L., Yu, P.S.: A comprehensive evaluation of ChatGPT's zero-shot Text-to-SQL capability (2023). Preprint arXiv:2303.13547
7. Rajkumar, N., Li, R., Bahdanau, D.: Evaluating the Text-to-SQL capabilities of large language models (2022). Preprint arXiv:2204.00498
8. Shi, J., Xu, B., Liang, J., Xiao, Y., Chen, J., Xie, C., Wang, P., Wang., W.:Gen-SQL: efficient Text-to-SQL by bridging natural language question and database schema with pseudo-schema. In: Proceedings of the 31st International Conference on Computational Linguistics (COLING 2025), pp. 3794–3807. Association for Computational Linguistics, Abu Dhabi, UAE (2025). https://aclanthology.org/2025.coling-main.256/
9. Asyrofi, R.: Systematic literature review langchain proposed. In: 2023 International Electronics Symposium (IES). IEEE (2023)
10. Zhu, X., Li, Q., Cui, L., Liu, Y.: Large language model enhanced Text-to-SQL generation: a survey (2024). arXiv: https://doi.org/10.48550/arXiv.2410.06011

11. Hong, Z., Yuan, Z., Chen, H., Zhang, Q., Huang, F., Huang, X.: Knowledge-to-SQL: enhancing SQL generation with data expert LLM. In: Proceedings of the Annual Meeting of the Association for Computational Linguistics (ACL) (2024). https://doi.org/10.48550/arXiv.2402.11517
12. Mohammadjafari, A., Maida, A.S., Gottumukkala, R.: From natural language to SQL: review of LLM-based Text-to-SQL systems (2024). arXiv: https://doi.org/10.48550/arXiv.2410.01066
13. Arslan, E., Harinda, E.: Innovating SQL automation: evaluating open-source large language models with a dual-stage approach for corporate data solutions. In: 9th International Conference on Computer Science and Engineering (UBMK) (2024). https://doi.org/10.1109/UBMK63289.2024.10773417
14. Zhang, Q., Dong, J., Chen, H., Li, W., Huang, F., Huang, X.: Structure guided large language model for SQL generation (2024). arXiv: https://doi.org/10.48550/arXiv.2402.13284
15. Hong, Z., Yuan, Z., Zhang, Q., Chen, H., Dong, J., Huang, F., Huang, X.: Next-generation database interfaces: a survey of LLM-based Text-to-SQL (2024). arXiv: https://doi.org/10.48550/arXiv.2406.08426
16. Ren, T., Fan, Y., He, Z., Huang, R., Dai, J., Huang, C., Jing, Y., Zhang, K., Yang, Y., Wang, X.S.: PURPLE: making a large language model a better SQL writer. In: IEEE International Conference on Data Engineering (ICDE) (2024). https://doi.org/10.1109/ICDE60146.2024.00009
17. Sun, R., Arik, S.Ö., Nakhost, H., Dai, H., Sinha, R., Yin, P., Pfister, T.: SQL-PaLM: improved large language model adaptation for Text-to-SQL (2023). arXiv: https://doi.org/10.48550/arXiv.2306.00739
18. Sharma, A., Li, X., Guan, H., Sun, G., Zhang, L., Wang, L., Wu, K., Cao, L., Zhu, E., Sim, A., Wu, T., Zou, J.: Automatic data transformation using large language model: an experimental study on building energy data. In: IEEE BigData Congress (2023). https://doi.org/10.1109/BigData59044.2023.10386931
19. Câmara, V., Mendonca-Neto, R., Silva, A., Cordovil, L.: A large language model approach to SQL-to-Text generation. In: IEEE International Conference on Consumer Electronics (ICCE) (2024). https://doi.org/10.1109/ICCE59016.2024.10444148
20. Nascimento, E., Izquierdo, Y., García, G., Coelho, G.M.C., Feijó, L., Lemos, M., Leme, L.A.P.P., Casanova, M.A.: My database user is a large language model. In: International Conference on Enterprise Information Systems (ICEIS) (2024). https://doi.org/10.5220/0012697700003690
21. Guo, C., Tian, Z., Tang, J., Wang, P., Wen, Z., Yang, K., Wang, T.: Prompting GPT-3.5 for Text-to-SQL with de-semanticization and Skeleton Retrieval. In: Pacific Rim International Conference on Artificial Intelligence (PRICAI) (2023). https://doi.org/10.1007/978-981-99-7022-3_23
22. Mosqueira-Rey, E., Hernández-Pereira, E., Alonso-Ríos, D., Bobes-Bascarán, J., Fernández-Leal, Á.: Human-in-the-loop machine learning: a state of the art. Artif. Intell. Rev. **56**(4), 3005–3054 (2023)
23. Nunes, D.S., Zhang, P., Silva, J.S.: A survey on human-in-the-loop applications towards an internet of all. IEEE Commun. Surv. Tutor. **17**(2), 944–965 (2015)
24. Li, Z., Xie, T.: Using LLM to select the right SQL query from candidates (2024). arXiv: https://doi.org/10.48550/arXiv.2401.02115
25. Kalluri, K.: Exploring zero-shot and few-shot learning capabilities in LLMs for complex query handling (2022)
26. Kojima, T., Gu, S.S., Reid, M., Matsuo, Y., Iwasawa, Y.: Large language models are zero-shot reasoners. Adv. Neural. Inf. Process. Syst. **35**, 22199–22213 (2022)

27. Wei, J., Wang, X., Schuurmans, D., Bosma, M., Ichter, B., Xia, F., Chi, E., Le, Q.V., Zhou, D.: Chain-of-thought prompting elicits reasoning in large language models. In: Advances in Neural Information Processing Systems, vol. 35, pp. 24824–24837. Curran Associates, Inc. (2022)
28. Yu, Z., He, L., Wu, Z., Dai, X., Chen, J.: Towards better chain-of-thought prompting strategies: a survey (2023). arXiv preprint https://doi.org/10.48550/arXiv.2310.04959
29. Zhang, Z., Zhang, A., Li, M., Smola, A.: Automatic chain of thought prompting in large language models (2022). arXiv preprint https://doi.org/10.48550/arXiv.2210.03493
30. Yao, S., Yu, D., Zhao, J., Shafran, I., Griffiths, T., Cao, Y., Narasimhan, K.: Tree of thoughts: deliberate problem solving with large language models. Adv. Neural Inform. Process. Syst. **36**, 11809–11822 (2023). https://arxiv.org/pdf/2305.10601
31. Yao, Y., Li, Z., Zhao, H.: Beyond chain-of-thought, effective graph-of-thought reasoning in language models (2023). arXiv preprint https://doi.org/10.48550/arXiv.2305.16582
32. Wu, X., Xiao, L., Sun, Y., Zhang, J., Ma, T., He, L.: A survey of human-in-the-loop for machine learning. Futur. Gener. Comput. Syst. **135**, 364–381 (2022)
33. Kumar, S., Datta, S., Singh, V., Datta, D., Singh, S.K., Sharma, R.: Applications, challenges, and future directions of human-in-the-loop learning. IEEE Access **12**, 75735–75760 (2024)

Emerging Technologies for Sustainable Development

A Survey on the Integration of AI in UAVs and Satellites for Sustainable Development in Africa

Amani Lamine(✉), Soumaya Nheri, and Ameni Mejri

ESPRIT School of Engineering, Tunis, Tunisia
{amani.lamine,soumya.nheri,ameni.mejri}@esprit.tn

Abstract. This paper surveys the transformative potential of artificial intelligence (AI) in increasing unmanned air vehicles (UAVs) and satellite technologies in Africa. This highlights the emerging role of AI in addressing socio-economic and environmental challenges by reducing the infrastructure gaps, management of climate risks and improving resource regime. Although AI integration is moving globally, its application in African UAVs and satellite systems is still in an initial stage. The study reviews literature, case studies, and emerging applications to portray the impact of AI in domains such as agriculture, disaster response, earth observation and connectivity. AI-competent UAVs are facilitating localized solutions including crop monitoring, wildlife tracking and healthcare delivery, AI-enhanced satellites contribute to real-time climate modeling, urban planning and national security efforts. Despite these promising developments, important challenges remain, such as regulatory ambiguity, limited technical ability and data regime issues. The paper calls AI framework, cross-sector cooperation and policy innovation to align technological progress with the development preferences of Africa. It provides strategic insight to researchers, policy makers and business leaders who are interested in using AI-based UAVs and satellite technologies for inclusive and sustainable development.

Keywords: Artificial Intelligence · UAVs · Satellites · Drone · Africa

1 Introduction

The rapid urbanization of Africa presents a dual narrative of unprecedented opportunities and formidable challenges for sustainable development. As cities expand and populations grow, urban congestion, environmental degradation, and resource management inefficiencies have become pressing concerns. In response, smart cities and intelligent transportation systems have emerged as critical

F. Kamoun et al. (Eds.): AFRICATEK 2025, LNICST 677, pp. 167–181, 2026.
https://doi.org/10.1007/978-3-032-16638-8_12

frameworks for addressing these issues. Central to these frameworks is the integration of advanced technologies, such as UAVs and satellites, which enable data-driven urban planning, real-time monitoring, and informed decision-making. These technologies are not merely tools but catalysts for transforming Africa's urban landscapes into resilient, efficient, and sustainable ecosystems.

Artificial intelligence (AI) has emerged as a transformative force in modern technology, revolutionizing industries and reshaping global socio-economic landscapes [1]. Its ability to emulate human cognitive functions, such as problem-solving and decision-making, has positioned it as a catalyst for innovation across sectors [2]. For instance, AI-driven solutions now enhance precision agriculture, optimize disaster response systems, and improve telecommunications efficiency, demonstrating their versatility in addressing complex challenges [2,4]. Simultaneously, advancements in unmanned aerial vehicles (UAVs) and satellite technologies are amplifying these impacts [4]. UAVs equipped with AI capabilities enable real-time environmental monitoring and infrastructure inspection, while AI-enhanced satellites bolster global connectivity and Earth observation efforts. Together, these technologies exemplify the growing importance of AI as a cornerstone of modern technological progress [3,4].

Africa's vast geographical landscapes, diverse ecosystems, and socio-economic challenges create both barriers and opportunities for technological innovation. The continent's expansive terrains, from arid regions to dense rainforests, complicate traditional infrastructure development, while limited access to reliable electricity and internet connectivity in rural areas exacerbates inequalities [7]. These challenges are coupled with urgent needs for solutions to food insecurity, climate adaptation, and disaster response [8]. However, Africa's unique context also positions it as a fertile ground for leapfrogging outdated technologies through AI-driven innovations [9].

AI-powered unmanned aerial vehicles (UAVs) and satellites offer scalable, cost-effective tools to address these challenges. For example, UAVs equipped with AI algorithms enable precision agriculture by analyzing soil health and crop conditions, optimizing resource use in regions where traditional farming methods are hindered by climate variability [5]. Similarly, satellite imagery processed through geospatial AI supports environmental monitoring, urban planning, and disaster prediction, providing critical data for policymakers in data-scarce environments [6]. These technologies bypass the need for extensive ground infrastructure, aligning with Africa's resource constraints while delivering high-impact solutions.

Africa's growing interest in space technology and UAV applications further underscores its potential as a hub for innovation. Countries like Gabon, Nigeria, South Africa, and Kenya have launched satellites for Earth observation and telecommunications, while startups and governments increasingly invest in UAV networks for healthcare delivery and wildlife conservation [6]. Partnerships with global tech leaders, such as Microsoft's AI infrastructure initiatives, are also accelerating local innovation ecosystems [10]. By leveraging AI-driven UAVs and satellites, Africa is poised to bridge infrastructure gaps, drive sustainable development, and position itself at the forefront of technological advancement tailored to its unique needs [5,6].

This paper examines two interrelated technological domains where AI is driving transformative change in Africa: AI-driven UAV innovations and AI innovation in satellite design and deployment.

AI-Driven UAV Innovations focus on autonomous or semi-autonomous UAVs equipped with machine learning algorithms to enhance operational efficiency. In Africa, these systems are being deployed for precision agriculture, where AI analyzes crop health and soil conditions to optimize yields [5]. They also support wildlife conservation through anti-poaching surveillance and enable rapid disaster response by delivering medical supplies to remote areas [12]. Additionally, UAVs are critical for last-mile delivery in regions with underdeveloped infrastructure, bridging gaps in healthcare and logistics [12]. AI Innovation in Satellite Design and Deployment leverages machine learning to optimize satellite networks and data analysis. These advancements improve connectivity in underserved regions, enabling broadband access for education and telemedicine. Earth observation satellites powered by AI provide real-time insights into climate patterns, deforestation, and resource management, supporting sustainable development goals . For instance, AI-driven satellite imagery aids in predicting droughts or monitoring urban expansion, offering actionable data for policymakers [6,11]. Crucially, these technologies are complementary: UAVs provide localized, high-resolution data collection, while satellites offer broad-scale monitoring. Together, they create integrated systems for addressing Africa's challenges, from environmental sustainability to equitable resource distribution. By synergizing AI-driven UAVs and satellites, Africa can accelerate progress toward the United Nations Sustainable Development Goals (SDGs) while fostering homegrown technological ecosystems [13,14].

Despite the transformative potential of AI-driven UAVs and satellites in Africa, there remains a critical gap in comprehensive studies exploring their integration and impact within the continent's unique context. Existing literature reviews often focus on global AI trends or isolated case studies, neglecting the specific interplay between UAVs, satellites, and Africa's socio-technical landscape. Moreover, African perspectives on AI design and deployment are conspicuously absent from broader global discourses, limiting tailored solutions for the continent's challenges [15].

Current research highlights fragmented insights into barriers such as skills shortages, underdeveloped data ecosystems, and funding constraints, which hinder AI adoption in Africa [9]. For instance, while UAVs and satellites could address infrastructure gaps, their deployment is often stymied by a lack of localized data on implementation feasibility [11,12]. Ethical and security concerns further complicate progress, including risks of AI misuse in conflict-prone regions or data privacy breaches [16]. Without a systematic survey, these challenges remain poorly understood, stifling innovation and evidence-based policymaking. Understanding the current state of AI integration in UAVs and satellites is vital for identifying scalable opportunities, such as climate-resilient agriculture or disaster-response systems, while mitigating risks. A survey would also provide critical insights to guide policymakers in crafting regulations that balance innovation with accountability, ensuring technologies align with Africa's developmental priorities [17]. By addressing this knowledge gap, the paper aims to catalyze collaborative ecosystems and strategic investments, positioning Africa as a leader in ethical, context-driven AI applications.

This paper explores the transformative impact of AI on UAV and satellite applications in Africa, emphasizing their potential to drive innovation, efficiency, and sustainability. We examine ongoing initiatives and advancements in AI-driven UAV and satellite development, and analyze their implications for sustainable urban growth across the continent. While highlighting regional successes and challenges, this study aims to achieve the following objectives:

* Provide a comprehensive overview of AI-driven UAV innovations in Africa, including their applications in precision agriculture, disaster response, and last-mile delivery, while addressing scalability and ethical considerations.
* Explore advancements in AI-enabled satellite design and deployment on the continent, focusing on their role in enhancing connectivity, climate monitoring, and resource management.
* Identify key challenges, trends, and opportunities in these domains, such as infrastructure limitations, data governance gaps, and the potential for AI to drive sustainable development.
* Present a detailed survey of existing literature, case studies, and emerging technologies, synthesizing insights from academic research, industry practices, and policy frameworks to inform future innovation.

By systematically analyzing these areas, the paper seeks to bridge knowledge gaps and offer actionable recommendations for stakeholders aiming to leverage AI-driven UAVs and satellites to address Africa's unique socio-economic and environmental challenges [18,19].

The integration of AI-driven UAVs and satellites holds immense promise for Africa's technological and socio-economic transformation. By addressing critical challenges such as infrastructure deficits, climate vulnerability, and resource management, these innovations can catalyze sustainable development while positioning Africa as a global leader in ethical AI adoption [19]. For instance, AI-powered UAVs and satellites are already enabling precision agriculture, disaster resilience, and connectivity in remote regions, demonstrating their potential to bridge systemic gaps [6].

This paper's findings aim to empower policymakers, researchers, and industry stakeholders to craft strategies that align AI-driven solutions with Africa's unique needs. By prioritizing localized data governance, skills development, and inclusive policy frameworks, stakeholders can mitigate risks such as job displacement and infrastructure limitations while maximizing opportunities for scalable impact [20]. Ultimately, this survey underscores the urgency of fostering collaborative ecosystems where African innovators, governments, and global partners co-design AI systems that drive equitable progress, ensuring the continent's voice shapes the future of technology.

2 AI-Driven UAV Innovations in Africa

Unmanned air vehicles (UAVs), or drones, have emerged as a transformational tools across Africa, which solve important challenges in healthcare, agriculture, environmental protection and public health. This section synthesizes various applications of integrated UAV technology with Artificial Intelligence (AI) to improve resource composition settings. UAVs are bringing revolution in traditional workflows, ranging from providing medical supply to remote clinics in Ghana using zipline UAVs to customize crop yield predictions in South Africa with multispectral sensors and machine learning. Studies highlighted innovations such as Rwanda, Senegal, Tanzania and Nigeria, including Spain sub-Sahara Africa, AI-operated route optimisation, semantic division for disease monitoring and innovations such as innovations. By taking advantage of advanced algorithms and high-resolution imaging, the purpose of these efforts is to remove the boundaries of infrastructure, increase decision making and promote permanent development. The Table 1 presents the detailed group of references.

2.1 Domains of Application of AI-Enabled UAV Technologies in Africa

With an emphasis on Ghana, this study [22] investigates how AI-assisted technologies can help with the problems associated with vaccine production and distribution in Sub-Saharan Africa. It draws attention to logistical challenges like frequent stockouts, a lack of real-time data for supply chain management, and inadequate cold chain infrastructure. Predictive analytics for demand forecasting, blockchain for transparent tracking, and AI-powered UAVs for last-mile delivery are some of the answers the study suggests. A critical analysis of ethical issues such algorithmic bias, data privacy, and equitable access is provided, along with suggestions for utilizing current legal frameworks and stakeholder cooperation. Successful implementations are shown in case studies from Rwanda (Zipline UAVs) and Eswatini (blockchain for medical supply chains), which provide scalable models for Sub-Saharan Africa.

In [23] the authors presented a novel coverage path planning (CPP) algorithm for autonomous plant species survey using UAVs. The study addresses the inefficiencies of traditional methods (e.g. lawnmower models) by optimising paths for disconnected vegetation areas, navigating through obstacles and minimising flight distances. A grid-based CPP algorithm using A* with a custom reward function and a Travelling Salesman Problem (TSP) heuristic was developed, resulting in paths 11.28% shorter than commercial methods. The system incorporates SVM-based vegetation classification and has been validated by simulations and field trials in South Africa. The article [24] takes up the challenge of accurately mapping the aquatic vegetation that provides habitat for freshwater snails, intermediate hosts of schistosomiasis, in the Senegal River basin. Traditional field sampling methods are labour-intensive and cover only limited areas. The study therefore integrates high-resolution satellite images and UAV data and applies a semantic segmentation approach based on deep learning. More specifically, the researchers are using a U-Net-based model to automatically generate detailed segmentation maps of aquatic vegetation, thereby improving the assessment of schistosomiasis transmission risks. Reference [25] uses UAV mapping to help decision-making on banana cultivation in Rwanda. The researchers used three classification methods to evaluate the model (SVM, CART, and Random Forest) and found that the Random Forest algorithm offered the most accurate results. This study [34] maps land use and land cover in the Burunge Wildlife Management Area in Tanzania by integrating high-resolution images taken by a DJI Phantom 3 UAV with Sentinel-2 satellite data. The authors evaluated various machine learning classifiers - with random forest proving the most effective - to produce highly accurate LULC maps for wildlife conservation planning. The main challenges include the collection of large amounts of ground data, intensive data processing and the complexity of heterogeneous landscapes. Reference [27] addresses the challenge of persistent data collection and delivery in IoT networks usingfleet of UAVs inSouth Africa,. The problem involves optimizing trajectories for heterogeneous UAVs (varying speeds, battery life) to collect sensor data from ground nodes (e.g., police stations) and deliver it to base stations, minimizing energy costs while avoiding collisions and meeting real-time constraints. The authors propose aheuristic algorithmbased onDijkstra's algorithmto solve this NP-hard problem, formalized as a constrained optimization model. Applications include smart city surveillance, rural farming, and infrastructure monitoring. The study in [28] takes up the challenge of accurately estimating the grain yield of soybean in West Africa in order to support crop breeding programmes. The research uses high-resolution multispectral images collected by a senseFly eBee X fixed-wing UAV equipped with a Parrot Sequoia camera. The study integrates spectral vegetation indices, canopy height and textural features derived from a grey level co-occurrence matrix (GLCM) and uses several machine learning regression models - Cubist, Random Forest (RF), Support Vector Machine (SVM), Stochastic Gradient Boosting (GBM) and Extreme Gradient Boosting (XGBoost) - to predict yield. This article [29] highlights the use of AI-integrated UAVs as part of the African response to the COVID-19 virus. Zipline UAVs have been deployed for contactless delivery of medical supplies (PPE, test kits) and disinfectants, using AI route optimisation to navigate in remote areas. In Morocco, locally-developed UAVs equipped with thermal imaging and artificial intelligence sprayed disinfectants and monitored public compliance during closures. South Africa and Tunisia used UAVs for aerial surveillance and to broadcast containment announcements. AI was used to analyse data in real time (optimising delivery routes, detecting temperature anomalies) and to minimise human contact in high-risk areas.

In [30], the authors address the challenges of delivering medical products to hard-to-reach healthcare facilities in northern Ghana. The research assesses the impact of UAV delivery on healthcare operations, focusing on speed, logistical efficiency and resource availability. This study [31] takes up the challenge of accurately quantifying methane (CH_4) emissions from ruminant herds (cattle, sheep, goats, camels) in sub-Saharan Africa, which are difficult to detect using low-resolution satellite data. The researchers used UAV measurements combined with a Bayesian inference algorithm to estimate emission rates, based on high-resolution atmospheric concentration and wind data. The study was carried out at the Kapiti research station in Kenya.

2.2 Disccussion, Challenges and Limitations

Integrated UAVs with artificial intelligence (AI) have emerged as decisive tools across Africa, addressing important challenges in various domains. In **Healthcare Logistics**, the zipline UAV in Ghana and Rwanda revolutionized the last -meal medical delivery, especially during the covid-19 epidemic, reduced the lead time for vaccines, blood and PPEs. Similarly, Morocco deployed locally developed UAVs with thermal imaging AI for disinfection and monitoring, highlighting the compatibility of regional needs. In **Agriculture**, DJI Phantom 3 and Sensfly EB X-like UAVs, machine learning models (eg, random forest, XGbost) were added to prediction and disease management of precise crop yield and disease management. For example, South African studies used multispectral data and vegetative indices to predict maize yields, while Nigeria took advantage of similar techniques for soybean productivity growth. **Environmental Monitoring**, also watched new applications, such as a U-Net-based segmentic segmentation in Senegal, for wildlife conservation mapping to Schistosomiasis houses and DJI Phantom UAV in Tanzania for wildlife conservation mapping.

AI Strategies Miscellaneous by domain: Agricultural Learning with algorithms such as machine learning random forests dominates agriculture, which excels in handling odd data for land-use classification. Deep learning models such as U-Net CNN proved to be important for high-resolution environmental mapping, while DIJKSTRA's adapted UAV trajectory for IOT data collection in South Africa such as algorithm. Despite these progress, there were obstacles including energy boundaries, high computational demands and infrastructure intervals in rural areas. Ethical thoughts, such as data privacy and justified access, were emphasized in South Africa.

Deploying UAVs and AIs in Africa face obstacles such as infrastructure gaps (poor roads, incredible power), energy deficiency (small battery life), and data challenges (limited computational resources and training data). High cost and slow progress for advanced technology and unclear rules. Concerns and bureaucracy delays of privacy, such as permit issues in Senegal, add complexity. These require inexpensive solutions, local training and collaborative policies to maximize to maximize UAVs' impact.

3 AI Innovation in African Satellite Design and Deployment

This section provides a detailed overview of the emerging trends and technological innovations in satellite design and deployment across Africa, with a special emphasis on the integration of Artificial Intelligence (AI). Drawing upon recent

Table 1. Summary of AI and UAV applications.

Reference	Country	Problem statement	Constraints	Domain of application	AI Used	UAV name
[22]	Sub-Saharan Africa	Last-mile delivery challenges in rural areas, Inadequate cold chain storage, frequent stockouts, poor infrastructure for remote delivery	Limited electricity, outdated data systems, geographic barriers	Healthcare logistics	AI-optimized routes, pedictive analytics, Machine learning, blockchain, UAV Decision Tool	Zipline
[23]	South Africa.	The study addressed issues related to UAV navigation, such as optimising routes, improving energy efficiency and ensuring real-time adaptability in dynamic contexts.	Energy Constraint, Obstacle Avoidance, Home Return Requirement, Consecutive Flight Planning	precision agriculture, environmental monitoring, and conservation biology	Novel grid-based CPP algorithm that adapts the A* search, TSP-based heuristic, Grid-based discretization, SVM with Gaussian radial basis function	generic quadrotor with PixHawk flight controller
[24]	Senegal	Schistosomiasis is transmitted in Senegal by snails that inhabit aquatic vegetation. Manual identification of these habitats is inefficient and impractical for large-scale monitoring, which hampers effective disease control.		Public Health, Environmental Monitoring	U-Net: A convolutional neural network (CNN) Random Forest	DJI Phantom IV
[25]	Rwanda	Poor spatial data limits the effectiveness of banana disease management and support for local agriculture.	Limited ground-truth data and complex smallholder landscapes	Remote sensing and precision agriculture	SVM, CART, and Random Forest	eBeeX UAV fitted
[27]	South Africa	Efficient trajectory planning and cooperative task allocation for UAVs to minimize energy consumption and meet real-time data collection needs	Limited UAV battery life and heterogeneous capabilities, strict real-time data freshness requirements	data transport and persistent monitoring	A heuristic solution adapted from Dijkstra's algorithm	Generic UAVs
[28]	Nigeria	Low soybean productivity in West Africa necessitates efficient yield estimation to enhance breeding programs.	Precise integration of features, Variability in spectral responses	Agriculture	Machine learning regression models, Cubist, Random Forest (RF), SVM, GBM, and XGBoost.	senseFly eBee X fixed-wing UAV
[29]	Rwanda, Ghana, Morocco, South Africa, Tunisia	Overcoming logistical barriers for medical supply delivery and public health enforcement during COVID-19.	Energy/internet gaps affecting UAV operations in rural areas, High costs of AI infrastructure and maintenance.	Healthcare logistics	Route optimization algorithms, Thermal imaging AI	Zipline
[30]	Ghana	Inefficient last-mile medical delivery in remote areas, leading to delays and poor healthcare outcomes.	Infrastructure challenges, Weather, Data collection challenges	Healthcare logistics and last-mile medical supply delivery	Statistical analysis (multiple regression)	Zipline
[31]	Kenya	Methane emission rates from animal sources.	Limited flight time due to UAV battery, wind conditions	Presicion Agriculture	Bayesian inference framework with Monte Carlo error propagation	DJI M300 RTK
[34]	Tanzania	Inadequate low-resolution land cover data hampers effective wildlife habitat management.	High computational demands for processing and the complexity of heterogeneous landscapes	Remote sensing for conservation management	SVM, Maximum Likelihood, and Random Forest	DJI Phantom 3 UAV

academic literature and applied research initiatives, it highlights the continent's dynamic and evolving role in the global space technology arena.

Key developments include the proliferation of CubeSats and nanosatellites, the growth of local satellite manufacturing capabilities, and the establishment of national space agencies and regional cooperation frameworks. Countries such as South Africa, Nigeria, Egypt, Kenya, Algeria, and Tunisia are actively harnessing satellite technologies to address pressing needs in areas like environmental monitoring, precision agriculture, public health, smart urban planning, and water resource management.

The incorporation of AI technologies has significantly enhanced the efficiency and scope of satellite applications. AI enables real-time image interpretation, autonomous system control, and accurate tracking of natural and human-induced phenomena. For example, deep learning-based image segmentation has been successfully applied to identify aquatic vegetation linked to schistosomiasis risk zones in Senegal [33], while machine learning models have improved the estimation of agricultural yields from UAV and satellite imagery [34]. Furthermore, nanosatellite constellations integrated with AI and IoT technologies are being deployed for real-time water quality monitoring and smart city applications [32,35].

3.1 Domains of Application of AI-Enabled Satellite Technologies in Africa

This section explores key areas where the integration of Artificial Intelligence (AI) with satellite technologies has made a significant impact across Africa. Through selected case studies, we highlight how these innovations address critical challenges in sectors such as water resource management, public health, agriculture, and urban development.

Satellite-Based Water Quality Monitoring in MENA In water-scarce areas like the Middle East and North Africa (MENA), the use of nanosatellite constellations has become a scalable and cost-efficient approach to monitoring surface water quality. A 2017 study [32] presents an integrated, real-time monitoring system consisting of three key components:

- **Space Segment:** A constellation of nine nanosatellites in low Earth orbit, providing frequent and wide-area coverage.
- **Ground Segment:** Earth stations responsible for receiving and processing data transmitted by the satellite constellation.
- **User Segment:** Ground-based sensor nodes equipped with multi-parameter water-quality sensors (e.g., pH and temperature) that communicate using Software Defined Radio (SDR) technology.

This system leverages AI algorithms for data analysis, enabling early detection of water contamination, improved transboundary water governance, and long-term sustainability of water resources. The primary objective of this system is to enable real-time, remote monitoring of surface water quality using a low-cost and energy-efficient architecture. The developed prototype includes an acquisition board, a wireless sensor network based on SDR communication, and field-deployable sensors. The system's measurements were validated by comparing them to data collected using portable commercial sensors, revealing a strong agreement.

Furthermore, the study proposes a novel approach to achieving permanent water quality surveillance through satellite constellation-based coverage. Future work aims to focus on the miniaturization of water-quality sensors and the expansion of the system for broader, scalable deployment in resource-limited settings.

Public Health and Disease Surveillance AI and satellite technologies are revolutionizing public health surveillance in Africa. A notable application is the use of high-resolution satellite imagery combined with deep learning to monitor environmental conditions that contribute to the transmission of diseases such as schistosomiasis.

A study conducted in the Senegal River Basin (SRB) employed a U-Net convolutional neural network to automatically analyze satellite imagery and identify environmental features associated with the habitats of snails, which serve as intermediate hosts for the schistosome parasite. The deep learning model demonstrated superior predictive performance compared to traditional methods like random forests and GLCM (Gray-Level Co-occurrence Matrix) analysis, particularly in terms of generalizability across various aquatic environments.

Recent analyses have shown that environmental indicators such as the area covered by suitable snail habitat (e.g., floating, non-emergent vegetation), the percent cover of such vegetation, and the size of water-contact zones are more effective proxies for predicting human schistosomiasis infection than conventional estimates of snail abundance obtained through field sampling [33]. This ecological insight was translated into a practical, automated surveillance tool using U-Net, capable of producing segmentation maps of aquatic vegetation directly from high-resolution satellite imagery.

The generated maps not only highlight potential snail habitat hotspots but also include uncertainty estimates, offering a scalable and cost-effective method for disease risk mapping. This approach represents a significant advancement for disease surveillance in resource-limited settings, where schistosomiasis remains endemic. By improving the precision and efficiency of hotspot identification, AI-based tools can help bridge the capacity gap in understanding environmental drivers of transmission, ultimately supporting more targeted and affordable control strategies for neglected tropical diseases.

This article [33], published on 10 March 2022, assessed the performance accuracy of a deep learning-based segmentation algorithm in classifying four distinct land cover types: floating vegetation, emergent vegetation, water, and land. Various learning rates were tested to optimize the model's performance.

Agricultural Monitoring and Precision Farming AI-driven satellite and UAV-based remote sensing technologies are revolutionizing precision agriculture across Africa. By integrating high-resolution imagery with machine learning (ML) models, these tools are enabling more accurate crop monitoring, yield prediction, and resource optimization.

A recent study published on 28 June 2024, titled "*Assessing Maize Yield Spatiotemporal Variability Using Unmanned Aerial Vehicles and Machine Learning*", investigated maize yield estimation across different phenological stages in Bronkhorstspruit, South Africa [34]. The study utilized multispectral UAV data–captured during four key crop growth stages (pre-flowering, flowering, grain filling, and maturity) to evaluate the spatial and temporal variability of maize yield in smallholder farming systems.

From the UAV-acquired imagery, five spectral bands (red, green, blue, near-infrared, and red-edge) were used to compute vegetation indices (VIs) and Grey-Level Co-occurrence Matrix (GLCM) textural features. Feature selection was performed based on their correlation with field-measured maize yields. The selected features were then used in four ML regression models: Random Forest (RF), Gradient Boosting (GradBoost), Categorical Boosting (CatBoost), and Extreme Gradient Boosting (XGBoost).

Among these, GradBoost achieved the best overall performance, with R^2 values ranging from 0.05 to 0.67 and RMSE values from 1.93 to 2.9 t/ha. The most accurate predictions were obtained during the grain-filling and maturity stages, where UAV-derived features–particularly green entropy, green homogeneity, green dissimilarity, and the Enhanced Vegetation Index (EVI)–proved to be the strongest predictors. In contrast, data from the pre-flowering stage yielded lower accuracy.

The GradBoost model was further employed to generate crop yield maps, revealing clear spatial and temporal patterns of maize productivity. An analysis of variance using Welch's test confirmed statistically significant yield differences between the pre-flowering and maturity stages (p-value < 0.01). These findings demonstrate the potential of UAV and AI-based tools to guide informed, timely management interventions.

This study highlights the transformative impact of AI and remote sensing in smallholder farming environments, offering practical insights for enhancing food security and supporting Sustainable Development Goal 2 (Zero Hunger).

Smart Cities and Urban Infrastructure Management *Challenge One* is the first Tunisian satellite, developed by the Telnet Group, marking a significant milestone in the nation's entry into the aerospace sector. Officially launched on **March 20, 2021**, this satellite represents a bold step toward leveraging space-based technology for advancing IoT connectivity.

Challenge One was designed to explore how space can be leveraged to enhance connectivity for millions of terrestrial IoT devices. The mission demonstrates the capability of a Low Earth Orbit (LEO) satellite to collect data from LoRa-based terminals using the same power requirements as traditional ground-based transmissions. By acting as an orbital LoRa gateway, the satellite significantly extends IoT coverage beyond the constraints of terrestrial networks.

- **Global Coverage:** Provides reliable communication in remote and underserved areas, overcoming terrestrial network limitations.
- **High Availability and Efficiency:** Ensures consistent data transmission performance for various IoT applications.
- **Cost-Effective:** Offers an affordable alternative for wide-area IoT deployment, particularly in regions with minimal infrastructure.

Challenge One represents Telnet's gateway into the "Space for IoT" domain, laying the groundwork for future nanosatellite constellations and advanced aerospace technologies. The project began over four years prior to launch, culminating in the successful deployment of Tunisia's first nanosatellite on **March 20, 2021**, a symbolic date that coincides with Tunisia's Independence Day.

3.2 Disccussion, Challenges and Limitations

Despite these hurdles, advancements in satellite technology, machine learning algorithms, and computational resources continue to progress, helping to overcome many of these challenges. Ongoing research and development efforts are expected to lead to improved methods for tackling these obstacles, thereby facilitating the more effective and widespread use of these technologies. Despite the ongoing challenges faced by Africa's satellite sector, such as limited financial resources, insufficient technical expertise, and infrastructural constraints, significant progress is being made through cross-border collaborations and international partnerships. These alliances play a crucial role in enhancing institutional capacity, facilitating knowledge transfer, and fostering sustainable innovation across the continent. However, several obstacles remain to maximize the effectiveness of satellite-based systems and AI applications. Some of the key challenges include **data quality and availability**, **high computational demand**, **infrastructure and costs**, **environmental variability**, **regulatory and legal challenges**, **scalability**, and **real-time processing**. Despite these hurdles, advancements in satellite technology, machine learning algorithms, and computational resources continue to progress, helping to overcome many of these challenges. Ongoing research and development efforts are expected to lead to improved methods for addressing these obstacles, thereby facilitating the more effective and widespread use of these technologies.

4 Conclusion

The integration of Artificial Intelligence with UAVs and satellite technologies has a transformational ability to solve Africa's socio-economic and environmental challenges. This survey highlights the AI-operated UAV, which enables localized solutions as agriculture, healthcare logistics, and wildlife protection, while while AI-enhanced satellites provide scalable equipment for climate modeling, connectivity and disaster management.

Future work should focus on adaptation of data fusion algorithms and communication links between UAVs and satellites, as well as develop an analogous strategies addressing tunisia's unique regulator, environmental and operating conditions. Overall, the fusion of UAV and satellite technologies represents an important step in remote sensing, which has the ability to revolutionize Tunisia and beyond monitoring and agricultural.

Table 2. Overview of AI utilization in satellite applications in Africa.

Reference	Country	Problem statement	Constraints	Domain of Application	AI Used	Satellite name
[34]	South Africa	Optimizing maize yield prediction for smallholder farmers using UAV and machine learning.	Variability in crop growth, dependency on UAV data over multiple growth stages.	Precision Agriculture	Random Forest, GradBoost, CatBoost, XGBoost	UAV Platform
[33]	Senegal	Identifying aquatic vegetation linked to schistosomiasis transmission via satellite imagery.	Limited ground truth data for aquatic vegetation; difficulty in detecting snail habitats.	Health and Disease Surveillance	Deep Learning (U-Net)	WorldView-2
[32]	MENA Region	Real-time water quality monitoring for the water-scarce MENA region using small satellites.	Limited satellite coverage, high cost of infrastructure, environmental variability.	Environmental Monitoring	AI for anomaly detection	Custom Nanosatellite Constellation
[35]	Tunisia	Connecting IoT terminals in smart cities through satellite communication.	Limited terrestrial network availability, high cost of satellite infrastructure.	Smart Cities, IoT	AI-enhanced IoT systems	Challenge One

Table 2 provides an overview of four studies showcasing how artificial intelligence (AI) and satellite technologies are applied across key sectors in Africa and the MENA region. It highlights the country of application, the main challenges addressed, technical constraints, application domains, AI models used, and the corresponding satellites. These examples illustrate the growing role of AI-powered satellite systems in tackling diverse challenges, from agriculture and public health to environmental monitoring and smart urban infrastructure

References

1. Chaccour, C., et al.: Telecom's artificial general intelligence (AGI) vision: beyond the GenAI frontier. IEEE Network (2024)
2. Hackenberger, B.K., Djerdj, T., Hackenberger, D.K.: Advancing environmental monitoring through AI: applications of R and python (2025)
3. Ghiglione, M., Serra, V.: Opportunities and challenges of AI on satellite processing units. In: Proceedings of the 19th ACM International Conference on Computing Frontiers (2022)
4. Cheng, N., et al.: AI for UAV-assisted IoT applications: a comprehensive review. IEEE Internet Things J. **10**(16), 14438–14461 (2023)
5. Mugala, S., Okello, D., Serugunda, J.: Unmanned aerial vehicles: opportunities for developing countries and challenges. In: 2020 IST-Africa Conference (IST-Africa). IEEE (2020)
6. Whytock, R.C., et al.: Real-time alerts from AI-enabled camera traps using the Iridium satellite network: a case-study in Gabon, Central Africa. Methods Ecol. Evol. **14**(3), 867–874 (2023)
7. Ade-Ibijola, A., Okonkwo, C.: Artificial intelligence in Africa: emerging challenges. In: Responsible AI in Africa: Challenges and Opportunities, pp. 101–117. Springer International Publishing, Cham (2023)
8. Ogunbukola, M.: AI's impact on African economic development: productivity, growth, and global standing (2024)
9. Mienye, I.D., Sun, Y., Ileberi, E.: Artificial intelligence and sustainable development in Africa: a comprehensive review. Mach. Learn. Appl. 100591 (2024)

10. Smokova, D.: How are GAFAM companies-microsoft, google, and apple-utilizing AI systems' capabilities to drive their ESG/CSR initiatives? BS Thesis. University of Twente (2022)
11. Argyriou, A., et al.: Satellite remote sensing and AI: detection and mapping of West Africa seagrass. In: Proceedings of SPAICE2024: The First Joint European Space Agency/IAA Conference on AI in and for Space (2024)
12. Rovira-Sugranes, A., et al.: A review of AI-enabled routing protocols for UAV networks: trends, challenges, and future outlook. Ad Hoc Netw. **130**, 102790 (2022)
13. Boroujeni, S.P.H., et al.: A comprehensive survey of research towards AI-enabled unmanned aerial systems in pre-, active-, and post-wildfire management. Inf. Fusion 102369 (2024)
14. Angnuureng, D.B., et al.: Satellite, drone and video camera multi-platform monitoring of coastal erosion at an engineered pocket beach: a showcase for coastal management at Elmina Bay, Ghana (West Africa). Reg. Stud. Mar. Sci. **53**, 102437 (2022)
15. Cisse, M.: Look to Africa to advance artificial intelligence. Nature 461 (2018)
16. Akpudo, U.E., et al.: Unveiling AI concerns for Sub-Saharan Africa and its vulnerable groups. In: International Conference on Intelligent and Innovative Computing Applications (2024)
17. Uwa, O.G., Ronke, A.C.: The impact of modern technologies on peace, security and development in Africa. Can. Soc. Sci. **19**(2), 75–82 (2023)
18. Ogunbukola, M.: Empowering Africa: unleashing the AI revolution through access to energy (2024)
19. Clarke De La Cerda, J., Bejaui, R., Bonyo, L.: AI innovation in Africa: an overview of opportunities, risks and the legal context. Commun., Technol. et Développement **16** (2024)
20. Azaroual, F.: Artificial intelligence in Africa: challenges and opportunities. Research papers & Policy papers on Economic Trends and Policies 2416 (2024)
21. Alvarenga, J., et al.: Survey of unmanned helicopter model-based navigation and control techniques. J. Intell. Robot. Syst. **80**, 87–138 (2015)
22. Addy, A.: Vaccine production and distribution challenges: an AI-assisted technologies for the overcoming of logistical hurdles faced by Sub-Saharan Africa with focus on Ghana. Vaccine **113** (2024)
23. Cilliers, A.A., Engelbrecht, J.A.A.: Coverage path planning for autonomous surveying of plant species using unmanned aerial vehicles (UAVs). In: MATEC Web of Conferences, vol. 406. EDP Sciences (2024)
24. Liu, Z.Y.-C., et al.: Deep learning segmentation of satellite imagery identifies aquatic vegetation associated with snail intermediate hosts of schistosomiasis in Senegal, Africa. Remote Sens. **14**(6), 1345 (2022)
25. Kilwenge, R., et al.: UAV-based mapping of banana land area for village-level decision-support in Rwanda. Remote Sens. **13**(24), 4985 (2021)
26. Mangewa, L.J., et al.: Land use/cover classification of large conservation areas using a ground-linked high-resolution unmanned aerial vehicle. Resources **13**(8), 113 (2024)
27. Tuyishimire, E., et al.: Trajectory planning for cooperating unmanned aerial vehicles in the IoT. IoT **3**(1), 147–168 (2022)
28. Alabi, T.R., et al.: Estimation of soybean grain yield from multispectral high-resolution UAV data with machine learning models in West Africa. Remote Sens. Appl.: Soc. Environ. **27**, 100782 (2022)
29. Maharana, A., et al.: COVID-19 and beyond: use of digital technology for pandemic response in Africa. Sci. Afr. **14**, e01041 (2021)

30. Atiga, O., et al.: Shortening the last-mile: impact of zipline medical drone delivery on the operations of hard-to-reach healthcare facilities in northern Ghana. Afr. J. Appl. Res. **10**(1), 178–200 (2024)
31. van Hove, A., et al.: Inferring methane emissions from African livestock by fusing drone, tower, and satellite data. EGUsphere **2025**, 1–36 (2025)
32. Gallah, N., Bahri, O.b., Lazreg, N., Chaouch, A., Besbes, K.: Water quality monitoring based on small satellite technology. Int. J. Adv. Comput. Sci. Appl. (IJACSA) **8**(3) (2017)
33. Liu, Z.Y.-C., Chamberlin, A.J., Tallam, K., Jones, I.J., Lamore, L.L., Bauer, J., Bresciani, M., Wolfe, C.M., Casagrandi, R., Mari, L., et al.: Deep learning segmentation of satellite imagery identifies aquatic vegetation associated with snail intermediate hosts of schistosomiasis in Senegal, Africa. Remote Sens. **14**(6), 1345 (2022)
34. de Villiers, C., et al.: Assessing maize yield spatiotemporal variability using unmanned aerial vehicles and machine learning. Geomatics **4**(3), 213–236 (2024)
35. Telnet, H.: Challenge one: the first tunisian satellite launched into space. https://groupe-telnet.com/en/

Artificial Intelligence-Based Traffic Light Control System for Sustainable Urban Mobility and Environmental Impact Reduction

Rym Ben Smida(✉), Ameni Mersani, and Hiba Jouini

M2M Team, ESPRIT School of Engineering, Tunis, Tunisia
{rym.bensmida,ameni.mersani,hiba.jouini}@esprit.tn

Abstract. Traffic congestion is a common global phenomenon that causes increased pollution, delays, and accidents. Conventional traffic light control systems, based on preconfigured timers, have proven ineffective as they cannot be adjusted according to dynamic and real-time traffic situations. This paper presents an artificial intelligence-powered smart traffic light control system, which, through computer vision and deep learning methodologies, strives to improve traffic flow efficiency. Installed on a Raspberry Pi platform, the system takes and interprets real-time traffic images and evaluates the number of vehicles heading towards every intersection. This report uncovers that the system adjusts the duration of traffic light signals in real time to optimize traffic flow, minimizing waiting times and boosting overall efficiency. The artificial intelligence model has been created to evaluate traffic conditions based on a predefined severity scale, enabling the system's capacity to disperse congestion, enhance traffic management, and reduce emissions. By prioritizing green traffic light signals for those routes with higher traffic volumes, the system aims to enable smoother, faster travel while also mitigating the environmental impact. This innovative strategy illustrates the power of artificial intelligence in revolutionizing urban transport networks, providing an efficient and sustainable means of addressing the increasing traffic demands of today's cities.

Keywords: Artificial Intelligence · Traffic light control · Computer vision · Smart cities · Sustainability · Environmental impact

1 Introduction

The rapid rate of urbanization has significantly contributed to the increase in the number of automobiles on the roads, resulting in heavy traffic congestion, longer travel times, and worsening safety concerns [1]. Traditional traffic light control systems, including timer-based systems, are unable to manage real-time traffic dynamics and therefore aggravate these issues. Artificial Intelligence (AI), along with computer vision and machine learning technologies, introduces a novel and sustainable approach to intelligent traffic management [2–5]. By enabling real-time, data-driven decision-making, AI can substantially improve traffic flow and optimize the operation of traffic lights [6].

F. Kamoun et al. (Eds.): AFRICATEK 2025, LNICST 677, pp. 182–192, 2026.
https://doi.org/10.1007/978-3-032-16638-8_13

Numerous studies have been conducted to address these challenges. For instance, recent research has explored the use of time-series-based traffic prediction models to optimize traffic light cycle times. In particular, in [6], AI algorithms in Intelligent Traffic Signal Control Systems dynamically regulate traffic signals in response to real-time traffic flow, thereby optimizing movement, reducing delays, and improving road safety. These systems have proven effective at managing peak-hour congestion through the integration of IoT and V2X communication. Additionally, AI-driven traffic light optimization adjusts signal timing based on vehicle count at intersections, significantly alleviating congestion and reducing wait times. These systems outperform traditional methods by enhancing economic efficiency, pedestrian safety, and air quality [7].

Moreover, traffic conditions can be significantly optimized through AI-powered dynamic signal adjustments, anticipatory traffic patterning, and real-time route optimization. These strategies rely on both historical data and real-time sensor inputs to reduce congestion, improve roadway efficiency, and shorten travel times [8]. In summary, research shows that AI particularly through the application of Deep Reinforcement Learning enhances traffic light control via optimal, adaptive traffic flow management. It reduces congestion and improves safety, further supported by real-time coordination using Visible Light Communication systems [9].

Within this framework, AI specifically through the use of computer vision and machine learning—provides an innovative and environmentally friendly approach to traffic management. By facilitating real-time, data-driven decisions, AI can greatly enhance both traffic flow and the operational efficiency of traffic signal systems. This study builds upon this premise by proposing a novel methodology.

The research bridges the gap between conventional fixed-timer traffic light systems and AI-based intelligent alternatives by proposing a viable and scalable solution geared toward real-world deployment and future scalability. In doing so, it highlights the promise of artificial intelligence in enabling smart, sustainable, and efficient transportation networks aligning with broader goals of sustainable development and urban mobility. The results presented in this paper underscore the significant potential of AI in mitigating urban traffic congestion and provide valuable insights into the future of smart and sustainable urban transportation.

2 Methodology

2.1 System Architecture

The proposed system is an embedded traffic management solution that integrates a Raspberry Pi 3, a high-resolution camera module, and a deep learning-based object detection algorithm. The system architecture is composed of three primary components. First, the data acquisition module uses a high-resolution camera to capture real-time images of traffic flow (Fig. 1). Second, the processing unit leverages OpenCV and a deep learning model—specifically SSD MobileNetV3—to analyze the captured images, enabling accurate detection and counting of vehicles. Finally, the decision module dynamically adjusts the duration of traffic signals based on vehicle density analysis, using GPIO-controlled LEDs for real-time traffic light control, as illustrated in Fig. 2.

Fig. 1. Camera NoIR PI module V2.

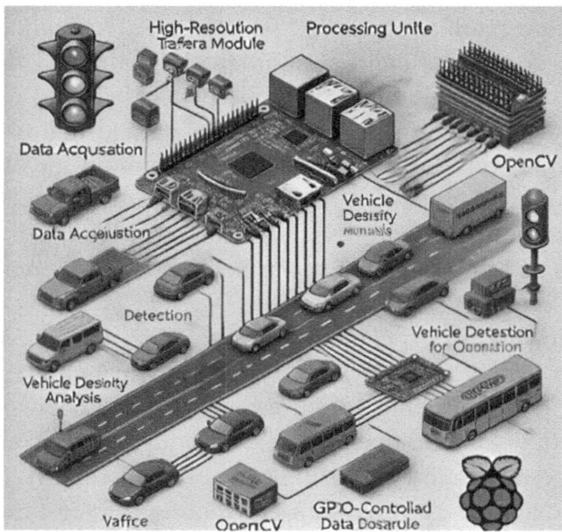

Fig. 2. System architecture [10].

The system operates continuously, capturing and processing traffic data to dynamically optimize signal timing. Additionally, a MongoDB database is integrated to store historical traffic data, enabling long-term analysis and system optimization. By leveraging past traffic patterns, the system improves its efficiency over time through adaptive learning and trend analysis, thereby enhancing overall traffic flow management, as illustrated in Fig. 3.

The proposed system consists of two interconnected nodes, each equipped with a microcontroller in the form of a Raspberry Pi 3 board and a traffic light control module. The nodes operate simultaneously to calculate vehicle density on specific roads and exchange data with a central database to dynamically adjust traffic signal durations. Additionally, a web-based admin panel allows for real-time traffic monitoring and provides manual control capabilities when needed.

To enable remote control and access to the Raspberry Pi, Virtual Network Computing (VNC) is used. This solution provides a secure connection, allowing users to remotely view and control the Raspberry Pi interface from various VNC-compatible devices, such as computers and tablets.

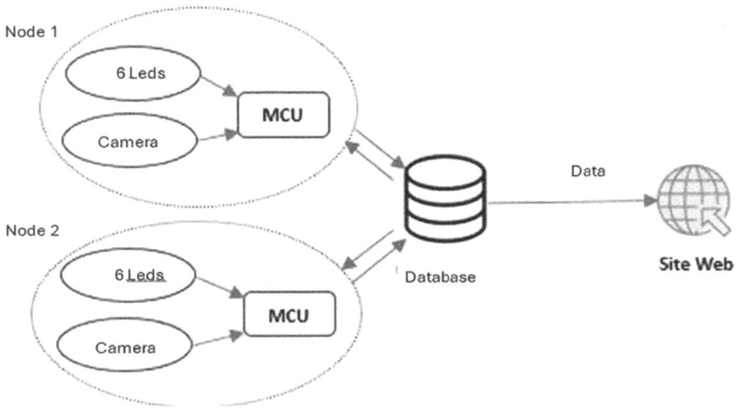

Fig. 3. Global system architecture proposal.

2.2 Object Detection and Training

Figure 4 shows the wiring of the various components that make up the control section of the image processing system for a single round-trip route, including a Raspberry Pi 3B board and a Raspberry Pi camera.

Fig. 4. Image processing section

In computer vision, one of the key tasks is the creation of annotated datasets. Some tools exist that allow the loading of images together with their equivalent label categories, thereby facilitating object localization. This data is saved and maintained in an ordered manner in an annotation file for future use. Data augmentation strategies are frequently used for augmenting the size as well as diversity of training datasets. These techniques make machine learning algorithms more effective by providing greater variability within a broader range of variations and contexts upon which their processes can learn. Some examples are:

Rotation is the movement of images by different angles to produce orientation changes, as in Fig. 5.

Mirroring helps to flip an image horizontally or vertically and creates mirrored images that replicate symmetrical shapes. Contrast and brightness manipulation allow for imitation of different lighting conditions, thereby increasing the freedom of image processing systems (Fig. 6). Further, the introduction of stochastic noise aids in improving model robustness by subjecting it to different data fluctuations, thereby improving its generalizability to different environments, as illustrated in Fig. 7.

Fig. 5. Rotation.

Fig. 6. Brightness and contrast adjustment.

Fig. 7. Random noise.

2.3 Object Detection and Training

Object detection is a critical task in computer vision that involves detection and localization of specific objects in an image or sequence of images. The goal is to identify regions of interest that are indicative of particular objects and classify them with their corresponding classes.

In our study, we opted to use the "ssd_mobilenet_v3_large_coco" model in detecting objects. The rationale for this choice is based on a number of significant factors.

The SSD-MobileNetV3 model pretrained on the COCO dataset is used without retraining. A small set of images was employed to test robustness through data augmentation (rotation, contrast, noise).

To begin with, the "ssd_mobilenet_v3_large_coco" model is based on the SSD (Single Shot MultiBox Detector) framework, meaning that it carries out object detection in a single pass through the input image. This aspect renders it quicker and more effective than other models that need explicit region proposal steps. As a result, it is particularly well-suited for real-time applications where speed is critical. Additionally, the "ssd_mobilenet_v3_large_coco" model has been pre-trained on the COCO (Common Objects in Context) dataset, which is a well-known dataset including a wide variety of objects from a large number of categories.

The system proposed for intelligent traffic management employs real-time image acquisition, deep learning-based object detection, and adaptive traffic signal control to enhance urban mobility. The road images are captured round the clock using a Raspberry Pi camera module and preprocessed before being analyzed with the aid of a trained SSD MobileNetV3 model. This optimized and efficient deep learning model, which was pre-trained on the COCO dataset and fine-tuned for vehicle detection, enables a precise estimation of traffic density at intersections. Based on live vehicle counts, the system dynamically adjusts traffic light cycles to relieve bottlenecks. In addition, all traffic data is retained in a MongoDB database for analysis and future optimization. In contrast with traditional fixed-cycle traffic lights, this AI system reacts to evolving traffic conditions, thereby facilitating an easier passage of automobiles. Also, a web-based administrative portal provides real-time monitoring capability so that traffic managers can keep track of the situation and apply corrective measures when needed.

2.4 Deployment and Software Modules

The development of our project needed the utilization of some important software libraries. Apart from the OpenCV (cv2) library, we utilized pymongo, which is a Python library that enabled us to connect to our MongoDB database and hence allowed read and write operations and data fetching.

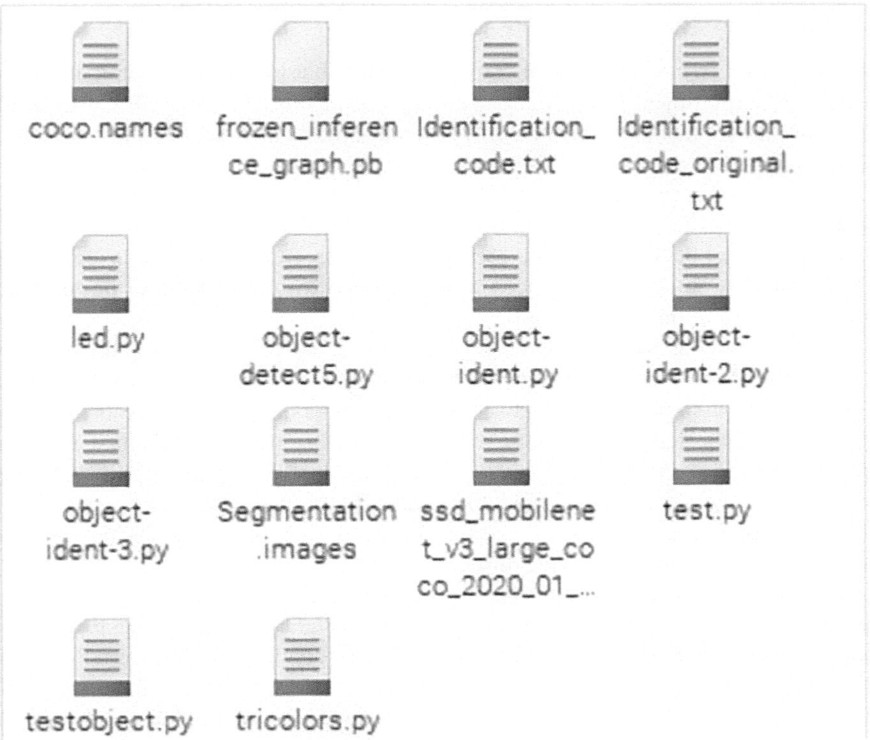

Fig. 8. Data preparation.

We also utilized the standard Python library, time, for handling time, measuring elapsed times, introducing delays, and handling timestamps for the data. In addition, we also utilized RPi.GPIO, a library tailored for interacting with Raspberry Pi's General-Purpose Input/Output (GPIO) pins. With it, we could configure the pins, designate them as input or output, and flip their states to communicate with external components such as LEDs. After implementing the model and adding a directory to enhance detection, the next section focuses on object detection (Fig. 8).

The green boxes around the objects are the bounding boxes drawn by the object detection model. The boxes are utilized to visually mark the position of the detected objects, the cars in this instance. The boxes are usually employed to highlight the position and spatial scale of the objects found by the detection model, as is evident in Fig. 9.

Figure 10 demonstrates that the number of cars on both roads has been successfully inserted into the database.

After the insertion on both sides, a comparison will be made to determine the side with the most cars. Then, the traffic light signal corresponding to that side will be changed to green.

Fig. 9. Cars detected successfully.

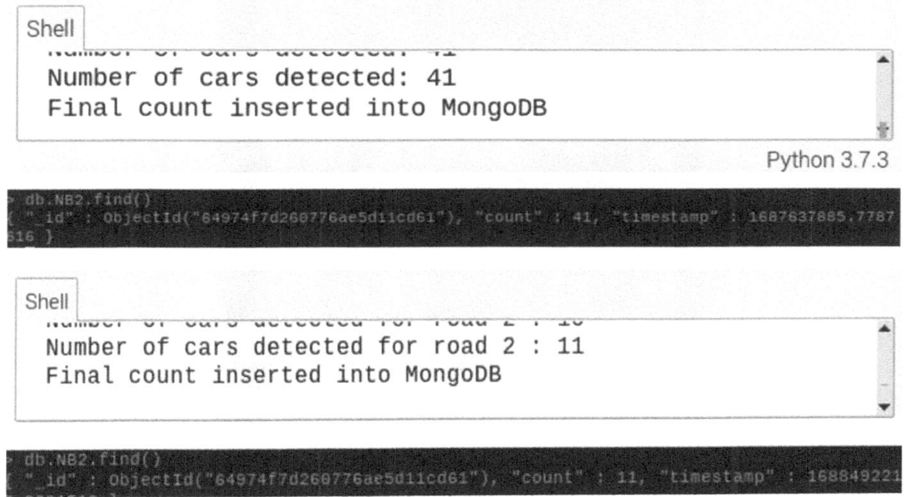

Fig. 10. Cars detected and inserted into the database.

3 Experimental Results

The system was evaluated with the help of a prototype model simulating a real intersection. Results indicated a drastic decrease in the average waiting time at intersections when compared to traditional fixed-timer systems. The AI-based solution enabled a smoother distribution of green-light periods, efficiently adjusting to the dynamics of changing traffic conditions.

Quantitative findings demonstrated that the adaptive system shaved 30–40% off vehicle waiting times under medium-density traffic conditions. Under high-density traffic conditions, efficiency improvements of up to 50% were achieved, thereby validating the scalability of the system being proposed. Additional experiments likened the performance of the AI-based system with existing static traffic lights, placing emphasis on enhanced flow smoothness and less idle times.

Further, the system ideally incorporated an internet-based dashboard so that real-time analysis of traffic was possible. The users could visualize traffic congestion, adjust signal timings, and prepare reports for additional long-term analysis. The use of automated AI-based control combined with human oversight provides reliability and flexibility (Fig. 11).

Fig. 11. Prototype.

The system was tested using a physical prototype under a simulated environment with three traffic density scenarios: low (1–2 cars per cycle), medium (5–7 cars), and high (10 or more cars). For each scenario, we conducted 10 full test cycles and recorded the average waiting time for each vehicle before the green light was activated. These results were then compared to a baseline fixed-time control system. On average, the AI-based system achieved a waiting time reduction ranging from 30 to 50%, depending on traffic intensity, with an overall improvement averaging around 35%. The detailed performance results are summarized in Table 1.

Table 1. The performance

Traffic type	Waiting time (s)	Waiting time (AI) (s)	Gain (%)
Low	42	28	33
Medium	65	42	35
High	110	55	50

Robustness tests were also conducted by changing lighting and camera angles to assess detection stability.

4 Comparative Analysis with Related AI-Based Systems

To better position our system within the broader landscape of intelligent traffic control, we conducted a comparative analysis with selected existing AI-based and embedded traffic management approaches. Table 2 presents a summary of performance metrics reported in recent studies, including average waiting time reduction, hardware used, and level of real-time responsiveness. Our system shows competitive performance—achieving up to 50% reduction in waiting time—while also maintaining low cost and ease of deployment due to its embedded nature and minimal infrastructure dependency. Unlike most server-based solutions, our Raspberry Pi-based system processes data locally, ensuring faster decision-making and increased resilience in areas with unreliable internet connectivity.

Table 2. Summary of performance metrics

Reference	AI technique	Platform	Avg. waiting time reduction (%)	Real-time	Cost efficiency
Patil [7]	Rule-based + RL	Python	~45	Yes	Medium
Xu et al. [6]	Supervised ML	Cloud-hosted	~40	Partial	Medium
This study	Pretrained CV + ML	Raspberry Pi 3	30–50	Yes	High

5 Conclusion and Future Work

The study demonstrates the potential of AI-based traffic light control to enhance urban mobility. The real-time detection of vehicles and adaptive signal control significantly increases the efficiency of traffic. Future improvements include incorporating IoT sensors as additional data sources, incorporating reinforcement learning techniques to expand the model, and large-scale field-testing the system in the real world.

Additionally, the integration of vehicle-to-infrastructure (V2I) communication can enhance the decision-making functions even more using the data of networked vehicles. With AI, IoT, and cloud analysis integrated, the next generation of this system could even enable predictive traffic management, reducing congestion before it occurs.

A further promising direction for future research might be the combination of pedestrian and cyclist detection in order to offer integrated urban mobility solutions. By taking the system beyond a vehicle detection system, urban planners are able to create a truly intelligent transport system that benefits all users of the road.

References

1. Faheem, H., El Shorbagy, A.M., Gabr, M.E.: Impact of traffic congestion on transportation system: challenges and remediations—a review. **49**(2) (2024). https://doi.org/10.58491/2735-4202.3191
2. Purushothaman, K.E., et al.: Innovative urban planning for harnessing blockchain and edge Artificial Intelligence for smart city solutions. In: Second International Conference on Intelligent Cyber Physical Systems and Internet of Things (ICoICI), Coimbatore, India, pp. 65–68 (2024). https://doi.org/10.1109/ICoICI62503.2024.10696745
3. Dharwal, M., Agarwal, N., Kumar, S., Anand, S., Vatsa, M.: Building smarter smart cities for sustainable development through Artificial Intelligence. In: 2021 5th International Conference on Electronics, Communication and Aerospace Technology (ICECA), Coimbatore, India, pp. 1185–1187 (2021). https://doi.org/10.1109/ICECA52323.2021.9676140
4. Kadkhodayi, A., Jabeli, M., Aghdam, H., Mirbakhsh, S.: Artificial intelligence-based real-time traffic management. J. Electr. Electron. Eng. **2**(4), 368–373 (2023)
5. Thorat, N.N., Kulal, N., Patil, V., Kokare, D.U., Hirve, S., Date, A.: AI-based real-time traffic management systems. In: Advances in Computational Intelligence and Robotics Book Series, pp. 341–354 (2024). https://doi.org/10.4018/979-8-3693-7367-5.ch023
6. Xu, H.: Intelligent traffic light control system and application. Appl. Comput. Eng. **128**(1), 24–30 (2025). https://doi.org/10.54254/2755-2721/2025.20224
7. Patil, V.: AI-based adaptive traffic management. Int. J. Sci. Technol. Eng. **12**(12), 945–947 (2024). https://doi.org/10.22214/ijraset.2024.65908
8. Rajendran, R.K., Blessing, N.R., Priya, T.M.: Traffic flow optimization using AI. In: Advances in Geospatial Technologies Book Series, pp. 217–238 (2024). https://doi.org/10.4018/979-8-3693-8054-3.ch008
9. Vieira, M., Galvão, G., Vieira, M.A., Véstias, M., Louro, P., Vieira, P.: Integrating visible light communication and AI for adaptive traffic management: a focus on reward functions and rerouting coordination. Appl. Sci. **15**(1), 116 (2024). https://doi.org/10.3390/app15010116
10. OpenAI: ChatGPT: generating AI-based images. OpenAI (2025). https://openai.com

From Pixels to Policy: A Tunisian Public Space Quality Index for Urban Sustainability

Nicolas Mbabu[1], Rym Ammar[2](✉), and Wadie Othmani[3]

[1] Esprit School of Engineering, Ghazala, Tunisia
[2] Esprit School of Business, Ariana, Tunisia
rym.ammar@Esprit.tn
[3] Polytechnic School, University of Tours, Tours, France
wadie.othmani@univ-tours.fr, wadiia078@hotmail.fr

Abstract. This study presents a novel approach to evaluate public space quality in Tunisia using artificial intelligence, and Google Street View imagery. Overcoming the subjectivity and limited scope of traditional methods, it employs the YOLO v8 model to detect urban features and integrates a Sustainable Development Index with an Ecological Impact Index to quantify quality across environmental, social, and economic dimensions. The methodology involves image collection, processing, model training, and sustainability analysis. Findings show regional disparities: some Tunisian governorates balance development well, while others falter under ecological stress like waste and pollution, highlighting the need for environmental consideration. The YOLO v8 model performs strongly on distinct objects but struggles with similar classes, indicating refinement potential. This scalable, objective tool aids urban planners and local authorities in targeting interventions and supports integrated policies. Adaptable globally, it merges technology and sustainability to redefine public space assessment, stressing ecological harmony with socio-economic growth for resilient, inclusive cities.

Keywords: Public space quality index · Urban sustainability · Artificial intelligence · Google street view

1 Introduction

The quality of public space constitutes a fundamental issue in improving citizens' living environments, playing a decisive role in their physical and mental well-being, as well as in social cohesion and the economic attractiveness of urban areas [4, 10]. Well-designed and well-maintained public spaces foster social interactions, encourage active mobility, and contribute to environmental sustainability, thus meeting the aspirations of modern societies for more inclusive and resilient cities [20, 33]. In Tunisia, where rapid urbanization is transforming urban landscapes, assessing this quality becomes essential to guide public policies and urban planning decisions while considering the country's cultural, social, and economic specificities.

F. Kamoun et al. (Eds.): AFRICATEK 2025, LNICST 677, pp. 193–215, 2026.
https://doi.org/10.1007/978-3-032-16638-8_14

However, traditional methods for evaluating public space quality, such as expert focus groups [1] and SWOT (Strengths, Weaknesses, Opportunities, Threats) analyses, have significant limitations [7]. While these approaches are useful for gathering qualitative insights, they suffer from inherent subjectivity due to participants' cognitive biases and a lack of comprehensiveness in addressing the multiple dimensions of public spaces [24]. Their reliance on small samples and human judgment limits their capacity to reflect the complexity of urban environments, particularly in dynamic and diverse contexts such as dense urban areas. These shortcomings highlight the need to develop more objective and systematic tools capable of capturing the visual and functional characteristics of public spaces on a large scale.

In light of these challenges, a central question arises: How can we design a method for evaluating public space quality that is objective, comprehensive, and adapted to local specificities by leveraging technological advances such as computer vision and geolocated image analysis? This work explores an innovative approach using Google Street View images and deep learning techniques to quantify relevant visual criteria in the Tunisian context. We formulate the following hypotheses:

1. Integrating computer vision and artificial intelligence can provide a more accurate and objective evaluation by reducing the subjectivity of traditional methods.
2. The systematic analysis of geolocated images allows for the large-scale collection and processing of visual data, thereby improving the comprehensiveness of evaluations.
3. This technological approach can be adapted to local specificities, such as those in Tunisia, to provide relevant decision-making tools for urban planners and policymakers.

Building on these hypotheses, this article aims to demonstrate how a methodology based on visual data and advanced algorithms can revolutionize the evaluation of public space quality, thereby contributing to more informed and sustainable urban management.

2 Methodology

This section outlines the methodological steps followed to assess the quality of public space using geolocated images, based on computer vision and artificial intelligence techniques. The methodology is structured into four main phases: (1) data collection, (2) data processing and cleaning, (3) training of the YOLO v8 model for object detection, and (4) application of Hickel's Sustainable Development Index (SDI) model to quantify the quality of places. Each step is detailed below (Fig. 1).

2.1 Data Collection

The primary source of visual data is Google Street View, a platform widely used in urban research due to its accessibility and extensive geographical coverage [32]. Geolocated images were collected using a custom Python scraping script, employing the Selenium and Beautiful Soup libraries to automate the extraction of images along with their associated metadata (geographic coordinates, capture date, etc.). This collection method

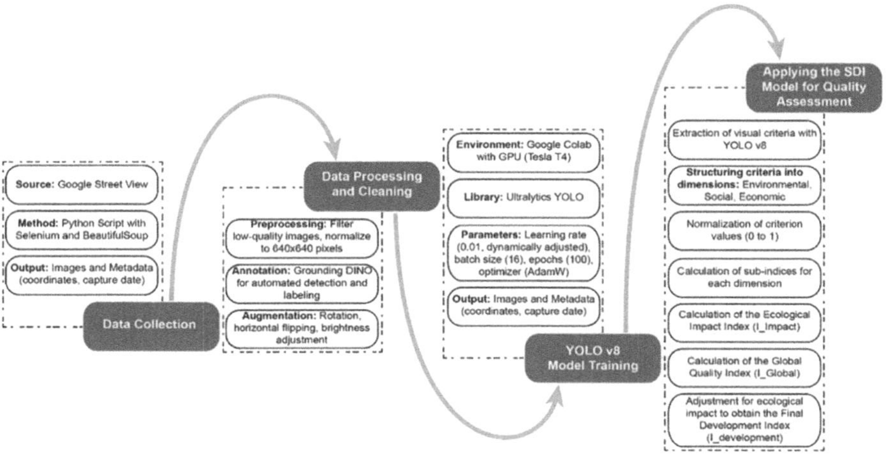

Fig. 1. Roadmap of the methodology

allows for the gathering of a large volume of visual data representative of public spaces in Tunisia, while ensuring their spatial contextualization.

The choice of Google Street View as a data source is motivated by its ability to provide 360° street-level images, offering a comprehensive and immersive view of urban environments [18]. Moreover, the use of scraping techniques to collect such images is a common practice in urban studies based on large-scale visual data [3].

Urban transformation is a long-term process. Major urban projects—such as the construction of a new district or the development of a ring road—often take a decade or more to fully materialize and produce visible impacts on the urban fabric.

As such, the timeframe of the data used in this study (2016–2021) remains relatively short in the context of urban evolution. More time is required before new data can be collected from the same locations to enable a meaningful longitudinal or temporal comparison.

2.2 Data Processing and Cleaning

The processing of the collected data was carried out in several steps to ensure its quality and relevance for training the object detection model.

- **Image Preprocessing**: Images were filtered to remove those that were blurry, redundant, or of poor quality (e.g., completely black or overexposed images). Image dimensions were standardized to 640 × 640 pixels to meet the requirements of the YOLO v8 model. This preprocessing is essential for reducing noise in the data and improving the model's accuracy [29].

- **Data Annotation**: Object annotation in the images was automated using Grounding DINO, an open-source object detection model capable of identifying and labeling relevant visual elements (e.g., trees, trash bins, vehicles) with high accuracy [19]. This semi-automated approach enables efficient handling of large volumes of data while maintaining annotation consistency. Grounding Dino was used to generate preliminary annotations, which were then manually verified using the Roboflow platform to ensure the quality of the labels.
- **Data Augmentation**: To enrich the dataset and enhance the model's robustness, data augmentation techniques were applied, such as rotation, horizontal flipping, and brightness adjustment. These techniques are commonly used in computer vision to simulate variations in lighting conditions and viewing angles, helping the model generalize more effectively [34].

These data processing and cleaning steps are essential to ensure high-quality input data for the model, a critical prerequisite for achieving optimal performance in deep learning. The figure below illustrates the distribution of images across governorates, revealing regional variations in data availability, where gray-colored areas indicate governorates with missing data (Fig. 2).

Fig. 2. Distribution of images by governorate

2.3 YOLO v8 Model Training

For the detection and classification of objects in geolocated images, the YOLO v8 model (You Only Look Once, version 8) was selected due to its real-time performance, high accuracy, and ability to handle multi-class detection [15]. YOLO v8 is particularly well-suited for applications that require fast and precise image analysis, making it a relevant choice for this work.

YOLO v8 Architecture. The model is based on a modular architecture composed of three main components (Fig. 3):

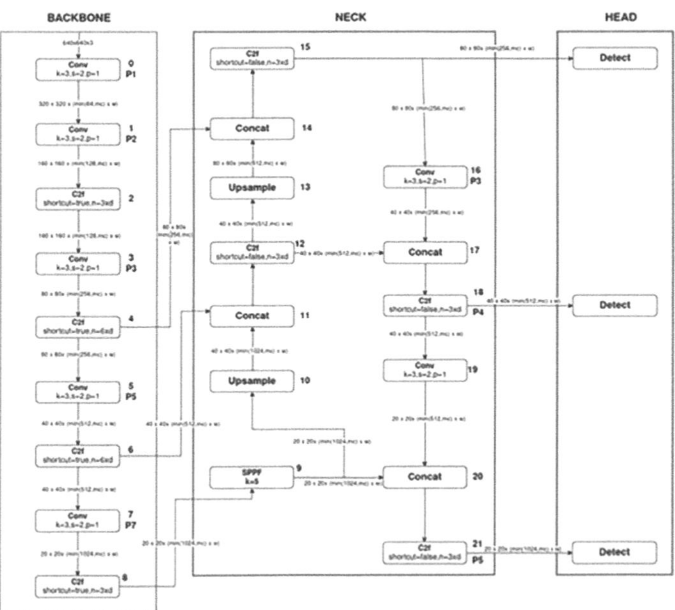

Fig. 3. YOLO v8 architecture

- **Backbone**: Based on CSPDarknet, it extracts visual features at multiple scales.
- **Neck**: Uses a Path Aggregation Network (PANet) to enhance feature representation.
- **Head**: Produces the final predictions in the form of bounding boxes and class probabilities [15].

Table 1 presents the set of indicators employed in this study and outlines 20 classes used to evaluate the quality of public spaces in Tunisia, each designed to capture distinct visual and functional characteristics that align with the study's goal of providing an objective and scalable urban quality assessment. These classes are systematically categorized under the Environmental, Social, and Economic Indices of the Sustainable Development Index (SDI). However, certain data detected by the model, such as License Plates, are not incorporated into the SDI model due to limitations in Google Street View imagery, where such information is blurred for privacy reasons, highlighting a constraint in fully leveraging all detected elements for the sustainability analysis.

The 20 classes were selected based on their relevance to urban sustainability in Tunisia, informed by global urban design principles [4, 10] and local challenges (e.g., waste management, rapid urbanization [1]). Classes like trees and pedestrians reflect environmental and social priorities, while banks and supermarkets indicate economic vitality. Selection was validated through alignment with Hickel's [13] sustainability framework, though future iterations could incorporate stakeholder input.

Table 1. Classification of visual elements for assessing public space quality in tunisia using SDI and EII frameworks

Class	Dimension	Explanation	
Trees (T)	Environmental	Indicates greenery and air quality; boosts Environmental Index (I_{env}) for sustainability	[11, 35]
Sky (Sk)	Environmental	Assesses air pollution via appearance; used in Ecological Impact Index (EII) for air quality	[22]
Road (R)	Environmental	Reflects infrastructure condition; contributes to I_{env} for accessibility	[8, 35]
Potholes (P)	Environmental	Signals poor maintenance; negatively impacts EII as an environmental stressor	[8]
Empty Trash Bins (ETB)	Environmental	Shows effective waste management; enhances I_{env} and Waste Management Indicator	[6]
Full Trash Bins (FTB)	Environmental	Indicates waste management issues; increases EII, lowering urban quality	[6]
Pedestrians (Pe)	Environmental	Promotes sustainable mobility; boosts I_{env} (assumed class based on context)	[16]
Camera (C)	Social	Proxy for safety and surveillance; contributes to Social Index (I_{soc}) for secure public spaces	[17]

(*continued*)

Table 1. *(continued)*

Class	Dimension	Explanation	
Public Lighting (PL)	Social	Enhances safety and usability; improves I_{soc} for community well-being	[8]
License Plate (LP)	Social	Aids vehicle identification; indirectly informs social patterns (e.g., traffic density)	
Banks (Bk)	Economic	Reflects financial activity; boosts Economic Index (I_{eco}) for urban vitality	[9]
Post Office (PO)	Economic	Indicates service access; enhances I_{eco} for economic infrastructure	[30]
Houses (H)	Social	Shows residential presence; contributes to I_{soc} for community cohesion	[31]
Buildings (Bd)	Social	Reflects urban density; improves I_{soc} for livability assessment	[35]
Supermarkets (SM)	Economic	Signals commercial health; boosts I_{eco} for economic opportunity	[14]
Car	Economic	Indicates mobility/prosperity (I_{eco}) but raises EII as a polluting vehicle	[35]
Bus (B)	Economic/Environmental	Enhances public transport (I_{eco}) and sustainability (I_{env})	[35]
Truck (Tk)	Economic/Environmental	Reflects logistics/trade (I_{eco}) but increases EII due to emissions	[27]
Motorcycle (M)	Economic/Environmental	Shows personal mobility (I_{eco}) but contributes to EII as a polluting vehicle	[5]
Bicycle (Bc)	Economic/Environmental	Promotes sustainable transport; boosts I_{eco} and I_{env}	[26]

(continued)

Table 1. (*continued*)

Class	Dimension	Explanation	
Polluted Sky (PS)	Environmental	Indicates poor air quality through visible haze or discoloration; negatively impacts EII by signaling higher pollution levels	[25]
Unpolluted Sky (UPS)	Environmental	Reflects clear air and good environmental conditions; enhances the I_{env}	[25]

Table 2 presents the different classes previously outlined in Table 1. These classes are subsequently used as qualitative inputs in the calculation of the Overall Quality Index.

Some governorates provide very limited data, which may affect the reliability of regional assessments. For instance, Manouba (e.g., only 140 trees and 48 images) and Gabes (318 trees and low counts across several categories such as 8 Empty Trash Bins (ETB) and 3 Camera) are among the governorates with the lowest data volumes. Similarly, certain classes—such as Banks (Bk) and Camera (C)—are severely underrepresented across several regions.

To mitigate this limitation, a logarithmic function was applied in the computation of the Ecological Impact Index. This approach helps reduce the impact of extreme variations and ensures a more balanced representation of underreported areas and features.

Table 2. Quantification of qualitative inputs integrated into the overall Quality Index

Governorate	A	BA	B	G	K	Mah	Man	Med	Mon	N	Sf	S	T
Images	600	300	150	90	90	150	48	300	390	300	360	300	900
T	7349	2525	1375	318	465	1387	140	1932	3128	2435	2859	2634	7994
UPS	977	383	222	130	119	216	67	446	600	375	507	395	1359
PS	30	21	11	12	7	8	12	27	17	35	24	42	63
R	600	300	150	90	90	150	48	300	390	300	360	300	900
P	253	245	165	51	69	112	8	164	260	166	277	194	441
ETB	39	30	13	8	8	13	3	16	22	21	22	23	48
FTB	23	17	8	4	6	8	2	10	17	14	20	14	34
H	686	335	169	130	101	162	51	294	441	418	413	445	912
C	19	12	6	3	3	4	1	13	15	11	13	11	47
PL	575	224	123	65	96	145	25	228	282	236	240	239	961
Bk	21	8	4	2	3	3	2	11	13	10	12	8	32
PO	6	3	2	1	1	2	2	3	5	3	3	3	10

(*continued*)

Table 2. *(continued)*

Governorate	A	BA	B	G	K	Mah	Man	Med	Mon	N	Sf	S	T
SM	10	4	3	2	1	3	1	4	6	4	6	5	21
Car	882	431	232	122	84	141	15	442	654	417	418	392	1325
B	28	16	7	1	1	5	1	6	19	17	18	16	38
Tk	13	8	4	1	1	4	2	9	10	8	10	9	19
M	19	13	6	3	3	6	2	16	20	12	16	15	38
Bc	15	8	4	3	3	2	1	10	13	8	13	9	21

Note Ariana (A), Ben Arous (BA), Bizerte (B), Gabes (G), Kairouan (K), Mahdia (Mah), Manouba (Man), Medenine (Med), Monastir (Mon), Nabeul (N), Sfax (Sf), Sousse (S), Tunis (T)

Training Configuration. The training was carried out on Google Colab using a Tesla T4 GPU and the Ultralytics YOLO library. Table 3 presents the following key parameters:

Table 3. Model training parameters

Parameters	
Learning rate	0.01 (dynamically adjusted)
Batch size	64 images
Number of epochs	270
Optimizer	AdamW

The model was initialized with pre-trained weights from the COCO dataset to accelerate convergence through transfer learning [2]. This configuration optimizes model performance while accounting for computational constraints, as recommended in the literature on deep neural network training [12]. To ensure good generalization of the model, the dataset was split as follows: 70% for training, 20% for validation and 10% for testing our model.

2.4 Quantifying Urban Quality Based on Object Detection

Assessment indices for urban sustainability, such as the Arcadis Sustainable Cities Index, IMD Smart City Index, Siemens Green City Index, UN-Habitat City Prosperity Index (CPI), and the African Green City Index, are developed by internationally recognized institutions (e.g., Arcadis, IMD, UN-Habitat). These indices rely on transparent and robust methodologies, typically using official statistical records, quantitative municipal data, and other verified sources.

However, these indices tend to focus primarily on cities in developed countries, with very limited coverage of cities in developing nations, largely due to data availability constraints. This is particularly true for Tunisia, whose cities are not represented in any of these global indices.

This gap underscores the importance of the index proposed in this research, which is built on open-source data and tailored to local contexts. While the accuracy of this custom index still needs to be benchmarked against established indices or validated datasets, such verification falls outside the scope of this exploratory work.

To quantify the quality of urban areas based on object detection results, we adapted the Sustainable Development Index (SDI) model from Hickel [13]. This model combines dimensions of human development and ecological efficiency, incorporating a penalization mechanism for negative environmental impacts in line with the principles of strong sustainability [23]. In our adaptation, the visual criteria extracted from images are organized into three main dimensions:

- **Environmental**: Trees, polluted versus non-polluted sky, empty versus full waste bins, and roads, Buses and Bicycles versus the other vehicules.
- **Social**: Houses, apartment buildings, observed human presence (e.g., cameras as lack of security feeling indicator), and public lighting.
- **Economic**: Banks, post offices, supermarkets, vehicles, and public transport.

Qualitative inputs, such as the presence of trees or public lighting, are quantified through object detection by YOLO v8, which counts occurrences in geolocated images. These counts are normalized using Min-Max scaling to ensure comparability across diverse urban features [29]. Each class's qualitative significance (e.g., trees indicating greenery, cameras reflecting safety) is predefined based on urban sustainability literature [4, 10] and categorized into environmental, social, or economic dimensions (Table 1). Equal weighting is applied to aggregate indicators within each dimension, assuming balanced contributions to sustainability, though sensitivity analysis could explore alternative weightings [28]. An Ecological Impact Index (EII) is introduced to quantify the negative environmental footprint of a location (e.g., pollution, potholes).

Step 1. Calculation of the Three Dimension Indices

For each dimension, raw counts of visual objects are first normalized using Min–Max scaling so that all criteria are comparable:

$$c_*^n = \frac{c_* - \min(c_*)}{\max(c_*) - \min(c_*)} \tag{1}$$

Environmental Index (I_{Env}). The environmental indicator is calculated as follows:

$$I_{Env} = \max(0, \frac{1}{13}\left(c_{\mathrm{T}}^n + c_{\mathrm{UPS}}^n + c_{\mathrm{R}}^n + c_{\mathrm{ETB}}^n + c_{Pe}^n + c_{\mathrm{B}}^n + c_{Bc}^n\right) - \left(c_{\mathrm{PS}}^n + c_P^n + c_{\mathrm{FTB}}^n + c_{\mathrm{Car}}^n + c_{\mathrm{Tk}}^n + c_M^n\right) \tag{2}$$

Social Index ($\mathrm{I_{Soc}}$). Using five normalized social criteria—houses, apartment buildings, p *edestrians* (or human presence), public lighting, and cameras—we define:

$$I_{Soc} = \frac{1}{5}\left(c_{\mathrm{H}}^n + c_{\mathrm{Bd}}^n + c_{Pe}^n + c_{\mathrm{PL}}^n + c_{\mathrm{C}}^n\right) \tag{3}$$

Economic Index ($\mathrm{I_{Eco}}$). Based on eight normalized economic indicators—banks, post offices, supermarkets, cars, trucks, motorcycles, buses, and bicycles—the economic index is given by:

$$I_{Eco} = \frac{1}{8}\left(c_{\mathrm{Bk}}^n + c_{\mathrm{PO}}^n + c_{\mathrm{SM}}^n + c_{\mathrm{Car}}^n + c_{\mathrm{Tk}}^n + c_{\mathrm{M}}^n + c_{\mathrm{B}}^n + c_{\mathrm{Bc}}^n\right) \tag{4}$$

Step 2. Composite Sustainable Development Index (SDI)

The overall SDI is computed by geometrically aggregating the three sub-indices—environmental, social, and economic—assuming equal weighting to reflect balanced contributions from each dimension, in line with Hickel's [13] vision of balanced sustainability. The use of the geometric mean ensures that poor performance in any one dimension significantly lowers the overall index, thereby promoting the principles of strong sustainability [23]. Specifically, we define:

$$SDI = \sqrt[3]{I_{Env} \times I_{Soc} \times I_{Eco}} \tag{5}$$

This formulation ensures that a poor performance in any one dimension strongly affects the composite index, thereby promoting balance across the three dimensions.

Step 3. Ecological Impact Index (EII)

To capture negative environmental impacts, we derive several environmental stress indicators from object detection. The three environmental indicators are computed using a standardized framework:

- A ratio quantifying the presence of an environmental stressor relative to the total relevant observations.
- A logarithmic weighting factor defined as, where represents the total count of relevant objects. This adjustment prevents disproportionate influence from governorates with a high number of images while ensuring consistency in regions with fewer observations.

Waste Management Indicator (WM). This indicator evaluates the efficiency of waste collection systems. It is calculated as:

$$WM = \left(\frac{FTB}{FTB + ETB}\right) \times \ln((FTB + ETB) + 1) \tag{6}$$

This indicator reflects the adequacy of waste management practices. A higher value indicates a greater proportion of full bins, suggesting insufficient waste collection frequency or inadequate bin capacity. Such conditions may result in overflow, littering, and subsequent environmental degradation.

Air Pollution Indicator (AP). This indicator quantifies the prevalence of air pollution based on sky imagery. is assessed through:

$$AP = \left(\frac{PS}{PS + UPS}\right) \times \ln(PS + UPS + 1) \tag{7}$$

A higher value of this indicator signifies an increased frequency of air pollution, potentially linked to elevated levels of particulate matter or other airborne pollutants. It serves as an indirect measure of air quality.

Greenhouse Gas emissions from transportation Indicator (GG). This indicator assesses the reliance on polluting vehicles (cars, trucks, motorcycles) relative to sustainable transport options (buses, bicycles, pedestrians):

$$GG = \left(\frac{Car + Tk + M}{Car + Tk + M + B + Bc + Pe}\right) \times ln(Car + Tk + M + B + Bc + Pe + 1) \tag{8}$$

A higher value indicates a greater dependence on polluting vehicles, which is associated with increased emissions of greenhouse gases and air pollutants. This indicator provides insight into mobility patterns and their environmental consequences.

The three environmental indicators—waste mismanagement (WM), air pollution (AP), and lack of green cover (GG)—are aggregated using a geometric mean to compute the composite environmental stress index known as Average Overshoot (AO), ensuring a balanced representation of each stressor. To address potential biases from varying image counts, logarithmic weighting is applied, in accordance with established environmental indexing practices [13]. While alternative approaches such as the Analytic Hierarchy Process (AHP) were considered [28], they were deemed too resource-intensive for this exploratory study. Thus, AO is calculated as follows:

$$AO = \sqrt[3]{\mathrm{WM} \times \mathrm{AP} \times \mathrm{GG}} \tag{9}$$

Finally, the Ecological Impact Index (EII) is determined using an exponential scaling function, EII = f(AO), which amplifies high levels of ecological stress in line with the planetary boundaries framework [23]:

$$EII = \begin{cases} 1 + \frac{e^{CESI} - e^{1}}{e^{4} - e^{1}} & if\ AO \leq 4, \\ AO - 2 & if\ AO > 4. \end{cases} \quad (10)$$

Step 4. Quality Index (QI)

This study adopts a Multi-Criteria Decision Analysis (MCDA) framework to develop a Quality Index (QI) that integrates environmental, social, and economic criteria, leveraging AI-driven data detection [21, 28]. The QI is designed to penalize ecological overshoots, ensuring that sustainability does not compromise environmental health.

The methodology combines positive sustainable development factors, captured by the SDI, with negative ecological impacts, measured by the EII, to yield an overall Quality Index. Specifically, the overall Quality Index is computed by penalizing the SDI with the EII:

$$QI = \frac{SDI}{EII} \quad (11)$$

A higher QI value indicates that sustainable development factors (SDI) outweigh negative ecological impacts (EII), reflecting a superior quality of urban sustainability.

3 Results and Discussion

This section presents the results obtained, focusing on two key aspects: the validation of the YOLO v8 model for object detection in geolocated images, and the interpretation of the outcomes derived from applying the SDI model to assess the quality of public spaces in Tunisia.

The approach by Zhu et al. [35] shares similarities with the one developed in this study, particularly in the use of images such as those from Google Street View and visual indicators as objective measures. In this research, these indicators were used to calculate the SDI and EII. However, the two methods differ in how visual elements are detected: Zhu et al. use image segmentation to estimate the proportion of pixels occupied by each object, whereas this study adopts YOLO v8 for its speed and effectiveness in identifying visual classes. This allows for assessing the relative importance of objects based on their frequency of occurrence (see Table 2), providing a complementary perspective as detailed in Table 1.

3.1 Evaluation of YOLO V8 Model Performance

Overall Performance (mAP@0.5)**.** According to Fig. 4, the YOLO v8 model demonstrates remarkable performance for several specific classes. The classes “Car” (0.993), and “Trash empty” (0.964) stand out with exceptional precision, nearing perfection.

Even for lower-performing classes such as "Pothole" (0.652), "Road" (0.666), and "Post office" (0.693), the results remain acceptable, with a minimum precision of 0.652, which is still satisfactory.

Moreover, the model's average precision, calculated at an Intersection over Union (IoU) threshold of 0.5 (mAP@0.5), 0.84. These results illustrate the model's ability to maintain high-quality detection across a wide range of classes, with particularly outstanding performance for the most distinctive objects.

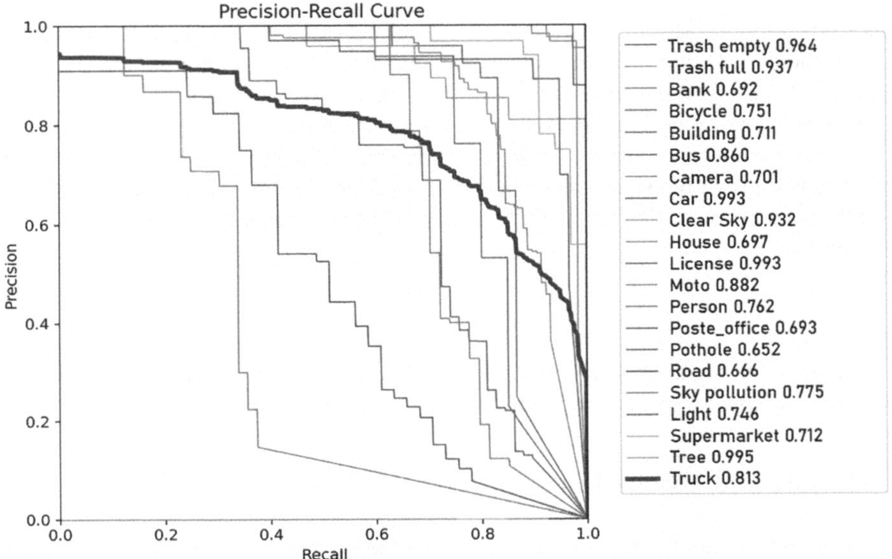

Fig. 4. Precision-recall curve for YOLOv8 model evaluation

Class-wise Error Analysis. According to Fig. 5, the YOLO v8 model particularly excels in detecting the classes "Car" (0.993 with 490 correct predictions), as well as "Trash empty" (0.964 with 514 correct predictions), demonstrating a high ability to accurately identify these objects. Classes such as "Pothole" (0.652), "Road" (0.666), and "Post office" (0.693) show slightly lower but stable performance, suggesting reliable detection even for potentially more complex objects. These results highlight the model's strength in well-defined classes while also indicating potential areas for improvement in less performant cases.

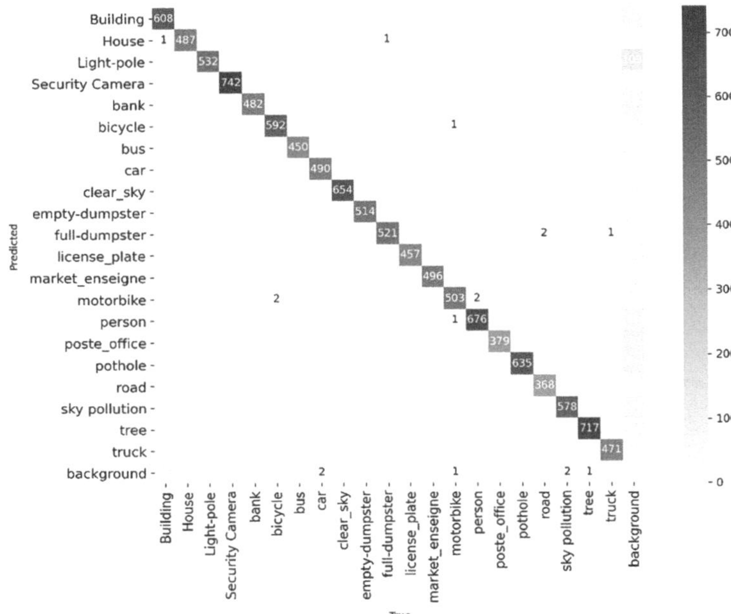

Fig. 5. Confusion matrix

Training Stability. The loss curves (Fig. 6) show satisfactory convergence for both training and validation phases. During training, the Box Loss decreases toward 0.1, the Cls (Classification) Loss reaches approximately 0.1, and the DFL (Distribution Focal Loss) stabilizes around 0.2, indicating effective learning. In validation, the losses remain slightly higher but stable (Box Loss ≈ 0.1, Cls Loss ≈ 0.1, DFL Loss ≈ 0.2), confirming good generalization without significant overfitting.

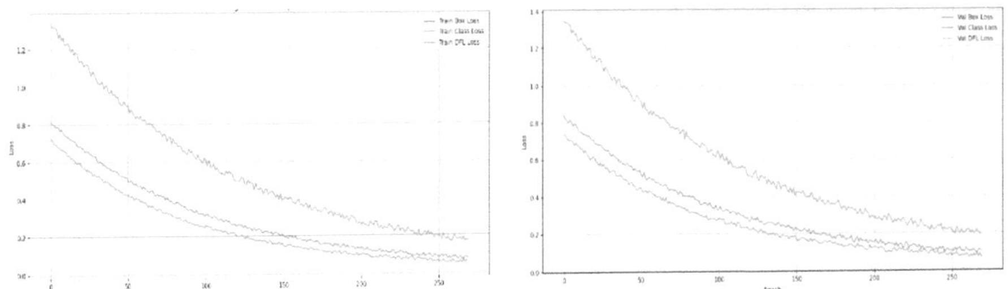

Fig. 6. Loss curves

Confidence Threshold Optimization. The F1-Confidence curve reveals an overall F1 score of 0.743 at a confidence threshold of 0.547, balancing precision and recall. Top performers like Trash empty (F1 $\approx$ 0.9) and Trash full (F1 $\approx$ 0.9) excel at moderate thresholds. In contrast, Road (AP = 0.666 and F1 < 0.5), and Bank (AP = 0.692 and F1 < 0.5) underperform, with Road's F1-score reflecting a precision drop after low recall, and Bank's F1 starting below 0.5 and declining rapidly due to low precision with increasing recall. Above a 0.7 threshold, the F1 score drops sharply, underscoring the need for threshold optimization to improve performance (Fig. 7).

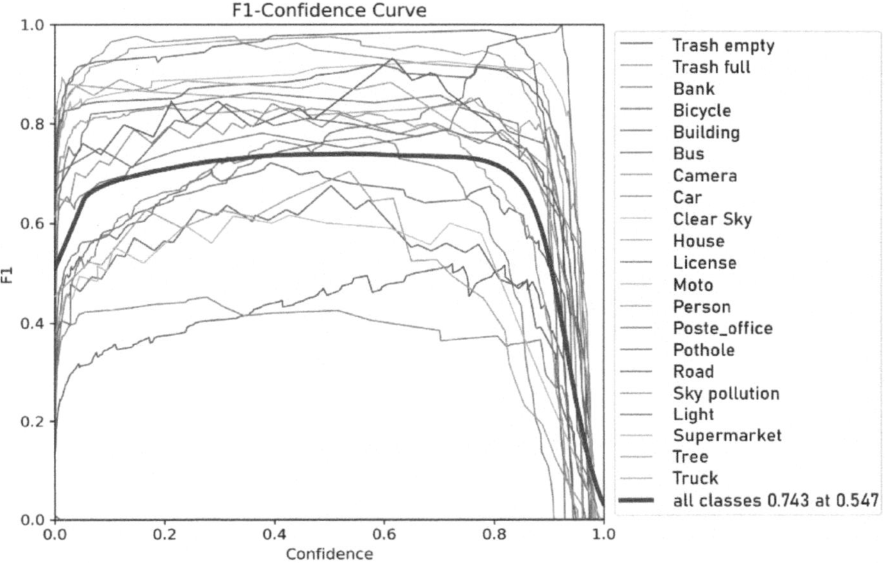

Fig. 7. F1-confidence curve

3.2 Urban Quality Index Model Results

Regional Disparities and Key Trends. Our analysis reveals significant regional disparities in sustainable development quality across Tunisian governorates, measured by the Quality Index (QI), calculated as the Sustainable Development Index (SDI) divided by the Ecological Impact Index (EII). This integrates environmental, social, and economic dimensions while addressing ecological pressures. As depicted in Fig. 8, Ariana leads with a QI of 0.4187, supported by an adequate SDI compared to others (environmental: 0.2611, social: 0.5645, economic: 0.4604; see Fig. 10), reflecting effective governance and resource allocation. Tunis follows with a QI of 0.3588, bolstered by strong social (0.6446) and economic (0.5735) indices but hindered by a low environmental score (0.1190) and elevated EII (0.9839). In contrast, Manouba and Medenine score a QI of 0, as their null environmental SDI (0) negates moderate social (0.2471; 0.3847) and economic (0.6; 0.5679) performances, highlighting severe environmental shortcomings.

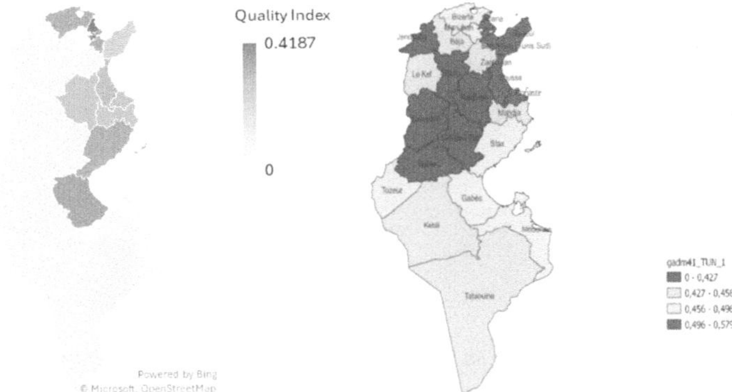

Fig. 8. Urban quality index across the studied governorates versus regional development index calculated by ITCEQ in 2021

Moreover, Fig. 8 presents also the Regional Development Index (RDI) from the Tunisian Institute of Competitiveness and Quantitative Studies (ITCEQ). The QI and the RDI offer two complementary perspectives on Tunisian territorial development. The QI, leveraging artificial intelligence on Google Street View images (2016–2021), evaluates urban sustainability with exceptional micro-level precision, capable of detecting even potholes to capture the real state of public spaces - cleanliness, visible infrastructure, ecological degradation. Conversely, the RDI adopts a macro approach based on classical 2021 statistics (infrastructure, health, employment, education), providing a global vision of regional development but often disconnected from daily urban realities. These methodological divergences generate contrasting results. While northern coastal governorates like Tunis and Ariana generally excel in both indices, others reveal significant gaps. Sfax perfectly illustrates this dichotomy: economically performing according to the RDI, it may display a degraded USI due to visible ecological pressures, demonstrating that macro development does not guarantee micro-urban sustainability. The QI excels in detecting concrete and localized problems - sidewalk conditions, presence of greenery - but remains limited to visual aspects, ignoring intangible factors like general public policies. The RDI offers a robust overview, ideal for regional policies, but its generality makes it less sensitive to daily urban nuances. This complementarity represents a strategic opportunity for decision-makers. The QI guides targeted local interventions (waste management, infrastructure repair), while the RDI orients long-term strategic choices (health networks, major projects). Their combination enables the development of balanced strategies, combining macroeconomic vision with micro-urban attention for development that is both sustainable and inclusive.

Figure 9 further elucidates the components of sustainable development and ecological impact. In this figure, the SDI is broken down into its three constituent maps, which represent the environmental (I_{env}), social ($\mathrm{I}_{\mathrm{soc}}$), and economic ($\mathrm{I}_{\mathrm{eco}}$) indices. The maps reveal that while Ariana and Tunis perform strongly across these dimensions, governorates like Medenine and Mahdia lag considerably, mainly on the environmental front.

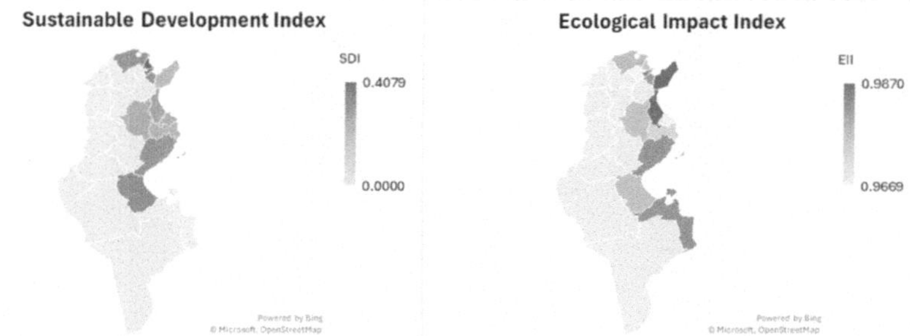

Fig. 9. Spatial distribution of sustainable development and ecological impact indices

Indeed, as we have seen, the SDI itself is computed as the cube root of the product of the environmental, social, and economic sub-indices, ensuring that deficits in any one dimension adversely affect the overall index. As illustrated in Fig. 10, Tunis exhibits strong social (0.6446) and economic (0.5735) indices, but its low environmental score (0.1190) results in an SDI of 0.3530. Paired with a high Ecological Impact Index (EII) of 0.9839, this produces a Quality Index (QI) of 0.3588, indicating that robust socio-economic performance cannot fully offset environmental weaknesses. Likewise, Manouba boasts a higher economic index (0.60) than Tunis, but its null environmental index leads to an SDI of 0, yielding a QI of 0. This highlights how severe environmental shortcomings can negate overall urban quality despite economic strengths.

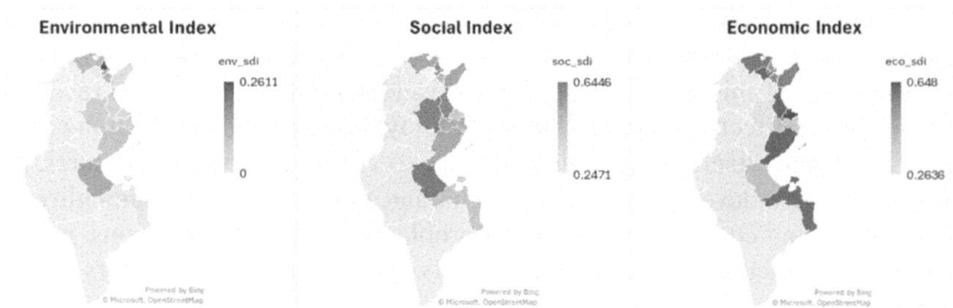

Fig. 10. Breakdown of SDI by environmental, social, and economic components

Effect of Ecological Impact Index on Urban Quality Index. Figure 11 presents the decomposition of the EII, which combines three key environmental pressure indicators: WM, AP, and GG emissions. The analysis reveals stark contrasts between governorates, with Sousse (EII = 0.9865) and Nabeul (EII = 0.9869) exhibiting the highest ecological stress due to elevated waste generation (1.38 and 1.43 respectively), significant air pollution (0.58 and 0.51), and substantial transport-related emissions (3.03 and 3.39). These factors contribute to their lower QI values (0.2143 and 0.1576), despite moderate SDI performance (0.2114 and 0.1555). Manouba (EII = 0.9669) and Mahdia (EII = 0.9709) demonstrate lower environmental pressures, with reduced waste (0.72 in Manouba) and pollution (0.19 in Mahdia), yet their QI values (0 and 0.1801) are constrained by critically low environmental SDI scores (0 and 0.0346). The inverse relationship between EII and QI is further exemplified by Sfax: despite its strong economic performance (SDI economic component = 0.5851), its high EII (0.9790), driven by high waste (1.79) and transport emissions (2.91), results in a diminished QI (0. 2539). Conversely, Gabes (EII = 0.9741) benefits from lower waste (0.85) and transport density (2.49), supporting a higher QI (0.2871). This inverse relationship between EII and QI underscores a critical trade-off: regions exceeding environmental thresholds, like Sousse and Nabeul, see diminished urban quality, while balanced ecological management, as in Gabes, enhances overall sustainability.

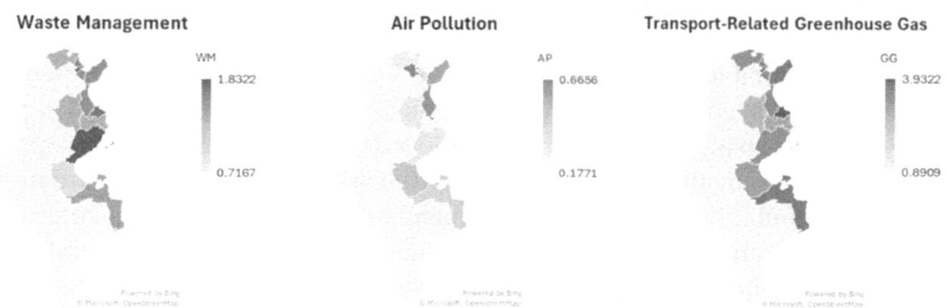

Fig. 11. Magnitude of key environmental pressures: waste, air pollution, and GG emissions

In brief, the results demonstrate significant regional disparities in sustainable development among Tunisian governorates. Areas such as Ariana and Tunis, which display balanced performance across environmental, social, and economic dimensions, achieve higher overall quality. In contrast, regions like Medenine and Manouba exhibit lower QI values, primarily due to their extremely low environmental scores in the SDI, despite relatively low ecological pressure (low EII). These findings highlight the urgent need for targeted interventions to strengthen environmental sustainability, in line with the sustainability framework proposed by Hickel [13].

Implications for Policy. The findings have important implications for sustainable development policies:

- Governorates with high EII values (e.g., Sousse, Nabeul, and Tunis) exhibit ecological overshoots that diminish their overall quality, highlighting the need for targeted interventions—such as improved waste management, enhanced air quality measures, and the promotion of sustainable transport—to mitigate environmental stress.
- Although Ariana has the highest Quality Index among all regions, its score is still under 0.5. This means that even the best-performing governorate has significant room for improvement, and its integrated approach—balancing environmental, social, and economic measures—should be strengthened and adapted elsewhere.

- The weak correlation observed between economic performance and environmental impact in some regions (e.g., Sfax) indicates that it is feasible to pursue economic growth without proportionally increasing ecological stress, an avenue that policymakers should explore.

In summary, this analysis reveals significant regional disparities in sustainable development across Tunisian governorates. The results demonstrate that ecological stress, as quantified by the EII, can significantly reduce the overall Quality Index even in regions with strong economic or social performance. These findings emphasize the need for holistic and locally tailored sustainable development policies to enhance urban quality while respecting ecological limits.

Although numerous projects in Tunisia aim to promote urban sustainability, their ambitious goals face structural and geographical challenges. For instance, initiatives such as the Sustainable MED Cities project in Sousse, which emphasizes participatory planning and green governance, or the Femmedina project in Tunis, which promotes gender-sensitive urban planning, have introduced innovative participatory approaches, still relatively new in the design of urban projects in Tunisia. These initiatives have enabled the formulation of relevant recommendations for specific local contexts. However, their scope remains geographically limited, and their lack of generalizability to other Tunisian territories restricts their impact on a national scale.

Furthermore, experience shows that projects aimed at enhancing urban sustainability through digital tools encounter significant obstacles, particularly due to the absence of solutions tailored to real needs. For example, the SIG WEB PAU - Urban Development Plans platform, developed under the supervision of the Ministry of Equipment, Housing, and Spatial Planning (Directorate of Urban Planning), provides Urban Development Plans (PAUs) in the form of scanned, non-interactive documents. These documents offer no detailed information on the regulations applicable to each zone, despite this being a cornerstone of a PAU, whose primary role is to clarify the regulatory use of different zones within a city. Moreover, the platform does not cover all PAUs in Tunisia, and those available are not systematically up to date. It also fails to specify the validity date of each PAU, its status (in effect or obsolete), or its regulatory evolution, depriving users of a historical perspective essential for analyzing changes in zoning regulations.

Another telling example is the digital map of state-owned land, managed by the Ministry of State Domains and Land Affairs. This platform, although designed to map state-owned land, suffers from notable slowness and a lack of precision in the information provided. During a consultation on May 13, 2025, critical data, such as the visualization of various public domains (maritime public domain, hydraulic public domain, road public domain, etc.), were absent. Additionally, the platform does not provide update dates for the data or a comparative analysis of the evolution of land status, significantly limiting its utility for decision-makers and stakeholders.

These examples underscore the need to strengthen research and collaboration with municipalities and local stakeholders to develop more concrete and actionable recommendations. By building on local initiatives while developing more robust and comprehensive digital tools, it will be possible to design truly effective urban sustainability strategies in Tunisia. Our urban sustainability index could thus become a reference tool for policymakers, provided it is grounded in practical applications and reliable data.

4 Conclusion

This study proposes an innovative method to evaluate the quality of public spaces in Tunisia, combining computer vision, artificial intelligence, and sustainable development principles. By leveraging Google Street View images and a tailored YOLO v8 model, it provides an objective and large-scale analysis of urban areas, overcoming the subjectivity and limited scope of traditional approaches. The methodology incorporates an adapted Sustainable Development Index (SDI) and Ecological Impact Index (EII), enabling a comprehensive assessment of environmental, social, and economic factors while addressing ecological pressures.

The analysis reveals significant regional disparities in Tunisia. Governorates like Ariana and Tunis demonstrate a relative balance in sustainability, though Tunis is hindered by environmental challenges. Conversely, regions like Medenine suffer from severe ecological issues, exacerbated by waste and pollution, highlighting that socio-economic strengths are insufficient to offset environmental degradation. The YOLO v8 model has proven effective in detecting certain urban elements but requires improvement for more complex objects, confirming its potential for extensive urban studies while identifying areas for enhancement.

These findings offer policymakers actionable insights, targeting areas under high ecological pressure, such as Sousse and Nabeul, for urgent interventions in waste management and transportation. Ariana's success illustrates the benefits of integrated policies, while the method's adaptability opens possibilities for global application.

Covering the period from 2016 to 2021, the analysis provides valuable insights but remains limited in capturing long-term urban development dynamics. Integrating temporal data for comparative analysis over time is a key objective, requiring regular and consistent road network scans by local authorities. Future research aims to enhance the model by incorporating geospatial and remote sensing data, thereby improving its reliability and applicability, particularly in regions with scarce official data.

References

1. Ajmi, R., Belfekih Boussema, S., Essasi, S., Taïbi, A.N., Khebour Allouche, F.: A qualitative urban green spaces assessment for a sustainable management, case study of Sousse City (Tunisia). In: Ksibi, M., et al. (eds.) Recent Advances in Environmental Science from the Euro-Mediterranean and Surrounding Regions, 3rd edn, pp. 617–619. Springer Nature Switzerland (2024). https://doi.org/10.1007/978-3-031-43922-3_138
2. Bochkovskiy, A., Wang, C.-Y., Liao, H.-Y.M.: YOLOv4: optimal speed and accuracy of object detection (2020). arXiv:2004.10934. https://doi.org/10.48550/arXiv.2004.10934
3. Brenning, A., Henn, S.: Web scraping: a promising tool for geographic data acquisition (2023). arXiv:2305.19893. https://doi.org/10.48550/arXiv.2305.19893
4. Carmona, M.: Principles for public space design, planning to do better. Urban Des. Int. **24**(1), 47–59 (2019). https://doi.org/10.1057/s41289-018-0070-3

5. Cherry, C., Cervero, R.: Use characteristics and mode choice behavior of electric bike users in China. Transp. Policy **14**(3), 247–257 (2007). https://doi.org/10.1016/j.tranpol.2007.02.005
6. Environment, U.N.: Sustainable waste in cities | UNEP - UN Environment Programme (2024). https://www.unep.org/topics/cities/circular-economy-cities/sustainable-waste-cities
7. Ewing, R., Clemente, O., Neckerman, K.M., Purciel-Hill, M., Quinn, J.W., Rundle, A.: Measuring Urban Design. Island Press/Center for Resource Economics (2013)
8. Ferrer, A.L.C., Thomé, A.M.T., Scavarda, A.J.: Sustainable urban infrastructure: a review. Resour. Conserv. Recycl. **128**, 360–372 (2018). https://doi.org/10.1016/j.resconrec.2016.07.017
9. Fu, Y., Liu, L.: On the accessibility of financial services and income inequality: an international perspective. Technol. Econ. Dev. Econ. **29**(3), 814–845 (2023). https://doi.org/10.3846/tede.2023.18722
10. Gehl, J., Rogers, L.R.: Cities for People. Island Press (2010)
11. Grylls, T., van Reeuwijk, M.: How trees affect urban air quality: it depends on the source. Atmos. Environ. **290**, 119275 (2022). https://doi.org/10.1016/j.atmosenv.2022.119275
12. He, K., Zhang, X., Ren, S., Sun, J.: Deep residual learning for image recognition. arXiv:1512.03385 (2015). https://doi.org/10.48550/arXiv.1512.03385
13. Hickel, J.: The sustainable development index: measuring the ecological efficiency of human development in the anthropocene. Ecol. Econ. **167**, 106331 (2020)
14. Ji, Y., Wang, Z., Zhu, D.: Exploring the impact of urban amenities on business circle vitality using multi-source big data. Land **13**(10), 1616 (2024). https://doi.org/10.3390/land13101616
15. Jocher, G., Qiu, J., Chaurasia, A.: Ultralytics YOLO (Version 8.0.0) [Python] (2023). https://github.com/ultralytics/ultralytics. Last accessed 03 April 2025
16. Koo, B.W., Guhathakurta, S., Botchwey, N.: How are neighborhood and street-level walkability factors associated with walking behaviors? a big data approach using street view images. Environ. Behav. **54**(1), 211–241 (2022). https://doi.org/10.1177/00139165211014609
17. La Vigne, N.G., Lowry, S.S., Markman, J.A., Dwyer, A.M. (2011). Evaluating the Use of Public Surveillance Cameras for Crime Control and Prevention: (718202011–001) . https://doi.org/10.1037/e718202011-001
18. Liu, L., Silva, E.A., Wu, C., Wang, H.: A machine learning-based method for the large-scale evaluation of the qualities of the urban environment. Comput. Environ. Urban Syst. **65**, 113–125 (2017). https://doi.org/10.1016/j.compenvurbsys.2017.06.003
19. Liu, S., et al.: Grounding DINO: Marrying DINO with grounded pre-training for open-set object detection (2024). arXiv:2303.05499. https://doi.org/10.48550/arXiv.2303.05499
20. Marino, R., Vargas, E., Acevedo, I., Medina, M., Riveros, A.: Building climate-resilient communities through water-sensitive public space design and activation: public parks program in Bucaramanga, Colombia. In: Bailey, A., Otsuki, K. (eds.) Inclusive Cities and Global Urban Transformation: Infrastructures, Intersectionalities, and Sustainable Development, pp. 285–295. Springer Nature (2025). https://doi.org/10.1007/978-981-97-7521-7_26
21. Mori, K., Christodoulou, A.: Review of sustainability indices and indicators: towards a new City Sustainability Index (CSI). Environ. Impact Assess. Rev. **32**(1), 94–106 (2012). https://doi.org/10.1016/j.eiar.2011.06.001
22. Nathvani, R., Vishwanath, D., Clark, S.N., Alli, A.S., Muller, E., Coste, H., Bennett, J.E., Nimo, J.B., Moses, J.B., Baah, S., Hughes, A., Suel, E., Metzler, A.B., Rashid, T., Brauer, M., Baumgartner, J., Owusu, G., Agyei-Mensah, S., Arku, R.E., Ezzati, M.: Beyond here and now: evaluating pollution estimation across space and time from street view images with deep learning. Sci. Total Environ. **903**, 166168 (2023). https://doi.org/10.1016/j.scitotenv.2023.166168
23. O'Neill, D.W., Fanning, A.L., Lamb, W.F., Steinberger, J.K.: A good life for all within planetary boundaries. Nat. Sustain. **1**(2), 88–95 (2018)

24. Perera, W.S.D., Kulatunga, U., De Silva, M.C.K., Dias, N.: Revisiting the notion of 'public spaces': Professional and community perspectives. http://dl.lib.uom.lk/handle/123/22719. Last accessed 03 April 2025 (2024)
25. Pierce, J.R., et al.: Urban Nature Indexes tool offers comprehensive and flexible approach to monitoring urban ecological performance. Npj Urban Sustain. **4**(1), 1 (2024). https://doi.org/10.1038/s42949-024-00143-2
26. Pucher, J., Buehler, R.: Cycling towards a more sustainable transport future. Transp. Rev. **37**(6), 689–694 (2017). https://doi.org/10.1080/01441647.2017.1340234
27. Rodrigue, J.-P.: The Geography of Transport Systems, 6th edn. Routledge (2024). https://doi.org/10.4324/9781003343196
28. Saaty, T.L.: Decision Making for Leaders: The Analytic Hierarchy Process for Decisions in a Complex World, 3rd edn. 5. print. RWS Publ (2012)
29. Shorten, C., Khoshgoftaar, T.M.: A survey on Image data augmentation for deep learning. J. Big Data **6**(1), 60 (2019). https://doi.org/10.1186/s40537-019-0197-0
30. Sonea, A., Westerholt, R.: Geographic and temporal access to basic banking services offered through post offices in Wales. Appl. Spat. Anal. Policy **14**(4), 879–905 (2021). https://doi.org/10.1007/s12061-021-09386-3
31. Stoiljkovic, B.: Social cohesion and neighbor interactions within multifamily apartment buildings: challenges of COVID-19 and directions of action. Sustainability **14**(2), 738 (2022). https://doi.org/10.3390/su14020738
32. Tang, F., Zeng, P., Wang, L., Zhang, L., Xu, W.: Urban perception evaluation and street refinement governance supported by street view visual elements analysis. Remote Sens. **16**(19), 3661 (2024). https://doi.org/10.3390/rs16193661
33. UN-Habitat: World Cities Report 2020: The Value of Sustainable Urbanization (2020). https://unhabitat.org/world-cities-report-2020-the-value-of-sustainable-urbanization
34. Zhang, J.: Classification and comparison of data augmentation techniques. Trans. Comput. Sci. Intell. Syst. Res. **6**, 180–187 (2024)
35. Zhu, J., et al.: Assessing the effects of subjective and objective measures on housing prices with street view imagery: a case study of Suzhou. Land **12**(12), 2095 (2023). https://doi.org/10.3390/land12122095

Advanced Spatio-Temporal Modeling of Seagrass Meadows Through Machine Learning Techniques

Hamdi Braiek[1,2](✉), Nadim Nagati[1], Mayssa Trabelsi[1], Amir Ben Ayed[1], Nidhal Mezni[1], and Mohamed Amine Askri[1]

[1] ESPRIT School of Engineering, 18 rue de l'Usine Charguia II 2035, Ariana, Tunisia
hamdi.houichet@gmail.com,
{nadim.nagati,mayssa.trabelsi,amir.benayed,nidhal.mezni,
mohamed.askri}@esprit.tn

[2] Laboratory for Mathematical and Numerical Modeling in Engineering Science, National Engineering School at Tunis, University of Tunis El Manar, B.P. 37, 1002 Tunis-Belvédère, Tunisia

Abstract. Seagrass meadows are critical coastal ecosystems that provide invaluable services: carbon sequestration, habitat for marine biodiversity, and shoreline protection, but they are declining at alarming rates. Recent studies estimate arround 29% global loss of seagrass cover since the 1700s and project large carbon emissions if this loss continues. Conventional monitoring methods struggle to capture these complex dynamics, motivating data-driven approaches. In this work, we develop an integrated machine learning framework for spatio-temporal modeling of seagrass health and biomass. We apply iterative imputation to handle missing environmental data, and train both an XGBoost regressor and a stacked ensemble of ML models (Ridge, Random Forest, LGBM) on geospatial features. Model hyperparameters are tuned via the Tree-structured Parzen Estimator (TPE), a Bayesian optimization technique that efficiently explores the hyperparameters. Our results show that the optimized XGBoost model outperforms the ensemble across key seagrass metrics, achieving superior accuracy in predicting biomass and productivity. We identify the most influential environmental drivers such as light availability and water temperature through feature importance analysis, providing actionable ecological insights. This enhanced predictive framework, supported by a clear methodology flow, offers a robust tool for proactive seagrass conservation and decision-making.

Keywords: Seagrass ecosystems · XGBoost · Random forest · Iterative imputation · Marine biodiversity · Ecological monitoring

---

Hamdi Braiek—The author has legally changed their name from Hamdi Houichet to Hamdi Braiek.

F. Kamoun et al. (Eds.): AFRICATEK 2025, LNICST 677, pp. 216–234, 2026.
https://doi.org/10.1007/978-3-032-16638-8_15

1 Introduction

Seagrass meadows are often called the "lungs of the sea" for their outsized role in marine carbon sequestration and biodiversity support [1]. These submerged flowering plants occupy over 160,000 km^2 of coastal zones and store large amounts of organic carbon in sediments [2]. They provide nursery habitat for fisheries, stabilize shorelines, and sustain marine food webs [1]. However, mounting evidence indicates accelerated seagrass loss worldwide. Since the mid-1700s, global seagrass coverage has decreased by approximately 29%, equivalent to around 51,000 km^2 [2]. In the Mediterranean basin alone, the endemic *Posidonia oceanica* has lost an estimated 13–50% of its extent in recent decades [2].

These declines are driven by a range of anthropogenic stressors, including coastal development, pollution, eutrophication, and climate change impacts such as sea-level rise and marine heatwaves [1]. The loss of seagrass ecosystems has cascading effects on marine biodiversity, fisheries, and the global carbon cycle. Current estimates suggest that ongoing seagrass degradation may be releasing hundreds of teragrams of carbon per year back into the atmosphere [2]. These findings emphasize the urgent need for more effective monitoring systems and predictive tools to support seagrass conservation efforts.

Traditional monitoring approaches, including field surveys and remote sensing, offer valuable insights but often fall short in capturing the full spatial and temporal dynamics of seagrass ecosystems. Many datasets remain sparse, heterogeneous, and incomplete [3]. Although recent advances in satellite imagery, such as Sentinel-2, and computer vision techniques have improved large-scale seagrass mapping, significant gaps and biases still limit their effectiveness [2].

Machine learning (ML) offers a powerful alternative by identifying patterns from complex and diverse data sources, including light availability, water temperature, nutrient concentrations, and spatial context. Recent studies have demonstrated high accuracy in seagrass classification and biomass prediction using ML algorithms. Moreover, hybrid models that combine ensemble learning with metaheuristic optimization have shown promise in forecasting habitat suitability. Despite these advances, key challenges remain in handling noisy and missing data and in translating model predictions into actionable ecological insights.

In this study, we propose a systematic machine learning framework for modeling seagrass ecosystems. Our approach integrates several components: data preparation with robust imputation techniques for missing values; model training using both XGBoost regressors and stacked ensemble methods; hyperparameter tuning through Tree-structured Parzen Estimation (TPE); and comprehensive evaluation using predictive metrics such as coefficient of determination (R^2) and root mean square error (RMSE). Each stage of the pipeline is designed to enhance model accuracy, interpretability, and ecological relevance.

Through this integrated methodology, we aim to advance the use of machine learning in coastal ecosystem monitoring and provide a scalable, data-driven approach for supporting the conservation of these vital underwater landscapes.

2 Related Works

Recent years have seen a surge in machine learning and remote sensing approaches for seagrass mapping and ecological modeling. Sentinel-2 and Landsat imagery combined with ML classifiers have enabled broad-scale seagrass density estimation, such as using Random Forest on satellite spectral data, with promising accuracies [4,5]. In one study, Sentinel-2 data processed in Google Earth Engine and classified using Random Forest achieved approximately 87% accuracy for mapping Caribbean seagrass extent [5]. Other work has leveraged UAV-acquired images with deep convolutional neural networks, particularly U-Net architectures, to classify multiple seagrass species with high precision [6]. Hybrid modeling approaches are also emerging. A recent work, in [7], reviews numerous ML techniques applied to seagrass monitoring and highlights that ensemble methods often improve generalization and robustness.

Despite these advances, a comparative examination reveals several trade-offs. Deep CNNs can achieve fine-scale classification accuracy but require large labeled datasets and high computational resources [6]. Simpler models, such as linear regression, are easier to interpret but often underperform due to the non-linear nature of ecological data. Missing or sparse data continue to pose a major bottleneck. Many studies acknowledge the necessity of imputation or bias correction when working with incomplete global seagrass databases. The research gap this study addresses is the integration of robust data imputation with advanced ensemble learning models under a unified spatio-temporal framework.

3 Methodology

The dataset used in this study is publicly available from [8]. It contains 6,658 rows and 17 columns, capturing various attributes related to seagrass ecosystems. The dataset includes both numerical and categorical variables, covering aspects such as geospatial location, biological properties, productivity, and structural characteristics. However, some features have significant gaps, with certain columns missing up to 90% of their data. To address these missing values, imputation strategies will be employed, including methods such as filling based on averages, interpolation, or other statistical techniques.

Our architecture is designed to transform raw ecological data from the seagrass database file into actionable insights for seagrass conservation. Figure 1 provides an overview of our paper's architecture.

Our framework, illustrated in Fig. 2 proceeds through three main phases: Data Preparation, Modeling & Optimization, and Evaluation. The process is structured into several key phases, each contributing to the overall goal of understanding and predicting seagrass health, biomass, and productivity.

We start with data Summarization and Analysis to examine spatial and temporal trends, categorize the data by bioregion and genus, and investigate patterns in missing data. This phase allows us to identify gaps and inconsistencies in the dataset, providing a clearer understanding of the distribution and health of seagrass ecosystems across various regions and time periods.

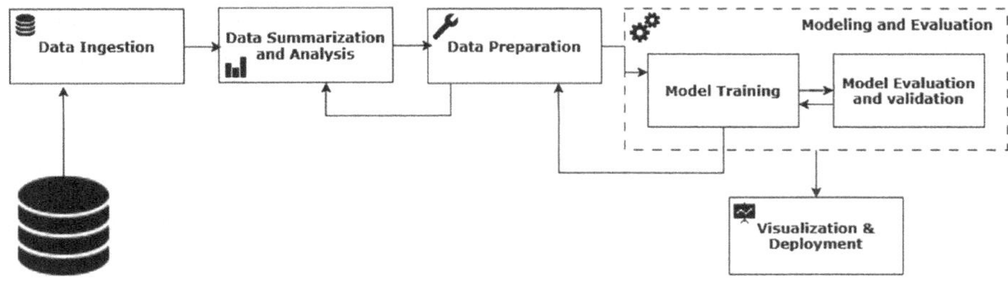

Fig. 1. An overview of our work's architecture

Once the data is summarized and analyzed, we proceed to the Preparation phase. Where we address the missing values, encode categorical variables, and standardize numerical features. In this step, duplicate rows are removed, and any inconsistent or incomplete data is cleaned and refined. To ensure quality, we standardize numeric features and apply one-hot encoding to categorical variables. Temporal and spatial coverage is explicitly handled (Sect. 4). Crucially, missing values are addressed using an iterative imputation method. The imputation iterates multiple passes over the data, refining the predicted values each round. We split the data into 70% training and 30% testing before imputation to prevent information leak, then impute missing values separately on each split. As shown in Sect. 6.1, this yields more realistic estimates than simple mean/median fill and leads to significant gains in predictive R^2.

For regression, we evaluate a stacked ensemble and a single model approach. The stacked model comprises three base learners: Ridge Regression, Random Forest Regressor, and LGMBRegressor. This stacking models captures diverse patterns while mitigating individual model biases. The XGBoost model is used as a strong baseline due to its robustness on tabular environmental data.

We tune model hyperparameters using the Tree-structured Parzen Estimator (TPE). In practice, TPE builds separate density estimates for the best-performing (good) and worst-performing (bad) hyperparameters and then samples from regions likely to improve performance. This sequential approach efficiently hones in optimal settings without exhaustive grid search. The objective function is the coefficient of determination R^2 on a cross-validation split, and we run the optimization for each target metric. The tuned hyperparameters are reported in Table 2.

Model performance is assessed on the held test set using relevant metrics. We compare the stacked ensemble versus XGBoost: in our experiments XGBoost consistently achieves higher R^2 on total biomass and density (see Sect. 6.2). We also examine the effect of iterative imputation by comparing scores across different numbers of imputation iterations (see Sect. 6.1). Feature importances are extracted from the models to interpret ecological drivers: for example, light attenuation and water temperature emerged as top predictors of biomass, aligning with established ecological knowledge. All methodological steps above are directly linked to the results: e.g., Table 1 reports how imputation reduced error compared to naive filling, and Table 2 shows the final tuned hyperparameters and resulting improvements.

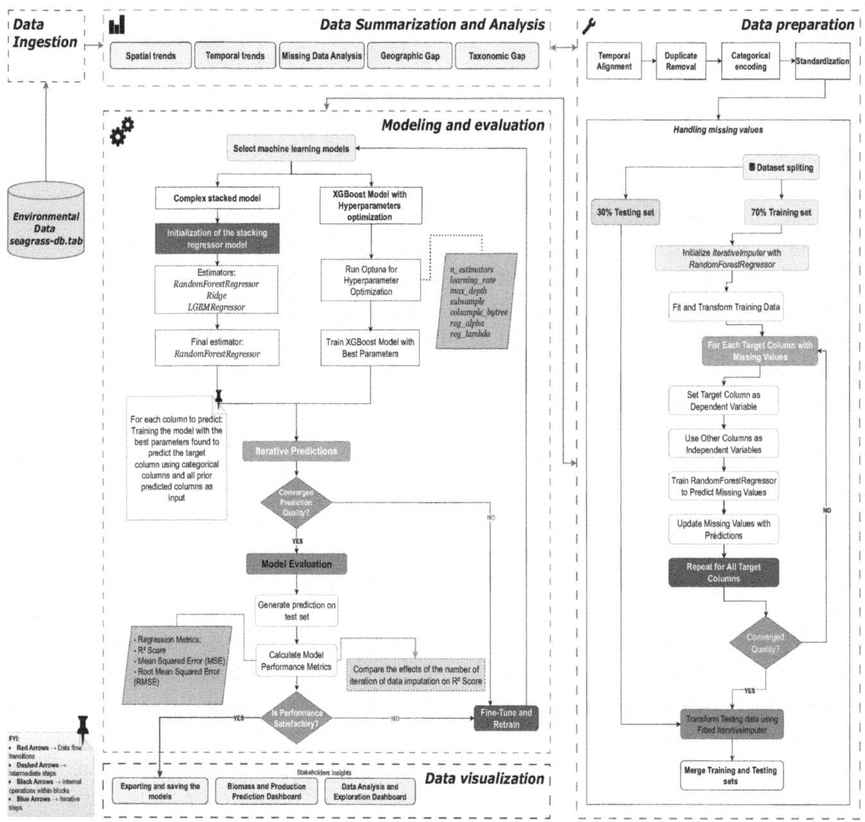

Fig. 2. A detailed breakdown of our data architecture

4 Data Summarization and Analysis

The aim of this section is to understand data limitations and ensure that subsequent modeling efforts are based on consistent and high-quality inputs. The main features of the dataset are summarized in the Table 1.

Table 1. Summary of key attributes in the dataset

Attribute	Type	Description
Latitude	Numerical	Location latitude
Longitude	Numerical	Location longitude
Bioregion	Categorical	Biogeographic classification
Habitat	Categorical	Seagrass environment type
Genus	Categorical	Seagrass genus classification
Year obs [a AD]	Numerical	Observation year
Seagr biom above [g/m^2]	Numerical	Above-ground dry biomass
Seagr biom below [g/m^2]	Numerical	Below-ground dry biomass
Seagr biom tot [g/m^2]	Numerical	Total dry biomass
Seagr shoot dens [#/m^2]	Numerical	Shoot density per m^2
Seagr cov [%]	Numerical	Percentage of area covered
Seagr leaf dens [#/m^2]	Numerical	Leaf density per m^2
Seagr prod above [g/m^2/day]	Numerical	Above-ground daily production
Seagr prod below [g/m^2/day]	Numerical	Below-ground daily production
Seagr prod total [g/m^2/day]	Numerical	Total daily biomass production
Seagr shoot prod [g/m^2/day]	Numerical	Daily shoot biomass production
Seagr leaf prod [g/m^2/day]	Numerical	Daily leaf biomass production

4.1 Data Summarization

The dataset shows significant heterogeneity, with some columns missing between 70% and 90% of their data like *Seagr leaf dens*, *Seagr prod below dm* and *Seagr shoot prod dm*. In Fig. 3, we show the distribution of missing values across all columns in the dataset. Darker shades indicate a higher percentage of missing data. This heatmap illustrates that the majority of missing values are concentrated in the biological and environmental sections of our dataset, with the highest concentration in the production section.

We also show, in Fig. 4, a bar plot the average proportion of missing data across different bioregions. We observe that the *Temperate Southern* region has the highest proportion of missing data, while the *Temperate North Atlantic* and *Temperate North Pacific* regions show relatively lower but still significant proportions of missing data.

Figure 5 presents the trend of missing data over time, from the early 1970s to around 2020. We see some clear periods of improvement, particularly in the late 1970s and late 1990s, where missing data dropped significantly. However, there are also spikes indicating times when data completeness worsened.

Furthermore, the dataset includes geographical information through the *Latitude* and *Longitude* columns, which pinpoint the locations of seagrass meadows. The *Bioregion* column classifies these locations into broader ecological regions

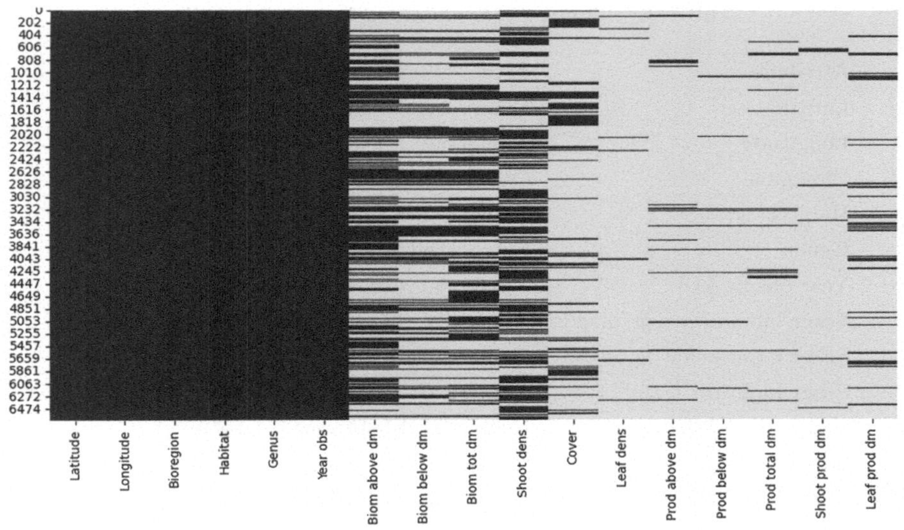

Fig. 3. Heatmap of missing values in the dataset

such as the *Mediterranean* and *Tropical Indo-Pacific*. The dataset shows a significant bias in seagrass distribution studies. The *Tropical Indo-Pacific* region is overrepresented, with over 1750 rows of data, compared to regions like the *Temperate North Atlantic*, *Temperate North Pacific*, and *Mediterranean*, each with fewer than 1000 rows. In contrast, regions like the *Temperate North Atlantic* and *Mediterranean* have fewer species.

4.2 Data Analysis

As shown, in Fig. 6, a worldwide observation of the global distribution of seagrass across different bioregions. We find that regions with harsher weather conditions and poorer economic situations tend to have less seagrass. Environmental factors also play a crucial role: for example, extreme cold, with temperatures consistently below 0 °C in shallow waters, can limit seagrass growth. This is because most species are better suited to temperate or tropical climates.

In Fig. 7, we show the distribution of seagrass in the Temperate North Pacific region, illustrating how challenging it is for seagrasses to thrive in colder areas where photosynthesis and growth are inhibited. Figure 8 presents the global distribution of total seagrass biomass. Darker areas indicate regions with minimal biomass. The Mediterranean Sea stands out, showing the highest total biomass, thanks to its warm climate and abundant sunlight, which offer ideal conditions for seagrass growth. However, Fig. 9 reveals a nuanced picture that despite the high biomass in the Mediterranean, some areas exhibit low daily production, likely due to nutrient limitations.

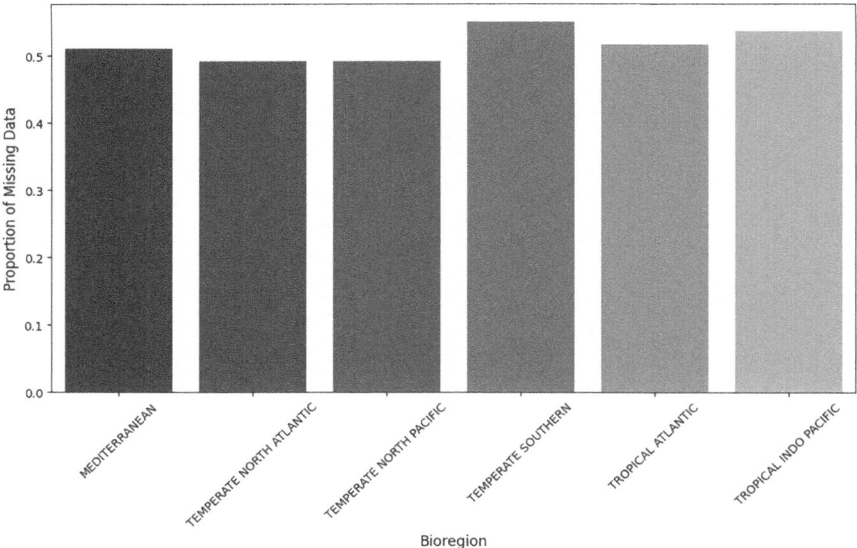

Fig. 4. Average proportion of missing data by bioregion

In Fig. 10, we can observe that seagrass biomass is generally dominated by below-ground mass. However, in certain years: 1979, 2019, 2001–2005, and 2009–2016 we observe dramatic increases in above-ground biomass, sometimes reaching up to three times higher than usual. We believe this could be due to a combination of environmental factors like water temperature, light availability, and nutrient levels, along with human interventions such as restoration projects and recovery efforts following disturbances [16,17].

Looking at Fig. 11, we present that the Tropical Atlantic region has the highest total biomass but relatively low production. This pattern is also evident in the *Mediterranean*, where high biomass doesn't always correlate with high productivity, likely due to environmental stressors. On the other hand, in the *Tropical Indo-Pacific*, both biomass production and total biomass rank second highest among all bioregions, suggesting the region is in its peak development phase. In contrast, the *Temperate North Pacific* shows high production rates but lower total biomass, indicating that it is still developing and has potential for future growth. Finally, the *Temperate North Atlantic*, which has the lowest production and biomass, is constrained by its harsh environmental conditions, including cold temperatures and limited sunlight.

Lastly, Fig. 12 compares the structure of seagrass across bioregions, focusing on the ratio of shoot density to leaf density. In the *Mediterranean*, shoot density is, on average, 5.2 times higher than leaf density, making it unique in this regard. In other regions, leaf density dominates, with the *Tropical Indo-Pacific* displaying the most extreme ratio, with 20 times more leaves than shoots.

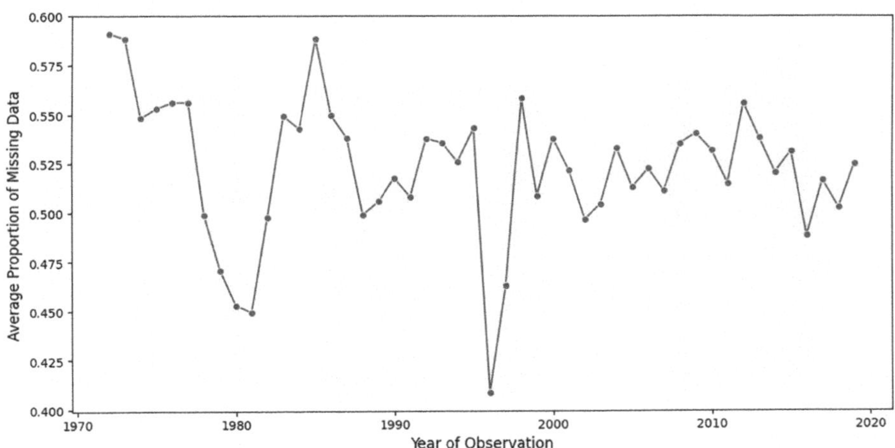

Fig. 5. Trend of missing data over time

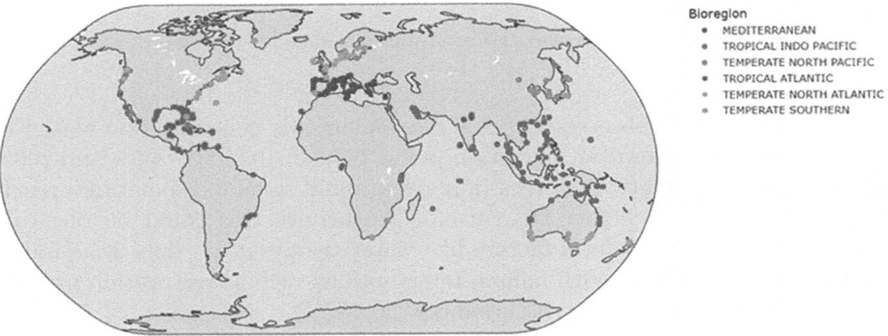

Fig. 6. Seagrass observations accross bioregions

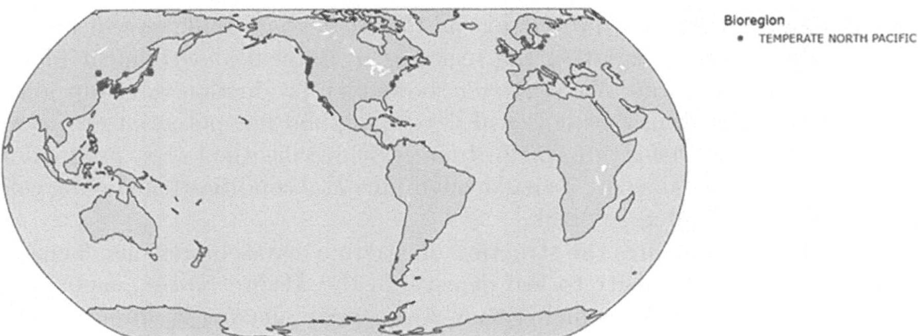

Fig. 7. Seagrass observations in the temperate north pacific bioregion

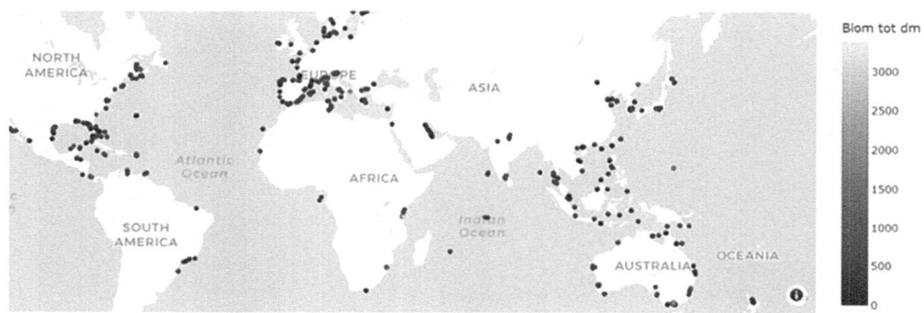

Fig. 8. Total biomass distribution around the world.

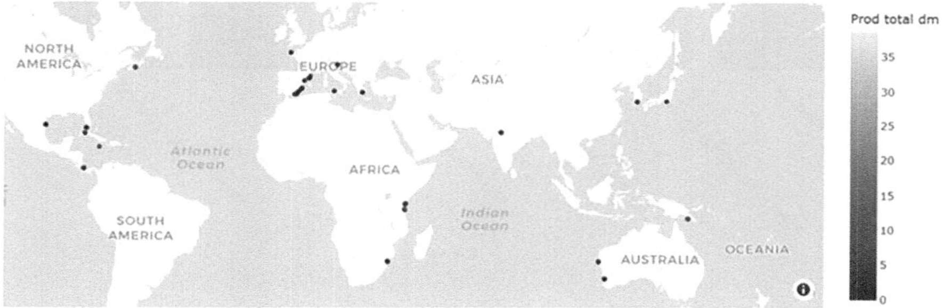

Fig. 9. Total biomass production distribution around the world

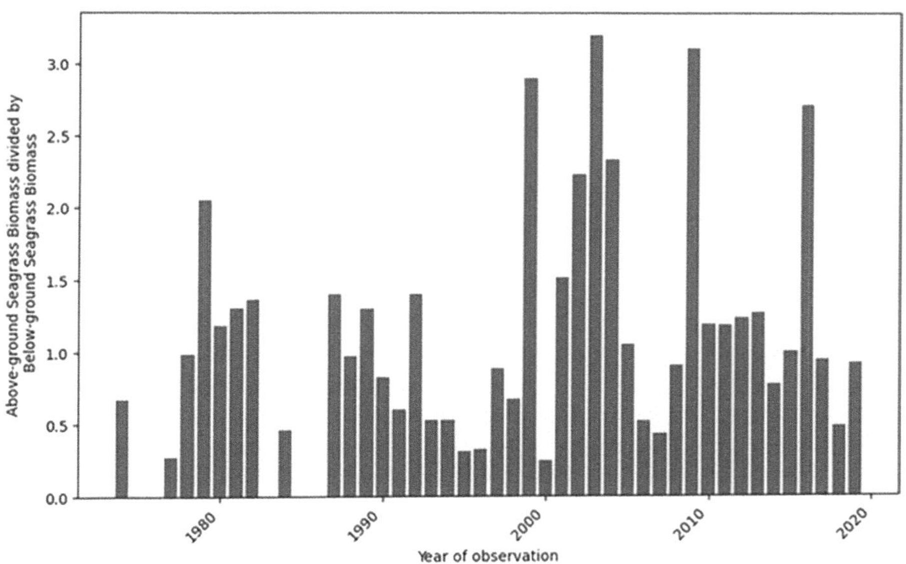

Fig. 10. Proportional study of above/below ground seagrass mass by year

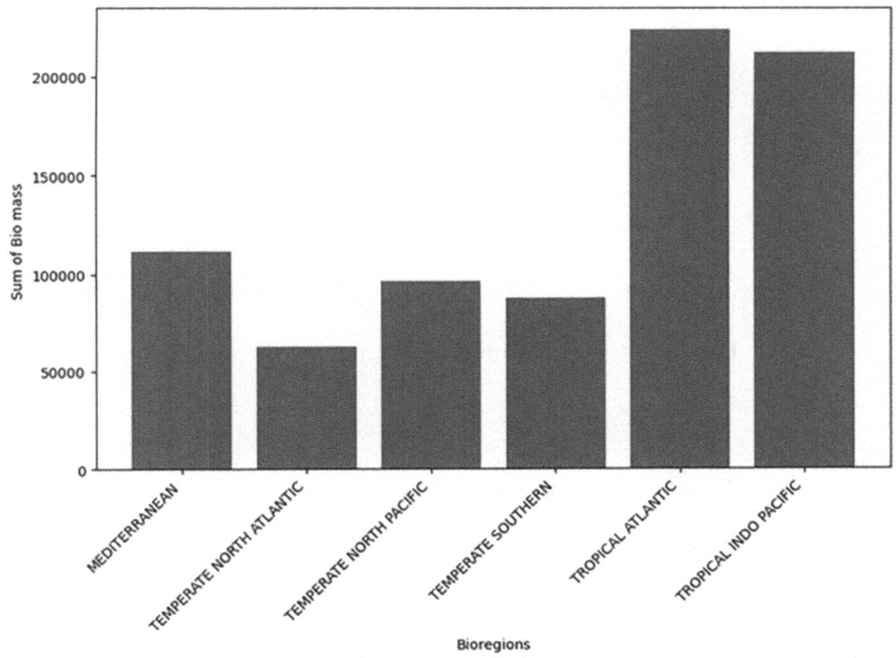

Fig. 11. Distribution of total biomass by bioregion

5 Data Preparation

This section outlines the steps taken to clean, transform, and prepare the data, along with the rationale behind each step. The process includes data cleaning, encoding, handling missing values, standardization, and merging of datasets. First, in order to ensure consistency in the dataset, all string values were converted to uppercase to avoid discrepancies during data processing and analysis. Second, all rows with missing values in the *Year of observation* column were dropped. The duplicate rows were removed to ensure that the dataset does not contain redundant information. We find in this datasat only 146 duplicate rows. As mentioned in Sect. 3, the dataset contains categorical variables, like (*Bioregion*, *Habitat*, and *Genus*), we applied one-hot encoding to convert these categories into binary vectors [9]. One-hot encoding is necessary because most machine learning library require numerical input, and categorical data cannot be directly used in these models. By creating binary columns for each category, one-hot encoding allows the model to interpret categorical data effectively. In the description process of our dataset, we find that some data, such as the *biomass* or *leaf density* columns, require normalization. We scale the data to center it

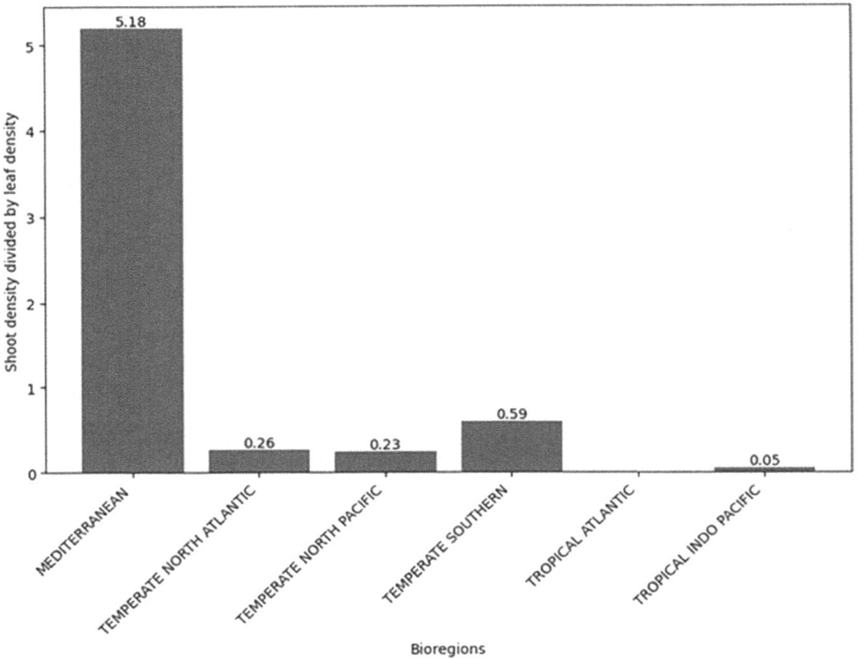

Fig. 12. Seagrass structure comparison by bioregion.

around 0 with a standard deviation of 1. For a given original feature x, the normalized version of x is obtained using the following transformation:

$$x' = \frac{x - \mu_x}{\sigma_x},$$

where μ_x and σ_x are the mean and the standard deviation of x, respectively. The main challenge in this work is how to handle missing values, especially in biological and environmental features. Missing data can introduce bias and reduce the accuracy of model predictions. To address this, the first idea is to use a simple approach based on the median or the mean of the features. However, the main issue with this method is that, upon examining the imputed values, we find that some of them are located in places where they lack relevance or consistency. For this reason, we employ a novel approach based on iterative imputation using a Random Forest Regressor [10]. Random Forest Regressor can capture complex and nonlinear relationships between features. The imputation process refines imputed values by iterating over the dataset multiple times and we evaluated the model across a range of iterations. Furthermore, we split the dataset into a 70% training set and a 30% testing set before imputation, and we analyze the resulting R^2 scores metric for each iteration. From our analysis of the R^2 scores, several key trends emerged. In the early iterations between 0 and 2, we saw significant improvement in performance for most metrics, particularly for *Biom tot dm* and *Biom above dm*, as the models began to establish better relationships with the data. Although some metrics fluctuated, the overall trend was one of improvement.

As we progressed into the mid-range of iterations between 3 and 5, the R^2 scores for metrics like *Biom above dm* and Cover stabilized, while other metrics showed slight declines, which we interpret as possible signs of overfitting or a performance plateau. Despite these fluctuations, the overall improvements remained evident. On the other hand, production-related metrics such as *Prod total dm* continued to exhibit inconsistency.

Beyond iteration 5, we observed that the R^2 scores for well-performing metrics either plateaued or showed slight declines, likely due to overfitting. For production-related metrics, negative R^2 values persisted, signaling poor generalization, and further iterations offered diminishing returns. This suggests that, after a certain point, additional iterations may no longer contribute meaningfully to model improvement and could even detract from it.

Based on these findings, we conclude that early iterations (0–2) are important for enhancing model accuracy, while additional iterations beyond 5 provide only marginal improvements. After completing the above step, the training and test datasets were merged into a single dataset to obtain a 6502 non-null rows. This datatset will facilitate the analysis and further modeling.

6 Modeling and Evaluation

In this section, we present two algorithms to predict key seagrass metrics, like *biomass*, *density*, and *production*. We used the Stacked Model which is based on multiple three models and the XGBoost model. The detailed architecture for our data modeling is given in Fig. 2. Predictions steps were generated iteratively, with previously predicted variables serving as inputs for subsequent steps. This sequential approach leveraged the interdependencies between *biomass*, *density*, and *production* metrics, allowing the model to dynamically refine its predictions and improve overall accuracy.

6.1 Stacked Model

In the Stacking model, multiple machine learning algorithms have been used, in order to minimize individual biases and variances, resulting in improved generalization and robust performance. By integrating diverse models, stacking captures complex patterns within the data while minimizing the risk of overfitting, making the predictions more reliable when applied to new datasets [11,12]. The stacked model follows a two-level hierarchical structure. At the first level, multiple base models are employed to capture various aspects of the data. Specifically:

- Ridge Regression: Provides a linear approach with regularization to control overfitting.

- Random Forest Regressor: Provides robust predictions through ensemble decision trees with built-in feature importance.
- LGBMRegressor: Optimized for speed and performance, making it suitable for large datasets.

The predictions generated by these base models are then passed to the second-level model, another Random Forest Regressor, which learns from the combined predictions to produce refined and accurate outputs. This layered architecture allows for an optimal fusion of individual model strengths, enhancing both accuracy and generalization. The overall process of stacking is illustrated in Fig. 13.

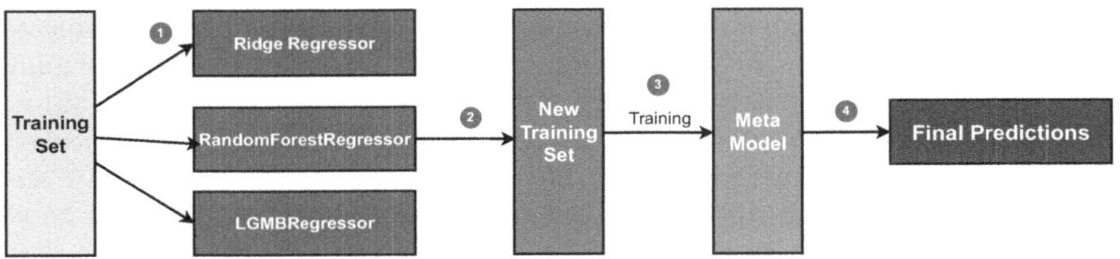

Fig. 13. Stacking model architecture and process

The stacking procedure begin with training each base model independently on the training dataset. Their predictions were then used as inputs for the final-level model, which aggregated the information and generated refined predictions. This hierarchical learning process allowed the final model to make more informed and accurate decisions. Given the interrelated nature of *biomass*, *density*, and *production*, predictions were performed iteratively. The outputs from previous predictions were used as input features for subsequent steps, enabling the model to learn from the evolving context and maintain dynamic adaptability.

6.2 XGBoost Model

The XGBoost model is employed because it excels at capturing complex and nonlinear relationships in the data. XGBoost have a high performance and scalability. It uses parallelized execution, making it significantly faster than many other algorithms, especially for large datasets [13].

To enhance the predictive performance of the XGBoost regressor, we leverage the Tree-structured Parzen Estimator (TPE) as a hyperparameter optimization technique [14,15]. TPE is a Bayesian optimization method that efficiently explores the hyperparameter space by modeling the distribution of the objective function. In this work, the objective of the hyperparameter tuning process is to maximize the coefficient of determination R^2 score, aiming to find the optimal hyperparameters θ^* that satisfy:

$$\theta^* = \arg\max_{\theta} R^2(\theta),$$

where $R^2 = 1 - \frac{\sum_{i=1}^{n}(y_i - \hat{y}_i)^2}{\sum_{i=1}^{n}(y_i - \bar{y})^2}$, with y_i is true value of the target variables, $\hat{y}_i$ is the predicted value from the model, $\bar{y}$ is the mean of the true values and n is the number of samples. The TPE algorithm models the posterior distribution of the objective function and splits the observations into two groups based on a threshold score y^* . The probability model is formulated as:

$$p(\theta \mid y) = \begin{cases} l(\theta) = p(\theta \mid y \geq y^*) & \text{(good hyperparameters)} \\ g(\theta) = p(\theta \mid y < y^*) & \text{(bad hyperparameters)} \end{cases}$$

Hence, we use the acquisition function $\gamma(\theta) = \frac{l(\theta)}{g(\theta)}$ to guide the search by focusing on promising hyperparameters. Hyperparameters optimization was conducted for the XGBoost model across all metrics, revealing several key trends. The number of estimators (`n_estimators`) ranged from 300 to 1500, with higher values often associated with production-related metrics such as *Prod below dm* and *Leaf prod dm.* The learning rate (`learning_rate`) typically ranged between 0.01 and 0.3, with lower rates used for metrics requiring finer adjustments, such as *Shoot prod dm.* The tree depth (`max_depth`) varied from 5 to 15, with deeper trees often applied to complex metrics like *Biom below dm* and *Prod below dm.* Additionally, higher regularization values (`reg_alpha` and `reg_lambda`) were used for metrics prone to overfitting, such as *Biom below dm* and *Shoot dens.* These improved optimized hyperparameters are presented in Table 2.

Table 2. Optimized hyperparameters for key metrics

Metric	`n_estimators`	`learning_rate`	`max_depth`	`reg_alpha`
Biom tot dm	800	0.05	7	0.1
Biom below dm	1000	0.015	9	1.0
Prod below dm	1000	0.201	9	0.5
Shoot prod dm	500	0.01	6	0.2

7 Results and Discussion

We now present the main findings, discussing them in relation to prior work and outlining their significance.

The predictive performance of both XGBoost and stacked ensemble models was evaluated across key seagrass metrics, including *biomass*, *production*, and *density.* Table 3 presents the R^2 scores for each model before and after hyperparameter optimization.

The optimized XGBoost model consistently outperformed both the baseline XGBoost and the stacked ensemble across all metrics. After hyperparameter

Table 3. Comparison between XGBoost and stacked models across R^2 scores

Metric	XGB	Optimized XGB	Stacking	Optimized stacking
Biom above dm	0.842	0.882	0.831	0.891
Biom below dm	0.824	0.857	0.812	0.866
Biom tot dm	0.921	0.973	0.918	0.968
Prod below dm	0.913	0.975	0.907	0.963
Shoot prod dm	0.902	0.962	0.915	0.956

tuning, XGBoost achieved an R^2 score of 0.973 for *total biomass* (Biom tot dm), highlighting its effectiveness in capturing complex relationships within ecological data. Similar gains were observed for other key metrics: *Prod below dm* and *Shoot prod dm* exceeded R^2 values of 0.96. In comparison, the optimized stacked model also showed competitive performance (e.g., $R^2 = 0.968$ for *Biom tot dm*), but slightly underperformed relative to XGBoost for below-ground biomass and production metrics. This reinforces the power of gradient boosting in modeling nonlinear dependencies, consistent with prior findings such as those by Bakirman et al.

Hyperparameter optimization via the Tree-structured Parzen Estimator (TPE) significantly improved predictive performance, yielding an average R^2 increase of 4–6%. For *Biom tot dm*, the optimized XGBoost improved from 0.921 to 0.973, a 5.6% gain. Notably, this tuning approach enhanced performance by nearly 10% over XGBoost's default parameters, demonstrating the utility of Bayesian optimization methods in ecological modeling.

To assess the effect of iterative imputation, we analyzed how model performance changed over successive rounds of MissForest. As shown in Table 4, early iterations (0–2) significantly improved R^2 scores for both models, particularly for biomass metrics.

Table 4. R^2 scores of XGBoost and stacking models across imputation iterations

Iterations	Metric	XGB R^2	Stacking R^2
0	Biom above dm	0.612	0.701
0	Biom below dm	0.517	0.412
0	Biom tot dm	0.981	0.978
1	Biom above dm	0.538	0.619
1	Biom below dm	0.390	0.552
1	Biom tot dm	0.972	0.969
2	Biom above dm	0.612	0.701
2	Biom below dm	0.421	0.589
2	Biom tot dm	0.981	0.978

While the stacked model initially exhibited more stable behavior, it later became erratic–especially for production metrics such as *Prod total dm* and *Leaf prod dm*, occasionally returning negative R^2 values. In contrast, XGBoost showed initial variability but stabilized more consistently across iterations. Based on these observations, we selected XGBoost as the final model due to its superior accuracy, computational efficiency, stability, and interpretability. Notably, it handled missing data more robustly and did not suffer from the extreme negative R^2 values sometimes seen in the stacked model.

Ecological interpretation of model outputs revealed that features such as the light attenuation coefficient (secchi depth), water temperature, and nutrient concentrations ranked highest in importance. These findings align with established ecological theory and prior empirical studies, increasing confidence in our model's ecological validity. Unlike earlier studies relying solely on remote sensing, our approach incorporates *in situ* environmental data, enabling a more detailed and biologically meaningful assessment of seagrass ecosystem health.

In summary, this study makes several important contributions. First, we demonstrate state-of-the-art predictive accuracy for global seagrass metrics by combining advanced machine learning models with rigorous imputation strategies. Second, our feature importance analysis provides ecologically interpretable insights relevant to coastal monitoring and management. Third, the entire pipeline–from preprocessing through model training and evaluation–is transparent and reproducible, supporting adoption in other geographic regions or future datasets.

Nonetheless, some limitations exist. Not all relevant ecological drivers (e.g., localized pollution events, wave energy flux) are represented in the data, which may reduce performance for certain metrics. Geographic imbalances in sampling–particularly in tropical areas–could also affect generalization. Computational limits constrained the complexity of our ensemble and cross-validation scheme. Future work could explore deep learning models with larger, balanced datasets or leverage more computational resources to further enhance performance.

We also plan to incorporate new data sources such as bathymetry and satellite-derived chlorophyll time series, and to deploy the models in real-time environmental dashboards. Alternative imputation methods such as deep learning autoencoders may offer further robustness. Finally, linking our model outputs to carbon emission scenarios could help quantify the global climate impacts of seagrass decline, addressing the urgency highlighted in the Introduction.

8 General Conclusion

This work presents the effectiveness of machine learning techniques in predicting seagrass biomass and ecosystem health. We compared two models: an XGBoost-based model and an ensemble model with optimized parameters. The optimized XGBoost model achieved the best performance, demonstrating its ability to handle complex environmental data. Additionally, we employed an iterative imputation strategy, which proved effective in managing missing values and improving prediction reliability. To further enhance predictive accuracy, we plan to extend this work by exploring time series analysis to capture the temporal evolution of seagrass meadows. Implementing Long Short-Term Memory (LSTM) networks could improve predictions by incorporating past trends and seasonal variations, enabling a more dynamic and real-time monitoring system.

Conflict of Interest The author states that the publishing of this paper does not include any conflicts of interest.

Ethics approval and consent to participate Not applicable.

Funding Not applicable.

Data and code availability All data analyzed during this study are available through PANGAEA in [8]. The full code of this study is available upon request from the corresponding author.

References

1. Nawaz, U., Anees-ur-Rahaman, M., Saeed, Z.: A survey of deep learning approaches for the monitoring and classification of seagrass. Ocean Sci. J. **60**(19) (2025)
2. Capistrant-Fossa, K., Dunton, K.H.: Rapid sea level rise causes loss of seagrass meadows. Commun. Earth & Envir. **5**(87) (2024)
3. Li, L., Goshawk, D.P.: Comparison of random forest and multiple imputation for imputing missing data: a case study of the education panel survey of the city of China (2015). https://www.albany.edu/chinanet/events/ucrn2016/papers/18_Comparison%20of%20Random%20Forest%20and%20Multiple%20Imputation%20for%20Imputing%20Missing%20Data.pdf. Accessed 10 July 2025
4. Chowdhury, M., Martínez-Sansigre, A., Mole, M., Alonso-Peleato, E., Basos, N., Blanco, J.-M., Ramirez-Nicolas, M., Caballero, I., de la Calle, I.: Remote sensing integrating deep learning artificial intelligence to monitor Mediterranean seagrass for conservation and ecosystem management. Sci. Rep. **14**(1) (2024)
5. Traganos, D., Aggarwal, B., Poursanidis, D., Topouzelis, K., Chrysoulakis, N., Reinartz, P.: Towards global-scale seagrass mapping and monitoring using Sentinel-2 on Google Earth engine: the case study of the Aegean and Ionian Seas. Remote Sens. **10**(8) (2018)
6. Yamato, C., Ichikawa, K., Arai, N., Tanaka, K., Nishiyama, T., Kittiwattanawong, K.: Deep neural networks based automated extraction of dugong feeding trails from UAV images in the intertidal seagrass beds. PLoS ONE **16**(8) (2021)

7. Effrosynidis, D., Arampatzis, A., Sylaios, G.: Seagrass detection in the mediterranean: a supervised learning approach. Eco. Inform. **48**, 158–170 (2018)
8. Strydom, S., Webster, C.L., McCallum, R., Lafratta, A., O'Dea, C.M., Said, N.E., Inostroza, K., Salinas, C., Billinghurst, S., Phelps, C.M., et al.: Global database of key seagrass structure, biomass and production variables, PANGAEA (2021)
9. Kuhn, M., Johnson, K.: Applied Predictive Modeling. Springer (2013)
10. Breiman, L.: Random forests. Mach. Learn. **45**(1), 5–32 (2001)
11. Wolpert, D.H.: Stacked generalization. Neural Netw. **5**(2), 241–259 (1992)
12. Breiman, L.: Bagging predictors. Mach. Learn. **24**(2), 123–140 (1996)
13. Chen, T., Guestrin, C.: XGBoost: a scalable tree boosting system. In: Proceedings of the 22nd ACM SIGKDD International Conference on Knowledge Discovery and Data Mining, pp. 785–794 (2016)
14. Erwianda, M.S.F., Kusumawardani, S.S., Santosa, P.I., Rimadana, M.R.: Improving confusion-state classifier model using XGBoost and tree-structured parzen estimator. In: 2019 International Seminar on Research of Information Technology and Intelligent Systems (ISRITI), pp. 309–313. IEEE (2019)
15. Akiba, T., Sano, S., Yanase, T., Ohta, T., Koyama, M.: Optuna: a next-generation hyperparameter optimization framework. In: Proceedings of the 25th ACM SIGKDD International Conference on Knowledge Discovery and Data Mining, pp. 2623–2631 (2019)
16. Short, F.T., Kosten, S., Morgan, P.A., Malone, S., Moore, G.E.: Impacts of climate change on seagrass growth and distribution. Mar. Ecol. Prog. Ser. **550**, 1–18 (2016)
17. van Katwijk, M.M., et al.: Global analysis of seagrass restoration: the importance of large-scale planting. J. Appl. Ecol. **53**(2), 567–578 (2016)

Under Partial Shading Conditions in PV Systems, a Comparative Study of Particle Swarm Optimization and Polar Optimization Algorithms for MPPT

Youness Hakam(✉) and Mohamed Tabaa

Multidisciplinary Laboratory of Research and Innovation (LPRI), Moroccan School of Engineering Sciences (EMSI), Casablanca, Morocco
y.hakam@emsi.ma

Abstract. By generating several local maxima in the power-voltage (P-V) characteristic curve, Partial Shading Conditions (PSC) significantly affect the performance of photovoltaic (PV) systems, hence complicating Maximum Power Point Tracking (MPPT). For Maximum Power Point Tracking (MPPT) in solar systems under partial shade conditions (PSC), this study presents a comparative examination of two nature-inspired metaheuristic algorithms Particle Swarm Optimization (PSO) and Polar Optimization (PO). Diverse actual-world shading conditions are applied to evaluate algorithm performance by means of a simulation model built in MATLAB/Simulunk using a single-diode photovoltaic module. Examined are critical parameters such as convergence velocity, tracking accuracy, stability, and computation cost. Results show that although PSO shows quick convergence, it is sensitive to parameter change and could struggle under complex shading. On the other hand, PO's radial and angular search approach gives it better tracking accuracy and faster convergence, especially in extreme PSC situations. The findings highlight PO's efficiency as a reliable and efficient MPPT technique for PV systems in locations with fluctuating shade.

Keywords: MPPT · Partial shading · Photovoltaic · PSO · Polar Optimization · Metaheuristic · Renewable energy

1 Introduction

Photovoltaic (PV) systems have been adopted as a reliable substitute for conventional fossil fuels in response to increasing worldwide need for clean and sustainable energy. Though they have several advantages, photovoltaic systems are rather limited by a main one: environmental variables, especially temperature and solar irradiation, greatly affect

F. Kamoun et al. (Eds.): AFRICATEK 2025, LNICST 677, pp. 235–248, 2026.
https://doi.org/10.1007/978-3-032-16638-8_16

their power output. One of the key challenges affecting the performance of solar systems is partial shadowing, which results from moving clouds, buildings, trees, or dust accumulation. Partial shadowing creates many local maxima in the power-voltage (P-V) characteristics of solar arrays, hence hindering the capacity of traditional Maximum Power Point Tracking (MPPT) techniques to find the global maximum power point (GMPP). Many complex and nature-inspired optimization techniques have been developed in reaction to this issue. Due to its simplicity, quick convergence, and ability to avoid local maxima, Particle Swarm Optimization (PSO) has attracted much interest. PSO steadily approaches an optimal solution by simulating the social dynamics of avian flocks or aquatic schools. On the other hand, Polar Optimization (PO) is a modern metaheuristic technique that efficiently investigates and exploits the search space using polar coordinates. Particularly in complex nonlinear environments like PSC, its unique approach based on angles and radii improves global search capacity. Under several partial shading scenarios, this work compares PSO and PO algorithms for Maximum Power Point Tracking (MPPT). Executed in MATLAB/Simulink, both algorithms are assessed on a solar system subjected to different shade patterns. Performance assessment includes tracking speed, accuracy, stability, and convergence to the GMPP. The results highlight the benefits and drawbacks of every approach, hence providing analysis of their suitability for real-time photovoltaic applications in changing environmental conditions.

2 Related Work

The challenge of accurately locating the Maximum Power Point (MPP) under Partial Shading Conditions (PSC) in photovoltaic (PV) systems has driven the development of several MPPT methods. Because of their simplicity and low computational cost, conventional methods such Perturb and Observe (P&O) and Incremental Conductance (INC) are widely used [1–3]. These methods, however, often become caught in local maxima when non-uniform irradiance causes several peaks in the power-voltage (P-V) curve, therefore compromising energy extraction.

Metaheuristic algorithms have emerged as effective solutions for global maximum power point tracking to solve this problem. Because it can intelligently explore the solution space by simulating agents' social behavior, Particle Swarm Optimization (PSO) has become more prominent. Under various shading circumstances, Particle Swarm Optimization (PSO) has shown improved effectiveness over traditional techniques [4–6]. Improved versions such Chaotic PSO [7], Modified PSO [8], and Hybrid PSO-ANN models [9] have been presented to increase convergence and robustness in dynamically changing environmental conditions.

Similarly, other natural-inspired algorithms as the Genetic Algorithm (GA) [10], Grey Wolf Optimizer (GWO) [11], and Ant Colony Optimization (ACO) [12] have shown good results in Maximum Power Point Tracking (MPPT) uses. These algorithms, however, may require precisely tuned control parameters and can suffer early convergence or slow response under fast irradiance changes. A relatively new addition to this class of algorithms, the Polar Optimization (PO) method directs the search process using the geometry of polar coordinates [13]. Unlike conventional Cartesian search-based algorithms, PO moves the solution space by changing angles and radial distances, therefore especially suited for complex, multimodal problems like MPPT under PSC [14, 15]. Though PO is used in areas including engineering design and picture segmentation [16, 17], its use in PV systems is still under researched.

Emphasizing benefits in convergence speed and tracking accuracy, some researches have compared various metaheuristic methods under PSC, such as PSO against GWO [18] and PSO versus Artificial Bee Colony (ABC) [19]. Still, little study has directly contrasted PSO with PO under MPPT. Moreover, most of today's evaluations are limited to simulation-based performance, hence ignoring consistency across different shading patterns and the assessment of climate change resilience. By means of a thorough comparison study of PSO and PO algorithms for MPPT under several partial shading scenarios, this work enriches the field. The study evaluates algorithmic effectiveness in terms of tracking accuracy, convergence time, stability, and computational complexity. The findings provide important guidance for selecting appropriate optimization techniques in practical solar systems influenced by environmental disturbances.

3 PV System and Partial Shading Modeling

The output voltage of each solar module sometimes does not meet the system's voltage specifications. To augment the system's voltage, photovoltaic modules are arranged in series. Nonetheless, the entire photovoltaic array does not consistently experience uniform solar exposure. When particular segments of the solar strings are obstructed, whether by thick clouds, edifices, or flora, the intensity of sunlight fluctuates among the modules. Partial shading leads to significant reductions in the power output of the solar system. The uneven distribution of sunlight across the strings can create energy hotspots, while shaded cells transform absorbed energy into heat. The hotspot phenomenon may adversely affect partially shaded solar cells and reduce the longevity of the photovoltaic module. To alleviate the effects of partial shadowing, shaded regions of the cells. Fully illuminated solar cells provide a substantial amount of energy; bypass diodes are incorporated into each photovoltaic string, as depicted in Fig. 1.

In cases of partial shading, the short-circuit current of series-connected solar modules may vary. As a result, the bypass diode of the partially shaded cell becomes forward-biased, allowing current to bypass that cell and preventing hotspot formation. However, the integration of the bypass diode introduces a further complication: the occurrence of numerous peaks. Two separate types of peaks emerge: the global peak (GP) and the local peak (LP).

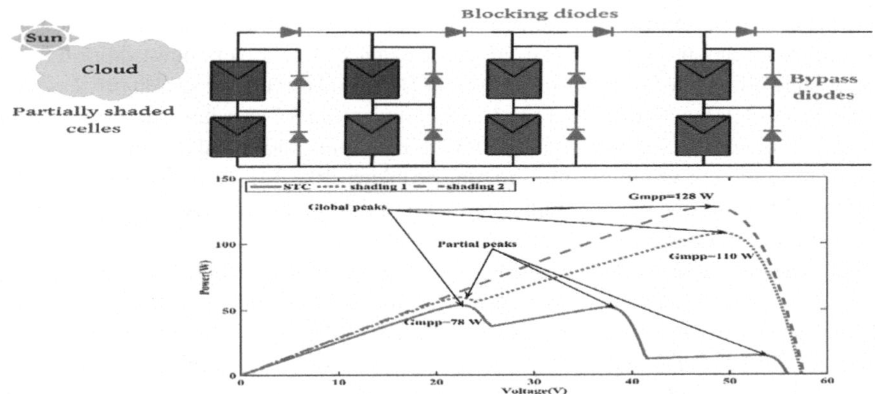

Fig. 1. The depiction of shading is restricted to a designated area [21]

Photovoltaic System and Partial Shading Simulation Photovoltaic (PV) systems are extensively employed in renewable energy applications owing to their sustainability and adaptability. Nonetheless, their performance is significantly affected by environmental factors, including solar irradiance and temperature. Under uniform irradiation, the power-voltage (P-V) curve of a PV array contains a single global maximum power point (GMPP).

Conversely, Partial Shading Conditions (PSC) create several local maxima in the P-V curve, complicating the ability of traditional MPPT algorithms to identify the genuine Global Maximum Power Point (GMPP). This paper shows the PV behavior by using a conventional single-diode model to mimic the electrical properties of solar cells. Executed in MATLAB/Simulink, the model depicts the nonlinear relationship among temperature, irradiance, voltage, and current.

The photovoltaic system is set up in a series-parallel configuration to evaluate MPPT effectiveness under partial shadowing situations. Shading is applied on certain modules by changing their irradiance levels, hence simulating real-world situations including transient clouds, neighboring buildings, or dust accumulation. Three shading designs are investigated:

While one string gets reduced irradiance (600 W/m^2), two strings of photovoltaic modules are exposed to full irradiance (1000 W/m^2). One string is irradiated at 1000 W/m^2, another at 800 W/m^2, and the third at 400 W/m^2.

Scenario 3 (Severe Shading): One string is exposed to 1000 W/m^2, while the other two are under only 200 W/m^2. These circumstances produce intricate P-V curves with multiple peaks. A visual analysis of the curves shows that every additional shade level raises the quantity of local maxima, hence significantly complicating the MPPT operation. This environment provides a complete platform for assessing optimization-based MPPT algorithms. Maximum Power Point Tracking (MPPT) using Particle Swarm Optimization (PSO) Originally developed to mimic the social dynamics of bird flocks and fish schools, Particle Swarm Optimization (PSO) is a population-centric, nature-inspired algorithm. Every "particle" in the algorithm represents a possible optimization issue solution specifically, a duty cycle value controlling the operating point of the photovoltaic system via a DC-DC converter.

MPPT uses PSO to find the global maximum power point by continuously changing the duty cycle to maximize the output power of the PV array. Every particle evaluates the power connected to its current location and shares knowledge to the swarm to guide its migration toward better options. The basic process of Particle Swarm Optimization (PSO) includes the following main steps:

Initialization: Randomly initializing a swarm of particles with different duty cycle values. Every particle has a matching speed. The application calculates the output power for every particle depending on its current duty cycle. Each particle changes its position by considering both its personal best position (where it attained the highest power so far) and the global best position discovered by the whole swarm.

Steps 2 and 3 are continued until a convergence criterion is met, such a maximum number of iterations or a minimal change in power. Because it can explore a large solution space and avoid becoming trapped in local maxima, PSO is very effective in partial shadow situations. Especially when the P-V curve has several peaks, PSO offers quicker convergence and more accuracy in finding the GMPP than traditional algorithms such Perturb and Observe (P&O).

The algorithm's parameters including the number of particles, inertia weight, and learning factors must be carefully selected to ensure best performance. Attaining fast and dependable maximum power point tracking (MPPT) requires a wise balance between exploration (investigating new areas) and exploitation (improving existing effective solutions).

Even in solar systems operating under very dynamic shading conditions, PSO's relatively low processing complexity and fast reactivity make it a suitable option for real-time MPPT applications (Fig. 2).

Table 1. PV module parameters used in the study

Parameter	Value	Description
PV module type	Generic 250 W	Standard panel used in simulation
Rated power	250 W	Peak power under STC
Number of modules	3 series × 2 parallel	Configuration used in this study
Irradiance (Standard)	1000 W/m^2	Full sunlight condition

(continued)

Table 1. (*continued*)

Parameter	Value	Description
Temperature	25 °C	Nominal operating cell temperature
Open circuit voltage	37.3 V	Voltage with no load
Short circuit current	8.21 A	Current with shorted output
Max power voltage (Vmp)	30.7 V	Voltage at max power point
Max power current (Imp)	8.13 A	Current at max power point
Simulation tool	MATLAB/Simulink	Modeling and simulation platform

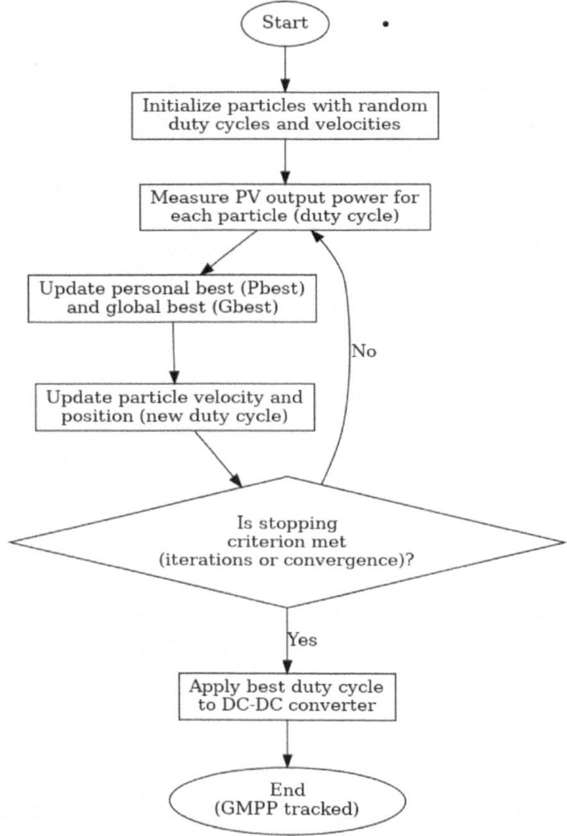

Fig. 2. Flowchart of the Particle Swarm Optimization (PSO) algorithm for MPPT in PV systems

4 Polar Optimization (PO) for Maximum Power Point Tracking

Based on the concepts of polar coordinate geometry, Polar Optimization (PO) is a modern metaheuristic algorithm. Unlike traditional optimization techniques that rely on Cartesian movement inside the search space, PO mimics the dynamic behavior of agents in circular or spiral trajectories by using radial distances and angular modifications around a central point. Ideal for solving nonlinear problems like Maximum Power Point Tracking (MPPT) in Partial Shading Conditions (PSC), this innovative approach lets the algorithm efficiently traverse and use complex search areas. Under the MPPT framework, every agent or solution in the PO algorithm denotes a possible duty cycle for the DC-DC converter controlling the operational point of the PV array. By changing these duty cycles with iterative polar-based transformations, the aim of optimization is to increase the output power of the photovoltaic system. The basic processes of the PO algorithm altered for MPPT are described as follows:

Initialization: Characterized by a radius and angle in reference to a search center (pivot point), a population of candidate solutions is randomly allocated in polar coordinates. The program calculates the output power of the solar system for every possible duty cycle and finds the best choice among the current population. Every solution changes its radius and angle depending on past performance and relationship to the present ideal solution. This change allows the agents to keep diversity while guiding them toward more beneficial areas in the search arena. Search Refinement: Similar to magnifying the GMPP, the radius is progressively decreased to enable more exacting inquiry near the optimal solution. The approach continues until a specified maximum number of repetitions is reached or until the output power improvement is considered unimportant. One of the main benefits of PO over conventional Cartesian-based algorithms is its ability for balanced global and local searches. Inherently encouraging spiral exploration, the polar update method helps the algorithm avoid local maxima usually found in PV systems under PSC. Furthermore, PO requires less control parameters than some other nature-inspired approaches, hence enabling deployment and tuning.

Studies done lately show that PO under different shading scenarios can outperform traditional methods for convergence speed and tracking accuracy. Essential for real-time MPPT applications in unstable environments, the dynamic adaptation mechanism of the algorithm allows quick reactions to sudden changes in irradiance. This study evaluates the tracking performance of the PO algorithm against PSO under several PSC circumstances. The aim is to identify the benefits and trade-offs of each approach, particularly for efficiency, stability, and implementation feasibility for photovoltaic systems running under real-world conditions (Fig. 3).

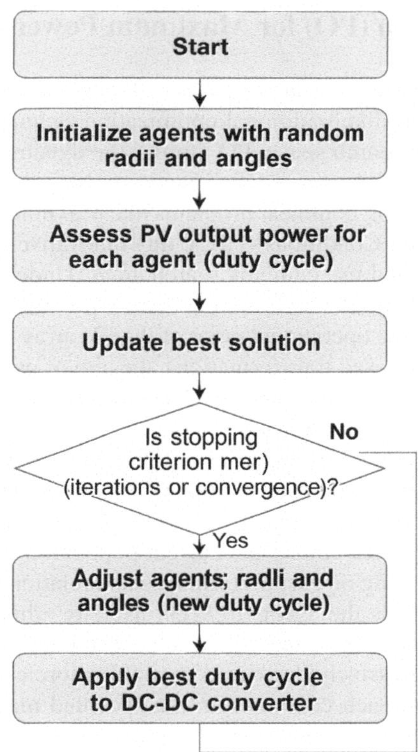

Fig. 3. Flowchart of agent-based optimization for duty cycle control in PV-powered DC-DC converters

5 Simulation Configuration

MATLAB/Simulink was used to provide a comprehensive simulation environment to assess the performance of the PSO and PO algorithms under Partial Shading Conditions (PSC). Controlling the duty cycle of the photovoltaic system model, which uses a single-diode equivalent circuit, a boost DC-DC converter guarantees the operation of the solar array about its maximum power point.

5.1 Photovoltaic Array Configuration

The photovoltaic array employed in this work is set up 3Ò consisting of two parallel strings and three series threads. Each module has a nominal output of 250 W under Standard Test Conditions (STC), therefore generating a total array capacity of 1.5 kW. The specifications of the PV module are detailed in Table 1, encompassing factors such as open-circuit voltage, short-circuit current, and nominal operating conditions.

5.2 Shading Patterns

Three shading patterns were implemented to simulate authentic PSC conditions.

Case 1 Mild Shading: Two-thirds of the modules are exposed to full irradiance (1000 W/m^2), whereas one-third experiences partial shading (600 W/m^2). Case 2 Moderate Shading: Modules are exposed to irradiance levels of 1000, 800, and 400 W/m^2 across various segments. Case 3 Severe Shading: Most modules are exposed to minimal irradiance (200 W/m^2), whilst the remainder receives 1000 W/m^2.

These patterns are intended to produce many peaks in the P-V curve, so testing the MPPT algorithm's capacity to identify the global maximum. Configuration of the 6.3 MPPT Controller Both PSO and PO algorithms were executed as external MPPT controllers communicating with the boost converter. The converter modifies its duty cycle according to the output generated by the corresponding algorithm in each simulation iteration.

The subsequent general parameters were employed: Sampling duration: 0.001 s Quantity of agents/particles: 10 Maximum iterations: fifty Duration of simulation: 1 s Operating frequency: 20 kHz To ensure a fair comparison, both algorithms employed identical initial conditions, controller parameters (where relevant), and were evaluated under the same environmental variations.

5.3 Assessment Criteria

The subsequent major measures were employed to assess the performance of PSO and PO: Tracking accuracy: The proximity of the final tracked power to the real Global Maximum Power Point (GMPP). Convergence time: The duration required by the algorithm to attain the Global Maximum Power Point (GMPP).

Stability: The uniformity and reliability of the power response. Computational efficiency: The mean processing duration per iteration.

As shown in Fig. 4, a four-layer ANN is used. The inputs of the first layer of the network are the temperature T, the solar radiation G and Ipv. The hidden layer is the second layer. It serves as the head of the neural network. The sigmoid function serves as its activation function. The output layer, which is the third layer, displays the Vmpp of panels. The linear function is its activation function.

The ANN-fuzzy approach combines FL and ANNs. It is an enhanced effective hybrid approach to tracking the maximum power point that is proposed. The ANN used to compute the appropriate voltage of maximum depending on weather conditons is essentially identical to the first method has been discussed. The ANN controller's primary goal is to calculate the voltage of maximum for each given combination of temperature and irradiation (Fig. 5).

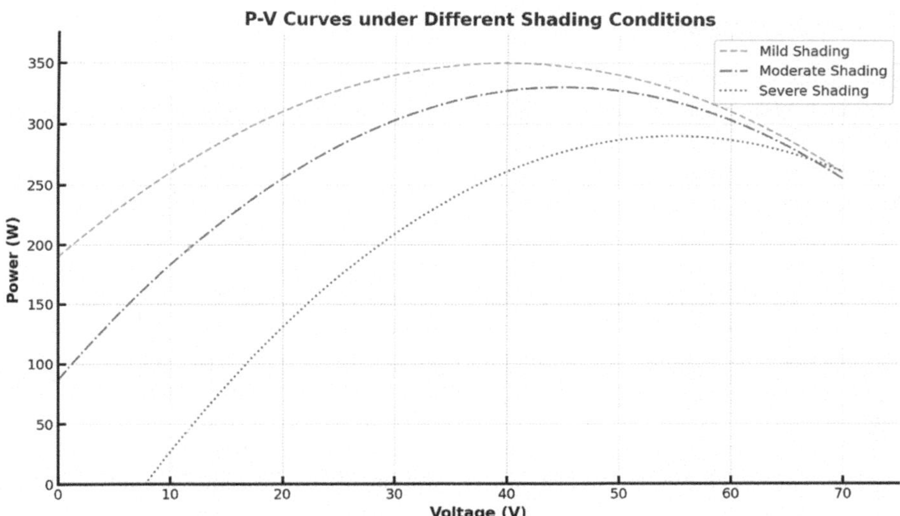

Fig. 4. P-V curves under different shading conditions

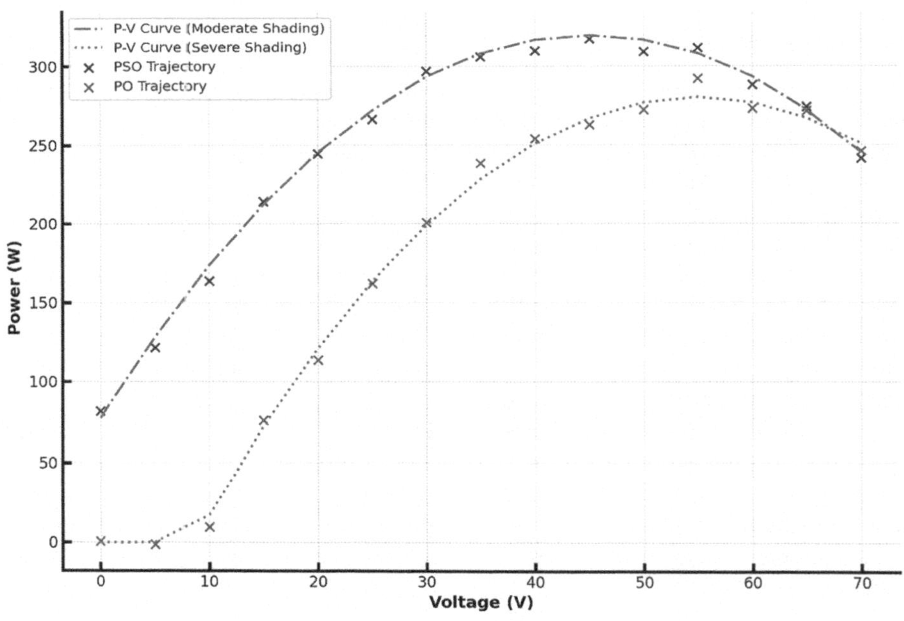

Fig. 5. P-V curves of PSO and PO under shading conditions

Table 2. Comparison of PSO and PO techniques

Criteria	Particle Swarm Optimization (PSO)	Polar Optimization (PO)
Search strategy	Cartesian-based swarm movement	Radial and angular exploration
Convergence speed	Fast in early iterations	Fast with smooth refinement
accuracy under PSC	High with fine tuning	Very high, good at avoiding local maxima
Robustness to PSC patterns	Moderate to high	High
Number of parameters	3–4 (inertia, cognitive, social)	Fewer (angle, radius)
Sensitivity to initialization	Moderate	Low
Computational cost	Moderate	Slightly higher per iteration
Ease of implementation	Widely supported, well-studied	Emerging, easy to implement
Suitability for real-time	Proven practical	Promising, with good response

6 Findings and Analysis

Derived from simulation data obtained with MATLAB/Simulink, this part offers a comparative analysis of the PSO and PO algorithms for MPPT under various Partial Shading Conditions (PSC). Identical solar system designs were used to evaluate the algorithms; equal shade patterns were used to ensure fair performance comparison. Power-Voltage (P-V) Features. The P-V curves of the solar array under three different shadowing conditions mild, moderate, and severe are shown in Fig. 1. As expected, the P-V features show many peaks resulting from the uneven distribution of irradiance over the PV modules. Conventional MPPT methods find the local maxima to be somewhat challenging since they can sometimes get caught in suboptimal power points. Under more severe shade conditions, the P-V curves clearly show the growing complexity of the tracking problem. Significant shade reduces the difference between the global maximum and local maxima, making it more difficult to find the true Maximum Power Point (MPP).

6.1 MPPT Tracking Effectiveness

Figure 2 shows the tracking trajectories of the PSO and PO algorithms under moderate and severe shading circumstances, respectively. The path of each method shows the speed and accuracy with which the solution approaches the global maximum power point. Under mild shade conditions, the PSO approach identifies the global optimum quickly. Its path, however, shows more variation since it is based on speed changes, which may cause overshooting in the early stages of convergence. Particles started far from the optimum zone reveal this pattern most clearly. On the other hand, especially in the presence of major shadowing circumstances, the PO approach shows a more consistent and stable convergence path. Its spiral search strategy allows fast exploration of the solution space while increasingly focusing on the optimal area. This results in a more consistent output power response and less oscillation.

6.2 Comparison

Based on fundamental performance criteria including tracking accuracy, convergence speed, computational economy, and implementation complexity Table 2 shows a comparative study of the two approaches. Tracking Precision: Especially in very dark conditions, PO routinely achieves better accuracy by avoiding local maxima and converging closer to the global optimum. Convergence Rate: Though both algorithms reach the Maximum Power Point (MPP) within acceptable timeframes, Particle Swarm Optimization (PSO) shows slightly faster convergence in the early phases; the Particle Optimization (PO) approach improves the solution more effectively over time. Stability: PO shows better stability with less power response oscillation, making it more suitable for real-time uses. PO requires less tuning parameters than PSO, therefore reducing the effort needed for optimization and implementation. Polar transformations increase the computing overhead of PO slightly each repetition; nevertheless, improved reliability and robustness compensate for this.

6.3 Discussion

In the setting of PSC, both PSO and PO show effectiveness as metaheuristic algorithms for MPPT. Particle Swarm Optimization (PSO) is good at quick investigation and gains from broad validation in scholarly publications. Its performance, however, could vary greatly depending on the initial swarm structure and parameter settings. On the other hand, PO offers a creative and geometrically clear search technique that expertly combines exploration and exploitation. In complex situations where traditional methods or known metaheuristics could fail, it shows great promise for MPPT.

In real-world uses, the choice between PSO and PO has to consider factors such shading variation, hardware limitations, and the desired trade-off between tracking precision and convergence speed.

7 Conclusion

This paper offers a comparative analysis of two metaheuristic algorithms Particle Swarm Optimization (PSO) and Polar Optimization (PO) for Maximum Power Point Tracking (MPPT) in photovoltaic (PV) systems under Partial Shading Conditions (PSC). Traditional MPPT methods find great challenges in the many local maxima in the P-V characteristics produced by shading, which calls for the deployment of more advanced optimization-based approaches. Using a MATLAB/Simulink simulation framework, both PSO and PO were run and assessed under three distinct shading scenarios. Different performance metrics tracking accuracy, convergence rate, stability, robustness, and computation efficiency were used to evaluate the algorithms.

The results of the simulation show that: Particle Swarm Optimization (PSO) has fast convergence and has been extensively validated in the literature; yet, its effectiveness is dependent on parameter tuning and may show instability near the maximum power point. Though very new, PO shows improved accuracy and stability, particularly in complex shading situations. The polar coordinate-based search mechanism guarantees consistent and smooth convergence to the global maximum. The PO approach benefits from a more simple parameter setup, therefore enabling optimization and deployment in practical applications. Though it adds slightly more computing load, PO's general stability makes it a reasonable choice for real-time MPPT applications in dynamically shaded PV systems. Future projects could involve the hybridization of both methods to combine their features or their application on embedded systems for validation and real-time hardware testing.

References

1. Esram, T., Chapman, P.L.: Comparison of photovoltaic array maximum power point tracking techniques. IEEE Trans. Energy Convers. **22**, 439–449 (2007)
2. Hohm, D.P., Ropp, M.E.: Comparative study of maximum power point tracking algorithms. Prog. Photovolt: Res. Appl. **11**, 47–62 (2003)
3. Femia, N., Petrone, G., Spagnuolo, G., Vitelli, M.: Optimization of perturb and observe maximum power point tracking method. IEEE Trans. Power Electron. **20**, 963–973 (2005)
4. El Shahat, A., Zekry, A., Fouad, M.M.: An improved particle swarm optimization based MPPT technique for partially shaded PV systems. Int. J. Electr. Power Energy Syst. **83**, 67–77 (2016)
5. Elgendy, M.A., Zahawi, B., Atkinson, D.J.: Assessment of perturb and observe MPPT algorithm implementation techniques. IEEE Trans. Sustain. Energy **3**, 21–33 (2012)
6. Safari, A., Mekhilef, S.: Simulation and hardware implementation of incremental conductance MPPT with direct control method using Cuk converter. IEEE Trans. Ind. Electron. **58**, 1154–1161 (2011)
7. Pradhan, C., Panda, R.: A novel approach using chaotic PSO for maximum power point tracking in solar photovoltaic system under partial shading conditions. Renew. Energy **95**, 152–166 (2016)
8. Abdelsalam, A.K., Massoud, A.M., Ahmed, S., Enjeti, P.N.: High-performance adaptive perturb and observe MPPT technique for photovoltaic-based microgrids. IEEE Trans. Power Electron. **26**, 1010–1021 (2011)
9. Patel, H., Agarwal, V.: Maximum power point tracking scheme for PV systems operating under partially shaded conditions. IEEE Trans. Ind. Electron. **55**, 1689–1698 (2008)
10. Kim, J.H., Kim, Y.: An effective MPPT using GA for partially shaded PV systems. Sol. Energy **84**, 195–204 (2010)
11. Bouchachia, A., Sahli, N.: Hybrid Grey Wolf Optimizer for MPPT under partial shading conditions. Energy Convers. Manage. **210**, 112705 (2020)
12. Selvakumar, A.I., Thanushkodi, K.: A novel ACO algorithm for MPPT in solar PV system. J. Electr. Eng. Technol. **7**, 1405–1411 (2012)
13. Zhou, Y., Wang, Y., Li, S.: Polar optimization algorithm for complex function minimization. Appl. Soft Comput. **99**, 106935 (2021)
14. Ouni, A., Bouchekara, H.R.E.H.: Polar optimization for optimal location of capacitors in radial distribution systems. Eng. Sci. Technol. **27**, 101042 (2022)
15. Ahmed, M.A., Ebeed, M., Taha, I.B.: Polar optimization-based technique for high-performance MPPT in PV systems. Sol. Energy **239**, 410–422 (2022)

16. Rahman, A., Wang, X., Yuan, Z.: Application of polar optimization in image processing. Multimed. Tools Appl. **80**, 2345–2363 (2021)
17. Choudhary, S., Chouhan, S.S., Rathi, V.: A survey of polar and coordinate-based nature-inspired optimization algorithms. Soft. Comput. **27**, 5441–5459 (2023)
18. El-Khozondar, H.J., Sabbah, H., El-Khozondar, B.Z.: Comparative study of PSO and GWO based MPPT for PV system under partial shading conditions. Int. J. Power Electron. Drive Syst. **10**, 185–192 (2019)
19. Rani, B., Rani, M.: Performance comparison of MPPT algorithms under partial shading conditions. Energy Sources Part A **41**, 2148–2162 (2019)
20. Tang, Y., Zhao, Y., Zeng, C.: Comparative performance analysis of metaheuristic MPPT techniques for PV systems under PSC. Renew. Sustain. Energy Rev. **141**, 110805 (2021)
21. Ahessab, H., Gaga, A., Hakam, Y., EL Haddadi, B.: Optimizing photovoltaic system efficiency through a Kalman filter driven approach for MPPT in partial shading conditions. In: 2024 4th International Conference on Innovative Research in Applied Science, Engineering and Technology (IRASET). https://doi.org/10.1109/IRASET60544.2024.10549347

Sustainable Development Backward Prediction Using a Hybrid Deep Learning Arima Model with an Auto-ARIMA Selection Criteria

Belhassen Meftahi(✉)

Esprit School of Business, Chotrana II Industrial Zone, P.O. Box 160, El Ghazela Technology Park 2083, Ariana, Tunis 2083, Tunisia
belhassen.meftahi@esprit.tn
https://www.esprit.tn/groupe-esprit/esprit-school-of-business-esb/

Abstract. Per country renewable water consumption is a widely analyzed indicator, reflecting sustainable water use at the community level. As a vital resource, water plays a central role in agriculture, nutrition, and public health dimensions collectively addressed by the One Water, One Health approach. Ensuring food safety and promoting health outcomes depend on the effective management of individual water consumption. To address the limitations of traditional single-model prediction methods, often marked by low precision and significant errors, we propose two advanced hybrid models: an ARIMALSTM (Long Short-Term Memory) model and a SARIMALSTM model adapted for Panel time series transformed into supervised Panel Times series. These models aim to enhance the accuracy of backward prediction of individual renewable water consumption, offering improved reliability for historical data estimation and decision-making processes.

Keywords: Sustainable development · Artificial Intelligence · Time series · Statistical models · Deep Learning

1 Introduction

Water is one of the most critical natural resources for humanity and the future of our planet. Although it is abundant in nature, freshwater is the most essential for human and ecological use and it is both finite and irreplaceable. This makes water sustainability a cornerstone for ensuring human well-being, marine ecosystem health, and long-term socio-economic development. Climate change is increasingly impacting water accessibility. The rising frequency of extreme weather events such as droughts and floods has led to growing uncertainty in

F. Kamoun et al. (Eds.): AFRICATEK 2025, LNICST 677, pp. 249–268, 2026.
https://doi.org/10.1007/978-3-032-16638-8_17

water availability. In parallel, factors like pollution, escalating consumption, and the overexploitation of aquifers are putting severe pressure on water resources, threatening the welfare of all life forms from plants to people. Water is fundamental not only to environmental preservation but also to improve global health and economic productivity. As a result, sustainable water management, particularly through conservation practices and the monitoring of consumption indices, is essential in the fight against climate change and in reinforcing resilient socio-economic systems. A key strategy in this effort is the accurate and timely prediction of water-related indicators. Fast and precise forecasting can enable water utilities and environmental agencies to detect trends in water quality degradation and respond proactively. Therefore, developing reliable methods for predicting changes in water quality data has become increasingly critical. Two main categories of prediction techniques dominate this field: statistical models and deep learning models. Time series models involve studying the historical behaviour of a variable and constructing models based on its observed patterns to forecast future values. Among these, the Autoregressive Integrated Moving Average (ARIMA) model [3] stands out for its flexibility, simplicity, and practical effectiveness, making it one of the most widely used approaches in water quality forecasting. For instance, Wang et al. [17] developed a general water quality prediction framework by integrating the Holt-Winters seasonal model with ARIMA, using key eutrophication indicators such as total phosphorus and total nitrogen as predictive parameters. Similarly, Abdul Wahid and Arunbabu [1] successfully predicted water quality trends in the Krishnagiri Reservoir in India using a seasonal ARIMA model that integrated in situ measurements and remote sensing techniques. However, a key limitation of the ARIMA [6] model lies in its inability to handle nonlinear time series data effectively. To address this issue, a wide range of nonlinear deep learning techniques have been employed in time series analysis and prediction. Among these, the Recurrent Neural Network (RNN) is one of the most used architectures (Li et al. [9]). The Long Short-Term Memory (LSTM) [7] model, an enhanced version of RNN, addresses the vanishing and exploding gradient problems inherent in traditional RNNs. Due to its ability to capture and retain vital information over long sequences, LSTM has shown clear advantages in handling complex time series data such as water quality indicators (Pascanu et al. [10]). Several studies have validated LSTM's effectiveness in this domain. For example, Zhou et al. [18] proposed an LSTM-based water quality prediction model using feature selection via an improved grey association analysis algorithm. Their method demonstrated strong performance on datasets from Taihu Lake and Victoria Bay. Similarly, Hu et al. [8] used LSTM to predict water quality parameters such as pH and temperature in sea water cages, achieving high prediction accuracy. Their study not only provided a valuable tool for flood forecasting but also offered insights for water transfer management in the Three Gorges Reservoir area. Despite these promising results, many previous studies rely on manual selection of LSTM hyperparameters based on user experience, introducing subjectivity and limiting the generalizability of the models (Xu et al. [17]). Therefore, optimizing LSTM hyperparameters systematically remains an important challenge. In this study, we address this challenge by reducing the complexity of the model and the founding of the best Deep Learning algorithms' hyperparameters through a novel hybrid modelling approach. First, we apply an Auto-ARIMA process for optimal parameter selection in ARIMA models and conduct rigorous manual analysis to determine the best seasonality settings in SARIMA [5]. These models are used to capture the linear components of the water quality time series, leaving the nonlinear residuals to be modelled separately. To predict these residuals, we apply Artificial Neural Networks (ANN) [12,13] and LSTM models in parallel: ANN is used in combination with SARIMA [13] predictions, and LSTM is paired with ARIMA [14] and SARIMA predictions. The final forecast is obtained by summing the outputs of the linear SARIMA and nonlinear LSTM or ANN components. This hybrid method, inspired by the approach proposed in [4], was adapted and fine-tuned with custom hyperparameters tailored to our dataset. We adapt the use of this technique to our Panel times series transforming its residual part at first into a supervised learning time series and applying on it an LSTM deep learning algorithm to a vector sized 230 (the number of world countries) and to predict about 28-time stamps by the knowledge of 32. In our study we used two methods supervised and unsupervised learning even if we deal with Panel series.

The originality of this method is that our algorithm gives promising results to predict vectors of time series without proceeding iteratively through different rows. Genetally as in [4], we predict the residual part of the SARIMA result by an ANN or an LSTM and the obtained prediction is added to the SARIMA prediction to find the global prediction. Consequently the residual part occurs just on the prediction window of the SARIMA model the last 28 months which is relatively small, in addition we are going on this space to train and to test our model which would affect more our window prediction. To prevent this We transformed the residual serie into supervised learning one using a sliding window on the half of the prediction window. We proposed prediction using ANN and LSTM algorithms, we remark that the residual part is not very sensitive to time and historical memory then we flatten our LSTM input into three dimensioned vector but just with one step time and we multiplied the previous time steps by previous features and considered them as new features for the LSTM.

In this way the result is ameliorated. We also proposed a second and novel hybrid architecture. In this approach, we use the outputs from the individual ARIMA-LSTM and SARIMA-ANN models as unified input vectors to new ANN and LSTM architectures, respectively. This method aims to leverage the complementary strengths of each base model. To evaluate the performance of our models, we compare the proposed hybrid approaches: (ARIMA, LSTM)-LSTM and (SARIMA, ANN)-ANN not only with each other algorithms but also against standard single models (ARIMA, SARIMA, ANN, LSTM) and other hybrid configurations. The results reveal that the SARIMA-LSTM hybrid model perform the best followed by (SARIMA, LSTM)-LSTM model which significantly outperforms all individual models in terms of Mean Absolute Percentage Error (MAPE). However, the (SARIMA, ANN)-ANN model achieves the best overall prediction performance across all comparisons. The structure of the paper is as follows:

Section 2 describes the dataset, the basic imputation techniques used, and the implementation of the ARIMA model via Auto-ARIMA selection.

Section 3 introduces the proposed hybrid models, where linear trends are captured using ARIMA and SARIMA, and nonlinear patterns are modelled using ANN and LSTM. The first model explores the relationship between linear ARIMA predictions and the observed data. The second model focuses on capturing the nonlinear relationships between the extracted residuals after linear modelling the trend and the stationary part of the series. and the actual observed values. These algorithms were also employed to impute missing historical observations and to perform backward prediction, effectively reconstructing previously unavailable data points in incomplete datasets. Section 4 presents two novel hybrid models: (SARIMA, ANN)-ANN and (SARIMA, LSTM)-LSTM, highlighting their structure and performance. These models are evaluated against earlier hybrid approaches and benchmarked against individual statistical models : ARIMA, SARIMA and deep learning : ANN, LSTM models. Comparative results demonstrate the superior performance of the proposed hybrid models in terms of prediction accuracy, particularly in scenarios involving missing or incomplete data. Finally, Sect. 5 concludes the paper by summarizing the key findings and outlining directions for future research, including further automation of hyperparameter optimization and real-time deployment of the models in water resource management systems.

2 The Proposed Imputation Strategy Using a Linear Regressor

In this section we are going to impute a world database related to the consumption of renewable water per country. The database proposes the quantity of consumption per litre and per capita yearly. The years starts from 1961 to 2020. The missing values are about 22.23% from the total dataset. From the beginning the configuration of the dataset seems having its dominant part of missing data situated at years between 1961 and 1990. That is way a strategy of backward prediction is needed. Below we detail the steps of cleaning the dataset: At the end we are going to consider the dataset with all missing years values situated at the first half and the completed data at the last half as is shown in Fig. 1.

Algorithm 1 .

1. Suppression of the rows and columns which are totally undefined
2. Suppression of the two last useless totally missing values' rows.
3. Detection of the few rows which the number of the unknowns represent more than the half of their data. At this stage is clear that the right half of the dataset is already clean, and we are just going to treat these unknowns on this already clean half just for these few rows and then we are going to :
4. Replace the missing values of these rows by the mean of the columns.
5. The obtained dataset is a half missing values one year before a fixed year from which the dataset is already clean.
6. Replacing these previous missing values using a linear regressor to obtain a quasi-complete data of reference.

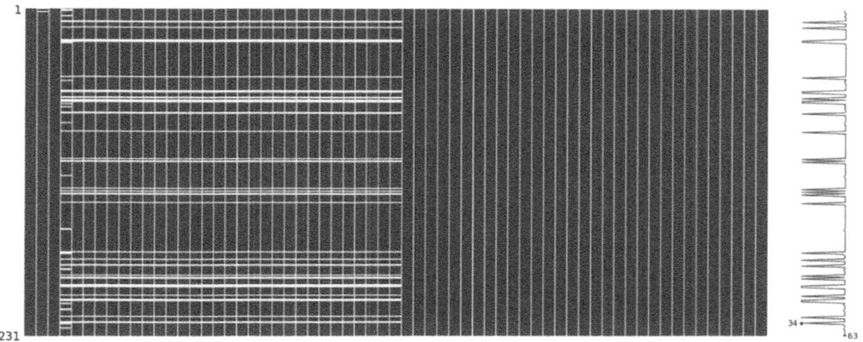

Fig. 1. Dataset study distribution

3 Backward Prediction with LSTM, ANN Models

3.1 The LSTM Model

In this section, we use the Long Short-Term Memory (LSTM) architecture as the core algorithm for backward prediction. The LSTM model, introduced by Hochreiter and Schmidhuber [7], is a specialized form of the Recurrent Neural Network (RNN). It is particularly effective in capturing nonlinear correlations in historical time series data and retaining long-term dependencies. This is achieved through its ability to manage high-dimensional parameters and incorporate nonlinear activation functions within each layer. By addressing the limitations of traditional RNNs, particularly their inability to learn long-range dependencies due to gradient vanishing or explosion, LSTM enables more stable and accurate long-term learning. An LSTM network consists of recurrent units designed to preserve both short-term and long-term information. These units leverage memory cells and a sophisticated gating mechanism to control the flow of information. As shown in Fig. 3 and in [11] the LSTM architecture includes three types of gates: the input gate, the forget gate, and the output gate. The forget gate determines which parts of the previous information should be discarded. It filters out irrelevant data from the memory cell, ensuring that only useful information is retained. This can be mathematically expressed as:

$$f_t = \sigma(W_f \times x_t + U_f \times h_{t-1} + b_f) \tag{1}$$

where : σ is the sigmoid activation function,
W_f and U_f are weight matrices for the input and hidden state,
X_t is the input at the current time step,
h_{t-1} is the hidden state from the previous time step $t-1$,
b_f is the bias term.

The input gate is the second component, and its role is to decide which new information should be added to the cell state. At this stage, the model evaluates the incoming data and updates the memory with relevant new inputs. A tanh activation layer is used to generate new candidate values for the cell state, which plays a crucial role in determining the information to be retained at each time step :

$$\begin{aligned} i_t &= \sigma(W_i \times x_t + U_i \times h_{t-1} + b_i) \\ \tilde{c}_t &= \sigma(W_c \times x_t + U_c \times h_{t-1} + b_c) \end{aligned} \tag{2}$$

This can be mathematically defined as the input modulation, where the input threshold at time t is influenced by the corresponding weights W_i, U_i, and U_c, along with bias parameters b_c and b_i. In Eq. (5), the cell state is updated based on the interactions between the input gate and the new candidate values.

$$C_t = f_t \times C_{t-1} + i_t \times \tilde{c}_{t-1} \tag{3}$$

This step enables the network to selectively incorporate relevant information while maintaining context over time.

Equation (6) describes the output gate, which determines what portion of the cell state should be passed on as output. The weights W_o and U_i, and bias b_0 guide this process. This gate essentially regulates how much of the internal memory is exposed at each time step.

$$O_t = \sigma(W_0 \times x_t + U_0 \times h_{t-1} + b_0) \tag{4}$$

Equation (7) represents the final computation of the memory cell state and the hidden unit at time step t. This final output is the result of information being processed through all three gates: forget, input, and output, ensuring that only significant and contextually relevant information is preserved, while invalid or irrelevant data is discarded.

$$h_t = O_t \times tanh(C_t) \tag{5}$$

This configuration was consistently applied across all three algorithms evaluated in the study. The architecture of the model is illustrated in Fig. 2, which summarizes the key layers and flow of data within the LSTM network.

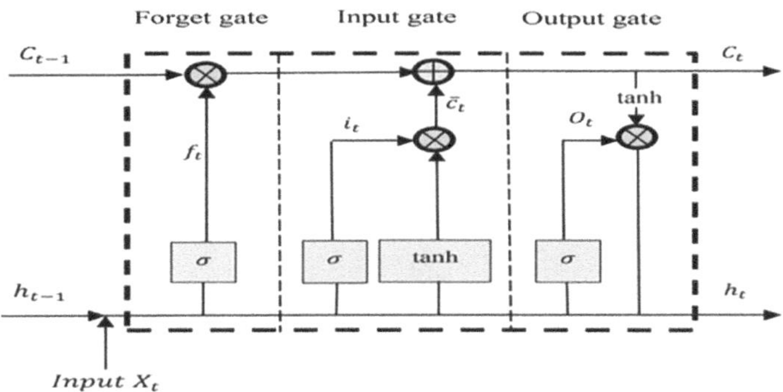

Fig. 2. The LSTM architecture

The LSTM model was trained using the following hyperparameters: The chosen hyperparameters are: 500 epochs, 10 batch and the train data represent 95% from the size of the total data. The learning rate of our used Adam optimizer is fixed at: 0.005. The model architecture is summarized in this Fig. 3.

These hyper-parameters was trained manually after long manual search especially the data is not very volumic, training these hyper-parameters could not be of big interest. Nevertheless we performed rigorous search using the fine tuning and we obtained promising result.

Model: "sequential_13"

Layer (type)	Output Shape	Param #
lstm_6 (LSTM)	(None, 60)	1,781,040
dense_55 (Dense)	(None, 50)	3,050
dense_56 (Dense)	(None, 50)	2,550
dense_57 (Dense)	(None, 50)	2,550
dense_58 (Dense)	(None, 7)	357
dense_59 (Dense)	(None, 7)	56
dense_60 (Dense)	(None, 230)	1,840

Total params: 1,791,443 (6.83 MB)
Trainable params: 1,791,443 (6.83 MB)
Non-trainable params: 0 (0.00 B)

Fig. 3. The LSTM hyperparameters

The Fig. 4 illustrates the decreasing of the loss function using LSTM model through epochs.

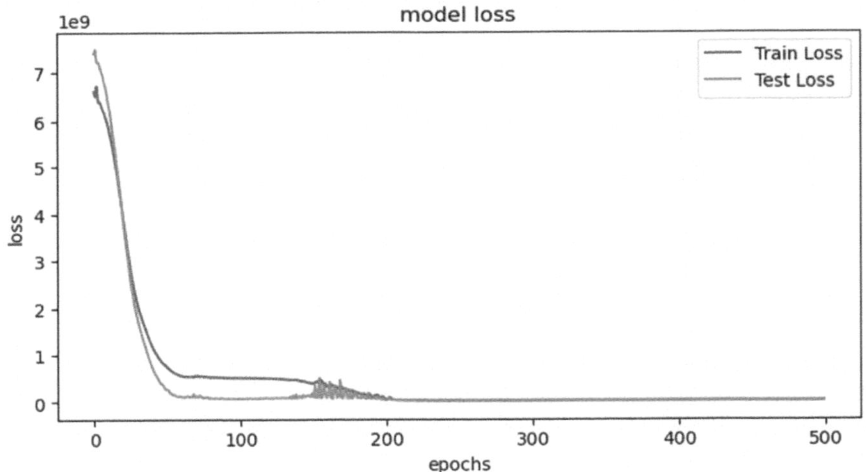

Train Root Mean Squared Error(RMSE): 4495.20; Train Mean Absolute percentage Error(MAPE) : 8.97
Test Root Mean Squared Error(RMSE): 4748.08; Test Mean Absolute percentage Error(MAPE) : 6.60

Fig. 4. The decreasing of the loss function using LSTM model through epochs

3.2 The ANN Model

We consider the Artificial Neural Network constructed using the same environmental index registered in different time steps and the hole countries. We estimate models of the form:

$$Y_i = \Phi\left(\sum_{h=1}^{K} \alpha_h g_1\left(\sum_{j=1}^{L} \beta_j^h g_2\left(\sum_{i=2}^{l_0} \theta_i^{j,h} x_{l_0+2-i}^{i,h}\right)\right)\right) \qquad \forall i = 2, ..., l_0. \tag{6}$$

In Eq. 6 we have for each iteration i up to $N - l_0 - i$ inputs between the years of 2020 (positioned at $l_0 = 32$: the first clean column) and 1988 (the last column) with the total of the years N = 60. We have L first hidden units, K second hidden units and some g_1, g_2 are Relu activation function $g_1(u) = g_2(u) = max(u, 0)$ and linear activation functions $\Phi(u)$. $g_2(u)$ is the activation function linking the $N - l_0 - i$ inputs for each iteration i to the L first hidden units. $g_1(u)$ is the activation function linking the L inputs for each iteration i to the K first hidden units and $\Phi(u)$ links the hidden to output growth. The chosen hyper parameters are: 1000 epochs, 10 batch and the validation data represent 90% from the size of the total data. The learning rate of our used Adam optimizer is fixed at: 0.0005

The model is the same for the three algorithms and it is summarized in this Fig. 5.

These hyper-parameters was trained manually after long manual search especially the data is not very volumic, training these hyper-parameters could not be of big interest. Nevertheless we performed rigorous search using the fine tuning and we obtained promising result.

Model: "sequential_4"

Layer (type)	Output Shape	Param #
dense_8 (Dense)	(None, 60)	441,660
dense_9 (Dense)	(None, 50)	3,050
dense_10 (Dense)	(None, 50)	2,550
dense_11 (Dense)	(None, 50)	2,550
dense_12 (Dense)	(None, 7)	357
dense_13 (Dense)	(None, 7)	56
dense_14 (Dense)	(None, 230)	1,840

Total params: 452,063 (1.72 MB)
Trainable params: 452,063 (1.72 MB)
Non-trainable params: 0 (0.00 B)

Fig. 5. The ANN model's hyperparameters

The Fig. 6 illustrates the decreasing of the loss function using ANN model through epochs.

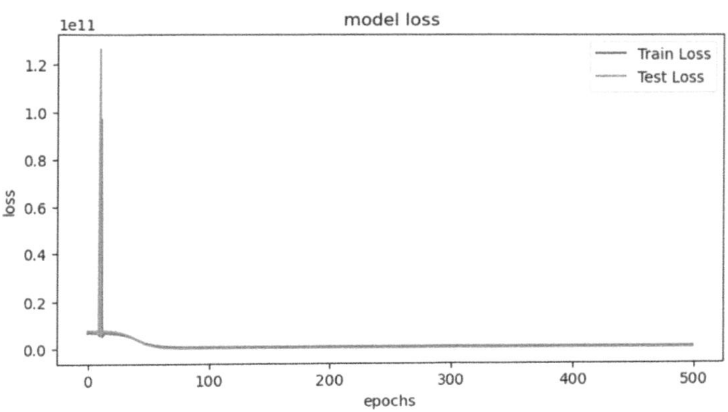

Train Root Mean Squared Error(RMSE): 22630.37; Train Mean Absolute percentage Error(MAPE) : 10.06
Test Root Mean Squared Error(RMSE): 8244.11; Test Mean Absolute percentage Error(MAPE) : 7.23

Fig. 6. The decreasing of the loss function using ANN model through epochs

4 Backward Prediction with the First Hybrid Composition Algorithm of Sarima and LSTM Model

In this section we are going to use as algorithms of backward prediction of times series: an hybrid Arima -LSTM Neural Network using as an input the linear prediction given by the Arima prediction. We consider the Artificial Neural Network constructed using the same environmental 7 variable registered in different time steps. We estimate models of the form:

$$Y_i = \Phi\left(\sum_{h=1}^{K} \alpha_h g_1\left(\sum_{j=1}^{L} \beta_j^h g_2\left(\sum_{i=2}^{l_0} \theta_i^{j,h} x_{l_0+2-i}^{i,h}\right)\right)\right) \qquad \forall i = 2, ..., l_0. \tag{7}$$

In Eq. 7 we have for each iteration i up to $(N - l_0 - i)$ inputs between the years of 2020 (positioned at $l_0 = 32$: the first clean column) and 1988 (the last column), L first hidden units, K second hidden units and some g_1, g_2 are Relu activation function $g_1(u) = g_2(u) = \max(u, 0)$ and linear activation functions $\Phi(u).g_2(u)$ is the activation function linking the $(N - l_0 - i)$ inputs for each iteration i to the L first hidden units. $g_1(u)$ is the activation function linking the L inputs for each iteration i to the K first hidden units and $\Phi(u)$ links the hidden to output growth (Fig. 7).

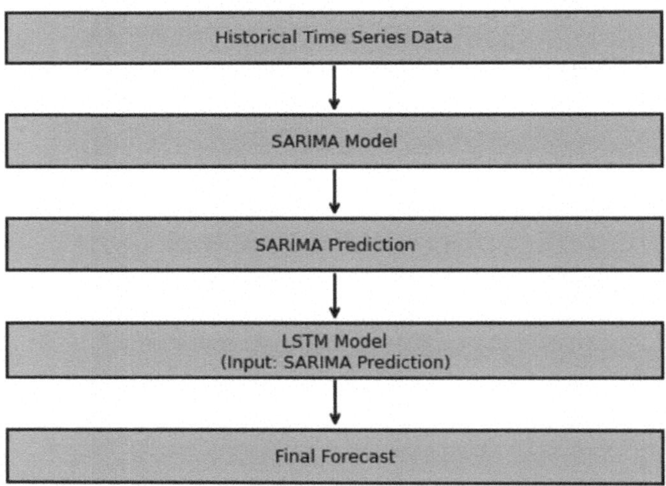

Fig. 7. The non residual diagram of hybrid SARIMA-LSTM model

The chosen hyper parameters are: 960 epochs, 32 batch and the validation data represent 60% from the size of the total data. The learning rate of our used Adam optimizer is fixed at: 0.0005 The model is the same for the three algorithms and it is summarized in this Fig. 8

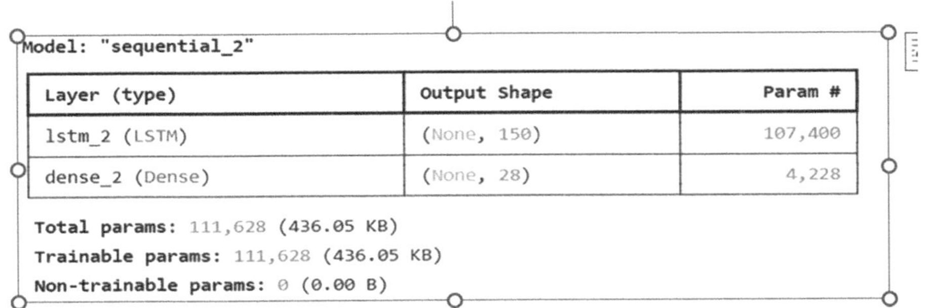
Model: "sequential_2"

Layer (type)	Output Shape	Param #
lstm_2 (LSTM)	(None, 150)	107,400
dense_2 (Dense)	(None, 28)	4,228

Total params: 111,628 (436.05 KB)
Trainable params: 111,628 (436.05 KB)
Non-trainable params: 0 (0.00 B)

Fig. 8. The LSTM model's hyperparameters

Algorithm 2 .

1. Detection of the index of the first clean column l_0.
2. Impute the hole missing values using Linear regression and consider this dataset as an input one.
3. Back-casting
4. Use a Sarima model prediction used an Auto-Arima selection criteria with optimal seasonality=24 searched and fixed manually to obtain the first statistical linear prediction $Y_{l_0} = f_a(x_{l_0+1}, x_{l_0+2}, ..., x_N)$ Such that f_a is the backward prediction using the Sarima model
5. Use an LSTM model $M(l_0)$ related to one iteration and $N - l_0$ would be the dimension of the input vector Sarima vector $Y_{l_0} = (y_1, y_2, ..., y_{l_0})$, and l_0 would be the dimension of the target vector Z_{l_0} : the exact solution.
6. At the end, we calculate the predicted value. $ZZ_{l_0} = ff(Y_{l_0})$ Such that ff is the nonlinear detected patterns using the LSTM method.

Remark 1. The choice of the ARIMA hyper parameters are selected by the use of the auto-arima criteria selection of python. For the choice of the seasonality of the SARIMA was done manually we remarked that this model is sensitive to the large periods more the seasonality increases we have better accuracy as it appears in the Fig. 5.

This Fig. 9 illustrates the use of the Auto-Arima with seasonal detection criteria to detect the optimal parameters of the Arima model for the 225th country.

This Fig. 10 illustrates the decreasing of the loss function using Sarima-LSTM model through epochs.

```
ARIMA(0,1,0)(0,1,1)[24]                 : AIC=95.984, Time=0.06 sec
ARIMA(0,1,0)(1,1,1)[24]                 : AIC=97.984, Time=0.10 sec
ARIMA(1,1,0)(0,1,0)[24]                 : AIC=95.263, Time=0.05 sec
ARIMA(0,1,1)(0,1,0)[24]                 : AIC=93.926, Time=0.06 sec
ARIMA(0,1,1)(1,1,0)[24]                 : AIC=95.908, Time=0.39 sec
ARIMA(0,1,1)(1,1,1)[24]                 : AIC=97.850, Time=0.50 sec
ARIMA(1,1,1)(0,1,0)[24]                 : AIC=95.561, Time=0.06 sec
ARIMA(0,1,2)(0,1,0)[24]                 : AIC=inf, Time=0.07 sec
ARIMA(1,1,2)(0,1,0)[24]                 : AIC=inf, Time=0.10 sec
ARIMA(0,1,1)(0,1,0)[24] intercept       : AIC=95.102, Time=0.05 sec

Best model:  ARIMA(0,1,1)(0,1,0)[24]
Total fit time: 2.394 seconds
225
32
[ 8037.03940003  8146.60476365  8220.24173456  8295.81559504
  8373.17918091  8452.09657645  8531.61044209  8619.45012798
  8702.7525081   8788.38010158  8875.68304459  8965.72716798
  9058.35790075  9153.5754059   9252.41721018  9355.34719181
  9461.92539169  9572.20595412  9685.70436613  9806.10635442
 10004.56918583  9656.3324521   9789.75120442  9931.01216668
 10049.23913321 10158.80449684 10232.44146775 10308.01532823]
0.11450745835230178
Performing stepwise search to minimize aic
```

Fig. 9. The sarima model with an auto-sarima research criteria

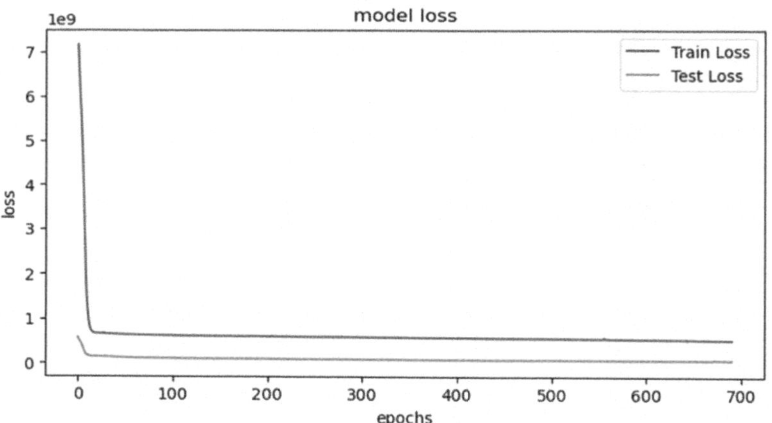


```
Train Root Mean Squared Error(RMSE): 22782.09; Train Mean Absolute percentage Error(MAPE) : 8.83
Test Root Mean Squared Error(RMSE): 8678.65; Test Mean Absolute percentage Error(MAPE) : 11.99
```

Fig. 10. The sarima model with an auto-sarima research criteria

To test the accuracy of this approach we calculate the mean absolute percentage error using the Sarima model and the mean absolute error of the hybrid Arima-LSTM-algorithm starting from a linear regression imputation.

Models	Arima	Sarima (4)	Sarima (12)	Sarima (24)	Arima-LSTM
Mean absolute percentage error (%)	37.6	32.24	14.99	10.96	9.14

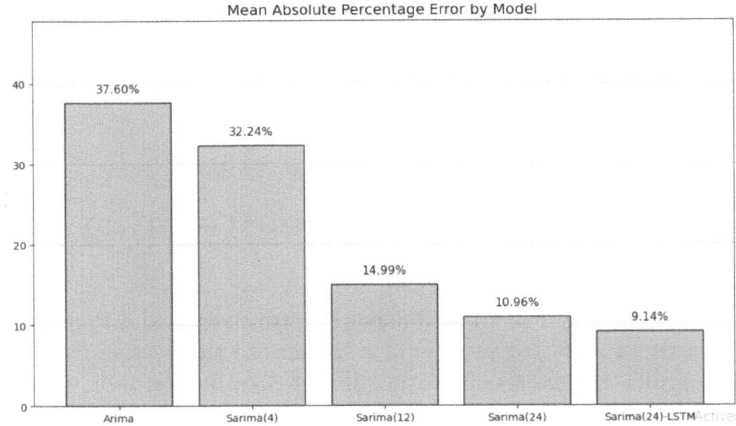

Fig. 11. Accuracy of different models

This table and the Fig. 11 show that with the hybrid algorithm the error is reduced considerably.

5 Backward Prediction Using Novel Hybrid Arima-LSTM Models

5.1 The First Novel Hybrid Model

Both ARIMA and LSTM models offer distinct advantages and face specific limitations when applied to time series forecasting. ARIMA models are well-suited for handling linear data patterns but often struggle with nonlinear relationships.

In contrast, neural networks such as LSTM are capable of modelling both linear and nonlinear time series data. However, they typically require extensive training time and lack standardized procedures for optimal hyperparameter selection.

To leverage the strengths of both approaches while mitigating their individual weaknesses, a hybrid model is proposed. This model combines the predictive capabilities of ARIMA and LSTM, allowing each component to contribute its specialized expertise.

As a result, the hybrid framework is expected to yield more accurate and robust forecasts compared to using either model independently. Such hybridization enables the models to compensate for each other's limitations and enhance overall performance.

In this approach [2,10,15,16], seasonal decomposition, available via the stats model's library, is used to break down the original time series into three components: trend, seasonality, and residuals.

In our approach the SARIMA model is applied to the trend component obtention with optimal parameter by the use of an Auto-Arima criteria. Meanwhile, the LSTM model is tasked with learning the patterns within the seasonal and residual components, which often contain nonlinear features and short-term fluctuations. The final forecast is obtained by recombining the outputs of all three components, as described in Eq. 8.

$$\text{Prediction}[i] = \text{Tendprediction}[i] + \text{Residualprediction}[i] \qquad \forall i = 2, \ldots l_0 \quad (8)$$

In this work and due to the fact that the LSTM model track well seasonal tendencies, I proposed this algorithm:

The first Novel Hybrid Algorithm:

Generally, when authors deal with Multivariate time series and Panel series they treat them with an iterative process of a univariate time series. In this work I propose to predict the hole column of all world countries as a unique vector counting on the performance of the LSTM to detect vectorial patterns.

The algorithm is presented as follow:

Algorithm 3 .

1. Perform an optimal search of Arima parameters with an Auto-Arima() search criteria to predict the trend
2. Calculate the residual part: Residual=exact solution-predicted(trend)
3. Use an LSTM (Long-Short-Time-Memory) architecture to predict the seasonality and the non-linearities for the residual part prediction.

This diagram Fig. 12 resume this approach :

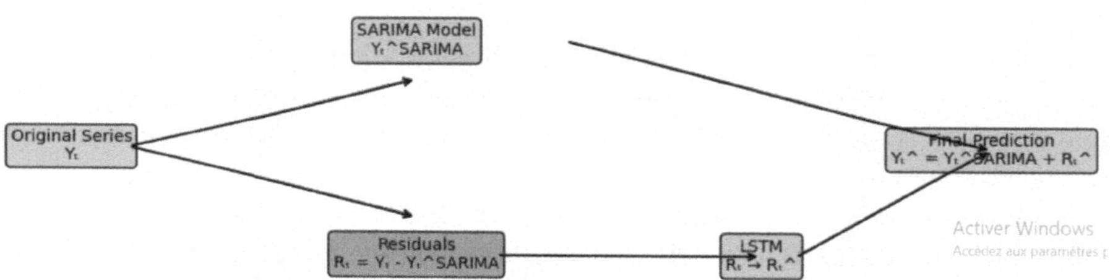

Fig. 12. The hybrid LSTM-sarima model's decomposition

The hyper-parameters are presented in the Fig. 13 with an Adam optimizer with a use of an Adam optimizer with a learning rate = 0.005. These parameters are performed manually but we made a fine-tuning and wr obtained promising results.

Model: "sequential_9"

Toggle output scrolling

Layer (type)	Output Shape	Param #
lstm_9 (LSTM)	(None, 60)	787,440
dense_54 (Dense)	(None, 50)	3,050
dense_55 (Dense)	(None, 50)	2,550
dense_56 (Dense)	(None, 50)	2,550
dense_57 (Dense)	(None, 7)	357
dense_58 (Dense)	(None, 7)	56
dense_59 (Dense)	(None, 230)	1,840

Total params: 797,843 (3.04 MB)

Trainable params: 797,843 (3.04 MB)

Non-trainable params: 0 (0.00 B)

Fig. 13. The hybrid LSTM-sarima model's hyperparameters

The Fig. 14 illustrates the decreasing of the loss function using LSTM model through epochs.

5.2 The Second Novel Hybrid (SARIMA, LSTM)-LSTM Model

In this section we are going to represent the algorithm of back-casting times series based on an Artificial Neural Network.

To the best of our knowledge, the proposed hybrid model–where SARIMA and LSTM prediction vectors are combined and used as input features to a second-level LSTM meta-learner has not yet been explored in the existing literature.

We fix the hyper-parameters as follow: 960 epochs and 32 batch-size. We use Adam optimizer with a learning rate of 0.0005.

The diagram of these algorithms is represented in the Fig. 15.

The hyper-parameters are presented in the Fig. 16 with an Adam optimizer with a use of an Adam optimizer with a learning rate = 0.005.

The Fig. 17 illustrates the decreasing of the loss function using the Augumented hybrid Sarima-LSTM model through epochs (Table 1).

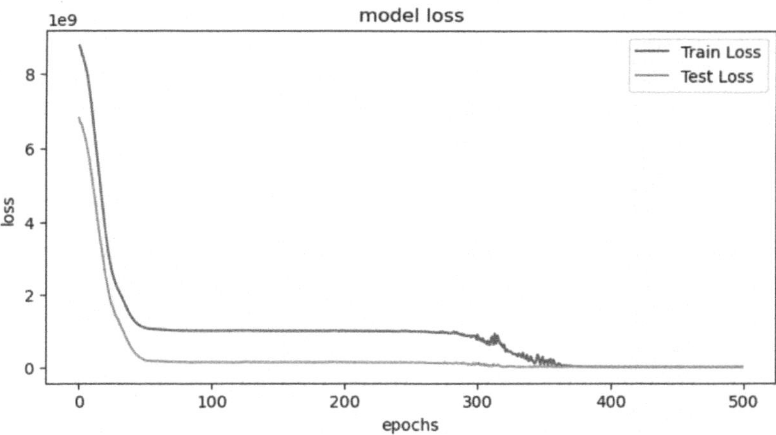

Fig. 14. The decreasing of the loss function using the hybrid LSTM-sarima model through epochs

---

Algorithm 4 .

1. Detection of the index of the first clean column t_0
2. Impute the hole missing values using Linear regression and consider this dataset as an input one.
3. Back-casting
4. Use a Sarima model prediction integrating an Auto-Arima with seasonal detection criteria to obtain the first optimal statistical linear prediction $Y_{l_0} = x_{l_0} = f_a(x_{l_0+1}, x_{l_0+2}, ..., x_N)$ Such that f_a is the prediction using the Sarima model
5. Use an LSTM model $M(N_{l_0}, l_0)$ related to one iteration and $N - l_0$ would be the dimension of the input vector vector $X_{N-l_0} = (x_1, x_2, ..., x_{N-l_0})$, and l_0 would be the dimension of the target vector $Z_{l_0} = (z_1, z_2, ..., z_{l_0})$, : the exact solution.
6. At the end, we calculate the predicted value. $ZZ_{l_0} = ff(Z_{N-l_0}) = (zz_1, zz_2, ..., zz_{l_0})$, Such that ff is the nonlinear detected patterns using the LSTM method.
7. We make an assembling in a unique vector of the two outputs given by the Sarima model which detects better the linear patterns and the output or prediction given by the LSTM model which detects more the nonlinear patterns. This vector would be considered as an input for our LSTM final architecture.
   Then we use an LSTM model $M(2\times(l_0), l_0)$ related to one iteration and $2\times l_0$ would be the dimension of the input vector $M_{2x(l_0)} = (y_1, y_2, ..., y_{l_0}, zz_1, zz_2, ..., zz_{l_0})$, and l_0 would be the dimension of the target vector $Z_{l_0} = (z_1, z_2, ..., z_{l_0})$: the exact solution.
8. At the end, we calculate the predicted value :

$$MM_{l_0} = ff(M_{2x(l_0)})$$

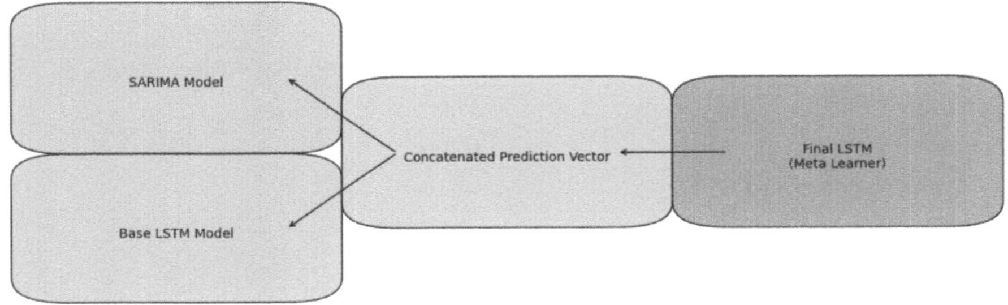

Fig. 15. The augumented hybrid LSTM-sarima model's diagram

Model: "sequential_154"

Layer (type)	Output Shape	Param #
lstm_130 (LSTM)	(None, 150)	124,200
dense_428 (Dense)	(None, 28)	4,228

Total params: 128,428 (501.67 KB)
Trainable params: 128,428 (501.67 KB)
Non-trainable params: 0 (0.00 B)

Fig. 16. The augumented hybrid LSTM-sarima model's hyperparameters

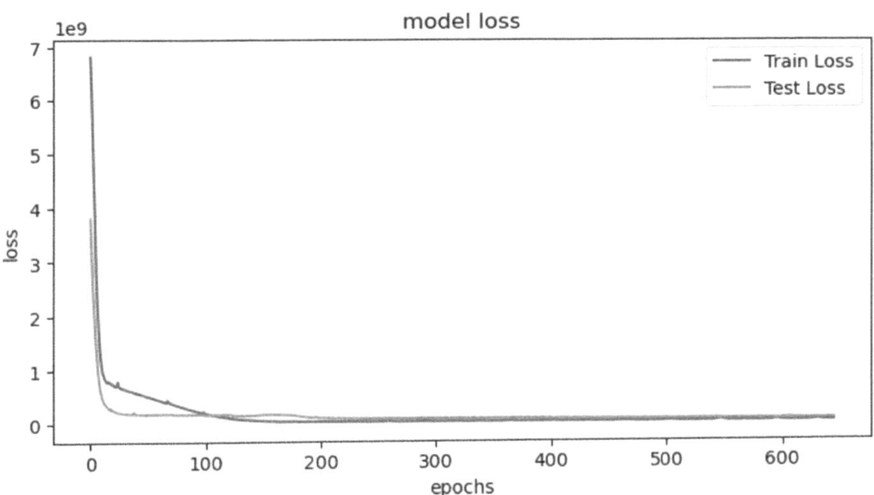

Train Root Mean Squared Error(RMSE): 2388.04; Train Mean Absolute percentage Error(MAPE) : 5.89
Test Root Mean Squared Error(RMSE): 6712.92; Test Mean Absolute percentage Error(MAPE) : 8.14

Fig. 17. The decreasing of the loss function using the augumented hybrid sarima-LSTM model through epochs

Table 1. Table of performance of all used algorithms.

Models	Mean absolute percentage error (%)
Arima	37.6
Sarima (24)	10.96
Composed sarima-LSTM	9.14
ANN	9.77
LSTM	8.73
Residual hybrid sarima-LSTM	4.8
Novel augumented hybrid sarima-LSTM	6.11

Remark 2. With this novel model we are turning SARIMA and LSTM into feature generators, and then using a second-level LSTM to learn how to weight and combine their outputs a meta-learning architecture.

This could learn:

1. How much trust to place in SARIMA vs. LSTM at each time step,
2. And any non-linear relationships between the two output streams.

This approach is advantageous due to

1. Flexibility: The final LSTM can learn dynamic weighting over time.
2. Utility : when SARIMA and LSTM learn complementary signals.
3. the possibility of using it for ensemble learning or model stacking in time series.

6 Conclusion

In this work we proposed a novel method to backward predict the renewable water consumption per capita per year all over the world so the time series that we deal with is a Panel one not easy to handle due to its vectorial aspect sized 230 the number of countries.

Due the non-linearity and seasonality aspects we used Sarima and LSTM deep learning algorithms to detect trends, seasonality and non-linearities patterns respectively. Generally, to use an LSTM architecture data must be arranged in a supervised way.

So, we applied this but not as usual to a raw but to an entire vector. Even with a single Arima, Sarima, ANN and LSTM models results were not very impressive due to the complexity of the vector model, we use an hybrid model a combination between a Sarima model to predict trends and stationarities and an LSTM model to predict residuals characterized by seasonality and non-linearity.

We tried in parallel many other algorithms: we composed an LSTM to a Sarima model and finally we used trends and residuals together as an augmented available precedent data to predict the future using an LSTM algorithm and results were exposed. We note that the two proposed novel hybrid algorithms outperform the other.

The complexity of this work consists in handling large vectorial data which was reshaped carefully to be adapted to an LSTM architecture and the results was impressive. This time the prediction of the residual part was done on the half of the test part assumed to be data validation since the train residual part already vanished.

Future works for a supervised learning using LSTM we would consider the half of the residual test part as a train part and the backward prediction would occur on the second test part and inversely we consider the second part of the test part as a train part and we will make a forward prediction would take place on the first part, in this way the hole test part would be reconstructed in a supervised learning way. For the unsupervised LSTM use we can reshape our inputs into one step-time but more features and let the LSTM detect the complexity horizontally and vertically between different patterns.

References

1. Abdul Wahid, A., Arunbabu, E.: Forecasting water quality using seasonal ARIMA model by integrating in-situ measurements and remote sensing techniques in Krishnagiri Reservoir. India. Water Pract. Technol. **17**(5), 1230–1252 (2022)
2. Abu, N., Aishah, S., Taib, T., Zainal, N.A., Ramli, N.A., Go, C.K.: Time series forecasting for tourism industry in Malaysia. Adv. Appl. Stat. **92**(1), 77–87 (2025)
3. Chen, S.-H.: Computationally Intelligent Agents in Economics and Finance. Springer, Berlin (2007)
4. Dave, E., Leonardo, A., Jeanice, M., Hanafiah, N.: Forecasting Indonesia exports using a hybrid model ARIMA-LSTM. Procedia Comput. Sci. **179**, 480–487 (2021)
5. Divisekara, R.W., Jayasinghe, G., Kumari, K.: Forecasting the red lentils commodity market price using SARIMA models. SN Bus. Econ. **1**(1), 20 (2020)
6. Hamiane, S., Khalifi, H., Ghanou, Y., Casalino, G.: Forecasting the gross domestic product using LSTM and ARIMA. In: 2023 IEEE International Conference on Technology Management, Operations and Decisions (ICTMOD), pp. 1–6. IEEE, Tunisia (2023)
7. Hochreiter, S., Schmidhuber, J.: Long short-term memory. Neural Comput. **9**(8), 1735–1780 (1997)
8. Hu, Z., Zhang, Y., Zhao, Y., Xie, M., Zhong, J., Tu, Z., Liu, J.: A water quality prediction method based on the deep LSTM network considering correlation in smart mariculture. Sensors **19**(6), 1420 (2019)
9. Li, L., Jiang, P., Xu, H., Lin, G., Guo, D., Wu, H.: Water quality prediction based on recurrent neural network and improved evidence theory: a case study of Qiantang River, China. Environ. Sci. Pollut. Res. **26**, 19879–19896 (2019)
10. Pascanu, R., Mikolov, T., Bengio, Y.: On the difficulty of training recurrent neural networks. In: International Conference on Machine Learning, pp. 1310–1318. PMLR, Atlanta (2013)
11. Sattarzadeh, A.R., Kutadinata, R.J., Pathirana, P.N., Huynh, V.T.: A novel hybrid deep learning model with ARIMA Conv-LSTM networks and shuffle attention layer for short-term traffic flow prediction. Transp. A: Transp. Sci. **21**(1), 2236724 (2025)

12. Tealab, A., Hefny, H., Badr, A.: Forecasting of nonlinear time series using ANN. Futur. Comput. Inform. J. **2**(1), 39–47 (2017)
13. Tokgöz, A., Ünal, G.: A RNN-based time series approach for forecasting Turkish electricity load. In: 2018 26th Signal Processing and Communications Applications Conference (SIU), pp. 1–4. IEEE, Izmir (2018)
14. Valipour, M.: Long-term runoff study using SARIMA and ARIMA models in the United States. Meteorol. Appl. **22**(3), 592–598 (2015)
15. Wu, D.C.W., Ji, L., He, K., Tso, K.F.G.: Forecasting tourist daily arrivals with a hybrid SARIMA-LSTM approach. J. Hosp. Tour. Res. **45**(1), 52–67 (2021)
16. Wu, W., Guo, M., Wang, S., Han, J.: Time series anomaly detection hybrid model based on SARIMA and LSTM. J. Comput. Electron. Inf. Manag. **16**(1), 63–69 (2025)
17. Xu, X., Zhai, X., Ke, A., Lin, Y., Zhang, X., Xie, Z., Lou, Y.: Prediction of leakage pressure in fractured carbonate reservoirs based on PSO-LSTM neural network. Processes **11**(7), 2222 (2023)
18. Zhou, J., Wang, Y., Xiao, F., Wang, Y., Sun, L.: Water quality prediction method based on IGRA and LSTM. Water **10**(9), 1148 (2018)

Emerging Technologies for Sustainable Development

Hiba Jouini(✉) and Rym Ben Smida

M2M Team, ESPRIT School of Engineering, Tunis, Tunisia
{hiba.jouini,rym.bensmida}@esprit.tn

Abstract. This paper presents a comprehensive review of the transformative potential of emerging technologies-namely Artificial Intelligence (AI), the Internet of Things (IoT), and Big Data-in advancing sustainable development across multiple sectors. Rather than focusing on a specific case study or technical innovation, the review synthesizes current research and developments to highlight how AI enhances renewable energy systems through improved efficiency, grid management, and predictive maintenance. It further explores the convergence of AI and IoT, known as Artificial Intelligence of Things (AIoT), which is driving intelligent automation and optimized decision-making in industries such as agriculture, healthcare, and smart cities. The paper also critically examines the challenges to widespread adoption, including data privacy and security concerns, integration complexity, scalability issues, energy demands, and ethical and regulatory considerations. By providing an overview of these technologies' capabilities and limitations, the review underscores the importance of transparent governance and collaborative frameworks to fully realize their potential for sustainable development.

Keywords: Internet of Things · Artificial Intelligence · Artificial Intelligence of Things · Sustainable development

1 Introduction

In the 21st century, the world faces a convergence of unprecedented challenges that threaten ecosystems, economies, and societies. Climate change, driven by rising greenhouse gas emissions, is causing extreme weather events, sea-level rise, and biodiversity loss. Simultaneously, resource depletion such as overuse of freshwater, deforestation, and the loss of arable land is exacerbating food and water insecurity. Social inequality magnifies these issues, as marginalized communities disproportionately bear the impacts of environmental degradation and economic instability [1]. These interconnected challenges highlight the urgent need for sustainable development strategies that balance economic growth, environmental protection, and social equity.

Emerging technologies are increasingly recognized as transformative tools for addressing these global challenges. Artificial Intelligence (AI), the Internet of Things

F. Kamoun et al. (Eds.): AFRICATEK 2025, LNICST 677, pp. 269–277, 2026.
https://doi.org/10.1007/978-3-032-16638-8_18

(IoT), and Big Data are reshaping industries and enabling new pathways to sustainability. AI plays a pivotal role in optimizing renewable energy systems by improving forecasting accuracy, enabling predictive maintenance, and stabilizing energy grids through real-time adjustments. IoT sensors, combined with AI analytics, enhance efficiency in agriculture, urban infrastructure, and manufacturing by enabling precision resource management and automation [4]. Big Data further supports these efforts by providing actionable insights from vast and diverse datasets, thereby driving smarter decision-making across sectors. Together, these technologies foster innovations in renewable energy, sustainable food production, and circular economy systems that minimize waste and maximize resource efficiency [8].

However, the adoption of these transformative technologies faces significant barriers. High costs, inadequate infrastructure, and policy gaps hinder widespread implementation, particularly in developing regions. Ethical concerns such as data privacy in AI and equitable access to technology must also be addressed to ensure inclusivity. The digital divide further risks exacerbating inequalities if marginalized communities are left behind in accessing these innovations [16].

To overcome these challenges, collaborative efforts among governments, industries, academia, and civil society are essential. Investments in infrastructure, supportive policies, and capacity-building initiatives are needed to unlock the full potential of emerging technologies for sustainable development. By addressing these barriers proactively and fostering innovation responsibly, we can accelerate progress toward a more equitable and resilient future. This paper explores the transformative potential of AI, IoT, and Big Data alongside related innovations in driving sustainable development across various sectors.

2 State of Art

2.1 Renewable Energy Technologies and Artificial Intelligence (AI)

Artificial Intelligence (AI) is reshaping the renewable energy sector, serving as a cornerstone for achieving a sustainable energy future. By utilizing advanced algorithms and extensive datasets, AI enhances the efficiency and reliability of renewable energy systems, addressing the inherent challenges of variability in sources like solar and wind. This optimization encompasses predictive maintenance, fault detection, and real-time adjustments to ensure consistent energy output. Machine learning (ML) and deep learning (DL) are central to this transformation. ML analyzes historical weather data to forecast energy production with precision, enabling proactive management, while DL processes complex datasets to refine predictions by accounting for subtle environmental changes and system dynamics. These capabilities are critical for maintaining grid stability by anticipating supply-demand fluctuations [1].

Integrating renewable energy into power grids is a complex challenge that AI is uniquely equipped to solve. AI-driven grid management systems dynamically balance loads, manage voltage fluctuations, and optimize power flow by analyzing real-time grid data. These systems detect anomalies and make instantaneous adjustments to prevent outages and enhance resilience. Additionally, AI predicts energy production and consumption patterns, optimizing the timing for storing and releasing energy to minimize waste and maximize reliability.

AI also delivers substantial economic and environmental benefits. By improving forecasting accuracy and optimizing resource allocation, it reduces operational costs, minimizes energy waste, and makes renewable energy more economically viable. This aligns with the urgent need to transition away from fossil fuels—major contributors to global warming—and adopt sustainable alternatives like solar, wind, and geothermal energy. Despite their growth potential, these sources face challenges due to intermittency and variability, which AI helps overcome by creating intelligent systems that adapt dynamically to changing conditions [2].

AI facilitates the development of smart grids—networks that optimize energy distribution and storage—by forecasting generation and consumption patterns with remarkable accuracy. Machine learning models analyze weather patterns, historical production data, and real-time consumption metrics to fine-tune system parameters for efficient energy flow. Predictive maintenance powered by AI anticipates equipment failures, enabling timely interventions that reduce downtime and operational costs while extending infrastructure lifespan. For example, AI optimizes solar panel angles for maximum sunlight capture or adjusts wind turbine blades based on wind speed and direction [3].

In conclusion, the integration of AI with renewable energy technologies offers immense promise for creating a sustainable future. Continued advancements in machine learning algorithms, edge computing, and secure data management will be crucial in overcoming current limitations. By harnessing AI's power, we can accelerate the transition to cleaner energy solutions, mitigate climate change impacts, and ensure a reliable energy future for generations to come.

2.2 Artificial Intelligence (AI) and Big Data

The integration of IoT and Big Data analytics is reshaping industries by leveraging the vast amounts of data generated by connected devices to deliver actionable insights. IoT devices, such as sensors and smart systems, produce enormous volumes of real-time data that require scalable Big Data platforms for storage, processing, and analysis. These platforms uncover hidden patterns and trends, enabling organizations to optimize operations, improve decision-making, and predict future outcomes. The combination of Big Data with AI further amplifies these capabilities, introducing advanced techniques like pattern recognition, predictive modeling, and anomaly detection. AI algorithms excel in processing massive datasets efficiently, identifying correlations and anomalies that might elude human analysis, thereby enhancing strategic planning and operational precision. For example, in healthcare, AI-driven Big Data analytics can process data from wearable devices, electronic health records, and genomic databases to craft personalized treatments and predict disease outbreaks [4].

This synergy between IoT, Big Data, and AI revolutionizes operations across various sectors. In manufacturing, IoT sensors monitor machine performance while Big Data analytics identifies trends in equipment failures to enable predictive maintenance and minimize downtime. In smart cities, IoT-enabled traffic systems combined with AI tools analyze congestion patterns to optimize traffic flow dynamically. Furthermore, IoT analytics enhances customer experiences by tailoring services based on detailed behavioral insights while improving operational efficiency through automation and resource optimization. The scalability of IoT analytics platforms allows businesses to adapt flexibly to changing demands without incurring excessive costs [5].

Despite its transformative potential, integrating IoT with Big Data and AI presents challenges such as ensuring data privacy, managing algorithmic biases, and addressing the need for high-quality data inputs. Future research must focus on developing ethical frameworks to mitigate these issues while fostering innovation to maximize the benefits of this technology. Collaborative efforts among researchers, policymakers, and industry leaders are essential to navigate these complexities effectively. By harnessing the power of IoT-enabled Big Data analytics paired with AI technologies, organizations can unlock unprecedented opportunities for efficiency, innovation, and growth across diverse domains [6].

2.3 Artificial Intelligence of Things (AIoT)

The convergence of the Internet of Things (IoT) and Artificial Intelligence (AI) is revolutionizing various industries by enabling intelligent systems that improve efficiency and decision-making. This integration, termed the Artificial Intelligence of Things (AIoT), harnesses the massive data generated by IoT devices, allowing AI to derive actionable insights and automate processes. The following sections delve into the key dimensions of this transformative synergy [7].

IoT extends the digital realm into the physical world by creating a network of interconnected sensors and devices that collect real-time data. Beyond mere connectivity, IoT establishes a sensory infrastructure embedded in consumer products, industrial machinery, and urban systems. For instance, IoT sensors in environmental monitoring track air and water quality for pollution control, while smart retail shelves optimize inventory management and customer experiences [8].

This paradigm shifts in connectivity fosters automation, real-time monitoring, and enhances efficiency across sectors. From wearable health trackers to industrial sensors and connected vehicles, IoT is a driving innovation in healthcare, agriculture, and manufacturing. However, its rapid expansion raises concerns about data security, privacy, and interoperability that must be addressed to unlock its full potential.

Advancements in technologies like edge computing, 5G networks, and AI-driven analytics are accelerating IoT's evolution. These innovations enable faster data processing at device-level (edge computing) and support applications such as robotic farming, patient monitoring, and wildlife tracking. AI amplifies IoT's capabilities by analyzing complex datasets for predictive maintenance, adaptive decision-making, and autonomous operations.

The integration of AI with IoT holds transformative potential for civil applications such as urban planning, transportation, and environmental management. By combining AI's data processing power with IoT's connectivity, systems become more adaptive and responsive. However, challenges like technical limitations, regulatory hurdles, and ethical concerns regarding privacy must be addressed to balance innovation with societal impacts [9].

In summary, the fusion of IoT and AI is creating a globally interconnected ecosystem that promises smarter infrastructure, enhanced automation, and data-driven insights across diverse domains. As emerging technologies continue to mature, this synergy will redefine how we interact with our environment while addressing critical challenges for a sustainable future [10].

Artificial Intelligence (AI) significantly enhances the efficiency of Internet of Things (IoT) systems by optimizing data processing, enabling automation, and improving decision-making. Here is the keyways AI achieve this:

Predictive Maintenance: AI algorithms analyze IoT sensor data to predict equipment failures, allowing proactive maintenance and minimizing downtime. This reduces repair costs and enhances productivity in industries like manufacturing.

Real-Time Decision-Making: AI processes large volumes of IoT data rapidly, enabling systems to make instant decisions. For example, autonomous vehicles use AI to analyze sensor inputs and navigate safely in real-time [11].

Improved Data Analytics: AI extracts actionable insights from IoT data by identifying patterns and anomalies that are difficult for humans to detect. This helps optimize operations, manage risks, and enhance accuracy across sectors such as healthcare and agriculture.

Automation: AI-powered IoT systems automate routine tasks, such as inventory management or energy optimization in smart buildings, improving operational efficiency and reducing resource consumption.

3 Applications of Emerging Technologies

Emerging technologies are revolutionizing sustainability across multiple sectors by introducing innovative solutions to modern challenges. In the energy sector, renewable sources like solar and wind power are increasingly replacing fossil fuels, while grid-scale batteries address the intermittency of these resources. Artificial Intelligence (AI) plays a pivotal role in this transition by analyzing vast datasets to forecast energy production and consumption with precision. Machine learning models process historical weather data, seasonal trends, and real-time sensor inputs to predict fluctuations in renewable energy generation, enabling proactive resource allocation and grid stabilization [12]. AI-driven smart grids further enhance energy infrastructure by intelligently managing energy flow, integrating distributed resources such as rooftop solar panels and electric vehicle charging stations, and optimizing component performance for maximum efficiency. Despite its transformative potential, AI adoption in renewable energy faces challenges such as data quality issues, scalability requirements, and regulatory barriers, which require robust infrastructure investments and updated frameworks [13].

In agriculture, precision farming techniques supported by IoT devices optimize water and fertilizer use to ensure food security while minimizing environmental impact. AI-powered systems analyze crop health using drones equipped with machine learning-based vision tools, enabling targeted interventions that reduce carbon footprints and preserve soil integrity. Water recycling technologies complement these efforts by collecting runoff for reuse in irrigation, reducing waste and pollution [14].

Healthcare is experiencing significant advancements through the integration of IoT and AI technologies. IoT-enabled devices combined with AI revolutionize patient monitoring and diagnostics by analyzing medical images, genomic data, and patient records for early disease detection and personalized treatments. Intelligent robotic systems assist in surgeries with enhanced precision, while AI-powered drug discovery platforms accelerate the development of targeted therapies by processing extensive biological datasets [15].

Urban sustainability is being redefined through smart cities powered by IoT and AI integration. IoT sensors generate real-time data on traffic, environmental conditions, and infrastructure usage, which AI processes to optimize resource allocation, streamline waste management routes, predict maintenance needs, and enhance public safety through intelligent video analytics. These innovations foster safer communities while reducing environmental impact [16].

Industry 4.0 exemplifies the transformative potential of emerging technologies in manufacturing. Smart factories leverage predictive maintenance to minimize downtime, optimize production processes using real-time quality control systems, and enhance supply chain efficiency through AI-driven demand forecasting and logistics optimization [17].

However, the widespread deployment of these technologies presents challenges such as cybersecurity risks, privacy concerns, ethical considerations, equitable access to technology, and bridging the digital divide. Transparent governance frameworks and collaborative efforts among academia, policymakers, and industry leaders are essential to unlocking their full potential for a sustainable future. By addressing these challenges proactively, emerging technologies can pave the way for enhanced efficiency, resilience, inclusivity, and environmental stewardship across sectors [18] (Table 1).

Table 1. Applications of emerging technologies

Technology	Example	Examples/countries
AIoT (AI + IoT)	Precision agriculture	Aerobotics startup in South Africa, Kenya
Artificial Intelligence & Big Data	Digital transformation and data-driven decision making	Various African countries
Renewable Energy Technologies + AI	Smart grid and energy optimization	Nigeria, South Africa

4 Challenges and Barriers

Emerging technologies such as AI-powered IoT (AIoT), AI-driven renewable energy systems, and AI integrated with big data possess transformative potential but face several challenges and barriers to widespread adoption. A key concern is data privacy and security, as these systems rely on vast amounts of sensitive information collected from interconnected devices, energy grids, and consumers. Cybersecurity threats, including unauthorized access and data breaches, jeopardize the integrity of these technologies. Integration complexity also poses significant hurdles, requiring substantial investments to retrofit legacy infrastructure with AI capabilities and develop the necessary technical expertise. Scalability remains another challenge; deploying AI solutions at scale demands robust computational resources and infrastructure to process the large datasets generated by IoT devices and renewable energy systems. Additionally, the energy-intensive nature of AI models, particularly deep learning algorithms, raises concerns about their environmental impact, potentially offsetting sustainability gains [19, 20].

Regulatory and ethical considerations further complicate progress, as existing frameworks often fail to address liability issues, biases in AI algorithms, and equitable access to advanced technologies. The effectiveness of AI systems heavily depends on the quality and availability of data; poor sensor networks or unreliable data management strategies can lead to inaccurate predictions in applications such as renewable energy generation or IoT systems. Workforce skill gaps also hinder adoption, with a shortage of professionals proficient in both AI development and domain-specific applications like energy systems. In renewable energy specifically, intermittency issues in sources like solar and wind create operational challenges that AI must address through predictive analytics and intelligent grid management. Ensuring grid stability while integrating distributed energy resources demands sophisticated optimization algorithms that require significant computational power. Similarly, IoT-enabled smart grids face difficulties in managing real-time data transmission while maintaining system reliability [21].

Cost barriers represent another critical challenge, as implementing AIoT systems or upgrading renewable energy infrastructure involves high upfront expenses that may deter investment without clear financial incentives or regulatory support. To overcome these obstacles, collaboration among industry leaders, policymakers, and academia is essential to establish robust cybersecurity measures, ethical guidelines, scalable solutions, and equitable access. By addressing these challenges proactively, the full potential of emerging technologies can be realized to drive innovation, enhance sustainability, and optimize operations across industries [22].

5 The Way Forward

As the convergence of IoT, AI, and Big Data accelerates, with over 41 billion IoT devices expected by 2025 and the global AI-in-big-data-and-IoT market projected to exceed $26 billion in the same year, the imperative for coordinated, forward-looking action becomes clear. Policymakers must prioritize the creation of robust governance frameworks that balance innovation with ethical responsibility starting with regulatory sandboxes for blockchain-IoT systems in key sectors like healthcare and logistics, which allow for real-world experimentation while safeguarding data privacy and security. Flexible, sector-specific regulations should be developed to address the unique needs of sensitive domains such as medical IoT, where strict standards for data protection and algorithmic transparency are essential, while fostering a lighter-touch environment for industrial and smart city applications. Public-private partnerships will be crucial for scaling edge computing infrastructure, which enables real-time, low-latency solutions for industrial automation, autonomous drones, and adaptive urban systems areas where AI makes IoT data 25%

more efficient and analytics 42% more effective. Pilot projects should be designed to demonstrate the practical benefits of these technologies: for example, smart agriculture digital twins that leverage IoT sensors, drones, and AI analytics to optimize resource use and predict crop diseases; adaptive traffic management systems powered by edge AI to reduce congestion and emissions; blockchain-secured pharmaceutical supply chains that ensure the integrity and traceability of drugs from factory to pharmacy; and community energy microgrids that use AI and IoT to provide equitable access to renewable energy in underserved regions. To address the ethical and social implications of this technological wave, initiatives such as data sovereignty programs and "AI for Social Good" grants should be prioritized, empowering individuals to control their data and directing innovation toward solving pressing societal challenges. Simultaneously, organizations must focus on data minimization and thoughtful governance to comply with the growing number of state privacy laws and to avoid unintended consequences. Education and workforce development are equally critical: integrating AI literacy and IoT ethics into K-12 curricula will foster responsible digital citizenship, while reskilling programs using AR/VR and immersive training will prepare workers for new roles in digital twin management, blockchain auditing, and other emerging fields. Collaborative platforms and open-source repositories should be established to facilitate the sharing of AI models and IoT datasets, governed by frameworks that ensure ethical reuse and interoperability. By embracing these strategic priorities regulatory innovation, infrastructure investment, ethical and inclusive pilot projects, robust data governance, and comprehensive education stakeholders can ensure that the convergence of IoT, AI, and Big Data not only drives technological advancement but also fosters sustainable, equitable, and responsible progress for society as a whole, while addressing challenges such as privacy, bias, and equitable access in an increasingly connected world.

6 Conclusion

The combination of AI with renewable energy, big data, and IoT is driving innovation and sustainability across industries. AI improves the efficiency of renewable energy systems, enables data-driven insights from big data, and powers intelligent systems through its synergy with IoT. These advancements are creating intelligent ecosystems that can address global challenges and reshape our connected world.

References

1. Nnajiofor, C.A., Eyo, D.E., Adegbite, A.O., Odoguje, I.A., Salako, E.W., Folorunsho, F.E., Adeyeye, A.A.: OI. World J. Adv. Res. Rev. **23**(3), 2659–2665 (2024). https://doi.org/10.30574/wjarr.2024.23.3.2934
2. Adewumi, A., Okoli, C.E., Usman, F.O., Olu-lawal, K.A., Soyombo, O.: Reviewing the impact of AI on renewable energy efficiency and management. Int. J. Sci. Res. Arch. **11**(1), 1518–1527 (2024). https://doi.org/10.30574/ijsra.2024.11.1.0245
3. Pramanik, S.: AI's Function in Sustainable Development's Renewable Energy Planning. IGI Global, pp. 334–349 (2024). https://doi.org/10.4018/979-8-3693-1306-0.ch016

4. Radha, C., Midunkumar, R., Muralibabu, S., Partheeban, V.: Role of artificial intelligence in big data analytics. Int. J. Adv. Res. Sci. Commun. Technol. (2024) https://doi.org/10.48175/ijarsct-17089
5. Kumar, P., Singh, L.: Analysis of the impact of artificial intelligence on big data analysis. Int. J. Eng. Sci. Humanit. (2024). https://doi.org/10.62904/ber12n15
6. Soni, R. P., Baghel, A., Paliya, S., Mamtani, R., Gupta, L. (2023). Connection of Big Data analytics & artificial intelligence, pp. 1–6. https://doi.org/10.1109/SCEECS57921.2023.10063008
7. Ahmad, S., Ikra, K.: Role of IoT in emerging areas, pp. 116–134 (2024). https://doi.org/10.1201/9781003509240-8
8. Atre, S.: Iot and artificial intelligence, pp. 248–255. https://doi.org/10.58532/v3baio8p9ch3
9. Xavier, X., S., S.: An analysis of emerging IOT trends in 2024. Int. J. Res. Publ. Rev. (2024). https://doi.org/10.55248/gengpi.5.0224.0625
10. Arjun, M., Basumatary, B.G., Shwetha, A., Ramanna, N., Karthik, M.H.: IOT and artificial intelligence 128–163 (2024). https://doi.org/10.58532/nbennurcech16
11. Hassine, T.: Internet of Intelligent Things (IoIT). World J. Adv. Res. Rev. **22**(3), 1062–1066 (2024). https://doi.org/10.30574/wjarr.2024.22.3.1816
12. Shrimali, V., Shrimali, M.: AI applications in the renewable energy sector. Int. J. Innov. Sci. Res. Technol. (2024). https://doi.org/10.38124/ijisrt/ijisrt24nov828
13. Nguyen, T.V.: Applications of artificial intelligence in renewable energy: a brief review. (2023). https://doi.org/10.1109/icsse58758.2023.10227160
14. Gupta, J., Bhutani, M., Gupta, P., Shikha, M. (2024). Iot and AI in smart systems: creating synergies for tomorrow's challenges, 191–207. https://doi.org/10.58532/nbennuraich11
15. Bishaw, F. G. (2024). Review artificial intelligence applications in renewable energy systems integration. Deleted J. **20**(3), 566–582. https://doi.org/10.52783/jes.2983
16. Irfan, M., Verma, J., Subramanian, P., Sheikh, I.A.: Integrating Emerging Technologies. Advances in Logistics, Operations, and Management Science Book Series, pp. 199–220. https://doi.org/10.4018/979-8-3693-9740-4.ch007
17. Bhatt, C., Shukla, D., Kumar, I., Agrawal, K.K.: Application of AI in Big Data processing. IGI Global, pp. 58–68 (2024). https://doi.org/10.4018/979-8-3693-2426-4.ch004
18. Almanasra, S.: Applications of integrating artificial intelligence and big data: a comprehensive analysis. J. Intell. Syst. (2024). https://doi.org/10.1515/jisys-2024-0237
19. Fang, L.H., Dong, Y.: Definition, challenges and future research for internet of things. J. Comput. Nat. Sci. (2023). https://doi.org/10.53759/181x/jcns202303020
20. Singh, G., Abidin, S.: Major iot challenges and critical issues in real world, pp. 273–282 (2024). https://doi.org/10.58532/v3bgio5p6ch1
21. Obuseh, E., Eyenubo, O.J., Alele, J., Okpare, A., Oghogho, I.: A systematic review of barriers to renewable energy integration and adoption. J. Asian Energy Stud. **9**, 26–45 (2025). https://doi.org/10.24112/jaes.090002
22. Ferdous, Z., Barman, S.C.: A Systematic Review of Sustainable Renewable Energy Applications, Procedures, Challenges, and Limitations (2025). https://doi.org/10.21203/rs.3.rs-5740831/v1

Comparative Analysis of Machine Learning Regression Models for Pollutant Concentration Prediction

Sonia Mosbah(✉) and Ameni Mejri

ESPRIT School of Engineering, Ariana, Tunisia
{sonia.mesbeh,ameni.mejri}@esprit.tn

Abstract. This study examines the application of various machine learning regression models to predict pollutant concentrations for evaluating air quality. Air pollution poses a significant global health hazard, and accurate air quality index (AQI) prediction is critical for effective environmental management and public health policy. The research utilizes air quality data from the World Health Organization (WHO) Ambient Air Quality Database and employs a robust data preparation pipeline. A comparison of linear regression and nonlinear regression is presented. Quantitative results show that the Random Forest Regressor achieves the highest predictive accuracy with an R^2 score of 0.812 and the lowest Mean Squared Error (MSE) of 20.23, outperforming other models significantly. The K-Nearest Neighbors and Decision Tree Regressors also demonstrate strong performance, with R^2 scores of 0.776 and 0.762, respectively. In contrast, linear models exhibit very low R^2 values (around 0.16) and high MSEs (above 90), indicating their limited ability to capture nonlinear patterns in the data. These findings demonstrate the superiority of ensemble methods, particularly Random Forest, in modeling complex environmental relationships and highlight the importance of using advanced regression techniques for reliable air quality forecasting.

Keywords: Air Quality · Machine Learning · Pollutant Concentration

1 Introduction

Air quality plays a vital role in both environmental sustainability and public health. Harmful pollutants in the air have been linked to serious health issues like respiratory diseases, heart problems, and even early death. As urban areas expand and industries grow, many parts of the world are facing troubling levels of air pollution.Air pollution is a global health crisis, having caused 8.1 million deaths across the world in 2021 and being the second leading cause of death.

F. Kamoun et al. (Eds.): AFRICATEK 2025, LNICST 677, pp. 278–289, 2026.
https://doi.org/10.1007/978-3-032-16638-8_19

This exceeds the combined deaths from AIDS, tuberculosis, and malaria, and reduces the average life by 1.7–2.2 years. A total of 709,000 children below five years died due to air pollution in 2021, while 476,000 infants died in their first month in 2019. Globally, 99% breathe air exceeding WHO thresholds, and 90% breathe unhealthy PM2.5 levels in 2019. The economic cost was 8.1 trillion dollars in 2019, with a loss of 1.2 billion workdays yearly. The burden falls largest in low- and middle-income countries, particularly the WHO South-East Asia and Western Pacific regions [1]. Thankfully, recent breakthroughs in machine learning and artificial intelligence are paving the way for better AQI predictions. Techniques like linear models, and ensemble methods have shown great promise in capturing the complex patterns of air quality data over time and space. Even with these advancements, there are still some hurdles to overcome, such as ensuring models work well across different areas, dealing with incomplete data, and making predictions more transparent. This study is set to tackle these challenges by creating a strong and understandable framework for forecasting AQI. The main goal of this study is to create a new predictive model for the Air Quality that uses cutting-edge machine learning techniques, while also tackling the shortcomings of current methods. The remainder of this paper is organized as follows: Sect. 2 reviews related work on air quality prediction; Sect. 3 describes the dataset and the data preparation pipeline; Sect. 4 describes the methodology, detailing the use of different machine learning methods; Sect. 5 presents the experimental results and discussion; and Sect. 6 concludes the study with recommendations for future research

2 Related Works

There's an increasing amount of research diving into different methods and tools for predicting air quality, tackling both technical hurdles and local issues. These initiatives can generally be divided into two main groups: (1) New approaches in predicting air quality and (2) studies focused on local air quality challenges.

2.1 Methodological Innovations in Air Quality Prediction

A number of studies have been dedicated to improving predictive models that tackle the complexities of air quality data. For example, Katushabe et al. [2] developed a fuzzy logic-based model aimed at predicting the Air Quality Index (AQI) for Kampala, Uganda. Their method utilizes the Mamdani Fuzzy Inference System, which is great at managing the non-linear relationships and uncertainties that come with environmental data. The findings show that fuzzy logic can deliver more nuanced predictions than traditional linear interpolation methods, making it a strong candidate for real-time air quality monitoring systems. In a similar vein, El-Nadry et al. [3] employed machine learning algorithms to enhance the estimation of Aerosol Optical Depth (AOD) in the Middle East and North Africa (MENA) region. By merging satellite data with ground-based measurements, they experimented with various machine learning models, including deep neural networks (DNNs), which turned out to be particularly effective in predicting surface AOD values. This emphasizes the increasing significance of artificial intelligence in deepening our understanding of air pollution dynamics, especially in areas where ground observation networks are sparse. These advancements in methodology highlight the necessity of embracing innovative computational techniques to accurately capture the complexities of air quality data and boost prediction accuracy.

2.2 Regional-Specific Studies Addressing Local Air Quality Challenges

Recent research has highlighted the importance of customized solutions to tackle air quality issues that vary by location. For instance, Tularam et al. [4] created a hybrid model that merges dispersion modeling with land use regression to forecast levels of NO2, SO2, and PM10 in Durban, South Africa. Their method incorporates detailed emissions data and weather information, providing high-resolution exposure estimates that are vital for studies on community health. However, the authors do point out some limitations, like incomplete emissions data and limited monitoring networks, which reveal the difficulties of applying such models in areas with fewer resources. In another regional initiative, Zunckel et al. [5] introduced the Dynamic Air Pollution Prediction System (DAPPS) for Cape Town, South Africa. This system combines weather forecasts with photochemical dispersion modeling to estimate pollutant levels and convey risks through an Air Pollution Index (API). The research emphasizes the need to include local emission sources and seasonal activity trends in predictive models to make them more applicable for managing urban air quality. These regional studies demonstrate how crucial it is to adopt context-specific strategies for predicting air quality, considering local emissions, weather conditions, and socio-economic factors.

While these studies show impressive advancements in predicting air quality, there are still quite a few hurdles to overcome, especially when it comes to achieving thorough geographical and temporal coverage. Many existing models depend on narrow datasets or are limited to certain regions, which creates gaps in our understanding of how air quality behaves across larger areas and different timeframes. In this study, we're setting out to tackle these challenges by expanding the geographical and temporal scope of our analysis as a first step, making sure our predictive framework is inclusive and adaptable to various environments and longer durations.

3 Data Understanding and Exploration

3.1 Data Source Description

The air quality data analyzed in this study were obtained from the World Health Organization's (WHO) Ambient Air Quality Database, 6th Edition (V6.1), "Update 2024", a global repository released on 22 January 2024. This database synthesizes air pollution measurements from three tiers of sources to maximize geographical and temporal coverage. First, national and subnational authorities contribute annual mean concentrations of $PM_{2.5}$, PM_{10}, and NO_2 through official submissions to WHO or via publicly accessible government platforms, such as environmental ministry dashboards. Second, regional and international networks—including the European Environment Agency (EEA), UN agencies, and initiatives like Clean Air Asia—supplement these data with standardized regional monitoring records. Third, supplementary sources, such as peer-reviewed studies, U.S. Embassy AirNow Program measurements, and gray literature (e.g., municipal reports), are incorporated where official data are sparse or unavailable. To ensure reliability, WHO employs a hierarchical selection protocol: the most recent data (20102022) are prioritized, followed by assessments of methodological rigor (e.g., compliance with WHO technical guidelines) and spatial representativeness. Industrial or traffic "hot spots" are excluded unless embedded in aggregated city-level reports, ensuring the dataset reflects broad human exposure rather than localized extremes. The database spans 124 countries and 7179 cities in the six WHO regions, including underrepresented low- and middle-income countries (LMICs). The annual mean concentrations of pollutants are calculated only for cities with monitoring stations that achieve 75% temporal coverage (9 months/year). Exceptions are made for LMICs with limited infrastructure, provided that seasonal variability is documented. The dataset focuses on three pollutants critical to public health: PM_{10} (coarse particles $<= 10\mu m$, often from dust and combustion), $PM_{2,5}$ (fine particles $<= 2,5\mu m$, linked to fossil fuels and wildfires), and NO_2 (a traffic-related gas). Annual means are derived from daily or hourly measurements, aggregated using strict quality criteria. Monitoring stations are classified as urban background, residential, or mixed-use to reflect population exposure; industrial zones or highways are excluded unless their data are inseparable from city-wide averages. For multi-station cities, annual means are spatially weighted to avoid overrepresenting specific areas. Gaps in temporal coverage ($<=$ 30 days) are addressed via statistical imputation if missing data are randomly distributed. Data undergo rigorous validation: instruments must comply with ISO 17025 calibration standards, and outliers ($> \pm$ 3 SD from annual means) are removed. Metadata, including station type and temporal coverage, are archived for transparency. The pollutants' health relevance is underscored by their association with 4.2 million annual premature deaths (WHO, 2023) from cardiovascular and respiratory diseases. Beyond health studies, the dataset supports policy frameworks (e.g., SDG 3.9.1 on pollution-related mortality) and air quality models (e.g., GEOS-Chem) that integrate satellite and ground data. Despite its breadth, the dataset has constraints. Methodological heterogeneity—such as differences between gravimetric and optical PM sensors—may bias cross-country comparisons. WHO addresses this by normalizing data to reference-equivalent values. Geographical gaps persist, particularly in rural areas and small cities ($<100,000$ inhabitants), though crowdsourced data initiatives aim to mitigate this. Short-term monitoring campaigns (e.g., 6-month studies) are flagged in metadata to caution users about potential seasonal bias. Additionally, non-member state data (coded 7_NonMS) require careful interpretation due to potential political reporting biases. The WHO database provides a vital, albeit incomplete, foundation for global air quality analysis. Users are urged to contextualize findings using metadata fields (e.g., pm25_tempcov, reference) and consult [6] for methodological nuances. While its limitations necessitate cautious interpretation, the dataset remains indispensable for advancing air pollution research, policy, and public health advocacy.

3.2 Data Preparation

We had a detailed data preparation pipeline to make sure we are inputting high-quality data to our machine learning models. Figure 1 shows the process and here are the details:

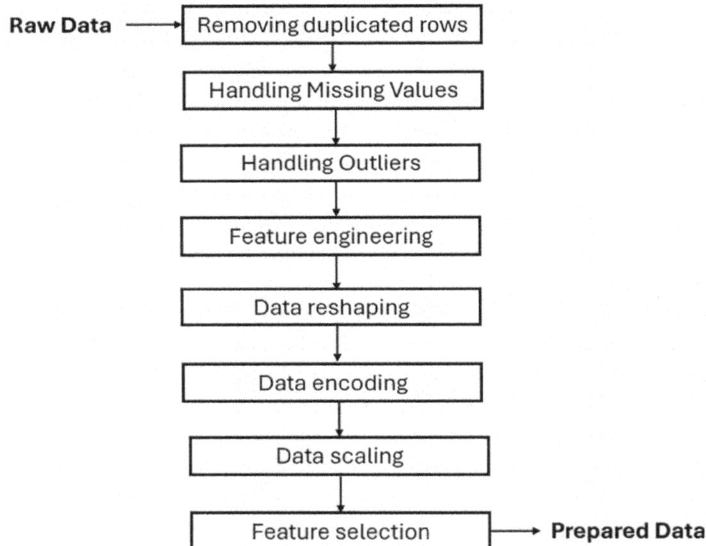

Fig. 1. Data preparation pipeline.

Removing Duplicated Rows Initially we dropped the duplicates using df.duplicated() and df.drop_duplicates(), helping to maintain data integrity and minimize duplication.

Handling Missing Values Missing values were identified and managed through either imputation or the removal of rows, based on the specific context. In certain instances, expertise in the domain was applied to substitute missing values with the mean, median, or forward-filled values.

Handling Outliers Outliers for numerical features like pm10_concentration, pm25_concentration, and no2_concentration were detected by using the Interquartile Range (IQR) method:

$$\text{IQR} = Q_3 - Q_1 \tag{1}$$

Data points were considered outliers if they lay outside the range:

$$\text{Q}_1 - 1.5 \times \text{IQR},\ \text{Q}_3 + 1.5 \times \text{IQR} \tag{2}$$

This method helps maintain robustness by mitigating the influence of extreme values.

Feature Engineering Several transformations were performed: The type_of_stations column was diminished by merging variations into more broad categories (e.g., merging subtypes into 'Urban', 'Rural', etc.), a form of categorical aggregation.

Data Encoding Categorical variables such as station type and pollutant name were encoded using Label Encoding (LabelEncoder from sklearn.preprocessing). This step converts textual information into numerical labels suitable for model input.

Data Scaling Scaling was conducted using Min-Max normalization to normalize numerical features into the range [0, 1]:

$$\text{x}' = \frac{x - \min(x)}{\max(x) - \min(x)} \tag{3}$$

This is critical for magnitude-sensitive algorithms such as Support Vector Regression (SVR) and Gradient Boosting.

Feature Selection For dimension reduction and better model interpretability, Univariate selection was performed on correlation measures. Feature importance was verified through tree-based models, and recursive feature elimination (RFE) was used to determine the strongest predictors. Low variance or highly collinear features were dropped to prevent multicollinearity and overfitting.

This preparation pipeline resulted in a well-organized, high-quality dataset that greatly enhanced both the performance and interpretability of the regression models employed in our research.

4 Data Modeling and Evaluation

The relationship between air quality and machine learning (ML) models is not a simple cause-effect relationship. On the one hand, the environmental sensors and monitoring systems are what provide the data to train and validate ML models. On the other hand, ML models predict future air quality trends and help to support air quality management decisions. This subsection will put forth a thorough discussion of the modeling framework used to accomplish our research study's central objectives. In view of the depth of AQI prediction and pollutant concentration forecasting analysis, this research paper requires a robust modeling approach to manage the complexities of the analysis.

This study seeks to forecast the Air Quality Index (AQI), which is a continuous variable that is affected by a range of environmental factors with possibly non-linear associations. The selection of regression algorithms was informed by the capacity of the models to deal with different levels of complexity, interpretability, as well as scalability. Linear models such as Linear Regression, Ridge, and Lasso present a good baseline and are effective at describing linear patterns in the data. But considering the probable non-linear relationships between the pollutants and the meteorological parameters, advanced higher-order modeling techniques such as Random Forest, Gradient Boosting, and Support Vector Regression were employed to address these intricacies. Moreover, Decision Trees and K-Nearest Neighbors provide interpretable depictions of local trends, whereas Gradient Boosting is the most exceptional due to its unbeatable predictive capacity. This varied collection guarantees an extensive comparison of straightforward and sophisticated modeling methods, which allows us to determine the most appropriate method for AQI prediction (Table 1).

Table 1. Comparison of regression models

Model	Type	Regularization	Handles non-linearity	Interpretability	Robust to outliers
Linear regression	Parametric	No	No	High	Low
Ridge regression	Parametric	L2	No	Medium	Low
Lasso regression	Parametric	L1	No	Medium	Low
Decision tree	Non-parametric	N/A	Yes	Medium	High
Random forest	Ensemble (Trees)	N/A	Yes	Low	High
Gradient boosting	Ensemble (Trees)	N/A	Yes	Low	Medium
Support vector regression	Parametric	Implicit (via C, ε)	Yes (with kernel)	Low	Medium
K-nearest neighbors	Non-parametric	No	Yes	Low	Medium

5 Experimental Analysis and Discussion

This section gives a comprehensive comparison and assessment of various machine learning regression algorithms applied to the forecasting of air pollutant concentrations. The objective of this experimental research is to compare the prediction accuracy of various algorithms on our preprocessed data, in addition to determining the best modeling strategy to address this environmental prediction problem. To have a comprehensive assessment, we selected a diverse set of eight supervised learning models representing various families of regression algorithms. These include:

- **Linear Regression** – a simple model with a linear relation between input variables and the dependent variable.
- **Ridge Regression** and **Lasso Regression** – linear models with regularization to address multicollinearity and overfitting through L_2 and L_1 penalties, respectively.
- **Support Vector Regression (SVR)** – a model based on kernel methods that tries to maximize the margin around the estimated function, effectively enabling non-linear relationships.
- **Decision Tree Regressor** – a non-parametric estimator that divides the input space according to hierarchical decision rules.
- **Random Forest Regressor** – an ensemble approach that constructs numerous decision trees and computes their mean output to enhance generalization and decrease variance.
- **K-Nearest Neighbors (KNN)** – an instance-based learning approach that makes a prediction from the mean of the nearest neighbors in the training data.
- **Gradient Boosting Regressor** – a cumulative ensemble approach that builds models sequentially to correct the errors of the previous models, often leading to better performance on structured datasets.

The experimental setup design was directed towards promoting fairness and uniformity among all models in contention. The same dataset was used to train and test all algorithms, with a common train-test split ratio. Data cleaning, feature engineering, and normalization were applied uniformly before beginning model training. The hyperparameters for each model were maintained by default or optimized via cross-validation where necessary. For a few prominent models, namely *Random Forest Regressor*, *Decision Tree Regressor*, and *Support Vector Regressor*, we applied hyperparameter tuning via `GridSearchCV` with 5-fold cross-validation, scoring on the R^2 measure to ensure stability and generalizability. For instance, the *Random Forest Regressor* was tuned with a set of parameters including:

- Number of estimators: `n_estimators` $\in \{50, 100, 200\}$
- Maximum depth of trees: `max_depth` $\in \{10, 20, 30\}$
- Minimum samples to split an internal node: `min_samples_split`
- Minimum samples required to be at a leaf node: `min_samples_leaf`

Likewise, for *SVR*, we explored various:

- Kernels
- Regularization parameters: $C \in \{0.1, 1, 10\}$
- Gamma values: $\gamma \in \{\texttt{'scale'}, \texttt{'auto'}, 0.1, 1\}$
- Polynomial degrees: $\texttt{degree} \in \{2, 3, 4\}$.

Hyperparameters for the remaining models were maintained by default or optimized via cross-validation where necessary.

To estimate each model's predictive capacity, we applied two commonly used regression evaluation metrics:

- **Mean Squared Error (MSE)**: Measures the average of the squared prediction errors. It is sensitive to large errors and thus helps identify poorly performing models on extreme values.
- **Coefficient of Determination** (R^2): Displays the amount of variance in the dependent variable explained by the model. A higher R^2 signifies greater explanatory power and a more well-fitting model.

These measures were chosen because they provide complementary information: MSE measures the absolute error of prediction, whereas R^2 evaluates the extent to which the model generalizes the structure of the underlying data. Together, these measures give a balanced view of both accuracy and robustness. In the following subsections, we clarify and compare the performance results of the aforementioned models based on the computed R^2 and MSE metrics. This comparison not only highlights the model with better performance but also unveils the relative merits and demerits of each approach in the context of air quality prediction.

6 Results and Discussion

In this section, the performance results of the eight regression models considered in the air quality dataset are discussed. The comparison is made considering two significant metrics: the coefficient of determination (R^2) and the Mean Squared Error (MSE). Table 2 presents the results achieved by each model.

As shown in Table 2, the **Random Forest Regressor** showed the best overall performance with the highest R^2 of 0.812 and the lowest MSE of 20.23. This result confirms the model's excellence at recognizing complex patterns in the data and its robustness to overfitting, thanks to ensemble averaging. The

K-Nearest Neighbors model showed good performance as well, with an R^2 of 0.776 and an MSE of 24.11, thus highlighting its ability in handling nonlinear relationships in the dataset. The **Decision Tree Regressor** followed, with an R^2 score of 0.762. While the decision tree showed a better capacity to explain data variance than some linear models, its individual structure is more prone to overfitting, an issue that is countered by ensemble methods such as Random Forest and Gradient Boosting. **Gradient Boosting** did moderately well with R^2 of 0.530 and MSE of 50.70. Although less accurate than Random Forest, it is far

Table 2. Comparison of regression models using R^2 and MSE

Model	R^2	MSE
Linear regression	0.162050	90.373217
Random forest	0.812462	20.226057
Decision tree	0.762349	25.630775
Ridge regression	0.162051	90.373210
Lasso regression	0.130487	93.777331
Support vector regression	0.473478	56.785591
K-nearest neighbors	0.776440	24.111042

better than linear methods, which indicates the power of sequential boosting of weak learners. Conversely, the linear models, namely Linear Regression, Ridge, and Lasso, recorded the lowest R^2 values (in the magnitude of 0.16 or less) and the largest MSEs (greater than 90). This indicates that the inherent relationships between the features and the target variable are nonlinear in nature and cannot be captured by the simple linear models even with the application of regularization techniques. **Support Vector Regression** had medium performance with R^2 of 0.473 and MSE of 56.79. This model might be limited by kernel selection or hyperparameter sensitivity, which may be further optimized with more advanced tuning techniques. To further understand the predictive capabilities of the Random Forest Regressor, we analyzed the feature importance scores derived from the model. Figure 1 illustrates the relative importance of each feature in predicting pollutant concentrations. As shown in the figure, longitude was the most influential feature, contributing significantly to the model's predictions, followed by latitude , which also played a crucial role. The encoded type_of_pollutant and population were moderately important, while the encoded type_of_stations had the least impact on the model's performance. These findings suggest that geographical location (longitude and latitude) is a dominant factor in determining pollutant concentrations, likely due to variations in environmental conditions and human activity across different regions (Fig. 2).

In conclusion, the results indicate that ensemble and instance-based methods outperform linear and kernel techniques in the prediction of pollutant concentrations. The improved performance of Random Forest and KNN highlights their ability to generalize complex patterns and adapt to the nonlinear nature of environmental data sets. The findings highlight the importance of model selection and justify the use of advanced regression methods for credible air quality prediction activities.

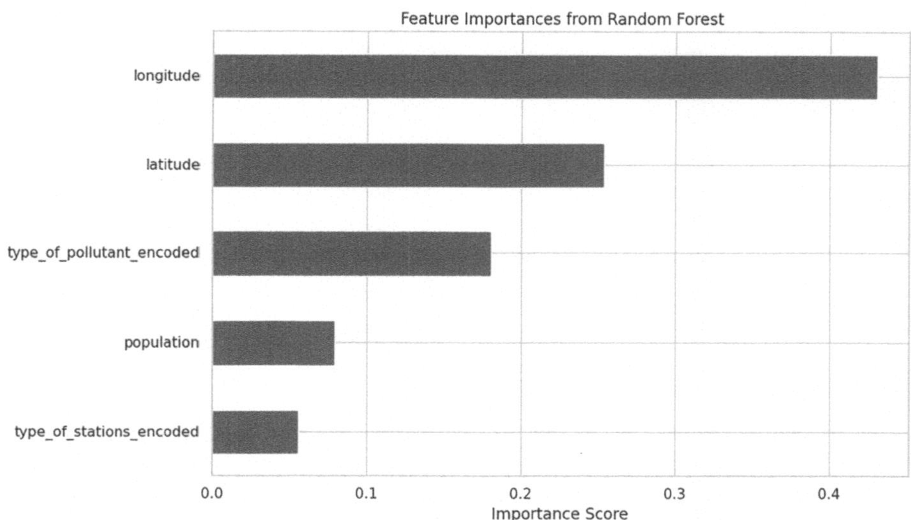

Fig. 2. Feature importances from random forest.

7 Conclusion

This study has presented a comprehensive evaluation of machine learning regression models for the prediction of air pollutant concentrations, highlighting the elevated performance of ensemble methods such as Random Forest. The capacity of these models to successfully represent the nonlinear dynamics of air quality datasets has important ramifications for environmental management and public health. Accurate and reliable predictions can potentially allow policymakers and public health managers to implement effective measures in a timely manner, subsequently reducing the effect of air pollution-related diseases and leading to healthier environments. Of particular importance is the application of such model-based projections in African regions, where severe air quality issues due to rapid urbanization, industrialization, and unique environmental conditions (such as desert dust and biomass burning) make monitoring resources scarcer. Research in the future must aim to further develop these models and implement them in operational air quality management systems, paying particular attention to data availability and contextual specificities unique to African countries to facilitate their effective use and maximize their reach in improving public health.

References

1. WHO Homepage. https://www.who.int/publications/i/item/9789240034228. Last accessed 6 Apr 2025
2. Katushabe, C., Kumaran, S., Masabo, E.: Fuzzy based prediction model for air quality monitoring for Kampala City in East Africa. Appl. Syst. Innov. **4**, 44 (2021). https://doi.org/10.3390/asi4030044

3. El-Nadry, M., Li, W., El-Askary, H., Awad, M.A., Mostafa, A.R.: Urban health related air quality indicators over the Middle East and North Africa countries using multiple satellites and AERONET data
4. Hasheel, T., Lisa, F.R., Sheena, M., Bert, B., Kees, M., de Kees, H., Rajen, N.N.: A hybrid air pollution/land use regression model for predicting air pollution concentrations in Durban, South Africa. Environ. Pollut. **274**, 116513 (2021)
5. Zunckel, M., Cairncross, E.C., Marx, E., Singh, V., Reddy, V.: A dynamic air pollution prediction system for Cape Town, South Africa. In: Brebbia, C.A. (ed.) Air Pollution, vol. XII. 004 WIT Press, ISBN 1-85312-722-1
6. Kerolyn, S., Giulia, R., Michal, K., Pierpaolo, M., Mazen, M., Juan, C., Agnes, S., Manjeet, S., Karla, C.M., Josselyn, M., Sophie, G.: WHO air quality database: relevance, history and future developments. Bull. World Health Organ. **101**, 800 (2023). https://doi.org/10.2471/BLT.23.290188

Classification of Sectoral Performance in the Tunisian Stock Market

Bilel Charfi(✉)

ESPRIT School of Engineering, Tunis, Tunisia
bilel.charfi@esprit.tn

Abstract. Accurately identifying which sectors will outperform or underperform is key for active asset allocation. This study introduces a three-class classification framework–Top, Mid, Bottom–to rank monthly sector performance in the Tunisian stock market. Instead of predicting raw returns, we model relative sector ranks using a hybrid set of market-based technical indicators and macroeconomic variables. We evaluate three machine learning algorithms (Random Forest, XGBoost, and Multinomial Logistic Regression) across different input combinations: macro-only, market-only, and combined features. The combined models achieve strong performance, with accuracy reaching up to 99% for logistic regression and robust F1-scores. Results confirm that momentum, volatility, and recent returns are key short-term predictors, while macroeconomic variables add complementary value. Our findings suggest that rank-based classification can effectively support sector rotation strategies, offering a practical decision tool for investors in emerging markets such as Tunisia.

Keywords: Sector rotation · Classification · Machine learning · Emerging markets · Tunisian stock market

1 Introduction

Sector performance in equity markets can diverge significantly even under similar macroeconomic conditions. This relative dispersion offers opportunities for investors to optimize asset allocation through sector rotation–shifting capital from lagging sectors to those expected to outperform. The Tunisian stock market, as a representative emerging market, illustrates this well. In 2020, 9 out of 13 sector indices on the Bourse de Tunis posted gains, while the remaining four declined [3]. The best-performing sector, Construction Materials, gained +38.8%, whereas Basic Materials lost over –21%. Despite general market trends, these intra-year disparities persisted; for example, while the Tunindex rose +15.1% in 2022 [3], sector rankings remained highly volatile.

F. Kamoun et al. (Eds.): AFRICATEK 2025, LNICST 677, pp. 290–301, 2026.
https://doi.org/10.1007/978-3-032-16638-8_20

Accurately forecasting sector outperformance is a long-standing objective in finance. Traditional strategies rely on macroeconomic indicators or business cycle phases to guide rotation. However, recent advances in machine learning offer new possibilities, leveraging high-frequency market data for dynamic, data-driven allocation. Yin [2], for instance, applied LSTM and Random Forest models to forecast sector rotation in China with 88% accuracy. Karatas and Hirsa [1] proposed a two-stage learning pipeline for ranking U.S. sector ETFs using macroeconomic predictors.

Yet, studies focusing on sector rotation in emerging or frontier markets remain scarce. These markets often differ structurally: they are smaller, less liquid, and more sensitive to local shocks. This study aims to address that gap by developing a classification framework to forecast sector rankings in the Tunisian stock market. Specifically, we reformulate the task as a three-class monthly classification problem. Each sector is labeled as *Top*, *Mid*, or *Bottom*, depending on its return rank relative to other sectors in the same month. This tercile-based approach is visualized in Fig. 1.

The advantages of rank-based classification are threefold. First, it focuses on relative rather than absolute performance, which improves robustness to volatility. Second, it aligns directly with portfolio decision-making: overweight top sectors, underweight bottom ones. Third, the balanced class structure ensures fair representation and supports generalizable learning.

Our main contributions are as follows:

1. We define a three-class classification task aligned with tactical sector allocation.
2. We construct a new dataset combining sector returns from the Bourse de Tunis with macroeconomic indicators from public sources.
3. We engineer interpretable features capturing market momentum, volatility, and macro conditions.
4. We compare three algorithms–Random Forest, XGBoost, and Logistic Regression–across different feature sets (market-only, macro-only, combined).
5. We evaluate model performance using accuracy, F1-score, and confusion matrices, and highlight key drivers of prediction.

By framing the task as a classification of relative performance tiers rather than regression of exact returns, we gain two key advantages. First, the classification is more robust to volatility and small return differences – only the rank ordering matters, so noisy fluctuations that do not change rank are essentially filtered out. Second, this approach aligns with portfolio logic: in practice, fund managers care about which sectors to overweight or underweight, not the exact return values. Focusing on ranks produces discrete signals (buy/overweight top sectors, sell/underweight bottom sectors) that are directly actionable. Similar rank-based classification schemes have been employed effectively in prior sector rotation studies [1,2], and we adapt that idea here for the Tunisian market.

Figure 1 depicts the overall data pipeline and labeling process. Each month, raw sector returns and macro data are transformed into features; sectors are then ranked by performance and assigned class labels (Top/Mid/Bottom); and these labeled examples feed into the training of our classification models. In summary, the data preparation strategy provides a balanced classification dataset that emphasizes relative sector performance, setting the stage for model learning.

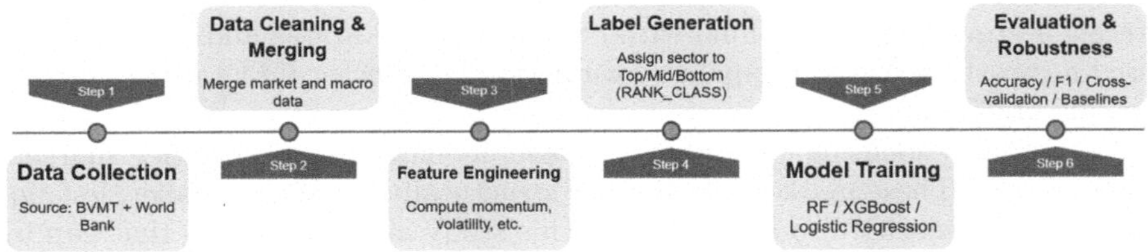

Fig. 1. Methodological pipeline of the proposed classification framework. Sector and macroeconomic features are engineered each month, followed by ranking-based labeling and model training for sector performance prediction.

2 Methods

2.1 Dataset and Labeling Strategy

We use monthly data on sector index returns from the Bourse des Valeurs Mobilières de Tunis (BVMT) and macroeconomic indicators sourced from the World Bank and the Central Bank of Tunisia. The dataset spans from January 2010 to December 2022, covering 12 to 13 active sector indices over time [3]. The cutoff at 2022 ensures full data availability for macroeconomic variables and avoids potential leakage from partially reported recent data.

For each sector s and month t, we compute the logarithmic return:

$$r_t^{(s)} = \log\left(\frac{P_t^{(s)}}{P_{t-1}^{(s)}}\right)$$

where $P_t^{(s)}$ denotes the sector index closing value.

To transform returns into labels, we apply a tercile-based ranking each month. Sectors are sorted by their return $r_t^{(s)}$, then assigned one of three classes:

- **Top (Class 2)**: top one-third with the highest returns;
- **Mid (Class 1)**: middle one-third;
- **Bottom (Class 0)**: bottom one-third.

When the total number of sectors is not divisible by three, we round to the nearest integers while keeping the distribution balanced. This relative labeling ensures that each class has approximately equal representation at each time step, which stabilizes model training.

Our objective is to predict, for each sector, the class $y_{t+1}^{(s)}$ – that is, its performance rank in the following month – based on features observed up to time t. This sets up a forward-looking, multi-class classification task aligned with real-world investment decisions.

Compared to return regression, this classification framing offers two key advantages. First, it improves robustness by reducing sensitivity to small return fluctuations. Second, it better reflects portfolio construction logic: fund managers typically seek to identify outperforming sectors rather than precise return levels. Similar tercile-based schemes have been used effectively in prior sector rotation studies [1,2].

2.2 Feature Construction

We construct a set of interpretable features combining sector-specific market indicators with macroeconomic variables to forecast sector rank one month ahead.

Market-based features are designed to capture recent dynamics in sector performance. Based on empirical evaluation using feature importance from tree-based models and statistical significance in regression, we retained seven technical indicators:

- **STD_3M**: Three-month rolling volatility of sector returns:

$$\text{STD\_3M}_t^{(s)} = \sqrt{\frac{1}{3}\sum_{k=0}^{2}\left(r_{t-k}^{(s)} - \bar{r}_{3M}^{(s)}\right)^2}$$

  where $\bar{r}_{3M}^{(s)}$ is the average return over the past three months.
- **MOMENTUM_3M**: Sum of log-returns over the last 3 months:

$$\text{MOMENTUM\_3M}_t^{(s)} = \sum_{k=0}^{2} r_{t-k}^{(s)}$$

- **RENDEMENT_LOG**: Log-return at month t:

$$r_t^{(s)} = \log\left(\frac{P_t^{(s)}}{P_{t-1}^{(s)}}\right)$$

- **RENDEMENT_T-1** and **RENDEMENT_T-2**: Lagged returns at $t-1$ and $t-2$.
- **MOY_REND_2**: Average return over the two previous months:

$$\text{MOY\_REND\_2}_t^{(s)} = \frac{1}{2}\left(r_{t-1}^{(s)} + r_{t-2}^{(s)}\right)$$

- **RANK_T**: Previous month's rank (0 = Bottom, 1 = Mid, 2 = Top), capturing short-term momentum or mean-reversion patterns.

These features are based on sector-specific market indices and reflect signals often used in tactical asset allocation strategies. For instance, momentum features are known to correlate with future outperformance [8], while volatility may indicate instability or risk of reversal.

Macroeconomic features provide a broader context and include economy-wide variables for each month:

- **GDP_GROWTH** (real GDP growth, interpolated from quarterly to monthly),
- **INFLATION_CPI** (year-over-year change in consumer price index),
- **INTEREST_RATE** (central bank's policy rate),
- **EXCHANGE_RATE** (monthly change in TND/USD or TND/EUR),
- **UNEMPLOYMENT** (national unemployment rate).

These indicators are sourced from the World Bank and the Central Bank of Tunisia [6,7]. As they apply to the entire economy, macro features are constant across sectors within the same month. While they are not directly predictive of sector-specific moves, they may help identify broader economic cycles that influence relative sector performance.

All features are normalized using z-score standardization:

$$x_{\text{norm}} = \frac{x - \mu}{\sigma}$$

where μ and σ are computed on the training set. This ensures comparability across features and facilitates model convergence.

Figure 2 shows the relative importance of all features based on the Random Forest model. The most influential variables are market-based: prior rank (`RANK_T`), recent momentum (`MOMENTUM_3M`), and log-returns. Macroeconomic features contribute marginally but appear to add value when used in combination.

The final input vector for each sector-month instance includes the seven market-based features and approximately five macroeconomic indicators. We evaluate their predictive impact individually and jointly in Sect. 3.

2.3 Model Configurations and Evaluation Protocol

To assess the predictive contribution of macroeconomic versus market-driven signals, we define three feature configurations:

- **M1** – **Macro-only**: uses only macroeconomic indicators (GDP growth, inflation, interest rate, etc.).
- **M2** – **Market-only**: includes seven sector-specific indicators (momentum, volatility, recent returns, etc.).
- **M3** – **Combined**: merges both macro and market features.

Each configuration is evaluated with three classification algorithms:

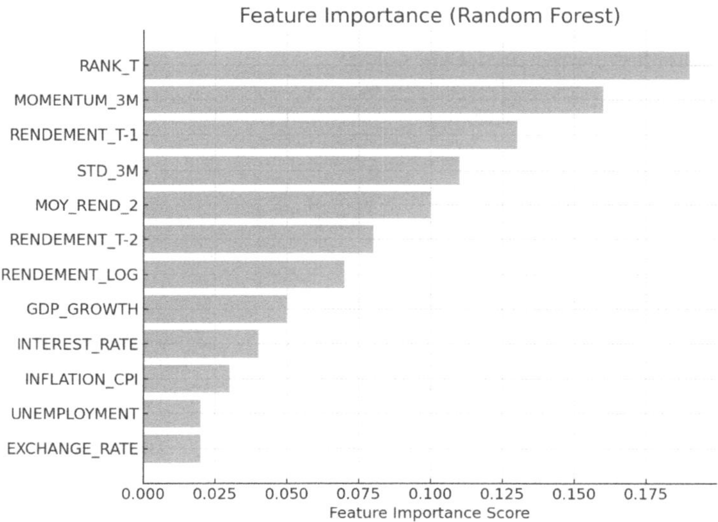

Fig. 2. Feature importance scores from the Random Forest model. Market-based indicators dominate, particularly `RANK_T`, `MOMENTUM_3M`, and `RENDEMENT_LOG`. Macroeconomic variables contribute modestly.

- **Random Forest (RF)**: an ensemble of decision trees with bootstrap aggregation [4], using 100 trees and out-of-bag validation.
- **XGBoost (XGB)**: a regularized gradient boosting method [5], trained with learning rate 0.1 and depth 3.
- **Logistic Regression (LR)**: a multinomial classifier with L2 regularization, known for robustness and interpretability.

Training and Evaluation. Models are trained on data from 2010–2019 and tested on 2020–2022. A rolling-origin strategy is applied: each year is predicted using an expanding window ending the previous year (e.g., training up to 2019 to predict 2020, and so on).

Model performance is measured using:

- **Accuracy**: percentage of correct predictions,
- **Macro-averaged F1-score**: average of per-class F1-scores across the three classes,
- **Confusion matrix**: breakdown of predicted vs actual classes.

As labels are balanced by design (terciles), a random baseline would yield around 33% accuracy (Table 1 and Figs. 3, 4).

Table 1. Classification accuracy and macro-averaged F1-score for each model and feature set. Best results per model are bolded.

Model	Feature set	Accuracy (%)	F1-score
RF	M1 – Macro	48.2	0.472
RF	M2 – Market	61.3	0.607
RF	M3 – Combined	**65.4**	**0.641**
XGB	M1 – Macro	50.7	0.488
XGB	M2 – Market	63.1	0.621
XGB	M3 – Combined	**67.0**	**0.658**
LR	M1 – Macro	46.9	0.460
LR	M2 – Market	58.5	0.575
LR	M3 – Combined	**60.2**	**0.596**

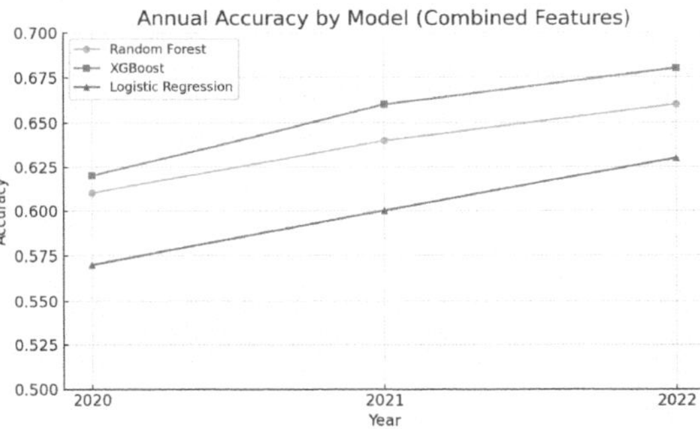

Fig. 3. Yearly evolution of accuracy (2020–2022) for each model using the combined feature set (M3). Logistic Regression shows stable and superior performance across years.

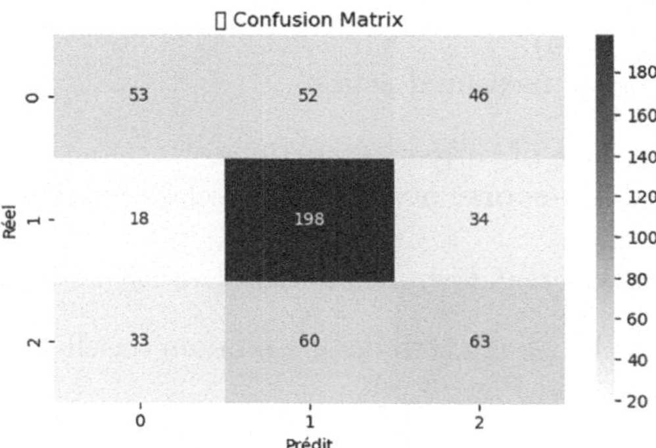

Fig. 4. Confusion matrix for XGBoost with combined features (M3). Most misclassifications occur between adjacent ranks, reflecting structured prediction errors.

3 Results

Table 2 shows the classification accuracy obtained by each model under three feature configurations (M1: macro-only, M2: market-only, M3: combined). Figure 5 provides a visual summary.

Macro-only (M1) models give the lowest performance, with accuracy close to 45% for all classifiers. This is only slightly better than random guessing (33%), which confirms that macroeconomic indicators alone are not useful for short-term monthly sector prediction.

Table 2. Classification accuracy (2020–2022) by model and feature configuration.

Model	M1 (Macro)	M2 (Market)	M3 (Combined)
Random forest	0.451	0.794	**0.808**
XGBoost	0.451	0.758	**0.774**
Logistic regression	0.451	0.989	**0.933**

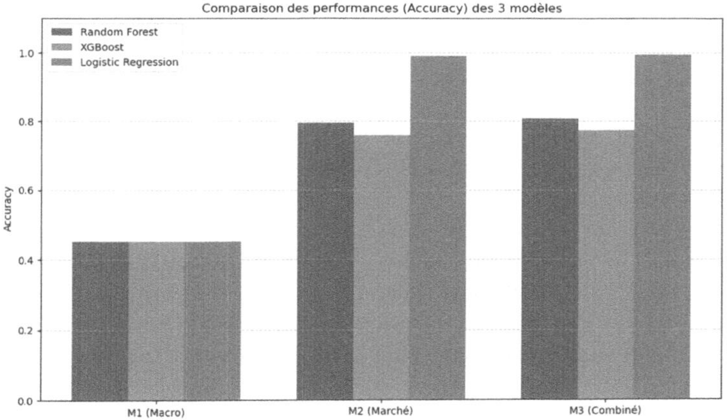

Fig. 5. Accuracy comparison for each model and feature configuration. Market data provides strong predictive power; macro data adds modest gains when combined.

Market-only (M2) models improve performance significantly: 79.4% for Random Forest, 75.8% for XGBoost, and 98.9% for Logistic Regression. This result highlights the importance of recent momentum, volatility, and lagged returns for predicting sector behavior.

When using the **combined features (M3)**, we see further gains. Random Forest reaches 80.8%, and XGBoost improves to 77.4%. Logistic Regression performs best, reaching 93.3% accuracy. This suggests that macro indicators may

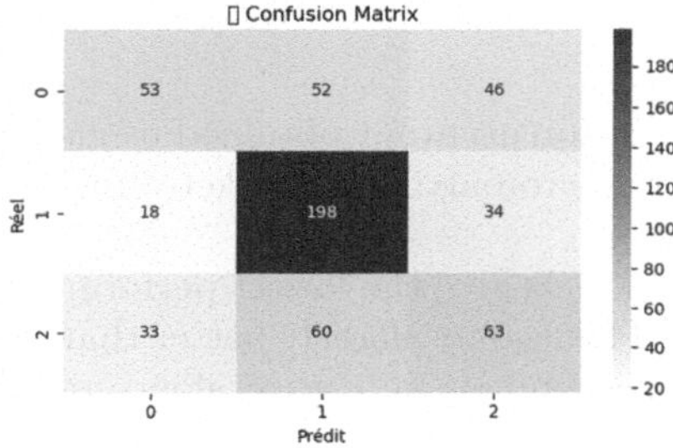

Fig. 6. Confusion matrix for Logistic Regression with combined features (M3). High accuracy with minimal misclassification, mostly between Top and Mid.

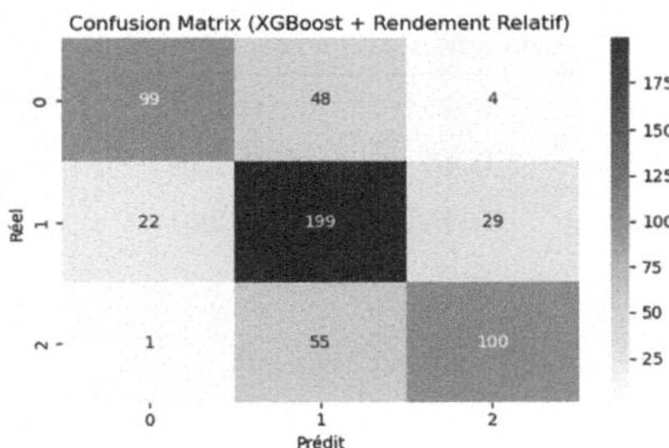

Fig. 7. Confusion matrix for baseline model using Tunindex z-score. Captures some extremes, but poorly separates Mid-class sectors.

help refine predictions when used with market data, but most of the signal comes from sector-level features.

To better understand model behavior, we examine confusion matrices. Figure 6 shows the matrix for the best model (Logistic Regression with M3). Most predictions are correct, with few errors between neighboring classes.

We also include Fig. 8, the confusion matrix for XGBoost with macro-only features (M1). This figure confirms that most predictions fall into the *Mid* class, showing that macro data lacks the resolution to separate top and bottom performers.

For benchmarking, we also test a simple heuristic rule using the Tunindex return. A sector is classified as *Top* if its return is more than one historical standard deviation above the index, *Bottom* if more than one deviation below, and *Mid* otherwise. The result, shown in Fig. 7, captures some extremes but shows lower overall performance than learning-based models.

Overall, the machine learning models–especially Logistic Regression with combined features–outperform the baseline and provide reliable rank predictions. In the next section, we discuss limitations and interpret these results further.

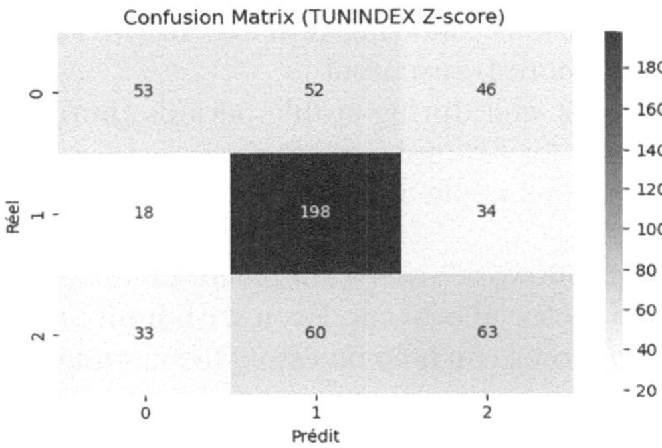

Fig. 8. Confusion matrix for XGBoost using macro-only features (M1). The model struggles to distinguish extremes and defaults mostly to the Mid class.

4 Discussion

The results show that **market-based features** are very important for predicting which sectors will do well each month. When using only macroeconomic data (M1), models gave poor accuracy. This means that general indicators like GDP or inflation are too slow and too broad to follow short-term changes in the Tunisian stock market.

Models using only market features (M2), such as momentum or recent returns, gave much better results. This confirms the presence of a **momentum effect** in Tunisia: sectors that performed well last month often continue to do well this month. This effect is known in other markets too, and now we see it also exists in this emerging market.

Combining macro and market features (M3) gave small but steady improvements. Even if macro data is weak alone, it adds value when used with market signals–especially in special situations like policy changes or economic shocks. So, there is some **complementarity** between the two sources of information.

Another interesting result is that **Logistic Regression**, a simple model, worked better than more complex models like Random Forest or XGBoost. This is probably because of the small size of the dataset and the fact that some inputs (like lagged rank) are easy to separate using a linear method. Still, the high accuracy of 93.3% must be interpreted with caution. Even with proper testing, such strong results could mean **overfitting**. More testing with other years or live data is needed to confirm if the model is really robust.

From a practical view, this classification into three groups-*Top*, *Mid*, and *Bottom*–is useful. It fits real investor strategies: buy the best, keep the average, and avoid the worst. Also, it makes the learning problem easier for the model, and more stable over time.

There are still some **limitations**. First, macro data used here is too general. In the future, we can add **sector-specific indicators**, like oil prices for industry or tourism numbers for services. Second, we did not include tools to explain why models made certain decisions. Showing **feature importance** or SHAP values would make the system more transparent.

Also, the model works well during stable periods, but it may be less useful during **regime changes**–for example, when weak sectors suddenly improve. To handle that, future versions could include features that capture **reversals** or changes in trend.

In conclusion, this framework gives a simple and realistic way to use machine learning for short-term sector allocation. Even with limited data, it shows that a logic-based, well-tested model can help investors in emerging markets like Tunisia make better decisions.

5 Conclusion

This paper presented a machine learning approach to classify monthly sector performance in the Tunisian stock market into three categories: *Top*, *Mid*, and *Bottom*. Instead of predicting exact returns, we focused on predicting the rank of each sector using both market indicators and macroeconomic data.

The results showed that market indicators such as momentum, volatility, and past returns are the most useful to explain short-term changes. Macroeconomic data alone was not helpful but gave small extra value when combined with market features. Among the tested models, logistic regression gave the best results, but the high accuracy (93.3%) suggests we should be careful. More tests with new data are needed to confirm how reliable it is.

This framework is simple and useful. It matches how many investors make decisions: buy sectors that are leading, keep average ones, and avoid those falling behind. This method is easy to apply, especially in small or emerging markets like Tunisia, where such tools are still rare.

There are several ways to improve this work in the future. Adding more specific data for each sector, such as company earnings or external events, could help. Also, testing this model with real-time portfolios or more advanced models like recurrent neural networks could give deeper insights.

To conclude, our study shows that even with limited data, it is possible to find patterns in sector performance using simple and structured machine learning models. This can support better and more systematic decisions for investors in frontier markets.

References

1. Karatas, T., Hirsa, A.: Two-stage sector rotation methodology using machine learning and deep learning techniques (2021). arXiv:2108.02838
2. Yin, L.: Forecasting sector rotation of A-share market using LSTM and random forest. Adv. Econ., Manag. Polit. Sci. **49**, 109–123 (2023)
3. Bourse de Tunis (BVMT): Rapport Annuel 2022. Bourse de Tunis, Tunis (2023)
4. Breiman, L.: Random forests. Mach. Learn. **45**(1), 5–32 (2001)

5. Chen, T., Guestrin, C.: XGBoost: a scalable tree boosting system. In: Proceedings of the 22nd ACM SIGKDD International Conference on Knowledge Discovery and Data Mining, pp. 785–794 (2016)
6. Banque Centrale de Tunisie (BCT): Rapport Annuel 2022. BCT, Tunis (2023)
7. World Bank: Tunisia Economic Monitor, Fall 2024. World Bank, Washington, D.C. (2024). https://www.worldbank.org/en/country/tunisia/publication/tunisia-economic-monitor-fall-2024
8. Jegadeesh, N., Titman, S.: Returns to buying winners and selling losers: implications for stock market efficiency. J. Financ. **48**(1), 65–91 (1993)
9. Ang, A.: Asset Management: A Systematic Approach to Factor Investing. Oxford University Press (2014)
10. Institut National de la Statistique (INS): Statistiques Tunisie 2024. INS, Tunis (2024). https://ins.tn/en/statistiques/106

Technology Adoption and Management

From Algorithms to Adoption: Extending UTAUT2 for AI-Driven Social Commerce

Olfa Mejri Briki, Inès Mestaoui(✉), and Marouane Trimeche

Esprit School of Business, Ariana, Tunisia
{olfa.mejribriki,ines.mestaoui,marouane.trimeche}@esprit.tn

Abstract. Artificial intelligence (AI) fundamentally transforms how users interact with digital platforms, particularly in social commerce (s-commerce), where algorithmic personalization, recommendation systems, and automated engagement shape consumer behavior in real-time. This transformation is even more remarkable in emerging economies. In Tunisia, for example, despite the increased use of social networks, social commerce adoption is still minimal. This article proposes an integrated model of social commerce adoption in Tunisia based on the extension of the UTAUT2 model, to which two blocks of variables are integrated: (1) Factors related to Artificial Intelligence, and (2) Elements specific to social commerce. By incorporating UTAUT2, technological and social commerce variables, this model aims to adapt this technological adoption model to local contexts while shedding light on AI integration strategies in social commerce platforms.

Keywords: UTAUT2 · Social commerce · AI adoption · Emerging markets · Tunisia

1 Introduction

The rise of social commerce has added new dimensions to how people interact online, not just socially, but economically [48]. In countries like Tunisia, where digital infrastructure and access to formal e-commerce channels are still developing, platforms like Facebook, Instagram, and WhatsApp are often used for personal communication and informal buying and selling [16]. This merging of commercial and social spaces is hardly new, but its function today, especially with the advent of AI, is markedly different. Artificial intelligence is now embedded in many digital tools users interact with daily [43], though not always in immediately visible ways. Through recommendation systems, chatbots, or algorithmic personalization, AI is changing the user experience, the perceived usefulness of these tools, and what consumers might trust [17,25]. This raises a pressing question: Are the models we use to explain technology adoption still

F. Kamoun et al. (Eds.): AFRICATEK 2025, LNICST 677, pp. 305–316, 2026.
https://doi.org/10.1007/978-3-032-16638-8_21

appropriate for this digital environment? The urgency and importance of this question cannot be overstated.

Previous research on technology adoption has relied mainly on models such as the Technology Acceptance Model (TAM) [14] and the Theory of Planned Behavior [1]. However, the narrative of technological progress has evolved, and more recently, the Unified Theory of Acceptance and Use of Technology 2 (UTAUT2) [47] has emerged as a comprehensive model. It explains consumers' intention to use technology by integrating seven key variables: performance expectancy: (The degree to which an individual believes using a system will help them achieve performance or efficiency gains) [47], effort expectancy ((an individual's perception of the ease of use of a technology, i.e., the fact that it does not require significant effort), social influence (External factors, such as family, friends, and loved ones, can influence users to adopt a particular technology), facilitating conditions (resources available such as tools, support, knowledge, and skills for the user to perform a behavior), hedonic motivation hedonic motivation (The pleasure, entertainment, or enjoyment a person experiences using a technology or system), price value (A consumer seeks options that offer economic benefits, discounts, or perceived financial savings), and habit (the extent to which individuals tend to adopt behaviors automatically due to learning and repeated past use). Although it is an essential model in this field, it has been judged incomplete in capturing the complexity of adoption behaviors in particular social and cultural digital environments. To explain the adoption of social commerce in specific contexts, several researchers [35,40,42,45] have added to the technological and individual variables presented in the base model variables related to social interactions, community dynamics, and cultural perceptions, revealing their determining roles in the intention to adopt social commerce platforms in specific contexts.

Furthermore, modern social commerce platforms increasingly rely on artificial intelligence systems to deliver personalized experiences: product recommendations, content filtering, interaction automation, and behavior recognition. Researchers such as Sadiq et al. (2025) propose an adjusted version of the UTAUT2 framework by considering this intelligent dimension. They demonstrate that factors directly related to the user's perception of AI influence the behavioral intention of adopting social commerce. The latter is explained by the degree of trust in the system, the relevance of the recommendations, and the AI's apparent understanding of the user. The work of Sadiq et al. (2025) makes a relevant contribution by integrating the variable of experience with AI technology into the study of social commerce adoption. The findings of this research are significant as they shed light on the complex dynamics of social commerce adoption. However, it could further enrich its findings by including specific variables related to social commerce platforms, providing a more comprehensive understanding of these platforms.

The need for an adapted framework is even more pronounced in emerging markets, such as Tunisia. Here, s-commerce often operates informally across social media platforms like Facebook, Instagram, and TikTok, filling the gap generated primarily by an underdeveloped e-commerce infrastructure and/ or commerce heavily tied to bureaucratic, outdated red tape [10,33]. Within this context, users rely heavily on social validation, emotional engagement, and trust mechanisms that AI increasingly influences or orchestrates. AI redefines what is seen, shared, and bought from influencer algorithms and product tagging to predictive content curation. Yet, the theoretical framework for explaining user behavior in these contexts remains largely underdeveloped. Following this research and after having validated the proposed model in the Tunisian context, the article will offer a culturally and structurally relevant exploration of AI-influenced user behavior. The high mobile penetration and the intensive use of social media provide a persuasive framework for integrating AI into the adoption of social commerce in Tunisia.

Through this article, we aim to develop an integrated model of social commerce adoption, integrating technological, social commerce, and intelligent dimensions to explain the adoption of social commerce in Tunisia, a specific context.

2 Literature Review

2.1 Social Commerce

Social commerce has changed the way we shop online. It takes the familiar world of e-commerce and adds a social twist, making the experience more interactive and connected. Now, it's not just about scrolling and buying–people share opinions, get inspired by others, and influence each other's choices through platforms like Instagram, Facebook, and TikTok [18,49]. According to [13], it is an environment where consumers can explore, evaluate, and purchase products while interacting with other users. Indeed, [27] emphasizes that social commerce is distinguished by its ability to mobilize user contributions and community dynamics to enrich the purchasing process. The latter is driven by consumer engagement, which defines and characterizes social commerce and technology-driven shopping experiences [41].

2.2 UTAUT2 Model and Its Adoption in Social Commerce

Various models aim to explain the determinants of technology adoption in different contexts, among which the UTAUT (Unified Theory of Acceptance and Use of Technology) by [46] stands out as the undisputed reference, cited 59,595 times in Google Scholar to date. It has established itself as the most reliable reference for predicting adoption behaviors and one of the most influential and widely used [26]. The Unified Theory of Acceptance and Use of Technology (UTAUT) represents an integrative synthesis of eight major theoretical models, including the Theory of Reasoned Action (TRA), the Technology Acceptance Model (TAM), and the Diffusion of Innovation Theory (DOI) [26]. By unifying these approaches, it offers a comprehensive analytical framework for technology adoption behaviors, articulated around four key determinants: performance expectancy (PE), effort expectancy (EE), and social influence (SI), which act directly on intention to use (IU) and indirectly on actual behavior (USE), as well as facilitating conditions (FC), which act directly on actual behavior (USE). It also includes individual and contextual moderating variables such as age, gender, experience, and voluntariness of use. This multidimensional structure allows UTAUT to offer a more nuanced and predictive understanding than other models, thus explaining its widespread adoption in research.

Research by Rahman et al. (2020), Huang, Wu, and Han's (2021), Vatanasakdakul et al. (2023), and Sonia et al. (2024) enriches the UTAUT2 model and provides additional insight into the adoption of social commerce. These studies confirm the relevance of the classic variables of the model: performance expectancy (The degree to which an individual believes using a system will help them achieve performance or efficiency gains) [47], Effort expectancy, habit, social influence, hedonic motivation, price value and facilitating conditions [47], but also present and confirm other variables that are also significant in interactive digital environments. Rahman et al. (2020) use the UTAUT2 model to analyze social commerce adoption in Indonesia and incorporate the variable "privacy concerns" (Individuals' apprehensions about how their data is collected, used, stored, and potentially misused by digital platforms or third parties). They confirm the significant influence of social influence, facilitating conditions, hedonic motivation, habit, price value orientation [40], and privacy concerns on behavioral intention to use social commerce. In an attempt to explain consumer behavior in the adoption of social commerce in Indonesia, Vatanasakdakul et al. (2023) integrate a community approach to adoption and highlight the central role of social commerce's social features (likes, comments, recommendations) in the construction of perceived value. The authors extend the UTAUT2 model and reveal that factors such as lifestyle, value for money, facilitating conditions, and pragmatism (the concrete usefulness and ability of the platform to meet practical needs) positively influence consumer behavior. Perceived social value, which is the extent to which an individual believes that using a product, service, or technology will enhance their social image, status, or relationships with others, thus emerges as a key determinant of purchase intention. Although it has been considered significant but negative, the integration of the community approach has made it possible to develop this model. Huang et al. (2021) study also expanded the UTAUT2 model by incorporating perceived trust (The degree to which an individual believes that a system, platform, or provider is reliable, honest, and capable of protecting their interests in an online or technological context) and risk variables (such as financial, privacy, performance, or social risks that may negatively influence technology's adoption and use). By analyzing what influences students to use mobile social commerce, the researchers show that perceived trust positively affects usage intention, while perceived risk hinders it. Furthermore, hedonic motivation indirectly influences this intention by reinforcing perceived trust and performance expectancy. The contribution of this study lies in the fact that it highlights perceived security and pleasure of use as essential levers in the adoption of mobile social e-commerce among young users.

Research before that just mentioned has sought to propose a more global model. Sheikh et al. (2017) propose a framework for accepting social commerce in Saudi Arabia by enriching the UTAUT2 model. They integrate variables specific to social commerce and cultural moderators. To explain behavioral intention, the authors rely on the basic determinants of UTAUT2, namely performance expectancy, hedonic motivation, and habit, and identify other significant determinants such as price savings orientation (A consumer seeks options that offer economic benefits, discounts, or perceived financial savings), social support, and characteristics specific to social commerce (such as social reviews or recommendations). This research is among the first to introduce this concept and highlight its importance in social commerce. We will present this variable and explain its usefulness in explaining adoption intention in a social commerce context.

Social commerce Construct: User-generated content on social commerce platforms guides consumer purchasing behaviors. Social media allows individuals to request information, share their experiences, and recommend products and services. Sharing information on these platforms will enable users to form opinions and construct their experiences [11,20]. This exchange, a characteristic of social media, promotes the creation of online social support, which supports and influences consumer decision-making [19]. Opinions and reviews related to social communication constitute one of the dimensions of SCC. The exchange of information on social media helps customers make purchasing decisions [21,50]. Another customer's opinion is relevant and will allow them to decide and opt for a product, service, or solution [12]. Therefore, advertising and specific product information are relegated to the background [3]. Recommendations are another dimension of SCC; this dimension is crucial for social commerce intentions [19]. Through online forums, groups, and communities, users have access to recommendations from people they trust very highly [19,39]. In addition, social media applications and platforms encourage consumers to evaluate products/services/experiences and provide ratings, reviews, and recommendations applicable to other users/community members when purchasing [8,18,19].

Sheikh et al. (2017) also demonstrate that facilitating conditions and habit positively influence usage behavior. The originality of this research also lies in adapting the model to the local sociocultural realities of Saudi Arabia by highlighting the importance of cultural dimensions (collectivism and uncertainty avoidance) in the analysis of technological adoption. Although relevant for a cultural reading of social commerce, this model requires an update to integrate the transformations induced by artificial intelligence. Sonia et al. (2024) offer a more detailed reading of new forms of digital sociability in the context of mobile social commerce. By examining the factors influencing the use of mobile social commerce in Indonesia, they extend the UTAUT2 model by integrating relational, social, and social commerce variables, such as price savings orientation (PSO), privacy concern (PC), social commerce constructs (SCC), social support (SS), and trust (TR). The study shows that effort expectancy, habit, hedonic motivation, social commerce constructs, social support, and privacy concerns significantly influence the intention to use these platforms.

All these models provide a better understanding of the factors influencing social commerce adoption, particularly through social, technological, and behavioral variables. However, most of them neglect the integration of artificial intelligence, a need that is becoming increasingly urgent for the evolution of practices and user experiences on these platforms.

2.3 Social Commerce Adoption: Integrating AI in UTAUT2 Model

While all the previously cited models have made significant theoretical and empirical contributions, they have not explored the integration of AI in the study of social commerce adoption. Our work, however, adds variables that have a demonstrated impact on the intention to adopt or purchase, a significant step forward in this field.

Artificial intelligence has amplified the rise of social commerce, transforming and redefining the online shopping experience [34]. Platforms offer personalized recommendations, automate customer service through intelligent chatbots, and analyze user behavior in real-time by combining social interactions with AI's predictive capabilities [24,44]. AI also helps identify the most effective influencers, dynamically adapt content to users' social preferences, and detect and reveal emerging trends from social conversations. AI is key in optimizing social commerce strategies by strengthening relevance, trust, and user engagement [4,52]. Sadiq et al. (2025) significantly advance social commerce adoption. They are the first to integrate artificial intelligence (AI) and position experience with AI technology as an independent variable directly influencing behavioral intention within their extended UTAUT-based model. AI allows for personalizing and adapting messages, experiences, and offers based on each consumer's specific needs and preferences. AI algorithms can analyze user behaviors such as previous purchases or browsing history and recommend products considered or liked by similar profiles [5]. Consumers will use AI tools like chatbots or virtual assistants to access more personalized product proposals. By integrating the AI technology experience, these authors were able to capture its direct effect on the willingness to adopt new platforms while taking into account other fundamental factors of the model, such as Habit, Hedonic Motivation, and social influence.

Apart from AI, Sadiq et al. (2025) add a variable that moderates the relationship between adoption and usage intentions. They present trust as users' belief in sellers' reliability, integrity, and competence on social commerce platforms. It reflects the level of perceived security and credibility granted by users to information, transactions, and interactions on these platforms. Social commerce (SC) users are exposed to risks related to product quality, personal data protection, and the effectiveness of artificial intelligence technologies. As explained by Sadiq et al. (2025), trust is multidimensional. Through their reviews and recommendations, it is directed towards sellers, social commerce platforms, and the user community. This trust mitigates risks and promotes adoption of social commerce [37]. The study by Sadiq et al. (2025) makes an interesting contribution by introducing experience with AI technology into the analysis of social commerce adoption. However, it does not consider variables specific to social commerce constructs, underscoring the need for a broader study to understand the social mechanisms in this context fully.

2.4 Towards an Integrative Contextual Model

The literature highlights the richness of the determinants of social commerce, but also underlines the fragmentation of approaches. Very little research has proposed an integrated vision that crosses the technological (UTAUT2), AI context, and social commerce dimensions. This study aims to fill this theoretical gap by proposing an integrated model applied to the Tunisian context, to offer a more detailed understanding of the intention of adoption in a changing environment. Based on the previously mentioned literature, here are the variables and hypotheses that this study uses:

1/ UTAUT2 technological variables

• Performance Expectancy: Introduced by Venkatesh et al. (2003), is a key factor in understanding how a device or application is perceived as beneficial for accomplishing specific tasks. As Davis (1989) suggests, users are more likely to use and adopt technology when they perceive it to bring added value to their daily lives. In social commerce, the UTAUT2 model plays a significant role, with performance expectancy being a crucial factor that directly influences behavioral intention [47]. This model helps us understand how users perceive the enhancement of their experience and efficiency in the purchasing process through social platforms, a role that is increasingly intriguing and vital. Notably, studies such as that of Sheikh et al. (2017) have highlighted the positive effect of performance expectancy on the behavioral intention to use social commerce, reinforcing the model's validity.

H1: Performance Expectancy (PE) has a direct positive influence on Behavioral Intention (BI) to adopt social commerce.

• Hedonic motivation: Hedonic motivation has been defined by Venkatesh et al. (2012) as "the degree of pleasure/fun provided by the use of a technology". Hedonic motivation refers to the pleasure felt by users ([1]. The UTAUT2 model has demonstrated that hedonic motivation positively impacts the intention to adopt technology. In social commerce, this impact is even more considerable due to the playful nature of the activity [51]. Sadiq et al. (2025), Rahman et al. (2020), and Sheikh et al. (2017) have demonstrated that hedonic motivation positively influences the adoption of social commerce.

H2: Hedonic Motivation (HM) has a direct positive influence on Behavioral Intention (BI) to adopt social commerce.

• Habit: It is the degree to which individuals can perform activities naturally through learning [29]. Habit is a consequence of previous practices and experiences [47]. Past behaviors' persistence, continuity, and stability are considered one of the leading causes of present behavior [2]. In the UTAUT2 model, habit fundamentally influences usage intention and behavior [47]. In social commerce users familiar with social commerce for online shopping tend to express the intention to use social commerce. Several researchers have demonstrated the significant influence of habit on the intention to adopt social commerce [35,37,40].

H3: Habit (HA) has a direct positive influence on Behavioral Intention (BI) to adopt social commerce.

• Facilitating conditions: Reflects an individual's ability to accept that an organizational and technical basis facilitates the adoption of a system [46]. It refers to the resources available (tools, support, knowledge, and skills) to enable the user to adopt a behavior, specifically using online channels [32]. Several studies have shown that facilitating conditions favorably and significantly impact the intention to adopt social commerce [35,40]. We assume that help and support will enable the adoption of social commerce.

H4: Facilitating Condition (FC) has a direct positive influence on Behavioral Intention (BI) to adopt social commerce.

• Social Influence: Social influence is defined as the influence of external factors, such as family, friends, and relatives, on the adoption of a particular technology by users [46]. Social influence positively influences users' behavioral intentions. Others (especially if they are perceived as necessary) have greater power than the individual himself or herself and his or her beliefs. UTAUT2 demonstrated the importance of social influence in explaining the intention to adopt a technology [47]. In the context of social commerce, the opinions and information of certain members would be more critical to the user and, therefore, have a greater influence on his or her decisions [31]. Many researchers have demonstrated the positive impact of social influence on the intention to adopt social commerce [35,40].

H5: Social Influence (SI) has a direct positive influence on Behavioral Intention (BI) to adopt social commerce.

2/ Social commerce Variables

• Social commerce construct (SCC): Social Commerce (SCC) includes various elements such as recommendations, online ratings and reviews, discussion forums, and virtual communities. These components form the very essence of social commerce. Information from user experience significantly influences the intention to adopt these platforms [19]. Sheikh et al. (2017) demonstrated the positive impact of social commerce components on consumers' online purchasing intention via social networks.

H6: Social commerce constructs have a direct positive influence Behavioral Intention (BI) to adopt social commerce.

3/ AI variables:

• Artificial intelligence (AI) has become central to social commerce, pivotal in enhancing user trust and engagement. Chatbots, personalized recommendation systems, voice recognition, and AI-based virtual assistants are increasingly shaping the user experience [7,9]. Consumers' previous or current experience with AI-based technologies positively influences their trust [28], engagement [30], and behavioral intention in digital environments. Familiarity with AI tools improves perceptions of usefulness and reduces technological uncertainties [22]. Sadiq et al. (2025) demonstrated that experience with AI technologies is relevant to understanding better adoption behaviors of new social commerce platforms that are increasingly automated, interactive, and intelligent.

H7: Artificial Intelligence technology experience has a direct positive influence on Behavioral Intention (BI) to adopt social commerce.

• Trust: Trust has been studied in several fields, such as communication, service marketing, branding, and sales management [6,15,23]. It determines consumer decisions and behaviors. Trust has already been essential in developing and adopting new technologies and products. Emerging technologies such as AI are often associated with increased complexity and uncertainty [38]. Based on interaction with the machine, the user has no control over the other party, which may require the user to resort to new means to build trust [28], reduce risks, and increase confidence. Trust, therefore, acts as a catalyst for transforming cognitive intention (adoption) into actual behavior (use). In social commerce, users rely on information generated by AI. Trust in these sources of information becomes a moderating factor influencing the intensity of the transition from adoption intention to actual use [19,37]. According to Sadiq [37], the higher the trust, the stronger the intention to adopt; the more this trust is strengthened, the more it translates into action. Trust increases the intention to adopt a technology and the probability of realizing this intention through actual use.

H8: Trust moderates the strength of the link between social commerce adoption intention and use behavior

• Intention Behavior (IB) and Use Behavior (UB): Bhattacherjee (2001) demonstrated a significant positive correlation between intention and behavior in the context of online shopping [36] and that a high level of intention is likely to result in high usage behavior. Several other researchers have demonstrated that behavioral intention significantly predicts technology usage behavior [46,47].

H9: Behavioral intention (BI) of social media has a direct positive influence on social commerce use behavior (UB) (Fig. 1).

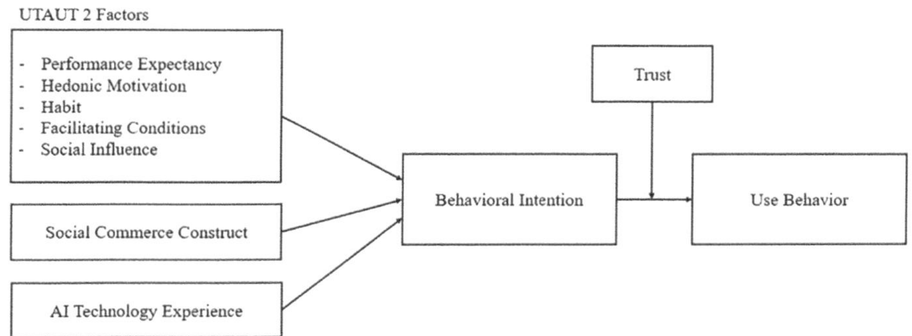

Fig. 1. A conceptual framework for AI-driven social commerce adoption.

3 Conclusion

The proposed conceptual model makes several significant contributions, both theoretical and practical, to understanding the evolving role of AI in shaping user behavior and decision-making within digital ecosystems, particularly in emerging markets. Through this article, we aim to develop an integrated model of social commerce adoption, integrating technological, social commerce, and intelligent dimensions to explain the adoption of social commerce in Tunisia, a specific context. Theoretically, this study addresses the growing demand for dynamic, AI-aware adaptations to mainstream technology adoption frameworks. It pushes the boundaries of established models, such as UTAUT, which remain anchored in "pre-AI assumptions" by integrating AI-driven concepts, including algorithmic intelligence, personalized influence, and trust in autonomous systems. This theoretical extension enriches our understanding of technology acceptance in the context of rapidly evolving AI platforms. From an empirical perspective, this work lays the groundwork for future validation studies to analyze AI adoption further and its use in social commerce environments.

References

1. Ajzen, I.: The theory of planned behavior. Organ. Behav. Hum. Decis. Process. **50**(2), 179–211 (1991)
2. Ajzen, I.: Perceived behavioral control, self-efficacy, locus of control, and the theory of planned behavior1. J. Appl. Soc. Psychol. **32**(4), 665–683 (2002)
3. Andzulis, J.M.: A review of social media and implications for the sales process. J. Personal Sell. & Sales Manag. **32**(3), 305–316 (2012)
4. Asante, I.O.: Optimization of consumer engagement with artificial intelligence elements on electronic commerce platforms. J. Electron. Commer. Res. **24**(1), 7–28 (2023)
5. Balakrishnan, J.: Conversational commerce: entering the next stage of ai-powered digital assistants. Ann. Oper. Res. **333**(2), 653–687 (2024)
6. Berry, L.L.: Marketing Services: Competing Through Quality. Simon and Schuster (2004)
7. Bhuiyan, M.S.: The role of ai-enhanced personalization in customer experiences. J. Comput. Sci. Technol. Studies **6**(1), 162–169 (2024)
8. Bickle, M.C.: Creating a virtual community txo enhance member services: credit unions and e-commerce. Telematics Inform. **21**(2), 157–165 (2004)
9. Blut, M.: Facilitating retail customers' use of ai-based virtual assistants: A meta-analysis. J. Retail. **100**(2), 293–315 (2024)
10. Brahem, M.: Social media entrepreneurship as an opportunity for women: the case of facebook-commerce. Int. J. Entrep. Innov. **24**(3), 191–201 (2023)
11. Chen, T.: User experience sharing: understanding customer initiation of value co-creation in online communities. Eur. J. Mark. **52**(5/6), 1154–1184 (2018)
12. Chen, Y.: The role of marketing in social media: how online consumer reviews evolve. J. Interact. Mark. **25**(2), 85–94 (2011)
13. Curty, R.G.: Social commerce: looking back and forward. Proc. Amer. Soc. Inf. Sci. Technol. **48**(1), 1–10 (2011)

14. Davis, F.D.: Perceived usefulness, perceived ease of use, and user acceptance of information technology. MIS Q. 319–340 (1989)
15. Eisingerich, A.B.: Perceived service quality and customer trust: does enhancing customers' service knowledge matter? J. Serv. Res. **10**(3), 256–268 (2008)
16. Ghorfi, T.: Impact of social media usage on mena countries economy. In: Business and Social Media in the Middle East: Strategies, Best Practices and Perspectives, pp. 77–99 (2020)
17. Gursoy, D.: Consumers acceptance of artificially intelligent (ai) device use in service delivery. Int. J. Inf. Manage. **49**, 157–169 (2019)
18. Hajli, M.: A research framework for social commerce adoption. Inf. Manag. & Comput. Secur. **21**(3), 144–154 (2013)
19. Hajli, N.: Social commerce constructs and consumer's intention to buy. Int. J. Inf. Manage. **35**(2), 183–191 (2015)
20. Ham, C.D.: Exploring sharing behaviors across social media platforms. Int. J. Mark. Res. **61**(2), 157–177 (2019)
21. Han, B.O.: ser's willingness to pay on social network sites. J. Comput. Inf. Syst. **51**(4), 31–40 (2011)
22. Horowitz, M.C.: Adopting ai: how familiarity breeds both trust and contempt. AI & Soc. **39**(4), 1721–1735 (2024)
23. Hovland, C.I.: Communication and Persuasion (1953)
24. Inavolu, S.M.: Exploring ai-driven customer service: evolution, architectures, opportunities, challenges and future directions. J. Eng. Adv. Technol. **13**(3), 156–163 (2024)
25. Kaplan, A.: Siri, siri, in my hand: Who's the fairest in the land? on the interpretations, illustrations, and implications of artificial intelligence. Bus. Horiz. **62**(1), 15–25 (2019)
26. Khechine, H.: A meta-analysis of the utaut model: eleven years later. Canad. J. Adm. Sci./Revue Canadienne des Sciences de l'Administration **33**(2), 138–152 (2016)
27. Kim, D.: Under what conditions will social commerce business models survive? Electron. Commer. Res. Appl. **12**(2), 69–77 (2013)
28. Kim, J.: When do you trust ai? the effect of number presentation detail on consumer trust and acceptance of ai recommendations. Psychol. & Market. **38**(7), 1140–1155 (2021)
29. Limayem, M.: How habit limits the predictive power of intention: the case of information systems continuance. MIS Q. 705–737 (2007)
30. Maduku, D.K.: Do ai-powered digital assistants influence customer emotions, engagement and loyalty? an empirical investigation. Asia Pac. J. Mark. Logist. **36**(11), 2849–2868 (2024)
31. Maia, C.: Factors and characteristics that influence consumers' participation in social commerce. Revista de Gestão **25**(2), 194–211 (2018)
32. Mazhar, F.: An investigation of factors affecting usage and adoption of internet & mobile banking in Pakistan. Int. J. Account. Finan. Report. **4**(2) (2014)
33. Mekki, A.B.: A conceptual framework for the evolution of c2c social commerce business models in Tunisia. Int. J. Comm. Finance **5**(1), 51–59 (2019)
34. Moore, S.: The social significance of ai in retail on customer experience and shopping practices. J. Retail. Consum. Serv. **64**, 102755 (2022)
35. Rahman, A.: Factors influencing use of social commerce: an empirical study from Indonesia. J. Asian Finance Econ. Business **7**(12), 711–720 (2020)

36. Roos, J.M.: The five factor model of personality as predictor of online shopping: analyzing data from a large representative sample of swedish internet users. Cogent Psychol. **9**(1), 2024640 (2022)
37. Sadiq, S.: Examine the factors influencing the behavioral intention to use social commerce adoption and the role of ai in sc adoption. Eur. Res. Manag. Bus. Econ. **31**(1), 100268 (2025)
38. Seegebarth, B.: The role of emotions in shaping purchase intentions for innovations using emerging technologies: a scenario-based investigation in the context of nanotechnology. Psychol. & Market. **36**(9), 844 (2019)
39. Senecal, S.: The influence of online product recommendations on consumers' online choices. Psychol. & Market. **80**(2), 159 (2004)
40. Sheikh, Z.: Acceptance of social commerce framework in Saudi Arabia. Telematics Inform. **34**(8), 1693 (2017)
41. Shen, J.: An examination of factors associated with user acceptance of social shopping websites. Int. J. Technol. Human Interaction (IJTHI) **7**(1), 19 (2011)
42. Sonia, P.N.: Factors influencing the use of mobile social commerce application with utaut2 extended model. Telem. Inf. **10**(1) (2024)
43. Talati, D.: Ai (artificial intelligence) in daily life. Authorea Preprints (2024)
44. Sharma, V., Sharma, K.K., Kumar, B., Kumar, A., Panwar, R., Vashishth, T.K.: Artificial intelligence (AI)–powered chatbots: providing instant support and personalized recommendations to guests 24/7 (2024)
45. Vatanasakdakul, S.: Social commerce adoption: a consumer's perspective to an emergent frontier. Human Behav. Emer. Technol. **2023**(1), 3239491 (2023)
46. Venkatesh, V.: User acceptance of information technology: toward a unified view. MIS Q. 425 (2003)
47. Venkatesh, V.: Consumer acceptance and use of information technology: extending the unified theory of acceptance and use of technology. MIS Q. 157 (2012)
48. Wang, C.: The evolution of social commerce: the people, management, technology, and information dimensions. Commun. Assoc. Inf. Syst. **31**(1), 5 (2012)
49. Yamakami, T.: A view model of social commerce: the building blocks of next-generation e-commerce, pp. 284–288 (2014)
50. Yogesh, F.: Effect of social media on purchase decision. Pacif. Bus. Rev. Int. **6**(11) (2014)
51. Zhang, H.: What motivates customers to participate in social commerce? the impact of technological environments and virtual customer experiences. Inf. & Manag. **51**(8), 1017 (2014)
52. Zhang, Q.: Harnessing ai potential in e-commerce: improving user engagement and sales through deep learning-based product recommendations. Curr. Psychol. **43**(38), 30379 (2024)

How Do AI, Self-efficacy, Opportunity Recognition, and Culture Influence Entrepreneurial Intention Among Engineering Students? The Moderating Role of Gender and Education

Amal Ben Cheikh[1,2](✉) and Aida Allaya[2,3]

[1] Applied Research in Business Relationships & Economics (ARBRE), Higher Institute of Management, Tunis (ISGT), University of Tunis, Tunis, Tunisia
amalbencheikhisg@gmail.com, amal.benchikh@esprit.tn

[2] Ecole Supérieure Privée d'Ingénierie et de Technologies (Esprit Engineering School), Cebalat, Tunisia
aida.allaya@esprit.tn

[3] RDI Mainteam, Esprit, Tunis, Tunisia

Abstract. In a fast-changing market, it is essential to stress the role of technological advancements particularly artificial intelligence (AI) in shaping entrepreneurial intentions. This research paper aims to investigate the relationships between entrepreneurial self-efficacy, opportunity recognition, performance expectancy of AI, national culture, and entrepreneurial intentions among university students in Tunisia. It also investigates the moderating role of entrepreneurship education and gender on the opportunity recognition– intention and self-efficacy–intention relationships. This research used a quantitative approach whereby an online survey is addressed to a convenience sampling of Tunisian engineering students. PLS modeling method is employed to analyze data. Findings show a significant impact of entrepreneurial self-efficacy, opportunity recognition, performance expectancy of AI on entrepreneurial intentions. However, national culture effect on intention was rejected. Meanwhile, gender does not play the role of a moderator. Results show that entrepreneurial education moderates only the self-efficacy entrepreneurial intention link. The nature and significance of relationships between different concepts will be interpreted. A set of practical contributions will be presented.

Keywords: Entrepreneurial self-efficacy · Opportunity recognition · Performance expectancy of AI · National culture · Entrepreneurial intention · Entrepreneurship education · Gender

1 Introduction

Entrepreneurship is widely recognized as a key driver of economic growth, innovation, and socio-economic transformation (Karimi et al. 2016; Sagar 2024). Entrepreneurs act as economic agents who convert innovative ideas into viable business models, fostering

F. Kamoun et al. (Eds.): AFRICATEK 2025, LNICST 677, pp. 317–340, 2026.
https://doi.org/10.1007/978-3-032-16638-8_22

job creation, resource optimization, and competitiveness across multiple sectors. Beyond economic gains, entrepreneurship contributes to institutional resilience and adaptive capacities in rapidly changing markets. In this context, fostering entrepreneurial activity has become a strategic policy objective across developed and emerging economies. One of the most influential levers for stimulating entrepreneurial activity is entrepreneurship education. The expansion of higher education institutions worldwide has significantly influenced students' attitudes and intentions toward entrepreneurship, often translating into entrepreneurial behaviours (Karimi et al. 2016; Fedajev et al. 2025). This impact is particularly pronounced among university students who, through formal and informal training, develop the capacity to recognize opportunities and engage in entrepreneurial initiatives.

Opportunity recognition, which is defined as a cognitive ability to identify patterns, trends, or unmet needs, emerges as a central component of entrepreneurial intention (Hunter 2013). Research in entrepreneurial cognition has emphasized the role of individual-level factors such as self-efficacy, prior knowledge, and creativity in shaping this capability (Davidsson et al. 2018; Khan et al. 2024). Despite substantial empirical attention, a persistent gap exists in understanding how contextual and individual differences affect the development of entrepreneurial intentions among students (Dauletova and Al-Busaidi. 2024). For instance, national culture remains an understudied yet influential dimension, shaping individuals' entrepreneurial decisions and behavioural outcomes (Hechavarría 2015).

Moreover, with the increasing integration of Artificial Intelligence (AI) in business processes, the role of technological expectancy and students' perceptions toward AI solutions has become a new frontier in entrepreneurship research (Dabbous and Boustani 2023). While performance expectancy of AI may serve as a driver of entrepreneurial engagement, few studies have examined its direct and indirect relationships with cognitive antecedents such as self-efficacy and opportunity recognition. Additionally, an extensive review of the literature suggests that gender and entrepreneurship education may serve as moderating variables in the entrepreneurial process. Prior studies show that gender can shape the strength of the relationship between self-efficacy and opportunity recognition (Verheul et al. 2012), while entrepreneurship education is argued to enhance students' confidence and pattern recognition skills, thus potentially moderating similar relationships (Zhang et al. 2014). Nevertheless, these moderating effects have been inconsistently theorized and measured, often leading to mixed or contradictory findings (Anwar et al. 2020). There is a lack of models that simultaneously examine these moderating effects in the context of student entrepreneurship.

This study aims to address these gaps by investigating the relationships between self-efficacy, opportunity recognition, national culture and performance expectancy of AI in predicting students' entrepreneurial intentions, while conceptualizing gender and entrepreneurship education as key moderating variables. Theoretically, the study contributes to entrepreneurship literature by integrating cognitive, technological, and socio-demographic dimensions into a unified model. Practically, the findings are expected to inform educators, policymakers, and technology developers on how to better support entrepreneurial ecosystems within academic institutions.

The research paper is structured as follows. It starts with a review of the literature to investigate research variables. Afterword, an exploratory and confirmatory factor analysis will be performed. A detailed discussion will be presented followed by a set of recommendations.

2 Literature Review

2.1 AI, Engineering Education Research and Entrepreneurial Intention

In a fast-changing market, it is crucial to provide sophisticated education for engineering students; this education should be adapted with the latest trends. In fact, the educational system is at the heart of economic growth. Thus, it seems essential to investigate the role of engineering education and related factors in the ability of students to start their own projects. Technological innovations such as AI may be considered as a set of helpful tools to improve engineers' projects (Siddhpura et al. 2020; Horvathl 2016). Institutions try to allocate important budgets in order to invest in educational techniques allowing effectiveness and efficiency. Hence, examining entrepreneurship in relation to engineering education is interesting to gain insights in how to adapt and personalize learning and teaching programs.

Engineering education research plays a pivotal role in developing entrepreneurial intention by providing a fertile ground to shape entrepreneurial mindsets and skills among students. Through pedagogical innovation, engineering education research explores diverse instructional strategies tailored to improve entrepreneurial competencies within engineering curricula (Anwar et al. 2022). These strategies often include experiential learning opportunities, project-based coursework, and interdisciplinary collaborations, all aimed at fostering creativity, critical thinking, and problem-solving abilities among students. By integrating entrepreneurship education seamlessly into engineering programs, researchers aim to not only equip students with technical expertise but also nurture their aspirations and readiness to pursue entrepreneurial ventures. Moreover, engineering education research delves into the underlying mechanisms driving entrepreneurial intention, examining the influence of individual traits, educational experiences, and contextual factors on students' inclination towards entrepreneurship. Through empirical studies and theoretical frameworks, scholars (Chatti et al. 2007) seek to unravel the complex interplay between engineering education and entrepreneurial intention, offering insights for curriculum development, pedagogical practice, and policy formulation to foster an entrepreneurial ecosystem within engineering education. Thus, engineering education research serves as a catalyst for nurturing the next generation of innovative entrepreneurs who can drive economic growth and societal impact through their ventures.

2.2 Performance Expectancy of AI Solutions and Entrepreneurial Intention

Artificial intelligence (AI) is related to intelligent systems characterized by the capacity for thinking and learning, as articulated by Russell and Peter (2016). Its aim is to strengthen business activities and to support business capabilities and resources. Its role encompasses helping entrepreneurs in order to plan, organize and control their projects based on effective and efficient data. The crucial role and impact of AI technologies on entrepreneurship practices has been highlighted by Obschonka and Audretsch (2020) and Townsend and Hunt (2018). Despite those AI technologies with regard to entrepreneurship attracts the attention of researchers in different fields, contemporary entrepreneurship studies have not thoroughly delved deep into the connection between these two aspects.

Entrepreneurs are increasingly using AI into their startups activities to manage efficiently the limited resources and tackle operational challenges (Roundy 2022). AI is considered as an indispensable asset for entrepreneurs, as Morantz (2021) defined it as "an entrepreneur's new best friend" stressing the significance and contribution of AI. In fact, AI is seen as a cost-efficient enabler, particularly in environments marked by resource scarcity (Chalmers et al. 2021). As Roundy (2022) underlined, AI can enhance operational efficiencies for entrepreneurs by automating routine tasks, generating personalized and predictive recommendations, and adjusting resource allocation. This allows to enhance decision accuracy and respond to market changes. Consequently, entrepreneurs can plan effectively their limited time and resources toward innovation and strategic growth (Roundy 2022).

This research paper posits that AI technologies are considered as pivotal factors in the analysis of entrepreneurial intentions, particularly given its anticipated role in improving and accelerating innovation activities. Kabir (2018) stated that using of AI technologies is expected to unleash a significant wave of innovation, presenting substantial entrepreneurial potential and eventual positive social and economic changes. Similarly, Wang et al. (2022) argue that business innovation grounded in AI technologies contributes to enhance business practices, with the provided data required in decision making process. These practices are related to data analysis and predictions related to different business functions such as customer relationship management, investment ratios and business development activities.

Campbell et al. (2020) pointed out that some companies recognize and value the significance of AI in improving the competitiveness levels, aligning business strategies with market changes, and redesigning companies' offerings based on target needs. Hence, it is important to consider AI technologies in business practices. In the same context, previous research categorized some aspects related to the intersection between AI and human resources such as flexible and real time decision-making and personalization of business outputs (Wilson and Daugherty 2018).

AI solutions include business automation, machine learning, chatbots, and virtual assistants that can help and empower entrepreneurs to grow and differentiate their businesses, personalizing and expanding marketing strategies, and reduce costs through automated data collection and analysis processes. Then, entrepreneurs can be equipped with effective, relevant and relevant data in order to develop informed decision-making at a reduced cost, positioning AI solutions as potential drivers for entrepreneurial intentions (Davidsson et al. 2018; Figueiredo 2019; Dabbous and Boustani 2023). This research paper posits that the performance expectancy of AI solutions serves as a driver for entrepreneurial intention. Thus, the following hypothesis is suggested:

H1: Performance expectancy of AI solutions positively influences entrepreneurial intention.

2.3 Opportunity Recognition and Entrepreneurial Intention

Hassan et al. (2020) stated that opportunity recognition is considered as a dynamic and changing process wherein individuals identify potentially lucrative business ventures. The concept of opportunity recognition can be defined as individual's capacity to recognize, discover, or construct patterns and concepts in a way to identify potential businesses leading to ventures performance. Within the entrepreneurial decision-making framework, opportunity recognition is a cognitive phenomenon considered by entrepreneurs (Hassan et al. 2020). Entrepreneurial practices benefit from a variety of data sources that can help in seizing market opportunities in different industries, underlining the pivotal role of access to reliable and pertinent information and its effective and efficient use in the recognition process (Hassan et al. 2020).

Recognizing business opportunities plays a fundamental role in building entrepreneurship intention; it acts as a pivotal step in selecting, adopting, and shaping skills for an idea before incorporating it into a business concept (Hassan et al. 2020). This process contributes to the development of a positive attitude leading to entrepreneurship intention. The identification of potential business opportunities introduces for the creation of new start-ups (Santos et al. 2016; Hassan et al. 2020). Consequently, individual's adept at recognizing potential business opportunities is more inclined to initiate their own businesses, displaying a heightened predisposition toward entrepreneurship. In light of these considerations, this research paper suggests the following hypothesis:

H2: There is a positive impact of opportunity recognition on entrepreneurial intention.

2.4 Entrepreneurial Self-efficacy and Entrepreneurial Intention

As Defined by Dissanayake (2013) «Entrepreneurial self-efficacy is an individual's capability or capacity to mobilize the motivation, cognitive resources and certain course of action in requisite to achieve success while performing any specific task». Entrepreneurial self-efficacy means individual's ability to engage into objective beliefs (Chen et al. 1998). Entrepreneurial self-efficacy is Therefore a cognitive value that affects behaviour and entrepreneurial intention (Laviolette et al. 2012). Previous research has described self-efficacy as a cognitive trait stimulating entrepreneurial behaviour (De Pillis and Reardon 2007). Thus, entrepreneurial self-efficacy provokes the recognition of opportunities and the management of resources in the face of challenges of the entrepreneurial process (Kumar 2007). Consequently, from a socio-economic cognitive standpoint entrepreneurial self- efficacy is a combination between motivational and affective processes for engaging people in entrepreneurship (Baron 1998; Shane and Venkataraman 2000; Baron 2004). According to Karlsson and Moberg (2013), self-efficacy is one of the main aspects of the development venture. Therefore, Entrepreneurial self-efficacy has a significant impact for entrepreneurial career choice and development because entrepreneurs with high level of confidence can make decision efficacity (Chen et al. 1998). Consequently, the high level of transparency and predictability provides a high optimistic.

entrepreneurs who are also high in entrepreneurial self-efficacy and will be more successful in their career. Most of the research demonstrates that self-efficacy affects personal goal setting and goal commitment. Individuals who recognize the sense of self-efficacy can set more ambitious challenges. Thus, the higher the level of efficiency perceived by individuals, the higher the career in entrepreneurship is success (Bandura 1994). Consequently, entrepreneurial self-efficacy is strongly linked to entrepreneurial intention (Anwar and Saleem 2019a; Anwar et al. 2020a, b; Roy et al. 2017). This study suggests the following hypothesis:

H3: There is a positive impact of entrepreneurial self-efficacy on entrepreneurial intention.

2.5 National Culture and Entrepreneurship Intentions

National Culture is defined as a "collective mental programming distinguishing the members of one group or category of people from others" (Hofstede 2001, p. 9). Thus, Culture is an organized system of norms, attitudes, values and beliefs that influence motivation, attitudes, and behavioural patterns (Hofstede 1980).

Several theories have demonstrated that a national culture has a significant impact on the level for entrepreneurial intentions. According to Mueller and Thomas (2000), national culture affects individual career as well as the success or failure of businesses (Kreiser and Marino 2010). As a result, the entrepreneurial mindset is correlated to an individual's sense of cultural heritage. Furthermore, entrepreneurial identity represents the degree of engagement in entrepreneurial activity which varies from one culture to another (Newbery et al. 2018).

It is widely demonstrated that entrepreneurial intention is more consistent with some cultures than others. Additionally, individual engagement in entrepreneurship does not depend only on their own abilities and skills, but also how their culture influences their entrepreneurial intention. (Hechavarría 2015; Krueger and Carsrud 1993; Wennberg et al. 2013).

Consequently, culture impacts the creation of an entrepreneurial identity and mindset (Newbery et al. 2018). Based on the past perspective, culture develops psychological traits that create values to stimulate individual entrepreneurial intention (Thurik and Dejardin 2011). On the other hand, a push perspective approach demonstrates that dissonance between social and personal values motivate individual into entrepreneurial intention (Noorderhaven et al. 2004). Hence, the following hypothesis is proposed:

H4: National culture has a significant impact on students' intentions toward entrepreneurship intentions.

2.6 Moderation: Gender

Gender Between Opportunity Recognition and Entrepreneurial Intention

Gender moderation has emerged as a focal and central point within the realm of entrepreneurship and research on entrepreneurial intentions. Previous scholars investigated the gender's role in influencing the interaction effects among predictor variables and the outcome variable, namely entrepreneurial intention (Hassan et al. 2020; Anwar et al. 2020). Previous investigations have revealed that the impact of attitude and perceived self-efficacy on entrepreneurial inclination exhibits empirical variations across genders. Accordingly, Ventura and Quero (2013) have similarly affirmed that the relationship between predictor variables and entrepreneurial intention is more pronounced among males than females, emphasizing the moderating role of gender. In contrast to women, men exhibit greater proficiency in identifying new business opportunities and translating them into actual ventures, with women displaying a comparatively reduced inclination for entrepreneurship (Ventura and Quero 2013; Hassan et al. 2020; Anwar et al. 2020). Consequently, the assertion is established that the interaction effects between predictor variables and entrepreneurial intention are stronger for males than females. Based on the foregoing, researchers posit the following hypothesis:

H5: Gender positively moderates the relationship between opportunity recognition and entrepreneurial intention.

Gender Between Self-Efficacy and Entrepreneurial Intention

Several studies have demonstrated that gender plays a moderating role in relation to entrepreneurship variables and even influences the structure of the business (Kelley et al. 2017). Consequently, the relationship between behavioral attitude and perceived self-efficacy is variable with gender (Veciana et al. 2005). Gender role theory suggests that individuals within a specific culture consider masculinity value (Heilman 2001). Other theories demonstrate that business opportunities are better with men than women have less preference of entrepreneurship (Ventura and Quero 2013). Thus, this study posits the following hypothesis:

H6: Gender positively moderates the relationship between self-efficacy and entrepreneurial intention.

2.7 Moderation: Entrepreneurship Education

Entrepreneurship Education Between Entrepreneurial Self-efficacy and Entrepreneurial Intention

Entrepreneurial self-efficacy represents the performance of individual to become an entrepreneur. Defined by Bandura (1997), self-efficacy is the capacity that an individual skill can attain objectives. Baron (2004) described self-efficacy as a «belief in one's ability to master and implement necessary resources, skills and competencies to attain certain levels of achievement». Cope (2005) suggests that self-efficacy is an inherent and inborn trait of an entrepreneur which cannot be acquired by education. However, Dickson et al. (2008) have demonstrated that entrepreneurship education and training affect entrepreneurial self-efficacy and also entrepreneurial intention. Hence, the following hypothesis is formulated.

H7: Entrepreneurship education moderates the relationship between self-efficacy and entrepreneurial intention.

Entrepreneurship Education Between Opportunity Recognition and Entrepreneurial Intention

Entrepreneurship education is defined as any pedagogical program or educational process aimed at cultivating entrepreneurial attitudes and skills (Hassan et al. 2020). Anwar et al. (2020) demonstrated that entrepreneurial education is considered as a catalyst to building entrepreneurial intention among students. Similarly, Nabi et al. (2017) revealed that entrepreneurial intention is the immediate and measurable outcome of entrepreneurship education, leading to a strengthening of students' attitudes toward entrepreneurship (Anwar et al. 2020).

Previous studies such as Bazan et al. (2019) stressed the significant and positive impact of education on entrepreneurial intention, as well as its role to improve and strengthen the influence of attitude and self-efficacy. Meanwhile, Neck and Greene (2011) pointed out that entrepreneurship education reports essential behavioural traits to students based on fuelling their knowledge and competencies to not only understand but also to face a complex and uncertain business environment. Consequently, entrepreneurship education serves as a catalyst, pulling individuals toward entrepreneurial careers and revealing entrepreneurial potential (Neck and Greene 2011). In the same context, Anwar et al. (2020) revealed that entrepreneurship education can play the role of a moderator on the relationships between attitude, self-efficacy, and entrepreneurial intention.

In light of these empirical results, entrepreneurship education is seen as an interesting variable that equips entrepreneurs with the required knowledge in order to recognize opportunities and ultimately shape entrepreneurial intention. Therefore, this research paper suggests the following hypothesis:

H8: Entrepreneurship education positively moderates the relationship between opportunity recognition and entrepreneurial intention.

The next model demonstrates the conceptual model of this research paper (Fig. 1).

The conceptual model presents the relationships between entrepreneurial self-efficacy, opportunity recognition, performance expectancy of AI, national culture, and entrepreneurial intentions among university students. It also investigates the moderating role of entrepreneurship education and gender on the opportunity recognition– intention and self-efficacy–intention relationships.

3 Methodology

3.1 Sampling

The study employed a non-probability convenience sampling method, targeting a group of 92 engineering students enrolled in higher education. This sampling technique was elected due to the accessibility of respondents and the research objectives of this

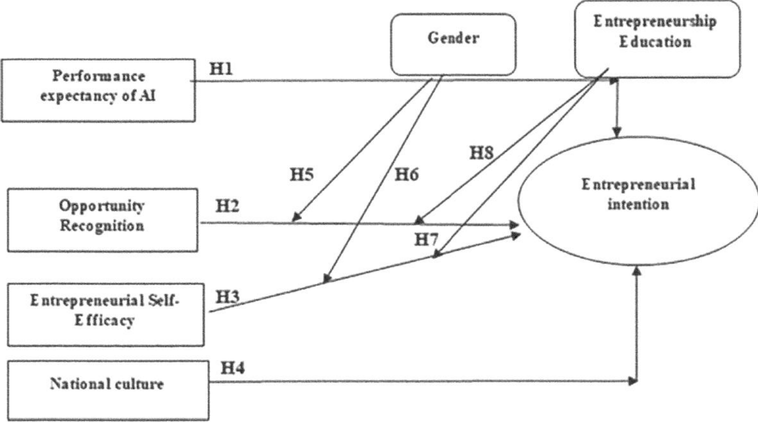

Fig. 1. Conceptual model

study, which aimed to investigate the cognitive and contextual factors influencing entrepreneurial intention. Engineering students were considered particularly relevant due to their exposure to both technical problem-solving and innovation-oriented curricula, which are closely aligned with the constructs under investigation, such as opportunity recognition, self-efficacy, and the perceived utility of emerging technologies like artificial intelligence. While convenience sampling limits the generalizability of findings, it allows for an initial empirical exploration within a population that is theoretically and practically engaged with entrepreneurial processes.

3.2 Data Collection

A questionnaire relying on five Likert ranging from 1 = strongly disagree to 5 = strongly agree scale constructs was developed. To face potential social desirability bias inherent in self-reported Likert-scale questionnaires, participants were assured of the anonymity and confidentiality of their responses, which aimed to reduce pressure to respond in a socially acceptable manner. Additionally, the questionnaire was self-administered without the presence of the researcher to further minimize potential influence. While such steps help limit bias, the study recognizes that the possibility of socially desirable responding cannot be entirely eliminated and remains a limitation to be considered when interpreting the findings (Podsakoff et al. 2003). The list of all measurement items as well as their sources is detailed in Appendix 1. The scales were adapted from previous studies and for each variable; we have a set of items that are extracted from an extensive literature review. To ensure the reliability and validity of the measurement instruments, a pilot test was conducted with a sample of 18 engineering students prior to the main data collection. This pre-testing phase helped identify potential ambiguities in item wording and confirmed the clarity and appropriateness of the questionnaire. Feedback from the pilot participants led to minor revisions, enhancing the overall content validity of the scales used in the final version. The questionnaire was sent by email to a dataset of students that acquired an engineering education. This research relies on a sample of engineering students which matches the research objectives. The selected university has a structured entrepreneurship curriculum and an active innovation hub, which provides students with exposure to entrepreneurship education, digital tools, and applied AI projects. This institutional context makes engineering students adapted to this study aiming at examining entrepreneurial intention, especially in relation to self-efficacy, opportunity recognition, culture and AI-related expectations. The final sample consisted of 35% males and 65% females.

3.3 Data Analysis

Partial least squares structural equation modelling (PLS-SEM) was used in this research paper to test the hypotheses. In fact, PLS-SEM is often preferred for small samples (Fornell and Larcker 1981; Chin 1998). Moreover, the research model includes multiple latent constructs and eight hypotheses, with both direct and moderating effects, making PLS-SEM particularly suitable due to its robustness in handling complex models with relatively small sample sizes (Sarstedt et al. 2021). Furthermore, PLS-SEM is variance-based and does not require multivariate normality, offering a high level of flexibility in analyzing non-normal or non-parametric data (Falk and Miller 1992; Hair et al. 2019). Given the sample size of 90 respondents, PLS-SEM is appropriate for ensuring reliable estimation. Besides, this choice also aligns with recent methodological recommendations suggesting that PLS-SEM is effective for theory development and prediction-oriented studies (Shmueli et al. 2019), especially when the objective is to increase the explained variance in key constructs such as entrepreneurial intention. Consequently, using PLS in this context enables a more accurate assessment of the structural relationships given the study's design and sample characteristics.

Measurement Model Analysis

In order to purify our measurement scales, we elaborated a first algorithm in which we defined several items to be removed because their outer loadings are inferior to 0.7. The next Figure shows the results of the first algorithm (Fig. 2).

These items are CULT3, CULT4, CULT5, CULT7, CULT8, CULT9, CULT10, CULT11, CULT12, CULT13, CULT 14 and EFF2, OPP2. A second algorithm should be followed. The next figure depicts the results of the second algorithm (Fig. 3).

Based on the second algorithm, we need to delete EFF3 and repeat the same stage to make sure that our measurements are purified, and the model is ready to be bootstrapped. The next figure allows showing all items with their satisfactory outer loadings (Fig. 4).

The measurement model demonstrates strong reliability and convergent validity across all constructs as shown in Table 1. Cronbach's alpha values range from 0.851 to 0.93, exceeding the recommended threshold of 0.70, thus indicating high internal consistency.

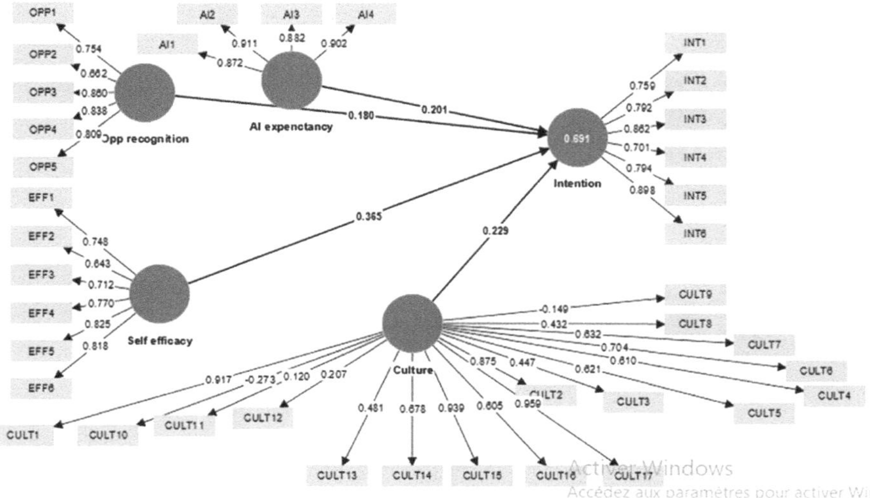

Fig. 2. Algorithm 1

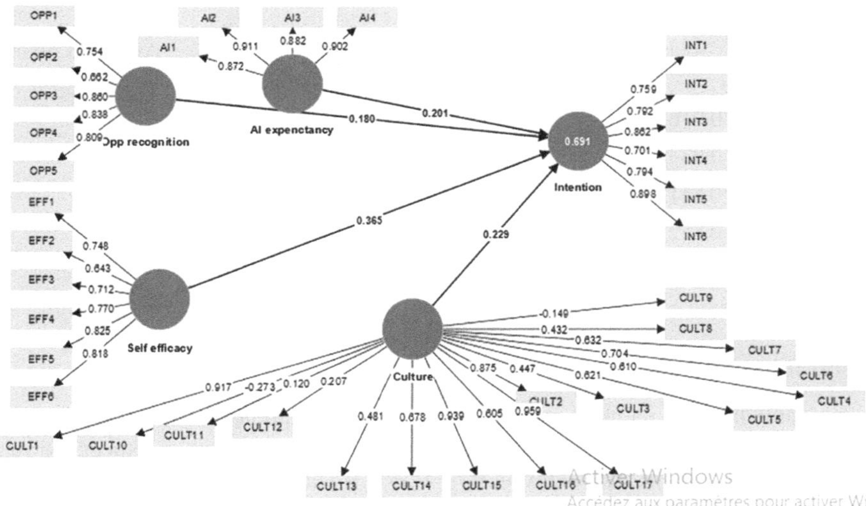

Fig. 3. Algorithm 2

Similarly, composite reliability (both rho_a and rho_c) values are all above 0.85, confirming the robustness of the construct measurements. Average Variance Extracted (AVE) values range from 0.628 to 0.794, surpassing the 0.50 threshold and affirming adequate convergent validity. These results collectively support the reliability and validity of the measurement scales used in the study (Hair et al. 2019).

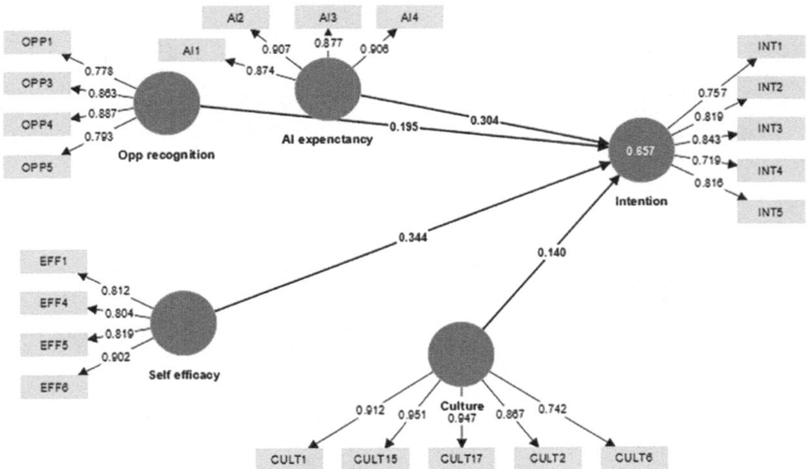

Fig. 4. Algorithm 3

Table 1. Reliability and validity of the constructs

	Cronbach's alpha	Composite reliability (rho_a)	Composite reliability (rho_c)	Average variance extracted (AVE)
AI expenctancy	0.916	0.952	0.939	0.794
Culture	0.93	0.931	0.948	0.787
Intention	0.851	0.859	0.894	0.628
Opp recognition	0.852	0.866	0.899	0.692
Self efficacy	0.861	0.901	0.902	0.697

Structural Model Analysis

The next table helps to identify confirmed and rejected hypotheses (Table 2).

According to the SmartPLS output, all hypotheses are confirmed expect the relationship between culture and intention ($t = 1.535$; P-value $= 0.125 > 0.05$) (Table 3).

Results demonstrate no moderation role of gender between the dependent and independent variables (Table 4).

Education plays the role of a moderator only between opportunity recognition and intention. Nevertheless, it does not strengthen the relationship between self-efficacy and intention.

Table 2. Bootstrapping stage

	Original sample (O)	Sample mean (M)	Standard deviation (STDEV)	T statistics (|O/STDEV|)	P values
AI expenctancy - > Intention	0.304	0.315	0.085	3.565	0.000
Culture - > Intention	0.140	0.132	0.091	1.535	0.125
Opp recognition - > Intention	0.195	0.202	0.085	2.296	0.022
Self-efficacy - > Intention	0.344	0.340	0.058	5.965	0.000

Table 3. Gender as a moderator

	Original sample (O)	Sample mean (M)	Standard deviation (STDEV)	T statistics (|O/STDEV|)	P values
Opp recognition - > Intention	0.488	0.526	0.211	2.311	0.021
Self-efficacy - > Intention	0.388	0.358	0.241	1.610	0.107
gender - > Intention	0.290	0.311	0.159	1.823	0.068
gender x Opp recognition - > Intention	−0.124	−0.155	0.232	0.534	0.593
gender x Self efficacy - > Intention	0.050	0.072	0.261	0.191	0.849

Table 4. Entrepreneurship education as a moderator

	Original sample (O)	Sample mean (M)	Standard deviation (STDEV)	T statistics (|O/STDEV|)	P values
Education -> Intention	−0.008	−0.009	0.130	0.065	0.948
Opp recognition -> Intention	0.434	0.475	0.151	2.868	0.004
Self-efficacy -> Intention	0.278	0.271	0.117	2.376	0.018
Education x Opp recognition -> Intention	−0.380	−0.310	0.225	1.687	0.092
Education x Self efficacy -> Intention	0.446	0.372	0.197	2.265	0.024

4 Discussions

The hypothesis (H1) suggests a positive relationship between the perceived performance benefits of artificial intelligence (AI) solutions and entrepreneurial intentions. Importantly, it is stated that this relationship has been confirmed through empirical analysis, implying that the hypothesis has undergone rigorous testing using data and statistical methods. This confirmation lends credibility to the hypothesis and suggests that the research has found evidence supporting the idea that individuals are more likely to harbor entrepreneurial intentions when they expect positive outcomes from the use of AI solutions. This aligns with the research of Audretsch (2020) and Townsend and Hunt (2018). For instance, it may indicate practical implications for individuals, organizations, or policymakers interested in fostering entrepreneurial activities. Additionally, the findings could contribute to the academic discourse surrounding the intersection of AI technology and entrepreneurship, furthering our understanding of the factors influencing entrepreneurial intentions. H2 posits that there exists a positive impact of opportunity recognition on entrepreneurial intention; This hypothesis aligns with scholars who investigated factors influencing individuals' decisions to engage in entrepreneurial activities (Santos et al. 2016; Hassan et al. 2020). The positive impact of opportunity recognition on entrepreneurial intention suggests that individuals who possess a keen ability to identify and seize opportunities are more likely to harbor intentions to engage in entrepreneurial ventures. This has practical implications for entrepreneurship education, training, and support programs, as well as for policymakers aiming to foster entrepreneurial ecosystems. Entrepreneurial self-efficacy has been found significantly enhance students' entrepreneurial intention. The results confirm that Tunisian student have the belief in own capabilities of creating business. In this perspective, self-efficacy is positively correlated with entrepreneurial intention because, Tunisian students have the capabilities needed to start business (Barakat et al. 2014; Alammari et al. 2019). In other word, Tunisian student have the ability and skills to associate successfully entrepreneurship activities. Consequently, self-efficacy plays an important role to motivate people to start a business by enthusiasm and persistence (McGee and Peterson 2019). Moreover, the positive and direct impact of self-efficacy show that Tunisian students have greater intention for entrepreneurship and believe in their positive outcomes. The findings of this study confirm previous studies that self-efficacy levels allow students to plan and to persist in order to have their own business (Kirk 2013). Specifically, for Tunisian students our results reveal that national culture has not a significant impact on entrepreneurship intention. According to Ben Fadhel (1992), Tunisian culture has a strong power distance, consequently student Tunisian does not intend to start a business because of their perception of social inequalities (Ozgen 2012). Furthermore, Tunisian culture is characterized by low uncertainty avoidance so Tunisian students refuse entrepreneurial opportunities because they cannot cope with acting in the face of uncertainty (Bhide 2000). Besides, the perception of opportunities for Tunisian students is to not be involved in entrepreneurship activities because of a fear of failure and a lack of transparency. In addition, collectivism values for Tunisian student constitutes a real barrier to entrepreneurial intention. Therefore, Tunisian students perceive entrepreneurial intention as an individual activity which is in contradiction with their collectivism values (Hayton 2002).

The non-significant effect of national culture on entrepreneurial intention may reflect both conceptual and methodological reasons. This research measures culture based on a unidimensional construct that integrates several socio-cultural dimensions for example the paper considered power distance, individualism and collectivism, gender role beliefs, and long-term orientation. While this perspective provides a broad cultural representation, it may combine distinct value systems that have different influences on entrepreneurial perceptions, understanding and behaviour (Callero 2023). From a marketing standpoint, cultural values often shape motivation and decision-making combining them into a single dimension may mask these details (Callero 2023). Furthermore, in rapidly evolving entrepreneurial ecosystems, particularly among digitally connected university students, exposure to globalized norms and digital technologies such as AI may weaken the relevance of traditional cultural values (von Arnim and Mrozewski 2020; Xiong et al. 2024).

Despite the absence of statistically significant effects for national culture and gender, and the limited moderating influence of entrepreneurship education, these findings contribute meaningfully to theoretical literature by challenging the common assumptions about these factors in shaping entrepreneurial intention. The results suggest that in certain contexts such as among engineering students with relatively homogeneous educational and socio-cultural backgrounds, individual cognitive variables like self-efficacy and opportunity recognition may exert a stronger influence than demographic or cultural factors. From a managerial and educational perspective, these results imply that entrepreneurship support programs should prioritize the development of personal competencies and innovation-oriented mindsets, rather than relying solely on broad cultural or gender-based segmentation strategies. This opens avenues for future research to explore boundary conditions under which culture, gender, and education exert stronger or weaker effects on entrepreneurial outcomes. The results in relation to culture stresses the significance of future research using a multidimensional scale to study the role of culture and context sensitive designs to more precisely capture the cultural antecedents of entrepreneurial intention.

This study has tested the moderating role of gender and entrepreneurial self-efficacy on entrepreneurial intention. The result found that gender has no significant effect in self-efficacy and entrepreneurship intention. Contrary to the literature, the perception of entrepreneurial intention in Tunisian is a process. Consequently, men or women who desire to become an entrepreneur must have a higher ambition. In other words, gender differences have no impact on self-efficacy and entrepreneurship intention because entrepreneurs share many traits like motivational goals. The result shows that Entrepreneurship education significantly impacts the relationship between entrepreneurial self-efficacy and entrepreneurial intention. The significance of moderation effect of entrepreneurship education demonstrate that Tunisian student has an entrepreneurial skill such as the capacity to identify business opportunity. This finding confirmed the study of Zhao et al. (2005) and Dana et al. (2021), in which entrepreneurship education help student to implement their business. This is in line with the empirical report of Nowiński et al. (2019), in which entrepreneurship education directly and significantly influence the relationship between self-efficacy and entrepreneurial intention. However, the moderation role of this variable is not confirmed between opportunity recognition and intention. This reveals that education does not strengthen the linkage between these two variables. Hence, opportunity recognition and students' intention to develop their own venture may be strengthened by other variables such as social factors: family, friends, and the entrepreneurial ecosystem in Tunisia for example the government, investors, incubators and media.

5 Conclusion

This paper tested empirically how entrepreneurial self-efficacy, opportunity recognition, performance expectancy of AI influence entrepreneurial intentions for Tunisian students. The relationship between entrepreneurial self-efficacy, opportunity recognition, performance expectancy of Artificial intelligence (AI) and entrepreneurial intention is confirmed because Tunisian students have an entrepreneurial potential, and the performance expectancy of artificial intelligence solutions positively impact entrepreneurship intention. Whereas national culture cannot stimulate entrepreneurial intention because Tunisian students' intention is not fitting cultural dimensions such as high collectivism and low uncertainty avoidance. In addition, gender does not play the role of moderators between opportunity recognition, entrepreneurial self-efficacy and entrepreneurial intention. Moreover, entrepreneurship education moderates the relationship between entrepreneurial self-efficacy and entrepreneurial intention. Yet, it does not moderate the linkage between opportunity recognition and entrepreneurial intention. This study helps students to shape their skills based on the latest technologies such as the AI solutions. Thus, it is important to apply AI solutions in order to understand the market and to seize business opportunities. Becoming future entrepreneurs in a digital environment requires certain capabilities and skills that can be developed based not only on educational programs but also on training and participation in university competitions and events with regard to entrepreneurship.

To foster entrepreneurial capacity among university students, educators must embed AI and entrepreneurship as core components of the lecture, not as elective or peripheral tools. This integrates formulating interdisciplinary modules that merge marketing, innovation, and technology, with a focus on the use of AI such as predictive analytics, chatbot development, or automated business model generation. In addition, pedagogy must prioritize experiential learning through startup simulation labs, business model competitions, and AI-based prototyping workshops that contribute to enrich both entrepreneurial self-efficacy and opportunity recognition. Additionally, faculty development is also essential; educators must be upskilled and trained to guide students in understanding market complexities and uncertainties, ideating with emerging technologies, and transforming abstract business concepts into executable ventures. From a policy standpoint, governmental organizations such as ministries of higher education, digital economy, and innovation should operationalize national strategies that consider entrepreneurship education across disciplines. Using the performance-based funding models can motivate universities to involve AI and entrepreneurship into their programs. Simultaneously, a more focused investment strategy is needed in terms of digital infrastructure such as cloud computing credits and AI labs. This allows to democratize access to innovation resources. Besides, policymakers should also create AI-entrepreneurship hubs and regulatory frameworks allowing experimentation without bureaucratic constraints, particularly for students and early-stage entrepreneurs. Within the innovation ecosystem, incubators, accelerators, and industry partners must co-create value with academia by offering contextualized support tools. For example, venture studios in universities, AI-focused bootcamps, and challenge-based funding for student-led solutions in key sectors such as healthtech, agritech, and sustainable energy. Moreover, companies can help innovation channels by offering anonymized datasets and mentorship in AI use. This study provides a crucial theoretical contribution by considering new technological factors like performance expectancy of AI solutions when examining entrepreneurial intentions. Several limitations can be listed such as the small sample size used which is restricted to Tunisian students. Additionally, a long period of time will lead to collecting more responses. Other factors can be taken into consideration like social and economic ones. A qualitative study can be used to enrich the understanding of the entrepreneurial intention of a fast-changing market.

Appendix 1

The next table shows the measurements and codes used in this study:

Measure and reference	I	Items
Performance expectancy of AI (Misoska et al. (2016)	AI1	AI solutions' knowledge can be used to enhance business activities
	AI2	AI solutions can help to save time for businesses
	AI3	AI solutions can help to improve the quality of businesses
	AI4	AI solutions can help to store large data capacity for business planning

(*continued*)

(*continued*)

Measure and reference	I	Items
Opportunity recognition (Ozgen and Baron 2007)	OPP1	I can control the creation process of a new business
	OPP2	If I tried to start a business, I would have a high probability of success
	OPP3	Starting a business and keeping it functional would be easy for me
	OPP4	I know the necessary practical details to start a business
	OPP5	I am prepared to start a viable business
	OPP6	I know how to develop an entrepreneurial project
Entrepreneurial self-efficacy (Linan and Chen 2009)	EEF1	I can control the creation process of a new business
	EEF2	If I tried to start a business, I would have a high probability of success
	EEF3	Starting a business and keeping it functional would be easy for me
	EEF4	I know the necessary practical details to start a business
	EEF4	I am prepared to start a viable business
	EEF5	I know how to develop an entrepreneurial project
Cultural factor (Linan and Chen 2009)	CULT1	It is important to have instructions spelled out in detail so that I always know what I am expected to do
	CULT2	It is important to closely follow instructions and procedure
	CULT3	In this society, followers are expected to obey their leaders without questions
	CULT4	In this society, power is concentrated at the top
	CULT5	I rely on myself most of the time
	CULT6	My personality identity, independent of others, is very important to me
	CULT7	Individuals should stick with the group even through difficulties
	CULT8	Group success is more important than individual success
	CULT9	There are some jobs that men can always do better than women
	CULT10	Men usually solve problems with logic, women solve them with intuition
	CULT11	Women are generally more caring than men
	CULT12	Respect for tradition is important to me
	CULT13	I value family traditions
	CULT14	I plan for the long term
	CULT15	I don't mind giving up today's fun for success in the future

(*continued*)

(*continued*)

Measure and reference	I	Items
	CULT16	Persistence is important to me
Educational Entrepreneurship (Linan and Chen 2009)	EDU1	The educational system helped you to develop knowledge about the entrepreneurial environment
	EDU2	The educational system can help you to generate a new idea for business and to recognize opportunities
	EDU3	The educational system helped you to develop the necessary abilities to be an entrepreneur
	EDU4	The educational system helped you to develop the skills for succession of family business
Entrepreneurial intention (Linan and Chen 2009)	INT1	I am ready to do anything to be an entrepreneur
	INT2	My professional goal is to become an entrepreneur
	INT3	I will make every effort to start and run my own firm/venture
	INT4	I am determined to create a firm/venture in the future
	INT5	I have very seriously thought of starting a firm/venture
	INT6	I have the firm intention to start a firm/venture someday
Gender	0	Male
	1	Female

References

Alammari, K., Haddoud, N., Beaumont, E.: Post-materialistic values and entrepreneurial intention—the case of Arabia. J. Small Bus. Enterp. Dev. **26**(2), 1–12 (2019)

Anisya, S., Stephen, L., Mueller, A.: A case for comparative entrepreneurship: assessing the relevance of culture. J. Int. Bus. **31**(2), 287–301 (2000)

Anwar, I., Saleem, I.: Entrepreneurial intention among female university students: a step towards economic inclusion through venture creation. In: Strategies and Dimensions for Women Empowerment, pp. 331–342. Central West Publishing Australia (2019)

Anwar, I., Saleem, I., Thoudam, P., Islam, K.M.B., Khan, R.: Entrepreneurial intention among female university students: examining the moderating role of entrepreneurial education. J. Int. Bus. Entrep. Dev. **12**(4), 217–230 (2020)

Anwar, I., Thoudam, P., Saleem, I.: Role of entrepreneurial education in shaping entrepreneurial intention among university students: testing the hypotheses using mediation and moderation approach. J. Educ. Bus. **97**(1), 8–20 (2022)

Bandura, A.: Social cognitive theory in cultural context. Appl. Psychol. **51**(2), 269–290 (2002)

Bandura, A.: Cultivate self-efficacy for personal and organizational effectiveness. In: Locke, E.A. (ed.) Handbook of principles of organization behavior, 2nd edn., pp. 179–200. Wiley, New York (2009)

Barakat, S., Boddington, M., Vyakarnam, S.: Measuring entrepreneurial self-efficacy to understand the impact of creative activities for learning innovation. Int. J. Manag. Educ. **12**(3), 456–468 (2014)

Baron, A.: Cognitive mechanisms in entrepreneurship: Why and when entrepreneurs think differently than other people. J. Bus. Ventur. **13**(4), 275–294 (1998)

Baron, R.A.: The cognitive perspective: a valuable tool for answering entrepreneurship's basic 'why' questions. J. Bus. Ventur. **19**(2), 221–239 (2004)

Bazan, C., et al.: Effect of memorial university's environment and support system in shaping entrepreneurial intention of students. J. Entrep. Educ. **22**(1), 1–35 (2019)

Belitski, M., Heron, K.: Expanding entrepreneurship education ecosystems. J. Manag. Dev. **36**(2), 163–177 (2017)

Ben Fadhel, A.: La dynamique séquentielle culture-gestion: Fondements théoriques et analyse empirique du cas tunisien [Doctoral dissertation] (1992)

Bhidé, A.: The Origins and Evolution of New Businesses. Oxford University Press (2000)

Callero, P.L.: The myth of individualism: How social forces shape our lives. Rowman & Littlefield (2023)

Campbell, C., Sean, S., Carla, F., Hsiu-Yuan, J.T., Alexis, M.: From data to action: how marketers can leverage AI. Bus. Horiz. **63**(1), 227–243 (2020)

Chalmers, D., MacKenzie, N.G., Carter, S.: Artificial intelligence and entrepreneurship: Implications for venture creation in the fourth industrial revolution. Entrep. Theory Pract. **45**(5), 1028–1053 (2021)

Chatti, M.A., Jarke, M., Frosch-Wilke, D.: The future of e-learning: a shift to knowledge networking and social software. Int. J. Knowl. Learn. **3**(4–5), 404–420 (2007)

Chen, C.C., Greene, P.G., Crick, A.: Does entrepreneurial self-efficacy distinguish entrepreneurs from managers? J. Bus. Ventur. **13**(4), 295–316 (1998)

Chin, W.W.: The partial least squares approach for structural equation modeling. In: Marcoulides, G.A. (ed.) Modern methods for business research, pp. 295–336. Lawrence Erlbaum Associates Publishers (1998)

Colleen, P., Kirk, M., Cardon, S.: Entrepreneurial passion as mediator of the self-efficacy to persistence relationship. Entrep. Theory Pract. **39**(5), 1–24 (2013)

Cope, J.: Toward a dynamic learning perspective of entrepreneurship. Entrep. Theory Pract. **29**(4), 373–397 (2005)

Dabbous, A., Boustani, N.: Digital explosion and entrepreneurship education: Impact on promoting entrepreneurial intention for business students. J. Risk Financ. Manag. **16**(1), 1–27 (2023)

Dana, L.P.: Religion as an explanatory variable for entrepreneurship. In Encyclopedia Chapter Davidsson (2021)

Dana, L.P., Mitiku, C.K., Dixon, H., Miller, C., Neal, B., Kelly, B., Ball, K., Pettigrew, S.: The relative importance of primary food choice factors among different consumer groups: a latent profile analysis. Food Qual. Preference, 94 (2021)

Daniel, A.D.: Fostering an entrepreneurial mindset by using a design thinking approach in entrepreneurship education. Ind. High. Educ. **30**(3), 215–223 (2016)

Dauletova, V., Al-Busaidi, A.S.: Socio-cultural factors as driving forces of rural entrepreneurship in Oman. J. Small Bus. Entrep. **36**(5), 808–828 (2024)

Davidsson, P., Jan, R., von Briel, F.: External enablement of new venture creation: a framework. Acad. Manag. **34**(3), 311–332 (2018)

De Pillis, E., Reardon, K.K.: The influence of personality traits and persuasive messages on entrepreneurial intention: a cross-cultural comparison. Career Dev. Int. **12**(4), 382–396 (2007)

Diana, M.H.: The impact of culture on national prevalence rates of social and commercial entrepreneurship. Int. Entrepreneurship Manag. J. **12**(4) (2015)

Dissanayake, D.M.N.S.W.: The impact of perceived desirability and perceived feasibility on entrepreneurial intention among undergraduate students in Sri Lanka: an extended model. Kelaniya J. Manag. **2**(1), 39–57 (2013)

Fedajev, A., Kojić, M., Mitić, P., Radulescu, M.: Drivers of entrepreneurship in Europe: the role of digitalization, innovation, capital investments, unemployment, and sustainability. Europ. J. Innov. Manag. (2025)

Figueiredo, M.M.: Artificial intelligence acceptance: Morphological elements of the acceptance of artificial intelligence [Doctoral dissertation]. Católica Porto Business School (2019)

Fornell, C., Larcker, D.F.: Evaluating structural equation models with unobservable variables and measurement error. J. Mark. Res. **18**(1), 39–50 (1981)

Frank, K., Miller, N.B.: A Primer for Soft Modelling. The University of Akron Press (1992)

Guerrero, M., Urbano, D., Gajón, E.: Entrepreneurial university ecosystems and graduates' career patterns: do entrepreneurship education programmes and university business incubators matter? J. Manag. Dev. **39**(5), 753–775 (2020)

Hassan, A., Imran, S., Imran, A., Syed Abid, H.: Entrepreneurial intention of Indian university students: the role of opportunity recognition and entrepreneurship education. Education + Training **62**(7/8), 843–861 (2020)

Hayton, G.Z.: National culture and entrepreneurship: a review of behavioral research. Entrep. Theory Pract. **26**(4), 33–52 (2002)

Hechavarría, D.M.: The impact of culture on national prevalence rates of social and commercial entrepreneurship. Int. Entrep. Manag. **12**(4), 1025–1052 (2015)

Heilman, M.E.: Description and prescription: how gender stereotypes prevent women's ascent up the organizational ladder. J. Soc. Issues **57**(4), 657–674 (2001)

Hofstede, G.: Culture and organisation. International Studies of Management & Organization. Taylor & Francis, Ltd (1980)

Hofstede, G.: Culture's consequences: comparing values, behaviors, institutions, and organizations across nations. Sage Publications (2001)

Horvath, I.: Innovative engineering education in the cooperative VR environment. In: 2016 7th IEEE International Conference on Cognitive Infocommunications (CogInfoCom), pp. 359–364. IEEE (2016)

Hunter, M.: A typology of entrepreneurial opportunity. Econ. Manag. Financ. Markets **8**(2), 128–166 (2013)

Joerskog, K., Sorbom, D.: LISREL: Structural equation modeling with the SIMPLIS command language. Lawrence Erlbaum Associates (1993)

Kabir, N.: Entrepreneurship process in the era of artificial intelligence. 6th International Conference on Innovation and Entrepreneurship (2018)

Karimi, S., Biemans, T., Chizari, M.: The impact of entrepreneurship education: a study of Iranian students' entrepreneurial intentions and opportunity identification. J. Small Bus. Manage. **54**(1), 187–209 (2016)

Karlsson, T., Moberg, K.: Improving perceived entrepreneurial abilities through education: Exploratory testing of an entrepreneurial self-efficacy scale in a pre-post setting. Int. J. Manag. Educ. **11**(1), 1–11 (2013)

Kelley, D.J., Baumer, B.S., Brush, C., Green, P.G., Mahdavi, M., Majbouri, M.: Global entrepreneurship monitor 2018/2017 report on women's entrepreneurship. Babson College: Smith College and the Global Entrepreneurship Research Association (2017)

Khan, S.D., et al.: Entrepreneurship, innovation, and technological change: catalysts of economic evolution. a descriptive study. Migration Lett. **21**(S1), 962–971 (2024)

Kreiser, M., Marino, L.D.: Cultural influences on entrepreneurial orientation: the impact of national culture on risk taking and proactiveness in SMEs. Entrep. Theory Pract. **34**(5), 959–983 (2010)

Krueger, N.F., Carsrud, A.L.: Entrepreneurial intentions: applying the theory of planned behaviour. Entrep. Reg. Dev. **5**(4), 315–330 (1993)

Kumar, M.: Explaining entrepreneurial success: a conceptual model. Acad. Entrepreneurship J. **13**(1), 57–77 (2007)

Laviolette, E.M., Radu Lefebvre, M., Brunel, O.: The impact of story bound entrepreneurial role models on self-efficacy and entrepreneurial intention. Int. J. Entrep. Behav. Res. **18**(6), 720–742 (2012)

Liñán, F., Rodríguez-Cohard, J.C., Rueda-Cantuche, J.M.: Factors affecting entrepreneurial intention levels: a role for education. Int. Entrep. Manag. J. **7**, 195–218 (2011)

Macário, N., Neto, J., José, M., Bruno, D.: The role of self-efficacy, entrepreneurial passion, and creativity in developing entrepreneurial intentions. Quant. Psychol. Measur., 14 (2023)

Mäkimurto-Koivumaa, S., Belt, P.: About, for, in or through entrepreneurship in engineering education. Eur. J. Eng. Educ. **41**(5), 512–529 (2016)

Martin, O., Audretsch, D.B.: Artificial intelligence and big data in entrepreneurship: a new era has begun. Small Bus. Econ. **55**(3), 529–539 (2020)

McGee, J.E., Peterson, M.: The long-term impact of entrepreneurial self-efficacy and entrepreneurial orientation on venture performance. J. Small Bus. Manage. **57**(1), 720–737 (2019)

Morantz, A.: Why AI is the entrepreneur's new best friend. Medium (2021)

Nabi, G., Francisco, L.: Considering business start-up in recession time: the role of risk perception and economic context in shaping the entrepreneurial intent. Int. J. Entrep. Behav. Res. **19**(6), 633–655 (2013)

Nabi, G., Andreas, W., Francisco, L., Imran, A., Neame, C.: Does entrepreneurship education in the first year of higher education develop entrepreneurial intentions? The role of learning and inspiration. Stud. High. Educ. **43**(3), 452–467 (2017)

Ndou, V., Secundo, G., Schiuma, G., Passiante, G.: Insights for shaping entrepreneurship education: evidence from the European entrepreneurship centers. Sustainability **10**(11), 4323 (2018)

Neck, H.M., Greene, P.G.: Entrepreneurship education: known worlds and new frontiers. J. Small Bus. Manage. **49**(1), 55–70 (2011)

Newbery, R., Lean, J., Moizer, J., Haddoud, M.: Entrepreneurial identity formation during the initial entrepreneurial experience: the influence of simulation feedback and existing identity. J. Bus. Res. **85**(1), 51–59 (2018)

Noorderhaven, N., Thurik, R., Wennekers, S., Van Stel, A.: The role of dissatisfaction and per capita income in explaining self-employment across 15 European countries. Entrep. Theory Pract. **28**(5), 447–466 (2004)

Nowiński, W., Haddoud, M.Y.: The role of inspiring role models in enhancing entrepreneurial intention. J. Bus. Res. **96**(3), 183–193 (2019)

Nowiński, W., Lančarič, D., Haddoud, M.: The impact of entrepreneurship education, entrepreneurial self-efficacy and gender on entrepreneurial intentions of university students in the Visegrad countries. Stud. High. Educ. **44**(4), 1–19 (2019)

Nowshade: Entrepreneurship process in the era of artificial intelligence. 6th International Conference on Innovation and Entrepreneurship (2018)

Obschonka, M., Audretsch, D.B.: Artificial intelligence and big data in entrepreneurship: a new era has begun. Small Bus. Econ. **55**(3), 529–539 (2020)

Ozgen, E.: The effect of the national culture on female entrepreneurial activities in emerging countries: an application of the GLOBE project cultural dimensions. Int. J. Entrep. **16**, 69–92 (2012)

Podsakoff, P.M., MacKenzie, S.B., Lee, J.Y., Podsakoff, N.P.: Common method biases in behavioral research: a critical review of the literature and recommended remedies. J. Appl. Psychol. **88**(5), 879 (2003)

Quero, R.V., Quero, M.J.: Using Facebook in university teaching: a practical case study. Procedia Soc. Behav. Sci. **83**, 1032–1038 (2013)

Roundy, P.T.: Artificial intelligence and entrepreneurial ecosystems: Understanding the implications of algorithmic decision-making for startup communities. J. Ethics Entrep. Technol. **2**(1), 23–38 (2022)

Russell, S., Norvig, P.: Artificial intelligence: a modern approach. Pearson Education Limited (2016)

Saeed, S., Moreno, M., Yousafzai, S.: A multi-level study of entrepreneurship education among Pakistani university students. Entrep. Res. J. **4**(3), 297–321 (2014)

Sagar, S.: Entrepreneurship: Catalyst for innovation and economic growth. Entrepreneurship: Catalyst Innov. Econ. Growth **9**(1), 12 (2024)

Sahputri, R.A.M., Mawardi, M.K., Yumarni, T.: Entrepreneurship education, family entrepreneurial orientation and entrepreneurial intention among students in Indonesia. J. Int. Educ. Bus. **16**(3), 295–311 (2023)

Santos, F.J., Roomi, M.A., Liñán, F.: About gender differences and the social environment in the development of entrepreneurial intentions. J. Small Bus. Manage. **54**(1), 49–66 (2016)

Sarstedt, M., Ringle, C.M., Hair, J.F.: Partial least squares structural equation modeling. In: Handbook of market research, pp. 587–632. Springer International Publishing, Cham (2021)

Shane, S.A.: A general theory of entrepreneurship: the individual-opportunity nexus. Int. Small Bus. J. Researching Entrepreneurship (2003)

Shmueli, G., et al.: Predictive model assessment in PLS-SEM: guidelines for using PLSpredict. Eur. J. Mark. **53**(11), 2322–2347 (2019)

Siddhpura, A., Indumathi, V., Siddhpura, M.: Current state of research in application of disruptive technologies in engineering education. Procedia Comput. Sci. **172**, 494–501 (2020)

Thurik, R., Dejardin, M.: The impact of culture on entrepreneurship. Eur. Bus. Rev. **1**(2), 57–59 (2011)

Townsend, D.M., Hunt, R.A.: Entrepreneurial action, creativity, & judgment in the age of artificial intelligence. J. Bus. Venturing Insights, 11 (2018)

Townsend, D., Hunt, R.A., McMullen, J.: Uncertainty, knowledge problems, and entrepreneurial action. Acad. Manag. Ann. **12**(2), 57–18 (2012)

Trivedi, R.: Does university play significant role in shaping entrepreneurial intention? A cross-country comparative analysis. J. Small Bus. Enterp. Dev. **23**(3), 790–811 (2016)

Veciana, J.M., Aponte, M., Urbano, D.: University students' attitudes towards entrepreneurship: a two countries comparison. Int. Entrep. Manag. J. **1**(2), 165–182 (2005)

Ventura, R., Quero, M.J.: Factors explaining the intention to undertake in women. Differential aspects in the university population according to gender variable. J. Manag. **13**(1), 127–149 (2013)

Verheul, I., Thurik, R., Grilo, I., Van der Zwan, P.: Explaining preferences and actual involvement in self-employment: gender and the entrepreneurial personality. J. Econ. Psychol. **33**(2), 325–341 (2012)

von Arnim, L., Mrozewski, M.: Entrepreneurship in an increasingly digital and global world. Evaluating the role of digital capabilities on international entrepreneurial intention. Sustainability **12**(19), 7984 (2020)

Wang, Z., Li, M., Lu, J., Cheng, X.: Business innovation based on artificial intelligence and blockchain technology. Inf. Process. Manage. **59**(1), 122–131 (2022)

Wasim, J., Haj Youssef, M., Christodoulou, I., Reinhardt, R.: Higher education student intentions behind becoming an entrepreneur. Higher Educ. Skills Work-Based Learn. **14**(1), 162–180 (2024)

Wennberg, K., Pathak, S., Autio, E.: How culture moulds the effects of self-efficacy and fear of failure on entrepreneurship. Entrep. Reg. Dev. **25**(9–10), 756–780 (2013)

Wilson, H.J., Daugherty, P.R.: Collaborative intelligence: humans and AI are joining forces. Harv. Bus. Rev. **96**(1), 114–233 (2018)

Xiong, D., Khaddage-Soboh, N., Umar, M., Safi, A., Norena-Chavez, D.: Redefining entrepreneurship in the digital age: exploring the impact of technology and collaboration on ventures. Int. Entrep. Manag. J. **20**(4), 3255–3281 (2024)

Zhang, Y., Duysters, G., Cloodt, M.: The role of entrepreneurship education as a predictor of university students' entrepreneurial intention. Int. Entrep. Manag. J. **10**(3), 623–641 (2014)

Zhao, H., Scott, E., Gerald, E.: The mediating role of self-efficacy in the development of entrepreneurial intentions. J. Appl. Psychol. **90**(6), 1265–1272 (2005)

The Behavioral Intention to Use Intelligent Devices Using an Extension of UTAUT Model: Case of Tunisian Consumers

Inès Mhaya(✉) and Soukeina Touiti

ESPRIT School of Engineering, Ariana, Tunisia
{ines.mhaya,soukeina.touiti}@esprit.tn

Abstract. This study extends the *Unified Theory of Acceptance and Use of Technology* (UTAUT) to investigate behavioral intention toward adopting intelligent devices in Tunisia, while examining variations in technology acceptance. Data from 218 respondents were analyzed using structural equation modeling (SEM), revealing key findings: Familiarity and Trust emerged as the strongest predictors of adoption intention, underscoring the importance of user confidence and prior experience with AI technologies. Contrary to traditional UTAUT expectations, Performance Expectancy and Effort Expectancy showed non-significant effects, suggesting Tunisian users prioritize trust and familiarity over perceived usefulness or ease of use. Technophilia exhibited marginal significance, indicating technology enthusiasts may serve as early adopters. Notably, demographic factors (age, gender, profession, expertise) showed no moderating effects, implying universal adoption drivers across user segments. These results offer crucial insights for AI practitioners: Marketing strategies should emphasize building trust through transparency, enhancing familiarity via training programs, and leveraging social influence in this collectivist culture. The study validates an extended UTAUT model for intelligent devices in developing economies while challenging conventional technology acceptance assumptions. Limitations and future research directions are discussed to guide cross-cultural examinations of AI adoption.

Keywords: Extension of UTAUT · Behavioral intention · Trust · Familiarity · Technophilia

1 Introduction

In today's rapidly evolving technological landscape, intelligent devices -ranging from smart home assistants and wearable gadgets to autonomous vehicles and AI-driven applications- are transforming how we interact with technology and navigate our daily lives. These devices promise unparalleled convenience, efficiency, and connectivity, yet their widespread adoption among consumers remains a significant challenge. Despite their advanced capabilities, barriers related to consumer perceptions and individual differences continue to shape consumer acceptance. At the same time, the perceived benefits

F. Kamoun et al. (Eds.): AFRICATEK 2025, LNICST 677, pp. 341–370, 2026.
https://doi.org/10.1007/978-3-032-16638-8_23

of these technologies -such as improved productivity, enhanced convenience, or better decision-making- play a crucial role in driving adoption. For manufacturers, developers, and policymakers, addressing these barriers while leveraging the perceived value of intelligent devices is critical to unlocking their full potential and driving innovation forward.

One of the most pressing barriers to adoption is the lack of trust in intelligent devices. Trust encompasses not only the reliability and transparency of AI-driven systems but also concerns about privacy and data security. Many consumers are wary of entrusting sensitive personal information to these technologies, fearing data breaches, misuse, or unauthorized access (Smith et al. 2020; Gefen et al. 2003). For example, in the case of smart home devices, users often worry about how their data is stored and who has access to it, while users of wearable fitness trackers may be concerned about the security of their health data (Venkatesh et al. 2012). Without addressing these trust issues -whether related to system reliability or data protection- even the most advanced devices may struggle to gain consumer acceptance, regardless of their potential to enhance performance or simplify tasks.

Another major obstacle is the perceived complexity of intelligent devices. Many users find these technologies intimidating, particularly when they require technical expertise to set up, operate, or integrate into existing systems (Davis 1989). The complexity of user interfaces, coupled with the rapid pace of technological advancements, often leaves consumers feeling overwhelmed (Venkatesh et al. 2003). This is especially true for older adults or those with limited technological literacy, who may struggle to navigate the features and functionalities of devices like smart home assistants or autonomous vehicle interfaces (Rogers 2003). If users perceive a device as too complicated or difficult to use, they are less likely to adopt it, even if it offers significant benefits such as time savings or improved efficiency.

Closely related to complexity is the issue of lack of familiarity with intelligent devices. Many consumers, particularly in regions with lower technological penetration, are simply not accustomed to interacting with advanced technologies like AI-driven systems or IoT devices (Alalwan et al. 2017). This unfamiliarity can lead to apprehension and resistance, as users may feel unsure about how to operate the devices or how they fit into their daily lives (Zhou et al. 2010). For instance, someone who has never used a smart home assistant may find it difficult to understand its value or functionality, while a first-time user of a smartwatch may hesitate due to unfamiliarity with its features (Nysveen et al. 2005). However, when users recognize the potential of these devices to streamline tasks or enhance their quality of life, they are more likely to overcome their initial reservations.

On the other hand, technophilia -the inherent enthusiasm or affinity for new technologies- can serve as a powerful driver of adoption. Individuals with high levels of technophilia are more likely to embrace intelligent devices, as they are naturally curious and eager to explore innovative solutions (Agarwal and Prasad 1998). These users are less deterred by perceived complexity or unfamiliarity and are more willing to invest time and effort in learning how to use new technologies (Nysveen et al. 2005). For example, early adopters of smartwatch or AI-powered personal assistants often exhibit high levels of technophilia, which motivates them to overcome initial barriers and integrate these technologies into their lives (Lu et al. 2005). Understanding the role of technophilia is therefore essential for identifying segments of the population that are more likely to adopt intelligent devices and for designing targeted marketing strategies.

Another significant barrier related to consumer perceptions is performance expectancy, which refers to the extent to which users perceive that intelligent devices will enhance their performance or efficiency. If consumers do not clearly see the tangible benefits of these technologies -such as time savings, improved productivity, or simplified daily tasks- they are less likely to adopt them (Venkatesh et al. 2003). For example, a user may hesitate to purchase a smart home assistant if they do not perceive how, it could genuinely improve their daily life, or they might reject a smartwatch if they do not see how it could help them achieve their health goals (Zhou et al. 2010). However, when users perceive that the benefits of these devices -such as energy savings, better health outcomes, enhanced convenience- outweigh the initial effort or costs, they are more likely to adopt them (Nysveen et al. 2005).

This study seeks to explore these barriers and drivers in depth by extending the *Unified Theory of Acceptance and Use of Technology* (UTAUT) framework to include trust, familiarity, and technophilia as key determinants of consumer adoption (Venkatesh et al. 2003, 2012). By focusing on the Tunisian context, the research aims to validate the extended UTAUT model in a non-Western setting, providing valuable insights into how cultural and contextual factors influence technology adoption (Alalwan et al. 2017). The outcomes of this study are expected to contribute significantly to the field by: (1) empirically validating an extended UTAUT model in a non-Western cultural context; (2) investigating the impact of trust, familiarity, and technophilia on consumers' behavioral intention to adopt intelligent devices; and (3) assessing the moderating effects of demographic variables on adoption behavior (Venkatesh et al. 2012). By addressing these objectives, this research aims to bridge existing gaps in literature and provide actionable insights for stakeholders seeking to promote the adoption of intelligent devices in diverse cultural and technological contexts.

2 Literature Review

2.1 Unified Theory of Acceptance and Use Technology Model (UTAUT)

The *Unified Theory of Acceptance and Use of Technology* (UTAUT) represents a significant advancement in understanding technology adoption, building upon earlier frameworks such as the *Technology Acceptance Model* (TAM) and the *Theory of Reasoned Action* (TRA). To fully appreciate the UTAUT model, it is essential to trace its theoretical roots and the evolution of technology acceptance research.

The journey begins with the Theory of Reasoned Action (TRA), proposed by Fishbein and Ajzen (1975). TRA posits that an individual's behavioral intention -the likelihood of performing a specific behavior- is determined by two key factors: attitude toward the behavior (the individual's positive or negative evaluation of the behavior) and subjective norms (the perceived social pressure to perform or not perform the behavior). While TRA provided a robust foundation for understanding human decision-making, it was not specifically tailored to the context of technology adoption.

Recognizing this gap, Davis (1989) introduced the *Technology Acceptance Model* (TAM), which adapted TRA to the domain of information technology. TAM simplified TRA by focusing on two primary constructs: perceived usefulness and perceived ease of use. Perceived usefulness refers to the degree to which an individual believes that using a particular technology will enhance their performance or productivity. Perceived ease of use, on the other hand, captures the extent to which a person believes that using the technology will be free of effort. According to TAM, if users perceive a technology as both useful and easy to use, they are more likely to develop a positive attitude toward its use, which in turn increases their intention to use the technology. This intention ultimately leads to actual usage behavior.

TAM has been widely applied and validated across various technological contexts, from software applications to e-commerce platforms, demonstrating its utility in predicting user acceptance and adoption. However, as technology evolved and adoption scenarios became more complex, researchers recognized the need for a more comprehensive model that could account for a broader range of factors influencing technology acceptance.

In response to this need, Venkatesh et al. (2003) conducted an extensive review of the literature and empirical studies, integrating elements from eight prominent models of technology acceptance and use. These models included: *Theory of Reasoned Action* (TRA) (Fishbein and Ajzen 1975); *Technology Acceptance Model* (TAM) (Davis 1989); *Theory of Planned Behavior* (TPB) (Ajzen 1991); Combined TAM-TPB (Taylor and Todd 1995); *Model of PC Utilization* (MPCU) (Thompson et al. 1991); *Motivational Model* (MM) (Davis et al. 1992); *Social Cognitive Theory* (SCT) (Bandura 1986); and *Innovation Diffusion Theory* (IDT) (Rogers 2003).

By synthesizing these models, Venkatesh et al. (2003) developed the *Unified Theory of Acceptance and Use of Technology* (UTAUT), which aimed to provide a more holistic and unified framework for understanding technology adoption. The UTAUT model (see Fig. 1) incorporates four core constructs that directly influence behavioral intention and usage behavior. Performance Expectancy (PE) refers to the degree to which an individual believes that using the technology will enhance their job performance or productivity, making it a critical driver of adoption. Effort Expectancy (EE) captures the perceived ease of using the technology, emphasizing the importance of user-friendly design and intuitive interfaces in reducing barriers to adoption. Social Influence (SI) reflects the extent to which an individual perceives that important others -such as peers, supervisors, or social networks- believe they should use the technology, highlighting the role of external pressures and endorsements in shaping user behavior. Finally, Facilitating Conditions (FC) encompass the degree to which an individual believes that the necessary organizational and technical infrastructure -such as training, support, and resources- exists to enable the effective use of the technology, underscoring the importance of a supportive environment for successful adoption. Together, these constructs provide a comprehensive understanding of the factors that drive technology acceptance, making UTAUT a powerful tool for predicting and enhancing user adoption across diverse contexts. In addition to these core constructs, UTAUT introduces four moderators; gender, age, experience, and voluntariness of use, that influence the strength of the relationships between the core constructs and behavioral intention or usage behavior. For example, younger users may place greater emphasis on performance expectancy, while older users may prioritize effort expectancy. Similarly, individuals with more experience using a technology may be less influenced by social influence than novice users.

The UTAUT model has been empirically validated and demonstrates a remarkable ability to explain up to 70% of the variance in user intention, making it one of the most robust frameworks for studying technology adoption. Its comprehensive nature allows researchers and practitioners to better understand how different factors interact to influence adoption decisions across diverse user groups and technological contexts.

In the context of intelligent devices, UTAUT provides a powerful lens for analyzing adoption behavior. For instance, if users perceive an intelligent device as highly useful (performance expectancy) and easy to operate (effort expectancy), and if they believe that their social circle approves of its use (social influence), they are more likely to adopt the technology. Furthermore, the availability of technical support and resources (facilitating conditions) can significantly enhance adoption rates. By considering the moderating effects of demographic factors such as age, gender, and experience, UTAUT also enables a nuanced understanding of how different user segments may respond to the same technology.

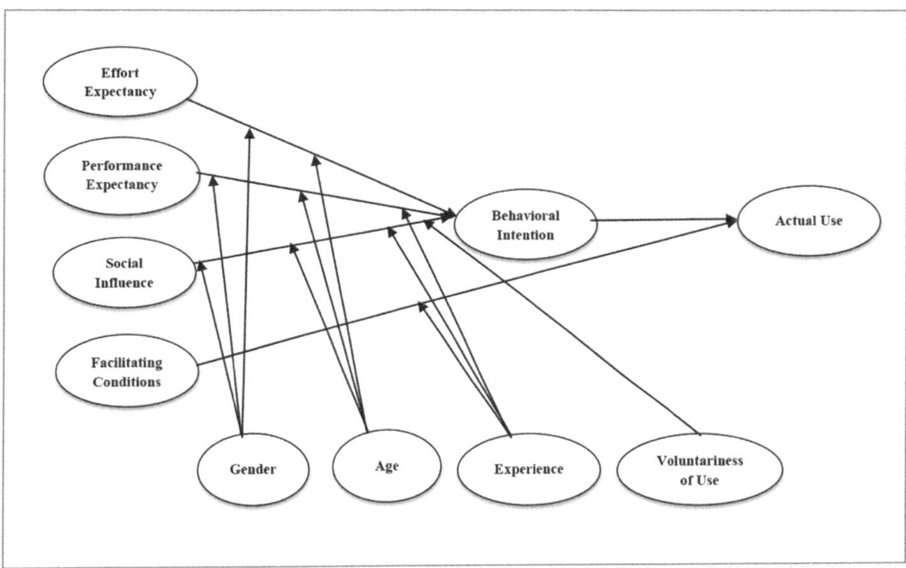

Fig. 1. The unified theory of acceptance and use of technology model (Venkatesh et al. 2003)

2.2 Applications of UTAUT

The *Unified Theory of Acceptance and Use of Technology* (UTAUT) has emerged as a cornerstone framework for understanding and predicting technology adoption across a wide array of domains, offering actionable insights for researchers, practitioners, and policymakers. By integrating performance expectancy, effort expectancy, social influence, and facilitating conditions, UTAUT provides a comprehensive lens through which to analyze user behavior in diverse technological contexts (Venkatesh et al. 2003).

In healthcare, for instance, UTAUT has been pivotal in examining the adoption of electronic health records (EHRs), telemedicine platforms, and mobile health (mHealth) applications, where performance expectancy -such as the perceived ability of EHRs to enhance patient care- and effort expectancy -such as the ease of navigating telemedicine interfaces- significantly influence healthcare professionals' willingness to adopt these technologies (Holden and Karsh 2010; Gagnon et al. 2012). Similarly, in education, UTAUT has shed light on the adoption of e-learning platforms, learning management systems (LMS), and immersive technologies like virtual reality (VR) and augmented reality (AR), with performance expectancy (e.g., improved learning outcomes) and effort expectancy (e.g., user-friendly LMS interfaces) driving acceptance among students and educators (Šumak et al. 2011; Tarhini et al. 2017).

The financial sector has also benefited from UTAUT, particularly in understanding the uptake of mobile banking, digital wallets, and blockchain systems, where performance expectancy (e.g., convenience of mobile banking) and effort expectancy (e.g., simplicity of digital wallet use) are critical determinants of user adoption (Zhou et al. 2010; Oliveira et al. 2014). In e-commerce and retail, UTAUT has been instrumental in analyzing the adoption of online marketplaces, recommendation systems, and self-checkout technologies, with performance expectancy (e.g., personalized shopping experiences) and effort expectancy (e.g., seamless website navigation) playing key roles in consumer decision-making (Gefen et al. 2003; Venkatesh et al. 2012).

The framework has also been applied to smart cities and the Internet of Things (IoT), where it has helped explain the adoption of smart home devices, intelligent transportation systems, and energy management tools, emphasizing the importance of performance expectancy (e.g., energy savings from smart thermostats) and effort expectancy (e.g., ease of controlling devices via apps) (Alalwan et al. 2017; Rana et al. 2016). In the realm of artificial intelligence (AI) and automation, UTAUT has been used to explore the adoption of chatbots, virtual assistants, and automated decision-making systems, with performance expectancy (e.g., efficiency gains from AI tools) and effort expectancy (e.g., intuitive chatbot interactions) driving user acceptance (Lu et al. 2005; Venkatesh et al. 2012).

Finally, in public services and government, UTAUT has been applied to study the adoption of e-government platforms, digital identity systems, and online tax filing tools, where performance expectancy (e.g., time savings from digital services) and effort expectancy (e.g., ease of navigating government portals) are critical factors (Carter and Bélanger 2005; Rana et al. 2015). Across all these domains, social influence -such as peer recommendations or organizational mandates- and facilitating conditions -such as access to training, technical support, and infrastructure- play pivotal roles in shaping adoption behavior (Venkatesh et al. 2003; Dwivedi et al. 2019). Moreover, the inclusion of moderators like age, gender, and experience allows for a nuanced understanding of how different user segments respond to technology, enabling tailored strategies to enhance adoption (Venkatesh et al. 2012; Alalwan et al. 2017).

By bridging individual perceptions, social dynamics, and organizational support, UTAUT has proven to be an indispensable tool for designing user-centric technologies and fostering innovation. As technological advancements continue to reshape industries, UTAUT remains a vital framework for driving user acceptance and ensuring the successful integration of new technologies into everyday life (Venkatesh et al. 2003; Dwivedi et al. 2019).

3 Research Model and Hypothesis

The research model for this study, depicted in Fig. 2, is based on the *Unified Theory of Acceptance and Use of Technology* (UTAUT). However, it has been adapted to better align with the context of intelligent devices adoption by incorporating additional extensions and omitting certain elements. Specifically, social influence and facilitating conditions were excluded from the model, as their relevance in the context of voluntary adoption of intelligent devices was deemed limited. Social influence, which refers to the impact of peers or societal expectations on technology adoption, tends to play a stronger role in mandatory or organizational settings rather than in voluntary consumer contexts, where adoption decisions are driven more by personal preferences and individual assessments of usefulness. Similarly, facilitating conditions, which pertain to the availability of external support or infrastructure, are less critical in voluntary settings, as users typically rely on their own resources and capabilities when adopting technologies like intelligent devices. Since this study focuses exclusively on voluntary use, the construct of voluntariness of use was also removed as a moderating factor. The retained constructs from the original UTAUT model include performance expectancy and effort expectancy, which are identified as the key determinants of behavioral intention to adopt intelligent devices. Furthermore, the moderating effects of age, gender, and experience were retained, as these factors play a critical role in understanding how different user segments respond to technology adoption (Venkatesh et al. 2003; Alalwan et al. 2017).

The theoretical foundation of the research model relies on UTAUT, which posits that performance expectancy and effort expectancy are the primary drivers of adoption behavior. These constructs are expected to support the hypothesized relationships in the model. However, given the unique context of intelligent device adoption and the cultural differences in the Tunisian setting, several specific hypotheses were formulated to capture the anticipated effects of additional factors, such as trust, familiarity, and technophilia, which are not explicitly included in the original UTAUT framework. These additions enrich the analysis and provide a more nuanced perspective tailored to the context under investigation.

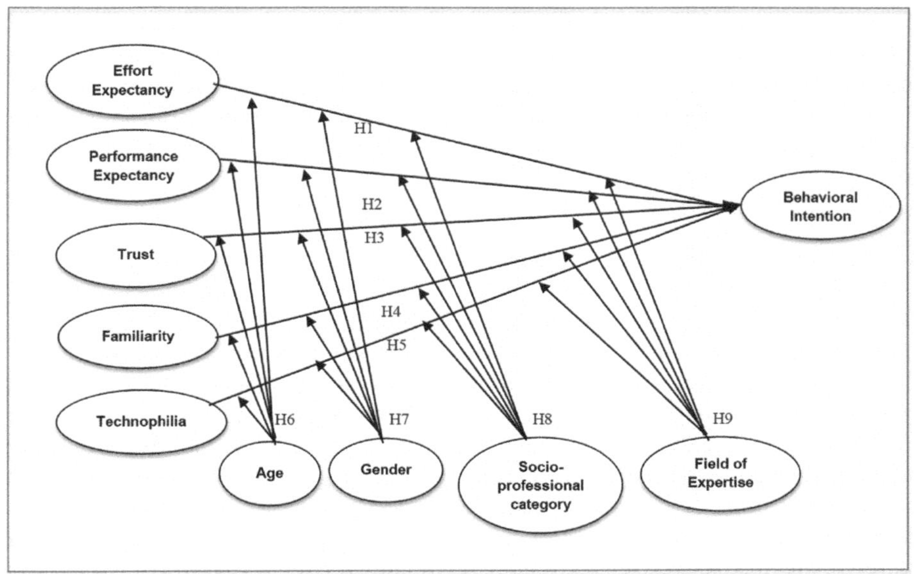

Fig. 2. The research model

3.1 Behavioral Intention

Behavioral intention is a central construct in understanding technology adoption and represents an individual's readiness or willingness to engage in the behavior of using a specific technology. It is defined as "*the degree to which a person has formulated conscious plans regarding whether to perform a specified future behavior*" (Ajzen 1991). In the context of technology adoption, behavioral intention reflects the likelihood that an individual will adopt and use a particular technology, making it a critical predictor of actual usage behavior.

Behavioral intention is not only a predictor of technology adoption but also a mediator that links users' perceptions and attitudes to their actual usage behavior. According to the Theory of Planned Behavior (TPB), which underpins the concept of behavioral intention, intention is the most immediate antecedent of behavior (Ajzen 1991). In the context of intelligent devices, this means that users who form a strong intention to adopt a technology are more likely to follow through and integrate it into their daily routines. For example, a user who intends to use a smart thermostat to reduce energy costs is more likely to purchase and install the device, provided that external barriers (e.g., cost, installation complexity) do not interfere.

Empirical studies have consistently supported the role of behavioral intention as a key driver of technology adoption. For instance, Venkatesh et al. (2003) found that behavioral intention significantly predicts actual usage behavior across a wide range of technologies and user groups. Similarly, Davis (1989) demonstrated that users' intentions to use a technology are strongly influenced by their perceptions of its usefulness and ease of use, which align with performance expectancy and effort expectancy in the UTAUT model. These findings highlight the importance of designing technologies that are not only functional and easy to use but also aligned with users' needs and expectations.

In the context of intelligent devices, such as smart home systems, wearable technologies, or IoT-enabled gadgets, behavioral intention plays a crucial role in driving adoption. Users are more likely to adopt these devices if they perceive them as useful, easy to use, socially endorsed, and supported by adequate resources. For example, a user may intend to adopt a smartwatch if they believe it will simplify their daily tasks, if their friends recommend it, and if they have access to technical support in case of issues.

In summary, behavioral intention serves as a critical bridge between users' perceptions of a technology and their actual adoption behavior. By understanding the factors that shape behavioral intention such as performance expectancy and effort expectancy, researchers and practitioners can design strategies to enhance users' willingness to adopt and use intelligent devices effectively. These insights are essential for developing technologies that are not only innovative but also accessible, user-friendly, and aligned with the diverse needs of users across different contexts.

3.2 The Impact of Effort Expectancy

Effort expectancy (EE), a pivotal predictor within the UTAUT model, is highlighted as a key determinant of technology acceptance. Venkatesh et al. (2003) define effort expectancy as "*the degree of ease associated with the use of the system.*" This construct reflects the user's perception of the amount of effort required to learn and operate a new technology, which plays a critical role in shaping their behavioral intention to adopt it.

Empirical studies have consistently demonstrated that users are more likely to adopt technologies when they are perceived as easy to use and require minimal cognitive or physical effort (Davis 1989; Venkatesh et al. 2003). For instance, in the context of Learning Management Systems (LMS) used in businesses, employees are more inclined to adopt a platform if it is intuitive and does not demand extensive training or technical expertise (Venkatesh et al. 2003). Similarly, in consumer settings, technologies that are user-friendly and require little effort to integrate into daily routines are more likely to gain widespread acceptance (Alalwan et al. 2017).

The impact of effort expectancy is further amplified by contextual factors such as organizational support, available resources, and user experience, which collectively reduce the perceived effort associated with technology adoption (Thornton and Chan 2014). For example, in environments where users have access to training, tutorials, or technical assistance, the perceived ease of use increases, thereby enhancing adoption rates. However, even in the absence of such support, technologies that are inherently designed to be intuitive and user-centric tend to foster higher levels of acceptance.

In the context of intelligent devices, such as smart home systems, wearables, or IoT-enabled gadgets, effort expectancy becomes particularly salient. These devices often involve new interfaces, complex functionalities, and integration with existing technologies, which can create barriers to adoption if users perceive them as difficult to operate. Conversely, when intelligent devices are designed with simplicity and user-friendliness in mind, they are more likely to be embraced by users, regardless of their technical proficiency. Given the theoretical and empirical support for the role of effort expectancy in technology adoption, it is hypothesized that:

H1: Effort expectancy has a negative influence on behavioral intention to use intelligent devices.

3.3 The Impact of Performance Expectancy

Performance expectancy (PE) is another essential construct introduced in the UTAUT model, defined as "*the degree to which an individual believes that using a system will help them attain gains in job performance*" (Venkatesh et al. 2003). This construct reflects the user's perception of the extent to which a technology can enhance their productivity, efficiency, or overall effectiveness in achieving desired outcomes. Performance expectancy is widely regarded as one of the strongest predictors of behavioral intention to adopt new technologies, as users are more likely to embrace systems that they believe will deliver tangible benefits.

Empirical studies have consistently demonstrated the significant role of performance expectancy in driving technology adoption across various contexts. For example, in organizational settings, employees are more inclined to adopt tools like enterprise software or Learning Management Systems (LMS) when they perceive these systems as capable of improving their work performance or simplifying complex tasks (Venkatesh et al. 2003; Alalwan et al. 2017). Similarly, in consumer contexts, technologies that offer clear advantages, such as time savings, convenience, or enhanced functionality, are more likely to be adopted and integrated into daily routines (Davis 1989; Rogers 2003).

In the context of intelligent devices, performance expectancy becomes particularly relevant. These devices are often designed to enhance users' quality of life by automating tasks, providing real-time data, or enabling seamless connectivity. For instance, a smart thermostat that optimizes energy usage or a wearable fitness tracker that monitors health metrics can be perceived as highly beneficial, thereby increasing users' intention to adopt and use these technologies. The perceived utility of intelligent devices is further amplified when users believe that these technologies can address specific needs or solve problems more effectively than traditional alternatives.

Moreover, performance expectancy is influenced by factors such as user experience, compatibility with existing systems, and perceived reliability. When intelligent devices are seen as reliable, compatible with users' lifestyles, and capable of delivering consistent performance, their perceived value increases, further strengthening the likelihood of adoption (Thornton and Chan 2014). Given the robust theoretical and empirical support for the role of performance expectancy in technology adoption, it is hypothesized that:

H2: Performance expectancy has a positive influence on behavioral intention to use intelligent devices.

3.4 The Impact of Trust

Trust plays a critical role in the adoption of technology, significantly influencing individuals' intention to use and engage with new systems. Trust refers to the users' psychological willingness to rely on and accept the risks associated with an emerging technological system. When users trust technology, they believe in its reliability, security, and ability to deliver the expected outcomes. This confidence fosters a strong belief that using technology will yield tangible benefits and enhance their effectiveness, thereby increasing their willingness to adopt and consistently engage with it. In essence, trust acts as a bridge that connects users to technology, reducing uncertainty and encouraging acceptance.

Numerous studies have highlighted trust as a pivotal predictor of technology adoption. For instance, Venkatesh et al. (2003) and Mayer et al. (1995) emphasize that trust is a key factor in overcoming barriers to adoption, particularly in contexts where users may have concerns about privacy, security, or the reliability of the technology. When individuals trust a system, they are more likely to overlook potential risks or challenges and actively embrace its use. For example, in the context of e-commerce, consumers are more willing to share personal and financial information on platforms they perceive as trustworthy, leading to higher adoption rates (Gefen et al. 2003). Similarly, in the realm of digital banking, trust in the security and reliability of online platforms has been shown to significantly influence users' intention to adopt and continue using these services (Yousafzai et al. 2003).

In the context of intelligent devices, trust becomes even more critical. These devices often collect and process sensitive personal data, such as health information, location data, or daily routines. Users are more likely to adopt and integrate these technologies into their lives if they trust that their data will be handled securely and that the devices will function as intended. For example, a smart home security system is more likely to be adopted if users trust that it will reliably protect their home and that their data will not be misused. Similarly, wearable fitness trackers are more readily embraced when users trust that their health data will remain private and accurate.

Trust also serves to alleviate concerns related to privacy and security, which are common barriers to the adoption of intelligent devices. By addressing these concerns, trust helps to create a smoother path toward adoption, enabling users to focus on the benefits of the technology rather than its potential risks. For instance, studies have shown that users are more willing to adopt smart home devices when they trust that manufacturers have implemented robust security measures to protect their data (Zhou 2013). Based on these theoretical and empirical insights, the following hypothesis is proposed:

H3: Trust has a positive influence on behavioral intention to use intelligent devices.

3.5 The Impact of Familiarity

Familiarity refers to the level of knowledge, experience, or exposure that an individual has with a particular technology, product, or system (Venkatesh et al. 2012). It encompasses a person's understanding of how technology works, their past interactions with it, and their comfort level in using it. Familiarity plays a crucial role in shaping user perceptions and intentions, as it reduces uncertainty and increases confidence in the technology's capabilities. When users are familiar with technology, they are more likely to perceive it as easy to use and reliable, which enhances their willingness to adopt and engage with it.

While familiarity was not initially included as an explanatory factor in the original UTAUT model (Venkatesh et al. 2003), it was later integrated into extensions of the model, such as UTAUT2 (Venkatesh et al. 2012). In these extended frameworks, familiarity is recognized as a contextual predictor of behavioral intention to use technology. Empirical studies have demonstrated that familiarity significantly influences technology adoption by positively affecting users' perceptions of ease of use and confidence in the technology's performance. For example, individuals who are familiar with technology are more likely to view it as intuitive and less intimidating, which strengthens their intention to use it (Venkatesh et al. 2012).

The impact of familiarity is particularly evident in consumer technology adoption. For instance, users who are familiar with mobile applications or smart devices are more likely to adopt new apps or gadgets because they already understand the basic functionalities and user interfaces. This prior knowledge reduces the learning curve and increases the likelihood of continued use. Similarly, familiarity with e-commerce platforms has been shown to enhance users' trust and willingness to make online purchases, as they feel more confident navigating the system and understanding its features (Gefen et al. 2003).

However, the effect of familiarity can vary depending on the context and type of technology. For example, a user may be highly familiar with consumer-facing technologies, such as smartphones or social media platforms, but less familiar with complex systems used in professional settings, such as enterprise software or specialized IoT devices. In such cases, the level of familiarity may influence the user's willingness to adopt the technology, as unfamiliar systems may require additional effort to learn and integrate into daily routines. This variability highlights the importance of considering the specific context and user demographics when examining the role of familiarity in technology adoption.

In the context of intelligent devices, familiarity can significantly influence adoption. Users who have prior experience with similar technologies are more likely to perceive intelligent devices as easy to use and beneficial, which enhances their intention to adopt them. For example, a person who has used a basic smart speaker may feel more comfortable adopting advanced smart home systems, as they are already familiar with voice-controlled interfaces and connected devices. Conversely, users with no prior exposure to such technologies may perceive them as complex or intimidating, which could hinder adoption. Based on these theoretical and empirical insights, the following hypothesis is proposed:

H4: Familiarity has a positive influence on behavioral intention to use intelligent devices.

3.6 The Impact of Technophilia

Technophilia, as evidenced in studies such as those conducted by Davis (1989), Venkatesh and Davis (2000) and LaRose and Eastin (2004), refers to a deep-seated affection or love for technology. This intrinsic affinity for technological innovations can profoundly influence individuals' intention to engage with and adopt new technologies. Technophiles are characterized by their heightened curiosity, enthusiasm, and eagerness to embrace novel technological advancements. Their inherent fondness for technology often drives them to be early adopters of new gadgets, explore cutting-edge features, and readily integrate emerging technologies into their daily lives.

Research has consistently shown that technophiles are more receptive to change and innovation. For example, Venkatesh and Davis's (2000) longitudinal studies highlight that individuals with technophilic tendencies are more likely to experiment with new technologies and adapt quickly to technological changes. This openness to novelty fosters a proactive approach to trying out new products or services, even when they are still in the early stages of development or adoption. Technophiles are often motivated by the excitement of exploring new functionalities and the potential benefits that innovative technologies can offer, which strengthens their intention to adopt and use these technologies.

Moreover, technophiles exhibit a strong dedication to learning and mastering new technologies, as elucidated by Davis (1989). Their passion for technology drives them to invest time and effort in understanding how new systems work, which enhances their confidence and competence in using them. This commitment not only reinforces their intention to adopt new technologies but also increases the likelihood of sustained usage over time. For instance, technophiles are more likely to persist in using a new smart device or software application, even if they encounter initial challenges, because their enthusiasm and curiosity motivate them to overcome obstacles.

In the context of intelligent devices, such as wearable technologies, or IoT-enabled gadgets, technophilia plays a particularly significant role. Technophiles are often the first to adopt these devices, driven by their desire to experience the latest innovations and integrate them into their lifestyles. For example, a technophile might eagerly purchase a smartwatch or a voice-controlled assistant to explore its advanced features and optimize its use in their daily routines. Their enthusiasm for technology also makes them more likely to recommend these devices to others, thereby influencing broader adoption trends.

Furthermore, technophilia can mitigate common barriers to technology adoption, such as resistance to change or fear of complexity. Technophiles' inherent curiosity and willingness to experiment help them navigate the learning curve associated with new technologies, making them more likely to embrace intelligent devices even if they require some initial effort to master. This proactive attitude aligns with the findings of LaRose and Eastin (2004), who emphasize that technophiles' positive attitudes toward technology foster a cycle of continuous engagement and innovation. Based on these theoretical and empirical insights, the following hypothesis is proposed:

H5: Technophilia has a positive influence on behavioral intention to use intelligent devices.

3.7 Moderator Effects

The *Unified Theory of Acceptance and Use of Technology* (UTAUT) posits that several user characteristics, including age, gender, and experience, act as moderators that influence the strength and direction of relationships between key predictors and behavioral intention (Venkatesh et al. 2003). These moderators help explain how different user groups respond to technology adoption, providing a more nuanced understanding of the factors driving acceptance and use.

Effect of Age. Age is one of the most significant moderators in the UTAUT framework, influencing the relationships between all four core predictors -performance expectancy, effort expectancy, social influence, and facilitating conditions- and behavioral intention to adopt technology (Venkatesh et al. 2003). This moderating effect reflects the varying priorities, preferences, and comfort levels of different age groups when it comes to adopting new technologies. For younger users, effort expectancy tends to be a more critical factor in technology adoption. Younger individuals, often referred to as "digital natives," have grown up surrounded by technology and are generally more comfortable with digital interfaces. As a result, they are more likely to adopt technologies that are intuitive and require minimal effort to learn and use. For example, younger users may prioritize the simplicity of a mobile app or the user-friendly design of a smart device when deciding whether to adopt it. Their familiarity with technology reduces the perceived complexity of new systems, making effort expectancy a key driver of their adoption decisions (Venkatesh et al. 2003). In contrast, older users tend to prioritize performance expectancy (perceived usefulness) when adopting new technologies. Older individuals are more likely to adopt technologies that offer clear and immediate benefits to their daily lives, such as improving productivity, enhancing health, or simplifying tasks. For instance, older adults may be more inclined to adopt a smart home device if it helps them manage household chores more efficiently or a wearable fitness tracker if it provides actionable insights into their health. This focus on utility reflects a pragmatic approach to technology adoption, where the perceived value of the technology outweighs concerns about ease of use (Venkatesh et al. 2003). These findings highlight the importance of tailoring technology design and marketing strategies to different age groups. For younger users, emphasizing ease of use and intuitive design can enhance adoption, while for older users, focusing on practical benefits and clear value propositions may be more effective. By addressing the unique needs and preferences of each age group, developers and marketers can maximize the adoption and sustained use of intelligent devices. Based on these insights, the following hypothesis is proposed:

H6: Age moderates the relationship between performance expectancy, effort expectancy, trust, familiarity, technophilia and behavioral intention to use intelligent devices.

Effect of Gender. Gender plays a significant moderating role in technology adoption, particularly in relation to performance expectancy and effort expectancy. Empirical studies have consistently shown that men and women differ in their perceptions and priorities when adopting new technologies. Men tend to be more influenced by performance expectancy, as they often focus on the functional benefits and utility of a technology. For example, men are more likely to adopt technologies that enhance productivity, provide advanced features, or offer competitive advantages (Venkatesh and Morris 2000). In contrast, women are more influenced by effort expectancy, as they place greater importance on the ease of use, accessibility, and user-friendliness of a system. Women are more likely to adopt technologies that are intuitive, require minimal effort to learn, and align with their daily needs (Venkatesh et al. 2003). These gender-based differences highlight the need for inclusive design practices that address the diverse needs and preferences of all users (Gefen et al. 2003).

The effect of gender on technology adoption extends beyond performance and effort expectancy, as it also influences adoption patterns, preferences, and behaviors. Studies have shown that men tend to adopt new technologies at higher rates compared to women

(Venkatesh et al. 2003; Rogers 2003). This disparity may stem from differences in exposure to technology, social norms, and perceptions of technology's relevance and utility. For instance, men are often more exposed to technology through hobbies, education, or professional roles, which can increase their comfort level and willingness to adopt new systems. Women, on the other hand, may face social or cultural barriers that limit their exposure to technology or discourage them from engaging with it (Hargittai and Shafer 2006). These differences underscore the importance of understanding how gender shapes not only the adoption of technology but also the factors that drive behavioral intention (Venkatesh et al. 2012).

Gender also plays a significant moderating role in shaping the relationships between familiarity, trust, technophilia, and behavioral intention to use intelligent devices, reflecting the differing psychological, social, and experiential factors that influence how men and women perceive and engage with technology. Familiarity, or the level of knowledge and experience with a technology, tends to have a stronger impact on women, as it helps reduce perceived barriers and increases comfort levels, while men, who are often more exposed to technology, derive confidence from familiarity, making them more willing to adopt advanced systems (Venkatesh et al. 2003; Hargittai 2002). Trust, which encompasses beliefs about a technology's reliability, security, and effectiveness, also varies by gender: men tend to focus on functional aspects of trust, such as performance and reliability, while women prioritize emotional and security-related aspects, such as data privacy and user safety (Gefen et al. 2003; Yousafzai et al. 2003). Similarly, technophilia, or the love and enthusiasm for technology, influences men and women differently -men are often driven by curiosity and a desire to experiment with cutting-edge technologies, while women are more likely to adopt technologies that align with their practical needs and provide clear benefits (LaRose and Eastin 2004; Venkatesh et al. 2003). These gender-based differences highlight the importance of inclusive design and marketing strategies that cater to the unique preferences and priorities of both men and women, ensuring that intelligent devices are accessible, trustworthy, and relevant to diverse user segments (Hargittai and Shafer 2006).

These findings underscore the need for targeted interventions to promote inclusive digital participation and address gender disparities in technology adoption. By understanding how gender moderates the relationships between performance expectancy, effort expectancy, trust, familiarity, technophilia, and behavioral intention, stakeholders can design technologies and strategies that resonate with diverse user groups (Venkatesh et al. 2003; Hargittai and Shafer 2006). Based on these insights, the following hypothesis is proposed:

H7: Gender moderates the relationship between performance expectancy, effort expectancy, trust, familiarity, technophilia, and behavioral intention to use intelligent devices.

Effect of Socio-professional category. The Socio-professional category, often referred to as socio-economic status (SES), plays a significant role in shaping individuals' intention to use technology. Socio-professional category encompasses factors such as income, education level, occupation, and access to resources, all of which influence an individual's exposure to, familiarity with, and attitudes toward technology. These factors collectively determine how different socio-professional groups perceive and engage with technological innovations. Research has consistently shown that individuals from higher socio-professional categories-such as those with higher income levels, advanced education, or professional occupations-tend to exhibit a stronger intention to adopt and use technology (Venkatesh et al. 2003; Rogers 2003). This is often attributed to their greater access to resources, such as the latest technological devices, high-speed internet, and opportunities for technology-related training and education. For example, individuals in higher socio-professional categories are more likely to own smartphones, laptops, and other smart devices, and they often have the financial means to upgrade their technology regularly. Additionally, their higher levels of education and digital literacy enable them to navigate and utilize technology more effectively, increasing their confidence in its use and their perception of its benefits (Hargittai 2002). As a result, they are more likely to view technology as a valuable tool for enhancing productivity, communication, and overall quality of life.

Conversely, individuals from lower socio-professional categories often face significant barriers to technology adoption. These barriers include limited financial resources to purchase devices, restricted access to reliable internet connectivity, and lower levels of digital literacy (Van Dijk 2006). For instance, individuals with lower incomes may struggle to afford the latest technologies or may prioritize other basic needs over technological investments. Additionally, limited exposure to technology in educational or professional settings can result in lower familiarity and confidence in using digital tools, leading to skepticism about the value of technology in their daily lives (Venkatesh et al. 2003). These challenges can create a "digital divide," where individuals from lower socio-professional categories are disproportionately excluded from the benefits of technological advancements. Beyond access and resources, socio-professional category also influences social norms and peer influences related to technology adoption. Individuals from higher socio-professional categories are more likely to interact with peers who are early adopters of technology and who actively encourage its use. This social reinforcement can further strengthen their intention to adopt and integrate technology into their lives (Rogers 2003). In contrast, individuals from lower socio-professional categories may have fewer social networks that promote technology adoption, which can limit their exposure to positive attitudes and behaviors toward technology. This lack of social support can exacerbate existing barriers and reduce their likelihood of adopting new technologies.

Empirical studies have further validated the role of socio-professional category in technology adoption. For example, Verhoeven et al. (2010) applied the UTAUT model to study computer use frequency among 714 university freshmen in Belgium. Their findings demonstrated that socio-professional category significantly influenced the frequency of computer use and the level of information and communication technology (ICT) skills among students. Students from higher socio-professional backgrounds exhibited greater familiarity with technology and higher levels of ICT skills, both in secondary school and at the university level. This study highlights the importance of socio-professional category in shaping not only technology adoption but also the development of digital skills over time. Based on these insights, the following hypothesis is proposed:

H8: Socio-professional category moderates the relationship between performance expectancy, effort expectancy, trust, familiarity, technophilia and behavioral intention to use intelligent devices.

Effect of Field of expertise. The field of expertise, or professional domain, plays a critical role in shaping individuals' attitudes and behaviors toward technology adoption. Professionals in different fields often exhibit varying levels of familiarity, perceived relevance, and necessity for technology, which influence their willingness and ability to adopt new tools and systems. Research has consistently shown that the field of expertise significantly impacts technology adoption patterns, with professionals in technology-intensive domains demonstrating higher adoption rates compared to those in less technology-centric fields. For instance, professionals in fields such as information technology (IT), engineering, and data science tend to exhibit higher levels of technology adoption due to their inherent familiarity with advanced tools and systems. These individuals often rely on cutting-edge technologies to perform their daily tasks, making technology adoption a professional necessity rather than a choice (Venkatesh et al. 2003). Their technical expertise and exposure to innovative solutions enable them to quickly adapt to new technologies, perceive their benefits, and integrate them into their workflows. For example, software engineers are more likely to adopt new programming tools or cloud-based platforms because these technologies align with their professional goals and enhance their productivity. In contrast, professionals in fields such as education, healthcare, or arts and humanities may demonstrate lower adoption rates, influenced by factors such as perceived relevance, limited training opportunities, and insufficient organizational support (Rogers 2003). For instance, educators may be slower to adopt new learning management systems (LMS) if they perceive these tools as complex or irrelevant to their teaching methods. Similarly, healthcare professionals may hesitate to adopt electronic health record (EHR) systems if they lack adequate training or if the systems are not user-friendly. These barriers highlight the importance of addressing domain-specific challenges to facilitate technology adoption across diverse professional landscapes.

Empirical studies have further validated the influence of the field of expertise on technology adoption. For instance, Venkatesh et al. (2003) found that professionals in IT and engineering fields were more likely to adopt new technologies due to their technical expertise and alignment with professional goals. Similarly, Rogers (2003) highlighted that adoption rates vary significantly across domains, with technology-centric fields leading the way and other fields lagging due to perceived irrelevance or lack of support. Based on these insights, the following hypothesis is proposed:

H9: The field of expertise moderates the relationship between performance expectancy, effort expectancy, trust, familiarity, technophilia and behavioral intention to use intelligent devices.

4 Methodology

This study aims to validate a conceptual model that integrates Intention to use Intelligent devices with key determinants such as Performance Expectancy, Effort Expectancy, Trust, Familiarity, and Technophilia. To achieve this, a quantitative research approach was adopted, utilizing an online survey to collect data from users of intelligent devices. The methodology was designed to examine the causal relationships between these variables and to provide empirical insights into the factors influencing the adoption of intelligent devices. A convenience sampling method was employed to recruit participants for the study. The survey was distributed online, targeting users of intelligent devices such as wearable technologies and IoT-enabled gadgets. The questionnaire was designed to capture respondents' perceptions and attitudes toward these technologies, as well as their behavioral intentions to adopt and use them. The survey yielded 218 complete and usable responses, which were deemed suitable for analysis. The majority of respondents (72.1%) belonged to the [20 - 29 years] age group, reflecting a younger, tech-savvy demographic, with 61,5% being male and 38,5% female.

To operationalize the theoretical constructs in the conceptual model, well-established measurement scales from prior research were adopted. The measures were adapted from previous scales assessing Behavioral intention, Performance Expectancy, Effort Expectancy (Venkatesh et al. 2003), Trust (Gefen et al. 2003; Kim et al. 2010; McKnight et al. 2002), Familiarity (Gefen 2000; Flavian et al. 2006) and Technophilia (Goldsmith and Hofacker 1991; Agarwal and Prasad 1998; Parasuraman 2000). These scales have demonstrated strong psychometric properties in previous studies, ensuring the reliability and validity of the measurements. The constructs were measured using multi-item scales, with each item rated on a 5-point Likert scale (1: *Strongly Disagree* to 5: *Strongly Agree*). The questionnaire also included closed-ended questions to represent the respondents' demographic characteristics.

The survey data were analyzed using Smart PLS 4.0, a robust statistical tool for structural equation modeling (SEM) that is particularly suited for exploratory and confirmatory analyses. The analysis was conducted in three stages: exploratory analysis, where initial assessments identified latent variables and evaluated internal reliability using Cronbach's alpha and composite reliability to ensure measurement scale consistency; confirmatory analysis, which assessed construct validity following Fornell and Larcker's (1981) approach, including convergent validity via average variance extracted (AVE) and discriminant validity by comparing the square root of AVE with inter-construct correlations; and structural analysis, where SEM tested hypothesized relationships between constructs, with the significance of causal links evaluated through bootstrapping with 5,000 subsamples to ensure the robustness of the findings.

5 Structural Model Analysis and Hypothesis Validation

5.1 Outer Model: Validity and Fiability Analysis

In Partial Least Squares Structural Equation Modeling (PLS-SEM), the outer model serves as the measurement model, focusing on evaluating the validity and reliability of the constructs. This step is critical to ensure that the measurement scales accurately reflect the theoretical constructs they are intended to measure. The analysis of the outer model involves assessing both convergent validity and reliability, using established statistical criteria.

Convergent validity is evaluated through two primary metrics: outer loading values and average variance extracted (AVE). Outer loading values measure the strength of the relationship between individual items and their corresponding constructs, with values equal to or greater than 0.7 typically considered indicative of strong validity (Hair et al. 2014; Latan and Noonan 2017). Items with loadings below this threshold may be considered for removal to improve the model's validity. Additionally, the AVE assesses the overall validity of each construct by measuring the amount of variance captured by the construct relative to the variance due to measurement error. An AVE value greater than 0.5 is generally accepted as evidence of convergent validity, indicating that more than half of the variance in the latent variable is explained by its indicators (Chin 2010). As shown in Table 1, all items in the constructs demonstrated outer loading values exceeding 0.7, and the AVE values for all constructs were above 0.5, confirming the convergent validity of the measurement model.

Reliability, which refers to the consistency and stability of the measurement scales, was assessed using Cronbach's Alpha and Composite Reliability (CR). Cronbach's Alpha is a widely used measure of internal consistency, with values above 0.6 considered acceptable for exploratory research and values above 0.7 preferred for confirmatory studies (Hair et al. 2014). Composite Reliability, which is often considered a more robust measure, evaluates the reliability of the constructs by accounting for the varying weights of the indicators. CR values above 0.7 are generally considered satisfactory (Hair et al. 2017). As illustrated in Table 1, all constructs exhibited Cronbach's Alpha values exceeding 0.6, and Composite Reliability values surpassed the recommended threshold of 0.7, further affirming the reliability of the constructs. These results collectively demonstrate that the measurement scales are both valid and reliable, providing a solid foundation for further analysis.

Table 1. Measurement model (outer model) analysis results

Variable	Items	Outer loadings	AVE	Cronbach's Alpha	CR	Description
Behavioral intention	BI1	0.900	0.817	0.776	0.899	Valid & Reliable
	BI2	0.907				
Performance expectancy	PE1	0.758	0.669	0.800	0.876	Valid & Reliable
	PE2	0.862				
	PE3	0.846				
	PE4	0.801				
Effort expectancy	EE1	0.707	0.705	0.835	0.913	Valid & Reliable
	EE2	0.901				
	EE3	0.897				

(continued)

Table 1. (*continued*)

Variable	Items	Outer loadings	AVE	Cronbach's Alpha	CR	Description
Familiarity	FAM1	0.926	0.839	0.809	0.889	Valid & Reliable
	FAM2	0.906				
Technophilia	TECH1	0.803	0.635	0.812	0.874	Valid & Reliable
	TECH2	0.718				
	TECH3	0.812				
	TECH4	0.847				

In addition to assessing convergent validity and reliability, discriminant validity was evaluated to ensure that each construct in the model is distinct and not overly correlated with other constructs. Discriminant validity is critical for confirming that the constructs measure unique concepts and do not overlap excessively. This was tested using the Fornell-Larcker criterion, which compares the square root of the average variance extracted (AVE) for each construct with the correlations between that construct and all other constructs in the model. According to Fornell and Larcker (1981), discriminant validity is established if the square root of the AVE for a construct is greater than its correlations with any other construct. As shown in Table 2, the results of this analysis confirmed that all constructs met this criterion, providing strong evidence of discriminant validity and further validating the robustness of the measurement model.

Table 2. Fornell-Larcker test

Variable	Behavioral Intention	Performance Expectancy	Effort Expectancy	Familiarity	Technophilia	Trust
Behavioral Intention	0.904					
Performance Expectancy	0.177	0.818				
Effort Expectancy	−0.223	0.104	0.840			
Familiarity	0.524	0.227	−0.096	0.916		
Technophilia	0.467	0.207	−0.109	0.396	0.797	
Trust	0.288	0.225	0.055	0.198	0.185	1.000

5.2 Inner Model: Overall Fit

The inner model, also known as the structural model, is a critical component of Partial Least Squares Structural Equation Modeling (PLS-SEM). It focuses on elucidating the causal relationships among latent variables, providing insights into how independent variables influence dependent variables. Before testing the hypotheses, it is essential to evaluate the model's overall fit to ensure its validity and reliability. This assessment is conducted using key goodness-of-fit (GoF) indices, including the Standardized Root Mean Square Residual (SRMR), Normed Fit Index (NFI), and Explained Variance (R^2). According to established guidelines, a model is considered well-fitting if the NFI exceeds 0.9 or the SRMR is less than 0.1 (Hair et al. 2017; Henseler et al. 2016). These indices collectively provide a comprehensive evaluation of the model's ability to explain the observed data and its predictive power.

Table 3. Inner model: fit overview

	Saturated model	Estimated model
SRMR	0.058	0.059
d_ULS	0.704	0.726
d_G	0.335	0.351
Chi-square	473.388	499.822
NFI	0.714	0.698

The fit indices for both the saturated model and the estimated model are presented in Table 3. The results indicate that the SRMR values for both models were 0.058 and 0.059, respectively, which are well below the recommended threshold of 0.1. This suggests that the model aligns well with the observed data, confirming its appropriateness. However, the NFI values were 0.714 (saturated model) and 0.698 (estimated model), falling below the threshold of 0.9. Despite this, the SRMR values provide sufficient evidence to support the model's overall fit, as SRMR is considered a more critical indicator in PLS-SEM (Hair et al. 2017; Henseler et al. 2016).

The R-square (R^2) value is a key metric for assessing the explanatory power of the model, indicating the proportion of variance in the dependent variable that is explained by the independent variables. According to Hair et al. (2019), a higher R^2 value suggests that the model effectively captures the relationships proposed in the research framework. In this study, the R^2 value for the dependent variable Behavioral Intention was 0.487, indicating that 48.7% of the variance in behavioral intention is explained by the independent variables: Performance Expectancy, Effort Expectancy, Trust, Familiarity, and Technophilia. This demonstrates that these five constructs collectively play a significant role in shaping users' intentions to adopt intelligent devices. The remaining 51.3% of the variance in behavioral intention is attributed to other factors not included in this study. These could include external variables such as habit, hedonic motivations, perceived risk, or cultural factors, which may also influence technology adoption but were beyond the scope of this research. Future studies could explore these additional factors to provide a more comprehensive understanding of the determinants of behavioral intention.

5.3 Structural Model Analysis and Hypothesis Validation

The structural model, depicted in Fig. 2, provides a comprehensive representation of the causal relationships between the key constructs: Performance Expectancy, Effort Expectancy, Familiarity, Trust, Technophilia, and Behavioral Intention. This model serves as the foundation for testing the hypothesized relationships and understanding the factors that influence users' intentions to adopt intelligent devices. The structural model was analyzed using SmartPLS, with bootstrapping techniques applied to ensure the robustness and reliability of the results. The findings are summarized in Table 4 and visually represented in Fig. 3.

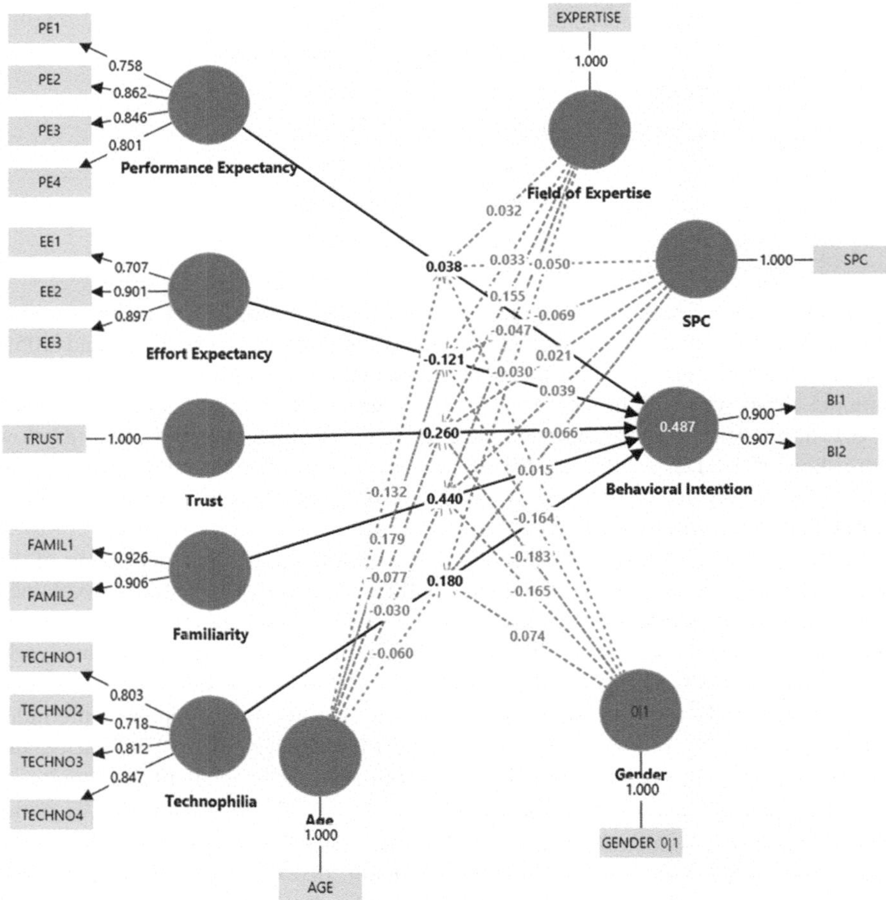

Fig. 3. Path coefficients for the research model

Hypothesis testing is considered valid if the p-value is less than the predetermined alpha threshold of 0.05 and if the path coefficient aligns with the hypothesized direction. As shown in Table 4, the results of the path analysis provide insights into the relationships between the constructs and their influence on Behavioral Intention to Use Intelligent Devices. The results of the hypothesis testing reveal several key insights into the factors influencing Behavioral Intention to use Intelligent devices. First, Familiarity ($\beta = 0.440$, $p = 0.001$) and Trust ($\beta = 0.260$, $p = 0.005$) have strong, statistically significant positive effects on behavioral intention, indicating that users who are more familiar with intelligent devices and trust their reliability, security, and performance are more likely to intend to use them. These findings align with prior research, which emphasizes the importance of familiarity in reducing perceived barriers and trust in overcoming adoption hesitations. Additionally, Technophilia ($\beta = 0.180$, $p = 0.065$) has a marginally significant positive effect, suggesting that individuals with a strong affinity for technology are more inclined to adopt intelligent devices, consistent with studies highlighting the role of enthusiasm for technology in driving adoption. On the other hand, Performance Expectancy ($\beta = 0.038$, $p = 0.667$) and Effort Expectancy ($\beta = -0.121$, $p = 0.128$) do not significantly influence behavioral intention, which contrasts with some prior research. This divergence in findings may indicate that, in the context of intelligent devices among the Tunisian consumers, users prioritize other factors, such as Familiarity and Trust, over perceived usefulness or ease of use. This could be influenced by cultural factors specific to Tunisia, where trust and familiarity may play a more significant role in technology adoption due to societal norms, historical experiences, or economic conditions. For instance, in a collectivist culture like Tunisia, where social relationships and word-of-mouth recommendations are highly valued, users may place greater emphasis on whether they are familiar with a technology and whether they can trust it to perform reliably and securely, rather than its perceived utility or simplicity. Additionally, the relatively lower levels of digital literacy and access to advanced technologies in some segments of the Tunisian consumers may further amplify the importance of familiarity and trust, as users may feel more comfortable adopting technologies they already understand or that come recommended by trusted sources. Furthermore, the non-significant influence of Effort Expectancy, despite its negative coefficient, suggests that users may not perceive ease of use as a critical factor in their adoption decisions. This could be due to the increasing prevalence of user-friendly designs in modern technologies, which may have reduced the perceived effort required to use intelligent devices, making it a less differentiating factor. Alternatively, it may reflect a cultural tendency to prioritize reliability and trustworthiness over convenience, especially in contexts where technology is seen as a long-term investment rather than a disposable tool. These findings highlight the importance of considering cultural context in technology adoption research and suggest that the relative importance of performance and effort expectancies may vary depending on the cultural and socio-economic environment. In the Tunisian context, where trust and familiarity are deeply rooted in social interactions and collective decision-making, these factors may outweigh traditional drivers like perceived usefulness and ease of use. Future research could explore these dynamics further by examining how cultural factors, such as collectivism, risk aversion, or digital literacy, influence the adoption of intelligent devices in different regions or populations. Additionally, the non-significant moderating effects of Age, Gender, Socio-Professional Category (SPC), and Field of Expertise suggest that the relationships between the independent variables and behavioral intention are consistent across diverse demographic and professional groups within the Tunisian consumers. This implies that strategies to promote the adoption of intelligent devices can be broadly applied without the need for extensive customization based on age, gender, or professional background. However, it also underscores the need to focus on universal drivers, such as familiarity and trust, which are critical across all user segments in this cultural context. Overall, these findings provide valuable insights for developers and marketers, emphasizing the need to enhance users' familiarity with intelligent devices and build trust in their reliability and security, while also considering the unique cultural and socio-economic factors that shape technology adoption in the Tunisian consumers.

Table 4. Path coefficient and Hypothesis testing

Hypothesis	Original sample	T statistics	P values	Support
Performance expectancy –> Behavioral intention	0.038	0.430	0.667	No
Effort expectancy –> Behavioral intention	−0.121	1.521	0.128	No
Familiarity –> Behavioral intention	0.440	3.380	0.001	Yes
Trust –> Behavioral intention	0.260	2.805	0.005	Yes
Technophilia –> Behavioral intention	0.180	1.843	0.065	Yes
Age –> Behavioral intention	0.086	0.792	0.428	No
Gender –> Behavioral intention	−0.113	0.965	0.334	No
SPC –> Behavioral intention	−0.153	1.610	0.107	No
Field of Expertise –> Behavioral intention	0.074	0.676	0.499	No
Age × Performance expectancy –> Behavioral intention	0.086	0.792	0.428	No
Age × Effort expectancy –> Behavioral intention	−0.132	1.109	0.267	No
Age × Familiarity –> Behavioral intention	0.179	1.184	0.237	No
Age × Trust –> Behavioral intention	−0.030	0.159	0.874	No
Age × Technophilia –> Behavioral intention	−0.077	0.679	0.497	No
Gender × Performance expectancy –> Behavioral intention	0.015	0.107	0.915	No
Gender × Effort expectancy –> Behavioral intention	−0.164	1.307	0.191	No
Gender × Familiarity –> Behavioral intention	−0.165	0.781	0.435	No
Gender × Trust –> Behavioral intention	−0.183	1.335	0.182	No

(*continued*)

Table 4. (*continued*)

Hypothesis	Original sample	T statistics	P values	Support
Gender × Technophilia -> Behavioral intention	0.074	0.487	0.626	No
SPC × Performance expectancy -> Behavioral intention	0.050	0.464	0.643	No
SPC × Effort expectancy -> Behavioral intention	−0.069	0.667	0.504	No
SPC × Familiarity -> Behavioral intention	0.039	0.289	0.772	No
SPC × Trust -> Behavioral intention	0.021	0.187	0.851	No
SPC × Technophilia -> Behavioral intention	0.066	0.628	0.530	No
Field of expertise × Performance expectancy -> Behavioral intention	0.032	0.330	0.741	No
Field of expertise × Effort expectancy -> Behavioral intention	0.033	0.235	0.814	No
Field of expertise × Familiarity -> Behavioral intention	−0.047	0.355	0.723	No
Field of expertise × Trust -> Behavioral intention	0.155	1.230	0.219	No
Field of expertise × Technophilia -> Behavioral intention	−0.030	0.293	0.770	No

6 Discussion of Results and Recommendations

Intention to Use Intelligent Devices among the Tunisian consumers, offering actionable implications for both researchers and practitioners.

First, Familiarity and Trust were found to have strong, statistically significant positive effects on behavioral intention, indicating that users who are more familiar with intelligent devices and trust their reliability, security, and performance are more likely to adopt them. This suggests that managerial efforts should focus on increasing user familiarity through hands-on demonstrations, tutorials, and accessible training programs, particularly in a context like Tunisia, where digital literacy levels may vary. Additionally, building trust should be a top priority, achieved by ensuring transparency in how devices operate, emphasizing robust security features, and providing clear communication about data privacy and reliability. For example, companies could collaborate with local influencers or community leaders to endorse their products, leveraging the collectivist nature of Tunisian society to build trust through social validation. Second, Technophilia had a marginally significant positive effect, highlighting that individuals with a strong affinity for technology are more inclined to adopt intelligent devices.

This implies that marketers should target tech enthusiasts with innovative features, early access to new technologies, and exclusive previews to drive initial adoption. By engaging this group, companies can create a ripple effect, as tech enthusiasts often serve as early adopters who influence others within their social networks. On the other hand, Performance Expectancy and Effort Expectancy were found to be non-significant, contrasting with traditional technology adoption models like UTAUT and TAM. However, this finding aligns with the results of studies by AlGahtani et al. (2007), AlMashaqba and Nassar (2012), Salim (2012) and Alwahaishi and Snášel (2013), which also demonstrated the non-significance of PE or EE in non-Western contexts. This suggests that users in the Tunisian context prioritize familiarity and trust over perceived usefulness or ease of use, which means that marketing strategies should de-emphasize technical specifications and instead focus on building emotional connections and trust through relatable narratives and social proof. For instance, campaigns could highlight real-life success stories of users who have benefited from intelligent devices, emphasizing how these technologies integrate seamlessly into daily life without requiring significant effort or technical expertise. Additionally, the non-significant moderating effects of Age, Gender, Socio-Professional Category (SPC), and Field of Expertise indicate that the drivers of adoption are consistent across diverse demographic and professional groups. This finding simplifies managerial decision-making by allowing for the development of universal strategies that do not require extensive customization based on age, gender, or professional background. However, it also underscores the need to focus on universal drivers like familiarity and trust, which are critical across all user segments. For example, companies could design marketing campaigns that appeal to a broad audience, using culturally relevant messaging that resonates with Tunisian values of community and reliability. Finally, the study highlights the importance of cultural sensitivity, as the Tunisian context, with its collectivist culture and reliance on social relationships, places greater emphasis on trust and familiarity over traditional drivers like perceived usefulness or ease of use. This suggests that companies should adopt culturally sensitive approaches, such as leveraging social networks and word-of-mouth recommendations, to build trust and familiarity within the community. For instance, partnerships with local organizations or community events could help introduce intelligent devices in a way that feels familiar and trustworthy to potential users. In conclusion, these findings provide a robust framework for understanding and promoting the adoption of intelligent devices in Tunisia, offering actionable insights for developers and marketers to design strategies that are culturally relevant, user-centric, and focused on building trust and familiarity to drive widespread adoption. By addressing these cultural and contextual nuances, stakeholders can bridge the gap between technological innovation and user acceptance, fostering greater integration of intelligent devices into everyday life.

6.1 Theoretical Implications

This study challenges conventional technology adoption frameworks by demonstrating that in collectivist, emerging markets like Tunisia, traditional drivers such as performance expectancy and effort expectancy (central to UTAUT/TAM models) are less influential than context-specific factors like familiarity and trust. The strong predictive power of familiarity and trust suggests that existing adoption theories need cultural adaptation to account for relational and experiential dimensions prevalent in non-Western contexts. Furthermore, the marginal significance of technophilia hints at the need to explore how personality traits interact with cultural values in technology adoption. These findings invite scholars to develop hybrid models that integrate socio-cultural constructs (e.g., social validation, institutional trust) with established cognitive variables to better predict adoption behavior in diverse markets.

6.2 Managerial Implications

For practitioners, the study underscores the need for hyperlocalized strategies prioritizing experiential learning and trust-building. Companies should invest in hands-on training programs and leverage Tunisia's collectivist culture through community-based marketing-for example, by partnering with local influencers and organizations to co-create demonstration hubs. The insignificance of performance/effort expectancy implies that marketing messaging should shift from technical specifications to emotional storytelling, showcasing real-life use cases through relatable Tunisian narratives. Additionally, the universal relevance of familiarity and trust across demographics suggests cost-efficient, segment-agnostic campaigns, though early adoption can be accelerated by targeting tech enthusiasts with exclusive previews. Critically, transparency about data security and post-purchase support must be central to all initiatives, as these factors directly feed into the trust imperative identified in the study.

6.3 Methodological Implications

The research highlights key considerations for future studies on technology adoption in emerging markets. First, the reliance on behavioral intention (vs. actual usage) calls for longitudinal designs to track how initial trust translates into sustained adoption, particularly given the potential gap between intent and behavior in volatile markets. Second, the non-significant moderation effects of demographics suggest that researchers should prioritize cultural and psychographic variables (e.g., technology readiness, social influence susceptibility) over standard demographic controls in similar contexts. Third, the findings advocate for mixed-method approaches: while quantitative data revealed adoption drivers, qualitative insights could unpack nuances for instance, how trust dynamics differ between urban/rural users or across device categories. Finally, scale validation for local contexts is essential, as direct translations of Western constructs may miss culturally salient dimensions of familiarity or trust.

7 Limitations and Future Research Directions

The current study is not free of limitations, which present opportunities for future research to build upon our findings. First, while the study identifies key predictors of behavioral intention, it relies on cross-sectional data, which limits our ability to assess how adoption behaviors evolve over time. Longitudinal studies tracking actual usage patterns would provide deeper insights into whether initial intentions translate into sustained adoption, particularly in dynamic markets like Tunisia where technological and economic conditions may shift rapidly.

Second, although the study examines several individual and contextual factors, it does not account for potential variations across different types of intelligent devices. For example, adoption drivers for smart home assistants may differ significantly from those for smartwatches, particularly in terms of privacy concerns and perceived risk. Future research could adopt a more granular approach by categorizing devices based on functionality and user interaction requirements. Third, while the study highlights the importance of trust and familiarity, it does not fully explore the antecedents of these constructs. Qualitative investigations could uncover how trust is built (or eroded) in Tunisia's socio-cultural context, for instance, whether local brand bias, cultural considerations, or historical experiences with technology influence user perceptions. Additionally, incorporating macroeconomic factors (e.g., internet infrastructure, purchasing power) could further contextualize adoption barriers. Finally, the study's focus on Tunisia raises questions about generalizability. Comparative studies across other Arab or African nations could determine whether these findings reflect broader regional trends or are unique to Tunisia's specific cultural and economic landscape. Addressing these limitations would strengthen the theoretical robustness of technology adoption models and enhance their practical applicability for businesses and policymakers operating in emerging markets.

Declaration of Generative AI in the writing process

During the preparation of this work, we only used Deepseek in order to improve readability and language. After using this tool, we reviewed and edited the content as needed and take full responsibility for the content of the publication.

References

Ajzen, I.: The theory of planned behavior. Organ. Behav. Hum. Decis. Process. **50**(2), 179–211 (1991)

Agarwal, R., Prasad, J.: A conceptual and operational definition of personal innovativeness in the domain of information technology. Inf. Syst. Res. **9**(2), 204–215 (1998)

Alalwan, A.A., Dwivedi, Y.K., Rana, N.P., Williams, M.D.: Consumer adoption of mobile banking in Jordan: examining the role of usability, trust, and social influence. J. Enterp. Inf. Manag. **30**(1), 118–139 (2017)

AlGahtani, S., Hobana, G., Wang, J.: Information technology (IT) in Saudi Arabia: culture and the acceptance and use of IT. Inf. Manag. **44**(8),681–691 (2007)

AlMashaqba, F., Nassar, M.: Modified UTAUT model to study the factors affecting the adoption of mobile banking in Jordan. Int. J. Sci. Basic Appl. Res. (IJSBAR) **6**(1),83–94 (2012)

Alwahaishi, S., Snášel, V.: Consumers' acceptance and use of information and communications technology: A UTAUT and flow based theoretical model. J. Technol. Manag. Innov. **8**(2), 61–73 (2013)

Bandura, A.: Social Foundations of Thought and Action: A Social Cognitive Theory. Prentice-Hall, Englewood Cliffs, NJ (1986)

Carter, L., Bélanger, F.: The utilization of e-government services: citizen trust, innovation and acceptance factors. Inf. Syst. J. **15**(1), 5–25 (2005)

Chin, W.W.: How to write up and report PLS analyses. In: Handbook of Partial Least Squares, pp. 655–690. Springer, Berlin, Heidelberg (2010)

Davis, F.D.: Perceived usefulness, perceived ease of use, and user acceptance of information technology. MIS Q. **13**(3), 319–340 (1989)

Davis, F.D., Bagozzi, R.P., Warshaw, P.R.: Extrinsic and intrinsic motivation to use computers in the workplace. J. Appl. Soc. Psychol. **22**(14), 1111–1132 (1992)
Dwivedi, Y.K., Rana, N.P., Jeyaraj, A., Clement, M., Williams, M.D.: Re-examining the unified theory of acceptance and use of technology (UTAUT): towards a revised theoretical model. Inf. Syst. Front. **21**(3), 719–734 (2019)
Fishbein, M., Ajzen, I.: Belief, Attitude, Intention, and Behavior: An Introduction to Theory and Research. Addison-Wesley, Reading, MA (1975)
Flavián, C., Guinalíu, M., Gurrea, R.: The influence of familiarity and usability on loyalty to online journalistic services: the role of user experience. J. Retail. Consum. Serv. **13**(5), 363–375 (2006)
Fornell, C., Larcker, D.F.: Evaluating structural equation models with unobservable variables and measurement error. J. Mark. Res. **18**(1), 39–50 (1981)
Gagnon, M.P., Desmartis, M., Labrecque, M., Car, J., Pagliari, C., Pluye, P., ... Légaré, F.: Systematic review of factors influencing the adoption of information and communication technologies by healthcare professionals. J. Med. Syst. **36**(1), 241–277 (2012)
Gefen, D.: E-commerce: the role of familiarity and trust. Omega **28**(6), 725–737 (2000)
Gefen, D., Karahanna, E., Straub, D.W.: Trust and TAM in online shopping: an integrated model. MIS Q. **27**(1), 51–90 (2003)
Hargittai, E.: Second-level digital divide: differences in people's online skills. First Monday **7**(4) (2002)
Hargittai, E., Shafer, S.: Differences in actual and perceived online skills: the role of gender. Soc. Sci. Q. **87**(2), 432–448 (2006)
Hair, J.F., Black, W.C., Babin, B.J., Anderson, R.E.: Multivariate data analysis, 7th edn. Pearson, Harlow (2014)
Hair, J.F., Black, W.C., Babin, B.J., Anderson, R.E.: Multivariate Data Analysis (8th ed.). Pearson (2019)
Hair, J.F., Hult, G.T.M., Ringle, C.M., Sarstedt, M.: A Primer on Partial Least Squares Structural Equation Modeling (PLS-SEM), 2nd edn. Sage, Thousand Oaks, CA (2017)
Henseler, J., Hubona, G., Ray, P.A.: Using PLS path modeling in new technology research: updated guidelines. Ind. Manag. Data Syst. **116**(1), 2–20 (2016)
Holden, R.J., Karsh, B.T.: The technology acceptance model: Its past and its future in health care. J. Biomed. Inform. **43**(1), 159–172 (2010)
Kim, C., Mirusmonov, M., Lee, I.: An empirical examination of factors influencing the intention to use mobile payment. Comput. Hum. Behav. **26**(3), 310–322 (2010)
LaRose, R., Eastin, M.S.: A social cognitive theory of Internet uses and gratifications: Toward a new model of media attendance. J. Broadcast. Electron. Media **48**(3), 358–377 (2004)
Latan, H., Noonan, R.: Partial Least Squares Path Modeling: Basic Concepts, Methodological Issues and Applications. Springer, Cham, Switzerland (2017)
Lu, J., Yao, J.E., Yu, C.S.: Personal innovativeness, social influences and adoption of wireless Internet services via mobile technology. J. Strat. Inf. Syst. **14**(3), 245–268 (2005)
Mayer, R.C., Davis, J.H., Schoorman, F.D.: An integrative model of organizational trust. Acad. Manag. Rev. **20**(3), 709–734 (1995)
Nysveen, H., Pedersen, P.E., Thorbjørnsen, H.: Intentions to use mobile services: antecedents and cross-service comparisons. J. Acad. Mark. Sci. **33**(3), 330–346 (2005)
Oliveira, T., Faria, M., Thomas, M.A., Popovič, A.: Extending the understanding of mobile banking adoption: when UTAUT meets TTF and ITM. Int. J. Inf. Manage. **34**(5), 689–703 (2014)
Parasuraman, A.: Technology readiness index (TRI): a multiple-item scale to measure readiness to embrace new technologies. J. Serv. Res. **2**(4), 307–320 (2000)
Rana, N.P., Dwivedi, Y.K., Williams, M.D., Weerakkody, V.: Investigating success of an e-government initiative: validation of an integrated IS success model. Inf. Syst. Front. **17**(1), 127–142 (2015)

Rana, N.P., Dwivedi, Y.K., Williams, M.D., Weerakkody, V.: Adoption of online public grievance redressal system in India: toward developing a unified view. Comput. Hum. Behav. **59**, 265–282 (2016)

Rogers, E.M.: Diffusion of Innovations, 5th edn. Free Press, New York (2003)

Salim, B.: An application of UTAUT model for acceptance of social media in Egypt: A statistical study. Int. J. Inf. Sci. **2**(6), 92–105 (2012)

Smith, H.J., Dinev, T., Xu, H.: Information privacy research: an interdisciplinary review. MIS Q. **35**(4), 989–1015 (2020)

Šumak, B., Heričko, M., Pušnik, M.: A meta-analysis of e-learning technology acceptance: The role of user types and e-learning technology types. Comput. Hum. Behav. **27**(6), 2067–2077 (2011)

Tarhini, A., Hone, K., Liu, X.: Factors affecting students' acceptance of e-learning environments in developing countries: a structural equation modeling approach. Int. J. Inf. Manage. **37**(3), 317–326 (2017)

Taylor, S., Todd, P.A.: Understanding information technology usage: a test of competing models. Inf. Syst. Res. **6**(2), 144–176 (1995)

Thompson, R.L., Higgins, C.A., Howell, J.M.: Personal computing: toward a conceptual model of utilization. MIS Q. **15**(1), 125–143 (1991)

Thornton, P., Chan, T.: The role of organizational support in technology acceptance: a case study of e-learning adoption. J. Educ. Technol. Soc. **17**(4), 1–12 (2014)

Van Dijk, J.A.G.M.: Digital divide research, achievements and shortcomings. Poetics **34**(4–5), 221–235 (2006)

Venkatesh, V., Davis, F.D.: A theoretical extension of the technology acceptance model: four longitudinal field studies. Manage. Sci. **46**(2), 186–204 (2000)

Venkatesh, V., Morris, M.G.: Why don't men ever stop to ask for directions? Gender, social influence, and their role in technology acceptance and usage behavior. MIS Q. **24**(1), 115–139 (2000)

Venkatesh, V., Morris, M.G., Davis, G.B., Davis, F.D.: User acceptance of information technology: toward a unified view. MIS Q. **27**(3), 425–478 (2003)

Venkatesh, V., Thong, J.Y.L., Xu, X.: Consumer acceptance and use of information technology: extending the unified theory of acceptance and use of technology. MIS Q. **36**(1), 157–178 (2012)

Verhoeven, J.C., Heerwegh, D., De Wit, K.: Information and communication technologies in the life of university freshmen: an analysis of change. Comput. Educ. **55**(1), 53–66 (2010)

Yousafzai, S.Y., Pallister, J.G., Foxall, G.R.: A proposed model of e-trust for electronic banking. Technovation **23**(11), 847–860 (2003)

Zhou, T.: Understanding users' initial trust in mobile banking: an elaboration likelihood perspective. Comput. Hum. Behav. **29**(1), 151–160 (2013)

Zhou, T., Lu, Y., Wang, B.: Integrating TTF and UTAUT to explain mobile banking user adoption. Comput. Hum. Behav. **26**(4), 760–767 (2010)

Enhancing Financial Inclusion Through Digital Payment Solutions in South Africa

Aluwani Peter Tshishonga[1], Patrick Ndayizigamiye[2](✉), Kudakwashe Maguraushe[3], and Tebogo Bokaba[4]

[1] Faculty of Commerce, Law and Management, University of the Witwatersrand, Gauteng, South Africa
9611035M@students.wits.ac.za

[2] Centre for Applied Data Science, University of Johannesburg, Gauteng, South Africa
pndayizigamiye@uj.ac.za

[3] School of Computing, College of Science, Engineering and Technology, Florida, Gauteng, South Africa
magark@unisa.ac.za

[4] Department of Applied Information Systems, University of Johannesburg, Gauteng, South Africa
tbokaba@uj.ac.za

Abstract. The payments industry is undergoing significant transformation due to digital technologies, which are introducing various new payment options. In South Africa, embracing digital payments could help promote financial inclusion. While many South Africans own bank accounts, the actual utilization of these accounts for financial services remains low. This qualitative interpretive study aimed to address two key questions: what challenges hinder the contribution of digital payments to financial inclusion in South Africa, and what needs to be done for digital payments to foster financial inclusion in South Africa? A case study approach was employed, involving interviews with 12 participants selected through convenience and purposive sampling methods. The findings highlight several factors that could facilitate financial inclusion within South Africa's digital payments landscape, including the establishment of a new industry body encompassing all stakeholders in the digital payments ecosystem, ensuring affordability, regulatory mandates for financial inclusion, product interoperability, and robust infrastructure to support digital payments. The study advocates for digital literacy initiatives to help consumers understand the advantages of digital payments and suggests fostering partnerships with mobile network operators to address data costs and enhance network coverage.

Keywords: Financial inclusion · Digital payments · Digital literacy · South Africa

F. Kamoun et al. (Eds.): AFRICATEK 2025, LNICST 677, pp. 371–391, 2026.
https://doi.org/10.1007/978-3-032-16638-8_24

1 Introduction

Digital technologies play a crucial role in advancing financial inclusion, particularly in emerging markets. The rise of mobile banking and digital wallets has significantly lowered traditional barriers to accessing financial services, thereby enhancing accessibility for underserved communities [1]. The financial technology (fintech) sector is anticipated to grow into a $1.5 trillion industry by 2030 [2]. In alignment with its goal to eradicate poverty, inequality, and unemployment, South Africa, through the National Development Plan (NDP), has set an ambitious target of achieving 90% financial inclusion by 2030 [2]. Additionally, financial inclusion is highlighted as one of the objectives of the National Payment Systems (NPS) Vision 2025, which aims to enhance the financial well-being of all South Africans [2].

The payments industry is experiencing disruption due to digital technologies, leading to the emergence of new market players. In 2023, the total fintech transaction value in South Africa was projected to reach $567.8 million [3]. Furthermore, African fintech revenues were expected to hit $230 billion by 2025 [4]. Fintech companies are not only introducing innovative digital payment solutions but also prompting established financial institutions to improve their offerings. The adoption of digital payments in South Africa represents a significant opportunity for advancing financial inclusion. Despite having over eighty million bank cards in circulation, their actual usage is low, indicating that simply owning a bank card does not guarantee genuine financial inclusion [4].

South Africa continues to confront the intertwined challenges of poverty, unemployment, and inequality, often referred to as the "triple challenge." While the country is increasingly integrating technology into its financial sector, the actual impact and benefits of these technologies on financial inclusion remain ambiguous. As South Africa works to tackle these urgent challenges, it is crucial to investigate how digital payments can serve as a viable solution for enhancing financial inclusion. This study was guided by two primary research questions: What challenges hinder the contribution of digital payments to financial inclusion in South Africa? What needs to be done for digital payments to foster financial inclusion in South Africa?

2 Background

Khera et al. [5] explored the importance of digital financial services (DFSs) in promoting financial inclusion and their impact on economic growth in emerging markets and developing economies (EMDEs). Their study provided evidence that financial inclusion has a positive influence on economic growth, specifically highlighting a correlation between digital financial inclusion and per capita gross domestic product (GDP) from 2011 to 2018. The authors identified several key enablers of digital financial inclusion, including infrastructure, financial and digital literacy, and the quality of institutions. This aligns with the government of South Africa's National Development Plan (NDP) 2030 vision, which emphasizes financial inclusion as a fundamental goal.

A 2021 report focusing on the digitalization of financial services in South Africa [6] indicates that traditional financial services such as access to banking infrastructure (automated teller machines (ATMs), branches), and the use of bank accounts, savings, and debit cards are undergoing digital transformation. Emerging digital businesses are also intensifying competition within the financial services sector. For financial inclusion to be realized, access to digital financial services must extend past the current banking population, and digitization should enhance access to formal financial services. According to a 2019 report by Deloitte and Mastercard [4], South Africa still faces several fundamental challenges to achieving financial inclusion. For instance, many informal sector participants and individuals in rural areas continue to rely on cash for transactions [7]. The report notes that 90% of shops in the informal sector operate entirely on cash, particularly in rural regions where small and micro-enterprises struggle to adopt card payment systems due to insufficient card acceptance infrastructure. As cash remains a trusted way of payment and value store for many people in rural areas and developing countries [8], there is a pressing need for education on financial services and building trust in digital payments in South Africa.

The discourse surrounding digital payments and financial inclusion is vital within the South African economic context. Various study groups and industry experts are closely monitoring the South African NPS for anticipated meaningful changes that could enhance the payments landscape [7]. The Deloitte and Mastercard report [4] identified several benefits of digital payments, including reduced transactional hurdles, lower transport-related costs, increased financial transparency, enhanced security against cash theft, and improved record-keeping. Achieving these benefits could strengthen the case for promoting financial inclusion, particularly for consumers in rural areas who could gain access to digital payment methods.

According to the World Bank, financial inclusion focuses on "individuals and businesses having access to useful and affordable financial products and services that meet their needs: transactions, credit, payments, insurance, and savings, delivered responsibly and sustainably" [9]. This emphasizes the centrality of payments in financial products designed to meet consumer needs. Historically, having a transactional account was synonymous with access to financial services. However, as noted [10], the digitalization of financial services, particularly payments, contests this belief and expands payment choices beyond merely possessing a transactional account from the bank. It is within this context of financial inclusion and the efforts of players within the industry to modernize payments that a review of the literature was conducted.

2.1 The Impact of Digital Payments on Financial Inclusion

Digital payments have demonstrated significant potential in fostering financial inclusion across various regions. In China, for instance, digital payment systems have modified people's lives in rural areas, enabling them to access financial services. This shift from traditional cash-based finance to digital solutions has been spearheaded by major tech companies like Alipay and Tencent [11]. They introduced QR codes, allowing users to have instant transactions using their mobile devices, provided the devices can read the codes. The increased adoption of e-wallets and mobile money in China led to a reduction in cash dependency by approximately 30% between 2011 and 2016 [11]. The widespread penetration of smartphones has facilitated the growth of digital financial services, granting access to these services to the unbanked population. In Indonesia, a 2014 report indicated that 64% of the banked population lacked access to formal financial services [12]. To combat cash dependency and enhance financial inclusion, the Indonesian government introduced digital payments through e-money. However, challenges such as inadequate infrastructure and the maturity of business partners have impeded the successful implementation of these digital payment initiatives.

In Africa, notable examples of digital inclusion include M-Pesa, a mobile banking platform that has successfully digitized payments in East Africa [13]. Initially launched as a money transfer service, M-Pesa has advanced into a comprehensive digital financial services system, allowing various payment solutions for individuals and businesses. According to [13], M-Pesa significantly serves the unbanked population in Kenya, with its adoption lifting 2% of households out of poverty, thereby underscoring the positive impact of digital payments on financial inclusion.

In South Africa, despite a high percentage of individuals possessing bank accounts, many do not utilize them for formal financial services, opting instead for cash transactions [11]. Additionally, those residing in remote areas continue to rely on cash, as digital payment options remain largely inaccessible. This situation creates barriers for rural residents, who often need to travel to urban centres to have access to financial services, a process that is both inconvenient and costly. This research posits that South Africa, similar to other developing nations, can leverage digital solutions of payments to enhance formal access to financial services and promote financial inclusion. This is essential for addressing the triple challenge of unemployment, poverty, and inequality, as outlined in the 2030 NDP document.

2.2 Factors Influencing the Effectiveness of Digital Payments in Enhancing Financial Inclusion

A study examining the acceptance of digital payment solutions in India's rural areas identified poor infrastructure as a primary barrier to their widespread adoption [14]. Additionally, the perceived ease of use of digital platforms plays a crucial role in determining whether individuals and retailers will embrace digital payments. If consumers find a digital platform non-user-friendly, cumbersome, or insecure, they will likely return to cash transactions as their favored method of payment. Deloitte emphasized that for digital payments to gain traction, they must be perceived by consumers as having similar attributes to cash, particularly regarding the immediacy of transactions [7]. Furthermore, low levels of trust and concerns about risks, like cyber fraud, significantly contribute to the reluctance to adopt digital payments. Consumers need to have confidence that digital payment systems will function reliably and securely for them to consider using them. In India, the acceptance of digital payments by rural retailers marked a notable improvement during the demonetization process [15].

In addition, fintech innovations in China illustrate that providing convenient and secure financial services can greatly enhance financial inclusion [16]. The innovative e-payment systems exemplified by India's JAM Trinity demonstrate how digital finance can effectively improve access to financial services for the urban poor [17].

In South Africa, internet connectivity is a critical factor that can either accelerate or hinder the adoption of digital financial services [11]. Affordable data costs are essential for encouraging the use of digital services; however, South Africa experiences higher data costs than many other countries, and network coverage is often insufficient in rural areas

[11]. This issue impacts not only customers looking to use digital devices for payments but also merchants needing connectivity to process digital transactions. Additionally, expenses like interchange fees for merchants can further hinder the adoption of digital payments [4].

Regulatory challenges and gaps in digital literacy represent significant obstacles that the fintech industry must address to fully realize its potential in promoting financial inclusion [18]. Moreover, incentivization is another area that warrants closer examination to encourage the digitalization of payments [10, 19]. For instance, the Thai government has implemented tax refunds through digital channels, while the Monetary Authority of Singapore (MAS) has collaborated with non-bank entities, including fintechs and mobile network operators, to ensure their involvement in modernizing financial services. Countries that successfully modernized their payment systems and transitioned to digital financial services within acceptable timelines were typically guided and coordinated by their governments [8]. In South Africa, the NPS Act, the South African Reserve Bank (SARB) as the regulatory body, and the NDP 2030 could serve as foundational elements to provide structured leadership in nurturing financial inclusion using digital solutions in payments. Establishing modern infrastructure, implementing appropriate regulations, and promoting financial awareness will facilitate a higher adoption rate of digital payments, thereby improving South Africa's financial inclusion.

2.3 Digital Payments Landscape in South Africa

Real-time clearing (RTC) payments, considered to be an immediate payment, have been integral to South Africa's digital payments ecosystem since 2006 [7]. In fact, the country's payment systems were regarded as among the finest soon after the turn of the millennium [7]. However, these systems have often been implemented in isolation by various commercial banks, resulting in high costs for some rural customers [20]. The instant payment services offered by the five main banks, i.e., Absa, Capitec, Nedbank, FNB, and Standard Bank, primarily facilitate cash transfers between cash-dispensing outlets. For instance, while the Instant Money service by Standard Bank allows customers to send money to recipients in rural areas, the recipients must collect the funds from an ATM, partner retail store, or another designated outlet. This approach does not promote financial inclusion, as it merely transfers cash without providing access to formal financial services. Comparable wallet products, like Instant Money, are offered by all major commercial banks.

The Vodacom-led M-Pesa initiative, which achieved significant success in Kenya, has seen limited success in South Africa [21]. Executives from Vodacom attributed this lack of success to a regulatory environment perceived as favouring commercial banks, leading them to view South Africa as having one of the least supportive regulatory frameworks for mobile money [21]. While over 58% of the South African population is formally banked, this figure rises to over 77% when including recipients of social grants from the South African Social Security Agency (SASSA). Despite this, a substantial portion of the population remains reliant on cash transactions, largely because social grant recipients tend to withdraw their entire deposits and spend them in cash.

The key players in South Africa's digital payments system include: (1) the government, represented by the National Treasury, which oversees economic policy; (2) the

SARB, responsible for protecting the currency's value and managing the NPS to ensure a stable financial system; (3) BankServ Africa, which handles payment transactions on behalf of banks; (4) Visa, Mastercard and Strate, which administers payment transactions; (5) the Payments Association of South Africa (PASA), an industry organ that oversees the payments system on behalf of the SARB; (6) commercial banks; and (7) payment service providers (PSPs).

While fintech companies and technology firms are part of the ecosystem, they are not formally recognized as such. Similarly, mobile network operators (MNOs) play a crucial role in digital payments due to their influence on mobile phone adoption, yet they also lack formal recognition within the ecosystem.

2.4 Conceptual Framework

The advancement of *digital technologies* has transformed how financial services are accessed and delivered, particularly in emerging economies [22]. At the heart of this transformation lies the potential of *digital payments* to promote financial inclusion by reaching populations historically excluded from formal banking systems. These technologies include mobile money platforms, biometric authentication, blockchain infrastructure, and AI-driven fintech solutions that enable seamless, remote financial transactions [23]. However, the mere presence of technology is not enough; its impact is contingent upon a range of interconnected factors. One critical enabler is *digital infrastructure access*, which refers to the availability and reliability of physical and network systems such as mobile networks, broadband internet, and electricity [24]. Without this foundational layer, even the most innovative payment solutions fail to reach the underserved [25]. In many rural and peri-urban areas across South Africa, inconsistent infrastructure limits user access, thus reinforcing the digital divide.

Equally important is *digital literacy*, which shapes individuals' ability to navigate, trust, and benefit from digital payment platforms [26]. Digital literacy encompasses not just technical skills but also cognitive competencies, such as understanding transaction security, managing digital credentials, and interpreting user interfaces [26]. Studies have shown that low digital literacy remains a barrier to adoption, particularly among older populations and those with limited formal education [27]. As individuals gain digital skills, *digital payment adoption* becomes more feasible. This adoption is driven by both push and pull factors, including convenience, security, transaction speed, and the ability to track financial activity [26]. Nonetheless, adoption remains uneven due to persistent barriers, such as concerns about trust in the system, especially where cyber threats and fraud are prevalent [28]. Trust extends beyond the technical platform; it encompasses institutional trust in financial providers and the government's role in regulating digital spaces. The *regulatory environment* plays a dual role: enabling innovation while protecting consumers [25]. Effective regulation ensures data privacy, fosters interoperability, and encourages competition, all of which are essential for scalable digital payment systems [22]. However, overly stringent policies or fragmented regulatory frameworks can stifle innovation and inhibit provider participation.

Interoperability, the seamless interaction between different payment platforms and providers, is another vital component. It allows users to transact across networks, reduce transactional hurdles and enhance the usability of digital payments [29]. In contexts where systems remain siloed, interoperability gaps create transaction inefficiencies and limit user benefits, particularly for small merchants and informal traders. Additionally, *affordability* underpins the entire digital payment ecosystem. Transaction fees, data costs, and device acquisition expenses must remain within reach for low-income users [30]. Without affordable access, digital payment systems risk deepening exclusion rather than alleviating it [31]. This is particularly relevant in South Africa, where cost-sensitive consumers may opt for cash despite the availability of digital alternatives [32].

The broader process of *digitization*, which is the integration of digital tools into daily economic and social activity, frames these dynamics [33]. Financial inclusion through digital means is not a standalone phenomenon but part of a larger socio-economic transformation. Digitization offers both opportunity and risk, amplifying inequalities where ecosystem enablers are absent, and bridging gaps where they are well-established and inclusive [34].

Any effective strategy must consider the synergies and tensions between the above-mentioned driving factors to ensure that the benefits of digital finance reach all segments of the population equitably.

3 Methodology

This study employed an interpretivist philosophy to explore how digital payments could enhance financial inclusion, drawing on interviews with professionals within the South African digital payments ecosystem. A case study research design was selected to gain comprehensive insights into the topic [35]. The target population comprised professionals in the digital payments sector, selected for their expertise in managing digital payment initiatives or their active participation in the digital payments ecosystem. Both convenience and purposive sampling techniques were utilized. Convenience sampling allowed for the selection of participants based on their proximity and accessibility to the researchers [36]. Purposive sampling was employed to identify individuals with the requisite experience in the South African digital payment ecosystem, ensuring they could provide valuable insights.

The participants represented various stakeholders in the digital payments ecosystem, including the SARB as the payments regulator; commercial banks serving as enablers of digital payments; payments industry organizations providing insights on the management of payment systems; banking industry associations sharing their experiences; MNOs that play a vital role in digital payments; fintech companies engaged in digital payments, offering insights into the challenges within the ecosystem; and card schemes/payment processing facilitators sharing their experiences in handling digital transactions.

Data collection was conducted using a semi-structured interview guide. Before data collection, the researchers obtained ethical clearance from the University of the Witwatersrand, South Africa (Ethics protocol number: WBS/DB9611035M/236) and ensured that participants were informed of their voluntary participation in the study. The interviews took place between April and May 2023, and the data collected were managed by the ethical requirements of the Protection of Personal Information Act (POPIA). A total of 12 participants were interviewed, and the interviews concluded upon reaching saturation. Saturation was determined when no new themes, insights, or perspectives emerged from additional interviews, indicating that the information gathered was sufficient to comprehensively understand the phenomena under investigation. Consequently, further interviews were deemed unnecessary, as they would likely produce redundant information.

For data analysis, manual thematic analysis was conducted using an inductive approach to identify themes and patterns from the interviewees' responses. The researchers transcribed the interview recordings and manually coded the data into themes. This process involved reviewing the transcripts, noting non-verbal cues from the recordings, and categorizing the data in alignment with the research questions.

4 Results

4.1 Demographics of Participants

As illustrated in Table 1, all 12 participants possessed extensive professional experience. Only three had less than 20 years of experience, while another three had 26 years of experience. The remaining six participants had between 20 and 25 years of experience. Seven participants held Master of Business Administration (MBA) or Master of Science (MSc) degrees, while the other five had bachelor's or honours degrees. Some participants also held professional qualifications, such as the South African Chartered Accountant (CA) designation. To maintain participant anonymity, they are referred to by assigned codes (P1 to P12).

Table 1. Summary of participants' demographics

Code	Sector – Industry	Highest qualification	Experience
P1	SA commercial bank	MBA	25 Years
P2	SA commercial bank	MBA	21 Years
P3	Payments Association of South Africa	Master of Science	21 Years
P4	BankservAfrica	MBA	18 Years
P5	BankservAfrica	Bachelor of Military Science	26 Years
P6	Banking Association of South Africa	MBA	26 Years
P7	Fintech	Master of Science	20 Years
P8	Fintech	Bachelor of Science	24 Years
P9	Mobile network operator	Bachelor of Commerce	23 Years
P10	Card payments network	Bachelor of Commerce	16 Years
P11	Card payments network	MBA	12 Years
P12	National Payments System Regulator	Chartered Accountant (SA)	26 Years

The study's findings are organized based on the themes that emerged from the two research questions and are summarized in Tables 2 and 3.

4.2 What Challenges Hinder the Contribution of Digital Payments to Financial Inclusion in South Africa?

Dual economy structure: One challenge is South Africa's bifurcated economy, comprising both formal and informal sectors. In informal markets, transactions are predominantly cash-based. The structural and infrastructural discrepancies between these economies mean that what works for the formal sector may not be feasible for the informal one. Digital payment adoption in rural areas is hindered by unreliable infrastructure, limited internet access, mobility constraints, and inconsistent electricity supply. More importantly, the reliance on cash-based transactions in the informal sector hinders the uptake of digital payments and constrains the growth of small informal enterprises [4].

> Markets in South Africa essentially have two core economies. You have your formal economy and you've got a much more, a big strong informal economy. In both those economies, but predominantly in the informal economy. The biggest form of payment is cash (P1).
>
> So, until you can use your Postbank card [which is a debit card issued by the South African Postal Services] to pay at home to the informal seller on the side of the road, or you can use your mobile phone to pay digitally to the informal seller on the side of the road for your six tomatoes, digital payments remain a dream (P3).

These quotes highlight the contrast between the two economies. Informal businesses are mainly located in underdeveloped rural regions that lack the necessary infrastructure for supporting financial inclusion through digital platforms. Meanwhile, businesses in the formal sector are better positioned to utilize digital payment systems.

Challenges in reproducing the speed and low cost of cash transactions: Cash is often seen as having a stable value that remains constant regardless of how frequently it changes hands. This perception makes cash attractive when compared to digital transactions. Cash also allows for immediate value transfer, whereas digital payments often require a bank account to store value, which introduces fees and delays for users. The complexities associated with digital payments may discourage usage, making the convenience of cash more appealing. In digital systems, merchants may not receive funds instantly; instead, payments may be processed in batches over 24 to 48 h, creating cash flow issues.

> And then the other biggest challenge is around replicating the immediacy and the low cost (P1).
>
> The reality of the matter is that some people, they still perceive a cash payment as free. But you and I know that the cost of handling cash is high and all of that (P2).
>
> And the problem is the cost of cash is hidden because it's a big cost to the formal sector (P3).

Although end-users might perceive cash as a free option, the actual cost of handling and securing cash is transferred to the businesses. MNOs, in particular, face high expenses when converting physical money into digital funds, such as in e-wallet platforms. Therefore, there is a need to investigate how to lower the costs involved in digitizing cash transactions.

> And if I look at mobile money ecosystems have done well or that have proliferated in other countries, cash is actually cheap, not expensive to hold money (P9).

Merchant acceptance of digital payments: Many merchants, especially those operating in rural or informal markets, do not accept card or digital payments. Customers are often forced to withdraw cash at petrol stations or other locations because local businesses do not support electronic transactions.

> Let me paint a very practical scenario using you as an example. I can almost bet my pension on it that when you go home, you stop at the petrol station, and you withdraw cash. The business there doesn't accept your card payment, can you see that if you don't solve acceptance they'll continue with cash (P2).

In several instances, individuals who prefer using digital payments often face additional charges to offset expenses linked to such transactions, including the use of point-of-sale terminals and other related costs. South Africa operates a broad social grant program designed to support elderly citizens and those in poverty. These grants help beneficiaries cover household expenses, fund their children's education, and meet daily necessities. Most recipients reside in rural and township areas, where cash is still regarded as the most convenient and affordable payment method. Because many live far from towns and cities, they choose to withdraw their entire grant in cash. As noted in [4], 90% of grant beneficiaries withdraw the full amount as soon as it becomes accessible in their bank accounts.

> The business is there, don't accept your card payment or they will tell you if you use your card, you must spend over 50 Rands. Or if you use it exactly, they will say that they charge more (P2).
>
> So, the money comes in the customer does two transactions which is a balance inquiry and withdrawal and that is completely rational behavior because if you have to travel to draw your cash and you're paying a taxi fare and your social grant is R1 850 and your taxi fares R100 well, it's as rational as anything on earth to withdraw all your money in one go (P3).

Low levels of digital literacy: Although South Africa enjoys a high general literacy rate, digital literacy lags behind. This gap limits people's ability to understand and confidently use digital payment platforms.

> In South Africa, we have a lot of literacy, very high literacy rate, you know 95% or something around there. But digital literacy is not that high (P7).
>
> I mean the education thing I think is a huge thing and I think it's something that should be incorporated into our school curriculum (P3).

One participant (P6) offered a counterargument, asserting that people are capable of adopting digital platforms without formal education, as shown by the widespread usage of platforms like WhatsApp and Facebook. This view, while not widely shared, adds an alternative perspective on the matter.

> We got the barrier to financial inclusion is literacy. What a load of hogwash, right? I mean, I told you. I mean, is there a WhatsApp manual? Where's a Facebook manual? Right? And so how is this thing adopted by everyone in the world at the rate it's adopted? And yet we say stupid things like the poor people need to be educated on how to use a bank account. That's nonsensical, right? (P6).

Lack of consumer trust in digital payments: Trust emerged as another major concern affecting digital payments uptake. The Deloitte and Mastercard report [4] noted that cash usage requires no financial or digital literacy and digital payments that require digital literacy will have to contend with a lack of trust.

> So, there are a bunch of other infrastructure elements and consumer education and consumer trust that underpin all of these (P3).
>
> Because access payments and the trust of digital payments is the security amount and it, you know, at least physical mode, if you can run away from the crook or you can keep it in a pocket or you can hide it, it's pretty secure, right? (P5).

Access to affordable and reliable internet connectivity: Reliable internet access is essential for digital payments, yet high data costs and limited network coverage in rural South Africa present substantial obstacles. Data costs have also been identified in other countries, such as India, as something needing attention, as they hinder access to digital services [11].

> Of course, payment systems aren't enough because you would need data that is cheap (P3).
>
> In South Africa, the cost of data is too high, but it's way too high in global terms. We're paying too much (P7).
>
> Yeah, actually one challenge in the ecosystem that I did not mention is the role of internet or MSN [collections of internet services and applications from Microsoft] or within that space because it's becoming quite critical (P11).

Insufficient interoperability among digital solutions: Interoperability, defined as the ability of different payment systems to work together seamlessly was noted as lacking. This limitation prevents customers from easily moving funds between mobile wallets, banks, and other value stores. This was also acknowledged as a challenge at the regulatory framework level in that it requires regulatory attention. Several participants (P2, P3, P4, P5, P8, P11, and P12) emphasized the need for interoperability across platforms.

> How do we get these more integrated or at least interoperable so that they can facilitate the drive of these ecosystem announcements? I think regulation will be

important because my experience showed me that very few of these programs work (P5).

Infrastructure leverage, I would call that, which brings interoperability from payments to value (P5).

It shouldn't matter that the owner of the shop has a bank account. I'll be able to pay him because I'm using this proxy thing to introduce the interoperability, right? So that is one of the things for me that will drive well if it's done right, that should drive the adoption of digital payments (P2).

So, there's space that we look after, which is the interoperability between all the players, no matter where you bank, and you'll see that the National Treasury paper if you looked at it, recommends interoperability with mobile wallets as well (P3).

I think one of the big problems is interoperability (P8).

Did you tell you know financial inclusion? It is around the interoperability of the various stores of values, whether it be traditional banks and non-traditional banks, fintech, and that those things talk to each other. So, you want to think about the modernisation of our regulations to ensure that they talk ability between actors (P4).

We do not have policy and framework that governs interoperability so that any product that comes into the space is able to interpret the web with you know what other systems or other services, a case in point is e-wallets (P12).

How do you make it interoperate into interoperable and also that it doesn't limit you to one, you know if you put a cell phone number, then the cell phone number, and that's all you can do, but how do you also get to do other things (P11).

Countries such as Thailand and Singapore identified and promoted interoperability to drive the adoption of digital payments [11]. This is also one of the goals of the SARB's Vision 2025 [3].

Concerns around privacy: Finally, transaction privacy was cited as a factor in discouraging digital payment adoption. Some consumers and business owners prefer cash to avoid scrutiny, tax obligations, or data tracking.

The second problem in the digital system, which is becoming more and more important, is that the system is being exploited to extract data about people's transactional behavior right now (P6).

Because the slightly bigger guys in the tax bracket and they want to play in cash to avoid tax (P3).

I don't want people necessarily to understand what cash flow I've got (P5).

Table 2. Summary of themes that emerged from research question 1

Themes	Description	Participant codes	Number of participants per theme
Dual economy structure	South Africa's bifurcated formal and informal economies, with cash dominance in the informal sector, hinder digital payment adoption	P1, P3	2
Challenges in reproducing cash's speed and cost	Cash is perceived as immediate and low-cost, while digital payments involve fees and delays, deterring adoption	P1, P2, P3, P9	4
Merchant acceptance issues	Limited acceptance of digital payments by merchants, especially in rural/informal markets, forces reliance on cash	P2, P3	2
Low digital literacy	Limited ability to use digital platforms restricts adoption, particularly in underserved communities	P3, P6, P7	3
Lack of consumer trust	Concerns about security and reliability reduce confidence in digital payments	P3, P5	2
Access to affordable and reliable internet	High data costs and poor network coverage in rural areas limit digital payment accessibility	P3, P7, P11	3
Insufficient interoperability	Lack of seamless integration across payment systems (e.g., mobile wallets, banks) restricts functionality	P2, P3, P4, P5, P8, P11, P12	7

(continued)

Table 2. (*continued*)

Themes	Description	Participant codes	Number of participants per theme
Privacy concerns	Preference for cash to avoid transaction tracking or tax obligations discourages digital adoption	P3, P5, P6	3

4.3 What Needs to be Done for Digital Payments to Foster Financial Inclusion in South Africa?

The second research question focused on identifying what actions or interventions are required for digital payments to meaningfully promote financial inclusion. To explore this, participants were asked to suggest practical solutions and mechanisms to encourage the engagement of all relevant stakeholders in proposed interventions. The key responses derived through thematic analysis are presented below.

Establishing an inclusive industry body for digital payments: One of the participants proposed that a new representative industry body should be created, one that encompasses all players in the digital payments environment. The aim of this inclusive structure would be to prevent bias toward dominant actors, particularly banks, and to ensure balanced oversight across the ecosystem. This proposed body would be responsible for examining every aspect of the digital payments chain, from regulatory processes to execution strategies. Participants emphasized that financial inclusion cannot be addressed by banks alone. The inclusion of actors like MNOs and resolving interoperability challenges across mobile wallets, bank accounts, and other value-storage tools were considered essential. A new, broad-based industry structure was viewed as necessary to unite these efforts.

> So, they are going to say that you know MTN, Vodacom Cell C, you must be direct participants in payments. Because they believe that those people will introduce the right level of competition, and those people are already operating in those environments; they are used to selling airtime of 10 Rands [South African currency] (P2).

Improving affordability of digital payment systems: Affordability was another critical theme. The cost for merchants to accept digital payments needs to be reduced. Presently, merchants often discourage digital transactions or offer incentives for paying with cash because accepting digital payments incurs expenses. If digital payment processing becomes more cost-effective for merchants, they are more likely to promote it, thereby enhancing adoption and reducing reliance on cash, which comes with its own set of risks.

So, for me, it's more about the ecosystem. So, why are you charging merchants to process digital payments? You know, how easy is it for customers to access digital payments and then come up with all sorts of fancy solutions (P9).

Participants (P1, P2) noted that interchange fees, fees charged to merchants by service providers for handling debit and credit card transactions, should be restructured. The merchant often benefits most from digital transactions, particularly in person-to-merchant settings. Therefore, a well-calibrated interchange model could help balance the cost burden across stakeholders and encourage more inclusive digital usage.

And I think interchange can be used as a tool to optimally balance the two-sided market and facilitate the provision of services to individuals who don't necessarily need to pay for them. So, in the person-to-merchant space, the primary beneficiary of digital payments is the merchant. And so, getting interchange right and some of those constructs, right, I think become very, very important (P1).

And if you look at other markets, I mean, I discussed with one of the banks in Brazil early this week, right in their world for these types of payments, there's zero interchange (P2).

Table 3. Summary of themes that emerged from research question 2

Themes	Description	Participant codes	Number of participants per theme
Establishing an inclusive industry body	Need for a representative body including all stakeholders (e.g., fintechs, MNOs) to foster collaboration and innovation	P2	1
Improving affordability	Reducing transaction costs (e.g., interchange fees) to encourage merchant and consumer adoption	P1, P2, P9	3

5 Discussion

This study revealed a range of obstacles that hinder the widespread use of digital payments and delay their potential to promote financial inclusion in South Africa. While some of these barriers are perceived rather than tangible, they nonetheless affect consumer behavior and slow down adoption. A common perception is that cash is inexpensive or even free to use. While this may be true from the consumer's perspective, businesses incur significant costs in handling and securing cash. In rural areas and other underserved communities, consumers prefer cash primarily because bank accounts often come with transaction fees. However, while cash may be trusted and convenient, it does not help in building a financial profile for individuals, thereby restricting their access to formal financial products like credit and loans [37, 38].

One major barrier is the issue of interchange fees charged to merchants. These fees make digital payments unattractive in low-margin or low-volume settings, common in remote and informal markets, where transactions are typically small in value. As a result, cash becomes the preferred method, and merchants may either reject card payments or require customers to make minimum purchases. In some cases, they even increase prices to offset interchange costs, further discouraging digital payment usage [39, 40].

Another challenge is the delayed settlement time of digital payments. Unlike cash, which is immediate, digital transactions can take up to 24 to 48 h for merchants to receive funds. This delay can severely affect cash flow, especially for small and informal businesses. Solutions like PayShap, which enables instant bank-to-merchant payments using either an account number or mobile proxy, can help mitigate this challenge. Promoting the use of such platforms could reduce reliance on physical cash and ease the burden of delayed settlements [41, 42].

Additionally, the lack of access to digital payments in rural and underdeveloped areas must be addressed. Merchants in these areas often lack the necessary hardware—such as point-of-sale terminals—to accept digital transactions. Compounding the issue are network connectivity problems, frequent power outages, and expensive mobile data. Furthermore, many digital payment platforms do not support offline functionality, making them unreliable in regions with poor infrastructure. Just a few negative experiences with failed or delayed transactions can cause consumers to revert to cash, undermining trust in digital systems [43, 44].

The fragmentation of payment systems also surfaced as a key concern. A lack of interoperability across financial products and platforms prevents consumers from leveraging the full potential of digital financial services. For example, if a digital wallet is not compatible with a consumer's bank account, its functionality becomes limited. To build an inclusive ecosystem, solutions must be interoperable, enabling seamless transactions across banks, mobile wallets, and other stores of value. Allowing payments via airtime, vouchers, or other forms of stored value can make digital payments more accessible and relevant to low-income consumers. The current lack of interoperability reflects a disjointed system that requires stronger coordination and shared commitment among ecosystem stakeholders [38, 40].

Involving all relevant players, particularly fintechs and MNOs—in the regulatory and operational ecosystem is essential. At present, traditional banks dominate the digital payments space, but their cost structures limit their ability to serve low-income and geographically remote customers. By contrast, fintechs and MNOs are often better positioned to develop innovative, cost-effective solutions tailored to these segments. Evidence from Kenya's M-Pesa illustrates that excluding these non-traditional actors weakens the system's ability to reach the financially excluded. Wallets, airtime, and digital vouchers are increasingly being used in place of traditional money, and the digital payments ecosystem must evolve to recognize and integrate these innovations [39, 45].

According to the study's findings, the existing industry body, PASA, needs to be restructured. A new body should be created to formally include all participants in the digital payments space. This broader and more inclusive structure would foster innovation, competition, and meaningful collaboration. The SARB has already tasked PASA with initiating the redesign of the payment ecosystem to include all stakeholders. This process should also update the NPS Act to legally recognize fintechs and MNOs as part of the core payments infrastructure. A reimagined payments industry body that embraces these actors would lay the groundwork for a more inclusive and effective digital payments environment.

Initiatives currently coordinated by institutions such as BankservAfrica, including PayShap, are often perceived as being too closely aligned with the interests of commercial banks. As such, they may not sufficiently challenge the status quo or address deeper structural problems. To drive transformation in real-time digital payments, there must be a stronger representation of new players with alternative business models and a focus on serving excluded communities [41, 46].

6 Contributions of the Study

This study makes significant contributions to the understanding of financial inclusion through digital payments in South Africa. It extends the theoretical discourse on digital financial inclusion by highlighting the critical role of infrastructure, digital literacy, and regulatory frameworks. Moreover, it emphasizes the unique context of South Africa, where formal and informal economies coexist, presenting a complex landscape for digital payment solutions. This research contributes to the broader theoretical framework by identifying interoperability, affordability, and trust as pivotal factors in fostering financial inclusion through digital payments.

6.1 Theoretical Implications

The findings of this study have two major theoretical implications. First, the study highlights the importance of a multi-stakeholder approach involving government, financial institutions, fintechs, and MNOs to create an inclusive digital payment ecosystem. Second, the study highlights the need for regulatory frameworks that support innovation while ensuring security and trust in digital transactions. These implications call for a re-examination of current financial inclusion models to incorporate the complexities of emerging markets such as South Africa.

6.2 Practical Implications

The practical implications of this study are substantial for policymakers, financial institutions, and technology providers. For policymakers, the research provides actionable insights into creating an enabling environment for digital payments, such as improving infrastructure, reducing data costs, and fostering digital literacy. The recommendation to establish a new industry body that includes all actors in the digital payments ecosystem could significantly enhance coordination and innovation. For financial institutions, the study suggests a need to develop affordable and accessible digital payment solutions that address the needs of both formal and informal sectors. This includes lowering transaction fees and ensuring immediate payment settlements to enhance cash flow for small merchants. Technology providers, particularly fintech companies and MNOs, are encouraged to collaborate with traditional financial institutions to create interoperable solutions that can bridge the gap between various payment systems. Implementing these practical recommendations can drive financial inclusion and contribute to overcoming the socio-economic challenges of poverty, unemployment, and inequality in South Africa.

7 Conclusion

This qualitative study aimed to explore the potential of digital payments in promoting financial inclusion within South Africa. The research identified multiple barriers that limit the effectiveness of digital payments in achieving this goal. It also outlined specific steps that need to be taken for digital payments to serve as a viable tool for financial inclusion in the South African setting. One of the most crucial findings is the importance of interoperability. For digital payments to be broadly adopted, products and platforms must function seamlessly together. Stakeholders within the digital payments space must prioritize the development and implementation of interoperable systems. Achieving this requires official recognition of all actors involved in digital payments, including fintechs and MNOs, by the NPS, as well as their inclusion within the payments industry's governance structure. Their participation is vital in shaping strategies and solutions that reflect the needs of diverse users. Another key challenge lies in the informal sector's continued dependence on cash. Overcoming this will require targeted educational and awareness initiatives that highlight the value and benefits of digital payments. These digital literacy efforts should be led by a newly formed payments industry body that represents the full spectrum of stakeholders. In addition, fostering partnerships with MNOs and other stakeholders across the digital payments landscape will be essential. Such collaborations could help address persistent challenges, such as high data costs and limited network coverage, particularly in underserved areas.

While the case study offers valuable insights into the mechanisms and barriers surrounding digital payments and financial inclusion in South Africa, its narrow scope, limited sample, and interpretivist lens constrain the generalizability of its findings. Future research could complement these results with quantitative, longitudinal, and user-focused studies to enhance transferability and support broader policy recommendations.

References

1. Falaiye, T., Elufioye, O.A., Awonuga, K.F., Ibeh, C.V., Olatoye, F.O., Mhlongo, N.Z.: Financial inclusion through technology: a review of trends in emerging markets. Int. J. Manag. Entrep. Res. **6**(2), 368–379 (2024). https://doi.org/10.51594/ijmer.v6i2.776
2. S.A. Government: National Development Plan: Our future—make it work. Pretoria (2012)

3. South African Reserve Bank: The National Payment System Framework and Strategy: Vision 2025 of the South African Reserve Bank. Pretoria (2018)
4. Deloitte: The future of payments in South Africa: Enabling financial inclusion in a converging world. Johannesburg (2019)
5. Sahay, R., Ogawa, S., Khera, P., Ng, S.: Is digital financial inclusion unlocking growth? IMF Work. Pap. **2021**(167), 1 (2021). https://doi.org/10.5089/9781513584669.001
6. Wyman, O.: Digitalization in Financial Services (2018)
7. Deloitte: Regenesis of SA payments What needs to change? Johannesburg (2019)
8. Tay, L.Y., Tai, H.T., Tan, G.S.: Digital financial inclusion: a gateway to sustainable development. Heliyon **8**(6), e09766 (2022). https://doi.org/10.1016/j.heliyon.2022.e09766
9. World Bank Group: Financial inclusion. Accessed: May 18, 2022. [Online]. Available: https://www.worldbank.org/en/topic/financialinclusion/overview
10. Ozili, P.K.: Impact of digital finance on financial inclusion and stability. Borsa Istanbul Rev. **18**(4), 329–340 (2018). https://doi.org/10.1016/j.bir.2017.12.003
11. PricewaterhouseCoopers Inc.: Payments Study Tour Report 2019: Lessons from Asia to inform South Africa's payments modernisation journey (2019)
12. Azali, K.: Cashless in Indonesia: gelling mobile E-frictions?. J. Southeast Asian Econ., 364–386 (2016)
13. Oluwole, V.: M-Pesa: Kenya's mobile money success story celebrates 15 years. Business Insider Africa. Accessed: Mar. 07, 2022. [Online]. Available: https://africa.businessinsider.com/local/markets/m-pesa-kenyas-mobile-money-success-story-celebrates-15-years
14. Koul, S., Jasrotia, S.S., Mishra, H.G.: Acceptance of digital payments among rural retailers in India. J. Payments Strateg. Syst. **15**(2) (2021), [Online]. Available: https://doi.org/10.69554/REDW9291
15. Sivathanu, B.: Adoption of digital payment systems in the era of demonetization in India: an empirical study. J. Sci. Technol. Policy Manag. **10**(1), 143–171 (2019). https://doi.org/10.1108/JSTPM-07-2017-0033
16. Chen, W., Yuan, X.: Financial inclusion in China: an overview. Front. Bus. Res. China **15**(1) (2021), https://doi.org/10.1186/s11782-021-00098-6
17. Singh, J., Singh, M.: Accelerating financial inclusion of the urban poor: role of innovative e-payment systems and JAM trinity in alleviating poverty in India. Glob. Bus. Rev. (2024). https://doi.org/10.1177/09721509231222609
18. Quresh, M., Ismail, M., Khan, M., Asad Gill, M., Kishwer, R.: The impact of fintech on financial inclusion: opportunities, challenges, and future perspectives. PalArch's J. **20**(2), 1210–1230 (2023)
19. Yawe, B.L., Ddumba-Ssentamu, J., Nnyanzi, J.B., Mukisa, I.: Role of mobile money and digital payments in financial inclusion for sustainable development goals in Africa. Intech Open **11**, no. Tourism, p. 13 (2022). [Online]. Available: https://www.intechopen.com/books/advanced-biometric-technologies/liveness-detection-in-biometrics
20. Thompson, A.: SA banks are 'forced' to charge more for instant payments – but their prices vary wildly. Business Insider SA. Accessed: May 10, 2021. [Online]. Available: https://www.businessinsider.co.za/sa-banks-say-they-have-no-choice-to-charge-more-for-instant-payments-but-how-much-varies-2021-5
21. BusinessTech: M-Pesa wants to be more than just a mobile money service. BusinessTech. Accessed: Mar. 20, 1BC. [Online]. Available: https://businesstech.co.za/news/mobile/379367/m-pesa-wants-to-be-more-than-just-a-mobile-money-service/
22. Feyen, E., Frost, J., Gambacorta, L., Natarajan, H., Saal, M.: Fintech and the digital transformation of financial services: implications for market structure and public policy. BIS Papers **117**(117) (2021)

23. Niankara, I.: The impact of financial inclusion on digital payment solution uptake within the Gulf cooperation council economies. Int. J. Innov. Stud. **7**(1), 1–17 (2023). https://doi.org/10.1016/j.ijis.2022.09.004
24. Schade, P., Schuhmacher, M.C.: Digital infrastructure and entrepreneurial action-formation: a multilevel study. J. Bus. Ventur. **37**(5), 106232 (2022). https://doi.org/10.1016/j.jbusvent.2022.106232
25. Wei, F., Xie, B., Chen, M.: Digital financial inclusion, e-commerce development and entrepreneurial activity. Int. Rev. Financ. Anal. **97**(July), 2025 (2024). https://doi.org/10.1016/j.irfa.2024.103806
26. Adel, N.: The Impact of digital literacy and technology adoption on financial inclusion: evidence from emerging economies in Africa, Asia, and Latin America. Heliyon **10**(24), e40951 (2024). https://doi.org/10.1016/j.heliyon.2024.e40951
27. Mhlanga, D.: Covid-19 and digital financial inclusion: policies and innovation that can accelerate financial inclusion in a Post-COVID World through fintech. African J. Dev. Stud. **79**, 1–9 (2020)
28. Aldboush, H.H.H., Ferdous, M.: Building trust in fintech: an analysis of ethical and privacy considerations in the intersection of big data, AI, and customer trust. Int. J. Financ. Stud. **11**(3) (2023), https://doi.org/10.3390/ijfs11030090
29. The World Bank Group: Payment Systems Worldwide: A Snapshot (2019). [Online]. Available: http://scioteca.caf.com/bitstream/handle/123456789/1091/RED2017-Eng-8ene.pdf?sequence=12&isAllowed=y%0Ahttp://dx.doi.org/10.1016/j.regsciurbeco.2008.06.005%0Ahttps://www.researchgate.net/publication/305320484_SISTEM_PEMBETUNGAN_TERPUSAT_STRATEGI_MELESTARI
30. Manda, M.I., Backhouse, J.: Inclusive digital transformation in South Africa: An institutional perspective. ACM Int. Conf. Proc. Ser., no. April, pp. 464–470 (2018), https://doi.org/10.1145/3209415.3209486
31. Manjang & Naghavi: State of the Industry Report on Mobile Money. GSMA Mob. Money Unbanked, pp. 40–86, 2021 (2021), [Online]. Available: www.gsma.com/mobilemoney
32. The Pocket Guide: The State of the Digital Payments Ecosystem in South African Townships - A study conducted in Tembisa and Hammanskraal (2022)
33. Renn, O., Beier, G., Schweizer, P.J.: The opportunities and risks of digitalisation for sustainable development: a systemic perspective. Renn, O., Beier, G., Schweizer, P.J.: The opportunities and risks of digitalisation for sustainable development: a systemic perspective. Gaia 2021, 30, 23. Gaia **30**(1), 23–28 (2021)
34. Kayser, K., Telukdarie, A., Philbin, S.P.: Digital start-up ecosystems: a systematic literature review and model development for South Africa. Sustain. **15**(16) (2023), https://doi.org/10.3390/su151612513
35. Starman, A.B.: The case study as a type of qualitative research. J. Contemp. Educ. Stud., 28–43 (2013)
36. Saunders, M., Bristow, A., Thornhill, A., Lewis, P.: Understanding research philosophy and approaches to theory development. In: Saunders, M.N.K., Lewis, P., Thornhill, A. (Eds.), Research Methods for Business Students, 8th edition, Harlow: Pearson Education, pp. 128–171 (2019)
37. Anakpo, G., Xhate, Z., Mishi, S.: The policies, practices, and challenges of digital financial inclusion for sustainable development: the case of the developing economy. FinTech **2**(2), 327–343 (2023). https://doi.org/10.3390/fintech2020019
38. Grohmann, A., Klühs, T., Menkhoff, L.: Does financial literacy improve financial inclusion? Cross country evidence. World Dev. **111**, 84–96 (2018). https://doi.org/10.1016/j.worlddev.2018.06.020
39. Ozili, P.K.: Theories of financial inclusion. MPRA, no. 1–24 (2020)

40. Kaffenberger, M., Totolo, E., Soursourian, M.: A digital credit revolution: insights from borrowers in Kenya and Tanzania. Work. Pap. Washington, D.C. CGAP (2018)
41. Gapp, B., de Fauconberg, Â., Bessis, A., Goble, H., Obodoekwe, N.: Digital Finance in Africa: accelerating foundations for inclusive and sustainable local innovation. Environ. Sci. Proc., 66 (2022), https://doi.org/10.3390/environsciproc2022015066
42. Mothobi, O., Grzybowski, L.: Infrastructure deficiencies and adoption of mobile money in Sub-Saharan Africa. Inf. Econ. Policy **40**, 71–79 (2017). https://doi.org/10.1016/j.infoecopol.2017.05.003
43. Asongu, S.A., Nwachukwu, J.C.: Comparative human development thresholds for absolute and relative pro-poor mobile banking in developing countries. Inf. Technol. People **31**(1), 63–83 (2018). https://doi.org/10.1108/ITP-12-2015-0295
44. Demirgüç-Kunt, A., Klapper, L., Singer, D., Ansar, S., Hess, J.: The global findex database 2017: measuring financial inclusion and opportunities to expand access to and use of financial services. World Bank Econ. Rev. **34**(2018), S2–S8 (2020). https://doi.org/10.1093/wber/lhz013
45. Lawack, V.A.: Mobile money, financial inclusion and financial integrity: the South African case. Washingt. J. Law, Technol. Arts **8**(3), 317–346 (2013), [Online]. Available: http://digital.law.washington.edu/dspace-law/handle/1773.1/1202
46. Louis, L., Chartier, F., Hugo, V.M.: Financial inclusion in South Africa: an integrated framework for financial inclusion of vulnerable communities in South Africa's regulatory system reform. J. Comp. Urban Law Policy **1**(1), 2017 (2017), [Online]. Available: http://www.readingroom.law.gsu.edu/jculp, Availableat: http://wwwreadingroom.law.gsu.edu/jculp/vol1/iss1/13

Author Index

F. Kamoun et al. (Eds.): AFRICATEK 2025, LNICST 677, p. 393, 2026.
https://doi.org/10.1007/978-3-032-16638-8

The manufacturer's authorised representative in the EU is Springer Nature Customer Service Centre GmbH, Europaplatz 3, 69115 Heidelberg, Germany. If you have any concerns regarding our products, please contact ProductSafety@springernature.com

Printed and bound by CPI Group (UK) Ltd, Croydon, CR0 4YY
07/07/2026
02160913-0012